ROUTLEDGE HANDBOOK OF SPORT HISTORY

The *Routledge Handbook of Sport History* is a new and innovative survey of the discipline of sport history.

Global in scope, it examines the key contemporary issues in sports historiography, sheds light on previously ignored topics, and sets an intellectual agenda for the future development of the discipline. The book explores both traditional and non-traditional methodologies in sport history, and traces the interface between sport history and other fields of research, such as literature, material culture, physical cultural studies, and the digital humanities. It considers the importance of key issues such as gender, race, sexuality, and politics to our understanding of sport history, and focuses on innovative ways that the scholarship around these issues is challenging accepted discourses. This is the first handbook to include a full section on Indigenous sport history, a topic that has often been ignored in sport history surveys despite its powerful upstream influence on contemporary sport. The book also reflects carefully on the central importance of sport history journals in shaping the development of the discipline.

This book is an essential reference for any student, researcher, or scholar with an interest in sport history or the relationship between sport and society. It will also be fascinating reading for any historians looking for fresh perspectives on contemporary historiography or social and cultural history.

Murray G. Phillips is a Professor of Sport History in the School of Human Movement and Nutrition Sciences at the University of Queensland, Australia, and President of the North American Society for Sport History.

Douglas Booth is the Dean of Adventure, Culinary Arts and Tourism at Thompson Rivers University, Canada, Emeritus Professor at the University of Otago, New Zealand, and Honorary Professor at the University of Queensland, Australia.

Carly Adams is a Professor in the department of Kinesiology and Physical Education and Co-Director of the Centre for Oral History and Tradition at the University of Lethbridge in Alberta, Canada.

ROUTLEDGE HANDBOOK OF SPORT HISTORY

Edited by Murray G. Phillips, Douglas Booth and
Carly Adams

LONDON AND NEW YORK

First published 2022
by Routledge
2 Park Square, Milton Park, Abingdon, Oxon OX14 4RN

and by Routledge
605 Third Avenue, New York, NY 10158

Routledge is an imprint of the Taylor & Francis Group, an informa business

© 2022 selection and editorial matter, Murray G. Phillips, Douglas Booth and Carly Adams; individual chapters, the contributors

The right of Murray G. Phillips, Douglas Booth and Carly Adams to be identified as the authors of the editorial material, and of the authors for their individual chapters, has been asserted in accordance with sections 77 and 78 of the Copyright, Designs and Patents Act 1988.

All rights reserved. No part of this book may be reprinted or reproduced or utilised in any form or by any electronic, mechanical, or other means, now known or hereafter invented, including photocopying and recording, or in any information storage or retrieval system, without permission in writing from the publishers.

Trademark notice: Product or corporate names may be trademarks or registered trademarks, and are used only for identification and explanation without intent to infringe.

British Library Cataloguing in Publication Data
A catalogue record for this book is available from the British Library

Library of Congress Cataloging-in-Publication Data
Names: Phillips, Murray G. (Murray George), editor. | Booth, Douglas, editor. | Adams, Carly, editor.
Title: Routledge handbook of sport history / edited by Murray G. Phillips, Douglas Booth and Carly Adams.
Description: Abingdon, Oxon ; New York, NY : Routledge, 2022. | Series: Routledge international handbooks | Includes bibliographical references.
Identifiers: LCCN 2021008149 (print) | LCCN 2021008150 (ebook) | ISBN 9780367331733 (hardback) | ISBN 9781032053615 (paperback) | ISBN 9780429318306 (ebook)
Classification: LCC GV571 .R685 2022 (print) | LCC GV571 (ebook) | DDC 796.09–dc23
LC record available at https://lccn.loc.gov/2021008149
LC ebook record available at https://lccn.loc.gov/2021008150

ISBN: 978-0-367-33173-3 (hbk)
ISBN: 978-1-032-05361-5 (pbk)
ISBN: 978-0-429-31830-6 (ebk)

DOI: 10.4324/9780429318306

Typeset in Bembo
by Taylor & Francis Books

CONTENTS

List of tables	*x*
List of contributors	*xi*
Sports photographs as historical documents Taylor McKee	*xix*
Foreword	*xxi*
Introduction *Murray G. Phillips, Douglas Booth and Carly Adams*	1

PART 1
History and representing the sporting past

7

1 History and representing the sporting past: Introduction   9
Douglas Booth, Carly Adams and Murray G. Phillips

2 Reflexivity in sport history   16
Malcolm MacLean

3 The last comparative review of sport history and sport sociology?   24
Richard Pringle

4 Writing macro and micro sport history   32
Mike Cronin

5 Sports history and the challenge of Physical Cultural Studies   41
Mark Falcous

6 Narrative/s in sport history   50
Daniel A. Nathan

Contents

7 Expanding repertoires inside and outside the archives: Methods 57
Gary Osmond

8 Sport and material culture 65
Maureen Smith

9 Why read historical fiction about sport? 74
Angie Abdou

10 Sport and activism 82
Russell Field

PART 2
New perspectives on old themes **91**

11 New perspectives on old themes: Introduction 93
Douglas Booth, Carly Adams and Murray G. Phillips

12 The origin and diffusion of modern sport 100
S.W. Pope

13 Time, space, and sport 110
Peter Donnelly

14 Sport and the body 119
Jaquelyn Osborne and Chelsea Litchfield

15 Sport and visuality 128
Mike Huggins

16 Sport and politics 136
Heather L. Dichter

17 Sport and international relations 144
Bruce Kidd

18 Sport and nationalism 152
Liam O'Callaghan

19 Race, racism, and racial entanglements 161
Sarah Barnes and Mary G. McDonald

20 Sport in post-apartheid South Africa: The race to class 169
Ashwin Desai

Contents

21 Women's sport history 180
Jaime Schultz, Michelle M. Sikes and Cat M. Ariail

22 Troubling sexuality and sport: Early histories of queer athletic visibility 188
Judy Davidson

PART 3
Emerging themes **197**

23 Emerging themes: Introduction 199
Carly Adams, Douglas Booth and Murray G. Phillips

24 Digital sport history: History and practice 204
Jennifer Guiliano

25 Teaching/learning sports history 212
Tara Magdalinski

26 Competitive gaming 219
Lu Zhouxiang

27 Sport and emotion 228
Barbara Keys

28 Sport heritage 235
Gregory Ramshaw

29 Towards new materialist sport history 243
Holly Thorpe, Julie Brice and Marianne Clark

30 Deaf and disability sport 251
Danielle Peers

31 Sporting borderlands 259
Colin Howell and Daryl Leeworthy

PART 4
Indigenous sport history **267**

32 Indigenous sport history: Introduction 269
Murray G. Phillips, Douglas Booth and Carly Adams

Contents

33 Settler colonialism and sport history 275
Murray G. Phillips

34 Māori and Indigenous sport histories: Hero/ine or dupe? 279
Brendan Hokowhitu

35 A critical discussion of history and Indigenous sport in Australia 287
Barry Judd and Gary Osmond

36 Indigenous sport history in Canada: Past and future considerations 295
Christine O'Bonsawin and Janice Forsyth

37 American Indian sport history 303
Jennifer Guiliano and Beth Eby

PART 5
Sport history journals 313

38 Sport history journals: Introduction 315
Murray G. Phillips, Douglas Booth and Carly Adams

39 Sport history journals and neoliberalism: Auditing the subdiscipline 323
Murray G. Phillips

40 Fifty years of *Sport History Review* 332
M. Ann Hall

41 The *Journal of Sport History* 339
Andrew D. Linden and Alison M. Wrynn

42 *STADION: International Journal of the History of Sport* 348
Manfred Lämmer and Markwart Herzog

43 The *Sport in History* Journal 353
Dave Day and Kay Schiller

44 *The International Journal of the History of Sport* 1984–2020: Twenty-four
million words and still counting 360
Wray Vamplew

45 The history of *Sporting Traditions: The Journal of the Australian Society for
Sports History* 367
Rob Hess

viii

Contents

46 Materiales para la Historia del Deporte: The journal on the History of
Sport, a reference for the Latin American world, with international scope   374
Teresa González Aja and Rodrigo Pardo

47 Recorde – Revista de História do Esporte: A Brazilian, Latin-American,
Ibero-American journal   381
Rafael Fortes and Victor Andrade de Melo

PART 6
Conclusion   **389**

48 Sport history: Past, present, future   391
Douglas Booth, Murray G. Phillips and Carly Adams

Index   395

TABLES

I.1	Content by chapters in key sport history books	2
5.1	Approaching the sporting past through Physical Cultural Studies	44
38.1	Sport history journals	316
39.1	Sport history journal Scopus average metrics (2015–2019)	327
39.2	Sport history journal altmetrics	328
39.3	Sport history journals SJR quartile rankings (2015–2019)	329
41.1	JSH Editors	342
46.1	Nationality of the Scientific Committee membership	377
46.2	Language of articles	377
46.3	National institutional affiliation of authors	378
46.4	Gender of published authors	378
46.5	Gender of management and administration	378

CONTRIBUTORS

Angie Abdou is an Associate Professor of Creative Writing at Athabasca University, Alberta. She is the author of eight books, including short prose, novels, and creative nonfiction. Her main scholarly interest is Canadian Literature, particularly writing about the body, and she is a long-standing, active member of the International Sport Literature Association.

Carly Adams is a Professor in the department of Kinesiology and Physical Education and Co-Director of the Centre for Oral History and Tradition at the University of Lethbridge in Alberta, Canada. In collaboration with Dr Darren Aoki, she is currently working on the Nikkei Memory Capture Project, a community-based oral history project focusing on Japanese Canadian histories in southern Alberta.

Cat M. Ariail is a History Instructor at Middle Tennessee State University, United States. She researches issues of race, gender, sexuality, and nationalism in twentieth-century women's sport in the United States and Caribbean.

Sarah Barnes is Post-Doctoral Visitor at York University in the School of Kinesiology and Health Science. Barnes' research focuses on athlete health and welfare in a rapidly changing society and she is working on several manuscripts that explore how sleep enhancing products and technologies are taken up in athletic settings.

Douglas Booth is the Dean of Adventure, Culinary Arts, and Tourism at Thompson Rivers University (Canada), Emeritus Professor at the University of Otago (New Zealand), and Honorary Professor at the University of Queensland (Australia). His books include *The Race Game* (1998), *Australian Beach Cultures* (2001), *The Field* (2005), and *Bondi Beach* (2021). Douglas serves on the editorial boards of *Rethinking History* and the *Journal of Sport History* and is an executive member of the Australian Society for Sport History.

Julie Brice is a doctoral candidate in Te Huataki Waiora/School of Health at the University of Waikato in Hamilton, New Zealand. Julie's research focuses on new materialist theories and conceptual practices regarding women's embodied experiences of fitness and the athleisure phenomenon.

List of contributors

Marianne Clark is a Postdoctoral Fellow in the Vitalities Lab at the University of New South Wales, Sydney, Australia. Her research interests include women's health, the physically active body, and the embodied dimensions of human engagements with digital health technologies. She is inspired by social theoretical frameworks and innovative methodologies that capture the complexities and capacities of moving bodies.

Mike Cronin is the Academic Director of Boston College in Ireland. He has published extensively on the history of sport, in particular questions relating to identity, as well as a series of major public history projects based around Irish topics. He is a regular media commentator on aspects of Irish and sporting history.

Judy Davidson is Associate Professor in the Faculty of Kinesiology, Sport and Recreation at the University of Alberta, Canada. Her research interests include queer and feminist approaches to sport and leisure phenomena. She has published on homonationalism, the international LGBT sport movement, and arena gentrification projects as forms of settler colonialism. She is an avid skier, mountain biker, and hiker.

Dave Day is Professor of Sports History at Manchester Metropolitan University, UK, where his research focuses on the history of coaching and training, the development of swimming and swimming communities, and the gendered nature of nineteenth and twentieth century sport and leisure. He has served in the past as editor of the *Sport in History* journal and as Chair of the British Society of Sports History.

Ashwin Desai is Professor of Sociology at the University of Johannesburg, South Africa. He is a wide-ranging writer whose work has been published in academic and popular books and journals around the world, and his research interests are the sociology of sport, social identity, and social movements.

Heather L. Dichter is an Associate Professor of Sport History and Sport Management at De Montfort University, Leicester, and a member of the International Centre for Sports History and Culture. She is the co-editor of *Olympic Reform Ten Years Later* (2014) with Bruce Kidd. She has published articles on sport in occupied Germany, sport and diplomacy, the winter Olympics, and Olympic bidding, and is the Europe regional editor for *The International Journal of the History of Sport*.

Peter Donnelly is a Professor Emeritus in the Faculty of Kinesiology and Physical Education, University of Toronto, Canada. His research interests include sport politics and policy issues, sport subcultures, and mountaineering (history) and he is the author of *Inside Sports* (1999). Peter served as the editor of the *Sociology of Sport Journal* (1990–94) and as the acting-editor of the *International Review for the Sociology of Sport* (2004–6).

Beth Eby earned her PhD in History from the University of Illinois at Urbana Champaign. She is currently a Postdoctoral fellow in the Center for Women's and Gender Studies and Native American and Indigenous Studies at the University of Texas at Austin. She is currently revising her dissertation, *Building Bodies, (Un)Making Empire: Gender, Sport, and Colonialism at Haskell Institute, 1880–1930*, into her first monograph. Her research and teaching interests include Indigenous History, Histories of Sport, Women's and Gender History, and Histories of Empire and Colonialism.

List of contributors

Mark Falcous is Associate Professor in the Sociology of Sport at the University of Otago, New Zealand. His research focuses on intersections of sport, globalization, national identity, and media. His work has appeared in *Sociology of Sport Journal, Continuum: Journal of Media and Cultural Studies, International Review for the Sociology of Sport, Studies in Ethnicity and Nationalism, Journal of Sport and Social Issue, Media and Cultural Politics*, and *Sites*. He co-edited (with Joseph Maguire) *Sport and Migration: Borders, Boundaries and Crossings* (Routledge, 2011).

Russell Field is an Associate Professor in the Faculty of Kinesiology and Recreation Management at the University of Manitoba, Canada. His recent research focuses on global sporting events as sites of resistance and protest, with recent publications examining the ideological origins of sport-for-development and the anti-colonial/anti-imperial origins of the 1963 Games of the New Emerging Forces in Jakarta, Indonesia.

Janice Forsyth, Cree scholar (Fisher River Cree Nation, Manitoba), is an Associate Professor in Sociology and the Director of Indigenous Studies in the Faculty of Social Science at Western University, London, Ontario, Canada. Her research focuses on Indigenous sport development in Canada, where she has a 20-year history of volunteer involvement at the national level.

Rafael Fortes is an associate professor in the Department of Social Sciences at the Federal University of the State of Rio de Janeiro. He has been an executive editor of *Recorde: Revista de História do Esporte* since the journal's foundation in 2008, and is also affiliated with the Graduate Interdisciplinary Program in Leisure Studies at the Federal University of Minas Gerais. His publications include books, book chapters, and articles in Portuguese, English, and Spanish. His current research focuses on representations of Rio de Janeiro and Brazil in surf magazines edited in Australia, South Africa, and the United States.

Teresa González Aja is Professor at 'Facultad De Ciencias De La Actividad Física Y El Deporte', Polytechnic University of Madrid, Director of the research group 'Social and Humanistic Studies in Sport and Physical Activity' and the Educational Innovation Group 'Areté'. She is member of the College of Fellows of the European Committee for Sports History (CESH) and member of the ISHPES executive board. Her publications cover the impact of physical activity and sports in arts, the political use of sports such as football or the Olympic Games, among others. She is member of the Editorial Board of the journal *Materiales para la Historia del Deporte*.

Jennifer Guiliano is Associate Professor in the Department of History and affiliated faculty in both Native American and Indigenous Studies and American Studies at IUPUI in Indianapolis, Indiana. She received a Bachelor of Arts in English and History from Miami University (2000), a Master of Arts in History from Miami University (2002), and a Master of Arts (2004) in American History from the University of Illinois before completing her PhD in History at the University of Illinois (2010).

M. Ann Hall is an author and retired professor, who taught for over 30 years in the Faculty of Kinesiology, Sport, and Recreation at the University of Alberta in Canada. She has published extensively on gender and sport, and on the history of Canadian women's sport.

List of contributors

Markwart Herzog is director of the Schwabenakademie Irsee. He is the author of numerous academic publications on topics related to the history of sport and history of religion; his main research interests include sport in the National Socialist period, the cultural history of soccer, the commemorative and funeral culture of soccer clubs, the history of women's football, and the media history of sport. He is member of the International Society of Olympic Historians (ISHO), the International Society for the History of Physical Education and Sport (ISHPES), and the Rotary Club Kaufbeuren.

Rob Hess is an adjunct professor with the Institute for Health and Sport at Victoria University, where he taught sport history for more than two decades. He is also a former editor of *Sporting Traditions* and a past president of the Australian Society for Sports History. He recently served a term as managing editor of the *International Journal of the History of Sport*, before resuming his long-term commitment as a regional editor with the journal.

Brendan Hokowhitu of Ngāti Pukenga is Professor of Indigenous Studies in the Faculty of Māori and Indigenous Studies at the University of Waikato. Underpinned by critical Indigenous theory, Professor Hokowhitu's research has led to the creation of the sub-fields of Indigenous masculinities, and critical Indigenous sports studies. His publications include over 60 peer-reviewed journal articles and book chapters. He was lead editor of the *Routledge Handbook of Critical Indigenous Studies* (2020). Currently, Brendan is the President Elect for the Native American and Indigenous Studies Association.

Colin Howell is Professor Emeritus in History and recently retired Academic Director of the Centre for the Study of Sport and Health at Saint Mary`s University in Halifax. Dr Howell has published widely in the field of sport and health studies. He was co-editor of the *Canadian Historical Review*, Canada's senior historical journal, from 1988 to 1992.

Mike Huggins is Emeritus Professor of Cultural History at the University of Cumbria, UK. He has published widely on British sport and leisure during the eighteenth, nineteenth, and twentieth centuries, and on a range of themes such as gambling, visuality, and sports tourism. He is the current president of the European Committee of Sports Historians. His most recent books include *Match Fixing and Sport: Historical Perspectives* (Routledge, 2019), co-edited with Rob Hess.

Barry Judd is Professor and Director of Indigenous Studies at the University of Melbourne. He is recognized internationally for research on Aboriginal peoples in sports, particularly in the context of Australian (Rules) Football. Professor Judd is a founding Chief Investigator of the National Indigenous Research and Knowledges Network (NIRAKN). Since 2015, Professor Judd has worked extensively on issues related to Indigenous livelihoods, particularly where they relate to inland arid Australia.

Barbara Keys is Professor of US and Transnational History at Durham University. She is a Fellow of the Australian Society for Sport History. She has published several dozen articles and book chapters on topics ranging from the International Olympic Committee's United Nations diplomacy to the role of the landline telephone in social movements.

Bruce Kidd is a Professor Emeritus in the Faculty of Kinesiology and Physical Education, University of Toronto, Canada. He teaches and writes about the history and political economy

xiv

of Canadian and international sport. He has authored or edited 12 books and hundreds of articles, papers, lectures, plays, and film and radio scripts. Bruce has worked with numerous local, national, and international bodies to advance opportunities for physical activity and sport. He has been a lifelong advocate of human rights and athletes' rights. He competed in the 1964 Olympics and is an honorary member of the Canadian Olympic Committee.

Manfred Lämmer is a historian and classical philologist. From 1975–2010, Professor Lämmer was Director of the History Department of the German Sport University Cologne. His main areas of research are Ancient Greek athletics, history and ideology of the Olympic movement, sport and politics, and sport and Judaism.

Daryl Leeworthy is the Rhys Davies Research Fellow based at the South Wales Miners' Library, Swansea University. He has published widely on the history of sport, social democracy, and twentieth-century literature. He is currently writing a biography of the novelist and screenwriter Gwyn Thomas and a history of women in the Welsh labour movement, both to be published in 2022, as well as a history of popular culture and intellectual life in the South Wales Coalfield.

Andrew D. Linden is an Assistant Professor of Sport Studies in the Department of Kinesiology at the California State University, Northridge (CSUN). He researches the intersections between sport and politics, with a focus on social movements. His research has appeared in *The International Journal of the History of Sport*, the *Journal of Sport History, Communication & Sport*, and the *Journal of Sport and Social Issues*. Previously, he was a faculty member at Adrian College in Sport Management and received his PhD in History and Philosophy of Sport from the Pennsylvania State University.

Chelsea Litchfield is a senior lecturer at Charles Sturt University, Australia. Dr Litchfield completed her studies through Victoria University, Melbourne, and she holds a Bachelor of Applied Science degree in Physical Education and a Class 1 Honours degree in Human Movement. Her PhD research explored the culture of safe and affirming spaces in women's team sports in Melbourne. Her research focuses on gender, sport, and media in an Australian context, specifically on gender-based abuse and violence in social media spaces.

Malcolm MacLean is a settler scholar and interdisciplinary historian whose research focuses on the cultural and social experience and identities associated with movement, sport, and play, with a specific interest in colonial, imperial, and decolonial relations and in sport-related political activism. He is a cofounder of the Philosophy at Play network and co-editor of five volumes of essays exploring philosophy and/at play. His academic affiliations include The University of Queensland, Australia, De Montfort University, UK and the University of Gibraltar.

Tara Magdalinski currently serves as Pro Vice-Chancellor (Education and Quality) at Swinburne University of Technology in Australia. Her research focuses on historical, cultural, and sociological aspects of sport, including identity and performance-enhancing drugs. She is the author of *Sport, Technology and the Body: The Nature of Performance* (Routledge 2008). Tara also co-edited *With God on their Side: Sport in the Service of Religion* (London, Routledge, 2002) and wrote *Study Skills in Sports Studies* (Abingdon: Routledge, 2013).

List of contributors

Mary G. McDonald is the Homer C. Rice Chair in Sports and Society in the School of History and Sociology at the Georgia Institute of Technology where she also directs the Sports, Society and Technology Program. Professor McDonald's research focuses on sport and intersecting inequalities of gender, race, class, and sexuality. She has published more than 50 refereed journal articles and book chapters and has co-edited several anthologies.

Taylor McKee is an Assistant Professor at Brock University (Ontario) and an Adjunct Assistant Professor in Sociology at Western University (Ontario). His research focuses on media, violence, and Canadian history, and he is co-editor of *Duelism: Confronting Sport Through Its Doubles* (2021). Taylor is a member of the Indigenous Hockey Research Network, a contributor to IndigenousSportHistory.ca, and a managing editor of the *Journal of Emerging Sport Studies*.

Victor Andrade de Melo is a Full Professor at the Federal University of Rio de Janeiro, where he works in the Postgraduate Program in Comparative History and in the Postgraduate Program in Education. He is coordinator of Sport: Laboratory of History of Sport and Leisure. Author of several books and articles dedicated to the historical studies of sports, he has been a productivity researcher (National Research Council/Brazil) since 2003.

Daniel A. Nathan is a Professor of American Studies at Skidmore College and holds The Douglas Family Chair in American Culture, History, and Literary and Interdisciplinary Studies. He has published several books, as well as essays and reviews for many periodicals. Nathan has served as the Film, Media, and Museum Reviews editor for the *Journal of Sport History*, is on several editorial boards, and is Past President of the North American Society for Sport History.

Christine O'Bonsawin (Abenaki, Odanak Nation) is an Associate Professor of History and Indigenous Studies at the University of Victoria, located on Lkwungen, Wyomilth (Esquimalt) and W̱SÁNEĆ homelands. Her scholarship in sport history and Indigenous studies take up questions regarding the appropriation and subjugation of Indigenous peoples, identities, and cultures in Olympic history and the future programming of the Games.

Liam O'Callaghan is senior lecturer in sport studies at Liverpool Hope University, UK. His research interests include the social history of modern Ireland with a focus on issues such as intersections of class and culture, the comparative history of sport and leisure, and popular history and myth.

Jaquelyn Osborne is a lecturer and discipline lead in the School of Exercise Science, Sport, and Health at Charles Sturt University in Bathurst, Australia. Jaquelyn teaches in the psychosocial dimensions of sport and exercise, particularly in sport sociology, sport history and philosophy. Dr Osborne's research is predominantly in the area of gender and the sports media.

Gary Osmond is an Australian Research Council Future Fellow (2017–21) and associate professor in sport history in the School of Human Movement and Nutrition Sciences at the University of Queensland. His Future Fellowship project is titled *Sport, Stories and Survival: Reframing Indigenous Sport History*.

List of contributors

Rodrigo Pardo is Associate Professor at the Faculty of Physical Activity and Sports Sciences – INEF (Universidad Politécnica de Madrid) and tenured member at Research Group ESHAFYD (Humanist and Social Studies in Physical Education and Sport). His main researches focuses on sport as a means of education and socialization, doping analysed from the perspective of Social Sciences, and educational innovation applied to Secondary Education and Universities. He is member of the Editorial Board of the journal *Materiales para la Historia del Deporte*.

Danielle Peers is a Canada Research Chair in Disability and Movement Cultures in the Faculty of Kinesiology, Sport and Recreation at the University of Alberta. Their research focuses on how movement cultures of all kinds can deepen or challenge social inequalities. Their research builds from their experiences as a Paralympic athlete, coach, and sport administrator in Wheelchair Basketball, as well as their experiences as a queer, disabled, non-binary athlete, artist, and scholar in Treaty Six territory.

Murray G. Phillips is a Professor of Sport History in the School of Human Movement and Nutrition Sciences at the University of Queensland, Australia. He is President of the North American Society for Sport History, former President of the Australian Society for Sport History, and former Editor of the *Journal of Sport History*. He is the author of *Representing the Sporting Past in Museums and Halls of Fame* (Routledge, 2012).

S.W. Pope is a visiting lecturer at Jilin International Studies University in northeastern China. He is co-editor (with J. Nauright) of the *Routledge Companion to Sports History* (2010). Pope received a PhD in History from the University of Maine in 1993.

Richard Pringle is a professor of socio-cultural issues in sport, health, and movement at Monash University in Melbourne. He is the co-author of *Foucault, Sport and Exercise* (2006) (with Pirkko Markula) and *Sport and the Social Significance of Pleasure* (2015) (with Bob Rinehart & Jayne Caudwell), and co-editor of *Critical Research in Sport, Health and Physical Education* (2018) (with Håkan Larsson and Göran Gerdin). He has served as the associate editor for the *Sociology of Sport Journal* and is currently on the editorial board of four international journals.

Gregory Ramshaw is a Professor in the Department of Parks, Recreation, and Tourism Management and a Fellow of the Robert H. Brooks Sports Science Institute at Clemson University in Clemson, South Carolina. His research explores the social construction and cultural production of heritage, with a particular interest in sport-based heritage.

Kay Schiller is Professor of Modern European History at the University of Durham, UK. He has published widely on modern Jewish-German history, German cultural history, and the modern history of sport. He is currently editor-in-chief of *Sport in History*.

Jaime Schultz is a Professor of Kinesiology, with an affiliate faculty appointment in Women's, Gender, and Sexuality Studies, at Pennsylvania State University. An award-winning teacher and scholar, she studies issues of sex, gender, sexuality, 'race', and sport. Schultz currently serves as editor of the *Sport and Society* series at the University of Illinois Press.

Michelle M. Sikes is an Assistant Professor of Kinesiology, African Studies, and History at Pennsylvania State University. She received her D.Phil. from the University of Oxford.

List of contributors

Before joining the faculty at Penn State, she taught at the University of Cape Town and Stellenbosch University in South Africa. As a former professional runner, Sikes represented the United States in the 5,000 metres at the 2007 World Athletics Championships.

Maureen Smith is a professor in the Department of Kinesiology at California State University, Sacramento. Smith is a former president of the North American Society for Sport History and currently serves as the Editor of the *Journal of Sport History*. Smith co-authored *(Re)Presenting Wilma* (Syracuse University Press, 2015), winner of the NASSH Monograph Award (2016). She is currently working on a book project examining sport statues and material culture in the United States.

Holly Thorpe is Professor in Te Huataki Waiora/School of Health at the University of Waikato, New Zealand. Her research interests include the moving body, gender, and women's health. She continues to find much inspiration in the challenges of working across disciplines, engaging with social theory and exploring feminist methodologies.

Wray Vamplew is Emeritus Professor of Sports History at the University of Stirling and Global Professorial Fellow at the University of Edinburgh. Previously he has been Pro-Vice-Chancellor at Flinders University and Foundation Director of the International Centre for Sports History and Culture at De Montfort University. Author or editor of 34 books, he has also published 148 articles and book chapters as well as over 100 other publications.

Alison M. Wrynn is Associate Vice Chancellor, Academic Programs, Innovations, and Faculty Development at the CSU Office of the Chancellor. Her PhD is in Human Biodynamics from UC, Berkeley and her area of scholarly research is in the History of Sports Medicine and Exercise Science. Alison served as the editor of the *Journal of Sport History* for the North American Society for Sport History from 2011–2014.

Lu Zhouxiang is a Lecturer within the School of Modern Languages, Literatures, and Cultures at National University of Ireland Maynooth. His main research interests are nationalism, national identity and sport history, and he has published extensively in these areas. His recent publications include *A History of Shaolin: Buddhism, Kung Fu and Identity* (Routledge, 2019) and *Politics and Identity in Chinese Martial Arts* (Routledge, 2018).

SPORTS PHOTOGRAPHS AS HISTORICAL DOCUMENTS

Taylor McKee

Cover photo: Native American football team, Haskell Institute, Kansas, date unknown
Source: George Rinhart/Corbis Historical via Getty Images.

With thousand-yard stares reminiscent of trench-weary conscripts, these football players tell their story without words. Hair cut, they are costumed in the trappings of a sport whose ancestry lies on the well-manicured fields of the Ivy League and British public schools. This game is one steeped in the traditions of collegiality and sociability, for a chosen few. Lawrence, Kansas, home of the Haskell Institute, formerly known as the United States Indian Industrial Training School, is a great distance from those Elysian fields, both in distance and demography. The lessons remain the same, at Eton, Harvard, or Carlisle: culture is learned, and can be un-learned, through sport.

There are no spectators, officials, or parents, and the focus of the image is simply the team; a team picture in the tradition of thousands of sports teams before and since. Except, the story of these athletes is far more complex. Athletes at boarding and residential schools, like the ones in this photograph, were positioned as thriving representatives of the government programmes designed to erase and replace Indigenous culture. A stark juxtaposition, these players are tightly posed, arranged as ideal representations of an assimilative system of sport and education, standing on a field devoted to a concept that appears so distant from the hardened exteriors of the young athletes: *play*.

There are many images left unseen of their time at the Haskell Institute, unable to be captured by photographs but likely seared into the minds of these attendees. The images that do survive need to be rigorously examined as historical documents, and critically analysed for their cultural context; the very survival of images, such as this one, demonstrates their perceived value to those that stage these photos. This particular image, like many from similar schools throughout North America, was meant to broadly demonstrate the successes of the institution and its ability to create pupils in the image of their schoolmasters: white, Anglo, and Christian.

The evocative power of photographs is magnified when viewers are able to identify a sense of familiarity, to see themselves in the eyes of the subjects. In that sense, images of sport and schooling are even more potent, inviting observers to superimpose their own experiences into the subject matter of the photograph. Enforced participation can be misread as youthful camaraderie and one field can be substituted for any other in the mind's eye. Therein lies the need for extra care when dealing with images of Indigenous athletes in forced schooling. This image, replete with piercing, haunting gazes, can easily represent the horrors of the forced schooling model applied broadly in North America to Indigenous people. However, had the players been bright-eyed and beaming, the images alone would not be sufficient to tell their full story. Images have the power to elucidate, as well as sublimate, the experiences of their subjects. This photograph is haunted by insights and accusations, questions and answers, stories and silences.

FOREWORD

I am very fortunate. Although not a member of the first generation of sport historians who laid the foundation for the field by conducting research and establishing organizations devoted to the topic, I followed closely behind and gained close access to many of them that in hindsight seem decidedly serendipitous in nature. While a graduate student at San Diego State University in the early 1970s, I took my very first sport history course from Reet Howell, a newly minted PhD from the University of Alberta who would have an outstanding career in the field until her untimely death in 1993 from cancer at the age of 48. A frequent guest lecturer in her course was her husband Max, at the time Dean of Professional Studies at the school who was a prolific author and one of the earliest proponents of sport history as a serious area of academic study and influential in implementing sport studies curriculums at both the University of British Columbia and University of Alberta before finishing his distinguished career at the University of Queensland.

The same semester I took Reet Howell's sport history class, I enrolled in a new sport sociology course being taught by Lyle Olsen, the former Brooklyn Dodger minor leaguer and San Diego State University baseball coach, who would ultimately spearhead the founding of the Sport Literature Association. The courses by Howell and Olsen, which I remember in great detail to this very day, were transformative for me personally and from a career perspective. Although I had been a voracious reader of sport and history from a very early age, this was the first time I had taken formal courses that examined in a serious way sport and its impact on culture and society. I knew almost immediately I wanted to do what Reet and Lyle did: spend my professional life teaching and writing and thinking seriously about sport and its relationship to other societal institutions. To do so at university level, I had to have a doctorate, so I set off for the University of Maryland to take my PhD under the guidance of Marvin H. Eyler, a founding member and first president of the recently created North American Society for Sport History (NASSH). This was another significant point in my life as Eyler was an extraordinary mentor, teaching me the ways of the academic world, requiring me and my fellow graduate students to learn the parent discipline by taking the majority of our coursework in the department of history rather than in kinesiology where we were officially taking our degree, and introducing us to scholars, many of them his former advisees, who were actively engaged in conducting research on the history of sport. It was an exciting time for many of us, largely because we were in the midst of the disciplinary movement in which a number of scholarly organizations were created to promote and encourage the serious study of sport from different vantage points. These organizations all created their own scholarly journals and yearly conferences so as to disseminate the latest research in their respective disciplinary areas.

Like all graduate students, much of my time at Maryland was spent trying to learn as much as I could about the secondary literature on sport history. I spent hours canvassing the holdings at the university library and Library of Congress looking for books on sport, searched for the latest scholarly articles on sport, and tried to stay abreast of professional presentations dealing with sport-related topics. In hindsight, I now realise how relatively little scholarly research had been completed at the time in sport history as well as the dearth of publication outlets devoted to the topic. The only two scholarly journals that focused on sport during my time at Maryland were the *Canadian Journal of the History of Sport and Physical Education* (1970) (now *Sport History Review*) and *Journal of Sport History* (1974). Only occasionally could I find an essay on sport in a journal in the parent discipline as the topic was deemed trivial and frivolous in the grand scheme of things by many trained historians. Serious scholarly books on the history of sport were particularly hard to find, although Eyler did all of us a favour in my view by requiring us to read Dennis Brailsford's *Sport in Society: Elizabeth to Anne* (1969) and I will forever be impacted by poring over Edwin B. Henderson's *The Negro in Sports* (1939, 1949) and C.L.R. James, *Beyond a Boundary* (1963) before departing Maryland and heading first to Kansas State University and then George Mason University for my nearly 40-year academic career.

How times have changed. Sport history has realized enormous growth and a measure of prestige over the last several decades that I could never have imagined as a young graduate student. No longer are there just two scholarly journals devoted to the history of sport, but now 16 published in different languages and, in some cases, with broad distribution. The overall quality of journal articles, by any measure employed, has steadily improved over the years along with an obvious willingness to broach a broad range of topics and utilise diverse methodological approaches. The number of quality books published on sport history has also increased dramatically over the last number of years with university and commercial presses soliciting and welcoming submissions of both monographs and anthologies dealing with the topic. Recognizing the general public's fascination with the topic and potential for increased sales because of the large number of sport-oriented university courses now being offered, publishers of all stripes are churning out books at an increasingly fast rate.

Examples of the increasing number of sport history books being published are many and varied, but two obviously important ones will suffice. Although once adverse to publishing books on the topic because of being perceived as trivial and frivolous, university presses are now so enamoured with the subject, and admittedly view it as a way to help keep them afloat financially, that they have established special series devoted specifically to sport. The University of Illinois Press was the first to implement such a series and now similar types of series are operating at such publishers as Syracuse University Press, University of Nebraska Press, The University of Arkansas Press, Temple University Press, Rutgers University Press, University of Texas Press, University of California Press, University of Tennessee Press, and University Press of Kentucky. The quality of the books published by these presses is generally quite high as evidenced by the awards some of them have garnered from prestigious national organizations.

Equally impressive for the large number of sport history books they have published have been commercial presses. These include such publishers as McFarland, Human Kinetics, Rowman & Littlefield, and Routledge. Among these, it is Routledge who has dominated the field regarding the sheer number of sport history titles they have published. The pace at which they have done so is impressive as are the different formats and voluminous nature of their books, as well as the large number of outstanding sport historians from around the world who have been persuaded to be involved in their projects. An interesting and effective format Routledge has used to disseminate research in sport history, and other aspects of sport and many other subjects for that matter, is through a series of handbooks typically edited by scholars prominent in their respective fields. There is a plethora of published handbooks, ranging from such titles as *Routledge Handbook of Global Sport* and *Routledge Handbook of Sport, Race, and Ethnicity* to *Routledge Handbook of Sport Development and Peace* and *Routledge Handbook of Youth Sports*.

One of the most recent of these books is the *Routledge Handbook of Sport History* edited by Murray Phillips, Douglas Booth, and Carly Adams. You could not ask for three more qualified people to co-edit this project as each of them has made important contributions to the field of sport history. Phillips, professor in the School of Human Movement and Nutrition Sciences at the University of Queensland, has an extensive publication list and is former editor of the *Journal of Sport History*. He has garnered multiple awards for his scholarship, including twice being recipient of NASSH's outstanding anthology awards for his books *Deconstructing Sport History* (2006) and *Representing the Sporting Past in Museums and Halls of Fame* (2012). Booth, the Dean of Adventure, Culinary Arts, and Tourism at Thompson Rivers University, has published a plethora of articles, book chapters, and books that have revolutionized the field. He has twice garnered the *NASSH Award for Outstanding Monographs* for his books *The Race Game: Sport and Politics* in *South Africa* (1998) and *The Field: Truth and Fiction in Sport History* (2005). Adams, Board of Governors Research Chair and professor of Sport History in the Department of Kinesiology at the University of Lethbridge, is the editor of *Sport History Review* and founding member of the Centre for Oral History and Tradition. She has a long list of publications in very prominent scholarly journals and anthologies.

The individual scholarly accomplishments of Phillips, Booth, and Adams are enough to warrant their selection as co-editors of the *Routledge Handbook of Sport History*. I would contend, however, that what makes them eminently qualified to co-edit this project is the interest all three have in epistemological issues, theory, methods, and historical analysis. While many of us write history, Phillips, Booth, and Adams are very interested in how knowledge is produced, the relationship between historians and their chosen topic, how evidence is collected and used, and how and what people choose to remember. This interest is certainly reflected in their focus on the latest cultural turn that places an emphasis on such factors as images, symbols, emotions, and meaning in historical analysis. It is also reflected in their choice of topics and who they selected to write about them.

Phillips, Booth, and Adams have designed a book that takes a fresh perspective on topics that have either been written about with some regularity or those that have received scant attention, and assembled an impressive list of contributors representing diverse disciplinary backgrounds and varying levels of experience, but all with a firm commitment to the field and solid scholarly backgrounds. What topics in the book readers will find most appealing, of course, is always contingent on personal preferences and scholarly interests. I have little doubt, however, that readers will be fascinated by the sections on Indigenous sport history and sport history journals. The latter topic, particularly for those of us who have been around awhile, is both a reminder of our limitations and the giant leap forward we have made as a scholarly field of study. Although there is still much to improve upon regarding the historical study of sport, the number, quality, and far-reaching nature of the scholarly journals in the field are very impressive and should be encouraging even for the most critical among us.

My mentors, all of whom have now passed, would be thrilled by this turn of events as well as the fact that journals in the parent discipline are more receptive to articles on sport and publishers of all stripes not only welcome but encourage sport history manuscripts. They would, I am sure, also encourage us not to rest on our laurels and continue to find ways to improve our scholarship and think creatively and imaginatively about the historical connection among sport and society. This is why I have no doubt they would be as appreciative and enthusiastic as I am about the *Routledge Handbook of Sport History* because it is as much a book about the future as anything else. Phillips, Booth, Adams, and their band of contributors have provided guideposts and a map to help us find our way forward as we proceed in our quest to gain a better understanding of the phenomenon of sport and how it has been represented and impacted the world. In all, those with a serious interest in the history of sport, irrespective of stage of career and area of specialty, would benefit from a close reading of the book as it is full of nicely crafted and thoughtful essays that cause one to think both differently and more deeply about a relatively young scholarly field of inquiry still searching for a place at the table among other important disciplines.

David K. Wiggins

INTRODUCTION

Murray G. Phillips, Douglas Booth and Carly Adams

As the editors of the *Routledge Handbook of Sport History*, we are delighted to welcome readers to what we conceptualize as a selective overview of the field, its diverse themes and topics, and its methods, theories, approaches, sources, problems, and issues. Since its inauguration as an academic field, sport history has experienced what many scholars now refer to as turns, or shifts, in their analytical, epistemological, and ontological approaches. One of the most important turns in the last 20 years in sport history has been the cultural turn which placed meaning, symbols, images, affects, emotions, voices, and experiences at the heart of analysis. The cultural turn has been critical to drawing historians' attention to the distinction between the past and history. The past and history are now recognized as two different things; so different that history cannot purport to be the past, but rather a selective and positioned representation of the past. Historians cannot recover the past for a number of reasons, but one of the most salient explanations is that the past is limitless. This means that historians are making choices from the moment a topic is chosen, the research approach is considered, empirical evidence is gathered, analytical concepts are applied, and the story is written not as mimesis (the past-as-history) but as a positioned narrative replete with metaphors, tropes, plots, arguments, and voices.

The organization, planning, and selection of topics for this *Handbook* reflect a very similar process to the challenges individual historians face as they confront a limitless past. We simply could not cover all of the content that constitutes the subdiscipline of sport history in one book. As a consequence, we made decisions, many conscious and perhaps some subconscious, about what should be included in this volume. In this *Handbook*, we only provide a slice of sport history, but what we consider to be an informative slice that demonstrates the adaptive, dynamic, and sophisticated qualities of the subdiscipline.

In the spirit of the cultural turn, that promotes a heightened state of authorial self-awareness, we explain and rationalize our decisions about what topics are chosen, and which ones are excluded. A productive way to demonstrate our decisions is by comparing and contrasting the content of this *Handbook* with two previous, prominent volumes. These are S.W. Pope and John Nauright's *Routledge Companion to Sports History* (2010) and Robert Edelman and Wayne Wilson's *Oxford Handbook of Sports History* (2017). Both are excellent books and recognized as landmark volumes in sport history. Indeed, Pope and Nauright's *Companion* and Edelman and Wilson's *Handbook*, like our current volume, represent the

DOI: 10.4324/9780429318306-1

1

interests, preferences, and priorities of the editors, and their perceptions of sport history as a subdiscipline and how it relates to other academic disciplines.

One prominent difference between our volume and Pope and Nauright's *Companion* and Edelman and Wilson's *Handbook* is content. Their volumes are devoted to telling stories about the role of sport in different historical epochs and in regional/national/continental contexts. Edelman and Wilson's volume, for instance, examines pre-modern sport, the establishment of modern sport, and patterns of diffusion and globalization. Readers are provided with summaries about sport in Ancient Greece, the Roman Republic and Empire, and the Medieval period. These premodern contexts are followed by chapters on key features of modern sport: industrialization, urbanization, communication, and the diffusion of international sports – football, baseball, cricket, and surfing – through both empire and globalization. The content focus of Edelman and Wilson's volume continues with histories of nations – China and Russia – and regional/continental areas including South and North Asia, the Middle East, Africa, North, South, East and West Europe, Latin America, and Australasia. Pope and Nauright's *Companion* is less concerned with providing content on premodern sport, but commissions 20 chapters – over half of the content of the book – on regional/national/continental histories of sport. Clearly the editors of these volumes were in agreement about the value of regional/national/continental histories of sport, but differed about the need to include chapters about premodern sport.

The chapters in these volumes produce excellent and comprehensive resources detailing changes in sport over time as well as the unique and defining development of sports in regional/national/continental contexts. The chapters are intended to be relatively short in length, but comprehensive in nature. Their readerships range from interested members of the general public, to undergraduate students, to scholars in the academic community. Writing these kinds of encyclopedic chapters requires knowledge, skills, and expertise, but there is a trade-off: authors need to prioritize comprehensiveness in relatively few words over engaging with theoretical or conceptual debates. In this structure there is little opportunity to address methodology, theory, epistemology, or ontology. In other words, the emphasis in these chapters is on content – what happened when, how are we to understand that, and what does it mean – rather than questions about history making: what shapes how history is researched, conceived, and written?

In this *Handbook*, as indicated in Table I.1, we deemed that sport history is already well served by a sway of comprehensive regional/national/continental histories and histories on premodern sport. On this basis, we only commissioned one chapter with a regional/national/continental focus and two on the emergence of modern sport. This *Handbook*

Table I.1 Content by chapters in key sport history books

	Regional/ national/ continental	Premodern sport	Emergence of modern sport	Themes	Critical historiography	Indigenous sport history	Sport history journals
Pope & Nauright	21	1	—	13	3	—	—
Edelman & Wilson	10	3	4	13	4	—	—
Phillips, Booth, & Adams	1	—	2	16	14	5	9

Introduction

includes a chapter on post-apartheid South Africa because this nation remains the archetypal example of sport and politics where recent social, political, and cultural changes continue to dramatically shape sport domestically and internationally. The other two chapters on the origins and diffusion of modern sport address a foundational theme in our understanding of how particular forms of physical activities emerged in their current forms. The origins and diffusion of modern sport remain a dominant and contested topic in sport history that continues to be reconceptualized.

Another defining feature of Pope and Nauright's *Companion* and Edelman and Wilson's *Handbook* is the attention devoted to key historical categories – particularly class, race, gender, religion, and nationalism – and other organizing concepts that are deemed to have considerably influenced sport such as urbanization, industrialization, communication, science and technology. In Pope and Nauright's *Companion*, these topics make up just under one half of the content, while in Edelman and Wilson's *Handbook*, these topics constitute just over one third.

In this *Handbook* we have continued to explore these key categories and concepts. Their inclusion is important because these topics move very quickly in terms of new paradigms, methods, theories, and concepts. While the cultural turn has shaped the introduction, and much of the content in this volume, there are a host of other turns – animal, archipelagic, digital, experimental representational, geographical, intersectional, linguistic, material, neuroscientific, quantitative, spatial, and transnational – across the humanities and social sciences that have in varying degrees impacted scholarship in sport history. There is healthy scepticism about the proliferation of these turns, and particular concerns that these turns may erase or obscure appropriate, existing paradigms of knowledge formation. Nevertheless, the insights from some of these turns are profoundly shaping how sport historians engage with key categories and concepts: borderlands, class, race, gender, politics, nationalism, international relations, science, sexuality, the visual, and the body. What stands out collectively about the chapters on these pivotal topics (see especially Parts 2 and 3) is their focus on new arguments, their identification of themes that cross traditional categories and conceptual boundaries, and their acknowledgement of the ways in which politics and sport intersect with the sporting past and present.

We also commissioned chapters on emerging topics that have not been covered in previous companions and handbooks of sport history. These topics represent recent shifts in disciplinary knowledge and include sport and emotion, online gambling, sport heritage, disabled sport, digital sport history, sport and material culture, and sport and activism (see Parts 2 and 3). These chapters represent the intersection of emerging interest areas in sport history and broader social and cultural shifts in sport and society. Foremost among these cultural shifts is the growing recognition that sport is a political practice and that professional athletes can, and in some cases should, use sport as a platform for change just as entertainers use the stage and as priests use the pulpit. By logical extension, the growing politicization of sport has given women, people of colour, and ethnic minorities a legitimate and accepted platform to challenge discrimination and inequities. In the same vein, there is an increasing recognition that sport historians should not shy away from politicizing their historical narratives (see the discussion below on self-reflexivity and authorial intent).

The chapters in Part 3 are grouped under three themes: the digital, the affective and the (trans)national. These chapters demonstrate the vibrancy, sophistication and dynamic nature of the subdiscipline and the ability of sport historians to cross disciplinary boundaries, to engage and explore new topics, to recognize and challenge their complicity in reproducing the taken-for-granted assumptions of the subdiscipline, and to contribute to current debates about sport, culture, and society.

Another defining feature of this *Handbook* is that it specifically addresses issues related to the cultural turn in history that have been previously articulated in scholarship about sport history. As Table I.1 indicates, issues driven by the cultural turn surfaced only tangentially in Pope and Nauright's *Companion* and Edelman and Wilson's *Handbook*. The editors of these volumes sparingly addressed the cultural turn through chapters on theory and the historical profession. Pope, Nauright, Edelman, and Wilson were certainly aware of the cultural turn, and their individual scholarship demonstrated an appreciation of historiography, but their emphasis was elsewhere, shaped by their perceptions about sport history, what they valued, and how they wanted to project the subdiscipline to the readership.

For the editors of the current volume, the cultural turn is far more central to sport history. It is a seismic shift that denotes a reversal of epistemological and ontological thinking about the relationship between history and the past. On this basis, we commissioned authors to write with the broad mandate to critically address how sport historians represent the past. Their work covers key issues that have emerged out of debates generated by the cultural turn: reflexivity, narrative, authorial choices, and ethics. Contributors in this *Handbook* tackle reflexivity in history against the background of a widespread acceptance in the profession of authored texts. With different perspectives and in different ways, they demonstrate how historians can work with a heightened state of self-awareness and authorial intent. Narrative is addressed through recognition of its status as the preferred discourse employed by historians: a discourse that represents the past rather than being the past itself; a discourse that is carefully staged with a beginning, middle, and end; and a discourse that is inescapably shaped by the author's ideology, trope, employment, and argument. Authorial choices refer to the seemingly obvious dimension of history: stories do not tell themselves. In this context, the historian takes on a critical role as the storyteller replete with options and decisions about evidence, concepts, voice, perspective, and ideology. Finally, Part 1 of the *Handbook* addresses the ethics of history making. Picking up a theme that resonates through many chapters elsewhere in the volume, sport historians are encouraged to position themselves politically and ideologically so that they produce not only socially responsible history, but socially responsible historical narratives.

A unique feature of this *Handbook*, identified in Table I.1, is the Part dedicated to Indigenous sport history (Part 4). There is a growing body of knowledge, and excellent books, about Indigenous sport history written by sport historians and scholars in other fields of Indigenous studies. Janice Forsyth and Audrey R. Giles's *Aboriginal Peoples and Sport in Canada: Historical Foundations and Contemporary Issues* won the North American Society for Sport History Book Award for Edited Collections (2014) and Allan Downey's *The Creator's Game: Lacrosse, Identity and Indigenous Nationhood* won the English-Language Canada Prize (2019). However, this body of knowledge of Indigenous sport history has not typically been represented in significant volumes in the field. Neither Pope and Nauright's *Companion* nor Edelman and Wilson's *Handbook* contained dedicated chapters on, or extensive references to, the historical relationship between Indigenous people and sport. We specifically address this lack of recognition through the conceptual and analytic framework of settler colonialism that helps explain how Indigenous history has been largely buried in sport history, ironically, through the burgeoning literature on race and sport that is consumed with issues related to African American involvement in North America sport and apartheid sport.

In order to address the silence, this *Handbook* includes a Part on settler colonialism and Indigenous sport in countries which became known as Australia, Canada, Aotearoa/New Zealand, and the United States of America. The chapters in Part 4 collectively acknowledge

Introduction

the centrality of sport to Aboriginal and Torres Strait Islanders in Australia, First Nations, Metis, and Inuit peoples in Canada, Māori in Aotearoa/New Zealand, and Native Americans in the United States of America. Indigenous peoples engage with sport for a wide variety of cultural, social, and political reasons and they do so under the various conditions created by unique formations of settler colonialism. Sport historians, however, are challenged to properly engage with Indigenous history. The traditional training of sport historians, either in schools of history or through kinesiology programmes, does not necessarily provide an appropriate understanding of what is required to work effectively and responsibly in Indigenous communities. This is especially true with regard to sharing knowledge, to collaborating in the process of knowledge production, and to understanding the perspective of voice in historical narratives. With regard to the last-mentioned point, there is a chasm between citing a voice – whether found in the archive or obtained in an interview – and giving a voice authorial control over the narrative. It is thus important that sport history as a subdiscipline gives Indigenous voices the opportunities to both tell their stories and to prefigure and configure narratives. This means encouraging Indigenous voices and authors into sport history; we believe that this *Handbook* makes clear inroads in these respects.

The chapters about Indigenous sport coalesce around a central message that implores sport historians to consider new methodologies, epistemologies, and ontologies with the ultimate objective of meaningfully contributing to decolonization. The kind of critical Indigenous sport history written by the authors in this Part stresses ethically and socially responsible scholarship in the subdiscipline. Similar to other scholarship in this volume about class, race, gender, and sexuality, Indigenous-focused chapters employ the history of sport as a forum to identify inequalities in society and to understand how sport perpetuates, or in some cases, challenges, these inequalities.

The remaining unique feature of this volume is the Part dedicated to sport history journals (Part 5). The initial suggestion for this Part came from Douglas Booth and was fully supported by the co-editors, but there was push back from the commissioning publisher. Routledge asked: Sport history is a relatively small subdiscipline, do journals really play a big part? Are individual chapters on specific sport history journals necessary? Could we not cover journals in a single chapter of the handbook? These were valid questions, and they forced us to carefully think through the value of a whole Part dedicated to journals.

We argue that journals have played and continue to contribute a central role in establishing, defining, and sustaining sport history. Early sport history journals initially provided outlets that evaluated submissions on their scholarly merit, rather than being cursorily dismissed by mainstream journals, which considered sport a trivial and unworthy academic topic. Furthermore, for almost 50 years, sport history journals have provided insights into the breadth and depth of scholarship in the subdiscipline. They present a portal into the subdiscipline and a critical forum of scholarly discourse, capturing shifting interests and fashions, historiographical debates between scholars, and in-depth evaluations of key conceptual issues that have been pivotal in sport history. Analysis of the contents of sport history journals reveal a number of key dimensions: the relationship between scholars and the diverse range of other fields in history; the influence of prominent theorists – from Bourdieu to Foucault to Gramsci; and the interaction with related disciplines – anthropology, cultural studies, geography, kinesiology, and sociology. Looking at the contents of any one of the long-established sport history journals from the 1970s into the new millennium is a reminder of how much the subdiscipline has changed, how much it has matured to become more intellectually sophisticated, and, as recent bibliometrics demonstrate, how successful sport history journals are in a competitive scholarly marketplace.

One interesting, and perhaps defining, feature of sport history is the internationalization of its journals. While English is the *lingua franca* for the vast majority of journals, one third embrace languages other than English. Sport history journals are published in Brazil, Germany, Italy, Spain, and Japan and in their native languages. Examining sport history journals, and soliciting chapters from these non-English journals, expands our understanding of the international scope of sport history as a subdiscipline. It also challenges those of us who only read English language journals to recognize the consequences of privileging a single language and to consider initiatives to break down barriers for our non-English speaking colleagues. Initiatives with this intention will enable the subdiscipline of sport history to fully realize its global potential.

Journals are also a barometer about the health and reach of a scholarly discipline, which also sits beside a very healthy commercial market in the popular history of sport, especially biographies of sports stars. There have been 19 sport history journals since the 1970s and 17 of these are still in existence. The most recent of these journals were created in 2020. From a scholarly production perspective, as well as the academic workforce needed to support this range of journals, sport history looks to be in good shape. This impressive journal footprint and the equally notable quantum of academic output, however, have to be reconciled against the impact of the world-wide constriction of the humanities and, more narrowly, the challenges to sport history as a foundational subdiscipline in kinesiology departments. As the humanities suffer on a global scale, and as kinesiology departments and schools prioritize science, health, and management, sport history is continually required to defend its centrality to sport-related curriculum and its contribution to the humanities. No doubt, in the future, the prevalence of sport history journals and the associated academic output will continue to be a barometer indicating the state of the subdiscipline as it faces ongoing challenges.

In summary, we have approached the introduction to the *Routledge Handbook of Sport History* with a specific purpose. We have endeavoured to be transparent about decisions, selections, and priorities, in order for the reader to get insights into our thinking processes, for all of its strengths and weaknesses. We have deliberately and overtly compared and contrasted this *Handbook* with previous similar volumes as an extension of our thoughts, preferences, and priorities, but equally importantly to highlight the dynamic, sophisticated, and increasingly reflective features of the subdiscipline. As Table I.1 indicates, sport historians are reconceptualizing key content areas, pursuing new areas of knowledge, and taking on the philosophical and practical challenges posed by the various historical turns, most notably the cultural turn and its impact on history making. The subdiscipline is also well served by national associations across the world and a large number of long-established journals emanating out of every continent except Africa and Antarctica, which are published in English, French, Italian, German, Portuguese, Spanish, and Japanese indicating a diverse range of scholars and readers around the world.

PART 1

History and representing the sporting past

1
HISTORY AND REPRESENTING THE SPORTING PAST

Introduction

Douglas Booth, Carly Adams and Murray G. Phillips

Prompted by an amalgam of feminism, postmodernism, and the cultural turn in the humanities and social sciences, historians are increasingly reflecting on, and explicitly addressing, their understanding of, and relationship with, the past. Today, historians working across various subdisciplines are more willing to acknowledge the fallacy of trying to reconstruct the past-as-it-was – whether by assembling remnants from the past or by applying theoretical concepts to the interpretation of empirical evidence. Historians of sport are among those who are engaging with these issues. Collectively, their musings constitute one of the more pronounced shifts in the subdiscipline in recent times and signal the emergence of representational approaches in history or history as a representation of the past.[1] Many of those historians are contributors to this *Handbook*. The opening Part of the *Handbook*, 'History and Representing the Sporting Past', comprises chapters from those who are thinking about, and engaging with, the presentation of the past. Drawing on these contributions, and referring to others in the second Part of the *Handbook*, 'New Perspectives on Old Themes', our introduction to the Part outlines the key issues associated with representations of the sporting past under four headings: reflexivity, narrative, authorial choices, and ethics.

Reflexivity

As a prerequisite for understanding the different ways in which historians subconsciously and consciously present the past, reflexivity refers to a heightened state of self-awareness in which practitioners make continual references to their own involvement in their histories. A reflexive historian explains how they represent the past as history and the different ways they unavoidably influence their presentation of the past; the reflexive historian enters into dialogues with other viewpoints. Reflexivity is a hallmark of all the contributors in this Part. However, reflecting wider paradigmatic and methodological debates in sport history, the contributors offer different perspectives and, in some instances, resolutions.

Malcolm MacLean (Chapter 2) contends that historians 'borrow ideas, techniques, questions, and answers from other subdisciplines', but he also recognizes an absence of broader reflexivity within the subdiscipline. He identifies two persisting structural barriers. The first is

DOI: 10.4324/9780429318306-3

the nature of History (as the discipline of the grand narrative of human time), which tends to discourage self-awareness among its practitioners. MacLean identifies a 'distinctive form ... of knowingness' within the history of sport as a second obstacle. Grounded in 'fandom', this form of knowing, MacLean argues, is unconducive to the reflexivity or critical awareness of the field which is necessary if sport history is to become 'its own object'.

Richard Pringle (Chapter 3) expands MacLean's arguments concerning the absence of critical awareness in sport history in his discussion of the enmity between sport historians and sport sociologists. The ontological, epistemological, theoretical, and methodological antagonisms between the two subdisciplines, Pringle argues, actually belie their 'common political and ideological ground', which he maintains is also shared across the social sciences.[2] As a case in point, Pringle refers to the 'fundamental preoccupations' of feminist sport history and feminist sport sociology; both advocate cultural intervention as an avenue to a 'future beyond patriarchy'.

Like MacLean, Mike Cronin (Chapter 4) discerns historians of sport who have moved past traditional 'empiricism' and who are thinking about 'form, content, value, and narration', and who are questioning 'historic meaning'. However, as with Pringle, Cronin believes that historians of sport have much to learn about historical meaning and that they can profit from a closer engagement with the debates and issues in the broader discipline. Cronin illustrates his case with an insightful survey of the current debates around microhistory and microhistory in the mainstream of the discipline. His crucial point is not that the methodologies of microhistory and microhistory per se are the avenues to an enlightened understanding of historical meaning. On the contrary, Cronin cites examples of historians of sport who have produced quality microhistory and who have engaged with macrohistory.[3] Rather, the lesson comes from the self-reflexive mindsets of the historians who are debating these approaches and who are consciously explaining how they choose their themes, level of detail, contexts, and comparisons (see also Jaime Schultz, Michelle Sikes, and Cat Ariail's Chapter 21 in Part 2 and their discussion of a 'global perspective' and their 'Top 10' list of turns).[4]

Mark Falcous (Chapter 5) agrees with Pringle's and Cronin's propositions that historians of sport can profit from venturing beyond the somewhat narrow confines of the subdiscipline. Falcous directs attention to the newly emerging intellectual stream of physical cultural studies.[5] As well as offering a useful overview of physical cultural studies and its key methodological, theoretical, and political debates, Falcous points historians of sport to a kindred subdiscipline that promotes self-reflexivity, that resides on the fringes of a mainstream field, that is simultaneously vying for a place in the broader scholarly conglomerate of kinesiology/sports studies, and that confronts a generally hostile, anti-intellectual and political climate.

Daniel Nathan (Chapter 6) is another contributor who draws on the literature beyond the immediate realm of sport history. Nathan's references include the philosopher Alex Rosenberg, the critical theorist Linda Hutcheon, mainstream historians Hans Kellner, Peter Novick, and Alan Spitzer, and the philosopher of history, Hayden White. Their works underscore Nathan's argument about the centrality of narrative to our understanding of both sport and the past, and, more fundamentally, to the way we present the sporting past.

Narrative (story)

In his contribution 'Narrative/s in Sport History', Nathan (Chapter 6) encapsulates perhaps the most pronounced shift in the subdiscipline in recent times, namely, the growing

History and representing the sporting past

recognition that history is 'the discourse used to represent and analyse the past, rather than the past itself' with narrative assuming the preferred discourse among historians. A typical narrative, Nathan explains, has a beginning, middle, and end, and each stage prepares and produces what follows. A coherent, effective narrative aligns the parts into a whole and resolves tensions between, or contradictions within, the parts. Crucially, a narrative contains a plot, a mode of organizing the evidence as a genre of story (for example, romance, tragedy, comedy, satire) in order to, in the words of White, 'add meaning – usually a moral meaning' – and to 'wrap' the subject up 'in an account ... from which instruction can be derived'.[6]

The implications of this formulation, which effectively translates history into a narrative representation of the past, are profound. Whereas the traditional idea of history as synonymous with the past emphasizes content and reduces narrative to prose style, the contemporary notion of historical narrative as the means by which historians create the past as history shifts the focus to content *and* form, and highlights the historian-author as an actor in creating our understanding of the past. No contributor offers a better example of the historian-author-actor than Gary Osmond. In Chapter 7, Osmond debunks the notions of history as synonymous with the past and the colonial and postcolonial archives as a locus of truth, objectivity, and neutrality. As he shows, there is increasing recognition that state archives generally exclude the memories and experiences of Indigenous communities. Osmond urges historians to take more care when contextualizing the archives. 'In order to understand individual documents,' he writes, 'we must know what the archive contains and understand how records are written, represented, and stored in terms of language, context, and categorization.' More importantly, Osmond proposes that historians can assist Indigenous communities to recover their pasts and construct alternative perspectives to those found in the written records. They can do this, he suggests, by taking archival material directly to communities or by annotating records. This brings us to authorial choices, the third of our key issues associated with representations of the sporting past.

Authorial choices

As Nathan reminds us, and as Osmond demonstrates, 'stories don't tell themselves – they are crafted by storytellers' who make choices at every turn. Authors select the content, including the empirical evidence and analytical concepts; they decide the form of the story including its metaphors, tropes, plots, arguments, and the narrator's voice and perspective. Nathan offers several examples of how those choices can change the way we understand and interpret the past. In the remainder of this subsection we comment on three choices: perspectives and conceptualizations, and theory.

Perspectives and conceptualizations

The second Part of the *Handbook* comprises chapters from contributors who offer new perspectives on enduring themes within the subfield. These include the origins of modern sport, sexuality, nationalism, race and racism, time and space, and politics. While new perspectives and conceptualizations can emerge along with fresh evidence and freshly formulated analytical concepts and theories, ultimately, their presentation depends on the choices made by historian-authors: the past does not produce perspectives and conceptualizations any more than it writes narratives.[7] Indeed, much of the impetus for recent perspectives and conceptualizations in the history of sport derives from a paradigmatic shift in the humanities and social sciences known as the cultural turn.[8] Somewhat arbitrarily, we include the chapters by Maureen Smith, Angie Abdou, and Russell Field in this Part. In their reconceptualizations of material culture (Smith and Abdou) and sports activism (Field), these authors illustrate our point about historians as authors who make choices about the past.

Smith (Chapter 8) offers two particularly clear examples of choices about the representation of the past in her discussions of sport museums and halls of fame, and cultural fragments. While the stories told in sport museums and halls of fame typically glorify and celebrate sports participants (players, administrators, spectators), professional historians tend to present a different genre of story based on critique, complexity, and nuance. It is not the past per se that dictates these forms of representation, rather it is the historian's perspectives, conceptualizations, and interpretations (see also Sarah Barnes and Mary McDonald's discussion on memorialization in Chapter 19, 'Race, Racism, and Racial Entanglements', in Part 2). Similarly, in her discussion of the increasing interest among historians in material fragments from the sporting past (e.g. ticket stubs, mascot figures, sports shoes, tape measures – the list is endless), Smith observes the important roles of the senses and emotions in attaching meaning to those fragments and ultimately 'how we tell stories and how we remember a story' (see also Barbara Keys' Chapter 27 in Part 3). Historians have, of course, always confronted incomplete and biased fragments from the past that have posed problems for analysis and interpretation; introducing human senses and emotions merely compounds the problem. However, the reconceptualization of material culture under the impetus of the cultural turn is, as Smith indicates, helping historians become more comfortable with ambiguity and doubt, and empowering them to write different types of stories that deal with an 'uncertain past'.[9] This is precisely the kind of reflexivity referred to by MacLean, Cronin, and Falcous.

Abdou (Chapter 9) adds weight to Smith's notions about the uncertain past and the importance of understanding and embracing human senses in her chapter about historical fiction. Abdou's example of Samantha Warwick's *Sage Island* (2008), a story about open-water swimming in the 1920s, is especially edifying, with the narrative 'combin[ing] the historical and the visceral'. Warwick, Abdou argues, 'capture[s] the physical sensations of the sport' including the initial immersion in the water, the '"underwater glide, the flying, weightless sensation of being suspended-free"' and others associated with the unfolding race: the '"racket of breaking water and muffled echo, a tumble of ache, throbbing shoulders, and smarting red eyelids"'. As Abdou demonstrates, fiction – the archetypal authorial choice – has been critical to bringing the human senses to representations of the past.[10]

In his big picture overview of sport as political activism in the twentieth and twenty-first centuries, Russell Field (Chapter 10) acknowledges that there are multiple ways to consider the subject. These include 'distinguishing between individual activists and social movements', and 'considering … activism that has focused on change both *in* and *through* sport'. Where the latter seeks to 'alter the landscape of and accessibility to sport', the former focuses on 'the platform sport affords to advocate for societal changes that extend beyond sport' (see also Heather Dichter, 'Sport and Politics', Chapter 16 in Part 2). Field offers a fresh conceptualization of the subject and a range of evocative examples. His reference to 'the judgement of history' touches, as does Smith, on a critical element of the representational approach to the past: historical narratives are cultural interventions.

Theory

The place of theory in history has been a source of endless debate within the discipline and no less so than among historians of sport and, in particular, between sport historians and sport sociologists.[11] Historians committed to the reconstruction of the past-as-it-was deem theory an unwanted intervention in the representation of the past and claim that it 'infuses predestined meaning' into history.[12] Others, however, insist that theory provides crucial blueprints for the interpretation of historical evidence. Jeffrey Hill, for example, notes that 'many of the influences that have come into history from theoretical sources have been invigorating, if only because ... they have forced ... historians out of the[ir] epistemological insularity'.[13] By putting the form of an historical presentation on par with its content, the representational approach to the past effectively renders the debates over theory 'pointless'.[14] Pringle veers towards this conclusion in his contribution. On the other hand, in their chapter on race and racism in sport, Barnes and McDonald (see Chapter 19, Part 2) illustrate the insights that can be gained when historians take an open approach and are prepared to reflect on, and recontextualize theory.[15] Employing the concept of entanglement, as put forward by the South African literary theorist Sarah Nuttall, Barnes and McDonald remind us that race and racism must be understood not only in the 'isolation or separation of groups' but also in the 'myriad of complex racial connections, interdependencies, intersections, memories, and intimacies'. Neither historical, political or sociological facts nor processes reside at the centre of entanglement; rather, it is a concept grounded in '"gaps, blind sports, mistakes, paradoxes, ironies, anomalies, and invisibilities"'. Ashwin Desai, too, displays a similar form of what might be called theoretical reflexivity in his discussion of non-racialism in South African sport (see 'Sport in Post-apartheid South Africa: The Race to Class', Chapter 20 in Part 2). Platoons of political and social theorists have unsuccessfully attempted to theorize the form of non-racialism adopted by the anti-apartheid South African Council on Sport (SACOS). Desai, who grew up in the world of SACOS, dispenses with the theory and reconceptualizes non-racialism as a 'felt principle', one that was 'internalized ... through ... participation in the struggle' where it 'came to possess a power and clarity that approached self-evidence', but which simultaneously proved extremely difficult to 'translat[e] ... into reality'.

If representational approaches to the past reduce historical narratives to cultural interventions, the question arises, can we tell the truth about the past?[16] For many of the contributors to the *Handbook*, this is a question about ethics which we discuss in the final part of this introduction.

Ethics

Social responsibility is at the fore in Pringle's, Osmond's, Barnes and McDonald's, and Desai's chapters; it is implicit in the contributions of Judy Davidson, Jaquelyn Osborne and Chelsea Litchfield, and Jaime Schultz, Michelle Sikes, and Cat Ariail in Part 2 of the *Handbook*. For these contributors, historical meaning 'flows', in the words of the philosopher of history Alun Munslow, 'from what is good or socially responsible to believe about the evidence of the past rather than to discover its true moral content'.[17] Hayden White agrees that the choices historians make with regard to their representations are fundamentally ethical issues, although he is less confident that historians always channel their narratives towards social responsibility and he is aware of the possibility of unpalatable alternative narratives.[18]

By raising the issue of socially responsible history and socially responsible historical narratives, Pringle and Osmond are encouraging the reflexivity advocated by MacLean, Cronin, and Falcous. Implicit in this reflexivity are questions about how historians position themselves politically and ideologically. While historians of sport have traditionally shied from these questions for fear of attracting the label of activist and the associated connotations of bias, they are an inextricable part of the emerging representational approach to the past. Indeed, one historian of sport has already lit the torch on the question of socially responsible narratives. 'My bias is clear,' declared Colin Tatz in *Obstacle Race: Aborigines in Sport*:

> it is pro-Aboriginal in most things and anti-racist in all things. I am not politically correct and do criticise some Aboriginal attitudes and behaviour. Every effort is made to be meticulous about matters of fact, but I cannot hide my anger or frustration at facts that by their nature embody either evil, moral turpitude or professional negligence.[19]

Tatz's words, and those of many of the contributors to this *Handbook*, are proof writ large that the history of sport is in the midst of change with regards to how it understands and represents the sporting past.

Notes

1 Dave Day and Wray Vamplew, 'Sports History Methodology: Old and New', *The International Journal of the History of Sport* 32, no. 15 (2015): 1715.
2 While better known for his sociology, Pringle has credibility in sport history as the co-author (with Murray Phillips) of the award-winning text, *Examining Sport Histories: Power, Paradigms, and Reflexivity* (Morgantown, West Virginia: Fitness Information Technology, 2013). In 2015, *Examining Sport Histories* received the ASSH award for best edited collection.
3 To Cronin's list, we cite Courtney Mason's recent work as an exemplary example of sport history that combines micro and macro approaches. See 'Colonial Encounters, Conservation, and Sport Hunting in Banff National Park', in *Sport and Recreation in Canadian History*, ed. Carly Adams (Champaign, IL: Human Kinetics, 2021), 77–100.
4 For an excellent example of how fresh context can change historical understanding, see Danielle Peers and Lisa Tink, 'Rereading Histories and Inclusive Recreation, Physical Education, and Sport', in Adams, *Canadian History*, 203–227.
5 Some readers may dismiss Falcous as a sport sociologist, an outsider. However, he has established his bona fides as an historian of sport. In 2010 the Australian Society for the History of Sport awarded him the Tom Brock Scholarship to research the issue of identity in New Zealand rugby league. See Mark Falcous, 'The Paradoxes of Provincialism, Nationalism and Imperialism: Otago Rugby Union(s), League and Amateurism', *Sporting Traditions* 30, no. 2 (2013): 15–31. See also, Mark Falcous, 'Rugby League in the National Imaginary of New Zealand Aotearoa', *Sport in History* 27, no. 3 (2007): 423–446.
6 Hayden White, *The Practical Past* (Evanston, IL: Northwestern University Press, 2014), 83.
7 For elaboration of this point see Alun Munslow's discussion of the distinction between reference and representation in *The Routledge Companion to Historical Studies*, 2nd edition (London: Routledge, 2006), 223.
8 The term cultural turn refers to the shift away from the social history approaches that dominated both mainstream history and sport history in the last quarter of the twentieth century and the embrace of culture as articulated through language, texts, and narratives. On the cultural turn see Victoria Bonnell and Lynn Hunt, 'Introduction', in *Beyond the Cultural Turn: New Directions in the Study of Society and Culture*, eds. Victoria Bonnell and Lynn Hunt (Berkeley, CA: University of California Press, 1999), 1–32.
9 Julia Laite, 'Radical Uncertainty', *History Workshop*, 16 September 2020, https://www.historywork shop.org.uk/radical-uncertainty/. For an example in sport history see Fiona McLachlan, '"You Can't Take a Picture of This – It's Already Gone": Erased Evidence, Political Parody, Postmodern Histories', *Sporting Traditions* 27, no. 2 (2010): 91–100, and Douglas Booth and Fiona McLachlan, 'Who's Afraid of the Internet? Swimming in an Infinite Archive', in *Sports History in the Digital Era*, eds. Gary Osmond and Murray Phillips (Urbana: University of Illinois Press, 2015), 227–250.
10 See also, Michael Oriard, *Reading Football: How the Popular Press Created an American Spectacle* (Chapel Hill: University of North Carolina Press, 2001), and Jeffrey Hill, *Sport and the Literary Imagination: Essays in History, Literature and Sport* (Oxford: Peter Lang, 2006).

History and representing the sporting past

11 See, for example, Douglas Booth and Mark Falcous, 'History and Sociology: Connections and Divisions in Critical Sport Studies', in *Routledge Handbook of the Sociology of Sport*, ed. Richard Giulianotti (London: Routledge, 2015), 153–163.
12 Geoffrey Elton, *Return to Essentials: Some Reflections on the Present State of Historical Study* (Cambridge: Cambridge University Press, 1991), 15.
13 Hill, *Sport and the Literary Imagination*, 11.
14 Alun Munslow, *The Future of History* (Houndsmills, UK: Palgrave Macmillan, 2010), 221.
15 See, for example, Jeffrey Nealon and Susan Searls Giroux, *The Theory Toolbox: Critical Concepts for the Humanities, Arts, and Social Sciences*, 2nd edition (New York: Rowman and Littlefield, 2012), which also contains a highly relevant chapter titled 'History'.
16 Yes, insist Joyce Appleby, Lynn Hunt, and Margaret Jacob in *Telling the Truth About History* (New York: W.W. Norton, 1994). They conjure a reconstructionist epistemology, which they call practical realism, to defend the traditional disciplinary project of representing the past-as-it-was. Practical realism is undoubtedly the default epistemology in the history of sport but few practitioners advance a convincing case.
17 Munslow, *Historical Studies*, 13.
18 White, *Practical Past*, 77.
19 Colin Tatz, *Obstacle Race: Aborigines in Sport* (Sydney: University of New South Wales Press, 1995), 23. Among his criticisms, Colin challenged Aborigines for not using sport as a political weapon especially in the lead up to the 2000 olympic games. Tatz, *Obstacle Race*, 24 and 347–348.

2

REFLEXIVITY IN SPORT HISTORY[1]

Malcolm MacLean

Speaking at the 2002 Cheltenham Literature Festival, Eric Hobsbawm suggested that for most historians engagement with theory came when they asked their questions.[2] This response is entirely consistent with Historians'[3] perceptions of our field as empiricist; Hobsbawm should probably be understood as suggesting that, rather than absent, theory is secondary to the evidence we adduce from explorations of settings, texts, documents and material, and other artefacts. In the more conventional modes of History writing, no doubt our theoretical and conceptual outlooks shape the form of our constructed plausible narratives that paper over the evidential gaps, while also shaping our understanding of the relationships between actors, parties, and others in our histories. It is probably reasonable to conclude that our implicit theoretical presence suggests a well-developed awareness of self by Historians – yet to a very large degree History remains remarkably self-unaware.

Sport history's academic genealogy makes it no better or worse at this self-awareness than most other sub-disciplines. For much of its first few decades sport history remained deeply grounded in the empiricist orientation Hobsbawm invoked in 2002, in this sense running parallel to most of the rest of the discipline in remaining 'silent concerning ourselves' and justified by a Popperian appeal to 'objective knowledge'.[4] Noting this persistent empiricist frame, critiques of sport history's early failures in terms of, amongst other analytical categories, gender and race should be seen as a quest for better evidence leading to comprehensiveness, and not necessarily an ontological critique. As with most other strands of historical practice, sport history's enhanced reflexivity and its becoming as if an object of study is linked to recent post-structuralist engagements and the 'cultural turn' in historiographical practice.[5] The upshot has been a limited demystification of practice and some heightened methodological explicitness, although the field still falls short of a systemic approach where it 'tak(es) itself as an object, [and] makes use of its own tools to understand and monitor itself'.[6] There is hope for enhanced reflexivity through an emerging endogenous historiography.

Sport history's ontological reflexivity

In becoming its own object, sport history's self-awareness turns on two subjects, both common to other forms of social and cultural history as structured social-cultural practice with a high degree of formalized organization. The first of these is an awareness of self, of the presence and

16

DOI: 10.4324/9780429318306-4

characteristics of the Historian in the object, while the second is the constructedness of the subject, of sport. As is the case with the study of many other cultural forms, those who study sport are often expected by both practitioners and critics, to be practitioners or followers, and seem to be slotted into the hierarchy of the popular and the 'serious' that Lawrence Grossberg criticized, where as a scholar of rock music he was classified as a 'fan', rather than labelled in the way 'aficionados' of opera might be.[7] Historians often seem expected to justify their work by emphasizing the importance of the field of study. Historians of sport tend to argue that the subject matters both in itself and in what it stands for, yet it seems often presumed that we are practitioners/players, struggling with a duality of being both fans *and* scholars.

This blurring of the distinctions between practitioners, fans, and scholars, thereby validating the analyst as experiential self, is not uncommon in other fields of study of popular culture, yet among those fields sport could, arguably, be seen as notable for the degree of its popular historicization (popular music scholars might make the same case). This may be seen in the 'sport' section of many bookshops, where the 'popular' historical treatments of sport are manifold, and much more common than 'scholarly' treatments, to the extent that distinction is clear.[8] The extent of sports' popular historicization however may best be seen in social spaces, especially those where men tend to congregate, although the male preserve seems to be weakening. In these settings we can expect to overhear or join in deeply argued, often arcane and detailed, discussions of aspects of sports' historical significance, pointing to the second way that sport history overlaps with other forms of the historicization of popular culture in that very often its historians and intellectuals are organic, and are in actuality fully fledged participants and practitioners. In this sense, the presumption of participation if not fandom may set sport history aside from many other forms of History but may not be unusual in the subject area and may be a sign of distinctive forms of knowing.

That sport history might be marked by a sense of organic knowingness that is distinctive must remain conjecture, largely because there is little in the way of cross field scholarship. The particular circumstances of the UK, where the subject is under pressure in higher education, and where changes in focus by scholarly societies meant that historians of leisure were seen as becoming adrift from a scholarly home, mean that steps have been taken towards a consilience of sport and leisure history.[9] For the most part and much like many other sub-fields of history, sport history has a tendency to be introspective. Some of this is driven by a desire of sub-disciplines to mark their own turf; other forces include the current political economy of higher education, an imperative to publish, and a commercially driven proliferation of academic journals, even among those most would not classify as predatory. In the Anglophone world this turf marking means that the reflexivity stimulated by engagements with close Others is often weak, whereas the discipline may borrow ideas, techniques, questions, and answers from other sub-disciplines, critical reflection on the subject prompted by cross-boundary analyses of leisure or of other cultural industries remains underdeveloped. Consequently, self-understanding and self-monitoring is less sophisticated than it might be.

A particular challenge for sport history may be the identification of those close Others, where there is some growing inter- and transdisciplinary analysis, especially between scholars grounded in history and in sociology. In part this might be a consequence of the home for both of these disciplines, more sociology than history, in sport studies and kinesiology programmes; equally significant is likely to be that sport history, as an off-spring of social history, traverses many of the same areas as sociology, although the extent to which the disciplines speak past each other needs further exploration. In the absence of a rigorous analysis, it seems that despite efforts such as the co-hosting of the 2007 congresses of the International Society for the History of Physical Education and Sport and the International

Sociology of Sport Association in Copenhagen, the relationship remains one of polite but mutual incomprehension. There are similar flirtations in other disciplines: the editors of the 'New Horizons in the Economics of Sport' series have included two volumes of essays in economic history.[10] For the most part, though, these external associations and therefore sites to encourage enhanced disciplinary reflexivity remain intermittent and subjects of study as close Others remain weakly recognized, let alone developed.

Sport history has in recent years become more aware of the artificiality of the stuff of its study, that not only is sport constructed, but the means of its construction has become an increasingly important area of inquiry. Engagement with constructedness, and with cross-disciplinary reflexive critique, has seen a growing awareness of not just who plays, but what plays, as analysts have focused on bodies in movement as essential to the comprehension of sport, and of changes in those moving bodies as vital to sport history. Much of that work has come from scholars exploring those players who are not the presumed norm of the field's practice – those players who are women, Indigenous, peoples of colour. Some of that work has challenged sport history to significantly rethink its silences about bodily practice, including ways that the presumptions of medicine were used to justify social constraints on women's physicality,[11] the kinds of developments that facilitated women's sport participation,[12] the production of comprehensible Indigenous bodies through sports' disciplining powers,[13] sports contested place in the maintenance of colonial power,[14] or the significance of bodily mediated (re)presentation in ideologies of 'race'.[15] That there are more and increasingly widespread voices pulling sport history away from its implicit characteristics suggests that they are making it more aware of its form.

This increasing self-awareness may be seen not only as a consequence of changes in questions, but also through changes in methods. Consider the rise of visually aware methodologies that may be seen in the pairing of methodological and empirical discussions as well as work across sport history and art history.[16] In this cross-disciplinary work we see engagements with near Others that help enhance awareness of sport history's limits. The consequent disciplinary self-awareness is articulated to a longer standing sense of reflexivity in visual cultural studies.[17] Along with these senses of constructedness is a growing but seldom articulated sense of the limitations of evidence, where in most cases inquiries into the development and growth of sport are limited to the innovations that worked; although sport is distinct among the cultural industries as performing its failures in public, this is not the case for all its innovations. Technological innovation, for instance, is often marked in the record only through success – although there is one notable exception to this, the development of rules, where often there is a record of the debates.[18] The predominantly social history orientation of the field however means that this absence of a record of failure has had only limited epistemological impact.

Sport history's epistemological reflexivity

The absence of attention to failure with its consequent epistemological certainty may be seen also in sport history's surety about the practices framed as sport in a tendency to treat them as consistent across cultural contexts.[19] Modernity's hierarchies construct modern sport as a 'civilized' (that is, regulated) development of 'raucous' folk sports, more so in the UK where an Eliasian 'civilizing process' discourse influences much of sport studies. Irrespective of the continuing debates over both the specifics and generalities of this approach, its overwhelmingly teleological ontology, in part a consequence of the failure to attend to failure, undermines disciplinary reflexivity and scepticism despite the doubts of many of the field's practitioners. Similarly, the tendency to authorial rather than disciplinary reflexivity common in more post-modern inflected approaches may also reinforce a tendency to teleology through a centring of the 'experiential self'. This boundary-reinforcing silence may be seen in two aspects of the field: the absence of play and the difficulties it has in discussing pleasure; and recent attention to Indigenous world-views and colonizing power in explorations of sport in colonial contexts.[20] The questions of play and of pleasure are likely to be an effect of sources and the challenges of writing the experiential,[21] while the issue of the Other as context and as in a dialogic relation to modern sport remains a largely unexplored question of the anthropological self. Where reflexive attention to the self has a tendency to focus on the authorial rather than the kinesiological-experiential, it would benefit from a wider anthropological disposition evaluating relative emphasis on the emic and the etic (that is, explicit attention to concepts relevant to and with meanings derived from units and distinctions *internal* and *external* respectively to the subject of inquiry).

Here sport history confronts a two-stranded constraint on its self-awareness, derived from the problems in identifying Others and from the question of the anthropological self. These two are further linked to the field's tendency to methodological nationalism[22] where at best comparative analyses stand in for transnational practice, resulting in an implicit universalization of experience. Consider the word 'football' with its multiple place-specific meanings, often contested in localities where more than one code is widespread, but often associated with the dominant code. Turning to Australia, in Melbourne 'footy' may mean the game played following the Australian rules yet in Sydney or Central Queensland it is likely to mean the 13-a-side version of rugby (although the social venue associated with the sport is as likely to be the Leagues Club, not the Footy Club).[23] Local histories of the game are unlikely to tease out this distinction; global histories tend to focus on a single code, noting the exception of Collins' recent global multi-code history.[24] The combined tendency to code and national specificity means that despite acknowledgement of variation, football's historians tend to talk past each other. The universalizing tendency applies to football's social articulations, where a sense of universal Whiteness presents 'soccer' in the United States as a predominantly women's sport (American Football having the masculinist associations of dominant football codes elsewhere) and in doing so writes out of many analyses the more prevalent associations of *futbal* with masculinity in the United States' Latinx communities, demonstrating a remarkable lack of a critical awareness of a disciplinary self. Notable exceptions aside, a more critically self-aware discipline could develop a transnational engagement with histories of sport as a cultural flow across various settings.[25]

This methodological nationalism may be seen in the field's dominant modes of periodization as an organizing tool for practice and comprehension. The field is framed by an overwhelmingly North Atlantic outlook that locates sport as a practice shaped by the key developments of capitalist modernity in western Europe and North America. An example of the limitations of this periodization may be seen in Sánchez García's recent historical sociology of Japanese martial arts.[26] This is an epistemologically complex text. Sánchez García develops his analysis fully within a Japanese context and draws powerfully on notions derived from Japanese body culture all of which is read through an Eliasian civilizing process. Despite the alertness to the Japanese frame, and the periodization of Japanese history via the relevant Shōgunates until the mid-nineteenth century, Sánchez García locates 'modern' martial arts coming together in the final third of the nineteenth century, resulting in a periodization that parallels the North Atlantic nexus that sees modern sport as a product of the same era. This periodization of sport seems at odds with the Japanese-centric evidential emphasis where source scepticism does not seem to have been accompanied by frame scepticism with the result that Japanese martial arts become sport not because of a demonstrable endogenous force, but because sport may be seen as those body cultures that concurrently cohered into an organized form at this time. Although this frame scepticism can be seen in sports history, in Hoberman's notion of Olympic Internationalism for instance, it remains less common than might be expected.[27] There have, in other settings, been suggestive analyses pointing to different periodizations and therefore different analytical frames. Schultz's exploration of women's sport in North America drawing on Gerda Lerner's notion of points of change suggests a very different frame through which to make sense of women in/and sport.[28]

Sport history, becoming its own object

Despite the value of reflexivity to the field's insights and meaningfulness, much of the recent debate about the ontology of sport history, its methodologies and its epistemic characteristics, has blurred into or conflated with the hard empiricist rejection of 'Theory', where Theory is seen as undermining the integrity of evidence-driven analyses. Many, but not all, of these debates have been spurred by responses to Booth's *The Field* and might be better seen as an expression of a disquiet widespread in the sub-discipline towards model building, exacerbated by Booth's deployment of work by Alun Munslow.[29] While Munslow, in particular, provided much of the initial basis and framing device for Booth's argument, equally important and often ignored in much of the debate was the influence of David Hackett Fischer's much more conventionally framed assessment of historiographical practice.[30] The relevance of Booth's analysis here lies not so much in its specifics than in the historiographical argument made.

To a large degree sports history has drawn on parent sub-disciplines for its historiographical frames, meaning that the field lacks an endogenous ontology. Historiography matters in these contexts because, until recently, it was by far the dominant way in which we taught historians' methodologies, where the focus on how arguments are made was the heart of the discipline's reflexive praxis. Just as Booth did, these were analyses of rhetoric, of evidential deployment, of epistemological orientation, of ontology, and of the veracity and origin of various texts, yet without a well-developed historiography of its own, sport history remains reflexively bound to other praxis, which might in part account for its difficulties in identifying and demarcating its near Others. These endogenous historiographies are both essential to and a product of an enhanced systemic reflexivity and therefore lie at the core of sport history becoming its own object.

A growing willingness to engage in historiographical discussions, most obviously since the later 2000s, has interwoven with assessments of the state of the field *including* its institutions. Alongside the discussions prompted by Booth's work, two sets of publications by leading figures in several of the scholarly societies set about unpacking the state of the field, exploring the kinds of political and academic responses that could or should be considered and sought ways to put the field on a more secure institutional and scholarly basis.[31] Along the way, an assessment of the place of sports history in the wider field of American history prompted further ontological and historiographical consideration, although in a replay of the subject's methodological nationalism this remained largely distinct from a parallel discussion in the UK.[32] Each of these discussions turned its gaze onto the field as a site of scholarly practice and as institutionalized in specialist scholarly societies or fractions within wider disciplinary bodies, university departments, or articulated to discussions and approaches beyond the academy. Even where the dominant Anglophone discourses are interrupted by

Reflexivity in sport history

interventions drawing on non-Anglophone contexts, pervasive methodological nationalism undermines much more than a cursory nodding towards other settings.[33] This largely taken for granted methodological nationalism – an assessment based on its pervasiveness and the silences that surround it – is becoming explicitly discussed in nascent moves towards transnational analyses and in the light of emerging decolonial themes.[34]

These developments since the mid-2000s mark sport history as becoming the object of its own study. The insights prompted by Booth's *The Field* and subsequent explorations of reflexive subjectivity and the emergence of a post-modernish cultural turn represent the best opportunity for the emergence of an endogenous historiography, acknowledging the social, economic, and cultural disciplinary homes of sport history while building its own self-aware approaches and understandings of its praxis.[35] Despite sport history's uncertain place in the academy, this emerging tendency to become an object of analysis is heartening, as is the growing presence of those discussions in pedagogically orientated texts.[36] Polley, in particular, highlights the distinctive methodological tropes of a subject rooted in the banalities of the everyday.[37] This emergence of an endogenous methodological awareness is an essential step in becoming an object of its study that, when considered alongside the need to engage more rigorously with close Others and the nascent hints of a move beyond methodological nationalism, points to circumstances where a more sceptical reflexivity might find a base for growth.

Notes

1 Limitations of space and my linguistic deficiencies mean this is a largely Anglophone assessment, although I have seen little to suggest that the situation is different in other national contexts or settings shaped by different colonial matrices of power.
2 From my notes, taken on the day.
3 I use upper case (History/Historians/Theory) to indicate a powerful dominant discourse shaping the practice of the discipline and an idealization of some of its practitioners; it indicates a semi-autonomous hegemonic force beyond any individual.
4 Emmanuel Kant, *Critique of Pure Reason* (London: Penguin, 2007); Karl Popper, *The Logic of Scientific Discovery* (London: Penguin, 2002).
5 As seen, for instance, in Keith Jenkins, *Re-Thinking History* (London: Routledge, 1991); Frank Ankersmit and Hans Kellner eds. *A New Philosophy of History* (London: Reaktion Books, 1995); Douglas Booth, *The Field: Truth and Fiction in Sport History* (London: Routledge, 2004); Mike Cronin, 'Reflections on the Cultural Paradigm', *Sporting Traditions* 27, no. 2 (2010): 1–13; Caroline Daley, '"The Ref's Turned a Blind Ear": The Cultural Paradigm and New Zealand's Sport History', *Sporting Traditions* 27, no. 2 (2010): 14–27; Daniel A. Nathan, 'Asking a Fish about Water: The Notes Toward an Understanding of "The Cultural Turn" and Sport History', *Sporting Traditions* 27, no. 2 (2010): 29–44; Jaime Schultz, 'Leaping into the Turn: Towards a New Cultural Sport History', *Sporting Traditions* 27, no. 2 (2010): 45–59; Murray Phillips, 'Commentary', *Sporting Traditions* 27, no. 2 (2010): 61–69.
6 Marco D'Eramo, 'They, The People' *New Left Review* 103 (2017): 134.
7 Lawrence Grossberg, 'Is There a Fan in the House? The Affective Sensibility of Fandom', in *The Adoring Audience: Fan Culture and Popular Media*, ed. L. Lewis (London: Routledge, 1992), 50–68. This section is based on my interpretation of the field after being in and around it for 25 years, having cut my historical teeth in the much less value laden field of urban and working class social history; even now that contrast remains viscerally felt.
8 Definitions are fraught here, and it would be nigh on impossible to count the number of historical books about sport published in any year, and numbers vary widely taking account of significant national events as well as global mega-events. It would not be unreasonable to assume many hundreds of these books are published each year. By way of comparison, the most wide-reaching scholarly sports history prize, the annual award by the North American Society for Sports History, would see around 50 titles submitted each year covering single subject books and anthologies.

9 See, for instance, the BSSH Sport & Leisure History seminar series at London's Institute of Historical Research (https://www.history.ac.uk/seminars/sport-and-leisure-history, accessed 8 May 2021).

10 Richard Pomfert and John K. Wilson eds. *Sport Through the Lens of Economic History* (Cheltenham, UK: Edward Elgar Publishing, 2017); John K. Wilson and Richard Pomfert eds. *Historical Perspectives on Sports Economics: Lessons from the Field* (Cheltenham, UK: Edward Elgar Publishing, 2019).

11 Patricia Vertinsky, *The Eternally Wounded Woman: Women, Doctors, and Exercise in the Late Nineteenth Century* (Urbana, IL: University of Illinois Press, 1994).

12 Jaime Schultz highlights tampons and sports bras as major factors in *Qualifying Times: Points of Change in U.S. Women's Sport* (Urbana, IL: University of Illinois Press, 2014).

13 Brendan Hokowhitū, 'Authenticating Māori Physicality: Translations of "Games" and "Pastimes" by Early Travellers and Missionaries to New Zealand', *The International Journal of the History of Sport* 25, no. 10 (2008): 1355–1373.

14 Allan Downey, *The Creator's Game: Lacrosse, Identity, and Indigenous Nationhood* (Vancouver: UBC Press, 2018); Janice Forsyth, *Reclaiming Tom Longboat: Indigenous Self-Determination in Canadian Sport* (Regina: University of Regina Press, 2020).

15 James E. Brunson III, *The Early Image of Black Baseball: Race and Representation in the Popular Press, 1871–1890* (Jefferson, NC: McFarlane and Co, 2009).

16 Mike Huggins and Mike O'Mahoney eds. *The Visual in Sport* (Abingdon: Routledge, 2014); Gillian Poulter, *Becoming Native in a Foreign Land: Sport, Visual Culture, and Identity in Montreal, 1840–85* (Vancouver: UBC Press, 2009).

17 Markus Stauff, 'The Assertive Image: Referentiality and Reflexivity in Sports Photography', *Historical Social Research* 43, no. 2 (2018): 53–71. https://doi.org/10.12759/hsr.43.2018.2.53-71

18 See, for instance, Tony Collins, *Rugby League in Twentieth Century Britain: A Social and Cultural History* (Abingdon: Routledge, 2006), 105–115; Lew Freeman, *Baugh to Brady: The Evolution of the Forward Pass* (Lubbock, TX: Texas Tech University Press, 2018).

19 This tension is woven through many of the contributions to *The Allure of Sports in Western Culture*, eds. John Zilcosky and Marlo A Burks (Toronto, University of Toronto Press, 2019).

20 Downey, *The Creator's Game*; Benjamin Sacks, *Cricket, Kirikiti and Imperialism in Samoa, 1879–1939* (Basingstoke: Palgrave, 2019); John Bale, *Imagined Olympians* (Minneapolis: Minnesota University Press, 2002); Carly Adams ed. *Sport and Recreation in Canadian History* (Champaign, IL: Human Kinetics Press, 2021).

21 For a case where writing the experiential works, see Jean-Philippe Toussaint, *Soccer* (New Brunswick, NJ: Rutgers University Press, 2019).

22 Ulrich Beck, 'The Cosmopolitan Condition: Why Methodological Nationalism Fails', *Theory, Culture, Society* 24, no. 7 (2007): 286–290.

23 An early effort to explore this question came with the Australian-based Football Studies Group and its journal *Football Studies* between 1997 and 2006. More recently, since 2015 the UK-based Football Collective has developed into a multi-code network after launching as a 'soccer'-specific research group that was subsequently joined by researchers exploring other forms of the game.

24 Tony Collins, *How Football Began: A Global History of How the World's Football Codes Were Born* (Abingdon: Routledge, 2019).

25 These rare and notable exceptions include Vertinsky, *The Eternally Wounded Woman* and Janelle Joseph, *Sport in the Black Atlantic: Cricket, Canada and the Caribbean Diaspora* (Manchester: Manchester University Press, 2017).

26 Raul Sánchez García, *The Historical Sociology of Japanese Martial Arts* (Abingdon: Routledge, 2019).

27 John Hoberman, 'Toward a Theory of Olympic Internationalism', *Journal of Sport History* 22, no. 1 (1995): 1–37.

28 Schultz, *Qualifying Times*.

29 Alun Munslow, *Deconstructing History* (London: Routledge, 1997).

30 David Hackett Fischer, *Historians Fallacies: Toward a Logic of Historical Thought* (New York: Harper-Perennial, 1970).

31 Mark Dyerson, 'Sport History and the History of Sport in North America', *Journal of Sport History* 34, no. 3 (2007): 405–414; Martin Johnes, 'British Sports History: The Present and its Future', *Journal of Sport History* 35, no. 1 (2008): 65–71; Thierry Terret, 'The Future of Sport History: ISHPES, Potential and Limits', *Journal of Sport History* 35, no. 2 (2008): 303–309. Tara Magdalinski, 'Sports History in Australia: Past Achievements, Future Challenges', *Journal of Sport History* 36, no. 1 (2009):

123–128; NASSH President's Forum, organized by Kevin Walmsley in 2016 (https://www.nassh.org/presidents-forum/ accessed 8 May 2021).

32 Amy Bass, 'State of the Field: Sports History and the "Cultural Turn"', *Journal of American History* 101, no 1 (2014): 148–172; Sarah Fields, 'Sport Studies: A Model for the Twentieth-first-century University', *Journal of Sport History* 43, no. 1 (2015): 56–65; Andrew Linden, 'Tempering the Dichotomous Flame: Social History, Cultural History, and Postmodernism(s) in the *Journal of Sport History*', *Journal of Sport History* 43, no. 1 (2015): 66–82. Maureen Smith, 'Will the Real Sport Historians Please Stand Up? Shadow Boxing with an Absent Presenter', *Journal of Sport History* 43, no. 1 (2015): 83–96; Duncan Stone ed. 'Special Issue: What Is the Future of Sport History in Academia?' *The International Journal of the History of Sport* 30, no. 1 (2013).

33 Pascal Delheye ed. *Making Sport History: Disciplines, Identities and the Historiography of Sport* (Abingdon: Routledge, 2014).

34 Noting a mid-2019 call for papers for a special issue of *Sport History Review* on transnational sport histories. See also, Samuel M. Clevenger, 'Sport History, Modernity and the Logic of Coloniality: A Case for Decoloniality', *Rethinking History* 21 (2017): 568–590; Malcolm MacLean, 'Engaging (with) Indigeneity: Decolonization and Indigenous/Indigenizing Sport History', *Journal of Sport History* 46, no. 2 (2019): 189–207.

35 Key other texts include, Murray Phillips ed. *Deconstructing Sport History: A Postmodern Analysis* (Albany, SUNY Press, 2006); Richard Pringle and Murray Phillips eds. *Examining Sport Histories: Power, Paradigms and Reflexivity* (Morganstown, WV, Fitness Information Technology. 2013).

36 Ryan Swanson, 'Theory and Method in American Sport History', in *The Routledge History of American Sport*, eds. Linda J. Borish, David K. Wiggins, and Gerald R. Gems (Abingdon: Routledge, 2017), 5–16; Jaime Schultz, 'New Directions and Future Considerations in American Sport History', in *Routledge History of American Sport*, eds. Borish et al., 17–29; Jeff Hill, *Sport in History: An Introduction* (Basingstoke, Palgrave, 2011).

37 Martin Polley, *Sports History: A Practical Guide* (Basingstoke: Palgrave, 2007).

3

THE LAST COMPARATIVE REVIEW OF SPORT HISTORY AND SPORT SOCIOLOGY?

Richard Pringle

Numerous scholars have written about the similarities and distinctions between the sub-disciplines of sport history and sport sociology.[1] These disparate reviewers often touch on similar themes and act to entrench ideas about what sport history and sociology 'are' and what they 'do' differently. These reviews have undoubtedly served a useful purpose in demarcating and, at times, blurring disciplinary boundaries and in questioning the strengths and weakness of various methodological and theoretical approaches. In this chapter, rather than replicating this comparative task, I adopt a Deleuze and Guattarian lens to reflect on how these scholars have contemplated the links between the two fields. I am particularly interested in examining the various authors' motivations and their related political aspirations. In other words, I reflect on their comparative efforts by thinking about 'who did they want to influence and why?' Such a task is highly subjective but through doing so, I hope to understand how these authors have conceptualized sport history and sport sociology and what they believe these fields of research can or should achieve. I then, relatedly, broaden my focus to question: 'What do these comparatives efforts do?' This prime question is derived from the theoretical musings of Gilles Deleuze and Félix Guattari.[2]

Deleuze and Guattari's interest in wanting to know what something 'does', as opposed to 'is', stems from the influence of Spinoza.[3] The philosophical view of Spinoza rested on the importance of examining the 'empirical real' with the understanding that all forms of reality, including material objects and human consciousness, exist within the same realm and therefore have possibilities for *affecting* each other. Affect relates to the capacity for 'force' or 'a capacity to multiply connections',[4] which can be understood as the ability of one body (such as a physical body, body of knowledge, or an idea or symbol) to augment or diminish the power of another body to act. In this manner, Deleuze and Guattari were interested to understand how objects and ideas influence each other and what these interactions do or produce. Their underpinning philosophy was not to reveal what is already known but to create new ways of thinking and feeling that they hoped would spur critical reflection and create potential change.

In a similar sense, I am interested in understanding how the comparative reviews of sport history and sociology *affect* the production of knowledge in each field and, respectfully, the producers or writers of these knowledges. This focus on sport history and sport sociology,

24   DOI: 10.4324/9780429318306-5

via the concept of affect, focuses attention on the interactions that sport history has with other 'bodies of knowledge', objects, or people and what is produced through these interactions. I am hopeful that through looking at sport history and sport sociology via a Deleuze and Guattarian lens that new ways of thinking about these sub-disciplines may emerge and this may inspire critical reflections that allow possibilities for doing sport history and sport sociology differently. I structure my chapter into three sections: first, an examination of what knowledge is produced via the comparative reviews, followed by an analysis of what these knowledges may then produce and, finally, ideas on how comparisons between sport history and other disciplinary subjects could be undertaken differently.

What do we learn from previous reviews of sport history/sociology comparisons?

A range of scholars have analysed the interconnections and points of difference between sport history and sport sociology: their erudite critical reviews are informative and imperative reading. These scholars acknowledge that the boundaries are blurred between these fields: with some sport sociologists recognizing the importance of the explicit historicization of sport and some historians drawing on sociological theories and postmodern concepts.[5] They also note the overlap between the social and/or socio-cultural historians and sport sociologists who have adopted a critical stance to explore social justice issues as related to class, race, and genders/sexualities.

The comparative scholars, nevertheless, have primarily focused their energies on revealing key ontological, epistemological, theoretical, and methodological differences between the two sub-disciplines. This focus on difference is often undertaken in a somewhat antagonistic manner. Douglas Booth and Mark Falcous, for example, stress that 'not even shared critical sentiments and perspectives could prevent skirmishes over methods, theories, politics and paradigms within and between sport history and sport sociology'. These 'skirmishes', they stress, 'have remained a source of endless ferment'.[6] At the same time as detailing key points of difference, many of these comparative scholars have stressed the advantages of increased interdependencies between the two fields.[7] Indeed, these scholars appear to be buttressed by a faith that closer sub-disciplinary connections would be beneficial for the academic standing of each sub-discipline, the production of 'better' knowledge, and, relatedly, the circulation of more insightful and critical findings that offer opportunity 'to link past to present to imagined futures'.[8]

The indirect strategy used by the comparative scholars to encourage greater interdependencies appears to rest on the assumption that through illustrating the comparative weaknesses and/or strengths of each field, researchers will become aware of their current shortcomings and will adopt new ways of doing research. Of importance, however, it appears that the key differences discussed are typically written about in a manner that lends support to the scholar's own preferred field of study and research paradigm. As Louise Mansfield and Dominic Malcolm noted: 'within existing debates about interdisciplinary relations there is a strong element of advocacy for the way individuals would like the two disciplines to be orientated'.[9] In other words, there is general agreement amongst these comparative reviewers of the necessity for a sport history/sociology fusion, yet typically only if the 'opposing' sub-discipline rejects their existing research paradigm, method, or theory in favour of what predominates in the other sub-discipline. Through pointing out existing weaknesses, as Allen Guttmann sardonically surmised, these researchers 'urge us to reflect upon our unhappy situation'[10] and invite us to change our research process: discussion of four of these reviews follows.

Richard Holt, a sport historian, advocated for the importance of blurring and boundary crossing between sport history and sociology.[11] Yet he also observed that sport sociologists, as a generalization, were apt to complain that sport historians lack a theoretical framework; whereas historians, he suggested, tend to critique sociologists for pandering to the artificial needs of rigid theoretical categories. Holt accordingly stressed that neither field respects how the other field undertakes research. Holt then revealed his biases by asserting that the complexity of socio-historic life could not be captured within the 'narrow confines' of a theoretical lens. Hence, he advocated for boundary blurring between the two sub-disciplines but only if the sociology researchers recognize the limitations with how they use theory.

Joseph Maguire's opening keynote address at the 1995 Australian Society for Sport History conference further encouraged boundary crossing between the sub-disciplines.[12] Yet in similar fashion to Holt, he focused on the differences between the two fields and, given his own sociological preferences, implored sport historians to adopt a theoretical perspective, as similar to how sociologists interpret data.

John Nauright also advocated for the need for closer interdependencies between the fields.[13] He stressed, pragmatically, that if sport historians were more closely connected to the sociology of sport, they would be more employable. Like Holt and Maguire, Nauright then highlighted the key differences between the two fields and advocated his preferred method to help the fields merge. He did this by urging sport historians to adopt critical theory so that they could challenge the 'conservative force'[14] of sport.

Booth and Falcous were similarly interested in the possibilities of 'closer relationships between the two disciplines'.[15] They also highlighted key differences between the fields; specifically, in relation to the adoption of a critical stance and postmodern theorizing. In contrast to previous reviewers, they eschewed the opportunity to tell readers of their preferred paradigmatic approaches in favour of insightful critiques of both fields. Sport sociology, for example, despite its turn to critical theory, has been vague in presenting a vision of 'social equality' and has become less focused on 'political engagement … in preference to theorizing'. Moreover, they noted that applied sport sociologists have moved away from sociology into the conservative world of sport management, whereas a large cohort of sport historians 'remain wedded to searching the archives for facts and have little desire to engage the concepts and philosophical ideas propagated by the social sciences'.[16] Thus, despite acknowledging that some sport historians are adopting postmodern theorizing (and are offering representations of the past rather than reconstructions), the notion that sport historians tend to be atheoretical was reinforced. Somewhat pessimistically, Booth and Falcous intimated that sport sociology and sport history appear united in their ineffectiveness to promote social change.

The comparative reviews between sport history and sport sociology have tended to produce knowledge that reinforces differences between the two fields and creates divisions.

What have these comparative efforts produced?

The comparative review focus on epistemological and methodological differences between the two fields had not *produced* the intended result of closer interdependency but 'revealed ongoing division and rivalry'.[17] Indeed, the highlighting of key differences between the fields has, somewhat ironically, worked in a way to hinder the bridging of the fields. Nauright, as an example, referred to the sport historians as 'antiquarians'[18] who were uncritically interested in revealing the facts and proffered conservative readings of sport that did little to produce social change. Critical sport sociologists *affected* by Nauright's reading would likely view sport historians as antithetical to their critical ambitions. Booth similarly suggested that sport historians used an 'antiquated methodology'.[19] And Mike Cronin, more staunchly, critiqued sport history by suggesting that the sub-discipline is 'still dominated by too many fans with typewriters'.[20]

In return, Guttmann melodramatically revealed his feelings of 'visceral horror' in witnessing how 'postmodernist theorists seized the field of sport sociology. And then … an advance guard of postmodernist theorists, led by Sydnor, Booth and Phillips, invaded and began to devastate the field of sports history'.[21] Guttmann informed fellow sport historians that the likes of Booth and Phillips espouse beliefs that sport historians are a 'rather dim-witted lot, averse to considering the epistemological questions that need to be answered before historical research can properly begin'.[22] The war theme employed by Guttmann and his subsequent discussion of the gut-wrenching horror of the theoretical invasion solidified a wall, not a bridge, between the two fields. The ongoing construction of the wall is evident in several recent commentaries offering comparative readings of sport history and sociological history, particularly as evidenced by the critiques and counter critiques surrounding figurational theory.

Wray Vamplew's comparison of empiricist versus sociological history, as an example, presented an attack on the use of Norbert Elias's theoretical concept of the civilizing process.[23] As a counter-critique to Malcolm's reading of cricket and the civilizing process, Vamplew summarized that Malcolm 'failed to define violence in a manner conducive to meaningful historical examination and, further, made historical errors of fact, relied too much on unchecked secondary sources, misinterpreted evidence, and argued by limited example'.[24] Malcolm responded by saying he could 'see little merit in Vamplew's critique',[25] that he 'vigorously' disputed his reading, suggesting it does not stand up to 'scrutiny'[26] and, given that Vamplew's critique has no redeeming methodological or epistemological points, he suggested that it can be read as 'simply an attack on one person's work'.[27] Yet Malcolm underestimated the scale of Vamplew's attack, as it is not directed just at Malcolm, but at figurational sociologists and, more broadly, sociologists who employ theory.

As perhaps already evident, these comparative reviews appear to result, on the one hand, in the production of unproductive feuds, and on the other, dissension between the fields. Recent discussion of a fusion between the two fields is, not surprisingly, underpinned by a reluctant pessimism of the possibility of greater interdependency, as Booth and Falcous state:

> Notwithstanding the fact that the critical streams of sport history and sport sociology share common political and ideological ground, we maintain that the traditional disciplinary foci of empirical evidence (history) and theory (sociology) and associated differences in methodological traditions constrain closer subdisciplinary connections. Moreover, we suggest that the recent intellectual turn towards postmodernism and scepticism of realist epistemologies compounds divides between the two subdisciplines.[28]

Another concern related to these comparative reviews is that they tend to omit discussion about what each field has achieved or what impact the knowledge has. In other words, there is an absence of discussion of what differences these fields have made to social and material realities, to issues of social justice or to the sporting world more broadly. If these fields are important in academia then who do they affect and in what way? The 'impact agenda', according to Simon Bastow, Patrick Dunleavy, and Jane Tinkler,[29] is set to influence the way in which researchers prioritize their work, where they publish, and the methods they use: hence, the growing interest in examining the 'difference' a field of research can make.[30] Yet analysis of the impact of sport history research is currently lacking.

Rather than looking at what is produced and the associated affects, these reviews tend to look at how the research process has been undertaken. They focus, as examples, on specific issues relevant to the two fields, such as the use of theory,[31] issues of researcher reflexivity or objectivity,[32] and data collection techniques such as interviewing. Malcolm, relatedly, examined interview techniques in the history of sport and sport sociology and concluded that the 'underpinning differences' in how interview data is presented is reflective of 'divergent conceptual views'.[33] Malcolm accentuated the differences to argue that the tendency of sport historians to cite personal names from interview data is problematic as it reduces the social to the individual and focuses 'attention on relatively insignificant information, and concomitantly detracts from asking more expansive questions about social structure'.[34]

The focus on specific research process issues within these comparative reviews suggests that they are written primarily for other researchers within the two sub-disciplines. The comparative reviews, relatedly, tend to ignore other disciplines, such as mainstream history or other sport disciplines, and therefore miss opportunities to build connections more broadly. Alan Tomlinson and Christopher Young have previously noted that sport historians operate 'in a narrowly defined academic world'[35] and that their published work is rarely cited in journals outside of sport history. Future reviews should not simply compare sport history and sport sociology, but recognize that there is a growing overlap between all social science disciplines. Hence, rather than comparing disciplines with assumed boundaries and points of difference, comparative reviews could focus on research across the disciplines that adopts similar methodologies, axiologies, or theoretical concepts. I expand on this idea in the following section.

What could future comparative efforts produce?

Despite the focus on differences, the comparative reviews should not be simply dismissed as narrowly acting to entrench irreconcilable difference between the fields. Indeed, as I have already noted, the reviews also point to existing blurring between the fields and they illustrate that change is taking place within and between sport history and sport sociology. Hence, these reviews are possibly acting as inspirations for some of the changes that are being enacted. Booth and Falcous further noted that particular historians and sociologists are in fact doing similar work and 'share common political and ideological ground'.[36] This focus on interdisciplinary similarities and shared political intent could be a more promising way to envisage and facilitate greater interdependency between the fields.

Deleuze and Guattari offered ideas on how such an examination could proceed.[37] First, as influenced by Spinoza, they recommend undertaking empirical examinations by rejecting the notion that any forms of reality have inner essences or exist with pre-conceived meanings. In this respect, they would not initiate a comparative review of sport history and sport sociology by drawing on 'pre-existing' definitions of the two disciplines. For example, existing definitions tend to divide the two disciplines via temporal factors: sport history referring to the study of sporting issues related to events or people in the past, whereas sport sociology is allegedly focused on contemporary issues. Yet, Mansfield and Malcolm argue that 'the divide between sociology and history can be too sharply drawn' and suggest that there is 'considerable overlap between the two fields.'[38]

Review of sport history and sociology

In contrast to searching for existing meanings or definitions of the two disciplines, Deleuze and Guattari[39] would focus on what the disciplines do, because they accept that concepts, such as the concept of sport history, only exist as a response to a problem. And to answer the rhetorical question, 'What problem does sport history aim to solve?', they would focus on what sport history does. As an example, Deleuze and Guattari compared horses and oxen without reference to pre-existing animal classifications or taxonomic rankings by focusing on what these animals 'did'. This focus allowed them to argue that a 'racehorse is more different from a workhorse than a workhorse is from an ox'.[40] They explained this assertion by illustrating that a workhorse and an ox 'do' similar tasks, such as carrying loads, and therefore they have a similar affect or influence on humans.

Through focusing on what things 'do', comparative researchers can similarly escape existing meanings and avoid the risk of re-presenting prevailing ideas (e.g. as illustrated within the comparative reviews that discussed the place, or lack, of theory in sport sociology and sport history). Such a focus allows possibilities to view the sub-disciplines afresh.

For example, I could argue that reconstructionist sport history is more different from constructionist sport history than critical feminist sport history is from feminist sport sociology. In other words, rather than focusing on alleged temporal differences, feminist sport history and feminist sport sociology could be recognized as having the same aims and therefore producing a similar *affect* on readers. To paraphrase Phillip Abrams, there is no relationship between feminist sport history and feminist sport sociology 'because in terms of their fundamental preoccupations' they 'are and always have been the same thing'.[41] Feminist sport historians aim to produce a 'future beyond patriarchy'[42] via critical cultural interventions as do feminist sport sociologists. Thus, what these critical researchers 'do' is aim to create change related to gender inequities.

The comparative focus on researchers with similar intent, such as feminist historians and sociologists, is a more fruitful comparison as it does not aim to reveal differences via competitive evaluations, but seeks to understand the critical effectiveness of differing approaches. This focus on critical effectiveness, or in Patti Lather's terms 'catalytic validity',[43] is never an objective task yet the value is of importance, as reflecting on the effectiveness of critical research allows researchers to think about what methodologies or theoretical approaches offer greater possibilities for enacting social change. In other words, this comparative task encourages a comparative sharing of research approaches to improve possibilities for achieving mutual political goals: a search for what works rather than a revelation of problematic differences. This comparative task, accordingly, encourages a blurring of disciplinary boundaries that allows possibilities for greater interdependencies to occur. Indeed, rather than thinking that sport history and sport sociology are different sub-disciplines, this comparison encourages the view that they are simply differing 'methods' of the same form of research. It is in this quixotic light that I wonder whether this chapter will be the last comparative review of sport history and sport sociology.

Notes

1 See, for example: Douglas Booth and Mark Falcous, 'History, Sociology and Critical Sport Studies', in *Routledge Handbook of the Sociology of Sport*, ed. Richard Giulianotti (London: Routledge, 2015), 153–163; Mark Falcous and Douglas Booth, 'Contested Epistemology: Theory and Method of International Sport Studies', *Sport in Society* 20, nos. 12 (2017): 1821–1837; Richard Holt, *Sport and the British: A Modern History* (Oxford: Oxford University Press, 1989); John Horne, Alan Tomlinson, and Garry Whannel, 'Socialisation–Social Interaction and Development', *Understanding Sport* 1 (1999): 129–155; Joseph Maguire, 'Common Ground? Links Between Sports History, Sports Geography and

the Sociology of Sport', *Sporting Traditions* 12, nos. 1 (1995): 3–25; Dominic Malcolm, 'A Response to Vamplew and Some Comments on the Relationship Between Sports Historians and Sociologists of Sport', *Sport in History* 28, nos. 2 (2008): 259–279; Louise Mansfield and Dominic Malcolm, 'Sociology', in *Routledge Companion to Sport History*, eds. Stephen Pope and John Nauright (London: Routledge, 2010), 99–113; Richard Pringle and Murray Phillips, *Examining Sport Histories: Power, Paradigms, and Reflexivity* (Morgantown, WV: Fitness Information Technology, 2013); David Rowe, Jim McKay, and Geoffrey Lawrence, 'Out of the Shadows: The Critical Sociology of Sport in Australia, 1986 to 1996', *Sociology of Sport Journal* 14, nos. 4 (1997): 340–361; Wray Vamplew, 'Empiricist Versus Sociological History: Some Comments on the "Civilizing Process"', *Sport in History* 27, nos. 2 (2007): 161–171.

2 Gilles Deleuze and Félix Guattari, *A Thousand Plateaus: Capitalism and Schizophrenia* (Minneapolis, University of Minnesota Press, 1988).

3 Deleuze and Guattari, *A Thousand Plateaus*.

4 Brian Massumi, 'Notes on the Translation and Acknowledgements', in Deleuze and Guattari, *A Thousand Plateaus*, xvi–xix.

5 Falcous and Booth, 'Contested Epistemology'.

6 Booth and Falcous, 'History, Sociology and Critical Sport Studies', 255.

7 For example, Holt, *Sport and the British*; Maguire, 'Common Ground?'; John Nauright, '"The End of Sports History?" From Sports History to Sports Studies', *Sporting Traditions* 16, no. 1 (1999): 5–14.

8 Patricia Vertinsky, 'Is There a "Beyond Patriarchy" in Feminist Sport History?' *Journal of Sport History* 39, no. 3 (2012): 479.

9 Mansfield and Malcolm, 'Sociology', 100.

10 Allen Guttmann, 'Review Essay: The Ludic and the Ludicrous', *The International Journal of the History of Sport* 25, no. 1 (2008): 100–112, 102.

11 Holt, *Sport and the British*.

12 Maguire, 'Common Ground?'

13 John Nauright, 'Towards the Next Generation: A Response to Bob Stewart and Roy Hay', *Victorian Bulletin of Sport and Culture* 6 (1996): 14–15.

14 Nauright, 'Towards the Next Generation', 15.

15 Booth and Falcous, 'History, Sociology and Critical Sport Studies', 153.

16 Booth and Falcous, 'History, Sociology and Critical Sport Studies', 156, 160, and 161.

17 Falcous and Booth, 'Contested Epistemology', 1828.

18 Nauright, 'Towards the Next Generation', 15.

19 Douglas Booth, 'Response to Bernard Whimpress', *Victorian Bulletin of Sport and Culture* 6 (1996): 13–14.

20 Mike Cronin's comments on the filed appeared on the SPORTHIST Internet list, 23 October 2007.

21 Guttmann, 'Review Essay', 101.

22 Guttmann, 'Review Essay', 102.

23 Vamplew, 'Empiricist Versus Sociological History'.

24 Vamplew, 'Empiricist Versus Sociological History', 161.

25 Dominic Malcolm, 'A Response to Vamplew', 259.

26 Dominic Malcolm, 'A Response to Vamplew', 271.

27 Dominic Malcolm, 'A Response to Vamplew', 271.

28 Booth and Falcous, 'History, Sociology and Critical Sport Studies', 153.

29 Simon Bastow, Patrick Dunleavy, and Jane Tinkler, *The Impact of The Social Sciences: How Academics and Their Research Make a Difference* (Thousand Oaks, CA: Sage, 2014).

30 For a recent example within sport sociology and health and physical education research see: Richard Pringle, Hakan Larsson, and Göran Gerdin, *Critical Research in Sport, Health and Physical Education: How to Make a Difference* (London: Routledge, 2018).

31 For example, Vamplew, 'Empiricist Versus Sociological History'.

32 For example, Richard Pringle and Murray Phillips, *Examining Sport Histories*.

33 Dominic Malcolm, 'Durkheim and Sociological Method: Historical Sociology, Sports History, and the Role of Comparison', *The International Journal of the History of Sport* 32, no. 15 (2015): 1809.

34 Malcolm, 'Durkheim and Sociological Method', 1809–1810.

35 Alan Tomlinson and Christopher Young, 'Sport in History: Challenging the Communis Opinio, *Journal of Sport History* 37, no. 1 (2010): 5–17, 6.

36 Booth and Falcous, 'History, Sociology and Critical Sport Studies', 153.

37 Deleuze and Guattari, *A Thousand Plateaus*.
38 Mansfield and Malcolm, 'Sociology', 100.
39 Deleuze and Guattari, *A Thousand Plateaus*.
40 Deleuze and Guattari, *A Thousand Plateaus*, 257.
41 Phillip Abrams cited in Mansfield and Malcolm, 'Sociology', 100.
42 Elizabeth Grosz, 'Histories of a Feminist Future', *Signs: Journal of Women in Culture and Society* 25, no. 4 (2000): 1017–1021.
43 Patti Lather, 'Issues of Validity in Openly Ideological Research: Between a Rock and a Soft Place', *Interchange* 17, no. 4 (1986): 63–84.

4

WRITING MACRO AND MICRO SPORT HISTORY

Mike Cronin

Intelligent readers of history, or so the lists compiled for the Internet by a host of online publications tell us, enjoy microhistory. In 2018, the online female-focused digital media company, Bustle, gave its readers (all 82 million of them) '9 Microhistory Books that Will Give You So Much to Think – And Talk About'. For its readers, Bustle defined microhistory as: 'an investigative exploration into a specific event or small unit of research'. By reading the nine listed books (which included histories of hair removal, blood, umbrellas, make up, and sea shells), Bustle assured its audience that they would 'find [themselves] talking about them at parties, on dates, and really to anyone who will listen'.[1] Microhistorical studies as popular and bestselling forms of history books are not, however, a new phenomenon.[2] While such books have their methodological genesis in scholarly studies of the medieval and early modern period, in landmark works such as *The Return of Martin Guerre, The Great Cat Massacre*, or *The Peasants of Languedoc*, it was, among others, Mark Kurlansky's *Cod: A Biography of the Fish that Changed the World*, published in 1997, that led to a long-running publishing phenomenon that has seen a large number of mass readership, single topic, deep interrogations of history being brought to sale each year since.[3] Lined up against the publishing success of in-depth research into a single topic have been those books which are marketed as taking a macrohistorical approach. Ranging from Jared Diamond's *Guns, Germs and Steel: The Fate of Human Societies*, Niall Ferguson's *The Ascent of Money: A Financial History of the World*, and, more recently, Yuval Noah Harari's *Sapiens: A Brief History of Humankind* and his follow up, *Homo Deus: A Brief History of Tomorrow*, these works are often classed as belonging to the stable of World or Big History.[4]

Clearly, holding up Kurlansky's work as an exemplar of microhistory, or that of Harari as the perfect illustration of macrohistory, would ignore the methodological complexity of what is meant by these specific approaches to historical research. The popularity of such works does though illustrate an interesting point. The public appears to like their history one of two ways: they either want an intimate history of a single item, person, or event, or else they want a grand sweeping history that embraces a breadth of both chronological and global possibility. What is absent from many of the myriad of lists online, of good and readable micro or macrohistory, are books that explore sport. And it's not because those books haven't been written. In 2019, for example, one could point to Prashant Kimbadi's *Cricket County: An Indian Odyssey in the Age of Empire* or David Goldblatt's *The Age of Football: The Global Game in the*

32

DOI: 10.4324/9780429318306-6

Twenty-First Century as examples of microhistory and macrohistory respectively.[5] There is a much larger issue, at the level of mainstream or popular publishing, that results in sporting titles, no matter how well researched and historically contextualized they are, being specifically placed on a separate list. They are sport books *not* history books. This chapter though is not concerned with the sale, marketing, and classification of books, but rather is specifically concerned with how two major historical methodological approaches or methods have been mobilized in the area of sport history. Effectively, have historians of sport embraced the potential of micro and macrohistory? Even though they may be considered, by the compilers of lists, as simply sport books, have the collective endeavours of sport historians produced good (or meaningfully engaged) micro or macro history? In answer, the chapter will argue, that while the historical study of sport should be the perfect subject for the application of methodologically informed and innovative micro or macrohistorical approaches – resulting from the structures of sport itself – this has not often been the case.

To begin with, the terms micro and microhistory require some interrogation. A study of the history of a single fish is not necessarily microhistory, and neither is a book about the history of humanity automatically a macrohistory. Scale is an important issue in both these terms (a shorthand dichotomy often reduces the two as: micro = small history, macro = big history), but the application of a concept, of a way of researching and reading history, and the use of specific methodological and narrative approaches is the real key. Distinguishing micro from macrohistory, and how they have functioned within the sport history space, is not simply a question of the magnitude of the subject under review. While size matters in this context, the methodological apparatus is the central issue.

Looking back, in 2017 Thomas V. Cohen, a foundational scholar in microhistory, argued that what he had spent his career as an historian doing, was not actually based around a field of historical research. He stated that the fields of history (economic history, art history, migration history, and so on) were 'defined and delineated first by subject'. Microhistory by comparison 'lacks a fixed subject [but] what it does possess is a method, or, to use a famous and perhaps better term, a practice'.[6] Cohen went on to argue, given his unease with the idea of microhistory as a method, that 'what it has instead is a habit – or, to dignify habit, a practice – of obsessive attention to detail. Microhistory practices close reading, looking for nuances in words, actions, and material conditions'.[7] He further defined microhistory as being concerned with the thick connectedness of things, the fractal nature of the unknown, a synergy between scholar and reader that acknowledges the failings and gaps within the historical record, the intimacy between scholar and subject, and the linkage between microhistory and story-telling.

To further this definition of microhistory, Jan de Vries agreed that 'its methodology is to reduce the focus of analysis, often to an individual or small group, a place or locality and, usually, a brief time period'. He went further in explaining the totality of microhistorical approaches, noting that 'microhistorians seek to contextualize the object of their interest as fully as possible, and often demonstrate a praiseworthy archive-based virtuosity in this respect'. Centrally he moved on to classify that a 'broad definition links microhistory to the larger cultural turn and microhistory's characteristic subversion of the triumphalism of grand narratives surely lies at the heart of both'.[8] And this is a huge issue for sport historians who, as has been rehearsed elsewhere, have been largely resistant to the idea of the cultural turn.[9] Rather than embrace a range of new theoretical opportunities, sport historians have, with a few notable exceptions, clung to the classic archive-driven empiricism of 'proof' over the potentially more exciting interrogation of meaning, cognition, affect, and symbols. Given that sport is such a powerful cultural form within societies across the globe, a lack of curiosity of how sport functions, and what it means *and* represents, has marked the effective failure of sport historians to move beyond a history that seems trapped somewhere between the Whig and Annales schools of the past.

Compared with the advanced methodological definition (and numerous examples) of what constitutes microhistory, macrohistory has been weakly defined. While there have been many historical works that can be understood as attempts at macrohistory, the lack of clarity of what it actually is (particularly in methodological terms), apart from its chronological and global reach, has meant that catch all terms such as big history or world history are also applied. Macrohistory has been defined as focusing on those 'diachronic and ideographic sciences', namely biography at the personal level, history at the social-systems level, and world-systems history at the global level, with microhistory, macrohistory, and world history as their counterparts.[10] In effect, macrohistorians are more concerned with a search for historical patterns and the ways in which history has been transformed over time. In the search for such patterns, macrohistorians are not bound by conventional (or modern) political geography (i.e. nation states), and neither are they constrained by historically constructed borders in time (medieval, pre-modern, modern, and so on).

The concept of macrohistory has been further broadened by two additional perspectives. First is the use of big data to fully explain human history. Championed by Peter Turchin,[11] among others, the collection and assessment of (ultimately) all available human historical data will allow 'historical theories [to be] be tested against large databases, and the ones that do not fit – many of them long-cherished – will be discarded. Our understanding of the past will converge on something approaching an objective truth'.[12] The search for a full understanding of 'truth' of human history has led many macrohistorians to argue that the past can therefore be used to predict the future course of humankind and the planet, or as Joseph Voros argued for historians: 'our perspective now turns from Big History's long view backwards to the macro-prospective long view forwards. In short, we now add a future dimension to our big historical thinking'.[13] The shift in macrohistorical process, from one concerned with the long history of humans to a forward *and* backward looking version has been a by-product of the influence of scientific and environmental/ecological thinking on the discipline. Marnie Hughes-Warrington stated that 'it is a common complaint that world history – as practiced by historians – does not live up to the scope of its terms' and argued that histories of a large scale, as written in the later twentieth century, essentially world and macrohistorical studies, 'could not withstand methodological and ethical scrutiny'. She outlined correctly that the reinvention of macrohistory in the twenty-first century would be one in which 'history must tell the biggest story of all, that of the origins and evolution of human beings, life, the earth, and the universe – hence, "big history"'.[14]

The quest to produce macro or big history has led, in recent years, to a turn against the nation state as the unit for historical study. John Paul A. Ghobrial stated that the trend away from national-based history has meant that

> if you are not doing an explicitly transnational, international or global project, you now have to explain why you are not. There is now sufficient evidence from a sufficiently wide range of historiographies that these transnational connections have been determinative, influential and shaping throughout recorded human history, for about as long as we've known about it.[15]

As macro or big history gains ever more popularity (despite its potential methodological instability), what then is the place of microhistory? Or, as the 2019 supplement of *Past &*

Present discussed, is the next major paradigm shift towards global history *and* (or perhaps through) microhistory. Furthering his argument against the dominance of macrohistory, whatever its virtues, Ghobrial warned against the embrace of the empiricism of the social sciences and argued, as Levi has done, that 'microhistory [is a potential] way of rejecting the too-general vision concealed in the concepts deployed by the social sciences in favour of practices of historical research that will ultimately contribute to the creation of new general questions'.[16] In this transition from micro to macro, with the inherent demands of research and evidence types (and the rejection of empiricism) is a call for microhistory to do, as its originators demanded from the 1960s, something different: not to seek evidence that proves or adds to existing orthodoxies of knowledge, but rather to allow new or different historical questions to emerge from the evidence at hand. For sport history, I would argue, this is the most complex challenge. How do sport historians move, or can they even move, beyond traditional concepts of empiricist history and the reverential search for archival truth?

So, how have sport historians used macro and microhistory in their work? At first glance, in terms of the way sport scholars have methodologically explained their outputs, the answer is not at all. A host of searches through various scholarly databases uncovered a solitary sport history title, in book or article form, that included the words macrohistory or microhistory.[17] This seems startling given the wide usage of both approaches across the broader discipline of history. So, have sport historians been doing macrohistory and microhistory, but not giving it a name, or have there been structural or conceptual issues in the way sport historians have tended to work which have meant that the macro or microhistorical approach has not been seen as desirable?

In many ways the historical study of sport has had a series of problems that have prevented the potentially fruitful methodologies of the macro and microhistorical approaches being applied. In general (but not exclusive) terms, the following perimeters can be thrown round the majority of work (including my own) in the sport history field. The study of sport history has been largely concentrated on the study of organized, codified sport and therefore histories of sport from the post–1860 period have dominated.[18] Given that codified sport has been traditionally constructed as a pursuit that emerges as a result of industrialization, urbanization, and modernization, it also follows that sport history has largely been concerned with the first or developed world. Also, as the concentration has been on modern codified sport (and as a result of how the *male* administrators of nineteenth-century sport organized themselves), the history of sport has primarily used the *masculinized* nation state as its organizational focus. Sport historians are often, in their published work, exactly that: historians of a single sport and have not often produced *sports* histories, and neither does their focus often broaden so as to contextualize sports more widely in terms of leisure or non-work time. Due to the concentration on single sports and the nation state as the organizational focus, there have been few histories of sport that have taken a wider geographical focus and shifted their lens to study at the continental or global level.[19] Indeed, even when the historical focus has shifted away from the west, the resultant work has been tightly focused on uncovering material and research from other nations (India and China, for example, have been well served in recent years by sport historians), but there has been little work that has moved in a comparative, transnational, or macrohistorical direction.[20] This has been especially surprising given that sport is a shared global culture, and has a number of world sporting organizations, such as FIFA and the International Olympic Committee, but these have been relatively poorly served by historians.[21] All these choices made by sport historians have resulted in very few macrohistorical (world or big) histories of sport. And there is little work that has taken on the additional challenges set by the macrohistorical agenda in terms of large-scale chronological works that explore the evolutionary, ecological, or future thinking themes in history.

A bigger problem perhaps, than the potential intellectual scope of work in sport history, has been an obsession with facts, truth, and the elevation of the archive. This critique of sport history, its need from the 1970s to establish itself as respectable by being hyper alert to the use of traditional empiricism (it was then a new area for the sub-study of history, not one which would be methodologically innovative), has been vocalized many times, but as Douglas Booth wrote:

> the mainstream of sport evinces virtually no interest in the cognitive status of studying the past; challenging questions about empiricist notions of certainty and veracity rarely surface. Rather, the field rests on the assumption – which has taken on rock-solid proportions – that there is a strong correspondence between words and the world, or between evidence and reality.[22]

With the tradition of empiricist study, governed by a focus on specific sports or nation states, sport history has largely failed to innovate. As such, potential new ways of thinking about, researching, uncovering, and explaining the history of sports, and their place in the world, have been mostly absent. And this is the problem. Sport history remains locked into a world-view from the 1970s, that empiricism is *the* way to *do* history. For all the potential fertility of the topic, for all the ways in which sport can excite and captivate, how it is represented and what it means, sport historians have been overly concerned with telling us how it was. And in that spirit, the potentially exciting approaches of macro or microhistory have remained largely unused.

Works that have attempted to explore sport history in the vein of macrohistory might include David G. McComb's *Sports in World History* and Allen Guttmann's *Sport: The First Five Millenia*. However, these works, while global in focus, still had as their chronological starting point the ancient Greek Olympics (although McComb's work is not strictly a traditional chronological in approach in the way of Guttmann's work). Not strictly a work of history, but one with a macrohistorical bent, was Besnier, Brownell, and Carter's *Anthropology of Sport: Bodies, Borders and Biopolitics*. Those works that have most successfully pursued a macrohistorical view are ones that have looked at the global history of a specific sport within the context of a long (but still modern) chronology. These include, for example, the works of Tony Collins, David Goldblatt, Stephen Hardy, and Thor Gotass.[23] What have largely passed for macrohistory in the sport studies and sport history arena are encyclopedias, such as *Sports Around the World: History, Culture and Practice* or the *Encyclopedia of World Sport: From Ancient Times to the Present*, but these are products of scale (there are entries on a raft of sports across geography and chronology) and are not methodologically informed in terms of creating a coherent, cogent macrohistorical work. While there have been works that have explored issues relating to sport and the environment, there has been little work, with the exception of Robert R. Sands and Linda R. Sands' *Anthropology of Sport and Human Movement*, that has examined sport and ecological history from a macrohistorical or evolutionary perspective.[24] There is a growing body of work that explores the possible future(s) of sport – particularly in light of the doping, medical technology, and transhumanism debates – but much of this fails to ground itself within an historical or macrohistorical framework and is driven, in disciplinary terms, by the specific concerns of sports ethics or sports medicine.[25]

Conversely, while the focus of sport historians and the structures of modern sport have therefore limited macrohistorical approaches and works, sport should be an ideal vehicle for microhistories.[26] Sport, while organized at the macro level around global structures, actually functions across the world in small, tightly focused units. Under each national federation, for whatever sport, are the micro units through which the majority of people experience sport: the league, the club, the team, the match. Within these smaller, localized units, all manner of specific groups are both represented or their presence contested (age, race, gender, sexuality, and so on). Sport, for all its omnipresence in the contemporary media world of rolling news and social media, exists primarily in small scale, local settings, and is also controlled by a highly specific set of rules that govern time, whether the length of a match or the frequency of games under season or tournament rules. But microhistory is not simply the application of a specific methodological approach that concerns limited scale as it has often been concerned with the way in which history is written. Microhistorians have often eschewed the traditions of historical narrative and commentary, and chosen instead to embrace different forms such as the first-person narrative as exemplified by Carlo Ginzburg's classic *The Cheese and the Worms*.[27]

István M. Szijártó wrote that microhistory, when successfully done, should reflect the best of 'microanalysis, the interest in general questions, agency, and the possibilities offered by the microhistorical approach for writing a better global history, gender history, or literary history'.[28] Szijártó did not include sport in their types of history that could be done better through the use of microhistory, but it is clear that it is an ideal methodology given the very nature of sport. But sport historians, while they may have unwittingly stumbled into microhistory by virtue of researching the localized and microanalysing it, have not often been informed by the specific methodology. This is particularly an issue in terms of evidence. Sport historians have overly relied on a combination of newspaper and some form of official (association, club, college, and so on) archive. Microhistory though demands the uncovering and interrogation of the slightest, most fragmentary sources, as if through a microscope. This search for small detail, for clues, challenges the perceived truth that has emerged from the official archive (however constructed), and allows microhistorians to unravel the meta narrative or what Ghobrial termed the 'triumphalism of grand narratives'. This in turn meant that microhistory challenges 'the large-scale paradigms that had come to influence the study of the past'.[29]

In this vein, Jan de Vries argued that 'a valuable and potentially powerful microhistory sets out to address a problem, or challenge a thesis. This necessarily brings the microlevel exceptional into contact with some model, or theory which, in turn, disciplines the interpretation of the microlevel sources'.[30] Sport history has not often sought to challenge a thesis. It has by and large functioned to establish orthodoxies of sport as a product of modernity, as an issue of class, as a symbol of gendered power, as a movement of bodily control, and so on. Where sport history has worked on the microhistorical level, the resulting work has been powerful and forces the reader to rethink how sport in history has been constructed. The major (although not only) architects of sporting microhistory (knowingly or unknowingly) have been Douglas Booth, Rita Liberti and Maureen Smith, Daniel Nathan, Gary Osmond, Murray Philips, Jamie Schultz, and Patricia Vertinsky.[31] There is not space to rehearse the value of their work, but the key point has been a willingness to study at the smallest level, to pursue evidence through the unfamiliar or non-official archive and, in doing so, play with form, meaning, and narrative. These scholars have acknowledged that much sporting activity (if not the majority around the world) is not wedded to the official record (be it sporting or state), but instead exists at the level of the local, the passing, the evanescent, and as such is forgotten within history. These sport historians, in the way of the best microhistory, have worked to uncover their subject, to reanimate it, and challenge and question its historic meaning. They have gone beyond empiricism to think about form, content, value, and narration (both historic and in their own contemporary re-presentation).

Christian G. De Vito wrote of the potential intersection of a microhistory, that is informed by a myriad of microhistories, that would allow for a broader and comparative perspective and study of the multiple traces that the processes of scaling have left across space. In this, he argued, it would be possible to 'investigate the shifting geographies of state power; and explore the construction of specific places at the crossroads of the areas of influence of multiple institutions'.[32] Sport history should be a space of intersectionality and transnationalism. It is a cultural artefact of human existence that allows us to microscopically investigate an activity that people across the globe have taken part in, the vast majority of which went unremarked and unrecorded. It is part of the human condition, to play and watch, and as such sport history should be a significant form in understanding the past. But so long as sport history clings to an outdated empiricism, that overvalues the archive and seeks to uncover and recount the official narratives of sport (at multiple levels), its contribution to knowledge beyond its own sub-field will be negligible. Through macrohistory sports history can bring together a massive shared past packed with meaning, and in microhistory it can potentially uncover the fragments, narratives, and significances attached to a long-forgotten sporting contest that was neither mediatized nor recalled but is significant because it happened. In asking bigger questions, in ignoring orthodoxies, in doing things differently, there can be a better version of sport history.

Notes

1 https://www.bustle.com/p/9-microhistory-books-that-will-give-you-so-much-to-think-talk-about-15 517826.
2 For an overview of microhistory, see *What Is Microhistory? Theory and Practice*, eds. Sigurour Gylfi Magnusson and Istvan M. Szijarto (London: Routledge, 2013).
3 Natalie Zemon Davis, *The Return of Martin Guerre* (Cambridge: Harvard University Press, 1983), Robert Darnton, *The Great Cat Massacre and Other Episodes in French Cultural History* (New York: Basic Books, 1984), Emmanuel Le Roy Ladurie, *The Peasants of Languedoc* (Urbana: University of Illinois, 1976), and Mark Kurlansky, *Cod: A Biography of the Fish that Changed the World* (London: Penguin, 1998).
4 Jared Diamond, *Guns, Germs and Steel: The Fate of Human Societies* (New York: W.W. Norton, 1997), Niall Ferguson, *The Ascent of Money: A Financial History of the World* (London: Allen Lane, 2008), Yuval Noah Harari, *Sapiens: A Brief History of Humankind* (New York: Harper Collins, 2015), and Yuval Noah Harari, *Homo Deus: A Brief History of Tomorrow* (London: Vintage, 2017).
5 Prashant Kimbadi, *Cricket County: An Indian Odyssey in the Age of Empire* (Oxford: Oxford University Press, 2019) or David Goldblatt's *The Age of Football: The Global Game in the Twenty-First Century* (London: Macmillan, 2019).
6 Thomas V. Cohen, 'The Macrohistory of Microhistory', *Journal of Medieval and Early Modern Studies* 47, no. 1 (2017): 54.
7 Cohen, 'The Macrohistory of Microhistory', 54.
8 Jan de Vries, 'Playing with Scales: The Global and the Micro, the Macro and the Nano', *Past & Present* 242, no. 14 (2019): 32.
9 See for example Douglas Booth, 'Escaping the Past: The Cultural Turn and Language in Sport History', *Rethinking History* 8, no. 1 (2004): 103–125; Amy Bass, 'State of the Field: Sports History and the Cultural Turn', *Journal of American History* 101, no. 1 (2014): 148–172; Jamie Schultz, 'Leaning into the Turn: Towards a New Cultural Sport History', *Sporting Traditions* 27, no. 2 (2010): 45–59; and Murray Phillips, 'Deconstructing Sport History: The Postmodern Challenge', *Journal of Sport History* 28, no. 3 (2001): 327–343.
10 Leif Littrup, 'Review: Macrohistory and Macrohistorians: Perspectives on Individual, Societal and Civilizational Change', *Journal of World History* 11, no. 1 (2000): 118.

11 Peter Turchin, *Historical Dynamics: Why States Rise and Fall* (Princeton: Princeton University Press, 2003).
12 Laura Spinney, 'History as a Giant Dataset: How Analysing the Past Might Help Save the Future', *Guardian*, 12 November 2019, https://www.theguardian.com/technology/2019/nov/12/history-as-a-giant-data-set-how-analysing-the-past-could-help-save-the-future, accessed 1 December 2019.
13 Joseph Voros, 'Big Futures: Macrohistorical Perspectives on the Future of Humankind', in *The Way that Big History Works: Cosmos, Life, Society and Our Future, Volume III*, eds. Barry Rodrigue, Leonid Grinin, and Andrey Korotayev (Delhi: Primus Books, 2017), 414.
14 Marnie Hughes-Warrington, 'Big History', *Historically Speaking* 4, no. 2 (2002): 16.
15 John-Paul A. Ghobrial, 'Seeing the World Like a Microhistorian', *Past & Present* 242, no. 14 (2019): 3.
16 Ghobrial, 'Seeing the World', 18.
17 Mike Cronin, 'The Gaelic Athletic Association's Invasion of America, 1888: Travel Narratives, Microhistory and the Irish American 'Other''', *Sport in History* 27, no. 2 (2007): 190–216.
18 The definitional clash between sport, something which is modern, and macrohistory which is in many ways timeless, is apparent in much sport history where the pre mid-nineteenth-century period can be 'avoided' by defining a limited concept of sport in relation to chronology, see for example, Mark Dyreson, 'Globalising the Nation-Making Process: Modern Sport in World History', *International Journal of the History of Sport* 20, no. 1 (2003): 91–106.
19 For an eccentric attempt to move beyond a Western conception of history see J.A. Mangan, 'Eurocentric Lens Removed: Wilsonian Impetus', *International Journal of the History of Sport* 30, no. 15 (2013): 1699–1708.
20 See for example Ramchandra Guha, *A Corner of a Foreign Field: The Indian History of a British Sport* (London: Picador, 2002), and Andrew D. Morris, *Marrow of the Nation: A History of Sport and Physical Culture in Republican China* (Berkeley: University of California Press, 2004).
21 Work on FIFA ranges from FIFA World Football Museum, *The Official History of the FIFA World Cup* (London: Carlton, 2019) through to the mass of work that has explored the recent history of FIFA corruption such as David Conn, *The Fall of the House of FIFA* (London: Yellow Jersey, 2018) and Andrew Jennings, *Foul: The Secret World of FIFA* (London: Harper, 2017). The IOC has an official history in the form of David Miller, *The Official History of the Olympic Games and the IOC: Athens to London, 1894–2012* (Edinburgh: Mainstream, 2012), and a host of city specific, legacy, and controversy studies, but lacks a macrohistorical treatment that is rooted in historical methodologies.
22 Douglas Booth, *The Field: Truth and Fiction in Sport History* (Oxford: Routledge, 2005), 2.
23 Tony Collins, *The Oval World: A Global History of Rugby* (London: Bloomsbury, 2015); David Goldblatt, *The Games: A Global History of the Olympics* (London: Pan, 2018); Stephen Hardy and Andrew C. Holman, *Hockey: A Global History* (Illinois: Illinois University Press, 2018), and Thor Gotaas, *Running: A Global History* (London: Reaktion, 2012).
24 See for example Rob Millington and Simon C. Darnell eds. *Sport, Development and Environmental Sustainability* (Oxford: Routledge, 2020) and Robert R. Sands and Linda R. Sands eds. *The Anthropology of Sport and Human Movement* (Lanham: Lexington Books, 2012).
25 See for example Kath Woodward, *Sporting Times* (Basingstoke: Macmillan, 2013; and in particular chapter 5), Andy Miah, *Sport 2.0: Transforming Sports for a Digital World* (Cambridge, MIT Press, 2017), P. David Howe, 'Sport, the Body and the Technologies of Disability' in *A Companion to Sport*, eds. David L. Andrews and Ben Carrington (London: Wiley, 2013), 210–222, and Michael J. McNamee, 'Transhuman Athletes and Pathological Perfectionism: Recognising Limits in Sports and Human Nature' in *Athletic Enhancement, Human Nature and Ethics: Threats and Opportunities of Doping Technologies*, eds. Jan Tolleneer, Sigrid Sterckx, and Pieter Bonte (Dordrecht: Springer, 2013), 185–200.
26 This is especially apparent if Brewer's 2015 article is read with sport in mind. John Brewer, 'Microhistory and the Histories of Everyday Life', *Cultural and Social History* 7, no. 1 (2010): 87–109.
27 Carlo Ginzburg, *The Cheese and the Worms: The Cosmos of a Sixteenth Century Miller* (London: Routledge and Kegan Paul, 1980).
28 István M. Szijártó, 'Probing the Limits of Microhistory', *Journal of Medieval and Early Modern Studies* 47, no. 1 (2017): 197.
29 Ghobrial, 'Seeing the World', 13.
30 De Vries, 'Playing with Scales', 36.

31 See for example Douglas Booth, 'Surfing: From One Cultural Extreme to Another' in *Understanding Lifestyle Sport: Consumption, Identity, Difference*, ed. Belinda Wheaton (London: Routledge, 2004), 94–110; Rita Liberti and Maureen Smith, *(Re)Presenting Wilma Rudolph* (Syracuse: Syracuse University Press, 2015); Daniel Nathan, *Saying It's So: A Cultural History of the Black Sox Scandal* (Champaign: University of Illinois Press, 2005); Gary Osmond, 'Photographs, Materiality and Sport History: Peter Norman and the 1968 Mexico City Black Power Salute', *Journal of Sport History* 37, no. 1 (2010): 119–137; Gary Osmond and Murray G. Phillips, 'Look at the Kid Crawling: Race, Myth and The Crawl Stroke', *Australian Historical Studies* 3, no. 127 (2006): 43–62; Jaime Schultz, 'Reading the Catsuit: Serena Williams and the Production of Blackness at the 2002 US Open', *Journal of Sport and Social Issues* 29, no. 3 (2005): 338–357; and Patricia Vertinsky, 'This Dancing Business is More Hazardous than any He-man Sport: Ted Shawn and his Men Dancers', *Sociology of Sport Journal* 35, no. 2 (2018): 168–177.

32 Christian V. De Vito, 'History without Scale: The Micro-Spatial Perspective', *Past & Present* 242, no. 14 (2019): 364.

5

SPORTS HISTORY AND THE CHALLENGE OF PHYSICAL CULTURAL STUDIES

Mark Falcous

The fragmentation of kinesiology/sports sciences/physical education departments and the concomitant privileging of the bio-sciences, the apparent political impotence of sociologists, and the sub-disciplinary diversification of critical sports studies over several decades have recently led some to question the pertinence of the sub-field of the 'sociology of sport'. The idea of a new transdisciplinary field under the aegis of Physical Cultural Studies (PCS) has subsequently been championed, chiefly by David L. Andrews, Michael Silk, and Holly Thorpe, as an antidote to these challenges.[1] This chapter considers the nexus of sports history with the nascent PCS. After briefly detailing its origins and tenets, I explore the implications and possibilities of PCS for those exploring the sporting past. Whilst it is beyond the bounds of this short chapter to excavate the full complexity of the debates and controversies surrounding the approach, I evaluate the framework towards the sporting past that it promotes and what versions it challenges. Such a discussion imbricates long-standing discussions around paradigms, theory, method, and activism across the entire sports studies field and, indeed, amongst sports historians.[2] This chapter first details the institutional, intellectual, and political contexts behind PCS. I then consider its relevance for sports historians; exploring what approaches to the sporting past PCS offers and consider its utility. Finally, I detail some of the controversies and criticisms that surround it in the context of debates about historical method, the place of theory, and politics/activism.

The intellectual and political contexts of Physical Cultural Studies

For several decades scholars have interrogated the social dynamics of sport – and increasingly physical cultures more broadly; to include exercise, fitness, health, leisure, recreation, the martial arts, and dance. While sociologists and historians have shared some intersections, differing approaches have predominated.[3] Within the sociology of sport, a critical qualitative turn cemented itself as orthodoxy in the 1980s. This constituted a shift from apparent neutrality towards explicitly ideologically committed analyses of sport intent on social change.[4] The primary emphasis within the critical canon was the workings of power and inequality, related to gender, race, class, sexuality, (dis)ability, the body, media representation, commerce, and nationalism.[5] The development of the field underwent (and continues to

DOI: 10.4324/9780429318306-7

undergo) struggles in its intellectual and institutional progress, marked by dialogue and disagreement between those oriented towards varying theoretical schools and methods. There have also been longstanding skirmishes between sports historians and sociologists oriented towards varying research paradigms and disciplinary traditions.[6]

The cross-disciplinary field of cultural studies came to predominate within critical scholarship that largely flourished under the label 'sociology of sport'.[7] Cultural studies emphasized historical and political contextualism, focused on the contested reproduction of power relations within (sport as) culture, and the narratives of marginal groups, while allowing for theoretical eclecticism. This approach was dynamic and contested. For example, early formulations were challenged by injunctions from gender theorists who argued for feminist-infused cultural studies approaches.[8] Contingent to this eclecticism, multiple disciplinary influences permeated an increasingly diverse 'sociological' sub field: urban studies, gender theory, media studies, queer theory, geography, history, post-colonialism, post-structuralism, post-Marxism, and anthropology. Lacking any single disciplinary security, the 'sociology of sport' sub-title was increasingly an inadequate descriptor of the field drawing on such diverse disciplinary traditions, methodologies, and subject matter. Simultaneously, the shifting tertiary education environment created new conditions and pressures in which critical exploration of physical cultures could exist.

Whilst it is fraught to identify any singular moment as an 'absolute beginning', David Andrews' 2008 paper was significant in advocating for the reformulation of thinking under the label 'Physical Cultural Studies'.[9] Andrews advocated for PCS as an antidote to 'kinesiology's current *crisis*', which he saw as characterized by: epistemological hierarchy, empirical ambiguity, and political impotence hindering the development of an integrated kinesiology, and hence limiting the field's potential. In particular, he problematized kinesiology's 'hyperfragmentation and hyperspecialization' that had rendered 'competing and seemingly irreconcilable factions with little or no interest in the field's potentially uniting empirical focus'. Furthermore, fragmentation, he noted, was associated with hierarchization that has privileged 'rationally conceived objective knowledge' and 'predictive over interpretive ways of knowing'. Consequently, those engaged in critical and interpretive research, he suggested, 'were forced to engage in a continuous struggle for their very existence'.[10] The solution, Andrews posited, was reformulation under the tenets of PCS.

Andrews promoted PCS on several interrelated grounds. First, a broadened focus on 'physical culture' over sport, which he deemed 'neither intellectually appropriate nor politically expedient'. Second, he advocated to 'reclaim' the human body from the bio-sciences to understand it as a site of social struggle; that is, as a means to bring into focus the way the active body 'is culturally regulated, practiced and materialized' and 'how dominant power structures become expressed in, and through, socially and historically contingent embodied experiences, meanings and subjectivities'.[11] This new focus, Andrews argued, necessitated transcending exclusive intellectual boundaries, which he said were themselves limiting. In a subsequent special edition of the *Sociology of Sport Journal*, Silk and Andrews summarized the premises of PCS as: a focus on the body or active physicality; an inclusive analysis of physical culture in its varied forms (dance, exercise, sport, outdoor recreation and health); the promotion of multi-method and inter-disciplinary approaches (designed, in part, to confront epistemological hierarchies); and an overt desire to challenge social injustices, and to support innovative types of qualitative research.[12] In a 2017 *Handbook of Physical Cultural Studies* Andrews and Silk offer a further formula detailing eight key characteristics of PCS: empirical, contextual, transdisciplinary, theoretical, political, qualitative, self-reflexive, and pedagogical.[13]

Physical Cultural Studies' relevance for sports historians?

The question of the utility of PCS to historians imbricates longstanding debates between those who explore sport/physical culture from differing paradigmatic and disciplinary perspectives. There have been numerous flashpoints *between* those advocating sociological and historical perspectives over several decades.[14] Furthermore, historians have adopted and debated varying positions towards paradigm, theory, and method.[15]

So what does PCS proffer for historians' approaches to sport? A specifically *historical* contextualism, although clearly elemental to the PCS framework is given little attention within the mapping of Andrews and colleagues. Indeed, they only once mention history as one of the multiple disciplines which make up a transdisciplinary approach.[16] This is perhaps unsurprising, given that, as Grossberg notes, cultural studies 'is about the future, and about some of the work it will take in the present, to shape the future'.[17] Given this 'future focus', historical contextualism appears largely implicit, and takes a back seat to the political terrain of the present. Whilst Andrews and colleagues don't specifically chart the place of approaches to the past in their vision of PCS other than to advocate historical contextualism, it is possible to take their mandate and consider its potential relevance for sports historians.

There are several features to approaching the past that PCS points towards. Foremost, it foregrounds an explicitly *politicized* approach. Most fundamentally, PCS sees the narrativization of the sports past as politicized, and it pushes against the banal, apparently *a*political (yet inherently power-laden) mythologization of the past. As Roland Barthes conceptualized, myth functions to construct phenomena both as 'normal' and 'inevitable' and hence, relatedly, as *a*historical. Myth, Barthes noted, 'deprives the object of which it speaks of all history'.[18] The denial of history works to leave things in the present as timeless, eternal and absolute, as opposed to sites of struggle and change between competing interests. The role of the critic of myths, Barthes continued, is to expose 'signs' and reveal their inner workings and show that what appears to be 'natural' is actually determined by historical struggle, constructed and power-laden. There are echoes of this signalled by the PCS approach. This fundamentally necessitates *contextualism*; that is, conceptualizing physical culture (including sport) within its broader social, economic, cultural, and political contexts. Whilst long germane for numerous historians as an explanatory paradigm, contextualization is typically ill-defined within sports history.[19] Contextualism for PCS entails seeing physical culture as a site in which power relations act, emerge, and can be contested. That is, it both understands sport as historically derived, and socially, politically, economically, and culturally contested. This accords with a *self-reflexive* approach to the writing of the sporting past, which is not viewed as a neutral, objective exercise.

In terms of Douglas Booth's oft-cited typology of sports history paradigms,[20] derived from the work of Alun Munslow, PCS reflects constructionist and deconstructionist influences. The constructionist elements appear in both the advocacy of theory as a tool to make sense of the power dynamics contouring the sporting past *and* the anti-relativist commitment to a meta-narrative of social justice.[21] The deconstructive influence rests on the position that instead of beginning with the past, historians must fundamentally interrogate the way the past has been represented; that is, historical method and writing are viewed as a power-laden enterprise. In short, PCS challenges the notion of sports history as an empirical project written by an unbiased, ideologically neutral, and objective historian, but simultaneously opposes postmodernist challenges to the legitimacy of 'meta-narratives' of modernist history. Andrews and Silk shun the philosophical relativism associated with postmodernist positions, describing PCS as an 'anti-relativist project'.[22] In Table 5.1, I elaborate on the eight features

Table 5.1 Approaching the sporting past through Physical Cultural Studies[23]

Elements of PCS	Implications for approaching the sporting past
Empirical	Approach to the past involves gathering evidence. Emphasizes doing so in a multi-scale way; encompassing a breadth of empirical sites ranging from the micro to the macro.
Contextual	Seeks to 'radically contextualize' the physical culture(s) of the present within the past, and avoid reductionist essentialism in its approach. A position that 'accepts nothing as given, nothing as final, nothing as fixed, nothing as permanent – everything as contingent'.[24] Thus, sceptical of acontextual sports history and of linear approaches to sporting development. Emphasizes mapping the wider historical context in and through which physical expressions (as contested products/expressions of culture) are made meaningful.
Transdisciplinary	Not confined to historical method/approach traditionally conceived; draws on a range of disciplinary approaches. Historians, thus, must be willing to engage other disciplinary methods, concepts, and theories.
Theoretical	Rejects a reconstructionist approach to the sporting past grounded in atheoretical objectivism. Leans towards uses of theory as sensitizing and as an explanatory tool. Draws upon a 'fluid theoretical vocabulary'.[25] Advocates a 'detour via theory'; that is, seeks to avoid totalizing, i.e. overly deductive uses of theory.
Political	Seeks to expose both the complexities, experiences, and injustices of the sporting past *and* its telling as 'sports history'. Approaches the past as contested and characterized by social divisions, inequality and hierarchy. Furthermore, approaches the recording of the past (the discipline of sports history) as power-laden and politicized. Therefore, problematizes the hierarchies of what topics are given prominence, whose voices are privileged, or what is marginalized or forgotten in sports history scholarship.
Qualitative	The recognition of history as an interpretive endeavour favours qualitative paradigms and data; that is, interpretation is a key theme/feature, not reductive quantified data often presented as linear timelines.
Self-reflexive	Recognizes that history is not the exclusive product of empirical endeavour; emphasizes the role of the historian in the creation of the past as narrative. Challenges the notion that history as an empirical project can be written by an unbiased, ideologically neutral and objective historian. Reflects a deconstructionist approach; yet does not retreat to a position of philosophical relativism. It retains evaluative criteria, unlike a 'hard relativist' position which rejects universal criteria for evaluating truth claims.
Pedagogical	Is associated with social justice advocacy and public intellectualism and aims at conscientization. Challenges dominant historical representations of sport/physical culture and the hierarchies they can sustain. Aims to facilitate individuals and groups to discern, challenge, and potentially transform power relations as they exist through orthodoxies of how sports history is hegemonically told.

of a PCS approach detailed by Andrews and Silk to consider its mandate for approaching the sporting past.

There are glimpses of how PCS approaches to the sporting past may look in Andrews' earlier work and in the work of Ben Carrington.[26] They demonstrate, for example, how corporate interests selectively (re)construct both Muhammed Ali and Martin Luther King within sport-themed television advertising. In doing so, they argue, marketeers strip these historical figures of their social and political complexity in line with present-day marketing priorities. Andrews similarly notes the faux-historical architecture which evokes collective memory in Niketown stores, or 'retro' baseball parks which fuel romanticized versions of baseball's 'authentic' past. He further critiques how corporate advertising featuring Manchester United stars of the past and present re-aligns the heritage of the club with the contemporary hyper-commodified game, asserting a seamless lineage between the two as a means to capitalize on the club's past. The critical issue in this case is obscuring the economic rationalities and media-centrism of the contemporary game by making connections with a nostalgic past phase of English football's commercial development. Likewise, Falcous and Newman have explored New Zealand sport as a site through which selective 'remembering' can be invoked and (re)entrenched in the present as national 'mythscape'.[27] They point to various cases that reveal how spectres of the sporting past circulate in selective and power-laden 'everyday' culture: on cereal boxes, within advertising campaigns, as memorial trophies and TV sports trailers. The effect is to consolidate national mythologies that imbricate economic and post-colonial power dynamics. Such works signal just some approaches to the past that PCS might foreground although there are also other possible trajectories.

Controversies and debates

Andrews and colleagues' advocacy of PCS has not been without debate.[28] Giulianotti commends the intent of PCS but offers four cautionary observations. First, as a 're-branding' exercise PCS may not offer anything substantively different from what existed previously in an already diversified field.[29] In this vein, Adams et al. aired reservations about the 'language of differentiation and emergence', which they suggest 'appropriates and territorializes concepts and commitments with long histories outside of PCS and that were being utilized within the sociology of sport and physical culture writ large'. Specifically, they comment that 'feminist histories tend to be unnamed and/or unacknowledged in PCS's [then] most frequently referenced works'. The effect of PCS as a 'boundary marking' project, Adams et al. contend, is to marginalize the existing field as 'lesser, dead or dying'.[30] This critique, however, is contested by Thorpe and Marfell, who advocate engagement with PCS, suggesting that Adams et al. ignore those feminist writers productively working within PCS.[31] Whether PCS is distinguishable from existing 'critical' approaches must be evaluated by historians already drawing on power-focused paradigms. Indeed, King has previously mapped an approach to history under the guise of 'contextual sports studies', identifying a focus on power relations, privileging 'marginal' voices, and avoiding a linear 'march of progress' genre which centres individual people, dates, and events.[32] King's 'cultural materialist' approach bears marked similarities to the approach to history that PCS ultimately signals.

Second, Giulianotti notes that the 'physical' side of PCS is not entirely convincing in that not all work under the umbrella focuses on the physical, moving body; for instance, much work examines mediated sport texts. This is highly pertinent to historians, many of whose work is focused on archives/documents rather than the lived, active body. Yet, Andrews counters that physical culture is 'ontologically complex' and might be considered to incorporate 'the reproduction and consumption of mediated representations of various forms of embodiment'.[33]

Third, Giulianotti notes that the apparent hostility towards quantitative paradigms could limit the capacity to create progressive social change. In his words, 'there are no obvious reasons why quantitative methods cannot be fully utilized; indeed, there are many critical social scientists who utilize these methods to make similar arguments to PCS regarding relations of power and progressive social change'.[34] This hostility has appeared to 'soften' in later writing where Andrews and Silk acknowledge 'the value of considered quantitative work'.[35] At times polemics and a crisis discourse have characterised PCS advocacy,[36] that is, championing an aggressively radical political agenda of progressive change designed to confront, agitate, and indeed (curiously) relish the marginalization that may emerge from this. This has been criticized as 'faux radicalism', whilst 'the often verbose, obtuse and inaccessible presentational style of work that characterizes the PCS tone of address' has also raised scepticism.[37] In more general terms, Vertinsky has observed that 'a full throttled social activist agenda can and often does alienate PCS from the science side of the house in kinesiology as well as the academy more generally'.[38] This is pertinent to historians who seek legitimacy amongst their mainstream history peers, where objectivist empiricism holds sway and the academic jargon that litters the social sciences is often distained.

Fourth, Giulianotti notes that to enhance the influence of the approach, there is a need to develop methodological and analytical diversity as a transnational approach to create a 'polyvocal, glocal and hybrid PCS'. Hence he cautions that 'PCS will require a decade or more of further research and publications in order for firm conclusions to be drawn on its significance and merits'.[39] In this sense, engagement from sports historians remains to be seen.

Conclusions

There is little doubt that PCS is an ambitious project yet to be fully realized. As I have detailed above, PCS has met with strong criticism, and indeed some previously embracing the title have moved away from it.[40] This criticism may be driven in part by the polemics of some of David Andrews and Michael Silk's earlier advocacy, rather than their apparent intent. As Giulianotti notes, its merits and significance remain to be seen over a longer timeframe. In a shift of tone, Andrews and Silk explain that their definitional effort 'should be considered generative as opposed to being definitive',[41] suggesting it as a dynamic project. My intention has been to provisionally consider the potential of PCS for sports historians.

Many historians of sport will find PCS writing to be abstruse, and some may dismiss the debates to be little more than academic status games. Indeed, some will likely view it as the product of a specific circumstance in relation to disciplinary fragmentation within kinesiology (or relatedly human movement studies, sports studies/sciences, physical education) departments, and even specifically the University of Maryland if Andrews' original trajectory establishing essay is borne in mind. Furthermore, the vagaries of 'social justice' as an ill-defined mantra in PCS loom large in any conversation about what a politicized sports history entails.

Yet, the original impetus of PCS is worth consideration, and that is about the vitality and relevance of the academic field in the current intellectual and political climate. The position of sports history at the fringes of both 'mainstream' historical debate and of kinesiology/sports studies suggest the debate is worth engaging. As Tomlinson and Young demonstrated a decade ago, sports historians' work has scarcely broken out of an extremely narrow enclave in over a quarter of a century.[42] The challenge for sports historians in this regard is to

History and Physical Cultural Studies

consider the ideas and, indeed, challenges that PCS foregrounds. This challenge resonates with long-standing debates within sports history and adds impetus to the likes of recent calls to 'decolonize' the discipline of sports history,[43] which echo similar calls in the parent discipline.[44] The marginalization of sports historians' work – within curricula, within the metrics of research productivity (privileging research grants and high impact factor, 'hard' science journals) that dominate neo-liberal universities, and the limited scope of a sports-centric purview alone is prescient in this regard. What sort of sports histories (and hence sports historians) can and will survive in this climate? Whether a PCS-infused approach may be valuable, even expedient, in undertaking what Vertinsky terms 'the tough disciplinary work of holding up your own methods of inquiry to constant scrutiny',[45] is a question for historians to consider seriously.

Notes

1 See David Andrews, 'Kinesiology's Inconvenient Truth and the Physical Cultural Studies Imperative', *Quest* 60, no. 1 (2008): 45–62; Michael Silk, Anthony Bush, and David Andrews, 'Contingent Intellectual Amateurism, or, the Problem with Evidence-based Research', *Journal of Sport and Social Issues* 34, no. 1 (2010): 105–128; David Andrews and Michael Silk, 'Physical Cultural Studies on Sport', in *Routledge Handbook of Physical Cultural Studies* eds. Michael Silk, David Andrews, and Holly Thorpe (London: Routledge, 2017), 83–93; Michael Silk, David Andrews, and Holly Thorpe eds. *Routledge Handbook of Physical Cultural Studies* (London: Routledge, 2017).

2 For an overview of the field, see Mark Falcous and Douglas Booth, 'Contested Epistemology: Theory and Method of International Sport Studies', *Sport in Society* 20, no. 12 (2017): 1821–1837. For sport history see Louise Mansfield and Dominic Malcolm, 'Sociology', in *Routledge Companion to Sports History*, eds. Steven Pope and John Nauright (London: Routledge, 2009), 99–113; Dominic Malcolm, *Sport and Sociology* (London: Routledge, 2012); Richard Holt, 'Historians and the History of Sport', in *Making Sport History: Disciplines, Identities and the Historiography of Sport*, ed. Pascal Delheye (Routledge: London, 2014), 29–58.

3 Falcous and Booth, 'Contested Epistemology', 1821–1837.

4 Significant to note, however, was that the focus of the emancipatory turn shifted emphasis towards theoretical/intellectual arguments rather than on practice within the sporting world – despite the emancipatory rhetoric of politicized frameworks.

5 More recently, concerns have expanded to include ecological and environmental justice.

6 See, for example, David Rowe, Jim McKay, and Geoffrey Lawrence, 'Out of the Shadows: The Critical Sociology of Sport in Australia, 1986 to 1996', *Sociology of Sport Journal* 14, no. 4 (1997): 340–361.

7 For reviews, see Robert Hollands, 'The Role of Cultural Studies and Social Criticism in the Sociological Study of Sport', *Quest* 36, no. 1 (1984): 66–79; David Andrews and John Loy, 'British Cultural Studies and Sport: Past Encounters and Future Possibilities', *Quest* 45, no. 2 (1993): 255–276. John Hargreaves and Ian McDonald, 'Cultural Studies and the Sociology of Sport', in *Handbook of Sports Studies*, eds. Jay Coakley and Eric Dunning (Sage: London, 2000), 48–60; David Andrews, 'Coming to Terms with Cultural Studies', *Journal of Sport and Social Issues* 26, no. 1 (2002): 110–117; David Andrews and Michael Giardina, 'Sport Without Guarantees: Toward a Cultural Studies that Matters', *Cultural Studies? Critical Methodologies* 8, no. 4 (2008): 395–422.

8 Cheryl Cole, 'Resisting the Canon: Feminist Cultural Studies, Sport, and Technologies of the Body', *Journal of Sport and Social Issues* 17, no. 2 (1993): 77–97.

9 Andrews, 'Kinesiology's Inconvenient Truth'.

10 Andrews, 'Kinesiology's Inconvenient Truth', quotes 45, 46, 47, 49, 50, 53–54, and 61.

11 Andrews, 'Kinesiology's Inconvenient Truth', quotes 53–54 and 61.

12 Michael Silk and David Andrews, 'Toward a Physical Cultural Studies', *Sociology of Sport Journal* 28, no. 1 (2011): 4–35.

13 Andrews and Silk, 'Physical Cultural Studies on Sport'.

14 See Rowe, McKay, and Lawrence, 'Out of the Shadows'; Falcous and Maguire, 'Interrogating Sporting Pasts and Presents: Whose Scholarship Will Count, and What Will It Count For?' in

Examining Sports Histories: Power, Paradigms and Reflexivity eds. Richard Pringle and Murray Phillips (Morganstown, VA: FIT Publishers, 2013), 251–271.

15 See Douglas Booth, *The Field: Truth and Fiction in Sport History* (London: Routledge, 2007); Pringle and Phillips, *Examining Sport Histories*; Allen Guttmann, 'Review Essay: The Ludic and the Ludicrous', *The International Journal of the History of Sport* 25, no. 1 (2008): 100–112.

16 Andrews and Silk, 'Physical Cultural Studies on Sport'.

17 Lawrence Grossberg, *Cultural Studies in the Future Tense* (Durham: Duke University Press, 2010), 1.

18 Roland Barthes, *Mythologies* (New York: Hill & Wang, 1957/2012), 264.

19 Booth, *The Field*.

20 Booth, *The Field*.

21 Andrews and Silk, in 'Physical Cultural Studies on Sport', note their 'anti relativism' 'acknowledges a multiplicity of truth claims, yet equally establishes that some truth claims are more methodologically sound, theoretically informed, and politically prescient – they are more interpretively insightful – than others, based on established criteria for assessing the rigour, relevance and quality of qualitative research' (92). Such a position is in opposition to the 'hard' relativism of the postmodern assault on universal truth claims as meta-narratives.

22 Andrews and Silk, 'Physical Cultural Studies on Sport', 92.

23 Adapted from Andrews and Silk, 'Physical Cultural Studies on Sport'.

24 Bryan Behrenshausen, 'Cultural Studies in the Present Tense', *Cultural Studies* 33, no. 1 (2019): 70.

25 Andrews, 'Kinesiology's Inconvenient Truth', 55.

26 David Andrews, 'Dead and Alive?: Sports History in the Late Capitalist Moment', *Sporting Traditions* 16, no. 1 (1999): 73–84. Ben Carrington, 'Postmodern Blackness and the Celebrity Sports Star: Ian Wright, "Race" and English Identity', in *Sport Stars: The Cultural Politics of Sporting Celebrity* eds. David Andrews and Steve Jackson (London: Routledge, 2002), 112–133.

27 Mark Falcous and Joshua Newman, 'Sporting Mythscapes, Neoliberal Histories, and Post-colonial Amnesia in Aotearoa/New Zealand', *International Review for the Sociology of Sport* 51, no. 1 (2016): 61–77.

28 Mary Louise Adams, Michelle Helstein, Kyoung-yim Kim, Mary McDonald, Judy Davidson, Katherine Jamieson, Samantha King, and Geneviève Rail, 'Feminist Cultural Studies: Uncertainties and Possibilities', *Sociology of Sport Journal* 33, no. 1 (2016): 75–91; Richard Giulianotti, *Sport: A Critical Sociology*, second edition (Hoboken, NJ: John Wiley and Sons, 2015); Richard Pringle and Mark Falcous, 'Transformative Research and Epistemological Hierarchies: Ruminating on How the Sociology of the Sport Field Could Make More of a Difference', *International Review for the Sociology of Sport* 53, no. 3 (2018): 261–277.

29 Giulianotti, *Sport: A Critical Sociology*.

30 Adams et al., 'Feminist Cultural Studies', 78. It's significant that Adams et al. note that: 'our comments about PCS are not directed at the many diverse projects that are given the PCS label … our concern lies primarily with a collection of recent writings that are intended to help establish PCS as a distinct approach to the study of physical cultures' (77). Thus, the criticism is of the 'canonization' of PCS, rather than the overall intent or merit.

31 Holly Thorpe and Amy Marfell, 'Feminism and the Physical Cultural Studies Assemblage: Revisiting Debates and Imagining New Directions', *Leisure Sciences* 41, nos. 1/2: 17–35.

32 Samantha King, 'Methodological Contingencies in Sports Studies', in *Qualitative Methods in Sports Studies*, eds. David Andrews, Dan Mason, and Michael Silk (Oxford, UK: Berg, 2005), 21–38.

33 Andrews, 'Kinesiology's Inconvenient Truth', 55–56.

34 Giulianotti, *Sport: A Critical Sociology*, 71.

35 Andrews and Silk, 'Physical Cultural Studies on Sport', 89.

36 For example, Silk, Bush, and Andrews, 'Contingent Intellectual Amateurism' is a polemic against the trend toward narrowly defined criteria of research evaluation that they argue is 'assaulting' higher education and increasingly evident in sport scholarship. They critique 'evidence based' objectivism and advocate prioritizing political investment and moral and ethical concerns as a criterion of research 'quality'. Although they don't cite examples, they claim that the sociology of sport is characterized by a 'growing preoccupation with evidence-based research (EBR)' (107). It is 'championed', they continue, 'among certain sections of the sociology of sport community' (108), but they provide no citations. Such an approach, they claim, 'is nothing short of collusion with, and explicit support for existing regimes of power' (108). In this way they are referring to the epistemological hierarchies that tend to be sustained by the evidence-based approaches advocated by public and private funding bodies.

History and Physical Cultural Studies

37 See John Sugden, Alan Tomlinson, and Belinda Wheaton, 'Joining the Dialogue: Challenging the PCS (Physical Cultural Studies) Positioning Within the Sociology of Sport'. Paper presented at the Crossroads in Cultural Studies Conference, Paris, France, 2012, see Abstract/Program, 234.

38 Patricia Vertinsky, 'Shadow Disciplines, or a Place For Post-disciplinary Liaisons in the North American Research University: What Are We to Do with Physical Cultural Studies', in *Playing for Change: The Continuing Struggle for Sport and Recreation*, ed. Russell Field (Toronto: University of Toronto Press, 2015), 400.

39 Giulianotti, *Sport: A Critical Sociology*, quotes 70 and 71.

40 The Florida State University, having launched a Centre for Physical Cultural Studies in 2012, subsequently changed its name in 2013 to the Centre for Sport, Health, & Equitable Development.

41 Andrews and Silk, 'Physical Cultural Studies on Sport', 87.

42 Alan Tomlinson and Christopher Young, 'Sport in History: Challenging the Communis Opinio', *Journal of Sport History* 37, no. 1 (2010): 5–17.

43 See Samuel Clevenger, 'Sport History, Modernity and the Logic of Coloniality: A Case for Decoloniality', *Rethinking History* 21, no. 4 (2017): 586–605.

44 See Vertinsky, 'Shadow Disciplines', 389–406.

45 Vertinsky, 'Shadow Disciplines', 398.

6

NARRATIVE/S IN SPORT HISTORY

Daniel A. Nathan

This chapter is a meditation on narrative and its relationship to history and sport history. One of its goals is to encourage sport historians and students to think critically about narrativity, the past, and historical narrative representations of it. But before considering narrative/s in sport history, I think we should discuss narrative/s in sports.

Most of us would agree that sports often tell great stories. Or more precisely, that some people tell great sports stories; after all, stories don't tell themselves – they are crafted by storytellers.

In sports, there are all manner of dramatic, exciting events and outcomes: last-second, game-winning shots are among our favourites. There are myriad historical and contemporary examples of people and teams working hard, making sacrifices, and overcoming hardships and odds to realize their athletic dreams. Sports fans around the world love those narratives and avidly consume them. They are certainly longtime staples of the sports/media complex. There are countless real-life (and fictional) sports comedies, romances, and tragedies. Every people, every culture, has its favourites, which neatly dovetail with the historical moment's cultural preferences and values.

In the United States, for example, for over a hundred years, millions of people have cherished baseball stories. 'More than any of our sports,' asserts the historian Elliott J. Gorn, 'baseball is about language. Each inning, each game, each season is a story, and some fine novelists have captured baseball's narrative art.'[1] There is considerable truth here. After much thinking, I have concluded that baseball is principally about narrative, that is, about the stories people tell and re-tell about the game.[2] For many of us, listening to, telling, and reading baseball stories is sometimes more interesting and valuable than playing or watching the game.

At the same time, Gorn's observation applies to most sports. In basketball and football (the hyperviolent version preferred in the United States and the 'beautiful game' the rest of the world loves), for instance, every possession of the ball is a very short story – a micro story, if you will – or perhaps a sentence in the larger narrative that is, say, a quarter or a half. If we put all the possessions in a game together, we get a longer, complete narrative. String all the games together and we get a season or a career. That is the way athletic and narrative accretion works. And yet just as clearly, this phenomenon is not unique to baseball, basketball, and football. To what sport does it *not* apply?

50   DOI: 10.4324/9780429318306-8

Narrative/s in sport history

Additionally, Gorn is correct that some novelists (such as Ring Lardner and Mark Harris) have done a first-rate job of exemplifying baseball's essential narrativity. And so have other people who traffic in words, such as journalists and historians, among others. When it comes to sports, baseball has no monopoly on the creative use of language and narrativity. It is far from the only sport that relies on narrativity to appeal to fans and to weave its way into the fabric of a culture.

In short, among the reasons many people love and are interested in sports is their capacity to tell deeply meaningful stories. This is also one of the reasons that sports constitute a multibillion-dollar globalized industry. Put differently, narrative is endemic to sports. Indeed, narrative and sports are inextricably intertwined. It is hard to imagine a sporting world that is not rooted in and fuelled by narratives about the games we play, watch, and cheer. Modern sports need narratives in order to exist as we know them.

History, by which I mean the discourse used to represent and analyse the past, rather than the past itself, is likewise heavily dependent upon narrative. From the first historian, and for some of us that means Herodotus, history has relied upon storytelling, which is 'the quintessential' vehicle for acquiring and transmitting understandings of the past'.[3] Of course, historical narratives must be evidence-based and avoid the 'narrative fallacies' that the historian David Hackett Fischer catalogues in *Historians' Fallacies: Toward a Logic of Historical Thought* (1970). 'Most historians tell stories in their work,' Fischer concedes. 'Good historians tell true stories. Great historians, from time to time, tell the best stories which their topics and problems permit.'[4] Fischer's last point is important, for historians frequently experience epistemological challenges and are constrained by disciplinary standards and conventions and by the availability of relevant evidence. Moreover, one does not need to be a narratologist (and I am not one) to recognize that historical narratives are often multifaceted and complex.

What are we talking about when we talk about narrative? Clearly, narrative means different things to people in different disciplines and walks of life. On the simplest level, though, a narrative is a story, and a complete story 'has a beginning, a middle and an end', contends Aristotle.[5] To be precise, Aristotle was referring to the nature of tragedy, which is a particular kind of narrative. Still, it seems reasonable to apply this criterion to other kinds of narratives, which come in all shapes and sizes, from multivolume novels to 30-second television commercials. Most narratives have characters, settings, a plot, and a point of view (and sometimes several of all of these things). In *The Nature of Narrative* (1966), Robert Scholes and Robert Kellogg explain: 'By narrative we mean all those literary works which are distinguished by two characteristics: the presence of a story and a story-teller.'[6] That obviously covers a lot of ground. And since I take 'literary' to mean simply the use of language, rather than traditional fictional works, it includes the work of historians.

The narratives that historians craft are necessarily retrospective. Always looking backward, historians sift through the past's textual (and sometimes physical) remains, which is often an arduous and sometimes unproductive process. Those remains or traces are the building blocks, the constituent parts of historical narratives. But this is not to suggest that historical narratives are somehow readymade if fragmentary, waiting to be put back together again à la Humpty Dumpty. The historian Hans Kellner puts it well:

> I do not believe that there are 'stories' out there in the archives or monuments of the past, waiting to be resurrected and told. Neither human activity nor the existing records of such activity take the form of narrative, which is the product of complex cultural forms and deep-seated linguistic conventions deriving from choices that have traditionally been called rhetorical; there is no 'straight' way to invent a history, regardless of the honesty and professionalism of the historian.[7]

Those 'complex cultural forms and deep-seated linguistic conventions' are themselves historically contingent and subject to contestation and change. But the larger point here is that historical narratives, like all narratives, exist in multiple contexts and are always crafted, put together by people.

There is, in fact, no choice in the matter, that is, if one wants to read historical narratives (and obviously not everyone does). Events do not unfold as narratives, stories just waiting to be told. As the folklorist and documentary filmmaker Bruce Jackson reminds us:

> Life itself has no narrative. It is serial and multiple: a million things happening at once, and then another million things happening at once, forever and ever. Narrative is one of the ways we apply order to that unimaginable overabundance of information.[8]

The desire for order, coherence, and meaning is understandable, but historical narratives (as well as many other kinds of stories) are always selective, incomplete, and partial (in both senses of the word). What, for example, would a truly comprehensive, objective history of, say, ice hockey or the ancient Olympics look like? These and innumerable other sporting subjects are so vast that such texts – no matter how massive – are inconceivable. The same is true of smaller, more obscure subjects.

Just as clearly, we do know many things about the sporting past. We know that James Naismith invented basketball in 1891 in Springfield, Massachusetts.[9] We know that the modern Olympics were inaugurated in 1896 in Athens.[10] We also know that Abner Doubleday did *not* invent baseball in Cooperstown, New York, which is where the National Baseball Hall of Fame is located.[11] There is a plethora of reliable evidence to support these facts. We know more complicated things, too, such as the complex, intertwined roles that industrialization, urbanization, immigration, race, ethnicity, gender, social class, the mass media, and technology had on the rise of modern sport in the late nineteenth and early twentieth centuries.[12] But knowing these things and being able to communicate them are different matters. 'Narrative,' the critical theorist Linda Hutcheon declares, 'is what translates knowing into telling.'[13] Narrative is something like a delivery system for all kinds of knowledge, not just history.

The human reliance on narrative, which allows us to know – and sometimes imagine and feel – things about the past (and the present), has deep roots and a long history. It predates literacy. Consider the prehistoric cave pictograms in France's Vézère valley, which are thought to be approximately 19,000 years old. Or the myriad indigenous creation stories, which were transmitted orally for untold generations. These and other examples suggest that we do not produce and consume narratives simply for entertainment. In *The Storytelling Animal: How Stories Make Us Human* (2012), Jonathan Gottschall argues, 'The human imperative to make and consume stories runs even more deeply than literature, dreams, and fantasy. We are soaked to the bone in story.'[14] There are many reasons for this, but one is that there is value and utility in narrative. Like a Swiss Army knife, narrative has many functions. It can do many things, including help us live richer, more well-informed and empathetic lives. For reasons that are difficult to pinpoint, Gottschall notes:

> Humans evolved to crave story. This craving has, on the whole, been a good thing for us. Stories give us pleasure and instruction. They simulate worlds so we can live better in this one. They help bind us into communities and define us as cultures. Stories have been a great boon to our species.[15]

These are all fine, defensible points, and not everyone agrees.

The philosopher Alex Rosenberg is among those who are critical of narrative's ability to represent the past meaningfully. In *How History Gets Things Wrong: The Neuroscience of Our Addiction to Stories* (2018), Rosenberg acknowledges that we can use language to document and chronicle that things happened in the past. He would surely accept that Naismith invented basketball in 1891. For Rosenberg, however, the problem is that historical narratives are 'almost always wrong. What narrative history gets wrong are its *explanations* of what happened'.[16] Drawing on cognitive science, evolutionary anthropology, and neuroscience, Rosenberg asserts that not only are historical narratives unreliable and lack explanatory power, but that most of them 'are harmful, damaging to people' because they provide a misleading sense of why things happened the way that they did.[17] A philosopher of science and a provocateur, Rosenberg argues:

> Stories are for children and for the child in us all. Nothing will ever stop us from loving them, at least not until natural selection radically changes our neurology. Narrative historians, like other storytellers, will never want for an audience. But we will all benefit by recognizing what narrative history at its best and most harmless actually gives us – not knowledge or wisdom, but entertainment, escape, abiding pleasure.[18]

There are problems here. First, some stories are of course unsuitable for children, and even our inner-children (at least my inner-child). Second, knowledge and wisdom are not always in contradistinction to 'entertainment, escape, abiding pleasure'. For some of us, being knowledgeable and receiving and earning wisdom give pleasure and joy. Undaunted and unafraid of hyperbole, Rosenberg concludes: 'Every national movement, religious tradition, regional culture, ethnic group, political party, and sports team has its own, often inflammatory narrative history. Some of them are entertaining. Few of them have any wisdom – and none, any knowledge – to impart.'[19] Really? No knowledge? No moral lessons? History is often 'distorted, politicized and badly mishandled', but to suggest that it never communicates any knowledge is not only implausible, it is wrong.[20] Many, indeed most, narrative histories do impart knowledge.

More incendiary than convincing, Rosenberg faults history for being unable to achieve the kind of replicable knowledge that is (sometimes) possible in the natural sciences. He seems vexed that different historians can look at the same evidence and write different kinds of narratives and arrive at different conclusions, a phenomenon with which I and many others are comfortable. Although Rosenberg pushes us to think more critically about the use of narrative to make causal judgments and historical arguments, he seems unwilling to acknowledge or accept that 'the study of the past is a constantly changing, never-ending journey of discovery'.[21]

Since the process of transforming lived experience and reality into prose and coherent narratives is fraught with challenges, it is unsurprising that many historians use familiar narrative forms, tropes, and strategies, including emplotment. According to the historical theorist Hayden White in *Metahistory: The Historical Imagination in Nineteenth-Century Europe* (1973), 'Emplotment is the way by which a sequence of events fashioned into a story is gradually revealed to be a story of a particular kind.'[22] Influenced by Northrop Frye's *Anatomy of Criticism* (1957), White identifies 'at least four different modes of emplotment: Romance, Tragedy, Comedy, and Satire'.[23] There are others, too, such as farce and tragicomedy. White contends:

Providing the 'meaning' of a story by identifying the *kind of story* that has been told is called explanation by emplotment. If, in the course of narrating his story, the historian provides it with the plot structure of a Tragedy, he has 'explained' it one way; if he has structured it as a Comedy, he has 'explained' it another way.[24]

Historians sometimes emplot their narratives self-consciously, with deliberation and care. One would be hard-pressed to read Ronald A. Smith's *Wounded Lions: Joe Paterno, Jerry Sandusky and the Crisis in Penn State Athletics* (2015) as something other than a tragedy. At the same time, despite how awful the Penn State-Sandusky scandal was (especially for the boys Sandusky victimized), it could be rendered as a (darkly) comedic narrative, with a cast of fools and moral imbeciles. Or as a horror story, with a grotesque monster roaming the hills of Happy Valley, with impunity, for years. White stresses that we should not mistake 'a narrative account of real events for a literal account thereof. A narrative account is always a figurative account, an allegory'.[25] That is, it is a discursive approximation, based on evidence, with a discernible moral of some kind. The final point is perhaps another way of saying that historical narratives are ideological.

This is another reason that some critics have decried narrative history as a practice: how can it be objective, neutral, or disinterested if it is ideological? I suppose it cannot. But objective, neutral, and disinterested history is chimerical anyway, a false ideal. 'As a practical matter,' the historian Peter Novick writes, the belief in and embrace of historical objectivity

> promotes an unreal and misleading invidious distinction between, on the one hand, historical accounts 'distorted' by ideological assumptions and purposes; on the other, history free of these taints. It seems to me that to say of a work of history that it is or isn't objective is to make an *empty* observation; to say something neither interesting nor useful.[26]

Amen. Of course, historians have a responsibility to get their facts correct, to the extent that is possible. This is an obvious prerequisite for writing history. Facts matter. Whatever one thinks about, say, baseball slugger Barry Bonds and his moral character and the context in which he played the last nine years of his career, however one emplots his biography, there is no denying that he hit a Major League record 762 home runs. This is empirical, verifiable, and indisputable. It is also a fact that needs to be carefully and critically assessed, contextualized, and communicated. All of which is to say, history can be and is an empirical-analytical discipline and it is also literary, in the sense that it is fashioned using language and 'employs all the devices of literary art (statement and generalization, narration and description, comparison and comment and analogy)', not that it is fictional.[27]

By this late date, I would hope that most people (but alas, not everyone) would be comfortable with this two-ness: history as an empirical-analytical discipline and a literary practice. Many years ago, the British historian and journalist A.J.P. Taylor declared that historians 'should not be ashamed to admit that history is at bottom simply a form of storytelling'.[28] A form of storytelling predicated on empirical documents, lowercase truths, reason, and analysis, but a form of storytelling and argumentation nonetheless.

All of which brings us back to Elliott Gorn, who sagely and self-reflexively notes:

> The stories we tell are constructed, and we know it (though there are a few who still won't admit it). Behind the confident prose and flowing narrative, a good historian is painfully aware of how much has to be left out of the story, how the

sources say contradictory things, how compelling other interpretations are, how eagerly our adversaries lie in wait to pounce on our weaknesses, how much must remain untold. We work with those problems as best we can, trying to capture as much nuance and complexity as possible. But, finally, we tell stories in little spaces that necessarily force us to leave out much more than they allow us to include; and we do it because the alternative is to not tell stories at all, at least not historical ones.[29]

Given our alternatives, we are better off with carefully documented, compelling historical 'stories in little spaces', despite their inevitable and inherent shortcomings, than the alternative, which would impoverish us all.

The argument here is that more historians should lean into narrative, run towards and embrace it. Sport history – all history – would profit from more self-reflexive, creative, sophisticated, engaging storytelling. The possibilities for sport history in particular are tremendous. Carefully studying the sporting past and telling well-documented, plausible, nuanced, historical stories about it is intellectually (and aesthetically) enriching, even if it lacks the scientific rigor and precision of neuroscience and mathematics. 'Of course people of goodwill, sharing the same standards, will continue to differ about the past,' muses the historian Alan B. Spitzer, 'which is to say that history is not mathematics – and even mathematics is fuzzy around the edges.'[30] Mature thinkers, I am convinced, can deal with the limits of historical knowledge, differences of interpretation, and some indeterminacy and fuzziness.

Notes

1 Elliott J. Gorn, 'Baseball As America: Seeing Ourselves through Our National Game,' *Journal of Sport History* 30 (Summer 2003): 276.
2 See, for example, Daniel A. Nathan, *Saying It's So: A Cultural History of the Black Sox Scandal* (Urbana: University of Illinois Press, 2003).
3 Robert Eric Frykenberg, *History and Belief: The Foundations of Historical Understanding* (Grand Rapids: W.B. Eerdmans, with the Institute for Advanced Christian Studies, 1996), 63.
4 David Hackett Fischer, *Historians' Fallacies: Toward a Logic of Historical Thought* (New York: Harper & Row, Publishers. 1970), 131.
5 Aristotle (translation by Anthony Kenny), *Poetics* (Oxford: Oxford University Press, 2013), 26.
6 Robert Scholes and Robert Kellogg, *The Nature of Narrative* (New York: Oxford University Press, 1966), 4.
7 Hans Kellner, *Language and Historical Representation: Getting the Story Crooked* (Madison: University of Wisconsin Press, 1989), vii.
8 Bruce Jackson, *The Story Is True: The Art and Meaning of Telling Stories* (Philadelphia: Temple University Press, 2007), 4.
9 James Naismith, *Basketball: Its Origins and Development* (New York: Association Press, 1941).
10 Allen Guttmann, *The Olympics: A History of the Modern Games*, Second edition (Urbana: University of Illinois Press, [1992] 2002).
11 David Block, *Baseball Before We Knew It: A Search for the Roots of the Game* (Lincoln: University of Nebraska Press, 2005).
12 Elliott J. Gorn and Warren Goldstein, *A Brief History of American Sports*, Second edition (Urbana: University of Illinois Press, [1993] 2013).
13 Linda Hutcheon, *A Poetics of Postmodernism: History, Theory, Fiction* (New York: Routledge, 1988), 121.
14 Jonathan Gottschall, *The Storytelling Animal: How Stories Make Us Human* (Boston: Houghton Mifflin Harcourt, 2012), 18. Along these same lines, in the introduction to the 1984 version of *Narration and Knowledge*, art critic and philosopher Arthur C. Danto argues, 'Narration exemplifies one of the basic ways in which we represent the world, and the language of beginnings and endings, of turning points

and crises and climaxes, is coimplicated [sic] with this mode of representation to so great a degree that our image of our own lives must be deeply narrational.' Arthur C. Danto, *Narration and Knowledge* (New York: Columbia University Press, 2007), xiii.

15 Gottschall, *The Storytelling Animal*, 197.

16 Alex Rosenberg, *How History Gets Things Wrong: The Neuroscience of Our Addiction to Stories* (Cambridge: MIT Press, 2018), 3.

17 Rosenberg, *How History Gets Things Wrong*, 6.

18 Rosenberg, *How History Gets Things Wrong*, 250.

19 Rosenberg, *How History Gets Things Wrong*, 259.

20 David M. Kennedy, 'What History Is Good For', *New York Times Book Review*, 19 July 2009, 10.

21 Eric Foner, *Who Owns History?: Rethinking the Past in a Changing World* (New York: Hill and Wang, 2002), xix.

22 Hayden White, *Metahistory: The Historical Imagination in Nineteenth-Century Europe* (Baltimore: Johns Hopkins University Press, [1973] 1975), 7.

23 White, *Metahistory*, 7.

24 White, *Metahistory*, 7.

25 Hayden White, *The Content of the Form: Narrative Discourse and Historical Representation* (Baltimore: Johns Hopkins University Press, [1987] 1990), 48.

26 Peter Novick, *That Noble Dream: The 'Objectivity Question' and the American Historical Profession* (New York: Cambridge University Press, 1988), 6.

27 Carl Becker, 'Everyman His Own Historian,' *American Historical Review* XXXVII (January 1932): 231.

28 A.J.P. Taylor, 'Fiction in History,' *Times Literary Supplement*, 23 March 1973, 327.

29 Elliott J. Gorn, 'Professing History: Distinguishing Between Memory and the Past', *Chronicle of Higher Education*, 28 April 2000, B4.

30 Alan B. Spitzer, *Historical Truth and Lies About the Past: Reflections on Dewey, Dreyfus, de Man, and Reagan* (Chapel Hill: University of North Carolina Press, 1996), 121.

7

EXPANDING REPERTOIRES INSIDE AND OUTSIDE THE ARCHIVES

Methods

Gary Osmond

Methodological experimentation is valued in sport history, with various historical 'turns' – including the digital, postmodern, and visual – triggering innovations. One area clamouring for methodological expansion is Indigenous sport history, especially given calls for greater recognition of, and engagement with, Indigenous research paradigms to acknowledge, address, and accommodate Indigenous epistemologies, methodologies, and ontologies. This chapter highlights one broad area – archives and archival uses – for expanding methodological approaches in Indigenous sport history. This focus recognizes the problematic relationship between the archive and history-making encapsulated by Australian historian Sue McKemmish and colleagues:

> As Indigenous and settler communities in various countries and regions have jointly reflected on their engagement with archives, there has been a growing recognition that western archival science and practice reflect and reinforce a privileging of settler/invader/colonist voices and narratives over Indigenous ones, of written over oral records.[1]

This chapter is concerned with expanding methodological repertoires for Indigenous sport histories inside *and* outside formal, public archives in ways that grapple with these issues of archival privileging. My underlying assumption is that archives are sites of power as well as knowledge, sites of exclusion as well as preservation.[2] This is not a new argument, but is one that has special resonance for Indigenous people and their histories. As sites of power, archives have abused, effaced, exploited, failed, and neglected Indigenous people. As sites of knowledge, however, they contain many records of concern and interest to Indigenous people. While these documents are almost always written from non-Indigenous perspectives, Indigenous people are finding increasing uses for this knowledge: in Australia, archives play a role in 'recovering identity and memory, reuniting families, seeking redress, and in the reconciliation process between Indigenous and non-Indigenous' citizens.[3] Sport historians

DOI: 10.4324/9780429318306-9

57

have the potential to contribute to recovery and reconciliation efforts. To do so, however, new repertoires are required beyond simple factual extraction from archives in order to better align research practices in sport history with Indigenous research paradigms and needs. Inside the archive, these include reading in new ways and contributing to archival reclamation. Outside the archive, oral history and, in particular, the methodology of yarning, offer under-explored potential. My focus is on Australia, however many of the arguments draw on the experiences of Indigenous people in other countries, are applicable beyond Antipodean boundaries, or may merit consideration in other Indigenous jurisdictions.

Indigenous archives

Archives are conceived in various ways: as physical institutions, as document collections within those edifices, or as metaphoric sites of remembering and forgetting – in Foucauldian terms, as 'the law of what can be said, the system of statements, or rules of practice, that give shape to what can and cannot be said'.[4] Knowledge is central to each of these. Whatever the conceptualization, recent decades have witnessed the increasing reframing of archives from simple sites of knowledge extraction to complex sites of knowledge production and power which acknowledges their contested nature rather than truth content. As anthropologist and historian Ann Laura Stoler has argued, archives have come under increased scrutiny as understandings of history have changed:

> A focus on history as narrative and history-writing as a charged political act has made the thinking about archives no longer the pedestrian pre-occupation of 'spadework' historians, of flat-footed archivists, nor the entry requirements of fledgling initiates compelled to show mastery of the tools of their trade. The 'archive' has been elevated to new theoretical status, with enough cachet to warrant distinct billing, worthy of scrutiny on its own.[5]

Carolyn Hamilton and colleagues have noted in the context of South Africa, with its colonial and apartheid figurations and biases, that archives are 'figured' and in need of 'transformation, or refiguring'.[6] The notion of 'figured', of the constructed nature of the archive, is central to revised understandings of its nature and of responses to working with archival institutions. Scholarship on the archive, driven by deconstructionism, calls for a refiguring of the archive to iron out hierarchical creases in source legitimacy: archives 'are just one of many vehicles – including newspapers, literature, oral testimony, photographs, films and so forth – for accessing the past'.[7] In this vision, archives are not monolithic, omniscient entities, but rather are 'slivers' in broad knowledge systems.[8] The call for refiguring is applicable to all settler-colonial states with Indigenous populations. It is certainly apt for the Australian context, where archives as sites of knowledge, sites of retrieval, and sites of power are all particularly problematic in the Indigenous context.

As sites of knowledge, institutional archives containing public documents can be useful to Indigenous people, as touched on in the introduction to this chapter, but that use is limited. Indigenous knowledges are primarily oral and therefore under-represented in physical archives.[9] Western vs Indigenous knowledges are privileged by these institutions, which serve state needs rather than those of Indigenous peoples and are often perceived as disserving those groups. As historian Lynette Russell has noted, many Aboriginal people see archives as 'the repositories of materials which are the result of surveillance'.[10] These materials are 'archival texts within which Indigenous people were the object (and subject) of the

Expanding repertoires

gaze of colonial authorities and "experts," and from which Indigenous knowledge, perspectives and voices were excluded'.[11] For this reason, there is a 'strong sense of distrust of archival institutions' among many Indigenous people.[12] This distrust is not widely shared by academic historians, among whom a 'cult of the archive' prevails.[13] Likewise, sport historians maintain a confidence in archives.[14]

Tensions over the knowledge worth of archives extends to their characteristics as sites of retrieval. The ability to extract knowledge from archives is valued highly in academia. Facts retrieved are often taken as having special truth status because they emanate from an archive, rather than being understood as privileged snippets of knowledge. For Indigenous people who may not trust their provenance or the circumstances of their collection, archival facts are problematic. And for Indigenous people who are aware of displaced knowledges – oral knowledge supplanted by written records, for example – archival offerings may be slim pickings.

As sites of power, archives are often both 'documents of exclusion and monuments to particular configurations of power'.[15] The wielding of power via the archives has been unkind to Indigenous people. Indigenous literatures scholar Evelyn Araluen Corr, for example, has argued that for Aboriginal women in Australia, the archive 'is a material and symbolic space of imperial violence', a discursive role visible in the treatment of Indigenous peoples within many archives.[16] Yet, as Corr observed, the role can be subverted as archives become a 'site of recovery' through, for example, provision of family histories.[17] McKemmish and colleagues make a similar point, deeming archives both 'instruments of oppression and of redress and reconciliation' for Indigenous people.[18]

Issues around archives as sites of knowledge, retrieval, and power were central to *Trust and Technology*, a research project on archives and Indigenous Australians conducted between 2003 and 2008 by a team of scholars, archivists, public servants, and Indigenous representative bodies.[19] Researchers on that project argued that 'archival sources of Indigenous knowledge and history are fragmented and dispersed, in many ways mirroring the dispossession, dislocation and disempowerment of colonialism and the post-colonial period'.[20] In specific response to this fragmentation and dispersal of knowledge, and to more general calls to refigure and reimagine the archive, the project broadens understandings of archival sources of Indigenous knowledge and history beyond the plaster-and-brick confines of institutional archives. In the process, it identified five sites for the location of these fragmented and dispersed archival sources, summarized below in the order in which they were reported:

1   Oral memory
2   Records created for and by Indigenous people, communities and organisations
3   Digital archives 'repatriated' from library, archive and museum collections
4   Research data archives
5   Records in all forms … created by non-Indigenous people and organisations about Indigenous people, including government records.[21]

Note here that the traditional conceptualization of the archive as a depot of documents features last in the list, and that oral memory appears first. These sites provide practical demonstration in an Indigenous context of the conceptual reframing of the archive that has been underway for some time, and are useful for extending methodologies for Indigenous sport history. I first discuss methodological changes possible within the conventional archive, followed by ways to expand our repertoire beyond those walls to include and address sites identified by the *Trust and Technology* project.

Expanding repertoires inside the archives

Stoler has noted in the context of the Dutch colonial archive in the Netherlands Indies that documents were not 'dead matter' once written and stored. What was 'left' was not 'left behind' or obsolete: 'Documents honed in the pursuit of prior issues could be requisitioned to write new histories [and] could be reclassified for new initiatives.'[22] These observations are true for all colonial archives. They are a reminder that, in addition to remembering and forgetting, archives are sites for imagining.[23] State documents, created and preserved for state purposes, can be used to write 'un-state-d' histories.[24]

For sport historians working within the traditional archive, two broad imaginative and innovative approaches require comment. Given that archives both conceal and reveal, consideration needs to be given to reading *against* the grain and *with* the grain, in what Stoler calls a turn from extraction to ethnography in the colonial archive.[25] Reading against the grain, or reading between the lines, is perhaps the more familiar. This 'art of inferring' aims to expose what is concealed or to allow productive speculation about what might have been concealed, what Corr calls 'investigating what the text (or archive) pushes against or seeks to conceal'.[26]

Reading between the lines is necessary in many areas of sport history with a dearth of written or other sources – the history of homosexuality is one such example where the historical record is marked by gaping silences, sheer absences, and elusive fragments. In such cases, 'often the historian is faced with little choice but to read the snippets and shadows, piecing together fragments and ephemera, often melding older historical concepts with newer historiographical and theoretical frameworks'.[27]

For Indigenous sport history, the problem is not (always) a dearth of records. There is (often) a wide range of sport records detailing events, discussing logistical arrangements, and situating these within official discourses and policies. The real problem is transparency. These records, as noted, were generated by white overseers, created within a context of surveillance, and reflected white administrator perspectives rather than those of the Indigenous people whose lives were documented. Sport offers particular issues because its records appear benign – records about athletic events are less likely to appear insidious than those on many other facets of Indigenous lives. It makes it easier for sport historians to simply extract and reproduce from the archive without deep analysis of lived reality.

One area where Indigenous sport history has questioned the transparency of archival records has been sport as a site of resistance. Following the lead of anthropologist and political scientist James C. Scott, who has studied the historic pathways of 'everyday forms of resistance' for subaltern groups, several historians have read between the lines of archival documents for alternative understandings of sporting experiences, including ways that apparent enthusiastic embrace of introduced sports can mask appropriation of those sports as means to exert agency and resistance against colonizing institutions.[28] Historian John Bloom, for example, analysed an oral history interview with a former Native American boarding school pupil to reveal 'hidden transcripts' of race, racism, and agency in the early twentieth century.[29] I have also explored 'hidden transcripts' of resistance in sporting contexts in Aboriginal reserves in Queensland to reveal examples of oppositional acts.[30] Reading against the grain in this way not only holds the promise of yielding new insights into the sporting past, as these examples indicate, but also respects research methodologies that rightfully insist on the inclusion of Indigenous perspectives on the past, including those that position Indigenous peoples as experiencing agency, autonomy, and selfhood in the face of settler-colonial oppression.

Reading *with* the grain requires a move from extraction towards archival contextualization. In order to understand individual documents, we must know what the archive contains and understand how records are written, represented, and stored in terms of language, context, and categorization. As Stoler has asked, 'How can students of colonialisms so quickly and confidently turn to "readings against the grain" without a prior sense of their texture and granularity?'[31] Anybody who has worked in archives understands the complexity of locating documents: transparency, Stoler reminds us, is not a hallmark of archives.[32] Initial catalogue searches often appear limited, yet prolonged exposure to those sources can give insight into the existence of other, less obvious, files. This opening up comes not only from dogged perseverance, but also from a developing understanding of the context of documents, of who they were written for, and of which institutions/bodies they were intended initially to serve. Admittedly, this is difficult to do. Without lengthy and total immersion in a particular archive, its boundaries are difficult to measure, its depths difficult to plumb, and the contextual contours difficult to gauge.

Some Indigenous scholars, reading with the grain, have adopted personal policies of archival exclusion – refusing to work with or cite certain sources because of their anonymity, unpublished or unapproved publication, or associations with colonial violence. As American Indian Studies scholar K. Tsianina Lomawaima has argued, such questions carry with them larger ethical issues.[33] For scholars who are interested in understanding Indigenous sport histories, contexts of creation and archiving are likewise important considerations.

Expanding repertoires outside the archives

Opportunities also exist outside the archive to extend the methodological palette in sport history. As the brief reference to oral histories above alludes, Indigenous voices on the sporting past have been rare in the public realm. While many sport historians have interviewed Indigenous people, few comprehensive accounts of these exchanges have been published. Yet within Indigenous cultures, oral memories are integral to the circuitry of Indigenous knowledges. Historian and anthropologist Lisbeth Haas, writing in the context of colonial Mexican California, defines Indigenous knowledges as 'material made, represented, and/or saved by native communities' that extends to artworks, dance, oral testimonies, ritual and song.[34] In this section, I focus on oral testimonies and opportunities for working with these to explore Indigenous sporting pasts in respectful cooperation with Indigenous knowledge holders.

In Indigenous communities worldwide, telling 'stories, constructing narratives and talking about the past is invariably regarded as part of knowing oneself, from where they come and to whom they are related'.[35] As historian William Bauer Jr. argues in the Native American context, but more widely applicable, individually oral histories reveal 'mundane' activities, but considered together they offer valuable collective memory capable of challenging and reinterpreting 'conventional understandings of the past'.[36] It is this collective potential that makes them important archival considerations.

Storytelling can fall into the epistemological divide between Western and Indigenous ways of knowing because of Western historians' wariness of memory, stories, and storytelling and their privileging of written accounts. In Australia, McKemmish and colleagues argue that this divide between orality and written text is a false dichotomy, not so different from what Adele Perry framed in the Canadian context as 'savage-orality-myth' versus 'literacy-civilisation-history'.[37] Aboriginal Australians have long used written records and written communication, and now oral and written records are 'flowing from one format to the other, constantly interacting and growing into a living archival continuum'.[38] For example, the 2008 national apology to the Stolen Generations – those thousands of Aboriginal and Torres Strait Islander people who had been forcibly removed from their families under settler-colonial rule – drew on both written archival records and on the memories and stories of those affected.[39]

To reduce power imbalances inherent in academic oral history projects on Indigenous themes – which are characteristically conducted by non-Indigenous interviewers in positions of power over their interviewee subjects – yarning offers methodological advantages. Yarning, a common term for conversing in Australian Aboriginal cultures, has been formalized into an appropriate and safe conversational research methodology by researchers across several fields. It has been defined as 'informal and relaxed discussion through which both the researcher and the participant journey together visiting places and topics of interest relevant to the research study'.[40] While yarning is idealized as involving groups of Indigenous people in time-unlimited, informal conversation, led by an Indigenous Elder, researchers have adopted tenets of respect, reciprocity, and cultural responsibility with more formal requirements of Western academic research as cross-cultural yarning. This recognizes the cultural requirements of both Indigenous participants and non-Indigenous researchers, such as formal human ethics requirements of universities; it may or may not involve groups and Indigenous facilitators.[41] Murray Phillips and I have employed cross-cultural yarning to collaborate with Aboriginal women from the former government-controlled Cherbourg Aboriginal Settlement in Australia to explore counter-narratives to those that dominate the archival record, for example, and the potential for sport historians to adopt yarning or its precepts for oral history research with Indigenous people appears strong.[42]

Conclusion

Working with archives, both inside and out, offers other modes of practice for sport historians beyond those discussed here. Globally, some archivists have begun to include Indigenous values and principles in their structures of governance, practice, procedures, protocols, and ethical guidelines.[43] Sport historians can contribute to these processes by helping to expand archival repositories. Russell has argued that archival materials can 'become Indigenous through reclamation processes'.[44] One possibility for contributing to reclamation efforts is to add oral memories, which are typically excluded from archival collections.[45] Hamilton and her colleagues refer to archival efforts launched in South Africa, for example, to 'document voices excluded from formal repositories in the past' via an oral history programme.[46] In Australia, various oral history projects have included Indigenous sport and, while there are limitations to our ability to fill gaps, these are worthy projects for discussion with archives. A second way that sport historians can help Indigenous communities reclaim archives is by bringing archival material directly to communities or, indirectly, to their notice.[47] Archives are increasingly important to Indigenous people, for example in terms of genealogies and land title yet, as Russell has argued, it is 'clear that some [Indigenous] communities do not know (or perhaps no longer remember) that there is material in the public domain relevant to their culture'.[48] This is as true for sport-related documents as in other fields. A third possibility is 'value adding' by annotating records and providing 'alternative perspectives' to written archival records.[49] While there may be no clear existing avenues for such initiatives, they may be worth considering in particular contexts.

Motivations for extending archival repertoires include the opportunity to enrich the historical record, to address Indigenous-specific issues around the archive as sites of knowledge,

Expanding repertoires

retrieval, and power, and to integrate archival practice with Indigenous research paradigms. This chapter has aimed to highlight some of the issues and opportunities; others are doubtless available and worth exploring as ways to expand methodological approaches in what, for many sport historians, is a valued but taken-for-granted institution.

Notes

1 Sue McKemmish, Shannon Faulkhead, and Lynette Russell, 'Distrust in the Archive: Reconciling Records', *Archival Science* 11, nos. 3–4 (2011): 218.
2 Douglas Booth, 'Sites of Truth or Metaphors of Power? Refiguring the Archive', *Sport in History* 26, no. 1 (2006): 100.
3 McKemmish et al., 'Distrust in the Archive', 218.
4 Carolyn Hamilton, Verne Harris, and Graeme Reid, 'Introduction', in *Refiguring the Archive*, eds. Carolyn Hamilton, Verne Harris, Jane Taylor, Michele Pickover, Graeme Reid, and Razia Saleh (Cape Town: David Philip, 2002), 9; Ann Laura Stoler, 'Colonial Archives and the Arts of Governance: On the Content in the Form', in *Refiguring the Archive*, ed. Hamilton et al., 87, 89. For definitions of archives, see Booth, 'Sites of Truth', 104–105.
5 Stoler, 'Colonial Archives', 86.
6 Hamilton, Harris, and Reid, 'Introduction', 7.
7 Booth, 'Sites of Truth', 103.
8 Hamilton, Harris, and Reid, 'Introduction', 10.
9 Lynette Russell, 'Indigenous Knowledge and Archives: Accessing Hidden History and Understandings', *Australian Academic & Research Libraries* 36, no. 2 (2005): 162, 168.
10 Lynette Russell, 'Indigenous Records and Archives: Mutual Obligations and Building Trust', *Archives and Manuscripts* 34, no. 1 (2006): 37.
11 McKemmish et al., 'Distrust in the Archive', 213; Russell, 'Indigenous Records', 36.
12 McKemmish et al., 'Distrust in the Archive', 219.
13 Ludmilla Jordanova, *History in Practice* (London: Hodder Arnold, 2nd ed, 2006), 161.
14 Booth, 'Sites of Truth', 97; Martin Johnes, 'Archives and Historians of Sport', *The International Journal of the History of Sport* 32, no. 15 (2015): 1784–1798.
15 Hamilton, Harris, and Reid, 'Introduction', 9.
16 Evelyn Araluen Corr, 'Silence and Resistance: Aboriginal Women Working within and against the Archive', *Continuum* 32, no. 4 (2018): 487.
17 Corr, 'Silence and Resistance', 487.
18 McKemmish et al., 'Distrust in the Archive', 214.
19 Monash University, *Koorie Archiving: Trust and Technology – Final report*, 2017 https://www.monash.edu/it/our-research/research-centres-and-labs/cosi/projects/completed-projects/trust/final-report accessed 5 June 2019.
20 McKemmish et al., 'Distrust in the Archive', 227.
21 McKemmish et al., 'Distrust in the Archive', 228.
22 Ann Laura Stoler, *Along the Archival Grain: Epistemic Anxieties and Colonial Common Sense* (Princeton, NJ: Princeton University Press, 2009), 3.
23 Verne Harris, 'A Shaft of Darkness: Derrida in the Archive', in *Refiguring the Archive*, ed. Hamilton et al., 75.
24 Stoler, 'Colonial Archives', 91.
25 Stoler, 'Colonial Archives', 86.
26 Johnes 'Archives and Historians of Sport', 1791; Corr, 'Silence and Resistance', 495.
27 Lisa Featherstone, 'Snippets and Shadows of Stories: Thoughts on Sources and Methods When Writing an Australian History of Sexuality', in *Intimacy, Violence and Activism: Gay and Lesbian Perspectives on Australasian History and Society*, ed. Graham Willett and Yorick Smaal (Melbourne: Monash University Publishing, 2013), 83.
28 James C. Scott, *Weapons of the Weak: Everyday Forms of Peasant Resistance* (New Haven, CT: Yale University Press, 1985), xvi.
29 John Bloom, *To Show What an Indian Can Do: Sports at Native American Boarding Schools* (Minneapolis: University of Minnesota Press, 2000). For 'hidden transcripts', see James C. Scott, *Domination and the Arts of Resistance: Hidden Transcripts* (New Haven, CT: Yale University Press, 1990).

30 Gary Osmond, 'Decolonizing Dialogues: Sport, Resistance and Australian Aboriginal Settlements', *Journal of Sport History* 48, no. 2 (2019): 288–301.

31 Stoler, 'Colonial Archives', 92.

32 Stoler, *Along the Archival Grain*, 8.

33 K. Tsianina Lomawaima, 'Mind, Heart, Hands: Thinking, Feeling, and Doing in Indigenous History Methodology', in *Sources and Methods in Indigenous Studies*, eds. Chris Andersen and Jean M. O'Brien (London: Routledge, 2016), 64.

34 Lisbeth Haas, *Saints and Citizens: Indigenous Histories of Colonial Missions and Mexican California* (Berkeley: University of California Press, 2014), 184.

35 Russell, 'Indigenous Records', 41.

36 William Bauer, Jr., 'Oral History', in *Sources and Methods in Indigenous Studies*, eds. Chris Andersen and Jean M. O'Brien (London: Routledge, 2016), 160, 165.

37 McKemmish et al., 'Distrust in the Archive', 225. The authors cite Adele Perry, 'The Colonial Archive on Trial: Possession, Dispossession, and History in *Delgamuukw v. British Columbia*', in Antoinette M. Burton ed. *Archive Stories Facts, Fictions, and the Writing of History* (Durham, NC: Duke University Press, 2005), 333.

38 McKemmish et al., 'Distrust in the Archive', 227.

39 McKemmish et al., 'Distrust in the Archive', 216.

40 Dawn Bessarab and Bridget Ng'andu, 'Yarning about Yarning as a Legitimate Method in Indigenous Research', *International Journal of Critical Indigenous Studies* 3, no. 1 (2010): 38.

41 Gary Osmond and Murray G. Phillips, 'Yarning about Sport: Indigenous Research Methodologies and Transformative Historical Narratives', *The International Journal of the History of Sport* 36, nos. 13–14: 1271– 1288.

42 Gary Osmond and Murray G. Phillips, 'Indigenous Women's Sporting Experiences: Agency, Resistance and Nostalgia', *Australian Journal of Politics and History* 64, no. 4 (2018): 561–575.

43 Bradford W. Morse, 'Indigenous Human Rights and Knowledge in Archives, Museums, and Libraries: Some International Perspectives with Specific Reference to New Zealand and Canada', *Archival Science* 12, no. 2 (2012): 121–124.

44 Russell, 'Indigenous Knowledge', 162.

45 Russell, 'Indigenous Knowledge', 168; Russell, 'Indigenous Records', 36.

46 Hamilton, Harris, and Reid, 'Introduction', 12.

47 Russell, 'Indigenous Knowledge', 167.

48 Russell, 'Indigenous Knowledge', 167.

49 McKemmish et al., 'Distrust in the Archive', 221.

8

SPORT AND MATERIAL CULTURE

Maureen Smith

A ticket stub from a New York Yankees game in 1977; a race singlet from the 1989 Empire State Games; 2018 Winter Olympic Games mascot figures; an Archie Griffin autographed football; a Billie Jean King bobblehead; second base used for three innings from the inaugural season at Citi Field in a game between the New York Mets and St. Louis Cardinals in 2009; a tape measure from the 1960s, made of plastic, a seemingly obsolete tool of measurement at the elite level of track and field, but still a handy device for a high school meet. Many of these objects sound like collectibles, and they are (to someone). They also represent a sliver of the infinite variety of objects that constitute the material culture of sport.

Understanding sporting cultures, both ancient and modern, has been greatly enhanced by the increasing reliance of scholars on utilizing material culture in their inquiries to tell the stories of the sporting past. Jules D. Prown defines material culture as 'the manifestations of culture through material production'. The 'values, ideas, attitudes, and assumptions' of a culture can be understood through the study of objects and artifacts from the past. Prown suggests that 'human-made objects reflect, consciously or unconsciously, directly or indirectly, the beliefs of the individuals who commissioned, fabricated, purchased, or used them and, by extension, the beliefs of the larger society to which these individuals belonged'.[1] Hardy, Loy, and Booth consider material culture of sport to be 'the artifacts of the arena', and offer their own typology to classify the 'vast material world of sport'. The nine categories, though not exclusive, are Playing Equipment, Venues, Training Equipment and Sport Medicine Technology, Sportswear, Prizes, Symbolic Artifacts, Performance Measurement Technology, Ephemera and Detritus, and Memorabilia.[2] Hardy and his colleagues contend that 'material culture both drives and reflects the meanings that humans attach to sports'.[3] This relationship, between humans and their objects, and the meanings we attach to these objects, is most certainly evident as we examine the material culture of sport. Hardy and his colleagues 'focus on forms of material culture that have had particularly strong associations with a particular long residual: prizes (*agon*), equipment (craft), colors (community), ephemera/detritus (gambling), sportswear (*eros*), and venues (framing)', making the connections between material culture and the six systems of practices and beliefs they identified throughout the lineage of sport history.[4]

These artifacts of sport serve to connect the present with the past in ways that go beyond the written word. Unlike other historical events, Prown suggests that 'an artifact is

DOI: 10.4324/9780429318306-10

65

something that happened in the past, but ... continues to exist in our own time'. These artifacts 'constitute the only class of historical events that ... survive into the present', according to Prown, adding that these artifacts, 'authentic, primary historical material' can be 'reexperienced'.[5] By engaging with these artifacts, we, the scholar, the student, the museum visitor, and the sport fan, can use our senses to engage with and better understand our sporting pasts.

Sport historians and material culture

Several scholars have critiqued their peers for not paying enough attention to material culture as sources to examine and understand the past, relying instead on the written word at the expense of a more extensive and inclusive primary source pool. Borish suggests to better understand the roles of women in the Olympic Games, both 'literary and non-literary sources ought to be explored in contemporary critical scholarship', and concludes that 'material culture approaches provide connections between ideology and artifact in the Olympic Games and the way women and men perceive the culturally constructed world of the Olympics'.[6] Vamplew aptly identifies that sport historians had been 'reluctant' to use artifacts in their research. In his work on sport museums, Vamplew challenges sport historians to 'step outside the archive room and into the exhibition galleries', seeing the artifacts on display as complementary to the 'literary text approach' relied on by most scholars.[7] Hardy and his colleagues, in creating their categories to consider various forms of material culture, echoed Vamplew; they inform their readers that material objects 'as forms of evidence and sources of inquiry ... are just as important as the minutes of powerful governing bodies, the recollections of hard-driving magnates and ingenious coaches, or the daily reports and scandals conveyed in the sporting press'.[8] Osmond addresses the lack of academic studies on sporting statues, stating 'despite their proliferation ... sporting statues are under studied by sports historians'. He suggests this is 'consistent with our preference for examining written sources, and statues are not alone among material objects as overlooked sources'.[9]

In the first decade of the twenty-first century, a handful of scholars published works that focused on the material culture of sport. These works focused on the material culture of sport as evidence to examine subjects, as well as cultural objects worthy of their own scrutiny. Olympics pins, equipment, stadiums, postage stamps, diaries, cemetery headstones, monuments and statues of athletes and sporting teams, and the birth of baseball received attention.[10]

Material culture, objects and artifacts related to sport, are a critical element in the storytelling of the past, sometimes even the focus of the story being told. Phillips, Osmond, and O'Neill, in writing about sport monuments, connect objects and narratives, positing:

> These artifacts communicate not just one version of the past, but multiple narratives that are seen, interpreted, and used by individuals and groups in myriad ways. Approaching them in this way will help sport history redress the dearth of monument studies in meaningful and relevant ways.[11]

Clearly, monuments can be a critical piece in storytelling, both in the story being told *by* the monument/artist/sponsor and the stories being told *about* and in reaction *to* the monument. Monuments, and others objects of material culture, are of little interest without a story or stories.

Perhaps in response to the growing number of sport historians examining material culture, several academic journals published special issues focusing on the material culture of sport.

Sport and material culture

Huggins and O'Mahony produced a special issue for *The International Journal of the History of Sport* in 2011, focusing on visual culture, including art, cartoons, and statues, bringing together some of the scholars whose works examined the material culture of sport. Cohen's analysis of early American political cartoons and the depictions of sports, and more importantly the cartoons themselves, serve as early evidence of the development of America's sporting culture.[12] Lisle's examination of photographs and illustrations of women in team programs, brochures, and advertising make clear that women have been targeted by professional sport teams as consumers to enjoy the stadium setting and its conveniences, promoting the idea that modern stadium spaces matter to women.[13] Fagg focuses on the paintings and photographs by Ben Shahn and their depiction of everyday life in America, which includes sport and fandom.[14] These three are among a collection of essays that delve into the visual material culture of sport and escort the reader through vivid examples of material culture at work. The editors conclude their collection claiming 'the visual materials of sport's heritage still remain marginal to both sport and visual culture historical research'.[15] Statues, stadiums, cartoons, photographs – the special issue presented a range of artifacts worthy of consideration as important pieces of evidence, as well as the subject of inquiry, in writing sport history.

A year later, in their introductory essay to a special issue of *Rethinking History*, Borish and Phillips, in their first sentence, claim the 'use, analysis, interpretation and expression of material culture typically exists as an underexplored source of history'.[16] Noting the 'ambivalence' of sport historians to focus on material culture as a subject or source of study, Borish and Phillips contend that their peers largely 'ignore the evidentiary and historical value of utilizing the theory and practice of material culture studies', preferring the 'written word over the object or thing in historical research'. In their view, and certainly the view of the authors in their special issue, 'objects ... yield a new and deeper interpretation of sport and history'.[17] Taking note of the Huggins and O'Mahony collection, they remind readers the 'intersection between visual culture theory and the sporting past has provided a legitimate forum for sport historians to explore material culture'.[18] Acknowledging published works on material culture in sport, the co-editors contend that sport historians have 'the potential to demonstrate innovative ways of making material culture matter'.[19] One example is Nathan's musings on three types of objects: a championship ring, baseball cards, and Johnny Unitas's jacket and the various emotions these objects that elicit from the holders of the objects.[20] This elicitation of emotions is an important, often overlooked, element. Objects matter to people, and they matter in how we tell stories and how we remember a story. Nathan's essay is a reminder of the important role objects play in historians' efforts to reconstruct the past.[21] Similarly, Huggins' examination of representations of sport on headstones indicates the role of sport in people's lives and how these individuals are remembered after their death.[22]

Sporting Traditions, Australia's leading sport history publication, devoted an issue to material culture in 2016. In this special issue, the articles largely focus on sport statues. Osmond and Phillips provide an introductory overview of the sport statue building trend in Australia and offer their assessments of the themes explored through sport statues. The subsequent essays provide further examples of both the building trend and various themes. Cashman examines 11 sculptures erected at Sydney Cricket Grounds between 2008 and 2011, viewing the sport statues as art and as a result writing about the material culture objects as sculptures rather than statues. Egan examines the project to build a statue of rugby player Steve Abala, a failed project, in part because civic leaders did not 'appreciate the value of the statue'. Osmond focuses his analysis on the Duke Paoa Kahanamoku statue at Freshwater, mining it to explore memory, identity, and motivations.[23]

Since the publication of these three special issues, as well as other publications focused on the material culture of sport, the argument that sport historians do not pay enough attention to material culture seems to have abated. Clearly, there is a body of work that focuses on various aspects of material culture. This growing body of literature focusing on the material culture of sport challenges readers and scholars alike to think about the multiple ways seemingly everyday objects can tell us stories about the sporting past.

Sport, material culture, and museums

Museums, specifically sport museums, are the greatest repositories of material culture related to sport. Many professional sport franchises, as they remodel or construct their sporting venues, have created their own team museums and halls of fame, using the material culture of their franchise's history to tell their athletes, owners, and team histories, in typical celebratory fashion. Snyder contends that the 'underlying purpose' of sport museums and halls of fame is the 'glorification of a sport heritage'.[24] Vamplew, writing about sport museums, contends that the 'philosophy of many sports museums is to "educate through entertainment"'.[25] Vamplew suggests that if the museum collections are 'properly utilized', they 'can tell us much about a nation's sporting culture and the social, economic, and political milieu in which it developed'.[26] Kidd echoes Vamplew on sport museums, contending that 'Hall of fame exhibits have much to offer the creative student and researcher'.[27] Sport museums utilize material objects to tell stories of the past to visitors through visual, auditory, and kinaesthetic exhibitions. Critical to thinking about material culture and their use as storytelling devices is to consider what stories are being told through these objects (as well as by the curators of the exhibits who select the objects and accompanying text).

Ramshaw and Gammon, in their work on the relationship of heritage and sport tourism, offer four categories in examining heritage, building on Ramshaw's work in this area. Two of the categories, tangible immovable and tangible movable, are inclusive of material culture. One important note of difference must be pointed out however. Ramshaw and Gammon claim: 'Like other forms of heritage, sport heritage seeks not to critique, but to celebrate; it seeks not to deliberate but to venerate.'[28] Thus, the purpose of material culture in heritage is often counter to that of sport historians. Brisbane and Wood, as cited by Ramshaw and Gammon, consider heritage to consist of 'those things of value we have inherited and wish to keep for future generations'.[29] Heritage producers, such as hall of fames or sport museums, do not share the same objective of 'knowing' history and will often use the material culture, these tangible objects, to tell their own stories, sometimes stories of celebration that might ignore relevant findings by sport historians. Thus, the work of sport historians with material culture takes on a new urgency and import in our understandings of the past and the stories and narratives about the past.

Prown contends that:

> by undertaking cultural interpretation through artifacts, we engage the other culture in the first instance not with our minds, the seat of our cultural biases, but with our senses. Figuratively speaking, we put ourselves inside the bodies of the individuals who made or used these objects; we see with their eyes and touch with their hands. To identify with people from the past or from other places empathetically through the senses is clearly a different way of engaging them than abstractly through the reading of written words.[30]

Kidd, applying Prown's sentiment to sport and the scholarship of sport history, suggests that material culture in sport museums and Halls of Fame could be sites where 'students could be helped to deconstruct artifacts', perhaps analysing an object on display 'in terms of the cycles of production, distribution, consumption, museum display, and discard, and through identifying meanings attributed to it by different groups of people'.[31] Kidd concedes that 'it will take such extra work to effectively analyze the information' presented in these spaces, adding that 'these popular "texts" may well provide the largest number of people their most important opportunity to reflect upon the place of sports in the elaboration and unraveling of late capitalist society'.[32] Borish and Phillips see the myriad potentials for the field of sport history and sport historians to 'demonstrate innovative ways of making material culture matter', and identify sport museums as a 'distinct genre of public history', where storytelling about sport has 'relied heavily on understanding material culture'.[33]

Several museums serve as illustrations of the critical role played by material culture in the study of the sporting past. Small town and skiing destination, Squaw Valley, host to the 1960 Winter Olympic Games, is home to the 1960 Olympic Museum. The museum's pamphlet reads, 'Guests can learn about Squaw Valley's Olympic Heritage with a visit to the resort's Olympic Museum'. The small museum, located at High Camp and accessible only by aerial tram (or a long uphill hike), tells the story of the city's acquisition of the event, as well as of the sporting events of those Olympic Games. The museum shares the story of Alex Cushing's bid to bring the international event to the small mountain town, with the walls and display cases adorned with equipment used in the Games, such as downhill and cross country skis and ice skates, results from the events, front pages of the *Sacramento Bee*, advertisements for the events, uniforms, and other gear worn in competition and ceremonies, and the Charles R. Blyth Memorial Arena plaque commemorating the rink atop a mountain that played host to an American ice hockey team who defeated Czechoslovakia for America's first gold medal in that sport. These artifacts from the VIII Olympic Games share stories that herald the small town's ability to play host to the world's greatest athletes amid a winter wonderland of snow that arrived at the last minute. Squaw Valley is a central character in the storytelling. In a picture frame, a narrative proclaims 'Against All Odds', and details Cushing's underdog winning bid, concluding with 'A unique idea, a strong personality and a commitment to his belief that "the Olympics belong to the world, not just one continent," won over the convention'. A display titled, 'The Olympics Go High Tech', details the use of the IBM RAMAC 305 data processing machine to calculate event scoring. Images of the machine surrounded by a small group of men, an image of the score sheet, and images of spectators looking at a scoreboard.

Browsing through the museum, one can easily fit the artifacts on display into the categories offered by Hardy and colleagues.[34] Skis and ice skates are Equipment, uniforms and opening ceremony jackets are Sportswear, programs and posters are Ephemera and Detritus, medals and trophies are Prizes, and even the display on the data processing machines falls into Performance Measurement Technology. While a visitor may not cognitively organize the objects as such, accompanying text and narratives can guide the visitor to interact with the materials from the past to engage with the 1960 Olympic Games. A visitor could easily imagine experiences of the past – what it might have been like skiing down the mountain on skis that appear almost ancient next to the technology of the twenty-first century, or how it might have felt to sit outside at the Blyth Arena watching an ice hockey game at the top of a mountain with Lake Tahoe in your periphery decades before the National Hockey League started hosting games in outdoor stadiums.

The newest Smithsonian museum, the National Museum of African American History and Culture (NMAAHC), represents a notable shift in the representation of sport, and thus material culture related to sport, as an important cultural institution. This museum marks a significant shift in how the material culture of sport is utilized and displayed in a museum setting for public consumption and understanding. Namely, this museum is focused on African-American history and culture; sport is directly identified as a cultural institution important to telling the stories of African-American experiences in the United States. Different from a sport museum or a sporting hall of fame, where a sport or team or event is celebrated, this newest museum of the Smithsonian Institute focuses on African-American history and culture and uses sport as one medium to understand the history and culture of African-Americans. Importantly, sport is among the permanent exhibitions of the museum. The inclusion of sport in such a central way to understanding culture, as presented in the NMAAHC, makes this museum unique among American museums. In this multi-floor facility, the NMAAHC has a permanent exhibit on sport on the third flood, sharing the floor with other cultural institutions, including the military, even seamlessly weaving sport and the military exhibits together physically with Muhammad Ali's refusal to be drafted into the Vietnam War.

In the sport exhibit, viewers are treated to a visual feast, with multiple videos playing on an endless loop, photographs enlarged with explanatory texts, and countless numbers of material objects selected to showcase individual athletes, sports, and events and the significances of the athletes, sports, and events and each's relationship with the African-American community. Sports have their own physical display spaces – football, baseball, basketball, and boxing – and a number of athletes are highlighted with their own small booths of visual space, including jockey Jimmy Winkle, tennis's Arthur Ashe, boxer Joe Louis, track and field great Wilma Rudolph among many. Several notable athletes with a profound impact on America's sporting culture, but more importantly African-American influence on American culture, are celebrated with statues, such as the William sisters, Jesse Owens, and Olympic medallists Tommie Smith and John Carlos. Items displayed include ticket stubs, a pair of skis worn by the first African-American to compete in skiing in the Winter Olympics, a pair of boxing gloves worn by Muhammad Ali, Rafer Johnson's Olympic torch, etc. The various uniforms and clothing worn fit with a theme expressed in video – 'style matters' and African-American athletes have been critical to shaping style in American sport and society. Walking among these objects and seeing them on display connotes to the audience – these items matter, these people matter, these accomplishments represented by these objects matter. These objects matter.

Similarly, the National Holocaust Museum, also located in Washington, DC, has an exhibit, both online and in their physical exhibitions, on the 1936 Summer Olympic Games hosted in Berlin, Germany, utilizing various forms of material culture to examine the role of sport in Hitler's Germany, as well as the American response to Germany's hosting of the sporting event within the social and political context of Nazi Germany.[35] Both museums present sport as critical to understanding culture and skilfully use material culture to help tell the stories of athletes and communities.[36] Similarly, both museums also offer online exhibitions for scholars and lay persons alike to examine items and objects from their eras and how each is part of the fabric of understanding the role of sport in broader cultural-political contexts.

Conclusions

As an academic subject worthy of investigation, the study of the material culture of sport is growing and appears to be quite robust. The reliance on material culture as a credible and worthy source by sport historians is just one indication that the academic study of material culture merits inquiry. From equipment and uniforms to game programs, ticket stubs, and posters, to larger items like monuments, statues, stadiums, the expanse of material culture continues to grow and provide scholars with rich materials to use in their historical research. Questions remain: will the typology developed by Hardy and his peers find room for expansion? Will the sporting heritage movement examined by Ramshaw introduce new forms of material culture or new ways to think about these objects? How do the stories told around said objects change? How does selection of objects shift as museum spaces shift to attract different viewers and technology demands change in how we tell stories and engage with audiences?

In considering the directions this field might take, we can look to expand upon material culture, or perhaps think about 'new' objects that might be considered part of the material culture, as we continue to tell stories about our sporting pasts that have implications for our contemporary lives. One recent example is the renaming of Monument Avenue in Richmond, Virginia for their native son, tennis great and pioneer Arthur Ashe. Previously honoured on Monument Avenue with a statue among a number of celebrated Confederate heroes, the renaming of this significant street indicates how contemporary Richmond is retelling a story of their past in a civic space, not confined to a museum, but rather with street signs. Perhaps not a traditional object of material culture, a street sign represents something much more than directions or locational information, rather it is a public display of material culture in the civic space, with the street itself is telling its own story.[37] As academicians, museum visitors, and sport fans muse about the sporting past and present, everyday and not so everyday objects of sport and civic life are critical pieces to understanding our evolving sporting culture.

Notes

1 Jules David Prown, 'The Truth of Material Culture: History or Fiction?' In *History From Things: Essays on Material Culture*, eds. Steven Lubar and W. David Kingery (Washington DC: Smithsonian Institution Press, 1993), 1.
2 Stephen Hardy, John Loy, and Douglas Booth, 'The Material Culture of Sport: Toward a Typology', *Journal of Sport History* 36, no. 1 (2009): 129–152.
3 Hardy, Loy, and Booth, 'The Material Culture of Sport, 146.
4 Hardy, Loy, and Booth, 'The Material Culture of Sport, 132.
5 Prown, 'The Truth of Material Culture', 2–3.
6 Linda Borish, 'Women at the Modern Olympic Games: An Interdisciplinary Look at American Culture', *Quest* 48 (1996): 49.
7 Wray Vamplew, 'Facts and Artefacts: Sports Historians and Sports Museums', *Journal of Sport History* 25 (1998): 276.
8 Hardy, Loy, and Booth, 'The Material Culture of Sport', 148.
9 Gary Osmond, 'Shaping Lives: Statues as Biography', *Sporting Traditions* 27, no. 2 (November 2010): 101.
10 Hardy, Loy, and Booth, 'The Material Culture of Sport'; Mike Huggins, 'Gone But Not Forgotten: Sporting Heroes, Heritage and Graveyard Commemoration', *Rethinking History* 16, no. 4 (2012): 479–495; Victoria J. Gallagher and Margaret R. LaWare, 'Sparring with Public Memory: The Rhetorical Embodiment of Race, Power, and Conflict in the *Monument to Joe Louis*', in *Places of Public Memory: The Rhetoric of Museums and Memorials*, eds. Greg Dickinson, Carole Blair, and Brian L. Ott (Tuscaloosa, AL: University of Alabama Press, 2010), 87–112; Johnathan Leib, 'The Witting Autobiography of Richmond, Virginia: Arthur Ashe, the Civil War, and Monument Avenue's Racialized Landscape', in *Landscape and Race in the United States*, ed. Richard H. Schein (New York: Routledge, 2006), 187–211; Tara Magdalinski, 'Creating History Ahead of Time: Olympic Collectibles and Marking Time', *Proceedings: International Symposium for Olympic Research* (2008), 413–417; Gary

Osmond, '"Modest Monuments?" Postage Stamps, Duke Kahanamoku and Hierarchies of Social Memory', *Journal of Pacific History* 43, no. 3 (2008); Jaime Schultz, 'Contesting the Master Narrative: The Arthur Ashe Statue and Monument Avenue in Richmond, Virginia', *The International Journal of the History of Sport* 28, nos. 8–9 (2011): 1235–1251; Maureen M. Smith, 'Frozen Fists in Speed City: The Statue as Twenty-First-Century Reparations', *Journal of Sport History* 36, no. 3 (2009): 401–420; Maureen M. Smith, 'Willie Mays Plaza, McCovey Point, and the Dominican Dandy in Bronze: (De)Constructing History at AT&T Park in San Francisco', *Journal of the West* 47, no. 4 (2008): 60–69. Also see David Block, *Baseball Before We Knew It: The Roots of the Game* (Place: Bison Books, 2005). In the case of baseball, Block relied on the diary of William Bray to re-establish the earliest games of baseball in the United States, helping to tell a new story about a sport whose origins have been written about ad nauseum. Also see John Thorn, 'Our Game: The Story of William Bray's Diary', *MLB.com*, 5 September 2013, https://ourgame.mlblogs.com/the-story-of-william-brays-diary-ff56a31de58d.

11 Murray Phillips, Mark O'Neill, and Gary Osmond, 'Broadening Horizons in Sport History: Films, Photographs, and Monuments', *Journal of Sport History* 34 (2007): 271–293.

12 Kenneth Cohen, '"Sport for Grown Children": American Political Cartoons', 1790–1850, *The International Journal of the History of Sport* 28, nos. 8–9 (2011): 1301–1318.

13 Benjamin D. Lisle, '"We Make a Big Effort to Bring Out the Ladies": Visual Representations of Women in the Modern American Stadium', *The International Journal of the History of Sport* 28, nos. 8–9 (2011): 1203–1218.

14 John Fagg, 'Sport and Spectatorship as Everyday Ritual in Ben Shahn's Painting and Photography', *The International Journal of the History of Sport* 28, nos. 8–9 (2011): 1353–1369. Also see Benjamin Flowers, 'Stadiums: Architecture and the Iconography of the Beautiful Game', *International Journal of the History of Sport*, 28, nos. 8–9 (2011): 1174–1185.

15 Mike Huggins and Mike O'Mahony, 'Epilogue', *The International Journal of the History of Sport*, 28 nos. 8–9 (2011): 1373. Also see Mike Huggins and Mike O'Mahony, 'Prologue: Extending Study of the Visual in the History of Sport', *The International Journal of the History of Sport* 28, nos. 8–9 (2011): 1089–1104.

16 Linda J. Borish and Murray G. Phillips, 'Sport History as Modes of Expression: Material Culture and Cultural Spaces in Sport and History', *Rethinking History* 16, no. 4 (2012): 465.

17 Borish and Phillips, 'Sport History as Modes of Expression', 476, 477.

18 Borish and Phillips, 'Sport History as Modes of Expression', 469.

19 Borish and Phillips, 'Sport History as Modes of Expression', 470.

20 Daniel A. Nathan, 'John Unitas's Jacket and Other Objects of Importance', *Rethinking History* 16, no. 4 (2012): 543–563. Nathan's essay is particularly helpful in thinking about the emotional meanings we attach to objects. For example, the objects listed at the start of this essay all reside in my work office, items I've collected over the years and have emotional memories linked to each object.

21 Nathan, 'John Unitas's Jacket'.

22 Huggins, 'Gone But Not Forgotten'.

23 Gary Osmond and Murray Phillips, 'Standing Tall: Memorialising Australian Sport Through Statues', *Sporting Traditions* 33, no. 1 (2016): 1–8; Richard Cashman, Reflecting on Sporting Sculptures at the Sydney Cricket Ground, *Sporting Traditions* 33, no. 1 (2016): 37–53; Ted Egan, 'The Proposed Steve Abala Role Model Statue', *Sporting Traditions* 33, no. 1 (2016): 93–96; Gary Osmond, 'The Duke Paoa Kahanamoku Statue at Freshwater: Motivations, Memory, and Identity', *Sporting Traditions* 33, no. 1 (2016): 67–91.

24 Eldon Snyder, 'Sociology of Nostalgia: Sports Halls of Fame and Museums in America', *Sociology of Sport Journal* 8 (1991): 229.

25 Vamplew, 'Facts and Artefacts', 274.

26 Vamplew, 'Facts and Artefacts', 268.

27 Bruce Kidd, 'The Making of a Hockey Artifact: A Review of the Hockey Hall of Fame', *Journal of Sport History* 23 (1996): 333.

28 Greg Ramshaw and Sean Gammon, 'More than Just Nostalgia? Exploring the Heritage/Sport Tourism Nexus', *Journal of Sport Tourism* 10, no. 4 (2005): 233. For more on heritage and sport, see Gregory Ramshaw, *Heritage and Sport: An Introduction* (Bristol, UK: Channel View Publications, 2020).

29 Ramshaw and Gammon, 'More than Just Nostalgia?', 231.

30 Prown, 'The Truth of Material Culture', 17.

31 Kidd, 'The Making of a Hockey Artifact', 333.

32 Kidd, 'The Making of a Hockey Artifact', 333.
33 Borish and Phillips, 'Sport History as Modes of Expression', 470.
34 In addition to the categories being easily identified, the six systems of practices and beliefs are also able to be discerned; what Hardy and colleagues define as residuals that have characterized sport over time. These residuals provide the framework for the classification of material culture. See Hardy, Loy, and Booth, 'The Material Culture of Sport'.
35 For more on the exhibit on the 1936 Olympic Games at the National Holocaust Museum, and the curation of sport exhibits in non-sport focused museums, see Vamplew, 'Facts and Artefacts', 272–275.
36 For an example of how material culture can be used to engage the public, see New York City's Tenement Museum, which offers online opportunities to examine and think about various pieces of material culture; for example, see https://www.tenement.org/objects-of-comfort/. Sport museums might consider following suit.
37 Kurt Streeter, 'Richmond Is at a Crossroads. Will Arthur Ashe Boulevard Point the Way?' *New York Times*, 21 June 2019.

9

WHY READ HISTORICAL FICTION ABOUT SPORT?

Angie Abdou

In 'Why Read?' Rowland McMaster, the long-time editor of *English Studies in Canada*, draws on great thinkers across the centuries, most closely echoing Matthew Arnold, to argue that the benefit of literary study is in 'the satisfaction of a scientific desire to see things as they really are and, by knowing others, to know ourselves'.[1] More traditional approaches to sport history also accomplish both the seeing and the knowing that McMaster ascribes to the literary arts. What do novelists add to the discussion of historical sporting events and figures? Drawing on the research and writing of historians, fiction writers can build multidimensional worlds and complex characters that pull readers into the lively world of story. Where traditional history tends to prioritize documentation, interpretation, and argument, story typically puts more emphasis on pleasure, immersion, embodiment, and empathy. Sport fiction, thereby, allows readers to (imaginatively) live past athletic lives in a sensory, personal, and immersive manner that complements – and could not exist without – more traditional approaches to sport history. Moreover, released from the pressure of putting forth a thesis, novelists can explore sport history in a way that leaves room for ambiguity, for open-endedness, for a variety of subjectivities, and for multiple, simultaneous interpretations of the same athletic lives, whether they be the lives of iconic sport legends or of historically marginalized figures.

As an academic field, the study of sport literature is young, gaining its first footing in 1983 with the creation of the Sport Literature Association and its journal *Arete: The Journal of Sport Literature*.[2] The introduction to *Upon Further Review: Sports in American Literature* offers sport literature as an antidote to the typical chatter that occurs in a sport-obsessed culture. The editors argue that, while sports remain partly a distraction in a superficial society, sport also functions as a place where we invest the most emotional, personal parts of ourselves: 'Deep emotion, of course, is also the province of literary artists – not the chauvinistic, rabble-rousing emotion of sports talk hosts or the feel-good emotion of so many popular artists, but an emotion that requires serious intellectual engagement.'[3] Just as Rowland McMaster credits fiction with an important combination of pleasure and intellectual rigour, Cocchiarale and Emmert emphasize a similar benefit of sport fiction: deep emotion existing alongside intellectual engagement. They assert:

> far from being a mere diversion or hobby [...] sport literature – and a sustained and serious critical attention to that literature – holds up a new and powerful lens to the

DOI: 10.4324/9780429318306-11

Why read historical fiction about sport?

[sports] figures and [sports] events that we may passively absorb on a weekend in front of the television set.[4]

With the aim of being more specific about what this powerful new lens brings to the study of sports, this chapter will focus on two Canadian sport history novels and offer an exploration of the mutually beneficial relationship these texts have with more traditional approaches to sport history, as well as a consideration of what fiction can add to sport history, particularly in terms of the emotive, empathetic, and immersive capacity of the literary arts.

During her twenties, novelist Samantha Warwick belonged to an open water swimming group in Vancouver. Debbie Collins and her husband Shane Collins coached the team, while Debbie also prepared to swim the Catalina Channel. After practice, Debbie and Shane spoke of the 1927 Wrigley Ocean Marathon. In response to Warwick's enthusiastic interest in the event's real-life drama and characters, the Collinses suggested Warwick track down a copy of *Wind, Waves, and Sunburn: A Brief History of Marathon Swimming* by Conrad Wennerberg, particularly chapter six: 'Catalina Island: The Chewing Gum Swim'. Warwick found the book the next day, and as soon as she read the recommended chapter, she knew it would be the basis for her debut novel.[5]

In drawing inspiration from female swimmers, Warwick entered a well-established genre, since 'the most notable literature of sport by women has taken swimming as its subject'.[6] The Wrigley Ocean Marathon, and the week leading up to the 22 mile race, supplied Warwick's first novel with an immediate foreground structure. *Sage Island*'s protagonist is the fictional Savi Mason who loses at the 1924 Olympic Trials to Trudy Ederle. Ederle goes on to great success at the Paris Olympics and then turns her attention to the English Channel. Defeated and searching for redemption, Savi also switches her focus to open water swimming, only to face another unexpected, preemptive defeat connected to Ederle. In a state of despair and unwilling to give herself over to the restricted life of working in her parents' bakery, Savi Mason learns of the famous Wrigley Swim. She worries that without swimming she will 'wake up to find [her]self in a vacant marriage, bored and irritated, up to [her] elbows in flour, with no way out'.[7] Desperate for athletic success to affirm her self-worth and save her from the limited options available to women in the 1920s, Savi Mason flouts the expectations of her society and flees unchaperoned to Catalina Island.

Despite the fully fictional nature of Savi Mason, the real-life swimming hero Trudy Ederle (based in New York) and the real-life Wrigley Swim (on Catalina Island) determined the novel's setting. Trudy Ederle served as a key inspiration for Warwick. Even before Warwick knew of this particular race, she knew of Ederle: the first woman to swim across the English Channel, on 6 August 1926 at the age of 19. Ederle finished in 14 hours and 34 minutes, two hours faster than any man before her, with a record that stood until 1950. Warwick incorporates Ederle into her fiction, making her the key rival of the fictional Savi Mason, also 19 years old and living in New York City. Warwick explains that the similarity allowed her to 'create a believable athletic rivalry' so Ederle would 'serve the story symbolically'. Even though Savi Mason is a product of Warwick's imagination and follows a fictional trajectory, the actual race is, because of Warwick's intensive historical research, a close depiction of how the marathon swim transpired. Explaining what her fictional representation of the Wrigley Ocean Marathon can add to the historical accounts of this well-documented swimming race, Warwick states: 'a dramatic story, told with creative licence and craft, has the power to bring historical sport events to life', and fiction has the 'potential to reach a wider audience because humans are wired for story'. *Sage Island* does, indeed, bring many elements of 1920s' swim culture to life through story.

75

Many sporting details place the book's events firmly in the era of the Roaring Twenties: pools are called 'chlorinated tanks';[8] freestyle is called 'the overhand crawl';[9] swim suits are called 'tank suits';[10] and an American woman can qualify for the Olympics in the 100 free with a 1:14.2.[11] The open-water swimmers struggle against the chafing of their water outfits made with *wool*. Even the language – in both the external and internal dialogue – sings with resonance of the flapper decade. From the earliest drafts, Warwick prioritized the importance of inhabiting vocabulary and rhythms of the 1920s:

> My narrator's voice – first person, present tense, 1927 – needed to resonate authentically and harness the voice of an unconventional-thinking 1920s quasi-flapper. There was a tremendous amount of slang and language play in the 20s which made this reading and research absorbing and fun.

Warwick insists that the research into what daily life looked and felt like for a young woman in the 1920s was time-consuming but not onerous because of her passion for the story, a passion she transfers to the reader.

In that playful 1920s' language, the novel makes references to the rarity of female coaches, the prevalence of injured and shell-shocked First World War veterans, and the fashion and social etiquette of the decade. The inclusion of the Wrigley prize money, $25,0000 for first place and another $15,000 for the winning woman, is also historically accurate. Warwick peoples the narrative with swimming legends like Trudy Ederle and Johnny Weissmuller, as well as with less remembered figures like Canadian George Young, a teenager who hitch-hiked the 3,000 miles from Toronto to Catalina Island to become the only swimmer to complete the race, in a time of 15 hours and 44 minutes, earning himself the nickname 'the Catalina Kid'.[12] Warwick includes a subplot focusing on Young's exploitation by his agent who took 40 per cent of Young's winnings, and *Sage Island* thus captures an early twentieth-century example of the corruption that inevitably accompanies the commercialization of sport. While Warwick is to be commended for her research and her skilful folding of historical details into her fictional story, the true strength of the novel comes in the way the narrative combines the historical and the visceral. Warwick's own personal, physical knowledge of open water swimming imbues the researched historical details with life and energy.

The most obvious approach to *Sage Island* is a feminist one, focusing on the way in which the novel tells an early story of new opportunities becoming available for women athletes even while they continued to struggle against inequality. In an exploration of mainstream American sports literature, feminist sport scholar Susan Bandy argues that the female tends to fill the 'quintessential outsider role' and 'she is nonexistent as an athlete, invisible in the arena, voiceless as a female character'.[13] Similarly, Christian Messenger argues that 'women never truly belong in any male ritual sports narrative except as a problem, prey, or potential sacrifice'.[14] In Warwick's novel, the female protagonist finds an athletic role for herself but decides that 'women are not yet viewed in the same league as men', and the female swimmers exist only as 'a bit of a sideshow'.[15]

The Wrigley Ocean Marathon comprised 89 male contestants and 13 female. Warwick admires the latter group especially for their resistance against cultural norms. The best historical example of this swimming-as-rebellion comes in terms of the women's competition gear. Warwick explains:

> the female swimmers realized that wearing heavy wool suits for over fifteen hours would chafe their skin and slow them down. The majority of them decided instead

to smear their naked bodies with black axle grease. Their nude swim became a huge news story. The Women's Christian Temperance Union was outraged.

Within the novel, some characters perceive the eschewing of swimsuits as a mere matter of practicality while others appear to enjoy the sensationalism and abandon their suits as a publicity stunt while others yet embrace the nude performance as a feminist, rebellious act. Savi's own struggles with wool and chafing and body grease bring this historical incident – with all of its nuanced and competing meanings – to life.

Jamie Dopp offers a thorough consideration of the ways in which this novel enters into dialogue with sport history, particularly the circumscribed nature of women's lives. Dopp stresses that Savi's limited choices stand out against 'the relative male privilege enjoyed by her brother, Michael'.[16] Dopp's analysis takes inspiration from Allen Guttmann's history of women's sport. Guttmann illustrates the way sexism in sport mirrors sexism in the larger society and claims that the halting progress of the women's movement manifested in an equally 'stops and starts' type of progress for women in sports.[17] Warwick – because of her careful research and reliance on sport scholars – sharply and with vivid, precise historical detail, captures this expanding and contracting nature of women's freedoms in sport.

What, though, does her novel capture that more traditional approaches to sport history do not? That answer has to do with *feel*, with immersion, with physical intelligence. The novel begins in the voice of Savi:

> That feeling when you first enter the water, straight as a needle, that underwater glide, the flying, weightless sensation of being suspended – free. You soar up to the surface and hit a rhythm, strike forward into a hypnotic swimming trance. That is where I feel right.[18]

During many sessions at the pool, Coach Higgins praises Savi for her 'physical intelligence'.[19] Readers ought to praise Warwick for the same. Warwick draws on her own swimming experience to capture the physical sensations of the sport: 'a racket of breaking water and muffled echo, a tumble of ache, throbbing shoulders, and smarting red eyelids'.[20] Deep in the pain of a race, Savi recounts: 'a nauseating burn began to hive in my body'.[21] Through poetic physical descriptions, Warwick offers a bodily inhabitation of the sport history. The first-person narration forces us as readers to experience events through the 'I' of Savi, to immerse ourselves in her body and feel the life of the marathon swimmer, to imagine our way into 1920s' marathon swimming.

Initially, Savi also imagines her way into the open water challenge, thus functioning as a role model for the reader. Intrigued by Trudy Ederle's attempt to cross the English Channel, Savi explains: 'the idea began to capture my imagination. I began to feel the ocean breathe inside me, luring me to the challenge, to the wildness it represented'.[22] Through Savi, readers can inhabit all the elements of the race in this same visceral manner. The research tells us that wool suits chafe, but living the novel with Savi we *feel* the intolerable burning chafe, the risk of infection.[23] During the long cold race – as fatigue, fear of sharks, and the sheer impossibility of the distance set in – readers dwell inside Savi's confused head space, a consciousness no longer renderable in coherent, literal language: '*Hello?* Is anybody there? There is nobody. Nobody. Nobody here: only pain coming at me in cold silver sheets. Got the icy mitts on me. White like Aspirin? Is that you? Aspirin?'[24] *Sage Island* creates a Catalina swim that exists beyond the historical record of rankings and prize money and finish times and winners and losers. Readers *become* Savi as she dissolves into the physical challenge of the swim and emerges reborn, not sure if she won or lost or even finished.

Early in the novel, Coach Higgins refers to Savi's entrepreneurial parents as 'such practical creatures',[25] completely unlike swimmer Savi and her novelist brother, both of whom Higgins classifies as 'dreamers, desperadoes'.[26] Warwick positions athletes and artists as people daring to exist outside society's predictable scripts. With a combination of historical research, physical intelligence, and emotive poetry, Warwick brings life to these dreamers and desperadoes of the 1920s. Inside the first-person narration of Savi, readers find themselves occupying a fully realized body and imaginatively living a life similar to those of the earliest recorded marathon swimmers. *Sage Island* thus stands as an example of the reciprocal relationship that can exist between sports history and the best sports novels.

Like *Sage Island*, Carrie Snyder's *Girl Runner* comes after the era of sport literature that Bandy describes with: woman 'is present, but she is not the player'.[27] Snyder does not relegate her female character to the role of spectator, cheerleader, or prize. Unlike much sport literature, Snyder also does not restrict herself to representing the athlete at the height of her sporting prowess. Instead, readers meet Aganetha ('Aggie') Smart, once an Olympic gold medallist, now 104 years old, all her friends dead, her medals collecting dust, her own athletic success forgotten. Far from podium top, this protagonist first appears 'propped in a wheeled chair in a room that smells of chicken fat and diapers'.[28] She has become an old woman with nobody left who remembers her even enough to write her obituary.[29] Aggie observes that her main achievement is to have lived long enough to see her life vanish.[30] Obituaries – of family members, coaches, friends, teammates – pepper the narrative as an example of the most meagre recording of a personal history. Significantly, after her athletic career (and after the brief spell of glamourous work her athletic success brings her), Aggie secures a position at a newspaper, writing obituaries. She describes the task: 'my job on obits is to collect the vicissitudes of life and to freeze them into sense. I work to make the facts stand still, stay put. I stop time. I sum a person up, beginning, middle, end'.[31] The obituary writer thereby serves as one of this novel's historians, a researcher dedicated to memorializing lives, giving them shape and meaning. But she is not the book's only historian. *Girl Runner*'s key preoccupation is recovering lives lost to time, particularly the lives of female athletes.

The novel begins when Kaley, a running star, comes to abduct Aggie from the nursing home. Readers learn that Aggie competed in the 1928 Olympics in Amsterdam. In an author's note, Snyder states that Canadian women's success at that Games served as inspiration. 'The Matchless Six', Canada's female track and field team, exceeded expectations, returning home with medals, including gold in the 4 X100 metre relay and the high jump.[32] Within the novel, Aggie's career gets cut short because she shines in the women's 800-metre run, an event historically axed from the Olympics after 1928. Snyder explains that contemporary news sources reported that 'at least half of the 800-metre finalists collapsed or failed to finish the race, a story whose accuracy was only recently called into question'.[33] At the time, an IAFF committee banned women from running distances longer than 200-metres in the Olympic Games. A 2012 *Runner's World* article, however, notes that 'film evidence exists that shows the entire field finishing the race'.[34] Nonetheless, based on assertions of the frailty of the female sex and speculation on the effect long distances might have on an athlete's uterus, women did not compete in the 800-metre run again until the 1960 Games in Rome. The misrepresentation of this event – and the way that representation restricted possibilities for female athletes for decades – illustrates the importance of accurate historical documentation and research. Past sport stories do shape the lives of future athletes.

Why read historical fiction about sport?

Kaley's 'kidnapping' exploit demonstrates her awareness of history's power to influence the future. Kaley recognizes Aggie as a trailblazer for generations of women runners but admits that the accomplishments of these Olympic athletes has been lost to time. Kaley expresses her desire in the simplest terms: 'I would like to tell your story.'[35] She wants to make a documentary film about Aganetha Smart, to bring her athletic life back into the light and thereby give Aggie and her teammates their rightful place in sports history. However, Kaley also has ulterior motives. A successful athlete, Kaley bemoans the fact that a runner's life has changed. In the 1920s, Aggie's offer of a position on the track team came with a job at a factory. While certainly not glamorous, the work gave her income and independence. Kaley explains the exorbitant expense involved in contemporary athletic life: 'It's different now, Miss Smart. You don't know how much it costs – there's coaching, physio, massage. There's vitamin supplements, travel expenses, gear, gym time, you have no idea, or I can't compete.'[36] Kaley wants to produce the film – and foster a connection to Aggie thereby gaining access to some expensive real estate that Aggie happens to own – to raise money for her own athletic endeavours, so she can compete in the future Rotterdam Olympics. Aggie hears her: 'The rules have changed from my day, she's saying. It isn't the same. The path is cluttered with obstacles. The obstacle are lit up in dollar signs.'[37] The revenue of the sport-history film (or at the least real-estate income that the film might help Kaley access) will allow for Kaley's athletic life in a very literal, financial way. Sport history will create sport future.

Aggie captures sport history through obituary, whereas Kaley hopes to do so through film. Carrie Snyder, as novelist, is *Girl Runner*'s third sport historian. Like Warwick, Snyder started this novel because of her own love of the sport:

> Since I'm a fiction writer, I wanted to express [my] newfound love of running through a character. I started to research the history of running, specifically long-distance running, and immediately came up against a problem: women had been actively prevented from running long distance until relatively recently – within my life-time. So I began to think about what it would be like to want to run and not be allowed to express that particular physical joy.[38]

Snyder lends her love of running to Aggie who recollects her first experience of the activity: 'I had not known that I could run so fast – I can fly, that's how fast. Now I know. I know that shock can spin itself into something near exhilaration, by mere application of speed.'[39] Pleasure of the sport permeates *Girl Runner* just as it does *Sage Island*.

Like Warwick, Snyder's pleasure of the sport came first and led to research, resulting in that combination of deep emotion and intellectual rigour wherein Cocchiarale and Emmert locate the value of sport literature. At first, Snyder thought the book would be set in the 1960s, a time 'when a few maverick women runners were sneaking into all-male races or running alongside the men in road races, even though they weren't allowed to enter officially'. But the character's voice that manifested in Snyder's mind 'was a good deal older than that – from a different era altogether'. From that voice, luck landed Snyder on the story of The Matchless Six. She fictionalized the characters, but took many of the events from history:

> the 1920s turned out to be a more open time for women athletes than many of the decades before or since. And one character seemed too important to fictionalize: Alexandrine Gibb [sport writer and chaperone], who leaped off the page as a remarkable behind-the-scenes force and support for Canadian women athletes of the era.

Though Gibb is the only historical figure in *Girl Runner,* Snyder's extensive primary research allows her to vividly create Gibb's era and immerse readers in an authentic, plausible world of 1920s' running culture.

How does Snyder's approach to sport history differ from that of traditional sport historians? In response to this question, Snyder returns to the imagination and to the potential for fictional texts to be 'immersive' in a manner that strictly factual works cannot. She asserts that she must give herself the 'freedom to re-imagine the past' in a way that might not be a 'precise or even entirely accurate rendering of the time' but with the goal of bringing the time to life 'so we can feel immersed there together'. Her interest, she says, is less on the big political events and more on domestic detail, saying of her primary research: 'it's the buttons and threads that I want to find'. She emphasizes that *Girl Runner* is a feminist version of history, with the aim being:

> to remind people that the past – and the specific restrictions on women's bodies detailed in the book – is not so far away. Humans have short memories. We tend to think we're moving in a naturally progressive arc through time, but in fact, progress can slip in an instant. The 1920s was a progressive period for women athletes [...] and that was lost in the decades that followed, and buried, forgotten.

Girl Runner reminds readers of the important work of unburying and un-forgetting these details – a task attempted by Aganetha and Kaley (in the fictional world) and Carrie Snyder (in the real one), all three of them runners and sport historians in their own way. Like Kaley, Carrie Snyder 'kidnaps' the past and brings it back into (imaginative) focus, with the ultimate goal of memorializing female athletes and thereby continuing to open the way for girls to run.

A fiction writer is not a historian. Novelists who peer into these past stories of sport do so only by standing on the shoulders of sport historians. With that boost, fiction writers can offer readers an immersive, visceral, emotional account of past athletic lives, one that complements and brings life to more factual historical accounts.

Notes

1 Rowland McMaster, 'Why Read?', *English Studies in Canada* 38, nos. 2–3 (2013): 45.
2 Sport Literature Association, accessed 5 December 2019, https://www.uta.edu/english/sla/lohistory. html Note: The SLA changed the journal name to *Aethlon* in 1988.
3 Michael Cocchiarale and Scott Emmert, *Upon Further Review: Sports in American Literature* (Connecticut: Praeger Publishing, 2004), xvii.
4 Cocchiarale and Emmert, *Upon Further Review*, xvii.
5 Samantha Warwick, Personal Interview, October 2019. Unless otherwise noted, the source for Warwick's statements are this personal interview.
6 Cocchiarale and Emmert, *Upon Further Review*, xiv.
7 Samantha Warwick, *Sage Island* (Victoria: Brindle and Glass Press, 2008), 56.
8 Warwick, *Sage Island*, 23.
9 Warwick, *Sage Island*, 20.
10 Warwick, *Sage Island*, 21.
11 Warwick, *Sage Island*, 36.
12 Warwick, *Sage Island*, 221.
13 Susan Bandy, 'The Female Voice in American Sports Literature and the Quest for a Female Sporting Identity,' in Cocchiarale and Emmert, *Upon Further Review*, 99.
14 Christian Messenger, *Sport and the Spirit of Play in Contemporary American Fiction* (New York: Columbia University Press, 1990): 154.
15 Warwick, *Sage Island*, 62.

16 Jamie Dopp,. 'From Tank to Deep Water: Myth and History in Samantha Warwick's *Sage Island*', in *Writing the Body in Motion*, eds. Angie Abdou and Jamie Dopp (Edmonton: Athabasca University Press, 2018), 142.
17 Allen Guttmann, *Women's Sports: A History* (New York: Columbia University Press, 1991), 135.
18 Warwick, *Sage Island*, 1.
19 Warwick, *Sage Island*, 9.
20 Warwick, *Sage Island*, 9.
21 Warwick, *Sage Island*, 31.
22 Warwick, *Sage Island*, 55.
23 Warwick, *Sage Island*, 170.
24 Warwick, *Sage Island*, 211.
25 Warwick, *Sage Island*, 81.
26 Warwick, *Sage Island*, 81.
27 Bandy, 'The Female Voice', 100.
28 Carrie Snyder, *Girl Runner* (Toronto: House of Anansi Press, 2014), 1–2.
29 Snyder, *Girl Runner*, 2.
30 Snyder, *Girl Runner*, 2.
31 Snyder, *Girl Runner*, 299.
32 Snyder, *Girl Runner*, 355.
33 Snyder, *Girl Runner*, 356.
34 Snyder, *Girl Runner*, 356.
35 Snyder, *Girl Runner*, 64.
36 Snyder, *Girl Runner*, 318–319.
37 Snyder, *Girl Runner*, 318.
38 Carrie Snyder, Personal Interview. October, 2019. Unless otherwise noted, the source for Snyder's quotations is this personal interview.
39 Snyder, *Girl Runner*, 23.

10

SPORT AND ACTIVISM

Russell Field

Two acts, separated by half a century; two people, fists raised, standing in defiance; one man, sitting alone, refusing to stand, but unbowed. John Carlos and Tommie Smith's protest at the Mexico City Olympics – most often interpreted as a gesture of 'Black power' – was a symbolic demonstration of the economic and racial injustices faced by African-Americans. It drew widespread condemnation and Avery Brundage, then-president of the International Olympic Committee (IOC), moved quickly to expel the pair from the 1968 Games.

Nearly 50 years later, Colin Kaepernick, of the National Football League's (NFL) San Francisco 49ers, was the highest profile of the players who, beginning in 2016, opted not to stand for the US national anthem before NFL games while African-Americans continued to face widespread abuse, racism, violence, and death at the hands of law enforcement agencies. Like Smith and Carlos, Kaepernick found himself ostracized by the power structures of sport. Essentially blackballed by the NFL – after having led the 49ers to the league championship game in 2013 – he remains without a contract as of 2020, his playing career all but over. Kaepernick also found himself the target of one of the US president's many racist Twitter-screeds, which sought to characterize the apparent disrespect of the US flag and anthem as unpatriotic.

Commentators drew strong parallels between the two protests. Jeré Longman called Kaepernick 'a direct descendant of Smith and Carlos, unyielding in his conviction, fully understanding of the risk and sacrifice and the power and dignity of silent gesture'.[1] While Carlos called Kaepernick 'my hero', there are differences between the Mexico City medal podium and the NFL sideline.[2] One is the judgement of history. Longman argues that Kaepernick can be comforted, in ways that Smith and Carlos could not, 'that history can act as sandpaper, smoothing abrasive denunciation into burnished acceptance'. Moreover, Kaepernick knelt at a time when other high-profile African-American athletes – including NBA star LeBron James – also protested in sympathy with Black Lives Matter.

There are multiple ways to consider such examples of sporting activism, including distinguishing between individual activists and social movements while also considering that activism has focused on change both *in* and *through* sport – the latter seeking to alter the landscape of and accessibility to sport; the former focused on the platform sport affords to advocate for societal changes that extend beyond sport. To illustrate these distinctions examples are drawn from a particular chronological/geographical nexus (American sport in the late 1960s), but ultimately a broad focus captures the diversity of sporting activism.

82   DOI: 10.4324/9780429318306-12

Framing activism

Activism and other acts of resistance involve a variety of actors utilizing a variety of tactics. Generally, activism is 'the coming together of people outside of formal political channels and demanding a say in the societies they inhabit – and even providing an alternative vision of what their societies *could* look like'.[3] While some examples of activism are individuals acting alone, such a definition suggests collective action or 'social movements': groups of people who share a vision for change, as 'participating in activism, protest, and social movements is one of the most important ways that human beings are able to express a voice about their own rights and the rights of those around them'.[4]

Nevertheless, social movements can be difficult to define in part because of the varied 'ways in which people express their desire for change'.[5] And, since the 1990s, modern social movements have been characterized by the use of a diversity of tactics to achieve their ends: from protests to direct action, from playful parody to destruction of property. That some of the more prominent examples of activism are protests that attracted media attention reflects the emphasis that social movement studies places on acts of protest, although Rodgers cautions not to overlook 'other forms of resistance that may be more related to multi-institutional targets, as well as everyday and less institutionalized forms of resistance'.[6] If targets of activism can 'include cultural, corporate, not-for-profit, and even religious authorities', the institution of sport is one of the 'cultural' institutions open to change and protest.[7]

Not only are the tactics diverse, so are the actors. In some cases, activists are 'individuals consciously and strategically creating products and materials and staging actions designed to raise awareness and challenge the ... "status quo"'.[8] Yet, self-identifying as an 'activist' is not, as Chris Bobel argues, a prerequisite for *doing* activism. Since activism challenges dominant power structures, perhaps activists can be most simply characterized as people who 'care enough about some issue that they are prepared to incur significant costs and act to achieve their goals'.[9]

Athlete activism

The seeming resurgence of athlete protests in the twenty-first century has renewed interest in the long history of sport and activism. Much of this has focused on high-performance sport, both professional and Olympic, in the United States, beginning in the late-1960s. The grievances and actions of athletes both reflected and contributed to the social unrest and civil rights assertions of the era. There are a number of examples of athletes who, motivated by their politics, risked their positions to critique the institutions of sport through activism.

Dave Meggyesy was a lineman with the NFL's St. Louis Cardinals. He increasingly found himself questioning the nature of football, where the players 'were the product, and the replaceable parts', which put him at odds with management and coaches.[10] Meggyesy also embraced the politics and lifestyle of the counter-culture movement. He grew his hair long, resisted the conformist nature of pro sports, and protested the US national anthem being played before games as part of his opposition to the war in Vietnam. The team chafed at his 'involvement in radical politics', while Meggyesy, according to his post-career autobiography, *Out of Their League* (1971), began to question 'what's really behind the video glitter of the game – the racism and fraud, the unbelievable brutality that affects mind as much as it does body'.[11]

Besides her remarkable success on the court, Billie Jean King is best known for her fight to achieve greater pay for female tennis players. King and eight other players ('The Original 9'), along with corporate support, organized a women's tennis tour in 1970 and by 1973 the US Open became the first major event to offer men and women equal prize money. This was also the same year that King's advocacy – and her symbolic affiliation with the women's liberation movement – had its greatest spectacle: the televised 'battle of the sexes' match against Bobby Riggs. Nevertheless, Susan Ware argues that 'feminist ideology was not the driving force behind the women's tour'.[12] Nancy Spencer notes, 'the majority of top-ranked women did not embrace the women's movement. Billie Jean King points out that although the women's liberation movement made the women keenly aware of their inequities in sport, not everyone on the tour saw herself as a feminist or a radical'.[13]

An all-star centerfielder, Curt Flood spent 12 seasons with the St. Louis Cardinals, winning two World Series championships and seven Gold Gloves. At the end of the 1969 season, the Cardinals traded Flood to the Philadelphia Phillies. Flood rejected being treated as 'a piece of property to be bought and sold irrespective of my wishes', and refused to report to the Phillies. He argued that his 'basic rights as a citizen and a human being' meant that he had 'the right to consider offers from other clubs before making any decisions'.[14] The commissioner of major league baseball, Bowie Kuhn, rejected this argument, maintaining that the 'reserve clause' in player contracts gave teams the right to control players' labour. Flood's career was all but ended by the incident, however his high-profile and principled stand was the beginning of the free agency system that would liberalize player movement and ensure that players earned a larger share of the sport's revenues.

Challenging the structures of sport

Such examples were attempts by the labour of sport to change the conditions of that industry to provide for more equitable compensation coupled with safer and more humane working conditions. Flood's activism also highlighted the links between the structural organization of sport and systems of oppression in the wider society. Unsurprisingly, athlete activism was prominent among groups marginalized both within and beyond sport: African-Americans and women. Their actions were inspired by and often linked to wider social movements.

Yet, like King and 'The Original 9', athlete activists, while remembered for the stands they took, often did not act alone. Flood was supported by Marvin Miller, head of the Major League Baseball Players Association, who would lead the players through a number of work stoppages (beginning in 1972), and helped the players realize free agency and an end to the reserve clause in 1976. Meggyesy and others were inspired by Jack Scott, author of *Athletics for Athletes* (1969) and *The Athletic Revolution* (1971). The latter title would become the phrase around which coalesced activism that focused on 'the rights, experiences, and opportunities of all athletes, involving the conditions of their participation as well as the broader symbolic meanings and values associated with their athletic performances and sport in general'.[15] Scott attempted to implement his vision of democratized sport during a brief stint as the athletic director at Oberlin College in Ohio in the early-1970s.

But perhaps the most influential organizer during the 'athletic revolution' was San Jose State University sociologist Harry Edwards, whose conception of sport was shaped by the social and material conditions of African-Americans in an era of heightened civil rights consciousness. This led him to organize Black athletes, primarily male track-and-field athletes, into what Edwards called the Olympic Project for Human Rights (OPHR). He argued: 'We must no longer allow this country to use a few so-called Negroes to point out how much progress she has made in solving her racial problems when the oppression of Afro-Americans is greater than it ever was'.[16] The OPHR programme for reforming sport included adding two Black coaches to the US Olympic track-and-field team and two Black decision makers to the US Olympic Committee.[17] While the OPHR failed to organize a boycott of the 1968 Olympics by African-American athletes, its efforts resulted in one of the most iconic moments in Olympic history.

As prominent as the actions of athletes such as Flood, King, and Meggyesy were, there is little doubt that the highest-profile athlete activism of the 1960s took place in Mexico City. Tommie Smith (gold) and John Carlos (bronze) accepted their medals for the men's 200-metre sprint at the 1968 Olympics by appearing on the medal podium wearing black socks, but no shoes. They also shared a pair of black gloves; Carlos wearing the right-hand glove, Smith the left. As the national flags were raised and the US national anthem played, Smith and Carlos each raised a black-gloved fist into the air. The two sprinters were symbolically highlighting – through their attire and the Black Power salute – the treatment of African-Americans and the US Olympic movement's willingness to reap the benefits of Black labour. The third runner on the podium, Peter Norman of Australia, had an OPHR button pinned to the chest of his track-suit top in support of Smith and Carlos. Nevertheless, Douglas Hartmann argues that 'African American athletes were both more sensitive to and uniquely empowered to speak out and act against mistreatment than their white counterparts' and sport 'provided them a powerful position from which to act'.[18] Other 1968 Olympians were politically engaged, including sprinter Lee Evans, and Wyomia Tyus dedicated her sprint and relay gold medals to Smith and Carlos.

The response of the sporting establishment was to assert that sport was inherently apolitical and that such demonstrations were 'an attack on sport itself, on everything sport stood for, everything it supposedly did best and contributed to American society'.[19] This notion that sport is apolitical has been widely debunked, but the defence also misses the larger message, as Hartmann argues: 'the ideological challenges the sporting establishment confronted had less to do with vexing questions about sport's role in social life than with the larger social struggles about equality and justice being played out in society at large'.[20]

Extending activism beyond sport

The now-iconic raised-fist protest, while prominent, was not the only example of sporting resistance by African-American athletes in the 1960s. No athlete had a higher profile than heavyweight boxing champion Muhammad Ali. His willingness to sacrifice his title and risk a jail sentence for his opposition to the war in Vietnam suggested the moral stances for which he would become celebrated later in life but which found him labelled seditious in the 1960s. Retired NFL star Jim Brown committed himself in part to economic empowerment in the Black community, starting the Negro Industrial and Economic Union in 1960s, later renamed the Black Economic Union.

Oftentimes activism directed beyond sport used the visibility and platform offered by the institution to effect change. While the OPHR called for the 'curtailment of participation of all-white teams and individuals from the Union of South Africa and Southern Rhodesia', in 1967, a group of sporting activists within South Africa, led in part by Dennis Brutus, had been operating the South African Non-Racial Olympic Committee (SANROC) since 1962.[21] As an alternative to the apartheid-government sanctioned Olympic committee, which was selecting whites-only teams for international competition, SANROC sought to influence the Olympic Movement – a struggle that eventually resulted in South Africa being banned from the Olympics – while continuing to build political support internationally against apartheid.

Following the Olympic ban, activism through sport against apartheid focused on sports beyond the reach of the Olympic Movement that also reflected South Africa's cultural ties to Britain and its dominions: specifically, cricket and rugby. Protesters focused on tours of South African teams in countries such as Britain, Australia, and New Zealand, as well as those nation's cricket and rugby squads playing matches in South Africa. Protesters called for a boycott of South Africa, with the goal of 'total political, economic, social and cultural isolation of South Africa's apartheid regime, and therefore of South Africa'.[22]

For example, 'Stop the Seventy Tour', working with the anti-apartheid movement, organized demonstrations and direct-action protests at each of the 23 matches played by South Africa's Springboks national rugby team during the 1969–70 tour of Britain, which led to the cancellation of a cricket tour scheduled for the following year. Even as the 1977 Gleneagles Agreement pledged the nations of the Commonwealth to discourage their citizens from sporting contact with countries where sport was organized on a racial basis, rugby and cricket tours persisted, as did the protests against them, for example, in New Zealand in 1981.

Such protests were not always supported by the populace interested in watching a cricket or rugby match and often faced considerable retribution from local authorities. Nevertheless, the tour protests resonated beyond sport, connecting activists to 'a global and a local anti-racist movement'.[23] As Malcolm MacLean argues: 'Although not the most significant factor in the collapse of apartheid, the sports boycott was responsible for a series of significant blows against the cultural security of apartheid's dominant groups'.[24]

The diverse nature of sporting activism

Other Black athletes were attuned to the politics of participating in sport with South Africa's apartheid government. The American tennis player, Arthur Ashe, after being denied a visa to play in the South African Open called for South Africa to be banned from the Davis Cup, among other sanctions, taking what Dave Zirin calls a 'bold stand' that 'began to raise the world's awareness of South Africa's apartheid government'.[25] For all of Ashe's bona fides as an activist, such an Americentric view overlooks the fact that sporting activism was (and is) more diverse than high-profile American and predominantly male examples would suggest. Moreover, 'it would be a mistake', Hartmann argues, 'to reduce the prominence of race with respect to the 1960s-era athletic unrest – or any other form of sixties social unrest and political activism, for that matter – simply to a matter of historical contingency or even powerful symbolic iconography'.[26] The 'deep material and symbolic underpinnings' of sport have engendered a wide array of activist actions within sport, since it emerged as a primarily white, male, middle-class Western practice in the nineteenth century. With sport suffused with messages about the physical and moral benefits of participation, activism for access to sporting opportunities has a long history among those implicitly or explicitly excluded. Additionally, sport became an institution through which larger grievances over exclusion could be articulated. Again, examples illustrate, but only scratch the surface of, the diversity of activism within and through sport.

Women's agitation for access to sporting opportunities did not begin in the 1970s during the women's liberation movement. French sporting feminists, including Alice Milliat, in the years after the First World War organized their own sporting events before creating an international organization: the Fédération Sportive Féminine Internationale

(FSFI). The FSFI organized Women's Olympic Games and agitated for inclusion within the IOC Games, which was achieved in track-and-field in 1928, although not to the satisfaction of all in the women's sport movement.[27] Nearly half a century later, the victories of the 1970s and 1980s were won not only in the court of public opinion, but in legislative bodies and the courts themselves: for example, the introduction of Title IX in the United States in 1972 and the successful challenges to human rights legislation in Canada in the 1980s. Yet these victories remain under attack, as evidenced by bans on religious and ethno-cultural head coverings (the hijab, in particular), which are a continuing reminder that activism has had to combat not only gendered but racialized prejudice as well.

High-performance sport has remained a platform for activism in and through sport, from mass demonstrations – such as student protests prior to the 1968 Mexico City Olympics to the widespread anti-government protests before the 2016 Rio Olympics – to individual acts of activism. Silver-medal winner Feyisa Lilesa crossed the finish line at the 2016 Olympics with his wrists crossed in an X, a symbol of protest used by the Oromo peoples of Ethiopia, the nation that Lilesa was ostensibly representing at the Games.[28] [FN] Cricketers Andy Flower and Henry Olonga used the occasion of the 2003 Cricket World Cup to wear black arm bands before Zimbabwe's first match to protest the human rights abuses endured by their fellow citizens under the regime of Robert Mugabe. Sport's apolitical nature was invoked to silence their demonstration, as their cricket careers were effectively ended and both had to leave Zimbabwe. Nevertheless, as Callie Batts argues, 'the narrative of the protest is relevant to broader histories of human rights and political struggle' and a further reminder that such struggles occur beyond the Global North.[29]

Indigenous athletes have similarly used high-performance sport as a forum to assert their indigeneity, which is often concealed by nation-state team jerseys, and protest the impacts of settler colonialism and racism faced by Indigenous peoples around the world. Mohawk canoeist Alwyn Morris from Kahnawake held an eagle feather aloft on the 1984 Olympic medal podium. Christine O'Bonsawin frames such a gesture as consistent with Indigenous athletes 'honoring their families and cultures and, thus, expressing their Indigeneity'.[30] But less than a decade later, a justifiably angrier demonstration was made by Australian Football League (AFL) player, Nicky Winmar. Following a victory in an April 1993 away match, he and another Aboriginal teammate received racial abuse from the home fans. In an unscripted moment, Winmar raised his shirt, pointed at his bare torso, and yelled, 'I'm black and I'm proud to be black' (where 'black' reads as Aboriginal), creating another iconic image of resistance through sport.

Conclusion

In December 2019, *Guardian Weekly* labelled the 2010s 'the decade of protest'. From the Arab Spring to Extinction Rebellion, from Black Lives Matter to #MeToo, 'millions of protesters have marched, sat down, sat in, camped out, occupied, filled jail cells, rioted, looted, chanted, petitioned, lobbied and hashtagged' most often in support of 'the demands of the poor, the young, students, workers, minorities, the indigenous, women, trade unionists and migrants'.[31] Perhaps it is not surprising then that, more than 20 years after Winmar's demonstration, another AFL star and Aboriginal athlete, Adam Goodes, took a high-profile stand, calling out abuse and choosing to sacrifice the final years of his career rather than withstand more racist taunting. Athletes like Goodes and Colin Kaepernick, while sacrificing much for their principles, also stand on the shoulders of generations of sporting activists – and do so with a level of social capital that ensures their actions will garner public attention and, in many quarters, sympathy. In 2018, Kaepernick was the voice of one of the most anticipated advertisements by the global apparel brand, Nike. In a narrative structured around athletes achieving their dreams against long odds, the camera focuses on someone in an overcoat. 'Believe in something,' the narrator asserts, as Kaepernick turns to reveal himself as the voice speaking, before continuing, 'even if it means sacrificing everything.'[32]

Notes

1 Jeré Longman, 'Kaepernick's Knee and Olympic Fists are Linked by History', *New York Times*, 6 September 2018, https://www.nytimes.com/2018/09/06/sports/kaepernick-nike-kneeling.html.
2 Cited in Longman, 'Kaepernick's Knee'.
3 Kathleen Rodgers, *Protest, Activism & Social Movements* (Don Mills, ON: Oxford University Press, 2018), 8.
4 Rodgers, *Protest, Activism & Social Movements*, 6.
5 Rodgers, *Protest, Activism & Social Movements*, 12.
6 Rodgers, *Protest, Activism & Social Movements*, 12.
7 Rodgers, *Protest, Activism & Social Movements*, 10.
8 Chris Bobel, '"I'm Not an Activist, though I've Done a Lot of It": Doing Activism, Being Activist and the "Perfect Standard" in a Contemporary Movement', *Social Movement Studies* 6, no. 2 (2007): 151.
9 Pamela E. Oliver and Gerald Marwell, 'Mobilizing Technologies for Collective Action', in *Frontiers in Social Movement Theory*, eds. Aldon D. Morris and Carol McClurg Mueller (New Haven: Yale University Press, 1992), 252, cited in Bobel, '"I'm Not an Activist"', 151.
10 Dave Meggyesy, *Out of Their League* (Lincoln: University of Nebraska Press, 2005), vi.
11 Meggyesy, *Out of Their League*, 6.
12 Susan Ware, *Game, Set, Match: Billie Jean King and the Revolution in Women's Sports* (Chapel Hill: University of North Carolina Press), 2011, 32.
13 Nancy E. Spencer, 'Reading between the Lines: A Discursive Analysis of Billie Jean King vs. Bobby Riggs 'Battle of the Sexes', *Sociology of Sport Journal* 17, no. 4 (2000): 399.
14 Cited in Dave Zirin, *What's My Name, Fool? Sports and Resistance in the United States* (Chicago: Haymarket Books, 2005), 104.
15 Douglas Hartmann, *Race, Culture, and the Revolt of the Black Athlete: The 1968 Olympics Protests and Their Aftermath* (Chicago: University of Chicago Press, 2003), 188.
16 Cited in Zirin, *What's My Name, Fool?*, 74.
17 Harry Edwards, *The Revolt of the Black Athlete*, cited in Jules Boykoff, 'Protest, Activism, and the Olympic Games: An Overview of Key Issues and Iconic Moments', *The International Journal of the History of Sport 34*, nos. 3–4 (2017): 168.
18 Hartmann, *Race, Culture, and the Revolt of the Black Athlete*, 199, 200.
19 Hartmann, *Race, Culture, and the Revolt of the Black Athlete*, 201.
20 Hartmann, *Race, Culture, and the Revolt of the Black Athlete*, 205.
21 Edwards, *The Revolt of the Black Athlete*, cited in Boykoff, 'Protest, Activism, and the Olympic Games', 168.
22 Malcolm MacLean, 'Anti-apartheid Boycotts and the Affective Economies of Struggle: The Case of Aotearoa New Zealand', *Sport in Society 13*, no. 1 (2010): 73.
23 MacLean, 'Anti-apartheid Boycotts', 74.
24 Malcolm MacLean, 'Revisiting (and Revising?) Sports Boycotts: From Rugby against South Africa to Soccer in Israel', *The International Journal of the History of Sport 31*, no. 15 (2014): 1832.
25 Dave Zirin, *A People's History of Sports in the United States: 250 Years of Politics, Protest, People, and Play* (New York: The New Press, 2008), 199.
26 Hartmann, *Race, Culture, and the Revolt of the Black Athlete*, 197.
27 See Florence Carpentier and Jean-Pierre Lefèvre, 'The Modern Olympic Movement, Women's Sport and the Social Order during the Inter-war Period', *The International Journal of the History of Sport 23*, no. 7 (2006): 1112–1127.

28 Cited in Boykoff, 'Protest, Activism, and the Olympic Games', 162.
29 Callie Batts, '"In Good Conscience": Andy Flower, Henry Olonga and the Death of Democracy in Zimbabwe', *Sport in Society 13*, no. 1 (2010): 55.
30 Christine O'Bonsawin, 'From Black Power to Indigenous Activism: The Olympic Movement and the Marginalization of Oppressed Peoples (1968–2012)', *Journal of Sport History 42*, no. 1 (2015): 202.
31 Gary Younge, 'Streets on Fire,' *Guardian Weekly* 202, no. 1 (2019): 35.
32 'Nike Releases Full Ad Featuring Colin Kaepernick', https://www.youtube.com/watch?v= -grjIUWKoBA.

90

PART 2

New perspectives on old themes

11

NEW PERSPECTIVES ON OLD THEMES

Introduction

Douglas Booth, Carly Adams and Murray G. Phillips

In a recent review of the history of sport, Dave Day and Wray Vamplew remind the field that it is an 'ever evolving ... organic discipline', responding to changes in material conditions and continually fracturing as individuals and groups adopt new paradigms, methods, theories, and perspectives. Not surprisingly then, historians of sport constantly engage and re-engage debates, approaches, and methodologies.[1] The contributions in this Part of the *Handbook* are evidence of an ever-evolving subfield. Arguably, the pace of change is accelerating as witnessed by the barrage of 'turns' across the humanities and social sciences. Indeed, we framed the introduction to Part 1 of the *Handbook* around the representational turn – a logical extension of the cultural turn and a phrase used to denote a reversal of epistemological and ontological thinking about the relationship between history and the past. And, as Jaime Schultz, Michelle Sikes, and Cat Ariail alert us in their chapter on women's sport history in this Part (Chapter 21), historians of sport should not expect any quick let up in new turns. Schultz and her colleagues identify a 'Top 10' list of turns for historians delving into women, power, and politics. Their list includes the intersectional turn, the geographical turn, the transnational turn, the experimental turn, and the digital turn. Critically, Schultz, Sikes, and Ariail frame turns as 'possibilities for ingenuity, innovation, and interpretation', rather than burdens. Turns will 'keep the field moving forward', in part by identifying new questions and new areas for research.

The contributors to Part 2, 'New Perspectives on Old Themes', provide copious examples of a dynamic and innovative field. Here we introduce these contributions under three inter-related headings: arguments, themes, and politics. Following the path chartered in Part 1, we are particularly interested in the sources of fresh perspectives as identified by the contributors whether they derive from new material conditions, evidence, theories, or turns. Irrespective of the source, we note the increasing sophistication of the field with historians of sport applying, in the words of S.W. Pope (Chapter 12), 'more conceptual and epistemological caveats'. In this regard, Pope's comments on the silencing of Indigenous voices in historical narratives dealing with the origin and diffusion of modern sport, the subject of his contribution in this Part, are especially apposite given the space devoted in the *Handbook* to the rapidly emerging theme of Indigenous sport history (see Part 4). While the emphasis in Part 2 is on new perspectives, we

DOI: 10.4324/9780429318306-14

are also mindful of the qualification offered by Sarah Barnes and Mary McDonald in their contribution (Chapter 19). Quite rightly, they warn of the dangers posed by new perspectives that can 'obscure other ways of being and knowing' and/or 'promot[e] a dichotomous framing that erases both the continuing salience of past approaches as well as paradigmatic differences and similarities that constitute the diverse ways to study[ing] and understand[ing]' the past.

Arguments

New arguments are a hallmark of the *Handbook*. We have already introduced some in Part 1: reflexivity as a prerequisite for disciplinary independence (Malcolm MacLean, Chapter 2), history as the discourse that represents and analyses the past (Daniel Nathan, Chapter 6), state archives as sites that exclude the memories and experiences of Indigenous communities (Gary Osmond, Chapter 7). This feature continues as we progress. For example, in Part 3 Colin Howell and Daryl Leeworthy (Chapter 31) point to the roles of transnational processes in the construction of cultural identities and in revealing the past through new eyes. In Part 4 Murray Phillips (Chapter 33) attributes the effacement of Indigenous sporting experiences to colonialism of a special type – settler colonialism, and in Part 5 Phillips (Chapter 39) makes the case that disciplinary specific journals have been as important as monographs, if not more so, in the development of the history of sport. Likewise, the contributors in this Part present new arguments, in this case concerning themes well established in the field. In this subsection we introduce the contributions of S.W. Pope ('The Origin and Diffusion of Modern Sport', Chapter 12) and Peter Donnelly ('Time, Space, and Sport', Chapter 13).

The origin and diffusion of modern sport is undoubtedly, in the words of Pope, a 'foundational theme in both the broad historical narrative and the corresponding historiography'. But as Pope and Donnelly reveal, it is also a dynamic theme in which new arguments continually arise. Pope, for example, proposes that the British may have introduced the world to modern sport and created many of the commonly held adages about the ethical practice of 'playing the game', but it was primarily Americans who taught the world how to package, sell, and consume sports. With regard to the origins of modern sport, Donnelly advocates for an analytical reconceptualization. Rather than instrumental approaches that focus on the broad processes which are considered to have shaped modern sport such as bureaucratization, commodification, and technology, Donnelly proposes that historians look more closely at the political and economic regulation of time and space as the driver of the emergence and development of modern forms of sport. As Donnelly reminds readers, pre-modern games were less bounded by time or space than modern versions which are spatially demarcated and played within fixed time limits. Pope and Donnelly are good examples of the reflective and reflexive historians identified by Mike Cronin (Chapter 4) in Part 1 who are consciously searching for, identifying, and exploring new contexts and comparisons.

Themes

Just as new arguments are a hallmark of the *Handbook* so too are new themes which appear in every Part. In this Part we introduce the body and visuality as two such themes.

The body

The sociologists of sport John Loy and Jay Coakley maintain that 'the body constitutes both the symbol and the core of all sport participation'.[2] Yet, notwithstanding the embodied essence of sport, Jaquelyn Osborne and Chelsea Litchfield (Chapter 14) observe that interest in 'the body per se' largely resides with feminist historians of sport. Osborne and Litchfield identify Patricia Vertinsky, Jennifer Hargreaves, and Roberta Park as early promoters of historical representations of the body who used the theme to 'redress the heavy bent in the early field towards the history of men's sports, male physical educators and male athletes'. In light of the discussions around authorial choice and theory in Part 1, Osborne and Litchfield's comments on Vertinsky's prolific contributions to theoretically informed representations of female gendered bodies are most apt. Similarly, their singling out of Jaime Schultz's recent contributions to representations of gendered bodies nicely fits the discussions below around political relationships in sport. Schultz, as Osborne and Litchfield point out, maintains that 'the physical is political' and that certain sporting bodies, especially female, are regulated by the political manipulation of biological, medical, and social divisions. Looking forward and taking cues from emerging material conditions, Osborne and Litchfield envisage historians of sport taking greater interest in 'cyber bodies and augmented bodies in sport' and embracing the paradigm of new materialism as a way to deal with what increasing numbers of scholars see as '"a messy, heterogenous and emergent social world"' (see also Chapter 29 by Holly Thorpe, Julie Brice, and Marianne Clark in Part 3).

Visuality

Like Maureen Smith in Part 1 of the *Handbook* (Chapter 8), Mike Huggins (Chapter 15) identifies a relatively recent interest among historians of sport in different, non-textual forms of representing the sporting past. Included in these forms are films, photographs, monuments, statues, museums, postage stamps, halls of fame, art, cartoons, and posters. Illustrating another of the historian's choices, Huggins bands these different forms under the heading of visuality and the turn to the visual. As well as a comprehensive overview of the principal works on each visual form in the history of sport, Huggins captures the methodological significance of visuality in his advice to readers to view visual material as 'mediated and contingent' and to engage it with 'imagination' and through 'self-reflexivity' and attention to detail. Emphasizing that sport is a visual experience, Huggins also reminds readers that the production and consumption of visual forms of representing the sporting past involves 'aesthetics, perception [and] sensation' and that these elements are not always readily accessible to historians.

Politics

The majority of contributors in Part 2 offer new perspectives on well-established themes that involve politics and political relationships. Politics is a distinctive type of action in response to those questions that guide us through the complexities of life: who am I, what should I do, how do I get what I want, and why do I suffer? While whole disciplines in the social sciences and humanities pursue answers to these questions, the distinctiveness of politics lies in the recognition that the solutions to the problems concerning one's self exist in a shared world of alliances, groups, collectives, and communities. Unique relations also mark politics, including power and powerlessness, domination and submission, authority and obedience, rights (liberty, equality, and justice) and responsibilities. Although these concepts are as abstract and contested as politics, they enable us to tease out the implications and interconnections between actions and practices that are not necessarily self-evident and which introduce questions about social identity, and social configurations and alignments. The history of sport is replete with such questions. Equally important in the context of socially responsible history (see Part 1), politics involves moral knowledge, opinions, and judgements, including evaluation of the principles, virtues, attitudes, and behaviours of others that inform visions of fair and just societies.[3]

Three contributors, Heather Dichter, Bruce Kidd, and Liam O'Callaghan, outline the breadth of political relationships in sport and the ways in which politics and sport have interweaved in the past and continue to entwine in the present. Dichter (Chapter 16) demonstrates how the relationships between sport and politics have transformed, and are transforming, the trajectory of sport history as well as shaping the emergence of new themes and topics. Among the themes identified and discussed by Dichter are community activism (see also Russell Field, 'Sport and Activism', Chapter 10 in Part 1), environmentalism, and diplomacy. Dichter proffers some rich examples. In response to grassroots protests and mobilization, the International Olympic Committee (IOC) now requires cities to hold referenda among citizens before a city can become an official candidate to host an olympic games. Athletes competing in winter sports have formed their own organizations to draw attention to climate change and its impact on their sports. In a move to force US Soccer to pay women members of the national soccer team the same money as their male counterparts, two congresswomen introduced the Give Our Athletes Level Salaries (GOALS) Act; the Act will halt federal funding for the 2026 International Federation of Association Football (FIFA) world cup and prevent FIFA officials from obtaining visas to enter the United States. These examples not only highlight the breadth of new political themes in the context of the historian as an author, they also logically (although not necessarily) encourage historians to reflect on their own positions as creators of socially responsible narratives.

Kidd (Chapter 17) explores the relationship between sport and politics at the international level with a focus on the IOC. He is refreshingly explicit about his viewpoint: 'I write from the perspective of a political economist and a lifelong participant in and enthusiast of the modern Olympic Movement and its ambition of intercultural understanding through sports.' Historians of sport who remain sceptical and critical of such authorial positioning – and who continue to instruct students to write in the third person and as omniscient narrators – will be hard pressed to fault Kidd's narrative. Kidd's chapter is balanced (i.e. 'objective' in the traditional language of reconstructing the past as it was) and socially responsible – in the language of representational approaches to the past. This is clear in his discussion of sport for development and peace (SDP) in the era of neo-liberal globalization, one of four distinct periods identified by Kidd and an example of a new perspective on the established theme of the relationship between sport and politics. SDP initiatives, Kidd notes, are mostly led by athletes, conducted by youth volunteers, and financed by first-world contributions. Wearing his hat as a participant in, and enthusiast of, sport and its political and cultural power, Kidd argues that SDP has brought 'the joys of sport to many' and has helped 'create and strengthen new relationships of intercultural understanding'. Wearing his hat as political economist, Kidd also observes that SDP initiatives 'rarely address the most pressing needs of the receiving societies, and often reproduce first-world cultural superiority among the volunteers, and feelings of subordination and impoverishment among the recipients'.

O'Callaghan (Chapter 18) offers a host of examples of the entanglement of politics in sporting nationalism. While sporting nationalism is a well-established theme in the history of sport, many of O'Callaghan's examples have received little attention in the mainstream of the field. Illustrating Pope's point above, about historians of sport increasingly applying 'conceptual caveats' to their work, O'Callaghan reminds readers of the 'imprecise and contingent' nature of nationalism. Rather than a concrete or unitary concept, O'Callaghan

New perspectives on old themes

argues that nationalism varies 'according to time period and geographical location' and changes with the 'political, economic, and technological context'. Echoing Cronin (Chapter 4) in Part 1 of the *Handbook*, O'Callaghan remarks on the lack of comparative examples of sporting nationalisms. O'Callaghan thus presents a fresh synthesis of sporting nationalism framed around three primary points: 'sport and the idea of the nation', 'sport and the failure of internationalism', and 'sportive nationalism in a global era'. O'Callaghan's synthesis reinforces a key precept of the *Handbook*, namely that sport history is a dynamic field in which the facts of the past impose no limits on fresh interpretations.

In addition to nationalism, the politics of sport also intersects with race and gender. Part 2 includes two essays on each. Sarah Barnes and Mary McDonald (Chapter 19), and Ashwin Desai (Chapter 20) explore race and racism in North American and South African sport respectively, while Schultz, Sykes, and Ariail (Chapter 21) and Judy Davidson (Chapter 22) discuss gender and sexuality in turn. We first referred to Barnes and McDonald's essay on race and racism in sport in Part 1, where we acknowledged their use of theory as a toolbox from which one selects ideas and concepts in order to question and think critically, rather than as a bulwark to defend narrow interpretations. Above, we highlighted their warning against rushing headlong towards new perspectives. Introducing Barnes and McDonald's chapter here, we recall the issue of new contexts raised in Part 1 (again by Cronin) and single out their broader contextualization of race and racism by aligning it with intersectionality. The concept of intersectionality, to which Schultz, Sikes, and Ariail, and Davidson also refer, 'entangles ... social categories, such as gender, class, and sexuality' in order 'to reveal interlocking systems' of social organization and relationships. As Barnes and McDonald show, contextualizing racism within a broader framework of adverse power relations can account more fully for the 'inequities, opportunities, and particularities that may exist between and within racial groups' than by examining racism as a 'singular' or 'isolated' issue. A broader context of intersectionality can also reveal how racialized people 'come to move through' society, including sporting systems, in 'intricate ways'. As an example, in Chapter 19, Barnes and McDonald cite Amira Rose Davis' representation of African-American women who were excluded from all-white professional baseball in the 1940s and subsequently joined teams in the black leagues. Davis, according to Barnes and McDonald, eschews 'a celebratory narrative'. In so doing, she 'maps out a far more complex story' of 'shifting and entangled racialized and gendered conditions of skill and labour'. Her story captures both 'a fuller presence of femininity in sport' and 'deep[er] ... scholarly understandings of the politics of race and racism as articulated through gender relations in the Civil Rights era'.

The dynamic nature of the history of sport is as apparent in case studies as it is in broad syntheses. Analyses of apartheid and post-apartheid South Africa, arguably the archetypal example of racial politics and sport, demonstrates this point.[4] In Chapter 20 Ashwin Desai places recent events in South Africa, including the nation's victory in the 2019 Rugby World Cup, under the captaincy of Siya Kolisi, the first black person to lead the national Springbok team, and questions of merit selection, in the socio-political context of an African National Congress government. In so doing, Desai brings the past into the present. However, Desai's contribution is much more than a chronology of the racial politics in South African sport and even a new perspective on an old theme. The chapter encapsulates key elements of the representational approach to the history of sport.[5] By positioning himself and his sporting world of apartheid South Africa in the late 1960s and early 1970s in the narrative, Desai reminds us that theory, in this case the theory of 'non-racialism' (see Chapter 1), is far from a universal panacea to historical interpretation and explanation. He also brings the past alive with some evocative first-hand accounts. In one powerful story, he describes his father being 'man-handled and unceremoniously pushed over the fence', back into space allocated to non-whites, during a Provincial cricket match. The lesson from Desai's work is that accounts of politics and sport in the past require knowledgeable and sensitive attention to complex geo-political issues, including human rights.

Like all the contributors to the *Handbook*, Schultz, Sykes, and Ariail (Chapter 21) emphasize the increasingly sophisticated, innovative, and new lines of inquiry emerging in the history of sport. Distinguishing between history, memory, and the past, Schultz, Sykes, and Ariail remind readers of the potential power of histories to construct identity and community. Referring to past examples such as female African-American track and field athletes, young Jewish American female professional tennis players, and Japanese American girls and women playing in basketball leagues, Schultz, Sykes, and Ariail encourage historians of sport to tell the stories of women 'beyond the global North'. They conclude their chapter with a call for more 'politically engaged histories'. Narratives and stories that 'speak to the concerns, contexts, struggles, and challenges of women' have the potential to emancipate women from institutionalized power in sport and the broader society; they are also articulate statements of social responsibility in the history of sport.

Davidson's narrative of sexuality in sport in North America – from 'the emergence of a nascent homosexual identity in the early twentieth century' to the beginnings of the 'gay and lesbian civil rights movement in the late 1960s and early 1970s' – is an accessible overview of a theme attracting increasing attention in the field (Chapter 22). Like Barnes and McDonald and Schultz, Sykes, and Ariail, Davidson stresses the importance of intersectional analysis and, in her case, the entanglement of sexuality with gender, race, and capital. As with many of the contributors in this Part, Davidson considers politics a key element in the representation of sexuality as well as lesbian and gay visibility in sport. Among her examples of political visibility are the launch of the gay games and its subsequent transformation from a primarily sporting event into a 'neoliberal, queer athletic mega-event spectacle'. Corresponding with the latter, 'anti-homophobia advocacy groups and LGBQ public education projects' for mainstream athletes added further to queer visibility. Davidson again highlights the value of intersectional analysis in her comments about 'neoliberal capital' that 'aggressively courted' queer visibility in order to access a very profitable 'pink' market. Here, too, Davidson reinforces the centrality of the representational approach to history. Notwithstanding the political mobilization of queer visibility and the 'celebration of successful and marketable athletes', she notes that sexual subjectivities are rarely made explicit in the prevailing representations of the mainstream media. Although such representations 'effectively mask' the gamut of structural and institutional relations of power that deny recognition of queer athletes (in all but the most contingent circumstances), as Davidson and other contributors to the *Handbook* demonstrate, they also invite new, alternative, and socially responsible representations of the sporting past and present. These representations will ensure that the history of sport continues to unfold and that it will embrace new content and fresh perspectives.

Notes

1 Dave Day and Wray Vamplew, 'Methodology in Sports History', *The International Journal of the History of Sport* 32, no. 15 (2015): 1716.
2 John Loy and Jay Coakley, 'Sport' in *Blackwell Encyclopedia of Sociology*, ed. George Ritzer (Hoboken, NJ: Wiley-Blackwell, 2007), 4643–4644.

New perspectives on old themes

3 Tracy Strong, *The Idea of Political Theory* (Indiana: University of Notre Dame Press, 1990), 3 and 18.
4 Historians are increasingly delving into the sporting past across the African continent. For a recent contribution see *More Than Just Games: Sports in Africa, Past and Present*, eds. Todd Cleveland, Tarminder Kaur, Gerard Akindes (Athens, OH: Ohio University Press, 2020).
5 Desai demonstrates his full skills as an ethnographer, social scientist, and oral historian in his recent book *Wentworth: The Beautiful Game and the Making of Place* (Pietermaritzburg: University of KwaZulu Natal, 2019).

12

THE ORIGIN AND DIFFUSION OF MODERN SPORT

S.W. Pope

The 'origin and diffusion of modern sport' is arguably the most foundational theme in both the broad historical narrative and the corresponding historiography of the field. While historians continue to utilize this basic framework in explaining change over time, they do so with more conceptual and epistemological caveats. What follows is a brief overview of several key historical processes which have individually and collectively transformed sport from a primarily local and regional pastime into a standardized, global phenomenon that we recognize today.[1] In this overview I employ the key roles and concepts of empire, industrial capitalism, cultural imperialism, and postcolonialism. These focus heavily upon Britain's monumental contribution to the origin and diffusion of modern sport in the eighteenth and nineteenth centuries and the United States' influence during the long twentieth century when the emergent world power eclipsed its former colonizer on both the global political and athletic stages.[2]

But my goal in this chapter is not to 'prove' or argue a specific thesis concerning the origin and diffusion of modern sport. Rather, I present what I identify as the basic historical processes which have individually and collectively transformed sport into a standardized, global phenomenon. In this sense, my authorial intentions are eclectic but intended to privilege the more recent scholarship on these historical contours. Underpinning this approach is my deconstructionist belief that any historical conclusion – much less 'truth' – is always provisional and relative to the differing and predisposing frameworks for interpreting a subject. In the end, as C. Butler notes,

> all we can have are competing stories, which are variously given coherence by their historical narrators, and the past is no more than what historians say it is. In this way, historiography usually stands in for history in most instances.[3]

I begin my chapter by revisiting the modernization model from which this topic emerged.

(A once) dominant paradigm

The concept of 'modern sport' derived originally from A. Guttmann's paradigm-shifting 1978 book, *From Ritual to Record: The Nature of Modern Sport* – a work informed by

The origin and diffusion of modern sport

modernization theory, which conceptually framed the scholarship and has continued to inform discussion ever since. The paradigm posited a relatively recent Western conception of sport which is unique in world history – fundamentally different from 'traditional' sports of Western and non-Western cultures alike. Whereas 'traditional' sport was loosely organized, tied to local religious customs, and connected to agrarian lifestyles, modern sport is secular, rational, specialized, bureaucratized, quantified in its obsession with records.[4]

The modernization paradigm *seemed* so natural and straightforward. It seemed to account for the most basic questions of how and when sports become what they are today. It not only became widely accepted among sport historians in the early development of the field but it continues to endure conceptually and as a clear narrative even four decades later. But according to R. Gruneau, the very terms 'sport' and 'modernity' are both conceptual abstractions which were invented, debated, and refined between the seventeenth and twentieth centuries by upper- and middle-class individuals in Europe and the Americas. As he writes, 'the study of sport and modernity is complicated by the fact that both terms have complex genealogies, multiple meanings, and contested histories' which did not evolve in a linear fashion. Gruneau goes on to demonstrate that sport 'involved the remaking of ... diverse gaming and sporting practices, into a more unified, regulated and purposeful social and cultural *field* of experience' and that this occurred 'unevenly and incompletely in different European societies and throughout European and North American colonies'. Thus, rather than modern sport arising from ancient practices, the process 'involved the *selective conjuring* [my emphasis] of images, aesthetic motifs, and the ideal from the past reworked and pressed into service of modernity'.[5]

While the 'origin and diffusion of modern sport' remains a useful heuristic tool for approaching the expansive landscape of sport throughout the past and present, it currently has a less talismanic hold on historians who have embraced other epistemological approaches which are less constricted to dualistic explanatory concepts (e.g. traditional-modern) and schematic models of social change (e.g. modernization) during the past two decades. One such suggestive direction directs our attention away from the characteristic *differences* between 'traditional' and 'modern' sports towards the *similarities* and *continuities*. S. Hardy argues that historians need to account for divergence (modern from traditional) and also convergence (persistence throughout time). In approaching this conceptual challenge, he discerned several key 'long residuals' which have 'extended throughout historical time and geographical space by means of endless repetitions of performance' – *agon, eros*, community, gambling, framing. In doing so, Hardy shows how one can embrace a longer comparative-historical trajectory to explain sporting development in an interdisciplinarily nuanced and self-reflexive manner. D. Booth characterizes such an approach as one that 'realizes the potential incongruity and transient nature of the knowledge produced'.[6]

The newer directions acknowledge that sport history is always subject to change and is forever being re-made. Scholars have utilized approaches such as social constructionism, discourse analysis, textualism, and narrative to interrogate sources as artefacts, the meaning of which exists in their reading and telling rather than their correspondence to an imagined past or a grand narrative of historical change (e.g. modernization). Despite the current unpopularity of grand narratives, I would suggest that modernization remains an active presence as a model to be approached or avoided but which still animates contemporary sports historiography.

Historians such as Booth and M. Phillips, for example, call for navigating away from 'modern' to a more reflexive, less certain engagement with the sporting past. As they and others have demonstrated, 'reflexivity requires historians to be more transparent about how they (re) present the past as history'. According to Booth, 'without reflexivity, historians contribute to the illusion that they have a firm grip on the past'.[7] D. Nathan reminds us that every historical 'moment' contains various interpretive versions and 'irrespective of our sources and evidence we tend to see what we want to see, believe what we need to believe'.[8] Nathan's self-reflexive appraisal of historical interpretation affirms H. White's argument that all historical narratives are 'verbal fictions, the contents of which are as much invented as found'. White believes that historians either consciously or subconsciously employ tropes to infuse their narratives with meaning and then plot them (e.g. tragic, comic, romantic, satiric) accordingly.[9] Deconstructionists maintain that reflexivity requires authors to admit that history is an interpretation rather than a recovery of the past.

The British Empire

The evolution and diffusion of early British modern sport is well-documented.[10] As such, the following sketch merely highlights some of the selective dynamics in this process.

Cricket was the first English ball game to be organized. The game was popular in both rural and urban areas but during the late seventeenth century wealthy landowners transformed an informal village pastime into a more organized sport. Aristocrats lavished their disposable wealth and time and codified the rules in 1744 (as they were motivated to ensure predictable gambling) and organized the Marylebone Cricket Club in London in 1787. The game evoked a romantic pastoral image and social class cooperation at the very time that the country was undergoing fundamental urban, industrial transformation. Professionals took the game on overseas tours to Canada and the United States (1859, 1862) and to Australia and New Zealand (1864), and commenced international competitions in 1877. From the outset, cricket served as a cultural bond of the British Empire.[11]

While cricket was promoted by aristocrats and professionals, rugby evolved out of the English public schools. In its various forms, football dates back to the fourteenth century. Between 1750 and 1830 the folk games were adopted to suit the environment of the English public schools and football was transformed into a rule-bound sport with specific codes governing behaviour by 1845 (simultaneous with the development of association football). At the time of the formation of the Rugby Football Union in 1871 the game was played primarily by upper middle-class boys and young men mainly in the schools and clubs in the south of England wherein amateurism flourished. By the end of the nineteenth century the rugby union game had spread throughout the British Empire's colonies and dominions.[12]

Initiated by the British, the international diffusion process featured a similar cast of characters and reflected a country's political-economic prowess through the spread of its sports. In his classic study, *Sport and the British*, R. Holt demonstrated that sport 'played a major role in the transmission of imperial and national ideas from the late nineteenth century onwards'.[13] The process featured a *horizontal diffusion* in which colonial officers (administrators, clergy, educators, military personnel) took cultural practices with them overseas and effectively 'sold' them to the indigenous whom they conscripted into their service. The indigenous – primarily cosmopolitan upper-class types presumably at one with their masters – were the early adopters of the foreign cultural form which typically followed trade and other capitalist routes of global entrepreneurialism. *Vertical diffusion* of the cultural formation followed, first at home, then abroad, and was the result of lower-class appropriation.[14]

Scholars drew upon the theoretical work in Cultural Studies to explain the power dynamics in this process. B. Stoddart posited 'cultural power' as a concept for understanding how ruling ideas and conventions became hegemonic throughout the empire and at home.

The origin and diffusion of modern sport

British domination was maintained through cultural ('soft') power – the ideas, beliefs, values, and conventions diffused throughout the empire by British administrators, military officers, educators, missionaries, and the like. 'The success of this cultural power,' Stoddart wrote,

> rested with the ability of the imperial system to have its main social tenets accepted as appropriate forms of behaviour and ordering by the bulk of the client population, or at least by those important sections of that population upon whom the British relied for the mediation of their ruling practices, objectives and ideology.[15]

Sport historians have profusely documented the role of the games culture of British public schools in culturally loaded brands of sport in which the overarching goal was the development of muscular Christians throughout the colonies. As a powerful ideology in the development of 'modern' sport, muscular Christianity, S. Brownell argues, was 'explicitly based on the convergence of masculinity, physical activity, asceticism, racial purity, and the white man's burden' and was used by its champions who sought to 'save' and 'civilize' 'the working classes and the impoverished at home as well as the colonial Others elsewhere in the world'.[16] Within this realm of spreading British sporting cultural practices, church missionaries figured prominently and their movement influenced the early twentieth-century playground movement and the beginnings of municipal recreation in Canada and the United States, the creation of the Young Men's Christian Association (YMCA), Boy Scouts, and other ethnic and religion-based sports programmes throughout the first half of the twentieth century as well as the cause of amateur sport more generally.[17]

In the end, coloniality and modernity are indivisible features of the history of industrial capitalism in the West as well as within other societies. The 'origin and diffusion of modern sport' within the British context was more than the sum of various descriptive, structural characteristics (e.g. 'rationalization'), or interpretive tropes (e.g. 'civilizing process'). Rather, it was inextricably shaped by a specific historical-economic configuration – merchant and industrial capitalism beginning in Britain during the eighteenth century. The process continued thereafter throughout the 'long nineteenth century' through the First World War – where the lasting characteristics were developed – and through the monopoly capitalist, post-Fordist, and neo-liberal phases. During these phases the canvas of sport was further coloured by nationalism, imperialism, racism, sexism, white privilege, and the like. The diffusion of modern sport was also structured by imperialism, which extended capitalist relations abroad and at home. Sport represented, as Collins summarized, the long history, 'the story of capitalism at play'.[18]

National and international associations

Scholars generally agree that the defining characteristic of modern sport is the standardization of rules. Prior to the mid- to late-nineteenth century, sports and athletic contests were played within local, face-to-face communities without codified rules. The emergence of what S. Brownell has termed the 'international sports system' emerged along two 'concurrent, interrelated strands': codified rules to facilitate wide-scale competitions and the proliferation of voluntary associations which were utilized by 'industrial and colonial elites and middle classes wherever they established themselves around the globe'.[19]

The process of linking thousands of local games and contests into a global system started in Western Europe. The British led the way in codifying the rules of boxing (1743) and cricket (1744) and with the formation of the International Football Association Board (IFAB) in

1886 they standardized the rules and coordinated relations between the soccer associations in England, Scotland, Ireland, and Wales. Between the 1840s and 1880s, the rules of baseball, soccer, rugby, swimming, track and field, skiing, cycling, tennis, badminton, and field hockey were codified. By 1900, 22 of the approximately 30 sports that had been, or would become, summer Olympic sports had written, internationally recognized rules.[20]

This crucial work of standardizing sports rules and regulations was the handiwork of elite and middle-class voluntary associations. Such organizations flourished initially at the national level between the 1860s and 1880s and then rapidly developed at the regional and international levels. For example, in Germany the Hamburg Turner Society was formed in 1816 and was succeeded by the German Turner Society in 1860; and in the United States, the Amateur Athletic Union was organized in 1888 and the National Association of Base Ball [sic] Players (amateurs) was organized in 1857 and was followed shortly thereafter by the National League (1876) and the American Association (1882) – the foundation of a national professional sport.

The vibrant growth of organizations and associations coalesced into a formidable international sports system which provided a viable structure for the further diffusion and development of global sport around the turn of the twentieth century. The two most powerful organizations that anchored the emerging global sports system were the International Olympic Committee (IOC) in 1894 and the *Fédération Internationale de Football* (FIFA) in 1904.[21]

J. Hoberman produced an evocative comparative analysis of this wave of international organizations and discovered crucial similarities amongst them. Most such organizations promoted a version of 'idealistic internationalism' – 'cultural projections of nationalist impulses employing cosmopolitan vocabularies rooted in ethnocentric ideas of national grandeur' – and were bound together by 'personal ties to more than one group'; moreover, all 'benefited from benign myths of origin rooted in reverential attitudes toward the personal qualities of their respective founding fathers and the salvational doctrines they created'.[22]

American postcolonialism

The North American context provided the first case study for the export of British sport. As Elliott Gorn and Warren Goldstein have written, 'settlers did not just transport English pastimes to the New World; they also brought their ideas about the role of play … across the ocean'. As such, the American colonists 'were heirs to England's bifurcated leisure heritage', which vacillated between Puritanical strictures regarding excessive physical and worldly pleasures and fantasizing upon how 'an easy, plentiful life could be recreated in terms of the old ideal of a leisurely paradise'.[23] In short, English colonists carried both traditions to North America and attempted to shape their lives with this cultural baggage.

During colonial and antebellum times Americans imported various British sports and games and, subsequently, transformed them with newly invented rules, conventions, traditions, and meanings after the Civil War. The maturation of American sport proved to be a decisive, resilient force of the postcolonial relationship. Symptomatic of more than a century of cultural rivalry, elite Americans were especially keen to initiate and test the 'mother' country. This sporting rivalry, which raged (especially) from the late nineteenth century through to the mid-twentieth, offers a window into transnational aspects of both American and British cultures. The development of an American sporting tradition was fundamentally incubated within the larger history of European colonialism that began in the fifteenth century – as its messianic sense of national destiny to transform the continent and conquer new territories abroad.[24]

The origin and diffusion of modern sport

The thrust of sports history in the United States during the nineteenth and early twentieth centuries was the adaptation and transformation of British ball games into uniquely *American* ones. This process of emulation and imitation began first with baseball (which derived from bat and ball games in seventeenth- and eighteenth-century England during the 1820s–1830s) and then with American football (developed out of the rugby code in the 1860s–1870s)—an exceedingly well-documented chapter of global sports history. Americans first staked their distinctive national sporting identity on the indigenous nature of baseball through a mytho-poetic creation story that the game was hatched in rural upstate New York in 1838 by a young man who later served as a general in the Civil War (1861–1865). Although this creation story was debunked in the 1940s, the notion that the game is a distinctly American creation persists to this day.

The development of baseball provides useful insight into the overarching themes of this chapter – the origin and diffusion processes as well as historical epistemology. In his impressively researched compilation, *Baseball Before We Knew It*, D. Block presents a 'theoretical flowchart of baseball's evolution' which traces the game's early history within the realm of medieval ball games, through 'trap ball' in the early seventeenth century to its status as a children's game in eighteenth-century England contemporaneous with North American colonization by English settlers.[25] By the time of the Revolutionary War (1770s) baseball (in its three common varieties) had moved beyond the exclusive purview of boys to become a diversion of young male soldiers; thereafter, a particular version, the Massachusetts version of the game, is popularized by Knickerbocker Club's distinctive adaptation of this variety in New York City during the 1840s, which would become the national version throughout the country by the end of the Civil War as soldiers returned home and transported the game.

While Block reassures his readers that his work is based on extensive documentation, he admits that his history of the 'roots of our beloved national pastime' is based upon evidence that remains 'somewhat selective' and thus, the resulting history is only a 'plausible' attempt to ascertain the origins of baseball. D. Booth uses this example to demonstrate how a deconstructionist account would not regard such matters as problematic. As Booth shows, in the hands of deconstructionists, 'the absence of certainties can be as fascinating as knowing the truth about the past, and equally powerful'.[26]

Baseball as the recognized American national pastime diffused to the Caribbean and Southeast Asia (Japan, China, Philippines) following the Spanish-American War of 1898 as the United States evolved into a major global power and later eclipsed Britain as the dominant empire of influence.[27] Like in Britain, American sport represented a type of cultural 'soft' power plied by Protestant missionaries and the YMCA. The trans-Atlantic ideology of muscular Christianity provided a crucial moral justification for sport as well as a sense of mission for the export of American and British sporting practices abroad. Baseball was the first which spread beyond continental borders (followed shortly thereafter by basketball after its invention in 1891). The sport diffused to the Caribbean as a function of an Americanized version of its British-styled predecessor imperialism. As A. Cobley notes, American sporting traditions 'spilled into the Caribbean basin – especially in the islands of the northern Caribbean' (Cuba, Puerto Rico, Dominican Republic) and in the countries of Central America that border the Caribbean (Costa Rica, Nicaragua, El Salvador and Panama) – 'in most of these places, baseball penetrated the popular culture to such an extent that it eventually achieved the status of the national sport'. T. Carter argues that baseball became the national sport in Cuba not because of American imperialism or colonialism, but because *criollos* – nineteenth-century island elites – made deliberate efforts to equate the game with a nascent

Cuban nationalism to differentiate themselves from the Spanish. As a distinctive practice, baseball provided a symbolic discourse for an independent Cuba.[28]

Just as the colonial American adoption and adaptation of various British children's games did not inevitably lead to a modernized version of baseball, neither did various versions of Irish and Scottish games automatically morph into the Canadian national sport of hockey. Irish hurling and Scottish shinty were traditional, pre-modern games played more than two millennia ago and numerous versions of field hockey were played throughout the New England, Quebec, and Atlantic Provinces region of North America into the mid-nineteenth century.[29] In their recent global history of the game, S. Hardy and A. Holman demonstrate how the most popular early version of this folk game played on ice in Montreal developed into the dominant version during the 1870s–1880s and diffused in *particular* ways 'through the efforts and struggles of entrepreneurs, reformers, bureaucrats, players, reporters, and everyday fans, who clashed over rules, technologies, representations, and meanings'.[30] The diffusion process was not a uniform one – exuding the linearity of 'modernization'. According to Hardy and Holman,

> if countries and cultures have occasionally embraced or adopted the games of another country they have just as often adapted and refashioned them to meet their own needs … cultural diffusion of any sort is never an even or predetermined process.

The process is very much based on contingency and chance.[31] In the case of hockey and baseball, as C. Howell has demonstrated, the borderland region of Atlantic Canada more closely replicated the sporting culture of urban, eastern New England than the rest of the Canadian nation. Sport diffusion cannot simply be portrayed as a top-down (centre-periphery) example of cultural imperialism without due consideration of the agency and creativity of peoples on the margins (within and between nations). As Howell writes, the 'relationship between metropolis and hinterland is a dialectical one, continually negotiated and re-negotiated, imagined and re-imagined. And nowhere is this fluidity more evident than in the production of culture in transnational borderland communities'.[32]

During the twentieth century, many sports adapted and diffused globally as the focus moved from nationalism and national worth to professionalism and commercialized, internationalized spectatorship. The British may have introduced the world to modern sport and created many of the commonly held adages about the ethical practice of 'playing the game', but it was primarily Americans who taught the world how to package, sell, and consume sports. While Americans were moderately successful at exporting (and facilitating the growth of) two of their nation's games (baseball and basketball), their most significant legacy to the development of global sport was in the promotion of sport as a commercial enterprise.[33]

Postcolonial cultural appropriation

Lacrosse is an example of the 'modernization' of a traditional, indigenous game that evolved in North America prior to European colonization and developed as a team sport within middle- and upper-class white society. From the seventeenth century onward, E. Gorn writes, English colonists and the native 'Indians' played apart within 'disparate cultural contexts [that] gave [their games] different meanings'.[34]

The earliest documented evidence of lacrosse dates to the mid-seventeenth century. Among the Huron, Iroquois, Sac, and Chippewa tribes it began much earlier and was considered a gift from the Creator who, it was believed, looked favourably on those who played it honourably.

The game was known among the natives as *Baggataway* (translated as 'little brother of war') and served key secular purposes such as military preparedness and diplomatic relations. The term lacrosse dates to 1636 when a Jesuit missionary named Jean de Brefeuf identified the similarity between the stick used in the game with the *crosier* which Catholic bishops carried in church ceremonies. La Crosse, eventually a single word, emerged by the 1790s as 'once standardized rules were created and the most overt war themes had been displaced'.[35]

As in the case of hockey, Montreal is considered the cradle of lacrosse for which the developmental timeline ran parallel to ice hockey. Anglo-Canadians competed against Native Americans during the 1840s–1850s; the Montreal Lacrosse Club was established in 1856 followed by the Canadian National Lacrosse Association in 1867 to effectively institutionalize the sport. Between the 1860s and 1880s the game expanded, predominantly in Montreal and Toronto and within the United States (mostly in US colleges and universities); eventually it appeared in Australia and New Zealand. In Canada, however, the established British public-school sports traditions of rugby and cricket inhibited its adoption.

Lacrosse provides a window into a rare case of Western emulation, adaptation, and 'modernization' of an indigenous game which was, in turn, expropriated into white, mostly middle-class sports culture. Within the literature on postcolonialism this process bespeaks 'cultural appropriation'. This calculated use of an external cultural practice to define another group's identity was exemplified by the activism of George Beers, a nationalist sportsman and lacrosse goalkeeper. Beers believed that by appropriating and transforming the Mohawk ballgame into a 'rational' sport, as D. Fisher surmised, the distinctly 'primitive' qualities exhibited by the 'noble savage' could benefit the 'civilized' white gentlemanly men who profess a *Canadian* national identity.[36] This practice of cultural appropriation of team names and mascots by non-Natives persists in the contemporary North American sports world despite protests from indigenous groups.

Indigenous sport remains a neglected area of study within the larger field of sports history. A recent special issue of the *Journal of Sport History* astutely highlights the skimpy quantity and quality of Indigenous sport history. The contributors argue that Indigenous pastimes have been 'relegated to European modernist notions' of traditional history and narrated with 'Western historical epistemologies which do not always recognize Indigenous ways of knowing concerning how history is told, recounted, transmitted, and understood'.[37] I fully concur with this critique. To date, sports historians have treated Indigenous sport within the conceptual frameworks of cultural imperialism, cultural hegemony, and the diffusion of modern sport – as I have done here and elsewhere.[38] As a result, settler colonialism, for example, has been 'often subsumed under the broader phenomena of colonialism in sport history' rather than as a specific practice that raises a set of unique questions, issues, and problems. A. Downey's 2018 book, *The Creator's Game*, demonstrates this vital new direction in the study of lacrosse through the tales of appropriation and re-appropriation which highlights the complex relationship between Indigenous and non-Indigenous people through the use of Indigenous epistemologies and sources such as oral history with Elders, Knowledge Holders, activists, writers, as well as academics.[39]

In this chapter I have adopted a deconstructionist sensibility by arbitrarily flagging selected pieces of the lush scholarly literature on sport and modernity and presenting them more like a bricolage than a traditional historical narrative. In so doing I have highlighted the conceptual limitations of traditional frameworks associated with cultural imperialism, cultural hegemony, and the diffusion of modern sport. Somewhat ironically, Indigenous epistemologies and sources not only reinforce these limitations but confirm the salience of deconstructionism.

Notes

1 For an excellent overview of this general topic see Susan Brownell's 'Sport Since 1750', in *The Cambridge World History, Vol. 7: Production, Destruction, and Connection,* Part 2: *Shared Transformation?* Eds. J. R. McNeill and Kenneth Pomeranz (Cambridge: Cambridge University Press, 2015), 343–377.

2 John Nauright and Steven Pope, 'The Twenty-first-century *SportsWorld*: Global Markets and Global Impact', *Sport in Society* 20 (2017): 1817–1820.

3 Christopher Butler, *Postmodernism: A Very Short Introduction* (Oxford: Oxford University Press, 2002), 35.

4 During the 1970s and 1980s, in particular, critics throughout the social sciences and within sports studies exposed 'modernization' as an ahistorical, anachronistic construct based upon a positivistic, ethnocentric Western worldview of 'progress', which fundamentally glossed over the relations of power between different social and economic groups; exaggerated social harmony; and often ignored the inevitable losers and outsiders in consensus building initiatives whether at the local, regional, national, or international levels. See Richard Gruneau 'Modernization or Hegemony: Two Views on Sport and Social Development', in *Not Just a Game: Essays in Canadian Sport Sociology*, eds. Jean Harvey and Hart Cantelon (Ottawa: Ottawa University Press, 1988), 9–32.

5 Richard Gruneau, *Sport and Modernity* (London: Polity Press, 2017), 1–14.

6 Stephen Hardy, 'Entrepreneurs, Structures, and the Sportgeist: Old Tensions in a Modern Industry', in *Essays on Sport History and Sport Mythology*, eds. D. Kyle and G. Stark (College Station, Texas: A & M Press), 45–82; S. Hardy, D. Booth and John Loy, 'The Material Culture of Sport: Toward a Typology', *Journal of Sport History* 36, no. 1 (2009): 129–152.

7 Douglas Booth, *The Field: Truth and Fiction in Sport History* (London: Routledge, 2005), 220.

8 Dan Nathan, *Saying It's So: A Cultural History of the Black Sox Scandal* (Urbana: University of Illinois Press, 2003), 210.

9 Hayden White, 'The Historical Text as a Literary Artifact,' in *Tropics of Discourse: Essays in Cultural Criticism* (Baltimore: Johns Hopkins University Press, 1985), 81–100.

10 J.A. Mangan, *The Games Ethic and Imperialism: Aspects of the Diffusion of an Ideal* (Harmondsworth: Viking, 1986) and J.A. Mangan, *Pleasure, Profit, and Proselytism: British Culture and Sport Abroad, 1700–1914* (London: Frank Cass, 1988).

11 Anthony Bateman and Jeffrey Hill, eds., *The Cambridge Companion to Cricket* (Cambridge: Cambridge University Press, 2011).

12 Tony Collins, *How Football Began: A Global History of How the World's Football Codes Were Born* (London: Routledge, 2018).

13 Richard Holt, *Sport and the British* (Oxford: Oxford University Press, 1989), 203.

14 Allen Guttmann, *Games and Empires: Modern Sports and Cultural Imperialism* (New York: Columbia University Press, 1994), 11, 178.

15 Brian Stoddart, 'Sport, Cultural Imperialism, and Cultural Response in the British Empire', *Comparative Studies of Society and History* 30 (1988): 649–673. See also Pope's essay 'Imperialism' in *Routledge Companion to Sport History*, eds. S.W. Pope and J. Nauright (London: Routledge, 2011), 229–247.

16 Susan Brownell, Niko Bernier, and Thomas F. Carter, *The Anthropology of Sport: Bodies, Borders, Biopolitics* (Berkeley: University of California Press, 2018), 45.

17 Simon C. Darnell, Russell Field, and Bruce Kidd, *The History and Politics of Sport for Development: Activists, Ideologues, and Reformers* (London: Palgrave, 2019), 41.

18 Tony Collins, *Sport in Capitalist Society: A Short Introduction* (London: Routledge, 2013), 13.

19 S. Brownell, *The Anthropology of Sport*, 41–42; Brownell, 'Sport Since 1750', *passim*.

20 Brownell, *Anthropology of Sport*, 41–42.

21 The scholarly and popular literature on the IOC and FIFA is substantial. See, for example, David Goldblatt, *The Games: A Global History of the Olympics* (New York: W.W. Norton, 2016); Jules Boykoff, *Power Games: A Political History of the Olympics* (London: Verso, 2016); and Matthew Llewellyn and John Gleaves, *The Rise and Fall of Olympic Amateurism* (Urbana: University of Illinois Press, 2016).

22 John Hoberman, 'Toward a Theory of Olympic Internationalism', *Journal of Sport History* 22 (1995): 10, 8, 3.

23 Elliott J. Gorn and Warren Goldstein, *A Brief History of American Sports*, 2nd edition (Urbana: University of Illinois Press, 2004), 16–17.

24 S.W. Pope, 'Rethinking Sport, Empire, and American Exceptionalism', *Sport History Review* 38 (2007): 92–120.
25 David Block, *Baseball Before We Knew It: A Search for the Roots of the Game* (Lincoln: University of Nebraska Press, 2005).
26 Booth, *The Field*, 59, 219. For a prime example of deconstructionist scholarship see Nathan, *Saying It's So*.
27 A.G. Hopkins, *American Empire: A Global History* (Princeton: Princeton University Press, 2019).
28 Alan Cobley, 'The Caribbean', in *Routledge Companion to Sports History*, 379.
29 For an excellent overview of this pre-modern history, see Hardy and Holman, *Hockey: A Global History*, 19–33.
30 Hardy and Holman, *Hockey: A Global History*, 11.
31 Hardy and Holman, *Hockey: A Global History*, 10, 98, 82. In their view, entrepreneurs were key figures in the four vectors of sporting development innovation, standardization, divergence, convergence process.
32 Colin Howell, *Blood, Sweat, and Cheers: Sport and the Making of Modern Canada* (Toronto: University of Toronto Press, 2001), 266, 259, 253. See also Howell and Daryl Leeworthy, 'Borderlands', in *Routledge Companion to Sports History*, 71–84.
33 Steven W. Pope and John Nauright, 'American-British Sporting Rivalries and the Making of the Global Sport Industry', *Comparative American Studies: An International Journal* 14, 3–4 (2016), 1170–1184.
34 Gorn and Goldstein, *A Brief History of American Sports*, 5.
35 Steven Jackson, 'Lacrosse', in *Encyclopedia of World Sport: From Ancient Times to the Present*, eds. D. Levinson and K. Christensen (New York: Oxford University Press, 1996), 219.
36 Donald Fisher, *Lacrosse: A History of the Game* (Baltimore: Johns Hopkins University Press, 2002).
37 Murray Phillips, Russell Field, Christine O'Bonsawin, Janice Forsyth, 'Indigenous Resurgence, Regeneration, and Decolonization through Sport History', *Journal of Sport History* 36, 2 (2019): 143–144.
38 S.W. Pope, 'Rethinking Sport, Empire, and American Exceptionalism', *Sport History Review* 38 (2007), 96–97.
39 Allen Downey, *The Creator's Game: Lacrosse, Identity, and Indigenous Nationhood* (Vancouver: University of British Columbia Press, 2018).

13

TIME, SPACE, AND SPORT

Peter Donnelly

> In the eighteenth and nineteenth centuries … representations of sport became sites for articulating competing discourses about … legitimate uses of time, space and the human body.[1]

Time and space are vast topics and concepts, each underlying at least one discipline in the social sciences – history and geography respectively – and the concepts, together and separately, have appeared frequently in analyses of the emergence of modern sport during the eighteenth and nineteenth centuries.[2] The emergence of modern sport was recently and extensively examined by Richard Gruneau, who describes its production as an autonomous cultural practice.[3] The qualities and values of this practice 'complemented parallel thoughts about knowledge, objectivity, universality, rational behavior, productivity and progress that collectively constituted a new conceptualization of modernity and which ideologically intertwined sport with modernity'.[4]

This chapter also focuses on the emergence of modern rationalized sport. However, previous studies have generally taken an instrumentalist approach, focusing on changes in sport in relation to more general processes such as bureaucratization, commodification, and the development of new technologies. This chapter focuses more specifically on the emergence and development of the *forms* and, to a lesser extent, the *meanings* of modern rationalized sport as a consequence of the political/economic regulation of time and space. This is not to imply that the form(s) and meaning(s) were determined by the regulation of time and space; rather, I argue that regulation, and resistance to regulation, provided a frame within which those forms and meanings were produced.

In keeping with the emergence of modern rationalized sport, this chapter focuses on the Global North, centred initially on the United Kingdom (UK) between the eighteenth and twentieth centuries, although similar patterns of change related to time, space, and sport were evident in many parts of the Global North. This does not mean that numerous sport-like alternative physical cultures do not exist or are not important. They are, to some extent, beyond the scope of a brief chapter, but their significance is acknowledged later in terms of cultural alternatives to the hegemony of modern rationalized sport.

The focus on this hegemonic form of sport is justified by its prevalence – it is the most widely recognized form of sport, with participants in every country. Modern sport spread

110

DOI: 10.4324/9780429318306-16

Time, space, and sport

from the UK as a consequence of colonization and trade. The cultural weight of colonization led to the erasure of many local languages, religions, customs, and physical cultures, which were largely replaced by the languages, religions, customs, and physical cultures of the colonizers. This process continued during the twentieth century with the addition of economic and cultural colonization (e.g. Americanization) to create what is essentially a global sport monoculture, variously described by McKay and Miller as 'corporate sport' and by Donnelly as 'prolympic sport'.[5]

The chapter begins with a brief examination of time and space as social constructions, focusing on the specific context of the UK, beginning during the 'age of enlightenment', which set the frame for the emergence of modern sport. This is followed by a more specific examination of the production of modern sport within the emerging spatial and temporal frames. The chapter concludes by outlining some physical cultural alternatives to the hegemony of modern rationalized sport.

Social construction of space and time

Time and space are both experiential and objective dimensions. They each lend themselves to precise, objective measurement, and they may be experienced through our senses and our consciousness. They are also social constructions such that, at different times and in different places, the forms and meanings of space and of time may also be different.[6] As with all social constructions, power is involved in establishing a dominant way, out of many possible alternatives, of organizing time and space. And, in Williams' terms, such hegemonies continually need to be negotiated and renegotiated but their success is evident in the widespread normalization of a specific conception of space and/or time.[7]

Space

Henri Lefebvre is perhaps best known for the representation of space as a social construction, but others such as David Harvey and Edward Soja have also developed the idea.[8] In what follows, I examine how a particular social construction of rural space in the UK, one that had been reproduced for perhaps 1,000 years, began to decline in the eighteenth century to be replaced by the enclosure of land in a new, privatized social construction of rural space.[9]

Before the eighteenth century, the traditional form of agriculture was based on a feudal system of land tenure. In the open field system villages were surrounded by large fields divided into small strips ('holdings') farmed and managed by the community. The surrounding 'waste land' (forest, heath, marsh) was also often held in common by villagers and used for gathering firewood, grazing animals, fishing, and hunting for small game.

The common lands were also used for games and recreations. Traditional games of football were played between villages across the common land, and the numerous festivals, feasts, fairs, and holidays that were an important part of the rural calendar frequently involved sporting contests in common spaces.[10] These customary practices declined as a result of enclosure – the hedging, fencing, and walling of fields and common land under private ownership.[11] Although enclosure was first sanctioned by an Act of Parliament in 1235, it proceeded at varying rates until the most intensive period of enclosure between 1760 and 1820, when the now familiar 'patchwork' pattern of countryside was developed.

Each enclosure required a privately introduced Act of Parliament, which were passed easily because of the significant representation of landowners in Parliament. Enclosures were routinely driven by economic interests such as intensive sheep farming in the thirteenth and fourteenth centuries, and by the increased profitability and efficiency of farming during the agricultural revolution (occurring simultaneously with the most intensive period of enclosure). Enclosures were not limited to farm land. With the growth of 'possessive individualism' enclosures increasingly included the privatization of forest and moorland (enclosed for logging and hunting), and the former 'waste land' commons of heaths and marshes.[12]

Nor was the privatization of space limited to rural land. The industrial revolution led to a significant movement of population from rural areas to towns and cities, where low-cost housing was rapidly built, but no provision made for recreational space. Stephen Hardy described how working people in Boston sought recreational space in cemeteries as the only green space available.[13] Even swimming in urban canals was banned by the owners following complaints from 'respectable females'.[14] Such social control measures continued with the newly emerging police forces helping to remove children's and adult play from the streets for reasons of morality and public order, but also to enable traffic and commerce on shopping streets.[15]

In his case study of mining towns and villages in East Northumberland, UK, Alan Metcalfe shows this regulation of public and recreational space continuing well into the latter part of the nineteenth century:

> Prior to the 1870s sport was played on public highways, beaches, the moors ... and on vacant land attached to inns. Reacting to increased mining activity and increased population, authorities moved to control access to and use of public space.[16]

Using just the control of roads as an example, authorities used prosecutions to end potshare bowling, then pedestrian contests, and then bicycle races. Thus, the nineteenth century was largely characterized by the social reconstruction of space, the political/economic privatization and regulation of spaces that were formerly used for sport and recreation.

Time

Tom Griffiths pointed out that, 'Historians often take time for granted, even though it is their medium. Time flows steadily; it dictates chronology; it lazily supplies causation.'[17] The effect of social constructionism on history was perhaps less overt than on geography since a recognition of the malleability of time had, to a great extent, been a part of historical discourse since before social constructionism.[18] For example, Fernand Braudel reorganized historical time into 'social time', 'geographical time', and 'individual time'.[19] However, E.P. Thompson's article, 'Time, Work Discipline, and Industrial Capitalism' had a powerful impact on the recognition of time as a social construction.[20]

Before the industrial revolution, and especially in rural areas, the temporal management of daily life was governed by church time (e.g. the Angelus bell to mark the midday meal break), daylight, seasons, and the weather. Much has been made of the invention of the clock on the regulation of time but, as Harvey noted, the hour was a thirteenth-century invention, but minutes and seconds did not appear until the seventeenth century.[21] Pastoral time was clearly flexible before the industrial revolution: 'free time' included Sundays and, as noted previously, the numerous festivals, feasts, fairs, and holidays that were an important part of the rural calendar.[22] Independent craftspeople such as hand loom weavers also kept flexible working days and times, taking time for both education and recreation.[23]

Thompson outlined the effects of industrialization on this customary use of time.[24] The imposition of clock-driven work discipline was key to the profitability of the new factories.

Time, space, and sport

In Marxist analyses of surplus value, profit is unpaid labour, and the more labour that could be extracted from workers, the higher the profit. The shift from a pastoral and customary understanding of time to 'work discipline' was not easy. Sunday was the only non-working day, and factories no longer recognized many of the traditional festivals and holidays. In the earlier days of industrialization, workers failed to go to work on Mondays so often that the days were referred to as 'Saint Mondays'.[25]

'Saint Mondays' came to an end as time/work discipline was increasingly imposed by punitive measures. However, it is generally acknowledged that the widespread introduction of public education had the most significant impact on establishing work discipline and preparing children who would be working in the new industrial order. They would learn to be in a certain place at a certain time (absence and lateness penalties) and to be obedient. Education was a double-edged sword in which 'educational arrangements for the children of the poor [combined] the notion of "moral rescue" [with] genuine educational intentions and ... the utilitarian concern for equipping children for industrial occupations'.[26]

Thus, the nineteenth century was also largely characterized by the social reconstruction of time, the political/economic regulation of times that were formerly used for sport and recreation. However, as Paul Glennie and Nigel Thrift have pointed out, Thompson – while important – is by no means the last word with regard to the social construction of time.[27] Barbara Adam refers to multiple aspects of time, all of which are critical:

> the physical universe, living nature, human social groupings, written language and symbolic knowledge, social records, technology, artifacts, clocks and calendars all form an integral part of our social life today, and since they are all implicated in a full understanding of time, it seems essential that they are explored in their own right.[28]

Glennie and Thrift point out that social theorists such as Elias, Foucault, and Giddens developed conceptions of time similar to Adam; and they (Glennie and Thrift) reformulated Thompson's approach under four headings: 'the multiplicity of times; the multi-faceted nature of the concept of time discipline; the skilled nature of time-competences; and the symbolic meanings of times'.[29]

Notwithstanding these theoretical and conceptual developments, a far stricter regime of time/work discipline was established, one that affected all but the 'idle rich'.

The production of modern sport in reconstructed space and time

Numerous commentators have examined the major changes in the forms of physical culture that occurred beginning in the mid nineteenth century, changes that are recognized as the emergence of modern rationalized sport:

> Modern versions of sport bear distinctive marks of the particular background in last century's England, 'the land of sport'. Their emphasis on exact measuring, comparison, and ranking of competitors according to strict, rule-governed standards of performance is seen as a clear expression of the values of capitalist industrialised societies.[30]

Interpretations are often descriptive and functionalist – sport *reflects* the changing society (e.g. John Betts and many others); and sometimes, like John Hargreaves' consideration of 'the repression and reform of popular sporting forms', insightfully critical.[31]

In many ways, 'repression and reform' echo the thesis of this chapter. Popular forms of physical culture were repressed in part as a result of growing moralistic concerns about cruelty to animals, gambling, and violence; but repression was mainly a result of the privatization of spaces where many of the folk sports and games took place, and by more rigorous demands on the time of the participants – most of whom were only free from work on Sundays, when participation was often forbidden by Sabbatarian 'Blue Laws'. Thompson recognized the losses in terms of both time and space: 'As important in this passing as the simple physical loss of commons and "playgrounds" was the loss of leisure in which to play and the repression of playful impulses.'[32]

The reform of popular sports was taken out of the hands of the former participants, and produced largely by middle- and upper middle-class professional and managerial men who reformed both the *form* of the sports and their *meanings*. The reconstructed sense of time and space, and resistance to it, provided the frame within which these reforms occurred. In the reformed sports, within the frame of restricted space and managed time, 'Time and space either constrain the participants into particular temporal or spatial slots or act as targets to be reached or overcome'.[33]

Dunning and Sheard's outline of 'The Structural Properties of Folk-Games and Modern Sports' provides one of the earliest and best summaries of the transformation that occurred. The theme of this chapter is addressed as follows: in *folk-games* there are 'No fixed limits on territory, duration or numbers of participants'. Thus, for example, early versions of ice hockey were played on naturally frozen ponds, bays, and rivers with banks as natural boundaries, early versions of lacrosse and football were played across open land, and early versions of cricket were played on commons/village greens of various sizes or on the lawns of country estates. *Modern sports* are 'Played on a spatially limited pitch with clearly defined boundaries, within fixed time-limits, and with a fixed number of participants equalized between the contending sides'.[34]

Metcalfe cleverly re-purposed the term 'enclosure' in his case study of East Northumberland to refer to the establishment of clearly defined playing boundaries, but also to the designation of specific spaces/places for playing specific sports: some private (e.g. golf courses on recently enclosed common land); some public (e.g. the development of municipal parks, swimming pools, and playing fields); and some enclosed for commercial purposes such as pay-to-play or for ticketed spectator entry.[35]

The spatial and temporal limits were not always rational in the transition from *folk games*, with their 'Simple and unwritten customary rules, legitimated by tradition', to *modern sports* and their 'Formal and elaborate written rules, worked out pragmatically and legitimated by rational-bureaucratic means'.[36] For example, the distance for the marathon race was established at the 1908 Olympics as the distance from Windsor to London's White City stadium; and the distances for many track races were adapted from horse racing.[37] Two furlong tracks, and their metric equivalents still create the standard distances in athletics. The standard sizes of fields, tracks, and playing surfaces established a spatial norm for sports.

The temporal norms also emerged slowly from the open-ended games that existed previously, games that may have ended with darkness or because of fatigue. For example, under the early written rules for lacrosse (George Beers' rules), a game ended when one team scored five goals or led by three goals.[38] Such rules could still lead to games not being completed, and more precise starting and ending times were developed to reach a conclusion, accommodate players' schedules, and to be able to advertise games and matches to paying spectators.

Time, space, and sport

Referring to space and time as social constructions suggests a normalization of the new regimes of time and space. Thompson comments on 'nostalgia for the pattern of work and leisure which obtained before the *outer and inner disciplines* of industrialism settled on the working man', but that discipline took time and, as with every hegemony, it 'has continually to be renewed, recreated, defended and modified. It is also continually resisted, limited, altered, challenged by pressures not all its own'.[39]

The frames established by the reconstruction of space and time limited the forms that emerging types of sports could take, and helped to shape them; but they did not determine precisely what those forms would be. Those forms, and the values and meanings of the *modern sports*, were determined by other social processes already well recognized in the academic literature.[40]

Residual cultures and resistance

The privatization of space was continually resisted, from trespasses onto formerly common land to hunt or to hike, to the re-purposing for adult sports of play spaces intended for children.[41] The Commons Preservation Society (now the Open Spaces Society) was a middle-class organization in the UK devoted to preventing enclosures in order to maintain the commons for rational recreation.[42] But the new urban poor was also instrumental in demanding parks and playgrounds for their children.[43] Those spaces were eventually won at the cost of having others imposing social controls and determining the forms of recreation that could take place.

Resistance to time restrictions took various forms, including 'Saint Mondays' and other forms of absenteeism, widespread violations of Sabbatarian rules against sport and recreation, and continual pressure, especially from organized labour, to reduce the length of the working day. The campaigns for paid vacations, for a five and a half day working week and eventually a five-day working week (now recognized as the invention of the weekend) were particularly successful in re-creating opportunities to participate in sports and recreation.[44]

Resistances to modern rationalized sports are still evident. It would be a mistake to think that *folk games*, or at least the playful elements that existed in *folk games* and in the early *modern sports* where amateurism determined an emphasis on process over outcome – what Williams referred to as *residual* cultures – had died out.[45] These are most evident in children's and pick-up games, where individuals come together to play ice hockey, baseball, cricket, basketball and soccer in informal circumstances. It is possible to find many elements that Dunning and Sheard attributed to *folk games* (those not related to violence) still in evidence: flexible time and rules (e.g. 'next goal/basket wins', games adapted to the space available, games officiated by the participants, and so on).[46] Similarly, the emphasis on process rather than outcome is evident in the ways that games are concluded (e.g. 'first to ten goals' or 'next basket wins') and in the ways that teams are selected in an attempt to establish equality, even to the point of switching players between teams in order to maintain a competitive balance.

In a world characterized by the time–space compression of globalization, where high-speed travel and digital communications have changed the landscape of modern competitive sports, and where electronic timing to 1/1000th of a second have made it possible to compete not just against those in the same race, but against all other athletes in the world who have a recorded time in a sanctioned race, it is gratifying to see playful alternative sports and games that have, in some ways, escaped the temporal and spatial frames that were constructed during the nineteenth century.[47]

Notes

1 Richard Gruneau, *Sport and Modernity* (Cambridge: Polity Press, 2017), 94.
2 For example, John Betts, 'The Technological Revolution and the Rise of Sport, 1850–1900', *Mississippi Valley Historical Review* 40, no. 2 (1953): 231–256; Eric Dunning, 'Sport in Space and Time: "Civilizing Processes", Trajectories of State-Formation and the Development Of Modern Sport', *International Review for the Sociology of Sport* 29, no. 4 (1994): 331–345; Allen Guttmann, *From Ritual to Record: The Nature of Modern Sports* (New York: Columbia University Press, 1978); Stefan Szymanski, 'A Theory of the Evolution of Modern Sport', *Journal of Sport History* 35, no. 1 (2008): 1–32.
3 Gruneau, *Sport and Modernity*.
4 Douglas Booth, 'Review of Richard Gruneau, *Sport and Modernity*', *Sociology of Sport Journal* 36, no. 1 (2019): 106.
5 Peter Donnelly, 'The Local and the Global: Globalization in the Sociology of Sport', *Journal of Sport and Social Issues* 20, no. 3 (1996): 239–257; Jim McKay and Toby Miller, 'From Old Boys to Men and Women of the Corporation: The Americanization and Commodification of Australian Sport', *Sociology of Sport Journal* 8, no. 1 (1991): 86–94; Peter Donnelly, '"Prolympism": Sport Monoculture as Crisis and Opportunity', *Quest* 48, no. 1 (1996): 25–42.
6 See David Harvey's essays on the social construction of space and time for an in-depth analysis of this point: David Harvey, 'Between Space and Time: Reflections on the Geographical Imagination', *Annals of the American Association of Geographers* 80, no. 3 (1990): 418–434; David Harvey, 'The Social Construction of Space and Time: A Relational Theory', *Geographical Review of Japan* 67, no. 2 (1994): 126–135.
7 See Williams' definition of hegemony for an explanation of the way in which the term is used here: Raymond Williams, *Marxism and Literature* (Oxford: Oxford University Press, 1977), 112–113. As in theoretical physics, many in the social sciences and humanities have recognized that time and space cannot be separated. The separation is maintained here for analytical purposes, but is gradually abandoned in the later sections.
8 Henri Lefebvre, *The Production of Space* (trans. D. Nicholson-Smith) (Oxford: Blackwell, 1991). Harvey, 'Between Space and Time: Reflections on the Geographical Imagination'; Harvey, 'The Social Construction of Space and Time: A Relational Theory'; Edward Soja, *Postmodern Geographies: The Reassertion of Space in Critical Social Theory* (New York: Verso, 1989).
9 Parts of the discussion of space in this and the following section are drawn from: Peter Donnelly, 'The Paradox of Parks: Politics of Recreational Land Use Before and After the Mass Trespasses', *Leisure Studies* 5, no. 2 (1986): 211–231; Peter Donnelly, 'The Right to Wander: Issues in the Leisure Use of Countryside and Wilderness Areas', *International Review for the Sociology of Sport* 28, nos. 2–3 (1993): 187–202; Peter Donnelly, '*Buen Vivir* [*Sumak Kawsay*]: Notes on the Consideration of Sport as a Cultural Commons', *Movimento* 20 (2014): 211–226.
10 Eric Dunning and Kenneth Sheard, *Barbarians, Gentlemen and Players: A Sociological Study of the Development of Rugby Football* (New York: New York University Press, 1979); Robert Malcolmson, *Popular Recreations in English Society, 1700–1850* (Cambridge: Cambridge University Press, 1973).
11 For more on these customary practices, including sports and games, and their erosion see, Hugh Cunningham, *Leisure in the Industrial Revolution, c.1780–c.1880* (London: Croom Helm, 1980); Malcolmson, *Popular Recreations in English Society*; Edward Thompson, *The Making of the English Working Class* (Harmondsworth, UK: Penguin, 1980), ch 7. New Game Laws also had the effect of privatizing woodland and moorland. See, Peter Munsche, *Gentlemen and Poachers: The English Game Laws, 1761–1831* (New York: Cambridge University Press, 1981); Edward Thompson, *Whigs and Hunters: The Origins of the Black Act* (New York: Pantheon, 1975).
12 See, C.B. Macpherson, *The Political Theory of Possessive Individualism: Hobbes to Locke* (Toronto: Oxford University Press, 1962). In the case of the 'Highland Clearances' in Scotland, another form of enclosure, inhabitants were evicted from their residences in mountain and moorland areas so that wealthy landowners could begin sheep farming.
13 Stephen Hardy, *How Boston Played: Sport, Recreation, and Community, 1865–1915* (Boston: Northeastern University Press, 1982).
14 Cunningham, *Leisure in the Industrial Revolution*, 79.
15 Peter Bailey, *Leisure and Class in Victorian England: Rational Recreation and the Contest for Control, 1830–1885* (London: Routledge & Kegan Paul, 1978); Cunningham, *Leisure in the Industrial Revolution*.

Time, space, and sport

16 Alan Metcalfe, 'The Development of Sporting Facilities: A Case Study of East Northumberland, England, 1850–1914', *International Review for the Sociology of Sport* 28, nos. 2–3 (1993): 110.

17 Tom Griffiths, *The Art of Time Travel: Historians and their Craft* (Carlton, Australia: Black Inc, 2016), 7.

18 Harry Bash, 'A Sense of Time: Temporality and Historicity in Sociological Inquiry', *Time & Society* 9, nos. 2–3 (2000): 187–204.

19 Fernand Braudel, *The Mediterranean and the Mediterranean World in the Age of Philip II,* 2 vols. (trans. Sian Reynolds) (New York: Harper and Row, 1949/1972). Social constructionism has been more evident in archaeology with a growing acknowledgement 'that social constructions of the past are crucial elements in the process of domination, subjugation, resistance and collusion'. George Bond and Angela Gilliam, eds., *Social Construction of the Past: Representation as Power* (London: Routledge, 1997), 1.

20 Edward Thompson, 'Time, Work-Discipline, and Industrial Capitalism', *Past & Present* 38, December (1967): 56–97.

21 Harvey, 'The Social Construction of Space and Time', 126–135.

22 Malcolmson, *Popular Recreations in English Society.*

23 Michael Sanderson, 'Social Change and Elementary Education in Industrial Lancashire', *Northern History* 3, no. 1 (1968): 131–154; Thompson, *The Making of the English Working Class.*

24 Thompson, *The Making of the English Working Class.*

25 Douglas Reid, 'The Decline of Saint Monday, 1766–1876, *Past & Present* 71 (1976): 76–101; Douglas Reid, 'Weddings, Weekdays, Work and Leisure in Urban England 1791–1911: The Decline of Saint Monday Revisited, *Past & Present* 153, no.1 (1996): 135–163; Thompson, 'Time, Work-Discipline, and Industrial Capitalism'.

26 Thompson, *The Making of the English Working Class*, 378. See also, Michael Katz, 'The Origins of Public Education: A Reassessment', *History of Education Quarterly* 16, no. 1 (1976): 381–407; Sanderson, 'Social Change and Elementary Education in Industrial Lancashire'.

27 Paul Glennie and Nigel Thrift, 'Re-working E.P. Thompson's "Time, Work-Discipline and Industrial Capitalism"', *Time & Society* 5, no. 3 (1996): 275–299; Thompson, 'Time, Work-Discipline, and Industrial Capitalism'.

28 Barbara Adam, *Time and Social Theory* (Cambridge: Polity Press, 1990), 47.

29 Glennie and Thrift, 'Re-working E.P. Thompson's "Time, Work-Discipline and Industrial Capitalism"', 282; Norbert Elias, *Time: An Essay* (Oxford: Blackwell, 1992); Michel Foucault, *The Birth of the Clinic* (London: Tavistock, 1973); Anthony Giddens, *Central Problems in Social Theory: Action, Structure and Contradictions in Social Analysis* (London: Macmillan, 1979); Anthony Giddens, *The Constitution of Society* (Cambridge: Polity Press, 1984).

30 Sigmund Loland, 'The Logic of Progress and the Art of Moderation in Competitive Sports', in *Values in Sport: Elitism, Nationalism, Gender Equality and the Scientific Manufacturing of Winners*, eds. Claudio Tamburrini and Torbjörn Tännsjö (London: Taylor & Francis, 2000), 39.

31 Betts, 'The Technological Revolution and the Rise of Sport, 1850–1900'; John Hargreaves, *Sport, Power and Culture: A Social and Historical Analysis of Popular Sports in Britain* (Oxford: Polity Press, 1986), ch. 2. See also, Gruneau, *Sport and Modernity.*

32 Thompson, *The Making of the English Working Class*, 408.

33 John Bale, 'Space, Place and Body Culture: Yi-Fu Tuan and a Geography of Sport', *Geografiska Annaler* 78B, no. 3 (1996): 164.

34 Dunning and Sheard, *Barbarians, Gentlemen and Players*, 33–4. Table 1.2 provides a direct comparison of the characteristics of *folk games* and *modern sports.*

35 Metcalfe, 'The Development of Sporting Facilities'.

36 Dunning and Sheard, *Barbarians, Gentlemen and Players*, 33.

37 In the rural roots of horse racing, steeplechasing across farmers' fields, a common measure of farmland was adopted. The furlong, 220 yards, was the length of a furrow in a 10-acre field. This was adapted to horse racing tracks, and the measure was then taken up by athletics for the one furlong, two furlongs (440 yards), four furlongs, and eight furlongs (one mile) races. The metric equivalents are still in use.

38 Alan Metcalfe, 'Sport and Athletes: A Case Study of Lacrosse in Canada, 1840–1889', *Journal of Sport History* 3, no. 1 (1976): 1–19; Robert Scott, *Lacrosse: Technique and Tradition* (Baltimore: JHU Press, 1978).

39 Thompson, *The Making of the English Working Class*, 357, emphasis added; Williams, *Marxism and Literature*, 112.

40 See, among many examples, Riesman and Denny's analysis of the development of American (grid-iron) football from British rugby by a process of culture diffusion. David Riesman and Reuel Denny, 'Football in America: A Study in Culture Diffusion', *American Quarterly* 3, no. 4 (1951): 309–325.

41 For trespasses and other resistances for access to land by hikers see, Peter Donnelly, 'The Paradox of Parks: Politics of Recreational Land Use Before and After the Mass Trespasses'; Howard Hill, *Freedom to Roam: The Struggle for Access to Britain's Moors and Mountains* (Ashbourne, UK: Moorland Publishing, 1980); David Hollett, *The Pioneer Ramblers, 1850–1940* (London: North Wales Area of the Ramblers' Association, 2002); Benny Rothman, *The Battle for Kinder Scout, Including the 1932 Mass Trespasses* (Altrincham, UK: Willow Publishing, 2012); Dave Sissons, Terry Howard, and Roly Smith, *Clarion Call: Sheffield's Access Pioneers* (Sheffield, UK: Clarion Call, 2017). For re-purposing children's play spaces for adults see, Metcalfe, 'The Development of Sporting Facilities'.

42 Open Spaces Society: https://www.oss.org.uk/.

43 Stephen Hardy and Alan Ingham, 'Games, Structure and Agency: Historians on the American Play Movement', *Journal of Social History* 17, no. 2 (1983): 285–301.

44 See Witold Rybczynsky, *Waiting for the Weekend* (New York: Penguin, 1991). By the second half of the twentieth century, sport itself was being critiqued for its complicity in establishing work discipline. See, for example, Jean-Marie Brohm, *Sport: A Prison of Measured Time* (trans. I. Fraser) (London: Ink Links, 1978); Bero Rigauer, *Sport and Work* (trans, A. Guttmann) (New York: Columbia University Press, 1981).

45 Williams, *Marxism and Literature*.

46 Dunning and Sheard, *Barbarians, Gentlemen and Players*, 33.

47 In addition to informal versions of established sports, newer sports such as Ultimate, hackey sack, skateboarding, BMX bicycling, and surfing also resist many of the characteristics of modern rationalized sports in their non-institutionalized forms.

14

SPORT AND THE BODY

Jaquelyn Osborne and Chelsea Litchfield

In sport, the human body is a common denominator. The body's capabilities are praised, celebrated, even coveted; moreover, the human body is the subject of much debate and regulation. From the contentious classifications of disabled bodies for competition to the seemingly insurmountable (and rigidly defended) nature of binary sex categorization, the body has shown itself to be the subject of innumerable debates about inclusion and, too regularly, exclusion. While sociologists and philosophers of sport have readily engaged in scholarship related to the body in all number of contexts, historians have been seemingly less enthusiastic. However, there is a solid body of work related to the body in physical education (and often, by extension, in sport) considered by educationalists and sport historians.[1] The history of the body in sport is necessarily underpinned by the philosophy and sociology of the body through time, and certainly on the value placed upon the body, or indeed certain bodies, at those times. There is a convergence of social science approaches in the examination of the body with philosophical, religious, and educational views and, of course, with intersecting histories of the body – political, sociological, economic, and medical among others.

The import of the body is evident. As Douglas Booth astutely recognizes, 'the body is the primary means by which individuals announce who they are to the world'.[2] In the immediate and present tense, the body (in person or mediated) is a central vehicle for self-identification, self-representation,[3] alignment with one or many ideologies, a mechanism for attracting like-minded individuals, and a means for expressing innumerable other messages. This chapter examines the body and sport as discussed by historians of sport, looking at influential authors and principal works. We explore the emergence of recent topics of interest as well as those areas which have, as yet, attracted little attention and which may benefit from further investigation.

Bodies in place and time

A significant amount of the literature on sport and bodies deals with specific locations and time periods: Ancient Greek athletic bodies, bodies in sport in nineteenth-century England, and works related to the first half of the twentieth century, concentrating on Nazi Germany and the regimented and superior Aryan body.[4]

DOI: 10.4324/9780429318306-17

There has been regular scholarly work on the subject of the Ancient Greeks' interest in athletics and the cultivating of male bodies in the image of the bodily perfection of the gods. One of the only known civilizations to encourage and embrace nudity during athletic performance, the Ancient Greeks also featured athletic bodies in art.[5] Much of the study of Ancient Greek athletics emerged from the work of classical historians with a penchant for sports and athletics.[6]

Nineteenth-century England is also the subject of much historical research on sport and the body. Sport, athleticism, and muscularity in the latter half of the Victorian era were entwined themes among sport historians in the last quarter of the twentieth century. In a movement that connected sport education and nationalism, the concept of Muscular Christianity underpinned notions of the strong, healthy, and, above all, manly body that could and should be produced via participation in sports. Team sports, flourishing in the English public schools, come to be embraced under this educational philosophy which also linked character development and appropriate religious beliefs to the appearance and performance of the body. This period and location fostered the interest of historians of sport (and education) in areas primarily related to the cultivation of the masculine body through sport.[7]

Sport and the body: key scholars

The body in relation to sport has been of interest to leading feminist sport historians including Patricia Vertinsky, Jennifer Hargreaves, and Roberta Park.

Patricia Vertinsky

In a career approaching half a century, the industrious and critical researcher, Patricia Vertinsky has published hundreds of papers, chapters, and books about sport. Although not specifically calling herself a sports historian as she is trained more broadly,[8] Vertinsky is overwhelmingly the most prolific contributor to the history of sport and the body, with her work on the history of sport, exercise, and physical education and the body. Many of Vertinsky's works relate to the gendered body, particularly to female bodies, and delve into highly theoretical sociological frameworks.

Ranging in scope from the body in school physical education[9] to the biomedicalization of aging female bodies[10] and the historical stereotypes of aging bodies (and even aging sport historians![11]), Vertinsky has published a plethora of work related primarily to the subjects of the history of the body, embodiment, and embodied culture. Her contributions address bodies in different sports (dance,[12] boxing,[13] bodybuilding[14]) and different cultures (Hong Kong, the United States, India, Canada, China, the United Kingdom, and Europe more broadly[15]). Her work broaches the topic of religious bodies,[16] and examines the contributions of significant women in the history of sport and physical education.[17]

Vertinsky's much cited book, *The Eternally Wounded Woman*, which examines exercise and medicine for women in the latter nineteenth century, can be considered a seminal work in understanding the medicalized and biologically based restraints and constrictions placed on women and their bodies during this period.[18] *The Eternally Wounded Woman* explores the responses of females to medical advice, and brought into view, for the first time, the reality of female physicians who endeavoured to challenge the pervasive view of women as fragile and anxious. The incorporation of women's voices and reactions, during a time of pervasive male discourse on the topic, positions this work as a critical addition to the history of this period. Of course, the restrictive ways of thinking about women, their bodies and exercise

Sport and the body

(which warned of the dangers of overexertion), underpinned a century or more of women's access to and acceptance in sport and exercise.

Jennifer Hargreaves

Through her socio-historical analyses of the multiplicity of women's experiences in sport and physical education and her 'intersectional analysis of women's active bodies', Jennifer Hargreaves has made a major contribution to sport and feminism.[19] Hargreaves' major work on the body is her monograph *Sporting Females*, which covers diverse periods including the First World War, the Inter war years, Victorian and Edwardian Britain, and the early modern Olympics. Hargreaves takes an intersectional approach to understanding bodies, which she conjoins with class, age, disability, ethnicity, and many other aspects of embodiment.[20]

Roberta J. Park

J.A. Mangan, in introducing an edited volume dedicated to Roberta J. Park, attests to one of her major missions, which was 'to win academic recognition for the study of the significance of the body in culture and cultures'.[21] Working at Berkeley in the Department of Physical Education, Park focused on the body, sport, physical education, and exercise with many pieces looking at gender. Investing herself in the history of education, Park introduced a contextualized view of the body using historical and sociological concepts. The sporting body, according to Park, was a landscape upon which a multitude of interconnected symbols and meanings were constructed. While investing heavily in the construct of gender as it relates to the body and sport, Park was not consumed by the study of any one aspect but instead was interested in all bodies and championed a diverse range of methods.

Park produced historical works related to sport and physical education on male bodies, female bodies, healthy bodies, fit bodies, and the medicalized body. Park's research touched on adaptations of Muscular Christianity in North America and the use of sport in defining masculine bodies, regularly comparing the differences (and similarities) in the development of desirable bodies (and persons) in Britain and America.[22] Sport history was a lifelong passion for Park, and she contributed much to help redress the heavy bent towards the history of men's sports, male physical educators, and male athletes that had previously dominated sport history. Overall, Park's contribution to the historical study of sport and the body ventured broad interpretation to an otherwise quite restricted view of sporting bodies.

Gendered and racialized bodies

Gendered bodies in sport have also been of considerable interest to sport historians since the 1970s. As mentioned above, Vertinsky, Hargreaves, and Park were leaders in the push to examine the female body; however, male bodies, masculinity, and the celebration of muscularity attracted significantly more attention in sport history. The Olympic Games, throughout the last century, provide prime examples of women being excluded by virtue of their feminine bodies. There have been several historical studies of women's inclusion and exclusion at the Olympic Games. From the complete exclusion of women at the 1896 Games, to the slow but regular addition of women's events in the marathon in 1984 and boxing in 2012 (over a century after the first men's Olympic boxing competition), there has been considerable examination of the reluctance of the International Olympic Committee (IOC) to include women in sports.[23]

Stemming from a supposed 'unsuitability' of women's bodies for sport and encompassing theories surrounding gender roles, the dual threats of infertility and a supposed 'masculinization' of women restricted women's participation. Avery Brundage, the longstanding president of the United States Olympic Committee (1928–1953) and the IOC (1952–1972), had advocated for women to confirm their sex in relation to the Olympic Games as early as 1936, but it was the sex testing (by visual inspection) of women athletes at the 1968 Mexico City Olympic Games that brought gendered bodies into the public sphere.[24] The IOC and the International Amateur Athletics Federation (IAAF), in particular, have displayed much anxiety over 'manly' women and the 'unnatural' masculine physiques that women may develop through sport. They coupled this with the contention that men pretending to be women posed a threat to sport.[25] The space between stereotypical male and female bodies and their biology is highly contentious and the IOC has struggled for over a century to set and maintain binary sex categorizations for human bodies. As Schultz astutely points out, 'the physical is political' and the regulation of bodies in sport by way of biological, medical, social, or political division contributes to the power and control that can be wielded for and against certain bodies in sport.[26]

The 'masculine' body and the 'manly' body were studied as far back as Classical times. Sports historians have shown close interest in the use of team sports, particularly the various football codes, to promote manly and muscular bodies.[27] Sport has been regularly employed for such purposes regardless of the definitional changes to what comprises 'appropriate' masculinity. From the designation of amateur and professional bodies, to the exclusion of effeminate bodies, particularly in male team sports, the appearance of the male body in sport has also been subject to restrictive sporting norms.

The history of the racialized body in sport, proffered predominantly by white scholars, is regularly but not exclusively considered from the perspective of another bodily binary, that being 'black' and 'white'. With its roots in the slave trading era, the segregation of black bodies from white bodies was a deplorable feature of European colonial outposts, in sport and often in all aspects of life.[28] Prior to the twentieth century, little investigation, historical or otherwise, of non-white athletic bodies was conducted. By the 1970s, the issues raised by sociologists relating to race in sport, accompanied by the interest in sport bodies more generally, resulted in a broadening scope regarding the historical study of the racial body in sport.[29] Historical studies ensued, primarily in relation to the segregation in the United States and to apartheid in South Africa (and the exclusion of that country from most international sport), and to the changes notable in specific sports, such as basketball and athletics.[30]

Dualistic narratives, so widely accepted in sports, were further solidified by the Victorian-era inspired focus on black bodies (rather than black intellect), which resisted holistic approaches. The black body was the subject of racialized scientific investigation by sports scientists. This fostered scientific imperatives to answer questions such as: why does this 'black' body run so fast or jump so high? The black body was discussed and investigated in physical terms and, as such, strengthened the body-as-machine (indeed a 'black body-as-super machine') narrative.[31] The racial body as a wholly physical entity was (is) persistent in sport long after other fields of science had debunked the 'natural superiority of whites' paradigm. The segregation of bodies is again linked to the 'look' or 'appearance' of the body,[32] which extended to variously superior and/or dangerous physical capacities.[33] Globalized sport, and the emergence of international competition as the pinnacle of elite sport, resulted in many in the white-dominated Western World to seek out 'black' sporting talent.

Sport body as object

Sport bodies (especially male sporting bodies) are athletic bodies first, and sentient bodies second (and occasionally not at all). The Merleau-Ponty vision of embodied consciousness,[34] and the notion of 'I am my body' rather than the dualistic 'I use my body', is perhaps preferable rhetoric at a time of concern about athletes' feelings, emotions, and selves. But the historical dominance of Cartesian dualism as appropriate in understanding the sport body has proven difficult to counter.[35]

The ideal body in any particular sport is also determined by social constructs and often changes over time.[36] Bodies in sprinting are muscular and appear strong; bodies in distance running and distance cycling are lean and wiry; and swimmers have broad shoulders (but not too broad if the body is female lest that body become the object of suspicion). Stereotypes abound: basketballers are tall, gymnasts are small, throwers are heavy, and divers are light. These stereotypes have historically led to the exclusion of some bodies from some sports and privileged others. In fact, the historical and current practice of sports talent identification is rarely about extant ability in the sport but instead is clearly linked to the stereotypes surrounding the ideal body type, or the potential for such an ideal, that is considered to be complementary to a particular sport.

Regardless of appearance, there is a prevailing belief that the body in sport must be able to be appropriated effectively for the purposes of sporting performance and success. The body is expected to be ever capable of the sporting feats for which it is employed.[37] The metaphor of the body-as-machine in sport[38] is relevant here. It relates to post-industrial concepts of maintaining a machine and the fuelling and repair of that (body-as) machine. Above all, it consolidates the resilient dualistic notions of the body. As athletes begin to gain control of some of the narratives around their own experiences (often in the social media space), there are resultant changes to the way historians conceptualize sport. As the result of inquiries into physical, sexual, and emotional abuse in sport, most recently in Women's Artistic Gymnastics,[39] there is clearly space for further investigation into the socio-historical foundations of such abuse, particularly in relation to the 'ownership' of sporting bodies.

The body-as-machine metaphor can also be related to disabled and Paralympic sport. The disabled body in sport has been well covered by sport historians.[40] The growing body of literature related to the disabled body in sport, welcome in itself, has the potential to merge with the growing interest in, and study of, cyber bodies and augmented bodies in sport.[41] Recent interest in the body in non-sport areas, such as the body as it is reimagined in relation to smart gadgets and cyberspace, perhaps heralds what may emerge in sport history.[42]

The socially conceived body and sport

Henning Eichberg examined the broad field of body culture, touching on areas of political and social theory to give a comprehensive account of the twentieth-century movements that underpinned and informed understanding of the human body. Eichberg touched on, *inter alia*, the constructed body as a 'matter of choice and self-construction'; the body as a 'field of dynamic human interaction', and human subjectivity 'in a world where the body had become increasingly acted upon by certain forces – production, consumption and reproduction'.[43] Sport historians have taken up Eichberg's work and explored these themes in relation to different settings, time periods, and cultures. In their edited collection of what they term Eichberg's 'provocative' essays in body culture, Bale and Philo (1998) suggest that

Eichberg's writings are particularly significant, so much so that notable sport historians such as Allen Guttmann and Richard Mandell have credited his influence on their own work.[44]

The relationship between class and the sporting body is an area of interest among sport historians. Booth and Loy argue convincingly that there is much potential for sport historians of any era in exploring the use of sport to increase status and prestige.[45] They suggest that the body is key to understanding how prestige and the accumulation of social distinction operate and that this is evident in sport. Day and Oldfield broach the historical importance of sport in one's ability to present the self as 'classed'. Writing of athletic (male) bodies in the nineteenth century, they show that sporting bodies carried with them the trappings of class.[46] The amateur ideal of the all-rounder, a leaner body with elegance and style coveted and cultivated by the middle classes, was to be contrasted with the working-class body (more muscular and specialized). In a more theoretical approach, drawing heavily on Weber and Bourdieu, Booth and Loy provide numerous examples of modern and postmodern sport that are shown to be incomplete without determining the contribution of said sport to class, particularly related to embodied social status, lifestyle, and consumption.[47]

Summary remarks

Recent historical examinations of sport acknowledge the flows of power and resistance from bodies as the result of a re-visioned, or re-versioned, understandings of gender, race, class, and sexuality. Aligning inquiry to these mechanisms overcomes some of the reductionist realities of examining 'the' body in sport by viewing the human as engaging and enacting multiple and sometimes contradictory 'bodies' in the context of sport.

It is evident that much more could be done. Sociologists of sport have long been investigating the body as a machine, as an object to be controlled, and as an embodied consciousness that experiences the joys, frustrations, and pains of the human engagement in sport. Sport historians have been slower to broach these topics. Their focus has been remedying the gaps in the sporting past rather than the body per se.

An examination of the body and sport readily lends itself to disciplines such as sociology and philosophy. As a result, sport historians who have researched the body move more fluidly between academic disciplines. The historical study of the body in sport involves multiple and intersecting narratives and understandings of the body in, and as, an accomplished athletic body, and in and outside sport. An array of postmodern perspectives allows the exploration of the meanings of bodies, and the representation of those bodies, by individual athletes. The interplay between bodily (self) representation, the marking (or indeed marketing) of one's body and the availability of social media in the twenty-first century opens this field of study for additional perspectives on understanding the history of the body. As sport scholars embrace New Materialism and respond to historically relevant changes in socio-political elements such as the rise of white supremacy, widening class issues, the Black Lives Matter movement, and the global reverberations of COVID-19, the future of historical and other research on sport and the body inevitably sits 'within a messy, heterogenous and emergent social world'.[48]

Notes

1 For example, a special issue of *History of Education* 36, no. 2 (2007) dealt with 'The Body of the Schoolchild in the History of Education'.

Sport and the body

2 Douglas Booth, *Australian Beach Cultures: The History of Sun, Sand, and Surf* (London: Routledge, 2001), 8.
3 And, indeed, the representation and interpretation of bodies by others. See for example, Jorn Eiben and Olaf Stieglitz, 'Depicting Sporting Bodies – Visual Sources in the Writing of Sports History. An Introduction', *Historical Social Research* 43, no. 2 (2018): 7–24.
4 Examples include Sandra Heck, '"A Blond, Broad-shouldered Athlete with Bright Grey-blue Eyes": German Propaganda and Gotthardt Handrick's Victory in Modern Pentathlon at the Nazis' Olympics in 1936', *Journal of Sport History* 38, no. 2 (2011): 255–274; John Hoberman, *Sport and Political Ideology*, (Austin, TX: University of Texas Press, 1984). See also Caroline Daley, *Leisure and Pleasure: Reshaping and Revealing the New Zealand Body 1900–1960* (Auckland: Auckland University Press, 2003); John Bale, *Imagined Olympians: Body Culture and Colonial Representation in Rwanda* (Minneapolis: University of Minnesota Press, 2002); Susan Bandy, Annette Hoffman, and Arnd Krüger, eds., *Gender, Body and Sport in Historical and Transnational Perspectives* (Hamburg: Verlag Dr. Kovac, 2007).
5 John Mouritidis, 'The Origin of Nudity in Greek Athletics', *Journal of Sport History* 12, no. 3 (1985): 213–232. See also James Arieti, 'Nudity in Greek Athletics', *The Classical World* 68 (1975): 431–436.
6 For example, Paul Christesen, 'Athletics and the Social Order in Sparta and in the Classical Period', *Classical Antiquity* 31, no. 2 (2012): 193–257; Mark Golden, *Sport and Society in Ancient Greece* (New York: Cambridge University Press, 1998).
7 See Eric Dunning and Kenneth Sheard, *Barbarians, Gentlemen and Players: A Sociological Study of the Development of Rugby Football* (Oxford: Martin Robertson, 1979), in particular the chapter 'Football in the Early Nineteenth-century Public Schools', 46–62; Timothy J.L. Chandler, 'The Structuring of Manliness and the Development of Rugby Football at the Public Schools and Oxbridge, 1830–1880', in, *Making Men: Rugby and Masculine Identity*, eds. John Nauright and Timothy J.L. Chandler (London; Frank Cass, 1996), 13–49. The work of Tony Mangan is also important here. See note 27.
8 As told to Beccy Watson in: Beccy Watson and Patricia Vertinsky, 'Patricia Vertinsky on Becoming and Being a Feminist Sport Historian: A Dialogue with Beccy Watson', in *The Palgrave Handbook of Feminism and Sport, Leisure and Physical Education*, eds. Louise Mansfield, Jayne Caudwell, Belinda Wheaton, and Beccy Watson (London: Palgrave Macmillan, 2018), 57–72.
9 Patricia Vertinsky, 'Reclaiming Space, Revisioning the Body: The Quest for Gender-sensitive Physical Education', *Quest* 44, no. 3 (1992): 373–396.
10 Patricia Vertinsky, 'Old Age, Gender and Physical Activity: The Biomedicalization of Aging', *Journal of Sport History* 18, no. 1 (1991): 64–80; Patricia Vertinsky, 'Stereotypes of Aging Women and Exercise: A Historical Perspective', *Journal of Aging and Physical Activity* 3, no. 3 (1995): 223–237.
11 Patricia Vertinsky, 'Aging Bodies, Aging Sport Historians, and the Choreographing of Sport History', *Sport History Review* 29, (1998): 18–29.
12 Patricia Vertinsky, 'Ida Rubinstein: Dancing Decadence and "The Art of the Beautiful Pose"', *Nashim: A Journal of Jewish Women's Studies & Gender Issues* 26, (2014): 122–146.
13 Ellexis Boyle, Brian Millington, and Patricia Vertinsky, 'Representing the Female Pugilist: Narratives of Race, Gender, and Disability in Million Dollar Baby', *Sociology of Sport Journal* 23, no. 2 (2006): 99–116.
14 Patricia Vertinsky, 'Bodymakers. A Cultural Anatomy of Women's Bodybuilding', *Journal of Sport History* 26, no. 1 (1999): 191–193.
15 Brad Millington, Patricia Vertinsky, Ellexis Boyle, and Brian Wilson, 'Making Chinese-Canadian Masculinities in Vancouver's Physical Education Curriculum', *Sport, Education and Society* 13, no. 2 (2008): 195–214; Patricia Vertinsky, '"Weighs and Means": Examining the Surveillance of Fat Bodies through Physical Education Practices in North America in the Late Nineteenth and Early Twentieth Centuries', *Journal of Sport History* 35, no. 3 (2008): 449–468; Patricia Vertinsky, Alison McManus, Cindy H.P. Sit, and Yuk Kwong Liu, 'The Gendering of Physical Education in Hong Kong: East, West or Global?', *The International Journal of the History of Sport* 22, no. 5 (2005): 816–839; Patricia Vertinsky, 'American Bodies: Cultural Histories of the Physique', *Journal of Sport History* 24, no. 2 (1997): 211–214.
16 Patricia Vertinsky, 'The "Racial" Body and the Anatomy of Difference: Anti-Semitism, Physical Culture, and the Jew's Foot', *Sport Science Review* 4, no. 1 (1995): 38–59.
17 Patricia Vertinsky, 'Sexual Equality and the Legacy of Catharine Beecher', *Journal of Sport History* 6, no. 1 (1979): 38–49; Patricia Vertinsky, 'A Militant Madonna: Charlotte Perkins Gilman – Feminism and Physical Culture', *The International Journal of the History of Sport* 18, no. 1 (2001): 55–72.

18 Patricia Vertinsky, *The Eternally Wounded Woman: Women, Doctors, and Exercise in the Late Nineteenth Century* (Urbana: University of Illinois Press, 2014). This book, first published in 1990, has been cited over 540 times (to August 2020).

19 Jessica Francombe-Webb and Kim Toffoletti, 'Sporting Females: Power, Diversity and the Body', in *The Palgrave Handbook of Feminism and Sport, Leisure and Physical Education*, eds. Louise Mansfield, Jayne Caudwell, Belinda Wheaton, and Beccy Watson (London: Palgrave Macmillan, 2018), 43.

20 Jennifer Hargreaves, *Sporting Females: Critical Issues in the History and Sociology of Women's Sports* (London: Routledge, 1994). See also Jennifer Hargreaves and Patricia Vertinsky, 'Introduction', in *Physical Culture, Power and the Body*, eds. Jennifer Hargreaves and Patricia Vertinsky (London: Routledge, 2007), 1–24.

21 J.A. Mangan and Patricia Vertinsky, eds., *Gender, Sport, Science: Selected Writings of Roberta J. Park* (London: Routledge, 2007), 2.

22 Roberta J. Park, 'Physiology and Anatomy are Destiny!?: Brains, Bodies and Exercise in Nineteenth Century American Thought', *Journal of Sport History* 18, no. 1 (1991): 31–63.

23 Jaime Schultz, 'Going the Distance: The Road to the 1984 Olympic Women's Marathon', *The International Journal of the History of Sport* 32, no. 1 (2015): 72–88.

24 Ian Ritchie, 'Sex Tested, Gender Verified: Controlling Female Sexuality in the Age of Containment', *Sport History Review* 34, no. 1 (2003): 80–98.

25 See, for example, Richard Holt, Ioulietta Erotokritou-Mulligan, and Peter Sönksen, 'The History of Doping and Growth Hormone Abuse in Sport', *Growth Hormone & IGF Research* 19, no. 4, (2009): 320–326; Jaime Schultz, 'Good Enough? The "Wicked" Use of Testosterone for Defining Femaleness in Women's Sport', *Sport in Society* 22 (2019): 1–21.

26 Jaime Schultz, 'The Physical is Political: Women's Suffrage, Pilgrim Hikes and the Public Sphere', *The International Journal of the History of Sport*, 27, no. 7 (2010): 1133–1153.

27 Dunning and Sheard, *Barbarians, Gentlemen and Players*; Nauright and Chandler, *Making Men: Rugby and Masculine Identity*; J.A. Mangan, *Athleticism in the Victorian and Edwardian Public School: The Emergence and Consolidation of an Educational Ideology*, (Cambridge: Cambridge University Press, 1981); J.A. Mangan, *The Games Ethic and Imperialism: Aspects of Diffusion of an Ideal,* (Harmondsworth: Viking, 1987).

28 See for example, Jeffrey Sammons, '"Race" and Sport: A Critical, Historical Examination', *Journal of Sport History* 21, no. 3 (1994): 203–278; and Peter Alegi, 'Beyond Master Narratives: Local Sources and Global Perspectives on Sport, Apartheid, and Liberation', *The International Journal of the History of Sport* 37, no. 7 (2020): 559–576.

29 Such as Patricia Vertinsky and Gwendolyn Captain, 'More Myth than History: American Culture and Representations of the Black Female's Athletic Ability', *Journal of Sport History* 25, no. 3 (1998): 532–561; and Patrick B. Miller, 'The Anatomy of Scientific Racism: Racialist Responses to Black Athletic Achievement', *Journal of Sport History 25*, no. 1 (1998): 119–151 on black bodies in the United States predominantly. Other notable studies on sport and racialized bodies include Colin Tatz, *Aborigines in Sport* (Sydney: University of New South Wales Press, 1995) and Andre Odendaal, 'South Africa's Black Victorians: Sport and Society in South Africa in the Nineteenth Century', in *Pleasure, Profit, Proselytism: British Culture and Sport at Home and Abroad 1700–1914*, ed. J.A. Mangan (London: Frank Cass, 1988), 193–214.

30 A 2020 Special Issue of *The International Journal of the History of Sport*, entitled 'Leveling the Playing Field: Histories of Apartheid Sport', shows the currency of interest in examining racial segregation by sports historians. Also see Samuel M. Clevenger, 'Transtemporal Sport Histories; or, Rethinking the "Invention" of American Basketball', *Sport in Society* 23, no. 5 (2020): 959–974.

31 For commentary on black women and perceived athletic prowess, see Vertinsky and Captain, 'More Myth than History'.

32 Douglas Booth and John Nauright, 'Embodied Identities: Sport and Race in South Africa', *Contours: A Journal of the African Diaspora* 1, no. 1 (2003): 16–36. For 'blacks' and 'coloureds' in South Africa, it was believed the body could be trained in the model of the 'Western elite' through sports. Cricket in particular was a vehicle to learn deportment, speech, etc. – in what they term as something of a 'finishing school'.

33 For instance, David Wiggins, 'Great Speed but Little Stamina: The Historical Debate over Black Athletic Superiority', *Journal of Sport History* 16 (1989): 158–185.

34 Maurice Merleau-Ponty, *The Phenomenology of Perception* (London: RKP, 1962).

35 Justin Bailey, 'The Body in Cyberspace: Lanier, Merleau-Ponty, and the Norms of Embodiment', *Christian Scholar's Review* 45, no. 3 (2016): 211–228.

Sport and the body

36 See for example, Natalie Barker-Ruchti, 'Ballerinas and Pixies: A Genealogy of the Changing Female Gymnastics Body', *The International Journal of the History of Sport* 26, no. 1 (2009): 45–62.

37 Gregory Quin, 'Perfect Bodies. Sports, Medicine and Immortality', *Sport in History* 33, no. 4 (2013): 614–615.

38 Jacques Gleyse, 'The Machine Body Metaphor: From Science and Technology to Physical Education and Sport, in France (1825–1935)', *Scandinavian Journal of Medicine and Science in Sports* 23 (2013): 758–765.

39 The allegations and subsequent inquiries into physical and sexual abuse in gymnastics, most notably in the United States, the United Kingdom, and the Netherlands, as well as the recent report by the international body Human Rights Watch entitled: '"I Was Hit So Many Times I Can't Count": Abuse of Child Athletes in Japan', indicates the currency and level of importance of examining bodily abuse in sport both contemporarily and historically. This report is available at: https://www.hrw.org/report/2020/07/20/i-was-hit-so-many-times-i-cant-count/abuse-child-athletes-japan.

40 See, most recently, Sylvian Ferez, Sébastien Ruffié, Hélène Joncheray, Anne Marcellini, Sakis Pappous, and Rémi Richard, 'Inclusion through Sport: A Critical View on Paralympic History from a Historical Perspective', *Social Inclusion* 8, no. 3 (2020): 224–235 but also works such as Steve Bailey, *Athlete's First: A History of the Paralympic Movement* (Chichester: John Wiley & Sons, 2008), and Ian Brittain, *From Stoke Mandeville to Sochi: A History of the Summer and Winter Paralympic Games* (Champaign, Il.: Common Ground Publishing, 2014).

41 Tomoko Tamari, 'Body Image and Prosthetic Aesthetics: Disability, Technology and Paralympic Culture', *Body and Society* 23, no. 2 (2017): 25–56.

42 A poignant example of this is the recent work by Justin Bailey, 'The Body in Cyberspace' see note 37 above.

43 Henning Eichberg, 'Body Culture', in *Routledge Companion to Sports History,* eds. S.W. Pope and John Nauright (London: Routledge, 2010), 162–181.

44 John Bale and Chris Philo, eds. *Body Cultures. Essays on Sport, Space & Identity by Henning Eichberg* (London: Routledge, 1998).

45 Douglas Booth and John Loy, 'Sport, Status, and Style', *Sport History Review* 30 (1999): 1–26.

46 Dave Day and Samantha-Jayne Oldfield, 'Delineating Professional and Amateur Athletic Bodies in Victorian England', *Sport in History* 35, no. 1 (2015): 19–45.

47 Booth and Loy, 'Sport, Status and Style'.

48 Nick J. Fox and Pam Alldred, *Sociology and the New Materialism: Theory, Research, Action* (London: Sage Publishing, 2016). For a recent anthology on sport and New Materialism (among other theoretical perspectives) see Joshua Newman, Holly Thorpe, and David Andrews, eds. *Sport, Physical Culture, and the Moving Body. Materialisms, Technologies, Ecologies* (Rutgers University Press: New Brunswick, NJ, 2020).

15

SPORT AND VISUALITY

Mike Huggins

Throughout his team's game against Collingwood in Victoria Park, Melbourne, in April 1993, Aboriginal AFL footballer Nicky Winmar had been subject to vehement racial abuse and barracking. At the end of the game he turned to the Collingwood crowd, lifted his jersey, pointed to his chest, and shouted, 'I'm black and proud to be black.' Two photographers managed to capture the moment on film. The image appeared on the front page of the *Sunday Age* the next day, quickly causing controversy, and subsequently became an iconic, culturally important Australian sporting image. More recently a bronze statue of Winmar making the gesture has been erected in front of Optus Stadium in Perth, in Western Australia, his state of origin, a permanent reminder of his defiant stance and pride in his indigenous origins. The original 'image', in the sense of its visual representation on a surface, has assumed particular importance in the context of changing Australian attitudes to sport, discrimination, race, and racism, and played a significant role in wider political, cultural, and social debate. Historians Gary Osmond and Matthew Klugman have used it as a starting point for a book examining the debates and shifts surrounding its purpose, meaning, and importance. More recently they followed up their study with a complex visual analysis of a much-less well publicized photograph, taken in 1994, of Australian athlete Cathy Freeman running past a mural showing scenes of Aboriginal elders in chains in the late nineteenth century, some two months before she famously carried an Aboriginal flag in her 400 metres victory lap at the Commonwealth Games.[1]

Such innovative approaches are still relatively new. Even a couple of decades ago such detailed attention to a single sporting image might have been thought strange, since many historians of sport still relied almost solely on written texts to shape their interpretations and understandings, often with their subjectivities unacknowledged. Visual material was treated with suspicion and circumspection and often relegated to a representational role as mere illustration of textual arguments, rather than, as Peter Burke put it, to 'give new answers or ask new questions'.[2]

This has been puzzling since, historically, actual experiences of sport by players and spectators have been dominated by the visual. In terms of mere vision, sports science research has always stressed the importance of visual search strategies, visual attention, and the encoding of visual information by players. Sports studies have explored the visual experience in the stadium, fan cultures, and sporting performance. By contrast, historians were slow to take

128

DOI: 10.4324/9780429318306-18

images seriously, and address 'visuality', the broader field of visual culture. Although the influential historian and literary critic Hayden White argued as early as 1988 that 'historiophoty' was a highly useful way of using images as historical sources *and* an important form of historical interpretation and narration,[3] sports historians largely stuck to textual material, leaving visual approaches under-theorized.

Yet visuality as a discursive practice for rendering and regulating 'reality' has been discussed in the historical mainstream in a number of different ways, from Michel Foucault's analysis of a controlling surveillance-focused and corporally disciplining 'panopticon' to Jacques Lacan's explorations of the pleasure in looking and the cultural construction of the gendered 'gaze'.[4] There has been a long cultural history of image-making and experiencing, and what the visual theorist John Berger called 'ways of seeing'.[5] As Mike O'Mahony has recently stressed, in a useful overview of the 'visual turn', the visual culture that surrounds sporting action has always contributed towards shaping our very subjectivity and behaviour.[6] This 'right to look', as Derrida famously described it, can be, for example, masculine, feminine, controlling or liberating, inventive or passive, and has helped to construct the sporting world.[7] Content, context, use, and meanings offered by audiences are all important.

The range of visual representations

Away from the events themselves, sport has long been variously visually exploited as media illustration, entertainment, spectacle, pedagogy, status or aesthetic marker, or catering for cultural notions of particular identities. By the nineteenth century this form of 'the sporting gaze' was being transformed by the new visual conventions of prints, commercial advertising posters, paintings, and sporting content in theatres and music hall, which might variously convey information, meaning, pleasure and entertainment or instruction.[8] The Irish playwright Dion Boucicault, for example, in the 1860s wrote two spectacular melodramas, one with a scene centred round the Derby and the other on the Oxford–Cambridge boat race, deploying theatrical technology stagecraft to demonstrate a response to the effects of modernity on male bodies.[9]

The rise of sport developed in parallel with the emergence of photography and film as key image-making media and was boosted by the new cinematic 'dream palaces' of the early twentieth century. Paintings too were loaded with symbolical significance. In the later nineteenth century and early twentieth century, some painters placed increased emphasis on idealized male bodies, utilizing iconography based on classical Greek antiquity, encouraging an association of sport with the civilized past. Engravings and photographs for working-class readers were more focused on celebrity and the drama of competitive sporting spectacle. The earliest photographers immediately embraced sport to encourage sales.[10] Across the world, a common cultural trope became the staged team photograph, a possible expression of fraternity, class, status, gender, race, localism, collectivity, or national unity. Players were briefly captured in often respectable, tranquil repose, providing a contrast with their vitality, aggression, and physicality. As exposure times shortened, magazines and newspapers included sporting action shots. From the 1880s cigarette manufacturers, first in the United States and then in Europe, began including cigarette cards, with a picture on the obverse and explanatory text on the reverse, to encourage sales, and sport was soon a central theme. Their topics around 1900 included (inter alia) 'champions of sport', 'sports of all nations', 'heroes of sport', 'captains', and 'sporting terms', as well as sets focusing on particular sports, especially soccer in Britain and baseball in America, often exploiting the promotional power of celebrity. Boys traded cigarette cards on Saturdays and after school with great enthusiasm.

The manufacture of sporting goods accelerated, as more amateur participants demanded them.[11]

Film was in its infancy in the late 1890s but early actuality local film footage often allowed filmgoers to see themselves in the crowds at sporting events, often gazing directly towards the camera.[12] Early films tended to show more static and unproblematic aspects, omitting controversial aspects such as player violence, disputes with officials, or aggressive crowd behaviour. Later newsreels showed national events with cross-class appeal, ensuring sport took firmer hold on the wider population, alongside the growth of an image-inundated society far more attuned to 'visual culture'. In the present time, as in the case of the Nicky Winmar photograph, visual residues of the past have been reused, reshaped, and re-represented in multiple reincarnations as they circulated globally in rapidly developing analogue, digital, and hybrid forms. New theoretical approaches are just beginning to address this paradigm shift.[13] As part of the 'sports heritage' movement, the recently founded and relaunched museums dedicated to specific sports, or local, national, or world sporting heritage, present their narratives predominantly through combinations of images, objects, and texts, which has led to a growth in museum studies within sports history.[14]

Recent work on the visual in sport

Historians of sport more generally were often initially slow to recognize that, as Douglas Booth put it in 2005,

> an understanding of sport, which is inextricably tied to corporality and movement, would be nigh on impossible without the testimony of the images that appear in numerous media such as paintings, lithographs, posters, coins and medals, ceramic arts, stone and metal sculptures, photographs and films.[15]

Booth stressed that all such rich and valuable, fragmented and partial, visual material should be viewed as mediated and contingent, treated analytically and critically, and engaged with in more nuanced ways using imagination, self-reflexivity, and an eye for detail. Images come in material form, and materiality is integral to their meaning and use. They also function in cultural form, often in relation to other images, as likenesses, concepts, or venerated icons. They are simply remnants and traces of the past in the present, and the ways in which they were produced and consumed are key aspects of their analysis, so responses can be those of aesthetics, perception, or sensation. Historians of sport are now increasingly aware of the multiplicity of concealed elements behind their creation. There is a growing fluency in visual literacy and using the language of visuality, although as with all understandings of sporting images, there is always much more in play that we initially realize.

In the course of the last two decades, this turn to the visual, with its specific epistemological, ontological, and phenomenological characteristics, has been seen as an exciting new area of investigation. It has opened up new methodological possibilities, and led to greater awareness by historians of sport of the potentialities of sporting images and visual phenomena, enhancing their ability to more critically historicize visual practices. With the development of the sub-field, visuality is now beginning to spawn narrative reviews or overviews of the topic as a whole.[16]

Studies of sport and visuality are rapidly increasing and now appear in a wide range of journals and books. Many of these however, are still disconnected individual case studies, insufficiently linked to the broader context of other studies, and lacking a clearly articulated theoretical basis and a more coherent set of understandings. Relatively few authors have produced more substantial and significant bodies of work. In Australia, Murray Phillips and Gary Osmond, separately and individually, have developed visuality's theoretical and empirical base through the exploration of sources such as film, photographs, monuments, statues, museums, postage stamps, and halls of fame. In Britain, Mike Huggins has produced studies of cartoons, newsreels, and works of art, and John Hughson cultural studies of sporting art and posters. Art historian Mike O'Mahony has produced monographs on representations of sport and physical culture in official Soviet art during the inter-war years; the visual culture of sport and the Olympic Games; and photography and sport, as well as related book chapters and articles. Malcolm Maclean has written on topics such as film and television. In recent years a growing number of scholars have become interested in the visual and material memorialization, commemoration, and celebration of sporting culture, and its links to heritage, nostalgia, and changing perceptions of the past. Chris Stride and his collaborators have produced a well-theorized body of work linked in part to the Sports Statues Project, in part a response to the increased international tendency to memorialize leading sports players in the form of public monuments. In America, Maureen Smith and Jaime Schultz have worked on topics such as statues and photographs. In France, Sébastien Laffage-Cosnier and Christian Vivier have been developing interesting research on comics and graphic narratives. In Germany, Markwart Herzog has published on memorial culture in soccer and Michael Krüger on sporting art.[17]

Methodologies and topics

Such studies presently draw on a range of approaches and methodologies, including those of mainstream writers on visuality such as W.J.T. Mitchell (who pointed out that pictures are 'ways of world making'),[18] Gillian Rose, Peter Burke, and Nicholas Mirzoeff.[19] An increasingly wide range of methodologies are available and have the potential to stretch the boundaries of the subfield. Such approaches can include art history's iconography and iconology, semiology, discourse analysis, psychoanalysis, audience and reception studies, and mixed studies.[20] Essays studying and researching visual culture are often particularly competent at setting visual material in its historical context. The deeper analysis of meaning, the ability to understand style and form, and the multiple ways in which visual materials circulate through time and across cultures are also engaging interest as writers take the 'sporting turn'.[21] Recent studies include histories of soccer in visual culture and art, and the ways in which the mediated and direct experience of sports such as cycling, cycling, motor racing, boxing, tennis, and rugby inspired the work of an international range of modernist artists in the early twentieth century.[22]

International conferences on the sporting visual slowly proliferate. An early example was a 2009 international conference on sport and the visual at the University of Bristol, attended by scholars from a diverse range of research disciplines including sport history, social history, art history, media studies, design history, architecture, and visual cultural studies. It stressed the constructed nature of sporting representations and resulted in a number of publications.[23] The 2010 men's soccer world cup generated further interest in visual themes, and a conference in Basel in 2012 focused on global perspectives, visualizing soccer in Africa as a social and cultural text, with topics ranging from media representations to the aesthetics of fandom.[24] In 2016 an international and interdisciplinary conference in Cologne on sports, bodies, and visual sources offered a wide range of papers likewise taking the intrinsic visuality of sport seriously.[25]

The range of topics and media covered is increasing. In terms of topics, for example, visual representations have increasingly attracted historians of the Olympics. For over a hundred years Olympic posters have been a prime means of visual communication, using eye-catching and memorable imagery, sometimes incorporating classical references and swirling banners. These helped to publicize, identify, and define each Olympiad to an increasingly international audience. As their study has shown, they linked art, politics, place, commerce, and culture.[26] In 2012 Mike O'Mahony provided a detailed cultural analysis of a wide variety of images of the Olympics, stressing the mediative role such images have played in terms of political, cultural, social, race, and gender issues. Among O'Mahony's examples are Leni Riefenstahl's *Olympia* (1938), Kon Ichikawa's *Tokyo Olympiad* (1965), and a variety of powerful photographs of figures such as Jesse Owens, John Carlos, and Tommie Smith.[27] The connections between art and sport, and most particularly the Olympic medals designed by Giuseppe Cassioli, were the subject of an exhibition in Sienna in 2018–2019.[28]

Photographs, films, and television

In terms of media covered, photographs, films, and television still battle for supremacy. Films are valuable pictorial sources for the history of sport's representation, articulating and shaping meanings about sport and temporality, and advancing complex interpretations of fictional or more actual sporting events such as Le Mans (*Le Mans*, 1971) or individuals such as British football manager Brian Clough (*The Damned United*, 2009). Sports films are almost reaching the stage of being a genre in their own right, with a consistent set of themes, images, and tropes, often but not always falling into four categories: biopics, historical dramas and themes, sports documentaries, and fictional films like *Raging Bull* (1980), *Hoosiers* (1986), or *Bend it Like Beckham* (2002).[29] As Sean Curran has adroitly shown, they can address issues such as gender, social class, and national identity.[30]

The ways in which sport has been represented in film have been of growing interest since the 1980s, when Roland Bergan's book *Sport in the Movies* (1982) appeared. The *Journal of Sport History* added film reviews to its book reviews and journal surveys in 1990 and film studies have become ever-increasingly nuanced and theoretically grounded, along with a generally rapid movement away from the simple collection of factual errors, and a notion of some fictional veracity. There is a clearer recognition that films, like other visual sources, are produced and consumed as constructed narratives that inevitably mediate the point of view of their creator, created in a particular context and time. Studies have included the ways sports films intruded on the landscape of American culture and the ways films have portrayed sporting celebrity.[31]

There has been much interest by media historians in the historical development of television and its transformation of sport, most especially from the 1960s, with its discourses from narrative fiction, show-business, and fashion, coupled with naturalized coverage which minimized audience awareness of the mediating effect. Indeed, David Rowe sees sport, culture, and the media as an 'unruly trinity … a dynamic metaphor of contested power and protean forms'.[32] Changes in commentary, screen coverage, and other presentational forms have seen representations move beyond terrestrial television to satellite, the Internet, and digital media.[33] A recent study of the impact of television on a single sport, cricket, showed how it undermined the pastoral fantasies of British radio broadcasts, while shaping the modern game and becoming its main source of revenue.[34]

Extending the field

Researchers need to be aware that where the camera lens points spatially and temporarily determines what is included and what is excluded. And for the onlooker, as Foucault reminds us, not all ways of visualizing are equally possible. There are cultural constraints, and any period lets some things be seen more easily, and casts others in the shade.[35] To cite one neglected topic, the visual culture of sporting colonialism had a significant role to play in explaining, defining, and justifying the colonial order and concealing from view the sports of indigenous peoples. Current research into visuality therefore needs to extend our analysis and interpretation beyond the confines of recent publications. There is most definitely a need for greater epistemological, methodological, theoretical, and conceptual robustness and diversity and more papers which make a stronger contribution to the development of the subfield more widely. One useful first step should be a rigorous systemic search and meta-evaluation of existing peer-reviewed literature. There is still an egregious gender imbalance. Studies thus far have focused on male sports, and visual sources produced by men. In her study of feminist art and women's soccer, Jennifer Doyle makes her point strongly: 'women athletes rarely appear on gallery walls', and coverage is 'highly asymmetrical'.[36] Exceptions are few.[37] There are opportunities to extend work on reception, and on the dissemination and circulation of images. Given that visual material can gain 'affective' value as it circulates and plays on our emotions, and serves as a gateway to broader somatic experience, much work still underplays affect and embodiment. And finally, the sheer range of potential sources is still under-explored. Soccer club badges and crests, to cite just one example, are covered in coffee-table books, but there has been no serious analysis of their deeply symbolical meanings, their cultural origins, or the ways they expressed the aspirations of clubs, owners, or fans.[38]

Notes

1 Matthew Klugman and Gary Osmond, *Black and Proud: The Story of an Iconic AFL Photo* (Sydney, NSW: New South Publishing, 2013); Gary Osmond and Matthew Klugman, 'A Forgotten Picture: Race, Photographs and Cathy Freeman at the Northcote Koori Mural', *Journal of Australian Studies* 43, no. 2 (2019): 1–15. Another iconic image, the San Jose statue of the human rights/black power salute of Carlos and Smith at the Mexico City Olympics was discussed in Maureen Smith, 'Frozen Fists in Speed City: the Statue as Twenty-First City Reparations', *Journal of Sport History* 36, no. 3 (2009): 396–414.
2 Peter Burke, *Eyewitnessing: The Use of Images as Historical Evidence* (Ithaca NY: Cornell University Press, 2001), 10.
3 Hayden White, 'Historiography and Historiophoty', *American Historical Review* 93, no. 5 (1988): 1193–1199.
4 Michel Foucault, *Discipline and Punish: The Birth of the Prison* (London: Vintage Books, 1995); Maria Scott, 'Lacan's "Of the Gaze as Objet Petit a" as Anamorphic Discourse', *Paragraph* 31, no. 3 (2008): 327–343.
5 John Berger, *Ways of Seeing* (London: BBC, 1972).
6 Mike O'Mahony, 'The Visual Turn in Sports History', in *The Oxford Handbook of Sports History*, eds. Robert Edelman and Wayne Wilson (Oxford: OUP, 2017), 510.
7 Nicholas Mirzoeff, *The Right to Look: A Counterhistory of Visuality* (Durham: Duke University Press, 2011).
8 Mike Huggins, 'The Sporting Gaze: Towards a Visual turn in Sports History', *Journal of Sport History* 35, no. 2 (2008): 311–329.
9 Shannon R Smith, 'Staging Sport: Dion Boucicault, The Victorian Spectacular theatre and the Manly Ideal', *Critical Survey* 24, no. 1 (2012): 57–73.
10 Mike O'Mahony, *Photography and Sport* (London: Reaktion Books, 2018) provides a useful overview of the changing relationship between the two.

11 Ellen R. Hughes, 'The People's Museum: George Brown Goode's Collection of Sporting Goods in the Smithsonian Institution of Victorian America', *The Historian* 64, no. 2 (2002): 295–315.

12 Vanessa Toulmin, Simon Popple, and Patrick Russell eds. *The Lost World of Mitchell and Kenyon: Edwardian Britain on Film* (London: British Film Institute, 2004).

13 But see Thomas Nail, *Theory of the Image* (Oxford: Oxford University Press, 2019).

14 Murray Phillips ed., *Representing the Sporting Past in Museums and Halls of Fame* (Abingdon: Routledge, 2012).

15 Douglas Booth, *The Field: Truth and Fiction in Sports History* (Abingdon: Routledge, 2005).

16 Huggins, 'The Sporting Gaze'; Mike Huggins, 'The Visual in Sport History: Approaches, Methodologies and Sources', *International Journal of the History of Sport* 32, no. 15 (2015): 1813–1830; O'Mahony, 'The Visual Turn in Sports History'.

17 Space constraints only permit single illustrative examples, e.g. Murray Phillips, Mark O'Neill, and Gary Osmond, 'Broadening Horizons in Sport History: Films, Photographs, and Monuments', *Journal of Sport History* 34, no. 2 (2007): 271–291; Mike Huggins, 'Projecting the Visual: British Newsreels, Soccer and Popular culture, 1918–1939', *International Journal of the History of Sport* 24, no. 1 (2007): 80–102; John Ewing Hughson, 'Ways of Seeing, Ways of Telling: From Art History to Sport History', *The International Journal of the History of Sport* 32, no. 15 (2015): 1799–1803; Mike O'Mahony, 'The Art of Goalkeeping: Memorializing Lev Yashim', *Soccer and Society* 20, nos. 5–6 (2017): 641–665; Chris Stride, J.P. Wilson, and F. Thomas, 'Honouring Heroes by Branding in Bronze: Theorizing the UK's Football Statuary', *Sport in Society* 16, no. 6 (2013): 749–771; Malcolm Maclean, 'Truth and Reality in Screening Sports Pasts: Sports Films, Public History and Truthfulness', *Journal of Sport History* 42, no. 1 (2014): 47–54; Maureen Smith, 'Mapping America's Sporting Landscape: A Case Study of Three Statues', *International Journal of the History of Sport* 28, no. 8 (2011): 1252–1268; Jaime Schultz, 'Contesting the Master Narrative: The Arthur Ashe Statue and Monument Avenue in Richmond, Virginia', *The International Journal of the History of Sport* 28, nos. 8–9 (2011): 1235–1251; Sébastien Laffage-Cosnier and Christian Vivier eds. 'Sports and Graphic Narratives: A New Topic for Sport Historians in Europe?', *European Studies in Sports History* 11 (2018): 1–234; Markwart Herzog ed. *Memorialkultur im Fussballsport: Medien, Rituale und Praktiken des Erinnerns, Gedenkens und Vergessens* (Stuttgart: Kohlhammer, 2012); Michael Krüger, 'German Sport History as Reflected in Sporting Art', *The International Journal of the History of Sport* 35, no. 1 (2019): 1–29.

18 W.J.T. Mitchell, *What Do Pictures Want? The Lives and Loves of Images* (Chicago: University of Chicago Press, 2005).

19 Burke, *Eyewitnessing*; Nicholas Mirzoeff, *An Introduction to Visual Culture* (Abingdon: Routledge, 2009); Gillian Rose, *Visual Methodologies: An Introduction to Researching with Visual Material* (London: Sage, 2014).

20 Huggins, 'The Visual in Sport History'.

21 Daniel Haxall, 'Pitch Invasion: Football, Contemporary Art and the African Diaspora', *Soccer and Society* 16, nos. 2–3 (2015): 259–281.

22 Daniel Haxall, *Picturing the Beautiful Game: A History of Soccer in Visual Culture and Art* (London: Bloomsbury, 2018); Bernard Vere, *Sport and Modernism in the Visual Arts in Europe c.1909–1939* (Manchester: Manchester University Press, 2018).

23 Mike Huggins and Mike O'Mahony eds. *The Visual in Sport* (Abingdon: Routledge, 2012).

24 Susann Baller, Giorgio Miescher, and Cirac Rassool, eds. *Global Perspectives on Sport in Africa: Visualizing the Game* (Abingdon: Routledge, 2013). A Special Issue of *African Arts* focused on art and the soccer World Cup of 2010: *African Arts* 44, no. 2 (2011), 1–79.

25 See the special edition of *Historical Social Research* 23, no. 2 (2018) edited by Jorn Eiben and Olaf Stieglitz on 'Visualities – Sports, Bodies, and Visual Sources'.

26 Margaret Timmers, *A Century of Olympic Posters* (London: V & A Publishing, 2008).

27 Mike O'Mahony, *Olympic Visions: Images of the Games through History* (London: Reaktion, 2012). For a more detailed analysis of Ichikawa's work see Ian McDonald 'Critiquing the Olympic Documentary: Kon Ichikawa's Tokyo Olympiad' in *Sport in Films* eds. Emma Poulton and Martin Roderick (London: Routledge, 2008), 182–194.

28 Museo Cassioli, *La Medaglia Olimpica di Giuseppi Casioli: Tra Arte e Sport* (Museo Cassioli: Asciano Siena, 2018).

29 Bruce Babington, *The Sports Film: Games People Play* (London: Wallflower, 2014).

30 Seán Crosson, *Sport and Film* (Abingdon: Routledge, 2013).

Sport and visuality

31 Dan Streibel, *Fight Pictures: A History of Boxing and Early Cinema* (Berkeley: University of California Press, 2008); Ron Briley, Michael Schoenecke, and Deborah A Carmichael, *All Stars and Movie Stars: Sports in Film and History* (Lexington: University Press of Kentucky: 2008).

32 David Rowe, *Sport, Culture and the Media* (Buckingham: Open University Press, 1999), 171; Garry Whannel, *Fields in Vision: Television Sport and Cultural Transformation* (London: Routledge, 1992).

33 Brett Hutchins and David Rowe, *Sport Beyond Television: the Internet, Digital Media and the Rise of Networked Media Sport* (London: Routledge, 2012).

34 Jack Williams, *Cricket and Broadcasting* (Manchester: Manchester University Press, 2011).

35 See John Rajchman, 'Foucault's Art of Seeing', *October* 44 (1988): 92.

36 Jennifer Doyle, 'Feminist Art and Women's Soccer', in Haxall, *Picturing the Beautiful Game*.

37 Alison Rowley, 'Sport in the Service of the State: Images of Physical Culture and Soviet Women, 1917–1941', *International Journal of the History of Sport* 23, no. 8 (2006): 1314–1340; Viridiana Lieberman, *Sports Heroines on Film: a Critical Study of Cinematic Women Athletes, Coaches and Owners* (Jefferson, NC, McFarland & Co., 2015).

38 For example, Martyn Routledge and Elsbeth Wills, *The Beautiful Badge: The Stories Behind the Football Club Badge* (London: Pitch Publishing, 2018).

16

SPORT AND POLITICS

Heather L. Dichter

Sport and politics have been intertwined from ancient Greece to the present day. Often this relationship (especially with modern sport) has focused on domestic politics within a country. Many regimes have incorporated sport as a central tenet of the state, from the Third Reich to the Soviet Union to the People's Republic of China.[1] Democratic states also became involved in their country's sporting matters during crisis points, such as to implement wartime physical training, to address education requirements, and to address perceptions that a country needed to enhance its international prestige.[2]

More recently, historical research has moved beyond a strictly national understanding of how sport and politics impact each other to address politics from international or transnational approaches. By taking these broader views of sport, this newer research on sport history overlaps with other historical subfields, including diplomatic history, security studies, and environmental history as just a few examples. These different and varied aspects of sport demonstrate that governments from across the political spectrum around the world have long been involved with sport. This extensive government engagement in sport appears at several levels: with international sport organizations, as the host country for a major international event, or as its own programme overseen by the government itself. Sport and politics have thus become more global in their scope and impact, often involving international sporting events or inter-state relations and rarely retaining a purely local or domestic context.

Sport and diplomacy

Countries have frequently used sport both informally and through government-supported programmes as part of diplomacy and state relations. Sport has played a large role in soft power or public diplomacy – an effort to win the hearts and minds of people living in other countries[3] – because it can incorporate so many different types of athletic activity in order to appeal to different groups of people across the world. With more countries having membership in the International Olympic Committee (IOC) than the United Nations, sport diplomacy can easily be adapted to fit the needs of, or appeal to, the country on the receiving end of these efforts. Geoffrey Pigman has defined the two major ways in which diplomacy incorporates international sport: as a government tool of diplomacy, and 'sport-as-diplomacy' between many different actors with the organization of international sport.[4] Both

136   DOI: 10.4324/9780429318306-19

of these types of sport diplomacy emerged in the twentieth century with more countries adopting them in recent decades.

As international sport expanded in the late nineteenth and early twentieth century, many athletes and teams went on overseas tours, often for commercial interests. These tours – whether they be by European soccer clubs or American baseball players – did not have an explicitly political purpose, yet the goodwill fostered by these trips often contributed to a state's diplomatic goals.[5] When the Cold War divided the globe into two distinct political camps, which then fought to pull non-aligned states into their orbit (or at least away from the other side), foreign ministries took a greater role in supporting these types of overseas tours as a formal tool of diplomacy. The US State Department sent African-American athletes abroad, often to newly independent African countries, to counter Soviet claims about the lack of equality in the United States.[6] Other countries similarly sent athletes overseas: Canadian ice hockey teams in eastern European states helped promote Canada's separate identity from its American and British allies, Chinese table tennis players contributed to opening Chinese–US relations and expanding Chinese relations with Africa and Latin America, and India's friendly cricket tours in Pakistan attempted to overcome tensions between the two rival states.[7]

In addition to sending prominent athletes to draw crowds at sport exhibitions and at meet-and-greet opportunities, foreign ministries have also incorporated a more grassroots approach to their sport diplomacy efforts. Some countries established programmes to establish or strengthen relationships during the Cold War, such as athlete and coach exchanges within the Soviet bloc, and Taiwan sending table tennis coaches to Latin America to counter Chinese efforts to have international sport rescind Taiwan's recognition.[8] Norway promoted Sport for All programmes in Tanzania in the 1980s.[9] These types of programmes have actually seen an expansion since the end of the Cold War, with the US State Department formalizing these grassroots or people-to-people exchange with the establishment of a sport diplomacy department in 2002 as just one example.[10] Scholars from other disciplines, many of whom have been involved in these types of sport for development and peace (SDP) programmes, have published articles about these programmes and experiences,[11] but historical examinations of these programmes are much needed to fully understand their scope and impact.

In addition to government-created or sponsored SDP programmes, other grassroots diplomacy programmes falling under the SDP umbrella have been established by non-governmental organizations (NGOs). This expansion of NGO involvement within sport diplomacy followed the United Nations' formal recognition of the use of sport to accomplish the organization's other goals in 2001.[12] Some of these efforts are the initiative of private charitable organizations, at times working in conjunction with international sport federations, whereas others might fall entirely under the auspices of the international sport community. The IOC's Olympic Solidarity funds a variety of programmes, including sessions to train new coaches or increase their qualifications and knowledge, as well as grassroots activities to increase participation in sport.[13] Particularly when the IOC, international federations, or other NGOs are involved in SDP programmes do they fall under Pigman's second category of sport-as-diplomacy.

Sport-as-diplomacy not only works at the grassroots level through SDP programmes but also through the organizing of large-scale sporting events, where governments work with local organizers as well as international sport organizations in the hopes of achieving broader diplomatic goals alongside the more basic function of simply hosting a sporting event. Cities use the Olympics and other major sporting events as a way to showcase themselves on a global stage, with national governments typically supporting these efforts as they can play a similar role for the country on a global stage as a form of public diplomacy. This 'place promotion' allows a city or a country to publicize a carefully curated narrative about itself to a global audience from the sustained media coverage and prestige which these events confer.[14] For cities and countries without the capacity to organize the Olympic Games or FIFA's men's World Cup, hosting smaller second-order events, such as continental games or world championships in other sports or junior levels, achieves the same goals.[15] The BRICS countries with major emerging economies in the twenty-first century – Brazil, Russia, India, China, and South Africa – all sought to host sport mega-events as part of their ability to demonstrate their arrival on the global stage, with each of them securing at least one if not more.[16] While this process appears not much different from Nazi Germany using the 1936 Olympics to demonstrate what the Third Reich had accomplished,[17] these more recent uses of sporting events as a form of place promotion are a concerted effort supported by governments during the candidature process,[18] in contrast to the IOC having awarded the 1936 Games two years before Hitler assumed power in Germany.

Hosting sporting events, sending athletes overseas, and sponsoring sport for development and peace initiatives all demonstrate the extent to which governments incorporate sport within their diplomatic endeavours. This area of sport and politics grew in the aftermath of the Second World War and continues to expand rapidly in the twenty-first century. These aspects are rich for further research, beyond the traditional great powers and states which have dominated both sport and sport politics literature, as they intersect with diplomatic history and humanitarian and human rights research.[19]

Activism

Local, state/provincial, and federal governments have increasingly provided the finances and other benefits for major sporting events. These massive financial outlays – particularly when it comes to the Olympic Games, FIFA World Cup, and other multi-sport international events – not only cost millions, if not billions, of dollars, they almost without fail far exceed the initial cost estimates. Grassroots activism against these efforts has become more widespread, with almost every Olympic bid today facing an anti-Olympics campaign, with these activists spread across the globe becoming more connected. The digital age has also fostered a new era of athlete activism, where athletes are more outspoken about issues which have both a local and international impact.

While Denver remains the only city to return the Olympic Games outside wartime, local populations have mobilized against bringing the biggest sporting event in the world to their communities, resulting in failed bids. Without public money, Denver could not move forward with its plans to host the Olympics. Increased security costs following the Munich Games and countries boycotting the Olympics allowed Los Angeles to organize the Olympic Games in 1984 entirely from private money, yet the Games could not happen without government involvement, including, at a bare minimum, allocating visas to athletes from communist countries, and provisions for security.[20] Los Angeles' success in turning a profit with the 1984 Olympics led to cities across the globe clamouring to host future Olympic Games. The glamour and appeal of hosting the Olympics encouraged cities and countries to cover many of these costs. Federal funding from the US government in support of the three most recent Olympic Games in the United States increased from $75 million for Los Angeles in 1984 to $609 million for Atlanta in 1996 to a staggering $1.3 billion for the much smaller 2002 Winter Olympics in Salt Lake City.[21] These amounts do not include local or state/provincial funding, further exacerbating how much public money is funnelled into the organization of mega-events.

These estimates for the 2002 Olympics were made a year before the September 11 terrorist attacks, which further increased security costs just months before the Winter Games as well as for the next Summer Olympics in Athens in 2004. The global media coverage of sport mega-events makes them ripe targets for terrorist groups, who know that their actions will receive extensive publicity – which was exactly what Black September achieved when they took Israeli athletes and coaches hostage at the 1972 Munich Olympics.[22] As a result, security costs for the next Olympics in Montreal skyrocketed.[23] Ensuring sporting events have the necessary security to prevent further terrorist attacks has involved a close relationship between sport organizers, governments, militaries, and global security firms.[24] Yet, as these security and surveillance apparatus expand, concerned citizens have expressed concern and actively campaigned against these actions.[25]

In addition to providing funding and security, government support has also become an essential component of winning the Games. Russian President Vladimir Putin participated in Sochi's final presentation to the IOC, speaking in Russian, French, and English – widely considered his first time speaking English in a public ceremony. Media accounts attributed his participation in Sochi's presentation as contributing to the Russian city's selection to host what ultimately became the most expensive Winter Olympics ever.[26] The final presentations before the vote for the 2016 Olympic Games host included Queen Sofia of Spain alongside the Spanish foreign minister supporting Madrid's bid, Brazilian President Luiz Inácio Lula da Silva promoting Rio de Janeiro, and United States President Barack Obama speaking on behalf of his former hometown of Chicago.[27] Further demonstrating their importance in the bid process, political leaders and royals participated in the presentations for all three final candidate cities for the 2020 Olympic race: Japanese Prime Minister Shinzo Abe and Princess Takamado, Spanish Crown Prince Felipe (a former Olympic athlete), and Turkish Prime Minister Recep Tayyip Erdoğan.[28]

With so much public money from both local and national taxes used to fund the organizing of Olympic Games, cities and provinces have increasingly been holding referenda to gauge public support for hosting the Olympics. At first the IOC appeared to punish cities which had lower support in referenda, such as selecting PyeongChang, South Korea, over Munich, Germany, to host the 2018 Winter Olympics when only 76.3 per cent of the German residents who voted in the Munich/Bavarian referendum supported the Games in contrast to 91.4 per cent of South Koreans.[29] Although a majority of the population was in favour of hosting the Olympics and the German bid did not require any new venues as the city and surrounding Alpine region already had world-class winter sports venues, the IOC nonetheless selected the South Korea region, which required almost every venue and several hotels to be built for the Games.

Anti-Olympic sentiment has been visible in host cities for decades but has become more pronounced during the candidature stage,[30] especially since that 2011 vote. Several cities have expressed interest in bidding for the Olympic Games, only to have local political action against these largely corporate-driven plans scuttle the bids. In the wake of the 2008 global financial crisis, polling revealed an overwhelming majority of the Czech population did not support Prague's bid for the 2020 Summer Olympics, leading to the demise of that bid before the city could submit formal materials to the IOC.[31] Rome's 2020 bid also ended because the Italian government decided not to provide financial support for the Games, and the city's 2024 bid collapsed from a lack of political support, particularly following the election of Virginia Raggi as the city's mayor in 2016.[32] The 2024 race also saw extensive opposition from Boston kill the Massachusetts city's bid shortly after it got off the ground.[33] Norway's parliament refused to agree to all of the IOC's stipulations, ending Oslo's very strong 2022 Winter Olympic bid. Referenda resulting in a majority of residents against hosting the Olympics ended bids from Hamburg, Germany (2024), three bids for the 2022 Winter Games (Krakow, Poland; Munich; and St. Moritz/Davos, Switzerland), and Calgary, Canada for the 2026 Winter Olympics.[34] As these anti-Olympic movements have become more effective in ending Olympic bids and sharing their arguments and tactics with their counterparts across the world, the IOC changed its candidature process in 2019 to require cities hold referenda prior to becoming an official candidate city,[35] demonstrating sport responding to this interjection of politics into sport.

Activism and the Olympics, however, is not limited to the anti-Olympic movement. The athletes themselves have become more vocal in advocating for causes and issues in which they strongly believe, using their visibility as global athletes. Athlete activism of course is not a new phenomenon in the twenty-first century, with sport playing a central role in the civil rights movement in the United States and the anti-apartheid movement in southern Africa.[36] Black athletes continue to fight racial injustice in the United States, from Colin Kaepernick to NBA and WNBA players. Athletes who compete in outdoor winter sports recognize the impact which climate change has on their sports, leading to several efforts to confront this global problem. Former snowboarder Jeremy Jones created Protect Our Winters (POW), a US-based non-profit organization with branches in several other countries, and dozens of elite athletes – many drawn from snow sports – are now involved in POW's work.[37] Nordic skiers competing on the World Cup circuit demonstrated their support and urged international leaders to come to an agreement during their 2015 meeting on climate change, which ultimately led to the Paris Climate Change Agreement.[38]

The future of sport and politics

For decades scholars have acknowledged the interconnected nature of domestic sport and politics, but recent research trends have demonstrated their close relationship at an international level as well. Building on the long-established field of diplomatic history as well as newer subfields has vastly expanded the understanding of what constitutes sport and politics. The international nature of sport – from competitions to media coverage to state relations – allows for this broader and richer view of sport and politics.

As more aspects of international sport are considered, the area of sport and politics will yield even more new themes for scholarly investigation. In support of the US Women's National Team's battle for equal pay from US Soccer following their victorious FIFA Women's World Cup run, two congresswomen introduced the Give Our Athletes Level Salaries (GOALS) Act, which would block all federal funding for the 2026 FIFA World Cup and prevent visa authorizations for FIFA officials from entering the United States until US Soccer provides equitable payment to the women's team.[39] For doping, bidding, and governance, international sport is rarely punishing individuals for violating their rules, and instead it is national criminal laws which are resulting in penalties. These experiences – from individuals transporting illegal doping substances across national borders to the widespread financial fraud and corruption of FIFA officials – demonstrates the broader implications within sport beyond a domestic legal system and simple criminal acts.[40] Taking the various aspects raised here and considering them from countries beyond the traditional sport powers will reveal greater nuances and new ways in which sport and politics impact one another and influence the trajectory of sport history.

Sport and politics

Notes

1 Barbara Keys, *Globalizing Sport: National Rivalry and International Community in the 1930s* (Cambridge, MA: Harvard University Press, 2006); Jenifer Parks, *The Olympic Games, the Soviet Sport Bureaucracy, and the Cold War: Red Sport, Red Tape* (Lanham, MD: Lexington Books, 2016); Xu Guoqi, *Olympic Dreams: China and Sports, 1895–2008* (Cambridge: Harvard University Press, 2008).

2 Lincoln Allison, *The Politics of Sport* (Manchester: Manchester University Press, 1986); Pierre Arnaud and James Riordan, *Sport and International Politics: The Impact of Fascism and Communism on Sport* (London: E & FN Spon, 1998); Christopher Hill, *Olympic Politics Athens to Atlanta*, 2nd edition (Manchester: Manchester University Press, 1996); Wanda Ellen Wakefield, *Playing to Win: Sports and the American Military, 1898–1945* (Albany: State University of New York Press, 1997); Tony Mason and Eliza Riedi, *Sport and the Military: The British Armed Forces 1880–1960* (Cambridge: Cambridge University Press, 2010); Thomas M. Hunt, 'Countering the Soviet Threat in the Olympic Medals Race: The Amateur Sports Act of 1978 and American Athletics Policy Reform', *The International Journal of the History of Sport* 24, no. 6 (2007): 796–818.

3 Joseph S. Nye, 'Soft Power and American Foreign Policy', *Political Science Quarterly* 119, no. 2 (2004): 255–270.

4 Geoffrey Allen Pigman, 'International Sport and Diplomacy's Public Dimension: Governments, Sporting Federations and the Global Audience', *Diplomacy & Statecraft* 25, no. 1 (2014): 96.

5 Peter Beck, *Scoring for Britain: International Football and International Politics, 1900–1939* (London: Frank Cass, 1999); Sayuri Guthrie-Shimizu, *Transpacific Field of Dreams: How Baseball Linked the United States and Japan in Peace and War* (Chapel Hill: University of North Carolina Press, 2012).

6 Damion L. Thomas, *Globetrotting: African American Athletes and Cold War Politics* (Urbana: University of Illinois Press, 2012); Kevin B. Witherspoon, '"Going to the Fountainhead": Black American Athletes as Cultural Ambassadors in Africa, 1970–1971', *International Journal of the History of Sport* 30, no. 13 (2013): 1508–1522; Ashley Brown, 'Swinging for the State Department: American Women Tennis Players in Diplomatic Goodwill Tours, 1941–1959', *Journal of Sport History* 42, no.3 (2015): 289–309.

7 John Soares, '"Our Way of Life against Theirs": Ice Hockey and the Cold War', in *Diplomatic Games: Sport, Statecraft and International Relations since 1945*, ed. Heather L. Dichter and Andrew L. Johns (Lexington: University Press of Kentucky, 2014), 251–296; Fan Hong and Lu Zhouxiang, 'Politics First, Competition Second: Sport and China's Foreign Diplomacy in the 1960s and 1970s', in *Diplomatic Games*, 385–407; Kausik Bandyopadhyay, 'Feel Good, Goodwill and India's Friendship Tour of Pakistan, 2004: Cricket, Politics and Diplomacy in Twenty-First-Century India', *The International Journal of the History of Sport* 25, no. 12 (2008): 1654–1670.

8 Evelyn Mertin, 'Steadfast Friendship and Brotherly Help: The Distinctive Soviet-East German Sport Relationship within the Socialist Bloc', in *Diplomatic Games*, 53–84; Chin-Fang Kuo, 'Sports, Diplomacy and Sense of Existence: The Table Tennis Coaches of the republic of China in Latin America during the Cold War, 1970–1980s' (paper presented at 20th Congress of the International Society for the History of Physical Education and Sport, 14–17 July 2019).

9 Solveig Straume, 'Norwegian Naivety Meets Tanzanian Reality: The Case of the Norwegian Sports Development Aid Programme, Sport for All, in Dar es Salaam in the 1980s', *International Journal of the History of Sport* 29, no. 11 (2012): 1577–1599.

10 'Sports Diplomacy', Bureau of Educational and Cultural Affairs, U.S. Department of State, https://eca.state.gov/programs-initiatives/initiatives/sports-diplomacy (accessed 16 April 2017).

11 Many articles about these programmes have been published in *The Journal of Sport for Development*, http s://jsfd.org/, which published its first issue in 2013.

12 Ingrid Beutler, 'Sport Serving Development and Peace: Achieving the Goals of the United Nations through Sport', *Sport in Society* 11, no. 4 (2008): 359–369.

13 Ian Henry and Mansour Al-Tauqi, 'The Development of Olympic Solidarity: West and Non-West (Core and Periphery) Relations in the Olympic World', *The International Journal of the History of Sport* 25, no. 3 (2008): 355–369. See also the Olympic Solidarity section of the IOC's website, https://www.olympic.org/olympic-solidarity.

14 John R. Gold and Margaret M. Gold, 'Olympic Cities: Regeneration, City Rebranding and Changing Urban Agendas', *Geography Compass* 2, no. 1 (2008): 301.

15 David Black, 'Dreaming Big: The Pursuit of "Second Order" Games as a Strategic Response to Globalization', *Sport in Society* 11, no. 4 (2008): 467–480.

16 Brazil hosted the 2007 Pan-American Games, 2014 World Cup, and 2016 Olympics; Russia the 2014 Winter Olympics and 2018 World Cup; India the 2010 Commonwealth Games; China the 2008 Olympics and 2022 Winter Olympics, and South Africa the 2010 World Cup. South Africa had also been awarded the 2022 Commonwealth Games but had them withdrawn after almost no progress had been made with plans.

17 Keys, *Globalizing Sport*.

18 Euclides de Freitas Couto and Alan Castellano Valente, 'The World Cup Is Ours! The Myth of Brazilianness in Lula's Diplomatic Rhetoric, 2007–2014', in *Soccer Diplomacy: International Relations and Football Since 1914*, ed. Heather L. Dichter (Lexington: University Press of Kentucky, 2020), 198–220; Brenda Elsey, '"Because We Have Nothing": The 1962 World Cup and Cold War Politics in Chile', in *Soccer Diplomacy*, 94–115; Nina Kramareva and Jonathan Grix, '"War and Peace" at the 1980 Moscow and 2014 Sochi Olympics: The Role of Hard and Soft Power in Russian Identity', *International Journal of the History of Sport* 35, no. 14 (2018): 1407–1427.

19 Barbara J. Keys, ed., *The Ideals of Global Sport: From Peace to Human Rights* (Philadelphia: University of Pennsylvania, 2019).

20 Stephen R. Wenn, 'Peter Ueberroth's Legacy: How the 1984 Los Angeles Olympics Changed the Trajectory of the Olympic Movement', *The International Journal of the History of Sport* 32, no. 1 (2015): 157–171; Robert Simon Edelman, 'The Russians Are Not Coming! The Soviet Withdrawal from the Games of the XXIII Olympiad', *The International Journal of the History of Sport* 32, no. 1 (2015): 9–36.

21 United States General Accounting Office, 'Olympic Games: Federal Government Provides Significant Support', September 2000, GAO/GGD-00–183, https://www.gao.gov/new.items/gg00183.pdf (accessed 2 August 2019).

22 Richard D. Mandell, *The Olympics of 1972: A Munich Diary* (Chapel Hill, NC: University of North Carolina Press, 1991); Simon Reeve, *One Day in September: The Full Story of the 1972 Munich Olympics Massacre and the Israeli Revenge Operation 'Wrath of God'* (London: Faber, 2001).

23 Philip Boyle, Dominique Clément, and Kevin D. Haggerty, 'Iterations of Olympic Security: Montreal and Vancouver', *Security Dialogue* 46, no. 2 (2015): 109–125.

24 Kristine Toohey, 'Terrorism, Sport and Public Policy in the Risk Society', *Sport in Society* 11, no. 4 (2008): 429–442; Colin J. Bennett and Kevin Haggerty, *Security Games: Surveillance and Control at Mega-Events* (London: Routledge, 2011); Pete Fussey, Jon Coaffee, and Dick Hobbs, *Securing and Sustaining the Olympic City: Reconfiguring London for 2012 and Beyond* (London: Routledge, 2016); Ramón Spaaij, 'Terrorism and Security at the Olympics: Empirical Trends and Evolving Research Agendas', *The International Journal of the History of Sport* 33, no. 4 (2016): 451–468.

25 Jules Boykoff and Pete Fussey, 'London's Shadow Legacies: Security and Activism at the 2012 Olympics', *Contemporary Social Science* 9, no. 2 (2014): 253–270.

26 'Sochi Given 2014 Winter Olympics', *BBC Sport*, 5 July 2007, http://news.bbc.co.uk/sport1/hi/front_page/6271122.stm (accessed 2 August 2019).

27 de Freitas Couto and Valente, 'The World Cup is Ours! in *Soccer Diplomacy*, 198–220; Larry Bennett, Michael Bennett, Stephen Alexander, and Joseph Persky, 'The Political and Civic Implications of Chicago's Unsuccessful Bid to Host the 2016 Olympic Games', *Journal of Sport and Social Issues* 37, no. 4 (2013): 364–383; 'Pain in Spain as Madrid Loses 2016 Olympic Vote to Rio de Janeiro at the Last', *Telegraph*, 2 October 2009, https://www.telegraph.co.uk/sport/olympics/6256044/Pain-in-Spain-as-Madrid-loses-2016-Olympic-vote-to-Rio-de-Janeiro-at-the-last.html (accessed 2 August 2019); Yunji de Nies, Karen Travers, and Huma Khan, 'Rio de Janeiro to Host Olympics 2016, Chicago Loses Despite Obama Pitch', ABC News, 2 October 2009, https://abcnews.go.com/Politics/rio-de-janeiro-host-olympics-2016-chicago-loses/story?id=8730822 (accessed 2 August 2019).

28 Owen Gibson, 'Tokyo Wins Race to Host 2020 Olympic Games', *Guardian*, 7 September 2013, https://www.theguardian.com/sport/2013/sep/07/tokyo-host-2020-olympic-games (accessed 2 August 2019).

29 Udo Merkel and Misuk Kim, 'Third Time Lucky!? PyeongChang's Bid to Host the 2018 Winter Olympics – Politics, Policy and Practice', *The International Journal of the History of Sport* 28, no. 16 (2011): 2365–2383.

30 Helen Lenskyj, *Olympic Industry Resistance: Challenging Olympic Power and Propaganda* (Albany: SUNY Press, 2008).

31 'Prague 2020 Olympic Bid in Trouble', GamesBids.com, 22 May 2009, https://gamesbids.com/eng/summer-olympic-bids/future-summer-bids/prague-2020-olympic-bid-in-trouble/ (accessed 2 August 2019); Jan Richter, 'Prague Drops 2020 Summer Olympics Bid', Radio Praha, 16 June 2009, https://

www.radio.cz/en/section/curraffrs/prague-drops-2020-summer-olympics-bid (accessed 2 August 2019).

32 'Rome's 2020 Olympic Bid Scrapped', ESPN, 14 February 2012, https://www.espn.com/olympics/story/_/id/7574333/rome-2020-summer-olympics-games-bid-scrapped-italy (accessed 2 August 2019); 'Rome 2024 Olympic Bid Collapses in Acrimony', BBC, 21 September 2016, https://www.bbc.co.uk/news/world-europe-37432928 (accessed 2 August 2019).

33 Eva Kassens-Noor and John Lauermann, 'Mechanisms of Policy Failure: Boston's 2024 Olympic Bid', *Urban Studies* 55, no. 15 (2018): 3369–3384.

34 Kassens-Noor and Lauermann, 'Mechanisms of Policy Failure', 3380; Chris Dempsey and Andrew Zimbalist, *No Boston Olympics: How and Why Smart Cities Are Passing the Torch* (Lebanon, NH: ForEdge, 2017).

35 Karolos Grohmann, 'Olympics: IOC Overhauls Bidding Process for Games to Stop Dropouts', Reuters, 26 June 2019, https://uk.reuters.com/article/uk-olympics-ioc/olympics-ioc-overhauls-bidding-process-for-games-to-stop-dropouts-idUKKCN1TR1M4 (accessed 3 August 2019).

36 Christopher Merrett, '"In Nothing Else are the Deprivers so Deprived": South African Sport, Apartheid and Foreign Relations, 1945–71', *The International Journal of the History of Sport* 13, no. 2 (1996): 146–165; Louis Moore, *We Will Win the Day: The Civil Rights Movement the Black Athlete, and the Quest for Equality* (Santa Barbara, CA: Praeger, 2017).

37 'The POW Alliance', https://protectourwinters.org/the-pow-alliance/ (accessed 2 August 2019).

38 Chelsea Little, 'Newell, Kalla, Brandsdal, and More Urge Binding Resolution at Paris Climate Negotiations', FasterSkier.com, 2 December 2015, https://fasterskier.com/fsarticle/newell-kalla-brandsdal-and-more-urge-binding-resolution-at-paris-climate-negotiations/ (accessed 2 August 2019).

39 Abigail Hess, 'House Bill Would Block 2026 Men's World Cup Funding Until Women's Team Receives "Equitable Wages"', CNBC, 24 July 2019, https://www.cnbc.com/2019/07/24/bill-would-block-world-cup-funds-until-womens-team-receives-fair-pay.html (accessed 29 August 2019).

40 Bastien Soule and Ludovic Lestrelin, 'The Puerto Affair: Revealing the Difficulties of the Fight Against Doping', *Journal of Sport and Social Issues* 35, no. 2 (2011): 186–208; Roy McCree, 'High Jack: Soccer and Sport Diplomacy in the Caribbean, 1961–2017', in *Soccer Diplomacy*, 178–197.

17

SPORT AND INTERNATIONAL RELATIONS

Bruce Kidd

The history of modern sports cannot be told without a fulsome account of the international relations that enfold them. From their very beginnings in the industrializing societies of nineteenth-century Europe and North America, the male organizers, advocates, and participants of modern sports exported and played them with peoples of other countries. At the same time, politicians, capitalists, and evangelists of all kinds, including Christian fundamentalists, first-wave feminists, and revolutionary socialists, sought to recruit sports to their international goals. Well before the end of the nineteenth century, there were international competitions, 'world' championships, and international tours in cricket, rowing, athletics, lacrosse, and baseball. In each case, the organizers, participants, sponsors, and those who wrote or read about them in the rising mass media, sought to influence or at least understand the experience in the context of what they knew or wanted to say about the peoples and countries involved and the relationships they desired between them. We can thus say that the very meanings and possibilities of sports – their ambitions, rules, events, and the 'representational status' of athletes and teams – have been inextricably bound up with the international relationships, and the myriad of economic, social, and political connections, that have been fostered through them.

International sports have not just been about competition, travel, and communication. They have often been mobilized for influence and power. In 1883, the Canadian George Beers, who refashioned the Haudenosaunee game of *tewaarathon* into the modern game of lacrosse, took two Montreal teams, one Euro-Canadian and the other Indigenous, to Britain to play a series of exhibitions. He sought to impart an enthusiasm for the game and a better understanding of its rules, use the occasion to advertise immigration to Canada – he distributed 150,000 pieces of promotional literature – and justify the newly independent settler state's subjection of the Indigenous Peoples. At the same time, the Indigenous Peoples joined these and similar tours to assert their own identity, both with foreign audiences and rulers like Queen Victoria and among themselves.[1]

Imperialism was a powerful vehicle for sports. Within the far-flung British Empire, soldiers, missionaries, and educators promoted sport, especially cricket and soccer, to impose deference to the British way of life upon nations and peoples they regarded as 'barbarous'. As Mangan has shown in his voluminous scholarship, the British Empire was in part an enormous sports complex, driven institutionally by the military and the church; 'sport travelled

144 DOI: 10.4324/9780429318306-20

the world with the bullet and the bible'.[2] The result was the presence of sports fields and clubs, organized teams, well-attended and reported competitions in every country the British ruled. In the emerging American empire and spheres of influence, baseball and basketball became the sports of influence and colonization, but the pattern was much the same. The American military introduced baseball to Japan and Cuba, while the entrepreneur Albert Spalding took the game (and the necessity to buy Spalding equipment) to Egypt, Italy, England, and Ireland.[3] YMCA missionaries took basketball to the Philippines, South America, and Europe.[4] Although less well studied, the imposition of the western way of playing in the countries thus colonized was often debated, even resisted. While the dominant culture in the capitalist countries assumes that the sports form is neutral of social and political influence, it was rarely understood that way in those countries whose traditional games and pastimes were being marginalized or eradicated in the process.[5]

One significant early project of sport and international relations was the modern Olympic Games established by Pierre de Coubertin. While Coubertin was deeply imbedded in the prevailing ethnocentrism and class and gender biases of his age, he sought to turn international sport into a pedagogy for intercultural understanding. Through the auspices of peaceful exchange and competition, he hoped that participants would gain respect for each other and, as a result, pressure their governments to resolve conflict through diplomacy and negotiation rather than war.[6] So successful did Coubertin's Games eventually become that they are now an important site for a wide range of other interventions intended to shape international relations – by international and national governments, non-state actors, and increasingly, corporations.

The history of sport and international relations has thus been extremely, even bewilderingly, complex, tumultuous, and far-reaching. The dynamic of sports and international relations has continually evolved in step with the increasing globalization and the tremendous economic, social, political, and technological transformations and ruptures of the last 200 years. In this short chapter, it will not be possible to give attention to all the ambitions, activities, achievements, and debates that should be covered under such a heading, but I hope to give sufficient introduction to encourage readers to undertake further study, even their own research. It's an important, fascinating subject.

My plan is to discuss the major developments in four distinct periods: (1) the decades prior to the First World War, when most of the important institutions of international sport were established: (2) the interwar period, during which time the Coubertin Olympics became highly politicized and strong feminist and socialist movements offered alternative visions: (3) the Cold War following the Second World War, when significant decolonization took place, polarized by super-power rivalries; and (4) the current period of neo-liberal globalization. I write from the perspective of a political economist and a lifelong participant in and enthusiast of the modern Olympic Movement and its ambition of intercultural understanding through sports.

Globalization and the modern Olympic Games

The men and boys who developed the first prototypes of modern sports in the all-male 'public schools', universities, and private clubs of industrializing Britain imbued them with ideologies of respectable masculinity (often known as 'Muscular Christianity'), self-improvement, nationalism, and progress. The new sports were expected to prepare participants for the responsibilities of family, career, and the British Empire, and help them build supportive networks of like-minded men. Sports were explicitly framed as a project of 'modernity'.[7]

As the known boundaries of the western world were pushed back through exploration, trade, immigration, settlement, imperialism and tourism, those at the forefront took sports with them. Elites and entrepreneurs in the United States, the British colonies, and Europe quickly adopted them, sent competitors to the new world championships, and added new sports of their own. Beers, for example, fashioned lacrosse as 'Canada's national sport'. Such was the excitement and popularity of the new sports that those excluded – the working classes, women, and the colonial populations in Africa, Asia, and the Caribbean – took them up as well, even if they had to do so 'outside the fence', or remodel them in their own cultural terms as the Trobriand Islanders did with cricket.[8] The tremendous investments in the new technologies of transportation and communication that drove the Industrial Revolution, especially the railroad, steamship, telegraph, 'stop action' photography, and the rotary press, significantly enabled and accelerated the standardization, promotion, and diffusion of sports. So did convergent projects of internationalization. Robertson has called the decades between 1870s and the 1920s the 'take off stage' of globalization, during which the ideas of an 'international community' and universal 'human rights' first gained widespread support, world's fairs became popular, international organizations (e.g. Red Cross) created, global awards (e.g. Nobel Prizes) celebrated, and the international language of Esperanto invented.[9] The internationalization of sports contributed to and benefited from these developments and relationships.

Pierre de Coubertin took advantage of and expanded these emerging ideas and networks when he established the International Olympic Committee (IOC) in 1894 and organized his first Games in 1896 in Athens. Others had organized modern events cloaked in the symbols of classical Greece, notably the French Revolutions' *jeux olympiques*, the Montreal Olympic Club's games of 1844, Evangelos Zappas' Athens Olympics of 1850, 1870, and 1875, and Penny Brookes' Olympics held between 1850 and 1890 in Much Wenlock, England. But they were all of a local or national character. Coubertin's innovation was to create *international* competitions in the name of the Olympics, governed by a small, self-selected body of sports leaders from around the western world. The combination of a storied classical pedigree with international competitions in the leading sports of the day resonated with the spirit of the early twentieth century, and gradually attracted many others to his project. Despite the fact that Coubertin had to stage the first three Olympics after Athens under the auspices of world's fairs in Paris (1900), St. Louis (1904), and London (1908), forcing him to share branding and scheduling with the fairs, his games gradually gained an international following. The breakthrough came in 1908, when the IOC and the London organizing committee insisted that National Olympic Committees (NOCs) field teams selected in national trials, so that the competitions took on a nation-to-nation character. (Previously athletes entered on an individual or club basis.) Linking the Olympics to the nation-state, with a national team march past in the opening ceremonies, national team uniforms, and victory ceremonies that celebrated national flags and anthems, proved an act of genius. It simultaneously embedded the Olympics in the two dominant narratives of the modern period – the importance of individual striving and accomplishment, and the strength, distinct character, and support of national communities. The new formula unleashed many new resources, including financial contributions from the state and massive media coverage. Never again did the IOC have to partner with a world's fair.

There are 'multiple narratives' at every Olympics, world championship, and international event, and a kaleidoscope of interactions between competitors, members of delegations, representatives of the host communities, and representatives of civil society. Major sporting events serve as sites for diplomacy, entrepreneurship, religious proselytizing, and espionage.

Sport and international relations

Yet ever since the 1908 Games, at least one major part of the story has revolved around nation–state relationships. Large and powerful nations compete to demonstrate their strength and accomplishments, smaller states and national communities with IOC-recognized NOCs without independent statehood participate to gain legitimacy on the world stage. It has been said that Finland 'ran its way to independence' because at a time when it was a grand duchy within the Russian Empire, Finnish athletes, notably the distance runner Hannes Kolehmainen, competed in the 1908 and 1912 Olympics with great *élan*, asserting their claim to recognition as a nation state.

The IOC also encouraged the creation and strengthening of International Federations (IFs) to govern their respective sports and organize them during the Olympics. By the outbreak of the First World War, a stable structure for international relationships in sports was in place.

The interwar alternatives

In the early twentieth century, Coubertin and his IOC colleagues, like many others in Europe, tried to halt the mounting arms race and the steady march to global conflict.[10] They awarded the 1916 Olympics to Berlin in the hope that the investment and preparations for the Games would distract the Germans from war. When fighting broke out, the IOC moved its headquarters to neutral Switzerland. After the Armistice, the bitterness emanating from the senseless slaughter and destruction was so great that there was little appetite to renew relationships as they were in 1914. The IOC banned the 'aggressor' nations of Austria, Bulgaria, Germany, Hungary, and Turkey from the 1920 Olympics in Antwerp and Germany from the 1924 Games in Paris.

The resentment within Germany against that country's harsh treatment after the war contributed to the rise of Nazism. Hitler turned the opportunity to oversee the hosting of the 1936 Olympics into a propaganda showcase for his regime and a cover for his brutal persecution of Jews, socialists, LGBTQ, and other minorities, prompting world-wide calls for an Olympic boycott and an attempt to hold counter-Olympics in Barcelona. He further politicized the narratives of international sport, making human rights and the auspices of staging games central issues ever since.

The international socialist movement had also opposed the arms race and the nation-state belligerence that led to the First World War. Yet when the fighting broke, most socialist parties and the trade unions that supported them encouraged their members to support their respective country's armies. Those who continued to oppose the war eventually split from the movement to create Communist parties and support the fledging Soviet Union. These politics triggered two very different approaches to international sport between the wars. The Socialist Workers' Sports International (SWSI), formed in 1913, regrouped after the war to hold winter and summer Workers' Olympiads every six years. The first Olympiads were held in Germany in 1925. The 1931 Workers' Olympiad in Vienna was arguably the largest international sporting event ever held, with 80,000 participants, 25,000 of whom were women. Instead of the overarching narratives of nation–state competition that characterized the IOC's games, the Workers' Olympics focused on international solidarity among the working people of all countries, 'no more war', and sport-for-all.[11] The Red Sport International, closely controlled by the Soviet Union, held multi-sport Spartakiads every four years to demonstrate the strength and militancy of the Communist working class. It was only with the rise of Nazism that the two internationals cautiously joined to oppose the 1936 Olympics and compete together in the 1937 Workers' Olympiad in Antwerp.[12]

The interwar period saw the creation of a feminist sports international as well, la Fédération Sportive Féminine Internationale (FSFI). Because Coubertin's Olympics excluded women, French feminist Alice Milliat organized Women's Olympics in Paris in 1922 and Gothenburg in 1926, and Women's World Games in Prague in 1930 and London in 1934. The emphasis of the Women's Olympics was vigorous women's participation and the encouragement of women's leadership. In 1928, Milliat agreed to change the name to the Women's World Games in exchange for ten athletics events on the IOC programme. She kept her part of the bargain but the IOC did not. After London, Milliat disbanded her games in the vain hope that the IOC would appoint an equal number of female members and create an equal number of women's events.[13]

The Cold War and decolonization

The geo-political, economic, and technological changes that followed the Second World War profoundly reshaped the international relationships and meanings of sports. Although the Soviet Union had fought the Axis powers in tandem with the western nations during the war, the 'grand alliance' fell apart when the Soviet Union consolidated control over the countries of eastern Europe immediately after the war and the United States initiated a strategy of containment. Within a few years, in what became known as the 'Cold War', most countries in the world were tightly aligned with either the Soviet Union or the United States, and the ideological, economic, and military competition between the two 'blocs' structured virtually every aspect of international relations. While the Soviet Union had previously railed against the Coubertin Olympics as 'bourgeois' and 'bosses' sport, it made peace with the IOC in the late 1940s and entered the 1952 Olympics in Helsinki. (Such were the tensions that a separate athletes' village was created for them.) The Soviets and their satellites (especially the German Democratic Republic and Cuba) invested heavily in science-led, professional sport development as a strategy of showcasing the strength of their political systems. They quickly enjoyed remarkable success. In six of the nine Olympics and seven of the nine Winter Olympics in which they competed, Soviet athletes won the largest number of gold medals. The first time they competed in Olympic ice hockey in 1956, with a remodelled bandy[14] team, they won the gold medal, relegating the vaunted Canadians to bronze.

The Soviet bloc success spurred western countries to follow suit. In 1961, the Canadian government created an entire state-driven programme to boost Canadian athletes, on the grounds (in the words of Prime Minister Diefenbaker) that Canadian performances in international competition 'shape the hearts and minds of people around the world'.[15] The ultimate effect of these changes, the significant increase in the number of international competitions and the global spread of television, was to intensify training and competition to the point where most athletes became fully paid full-time performers, trained to focus entirely upon their performances and expound upon the values and attributes of their nation states (and corporate sponsors). Coubertin's aspiration to intercultural understanding through international sport was largely forgotten.[16]

The webs of international sport were also significantly transformed by the decolonization that followed the Second World War, beginning with the independence of Indonesia from the Netherlands in 1945, of the Philippines from the United States in 1946, and of India and Pakistan from Britain in 1947. Whether it was through the peaceful transfer of power or military liberation, virtually all of the European and American colonies in Africa, Asia, and the Caribbean won their independence by the 1990s. Although many were hesitant to adopt

Sport and international relations

western sports, most of the newly independent nations created national sports federations and NOCs affiliated to the established international federations and the IOC. The opportunity to march into an Olympic Opening Ceremony as distinct nations under their own flags before a worldwide television audience proved a powerful incentive.

The post-colonial relationships were complicated by several factors. The established sports bodies were extremely reluctant to welcome the newly independent sports leaders as equals. When the IOC was created, it was the intention to appoint one or two new members for every new country admitted, but once those nations came from the Global South, the idea was dropped.[17] In 1976, there were 45 National Olympic Committees (NOCs) in Africa, but only seven IOC members from the continent; one of those was a white planter from Kenya, the other an unrepentant white representative of the expelled apartheid South Africa. To this day, almost twice as many IOC members come from Europe than any other region. These tensions fuelled two important opposition attempts. The first of these was the Games of the Newly Emerging Forces (GANEFO), established in 1963 by Indonesian president Sukarno to unify Asian, African, Latin American, and Socialist countries and to 'shake the world balance of power and weaken the economic domination of the world by industrialized countries'.[18] The first GANEFO were held in Jakarta in 1963, with both western sports and games indigenous to Asia. A prominent participant was the People's Republic of China, which at the time did not compete in the IOC's Games. Forty-eight countries participated, including Japan. But the IOC suspended the participating athletes, Sukarno was overthrown in a coup, and the Games were never held again.

A much more successful effort to transform international relations in sports was the campaign to isolate apartheid South Africa in sport, initiated by non-white sports leaders in the early 1960s to protest the brutal system of racist exploitation and repression that the tiny white minority forced upon every aspect of South African society, including sports. The campaign sought to persuade every country in the world to prevent its athletes from playing South Africa in any sport, and the IOC and other bodies to adopt strong anti-racist policies. It became a powerful rallying cry against the vestiges of colonialism. Drawing support from African, Asian, and Caribbean countries, the Soviet bloc, the anti-apartheid movements, and, eventually, many western governments, the campaign succeeded in expelling white South Africa from the Olympics and the major IFs, and by the mid-1980s ending all official sporting tours to South Africa. It thus contributed in dramatic, symbolic ways to the overthrow of apartheid in 1990.[19]

Both the Cold War and apartheid precipitated major conflicts. The 1980 Olympics in Moscow and the 1984 Games in Los Angeles faced tit-for-tat boycotts by western and Soviet bloc countries respectively, while the 1968, 1972, and 1976 Olympics were threatened or disrupted by issues emanating from apartheid and colonialism. In 1976, 29 African, Asian, and Caribbean countries walked out or stayed home from the Montreal Games after the IOC refused to take a position on a New Zealand rugby tour of apartheid South Africa. A previous generation of sports leaders, notably Avery Brundage who was IOC president from 1952 to 1972, had tried to wish away geo-political conflicts with the mantra that 'sport and politics do not mix'. But their successors concluded that they must actively navigate such conflicts to prevent or minimize major disruptions. Thus Juan Antonio Samaranch, who was IOC president from 1980 to 2001, repeatedly flew back and forth between western and Soviet-bloc capitals to ensure that the 1988 Olympics in Seoul, Republic of Korea (South Korea), which did not recognize the Soviet bloc, would occur without another boycott. Even then, while most of the Soviet bloc did participate, Cuba, Ethiopia, and Democratic People's Republic of Korea (North Korea) stayed away.[20]

149

Neo-liberal globalization and sport for development and peace

The collapse of the Soviet Union and its satellite states in 1990 significantly discredited the idea of state-led strategies of governance and development, accelerating the trends for reduced government, expanded free market capitalism, and unrestricted global trade that began in the United States and Britain under Ronald Reagan and Margaret Thatcher respectively in the 1980s. These ideas are known as neo-liberalism. Increasingly, athletes, teams, national and international federations, and major championships were encouraged/forced to commercialize their activities through marketing strategies, corporate sponsorships, for-profit recruitment, coaching and training camps, and media partnerships. While narratives and relationships grounded in the nation-state continue to dominate the Olympic Games, the run-away privatization of other forms of international sport has made the business side of sports – branding, production, market share, and so on – an integral part of the discussion.

Neo-liberalism eschews 'rights-based' approaches to the development of societies and insists upon private ventures as a way to deal with opportunities and social problems. To fill the gap left by the downsizing of government and to address the woeful inequality in the global provision of sports, a vast network of individuals, corporations, non-governmental organizations (NGOs), and sports bodies conducts programmes in every corner of the globe under the banner of 'sport for development and peace'.[21] The IOC, through Olympic Solidarity, and IFs like FIFA are major contributors. Many of the non-governmental activities have been athlete-initiated and are conducted by youthful volunteers, financed by the charitable contributions of first-world citizens. On the one hand, they bring the joys of sport to many who would never otherwise experience them, and create and strengthen new relationships of intercultural understanding and internationalism among the participants. On the other hand, they rarely address the most pressing needs of the receiving societies, and often reproduce first-world cultural superiority among the volunteers, and feelings of subordination and impoverishment among the recipients in the Global South.[22]

In summary, during the last 200 years, modern sports have become an indelible component of international culture, spinning countless, complex webs of economic, political, social, and sporting relationships. These relationships affect the experiences of the participants as much as the actual play on the field.

Notes

1 Don Morrow, 'The Great Canadian Lacrosse Tours of 1976 and 1883', in *Proceedings of the 5th Canadian Symposium on the History of Sport and Physical Education*, ed. Bruce Kidd (Toronto: School of Physical and Health Education, University of Toronto, 1982), 11–22; Gillian Poulter, *Becoming Native in a Foreign Land: Sport, Visual Culture and Identity in Montreal 1840–1885* (Vancouver: UBC Press, 2009); and Allan Downey, *The Creator's Game: Lacrosse, Identity and Indigenous Nationhood* (Vancouver: UBC Press, 2018).

2 J.A. Mangan, *The Games Ethic and Imperialism: Aspects of the Diffusion of an Ideal* (Portland, OR: Cass, 1995).

3 Thomas Zeiler, *Ambassadors in Pin Stripes: The Spalding World Tour and the Birth of the American Empire* (Lanham, MD: Rowan and Littlefield, 2006).

4 Robert Elias, *The Empire Strikes Out: How Baseball Sold US Foreign Policy and Promoted the American Way Abroad* (New York: New Press, 2010).

5 Gerald Glassford, *Application of a Theory of Games to Traditional Eskimo Culture* (New York: Arno, 1976); and Boria Majumdar, *Cricket in Colonial India* (London: Routledge, 2008).

6 Pierre de Coubertin, *Olympism: Selected Writings*, ed. Norbert Muller (Lausanne: International Olympic Committee, 2000); and John MacAloon, *This Great Symbol: Pierre de Coubertin and the Origins of the Modern Olympic Games* (Chicago: University of Chicago Press, 1981).

Sport and international relations

7 Richard Gruneau, *Sport and Modernity* (Cambridge, UK: Polity, 2017).
8 C.L.R. James, *Beyond a Boundary* (Kingston, Jamaica: Sangster's Book Stores, 1963); and Jerry Leach, *Trobriand Cricket* (Alexandria, VA: Filmakers Library, 1975).
9 Roland Robertson, *Globalization: Social Theory and Global Culture* (London: Sage, 1992).
10 Otto Schantz, 'Pierre de Coubertin's "Civilizing Mission"', in *Pathways. Critiques and Discourse in Olympic Research,* eds. Robert Barney, Michael Heine, and Kevin Wamsley (London, Ontario: International Centre for Olympic Studies, 2008), 53–62.
11 Kalevi Olin, ed., *Sport, Peace and Development: International Worker Sport 1913–2013* (Vienna: SportVerlag, 2013).
12 The SWSI and the Workers' Olympics continue to this day as the International Workers and Amateurs in Sport Federation (CSIT) and the World Sport Games. The Soviet Union disbanded the RSI following the Second World War and joined the IOC's Olympics.
13 Mary Leigh and Therese Bonin, 'The Pioneering Role of Madam Alice Milliat and the FSFI in Establishing International Track and Field Competition for Women', *Journal of Sport History* 4, no. 1 (1977): 72–83.
14 Bandy is a team sport, played with sticks and a ball on a large sheet of ice, mostly in northern Europe. It has many similarities to ice and field hockey.
15 Donald Macintosh, Thomas Bedecki, and C.E.S. Franks, *Sport and Politics in Canada: Federal Government Involvement since 1961* (Kingston: Queen's McGill, 1987).
16 Bruce Kidd, '"Seoul to the World, the World to Seoul" … and Ben Johnson: Canada at the 1988 Olympics', in *Toward One World Beyond All Barriers*, ed. Koh Byong-Ik (Seoul: Poong Nam, 1990), vol. 1, 434–454; and John MacAloon, *Intercultural Education and Olympic Sport* (Montreal: Olympic Academy of Canada, 1986).
17 Barbara Keys, 'The Early Cold War Olympics 1952–1960: Political, Economic and Human Rights Dimensions', in *The Palgrave Handbook of Olympic Studies*, eds. Helen Lenskyj and Stephen Wagg (New York: Palgrave Macmillan, 2012), 72–87.
18 Swanpo Sie, 'Sports and Politics: The Case of the Asian Games and the GANEFO', in *Sport and International Relations*, eds. B. Lowe, D. Kanin, and A. Strenk (Champaign, IL: Stipes, 1978), 279–296.
19 Douglas Booth, *The Race Game: Sport and Politics in South Africa* (London: Cass, 1998).
20 Richard W. Pound, *Five Rings Over Korea: The Secret Negotiations over the 1988 Olympics in Korea* (Boston: Little Brown, 1994).
21 Bruce Kidd, 'A New Social Movement: Sport for Development and Peace', *Sport in Society* 11, no. 4 (2008): 370–380; and Simon C. Darnell, Russell Field, and Bruce Kidd, *The History and Politics of Sport-for-Development: Activists, Ideologues and Reformers* (London: Palgrave Macmillan, 2019).
22 Simon Darnell, *Sport for Development and Peace: A Critical Sociology* (London: Bloomsbury Academic, 2012).

18
SPORT AND NATIONALISM

Liam O'Callaghan

It is a truism that the relationship between sport and nationalism is a complex one. This is due, in the main, to the complexity and multifariousness of nationalism itself. Nationalism has been described by scholars as, among many things: an idea, a sentiment, a form of politics, a call to political action, a cognitive phenomenon, and so on.[1] Accompanying this diversity of paradigms is the contradictory nature of how nations are perceived. Thus nations can be perceived as natural, organic entities, or the product of an elaborate process of invention.[2] Breuilly has pointed out that of all political ideologies, nationalism is 'through and through historical'.[3] A shared sense of history binds the people of any nation together. But this historicism is contradictory. While many nations claim ancient heritage, and some historians trace the origins of national traditions to the distant past, others dispute this apparent antiquity and argue that nationalism is a thoroughly modern phenomenon, a synthesis of eighteenth-century ideas and nineteenth-century technology.[4] One can view nationalism as being relatively benign or dangerously nefarious. Critics view nationalism, especially variants of it derived from ethnic identity, as illiberal and exclusivist. Nationalism, after all, is fascism's underpinning ideology. On the other hand, civic nationalism, with its grounding in liberal values, has a more benign reputation.[5] Though the categorization of nationalism into 'civic' and 'ethnic' variants may be simplistic, the important point holds: nationalism is the subject of both positive and negative moral judgment.

Nationalisms are at once universal and particular. Smith has argued that all nationalist ideologies will incorporate the goals of national identity, unity, and autonomy.[6] National identities, in turn, will include some of the following shared characteristics: language, religion, culture, a sense of history, a desire for sovereign statehood, and a territorial claim (whether realized or not), and so on.[7] The nation does not always achieve sovereignty. Thus along with nation states, we have stateless nations and multinational states. With all of these factors in mind, one cannot easily stray from the old platitude that nationalism is difficult to define.

Sport and nationalism

The one thing that we can be certain about when considering the historical relationship between sport and nationalism is that sport, like nationalism, is imprecise and contingent and varies greatly according to time period and geographical location. For the historian, developing a synthesis of the history of sporting nationalism thus presents a challenge. There is no unitary approach to sportive nationalism and its history.[8] We can find, without much effort, sport-related examples to support all theories of nationalism and to illustrate all variants. Moreover, a nation's sporting culture, in its totality, will rarely tell a singular version of its nationalist story. Mike Cronin, for example, has convincingly argued that Gaelic Games and soccer embody contrasting versions of Irish nationalism.[9]

The features of sport that make it a suitable vector for nationalism are easy enough to recognize. Sport is ritualistic and is thus easily embedded in national traditions. In this sense, sportive nationalism is partly self-perpetuating: the historical reference points that drive group cohesion might themselves be sporting ones. Sporting events put on display the full range of national symbolism: anthems are sung and flags waved. Sport's entanglement with the media ensures that the 'imagined community', postulated famously by Anderson,[10] is developed and nourished through national sports teams. Moreover, its competitive dimension can mimic national struggles.[11]

Yet developing an historical synthesis of sport and nationalism is challenging. A significant historiographical problem in this respect is that the great majority of academic sports history works dealing with the topic are 'national' histories lacking a comparative dimension.[12] Another outcome of the focus on individual nations is a lack of conceptual focus. This problem, one authority has noted, has afflicted the historiography of nationalism more generally.[13] Amid this conceptual fog, the historian can fall back on chronology. And that is the general model adopted in this chapter. Though no precise periodization is possible, the relationship between sport and nationalism evolved over time as the political, economic, and technological context in which the two phenomena intertwined changed.

Sport and the idea of the nation

The relationship between sport and nationalism had its first flourish in the early nineteenth century and had both political and cultural origins. Politically, the fallout from the French Revolution and the conflicts in Europe that followed provided the ideal context in which martial exercise movements with a nationalist inflection could grow. These, in turn, had a strong cultural dimension, typically encompassing elements of contemporary romantic nationalism and national revivalism.[14] The idea that games could have a social and ideological meaning – and in this case a nationalist one – was a British innovation. In the late eighteenth and early nineteenth centuries, in the context of economic and social change at home and conflict abroad, games, and conspicuously boxing, came to be seen as uniquely British. 'Pugilism,' one correspondent to the *Morning Chronicle* claimed in 1808, 'is not so much the cause as the effect, or rather sign or measure of English valour; and its professors may be considered the representatives of the courage of the nation.'[15] The narrating of the nation through sport was, from the outset, heavily leavened with myth. In England 'the tumult and conflict in Europe' led to cultural reaction at home, where 'a yearning for a Neverland of the rural past' became fashionable.[16] This romantic attachment to landscape was evident in the views of a *Bell's Life* correspondent in 1834 who asserted that 'The practice of athletic exercises has been from time immemorial held in just estimation by the inhabitants of this island. Natural, more or less, to all the human race, they are yet peculiarly so to the natives of Britain.'[17]

Further afield, the *Turner* (a form of gymnastics) movement was woven into the nationalist politics of nineteenth-century Germany, and was given initial impetus by the threat of

French hegemony. F.L. Jahn, the movement's founder, had an ethnic and organic view of German nationhood and saw in gymnastics an opportunity to revive the spirit of the Teutonic warrior.[18] Similarly the Czech *Sokol* movement and its associated events were also suffused with Czech nationalist mythology.[19] In Norway, a tradition of 'national' sports, with emphasis on skiing, was created that combined a characteristically romantic exaltation of the country's inhospitable winter landscape with a recollection of the glorious mythological past.[20] This process was sharpened by contemporary moves towards complete independence from Sweden. Martial gymnastic movements of different accents – but both possessing a racial tinge and a strong element of Germanophobia – also emerged in France and in Denmark in the late nineteenth century.[21] Anglophobia was the ideological imperative that drove the Gaelic Athletic Association. Founded in Ireland in 1884, it was also symptomatic of a transnational cultural nationalist trend, though this time embodied in the codified field sports of hurling and Gaelic football rather than gymnastics. The Association's use of pageantry, symbolism, its discursive links with Ireland's mythic past, and its moral dimension – signalled by its embrace of amateurism – were all characteristic of organizations that cropped up in national revivalist movements across Europe and beyond in the nineteenth century.

Historicizing, however anachronistic, was important if these athletic organizations were going to stimulate national consciousness. Yet, this was by no means confined to nations possessing a canon of epic and folkloric tales. In settler societies, for example, where no claims of an ancient national heritage are possible apart from those of the indigenous peoples, national sporting traditions were also nurtured by myth. In these cases, timelessness replaced antiquity. Baseball, for example, with its designation as the United States' national sport, and its embodiment of a rural, pastoral vision of American culture, has elements of nationalist rhetoric associated with romantic nationalism.[22] In New Zealand, an entire national myth has been forged around the 1905 All Black tour to the British Isles. The success of the 'invincibles' was evidence of the superiority of the settler colonial way of life over the urban degeneracy of the 'Mother Country'. This myth was heavily leavened with the language of masculinity: the virile frontiersman was the archetypal figure in New Zealand rugby. In terms of narrating the nation, the rugby player sat astride the ANZAC soldier of the Gallipoli battlefield.[23]

As evidenced by the New Zealand example, sportive nationalism, from the outset, had a fundamental gender dimension. Sport, and any meaning attached to it, was a male imperative, not least due to the simple fact that women were mostly excluded from taking part. In Britain discourses of sport, nation, and masculinity were fused in the doctrine of Muscular Christianity that flourished in the public schools. Cricket, according to the character George Arthur in *Tom Brown's Schooldays*, was the 'birthright of British boys old and young, as habeas corpus and trial by jury are of British men'.[24] The best qualities of the English were, by definition, masculine. One nineteenth-century commentator observed that 'the individual Englishman owes his superiority to the individual of every other country in courage, strength … [and] agility' to boxing. Contemporary criticism of the sport was dismissed as 'effeminate cant'.[25] It seems reasonable to deduce that contemporary ideas around female physiology and psychology ensured that national weakness was, in the views of some, associated with femininity.

Sport and the failure of internationalism

The dominant model eventually adopted in international sport was contests between teams representing *nation states* rather than nations per se. This framework was the sporting

Sport and nationalism

outgrowth of dramatic changes in political geography that began in the nineteenth century and gathered pace after the First World War. The fallout from the conflict put paid to the great multi-ethnic dynastic states that had dominated the continent's map for centuries and saw them replaced with smaller successor states. As the twentieth century progressed, European powers ceded their remaining colonial possessions and the nation state model came to dominate in Asia and Africa from the 1950s. The break-up of the Soviet Union in the early 1990s led to another round of nation state formation in Eastern Europe and in the erstwhile Soviet republics of Central Asia. The fall of socialist regimes in 1989 also led to the peaceful dissolution of Czechoslovakia and the traumatic sundering of Yugoslavia.

In assessing the growing presence of nationalism in sport, the Olympic Games warrants specific attention here, not least because of its theoretical commitment to internationalism. The Anglophile Pierre de Coubertin, writing in 1893, saw in the Olympic Games a means of bringing the nations of the world together and that the resultant 'peaceful, courteous confrontations' would be 'the best form of internationalism'.[26]

In this, he was proved wrong. International sport of the type pioneered by the Olympic Games was almost entirely incompatible with internationalism. An initial source of rancour at the Olympics was the criteria for what constituted a competing nation. At the 1908 Summer Olympics held in London, for example, there were anomalies and inconsistencies in this regard. The Russian Empire, apart from Finland, competed as one team. The Austro-Hungarian Empire had teams representing Austria, Hungary, and Bohemia. The settler societies of Canada, Australasia (Australia and New Zealand), and South Africa each sent a team, despite German assertions that they should all compete under the British flag. The Austrian International Olympic Committee (IOC) member, Prince Solms-Braunfels, furiously wrote to Coubertin pointing out that 'Bohemia is a mere Austrian province'.[27] The IOC eventually arrived at a compromise formula: 'A region will be regarded as a "country" if it is represented in the International Olympic Committee; where there is no such representation, any region under a single government will be regarded a "country".' Thus the semi-autonomous Finns and Bohemians each entered a team but the Irish, to whom the British Olympic Association denied IOC representation, continued to compete under the Union Jack.[28]

Internationalism, almost from the outset, was also undermined by ill-tempered, if initially relatively trivial, rivalries between states. The First World War was a key inflection point in the relationship between sport and nationalism and this was most apparent again at the Olympic Games where the winning of medals came to be conflated with power and prestige more generally. The United States was arguably the principal culprit. Representing a brash and rising power, American Olympic teams enjoyed the support of a bellicose press who, in turn, promoted the idea that the Olympics was a competition to be won. This led to the invention of the medal table.[29] After the Los Angeles games of 1932, and despite the dire prevailing economic context, the American press 'engaged in an orgy of nationalistic self-congratulation'.[30] Recognition of the broader political significance of sport was not confined to the Americans. Elements within the British sporting establishment, worried that their nation's relative paltry haul of medals at the 1920 games was undermining its claims to global sporting superiority, saw to it that their Olympic team were well-funded for the 1924 games in Paris.[31] And while the win-at-all-costs attitude of the Americans offended British amateur sensibilities, being upstaged in international sport came to be seen by some as a measure of national decline. Coubertin, reflecting wearily in 1928, lamented the lack of chivalry of contemporary spectators and 'those outbursts of crude nationalism that give our era a semi-barbaric stench'.[32]

155

Nationalistic controversies extended beyond squabbles between old and emerging powers. This was exemplified in that most volatile hotbed of nationalist disputes: East-Central Europe. Prior to independence, for instance, 'national' football associations were founded in the Czech and Polish territories under Habsburg dominion. These associations were not recognized by FIFA, where Austria held a veto. After the First World War, the alignment of state and ethnic boundaries was haphazard in the region and the nation-state model of international sport was arguably ill-fitting.[33] Moreover, the use of sport as a means of forging national cohesion proved a challenge as successor states had regions heavily populated with ethnic minorities. The Hungarians now living in the newly created Greater Romania, for example, often ignored Romanian sports governing bodies and organized sporting activities on their own terms. When Romania sent a team mainly composed of ethnic Hungarians from the Carpathian region to the 1924 Olympic football tournament, Romanian press commentators attributed the team's heavy defeat to their ethnicity.[34] Likewise, in multi-ethnic Czechoslovakia, the Germans of the Sudetenland maintained their own sporting culture and favoured, for example, *Turnen* over the local *Sokol* equivalent.[35] In post-war Poland, where there were significant German, Belorussian, Ukrainian, and Jewish populations, sport was also divided along ethnic lines. The football clubs of Silesia, East Prussia, and Gdańsk, for example, were labelled 'German clubs' by wary 'native' Poles.[36]

The scale and significance of international sport were revolutionized both by political and technological developments after the Second World War. The Cold War created a system of international rivalry in which sport became a surrogate battleground. Meanwhile the development of television ensured that these rivalries would reach an audience never before imaginable. The embrace, by communist states, of 'bourgeois' international sports was grounded in both pragmatic and ideological considerations. In the first instance, it fostered nation-building in multi-ethnic states. The Soviet Union, for example, was a country of bewildering ethnic diversity and the communist regime was eager to use sport to build a sense of patriotic Soviet citizenship. Sport also became a useful proxy measure of power and prestige on the international stage.[37] Mobilizing sport to these ends was easier, of course, in regimes where state intervention in civil society was the norm. The bitter rivalries that emerged in sports events between communist and capitalist states during the Cold War have been well documented. The systematic doping, the boycotts, the feverish race to the top of the medal table, the flashpoints on the skating rink and in the water polo pool, and so on, all provide eloquent evidence of the failure of internationalism in sport.

The attraction of nationalist one-upmanship, ultimately, has proven irresistible. The Pan-Arab games, for example, founded to promote regional unity, have been marked by fragmentation as western models of sportive nationalism were embraced by competing nations.[38] Even that most esoteric of states, North Korea, since its embrace of international sport in the 1960s, celebrates sporting success with media rhetoric heavily laden with the language of nationalism. Moreover, in a weird imitation of a nineteenth-century bourgeois trend, the North Koreans have embraced cultural nationalism in their veneration of taekwondo.[39]

Arguably the most violent fusion of sport and nationalism since the Second World War, or in any era, occurred just after the end of the Cold War. A particularly virulent strain of nationalism infected sport in the nations of Federal Yugoslavia as the latter collapsed into internecine warfare in the early 1990s. As ethnic nationalism spread across the state in the 1980s, football supporters in particular began to invest their loyalty with their own ethnic group. In Serbia, for example, the warlord Arkan famously used the terraces of Red Star Belgrade as a recruiting ground for his paramilitary group. Violent clashes in Zagreb in May 1990 between supporters of Dinamo Zagreb and Red Star Belgrade have entered popular myth as the day the Croatian War of Independence started. Franjo Tudjman, the first president of independent Croatia, was especially keen to harness the symbolic power of sport.[40] In October 1990, and in the midst of a full-scale insurrection by Croatian Serbs in the Krajina, Tudjman arranged an exhibition soccer match between Croatia and the United States, designed as an ostentatious display of Croat independence. The Croat team wore white and red chequered shirts – a dread symbol for the country's Serbs.[41] Bosnian football was similarly riven along ethnic lines.[42]

Sportive nationalism in a global era

The end of the Cold War signalled the triumph of capitalism. The neoliberal economic model, favouring unfettered markets, deregulation, and fewer restrictions on cross-border movements of capital had a profound impact on sport.[43] The commercialization of sport, largely fuelled by a deregulated television market, accelerated exponentially from the 1980s. The 'globalization' that followed broader economic and technological developments might, some scholars assumed, have led to the demise of the nation. In reality, however, the relationship between sport and nationalism persevered and adapted to prevailing economic orthodoxy. One symptom of this new dispensation was the migration and naturalization of athletes and the implications for notions of citizenship that followed from this process. This has been noted specifically in athletics where European and the Middle East states have 'acquired' African athletes to further their national teams' quest for medals.[44] This is market logic at its most basic. Individuals in a limited talent pool sell their potential to wealthy nations; these nations, in turn, measure prestige in accordance with the simplest of metrics – the medals table.

In ultra-competitive markets, branding and marketing acquired an importance not previously witnessed. Thus, what sociologists term 'corporate nationalism' – the use by large multinational corporations of national symbolism in advertising and promotional materials – became prevalent in sport. One good example of this global–local nexus was the relationship between the New Zealand's rugby union team, the All Blacks, and huge multinational corporations such as News Corporation and Adidas.[45] The *haka*, a traditional Māori challenge performed by the All Blacks prior to international fixtures, was brazenly commodified by Adidas in 2007 when it was included in a television advert. Thus a highly localized and idiosyncratic feature of national symbolism was appropriated to enhance the brand equity of a global sportswear company.

Sport in the neoliberal age also, in various ways, became a method of 'nation branding'. This was best exemplified, perhaps, by the feverish competition from the late 1980s to the mid-2010s between states and cities to host sport mega-events. Nations, competing with each other for mobile capital and attempting to acquire 'soft power', could engage in a process of 'brand management' through the staging of the Olympics or the FIFA World Cup. China, for example, attempted to use the occasion of the 2008 Beijing Olympics as an opportunity to soften its global image. In 2012 the UK, through the medium of the opening ceremony at the London Olympics, projected an overwhelmingly positive image of itself to a huge global audience.[46] In the post-Cold War era, ultimately, the organizing principle of the market and the effects of globalization tended to enhance as much as diminish sportive nationalism.

Despite the prevailing twenty-first-century context and talk of a postnationalist age, ancient hatreds still toxify sport. In 2014, for example, an international soccer match between Albania and Serbia was abandoned when the lowering of an Albanian flag onto the field led to fights between players and a pitch invasion by supporters. The proximate cause of the incident, of course, was the irredentist Serb claim on Kosovo, dating back over 600 years in folk memory. This is just one relatively high-profile example of the type of unresolved nationalist disputes that remain common around the world. In sport, stateless peoples have, for example, coalesced, formed football teams, and created tournaments. When the Confederation of Independent Football Associations (CONIFA) tournament took place in 2018, the Hungarian minorities living in Slovakia, Romania, and Ruthenia each entered a team – a reminder of the imperfect state-formation of the past. And while CONIFA is plainly only a semi-serious organization – Yorkshire, for example, has a representative association, while potential big-hitters such as Catalonia and the Basque Country do not – it has as members a plethora of teams from within the borders of the Ukraine and from the Caucuses, regions with serious separatist movements.[47]

In conclusion, the historical relationship between sport and nationalism is shapeshifting and contradictory. It is a relationship that has clearly adapted to the broader context in which it has evolved. Sport, when instrumentalized by powerful actors, can serve both to unite and to divide nations. It can create a sense of belonging among disparate groups in multinational states but it can highlight their differences as well. The experience of Yugoslavia is a terrifying lesson in all of this. Sportive nationalism is at once local and international. National sporting cultures persist, with their own vernaculars and rituals, while a more homogenized international sporting calendar attracts record audiences. One must remember, however, that while sport is a powerful mirror of political events, it does not generally direct them. Orwell, in his famous essay, cautioned readers that he 'did not, of course, suggest that sport is one of the main causes of international rivalry'; 'big-scale sport', he asserted, was 'merely another effect of the causes that have produced nationalism'.[48] And irrespective of how nationalism evolves, sport is likely to remain a sharp lens through which we can observe it.

Notes

1 U. Özkirimli, *Contemporary Debates on Nationalism* (Basingstoke: Palgrave, 2005); J. Breuilly, 'Introduction' in *The Oxford Handbook of the History of Nationalism*, ed. J. Breuilly (Oxford: Oxford University Press, 2016), 1–21.
2 See, notably, E. Hobsbawn and T. Ranger eds. *The Invention of Tradition* (Cambridge: Cambridge University Press, 1992).
3 Breuilly, 'Introduction', 1.
4 B. Anderson, *Imagined Communities: Reflections on the Origins and Spread of Nationalism* (London: Verso, 2006).
5 M. Tabachnik, 'Untangling Liberal Democracy from Territoriality: From Ethnic/Civic to Ethnic/Territorial Nationalism', *Nations and Nationalism* 25, no. 1 (2019): 191–207.
6 Anthony Smith, *Nationalism* (Cambridge: Polity Press, 2010), 2.
7 M. Goswami, 'Rethinking the Modular Nation Form: Toward a Sociohistorical Conception of Nationalism', *Comparative Studies in Society and History* 44, no. 4 (2002): 770–799.
8 'Sportive nationalism' is an inelegant term but is more accurate than alternatives and is therefore used throughout for ease.
9 See M. Cronin, *Sport and Nationalism in Ireland: Gaelic Games, Soccer and Irish Identity Since 1884* (Dublin: Four Courts, 1999).
10 Anderson, *Imagined Communities*.
11 John Hargreaves, *Freedom for Catalonia?: Catalan Nationalism, Spanish Identity, and the Barcelona Olympic Games* (Cambridge: Cambridge University Press, 2000), 13–14.
12 Alan Tomlinson and Christopher Young, 'Towards a New History of European Sport', *European Review* 19, no. 4 (2011): 487–507.

Sport and nationalism

13 Breuilly, 'Introduction'.

14 See Tony Collins, *Sport in Capitalist Society* (London: Routledge, 2013), 21–27.

15 *Morning Chronicle*, 9 November 1808.

16 Collins, *Sport in Capitalist Society*, 25.

17 *Bell's Life*, 27 April 1834.

18 P. Roubal, 'Politics of Gymnastics: Mass Gymnastic Displays under Communism in Central and Eastern Europe', *Body & Society* 9, no. 2 (2003): 1–25.

19 A. Gajdoš, M. Provazinokova, and S.J. Banjak, '150 Years of the Sokol Gymnastics in Czechoslovakia, Czech and Slovak Republic', *Science of Gymnastics Journal* 4, no. 2 (2012): 5–26.

20 M. Goksøyr, 'Taking Ski Tracks to the North: The Invention and Reinvention of Norwegian Polar Skiing: Sportisation, Manliness and National Identities', *International Journal of the History of Sport* 3, no. 6 (2013): 563–579.

21 R. Holt, 'Contrasting Nationalisms: Sport, Militarism and the Unitary State in Britain and France Before 1914', in *Tribal Identities: Nationalism, Europe, Sport*, ed. J.A. Mangan (London, Frank Cass, 1996), 39–54. H. Eichberg, 'Nationalism and the Culture of the Body: The Politicization of "Popular Gymnastics" in Nineteenth-century Denmark', *Tribal Identities*, 135–146.

22 S.W. Pope, *Patriotic Games: Sporting Traditions in the American Imagination* (New York, Oxford University Press, 1997).

23 C. Daley, 'The Invention of 1905' and G. Ryan 'Rural Myth and Urban Actuality: The Anatomy of All Black and New Zealand Rugby 1884–1938'. Both in *Tackling Rugby Myths: Rugby and New Zealand Society 1854–2004* ed. G. Ryan (Otago: Otago University Press, 2005), 69–88, 33–54.

24 https://www.gutenberg.org/files/1480/1480-h/1480-h.htm. Accessed, 20 September 2019.

25 *Morning Chronicle*, 9 November 1808.

26 N. Müller ed. *Pierre de Coubertin 1863–1937. Olympism: Selected Writings* (Lausanne: IOC, 2002), 299.

27 F. Kolár and J. Kössl, 'Origin and Development of the Czech and Czechoslovak Olympic Committee', *Citius, Altius, Fortius* 2, no. 3 (1994): 11–26.

28 K. Lennartz, 'The Olympic Games and Politics', *Proceedings: International Symposium for Olympic Research* (2010), 143.

29 D. Goldblatt, *The Games: A Global History of the Olympics* (London: Macmillan, 2016), 119.

30 M. Dyreson, 'Marketing National Identity: The Olympic Games of 1932 and American Culture', *Olympika* 4, (1995): 34.

31 M.P. Llewellyn, 'Chariots of Discord: Great Britain, Nationalism and the "Doomed" 1924 Paris Olympics', *Contemporary British History* 24, no. 1 (2010): 67–87.

32 Müller, *Pierre de Coubertin 1863–1937*, 562.

33 A. Hilbrenner and B. Lenz, 'Looking at European Sports from an Eastern European Perspective: Football in the Multi-ethnic Polish Territories', *European Review* 19, no. 4 (2011): 595–610.

34 F. Faje, 'Playing For and Against the Nation: Football in Interwar Romania', *Nationalities Papers* 43, no. 1 (2015): 160–177.

35 See S. Zwicker, 'Sport in the Czech and Slovak Republics and the Former Czechoslovakia and the Challenge of its Historiography', *Journal of Sport History* 38, no. 3 (2011): 373–385.

36 M. Lenartowicz and A. Karwacki, 'An Overview of Social Conflicts in the History of Polish Club Football', *European Journal for Sport and Society* 2, no. 2 (2005): 102.

37 See B. Keys, *Globalizing Sport: National Rivalry and International Community in the 1930s* (New York: Harvard University Press, 2006).

38 Ian P. Henry, Mahfoud Amara, and Mansour Al-Tauqi, 'Sport, Arab Nationalism and the Pan-Arab Games', *International Review for the Sociology of Sport* 38, no. 3 (2003): 295–310.

39 Jung Woo Lee and Alan Bairner, 'The Difficult Dialogue: Communism, Nationalism and Political Propaganda in North Korean Sport', *Journal of Sport and Social Issues* 33, no. 4 (2009): 390–410.

40 Dario Brentin, '"A Lofty Battle for the Nation": The Social Roles of Sport in Tudjman's Croatia', *Sport in Society* 16, no. 8 (2013): 993–1008.

41 Allen Sack and Zeljan Suster, 'Soccer and Croatian Nationalism', *Journal of Sport and Social Issues*, 24, no. 3 (2000): 305–320.

42 Richard Mills, 'Velez Mostar Football Club and the Demise of "Brotherhood and Unity" in Yugoslavia, 1922–2009', *Europe-Asia Studies* 62, no. 7 (2010): 1107–1133.

43 Collins, *Sport in Capitalist Society*, 120–125.

44 Joseph K. Adjaye, 'Reimagining Sports: African Athletes, Defection and Ambiguous Citizenship', *Africa Today* 57, no. 2 (2010): 26–40.

45 J. Scherer and S. Jackson, 'Sports Advertising, Cultural Production and Corporate Nationalism at the Global-Local Nexus: Branding the New Zealand All Blacks', *Sport in Society* 10, no. 2 (2007): 268–284.

46 J. Grix and B. Houlihan, 'Sports Mega-events as Part of a Nation's Soft Power Strategy: The Cases of Germany (2006) and the UK (2012)', *The British Journal of Politics and International Relations* 16 (2014): 572–596.

47 www.confia.org (accessed 15 September 2019).

48 George Orwell, *Shooting an Elephant and Other Essays* (London: Penguin, 2003), 195.

19

RACE, RACISM, AND RACIAL ENTANGLEMENTS

Sarah Barnes and Mary G. McDonald

To engage new perspectives on 'old' themes of race and racism is to confront an impossible task, as any discussion will inevitably obscure other ways of being and knowing. Such a standpoint also offers the danger of promoting a dichotomous framing that erases both the continuing salience of past approaches as well as paradigmatic differences and similarities that constitute the diverse ways to study and understand articulations of race and racisms.[1] Given this state of affairs, in this chapter we offer a highly selective account that briefly engages recent writings in the study of race, racism, and sport history while also acknowledging their indebtedness to previous scholarly insights. Specifically, we offer close readings of several analyses published over the past decade to highlight some ways in which several scholars conceptualize the porous character of race relations and racism, particularly within North American contexts. Our goal, then, is not to suggest any sense of comprehensiveness, but to instead offer a very brief provocation in an on-going conversation seeking to unlock the troubling place of race and racism within the sporting past.[2]

Entangled histories

We begin by recounting literary theorist Sarah Nuttall's notion of entanglement, a concept she uses to imagine and theorize contemporary and historical race relations in a post-apartheid South African context.[3] Scholars working in anthropology, sociology, literary studies, and science and technology studies have also deployed this concept of entanglement to various ends. For Nuttall, entanglement

> is a condition of being twisted together or entwined, involved with; it speaks of an intimacy gained, even if it was resisted, or ignored or uninvited. It is a term which may gesture towards a relationship or a set of social relationships that is complicated, ensnaring, in a tangle, but which also implies a human foldedness.[4]

The usefulness of this concept is found in its ability to both engage and move beyond familiar conceptual tools that privilege dominant understandings of 'difference' and 'sameness'. The analytic of racial entanglements is productive in drawing attention 'to

DOI: 10.4324/9780429318306-22

those sites in which what was once thought of as separate – identities, spaces, and histories – come together or find points of intersection in unexpected ways'.[5] This conceptualization suggests that apartheid is not only an entrenched structure but also always permeable and composed of unequal, but often shared spaces, experiences, identities, and histories.

Douglas Booth uses the concept of entanglement to rethink sport histories under apartheid, where South African black, coloured, Indian, and white male athletes had points of contact within physical activity settings.[6] Dominant narratives in sport history highlight how the world of sport often helped to separate racial groups. Booth acknowledges this state of affairs but instead explores moments where such intentions failed. This includes exposing incidents where men of different backgrounds formed cross-racial friendships and experienced affective sporting moments as 'examples of humanity, dignity and esteem'.[7] Rather than conceptualizing these episodes as moments of resistance, Booth, following Nuttall, argues the necessity of using a different standpoint to capture the 'complexity and contemporaneity' of racial 'formations'.[8] At the same time, Booth is interested in the methodological implications of how sport historians can tell stories differently to open up new possibilities for understanding physical activity and sport. Such a postcolonial focus has much in common with important sport histories analysed via feminist, critical race, and queer lenses, which offer related insights while seeking a 'defamiliarising way of reading' the past.[9]

Both Nuttall and Booth demonstrate that the conceptual use of racial entanglement has been enabled by scholarly contributions including critical approaches, which acknowledge the power of 'institutional racism, patterns of exclusion, and structurally marked patterns of access'.[10] Relatedly, approaches that document how race relations unfold differently are especially noteworthy in exposing the mythological status of the seemingly separate and fixed character of dominant racial categories such as 'black' and 'white'. Much sport history scholarship is embedded in uncovering the former structures, while less frequently adept at offering analyses aligned with the latter.

Nuttall introduces several rubrics or ways in which lenses of 'entanglement' have been implicitly or explicitly deployed in previous literary and critical scholarly writings to uncover the complicated porous workings of (post)apartheid South Africa. These include the recognition of: historical entanglements; temporal entanglements; and the entanglements of people and things. Importantly these various notions of entanglement are not simply significant conceptual tools for the study of South Africa – but similar dispositions operate within other geographies including within North American contexts.

In the remaining portions of this chapter we extend Nuttall's and Booth's theorizing around the porous character of racialized structures via illustrations drawn from North American sport history scholarship; instances that also reflect our own scholarly investments in regards to feminist cultural studies of sport. Given that the authors cited below rarely use the term 'racial entanglement', our explication is suggestive in seeking to highlight the often permeable and, at times, flexible structures that shape sport and sporting experiences. We additionally consider the ways our diverse applications of entanglements are aligned with previous conversations and scholarly conceptualizations.

Organizationally in what follows, we first engage three specific historical analyses that illustrate divergent aspects of racial entanglements. Next, we again draw upon contemporary scholarship to emphasize the affinities between the lens of entanglement and the concept of intersectionality. Before concluding this chapter, we very briefly discuss public sport memories as illustrative of how the past and the present are also entangled.

Disentangling sport history

Nuttall's use of historical entanglements in the context of apartheid implies the importance of both hierarchy and interconnection while also suggesting that, 'the more that dispossession occurred, the more blacks and whites depended on each other'.[11] Similar mutual, albeit exploitative, connections also operate within very different North American contexts across time.

Perhaps nowhere is this sensibility more evident than in the spaces where black labour served as the lifeblood for a given sport, while at times providing pleasurable experiences for white and black audiences. This dynamic frequently occurred within horseracing in the nineteenth and early twentieth centuries. *Race Horse Men* by Katherine Mooney covers the period from the late 1820s to the eve of the First World War, and explores how histories, identities, and allegiances were forged on racetracks as well as in barns, breeding sheds, pastures, and in back offices.[12] Wealthy, white horse owners came to rely on the knowledge, judgments, and competence of enslaved men – and, later, their descendants – who were trained as grooms, jockeys, and breeding supervisors to shoulder the care of race horses.[13]

While seemingly suggestive of Hazel V. Carby's book *Race Men*, which interrogates dominant images of black manhood and masculinity within African-American communities, the title of Mooney's book is instead taken from the official death notice of George Marshall, a black man born into the Kentucky horse business before emancipation. Marshall died in 1925 in Rock Island, Illinois and Mooney suggests that his life-long occupation as a 'race horse man' bespeaks a mixture of pride and dignity that often accompanied such occupations. Race horse men were highly skilled labourers who were indispensable to enterprise of racing. They often worked side-by-side with white owners and at times gained access to enhanced forms of mobility, autonomy, respect, and authority. But such close ties also frequently came at a cost. These specialized workers were also subject to intense scrutiny and oversight, even as they became an object and source of affection and companionship for their white owners. Mooney notes that both 'black talent and black subordination' where foundational to the success of any stable.[14] And yet, the brutal training regimes of jockeys offer a vivid example of the ensnaring intimacies and visceral racial interconnections that emerged against the backdrop of racing. On top of a general pedagogy that emphasized constant beatings and extreme physical discipline, jockeys were routinely exposed to malnutrition and denied food in order to keep off weight.

Mooney's stories of race horse men offer an entry point to better understand the insidious nature of racism and its quotidian character, which has always included more than policies, institutional frameworks, or the ballot box. The lives and fates of race horse men and their white patrons became entangled in ways that involved physical, material, and affective dimensions. Through encounters in racing arenas, we see the fragility of the privilege earned by race horse men and the potential for violence and punishment at every turn, a state of affairs which illustrates that 'intimacy does not necessarily exclude violation'.[15]

Writing about very different contexts and spaces, recreational swimming pools in Canada in the twentieth century, Ornella Nzindukiyimana and Eileen O'Connor document a different type of porousness within leisure spaces. While Canada contained segregated sites of exclusion, the absence there of Jim Crow laws that permeated the United States allowed for local conventions and laws to dictate interactions among the races. The resulting permeability of the colour line meant that 'one could be admitted in an establishment one day and turned away from that same establishment the next'.[16] Still, these public spaces often reified white fears of miscegenation in seeking to limit the interactions of men of color and white women in the water and around these spaces, suggesting the interlinked gendered and racial character of intimacy.

While distinctive, these two examples further reveal the decidedly unequal 'terrains of mutuality'.[17] Writing about the power of stadiums as spaces of interaction and community building, Frank Guridy offers yet another way to think about mutuality and entanglements via an examination of the cultural and political legacies of the Los Angeles Coliseum, a publically managed sport stadium that was erected in 1923.[18] His analysis of the LA Coliseum disrupts familiar narratives of sport stadiums and urban space by illuminating how this venue fostered cross-racial understandings, linkages, and solidarities, particularly among the city's Latino and racially marginalized groups. At a time when patterns of white racial exclusion shaped public life and official policy, the Coliseum welcomed racially diverse workers, audiences, religious and political leaders, athletes, and entertainers. From the 1930s onwards, the Coliseum hosted integrated college sporting events and showcased well-known athletes, including black and Mexican-born professional soccer players and boxers, who were respected and admired by white and racialized communities alike.

This is not to suggest that the Coliseum was ignored by the city's most privileged and affluent. Many of the city's white elite viewed the Coliseum as a vehicle to grow the influence and status of Los Angeles. Furthermore, these community gatherings did not escape the patriarchal and heteronormative parameters that have consistently shaped public life in North American society across the twentieth and twentieth-first centuries. Nevertheless, Guridy's work reminds his readers that current configurations of sport stadiums, which hinge on racialized athletic labour and corporatized, profit-driven major league sports are neither natural nor inevitable. It is possible to use stories about the past and iconic public venues like the LA Coliseum to imagine a utopian future where public spaces serve diverse, intertwined communities that promote a fuller sense of mutual connection and progressive agendas related to racial and gender equity.

Intersectionality and entanglements

Instead of imagining race as a something that can be isolated or fully grasped in singular terms, the aforementioned illustrations are also aligned with those histories which demonstrate that dominant understandings of 'race' are co-constituted or 'entangled' with other meaningful social categories, such as gender, class, and sexuality. First coined by critical legal theorist, Kimberle Williams Crenshaw, diverse conceptualizations of 'intersectionality' have been applied by sport historians to reveal that interlocking systems of racism, classes, and sexism articulate in unique ways with important consequences in terms of life chances. This concept helps account for inequities, opportunities, and particularities that may exist between and within racial groups while documenting how people, variously positioned, come to move through sport systems in intricate ways.[19]

For instance, Amira Rose Davis explores the baseball careers of three African-American women, Toni Stone, Connie Morgan, and Mamie 'Peanut' Johnson. During the 1940s, these athletes were excluded from playing in the all-white, All-American Girls Professional Baseball League (AAGPB), a league made famous years later in the 1992 movie 'A League of Their Own'.[20] They subsequently joined teams in the Negro Leagues. Rather than offering a celebratory narrative, Davis maps out a far more complex story by noting many of the contradictions surrounding these athletes. The popularity of the Negro Leagues eroded as the very best players started to find new opportunities in the de-segregating, formerly all-white Major Leagues. Major League Baseball owners sought black male talent to help bolster their

Race, racism, and racial entanglements

athletic labour force, which had been depleted during the Second World War, thus also opening the door for Stone, Morgan, and Johnson's entry into the Negro Leagues.

However, while these pioneering athletes received plenty of media attention, this coverage was often exploitative, presenting them as sporting novelties as opposed to serious athletes. Davis illuminates how these three women navigated sexist and racist environments where harassment from other players, the black and white press, and audiences was common. Yet, these athletes also attracted legions of female supporters and fought to create space for themselves to be seen as legitimate ball players. In dissecting the public memories of these trailblazing athletes, Davis suggests that prominent depictions have often extracted inspirational stories (and profits) instead of capturing a far more complex picture documenting the intersecting sexist and racist structural components that impacted these athletes' sporting experiences. Ultimately, this analysis shows shifting and entangled racialized and gendered conditions of skill and labour enabled a fuller presence of femininity in sport while deepening scholarly understandings of the politics of race and racism as articulated through gender relations in the Civil Rights era.

The ability to move back and forth into different racialized spaces, thus revealing the interdependence of segregated communities, is another theme that has been explored. One case in point is that of Mary Garber, a white female sportswriter from North Carolina who wrote primarily about black high school and collegiate sports from the mid-1940s to the 1960s. Dain TePeol shows how Garber drew upon the power of whiteness to provide a media platform through which she created dignified and complexly textured stories of non-dominant (re: not white, male) sport cultures that resisted racist stereotypes and offensive tropes.[21] Garber often noted the intelligence, work ethic, and American ideals she saw in many of the black men she covered. While also facing blatant sexist discrimination in her workplace, Mary Garber's vocation intertwined with the athletes she covered, revealing mutual interdependencies as the sportswriter produced counter-narratives for many sports fans.

Memory and temporal entanglements in sport history

A key aspect of Nuttall's conception of entanglement focuses on the nature of memory and the interdependency of the past, present, and future. She draws our attention to how specific ways of remembering (or forgetting) racism and discrimination may serve the needs and interests of those in the present and shape how it is possible to envision the future. Sport historians have similarly explored how racial dynamics impact shared mythologies and customs of remembering, and by doing so, leave us with a fuller appreciation of the evolving nature of racism in the current moment.[22]

Jaime Schultz, for instance, critically evaluates how today's political and racial climate shape recent efforts to commemorate the athletic achievements and injustices suffered by Jack Trice, Ozzie Simmons, and Johnny Bright, three black football players who competed at colleges in Iowa in the early-to-mid twentieth century. By studying 'why, when, and how' memorials to these men came about, Schultz illuminates what she calls 'racialized memory'.[23] This concept highlights an expanding collective willingness to re-narrate the past and to see how racism and discrimination shaped the unfolding of past events, experiences, and identities in the sporting arena. While some might see these changing racial sensibilities as evidence of a more tolerant or inclusive (white) society, Schultz cautions her readers against embracing such celebratory progress narratives. Even as communities become more eager to rectify past wrongs and to address the enduring legacies of racism, these efforts too frequently continue to serve the interests of dominant groups in society. This does not diminish the importance of publically acknowledging and celebrating the lives, struggles, and contributions of athletes like Trice, Simmons, and Bright. It does however require an understanding of the fact that histories are made by people embedded in social relations. It further compels communities to collectively grapple with the possibilities and limitations of these commemorative efforts in order to create new forms of racialized cultural memories that do not simply re-inscribe and naturalize social hierarchies.

Another view of racialized memory is seen in the scholarship of Rita Liberti and Maureen M. Smith, who explore the nature of remembrance in the cultural retelling of stories about track star and three-time Olympic gold medallist Wilma Rudolph.[24] The constant narration of Rudolph's life follows predictive scripts that reify dominant notions of individual achievement and perseverance while positioning racism, sexism, and classism as largely confined to the past. Alternative storylines, while fewer in number, celebrate black female athleticism while also highlighting Rudolph's advocacy, challenging norms of racism and sexism. In showing the diverse scripts that abound across times and spaces, the authors expose the temporal dimensions of entanglements. That is, against mythological depictions of linearity, the past, present, and future are intertwined.[25]

Adrian Burgos, Jr. also explores collective memory, and historical forgetting, connected to the role of Afro-Latino players in the Negro Leagues and in Major League Baseball.[26] Burgos, Jr. notes how historical revisions that attempt to capture the dynamics of the Negro Leagues often fail to account for the vibrant flow of people, expertise, and capital that existed in major America cities and places like Puerto Rico, Cuba, and Mexico as a part of black baseball circuits. He contends that many recovery efforts inadequately grasp the diasporic character of blackness and the necessity of a transnational framework that conceptualizes black identity beyond a US context.

For Burgos, Jr. the crux of the problem lies in how Afro-Caribbean identities confound dominant American racial and ethnic categories, which code people as either 'Black' or 'Latino' and not 'Black' and 'Latino'.[27] The inability to see blackness in relation to overlapping and intertwined social constructions of race obscures what segregation, and the slow process of integration, actually entailed for athletes like Orestes 'Minnie' Miñoso, who had a prolific professional career as one of the first Afro-Cuban players in the major leagues. Afro-Latino athletes faced a double burden. They were often treated with a degree of suspicion in the black community. Some Spanish-speaking players were accused of not being black 'enough' by teammates and white sportswriters, even as these men continued to be subject to segregationist policies and, later, racial prejudice.[28] Yet, language and cultural barriers also existed for these athletes in terms of their Latin identities. Stereotypes about the 'hot-blooded' nature of Latinos created a stifling atmosphere that made it almost impossible to express frustration at experiences such as being repeatedly hit by pitches or misrepresented in the press.[29]

The trajectories of Afro-Latino ball players through the Negro Leagues and Major League Baseball dispel oversimplified notions of a unified or essential black identity or the idea that blackness automatically translates into a shared sense of struggle. Burgos, Jr. broadens the terms of blackness in scholarly histories of baseball by acknowledging how this category is riddled with tensions, difference, and diverse understandings of how to respond and challenge racism. This analysis offers an additional take-away point suggesting that the stories which attach to bodies have afterlives that morph across time and place, again, revealing the temporal and spatial power of racial memories and entanglements.

Concluding thoughts

In this chapter, we have taken liberty to both use and expand upon Sarah Nuttall's conception of entanglement as an opening into ongoing conversations about the complicated character of race and racism in the field of sport history. Contrary to popular beliefs and dominant historical accounts, different scholarly writings disclose that race and racism do not exist simply through the forced isolation or separation of groups, although clearly segregation has been powerful in shaping the sporting past and present. Instead, we provided alternative accounts that detail the myriad of complex racial connections, interdependencies, intersections, memories, and intimacies as key social dynamics that are also evident in the sporting realm. That is, 'gaps, blind spots, mistakes, paradoxes, ironies, anomalies, ambiguities, and invisibilities'[30] further create particular seams of engagement and possibilities for thinking anew about the racialized sporting past. It is our hope that this chapter has provided sufficient information for provocation which helps to expand understandings of embodiment and racial formations, while also demonstrating the often non-linear, fragmented character of historical cultural processes and social change.

Notes

1 Andrew Linden, 'Tempering the Dichotomous Flame: Social History, Cultural History and Post-modernism(s) in the Journal of Sport History, 1974–2014,' *Journal of Sport History* 43, no. 1 (Spring 2016): 66–82.

2 This chapter joins a robust body of scholarship which maps out the diverse ways of being and knowing about racism within sport history scholarship. For an earlier overview see John Nauright and David Wiggins, 'Race', in *Routledge Companion to Sports History* ed. S.W. Pope and John Nauright (New York: Routledge, 2009), 148–161.

3 Sarah Nuttall, *Entanglement: Literary and Cultural Reflections on Post-Apartheid* (New York: NYU Press, 2009).

4 Nuttall, *Entanglement*, 1.

5 Nuttall, *Entanglement*, 11.

6 Douglas Booth, 'Disentangling Race: Re-Narrating Apartheid Sport?' *The International Journal of the History of Sport* 33, no. 15 (2016): 1866–1883.

7 Booth, 'Disentangling Race', 1877.

8 Nuttall, *Entanglement*, 47.

9 Nuttall, *Entanglement*, 12.

10 Nuttall, *Entanglement*, 9.

11 Nuttall, *Entanglement*, 2.

12 Katherine Mooney, *Race Horse Men. How Slavery and Freedom Were Made at the Race Track* (Cambridge: Harvard University Press, 2014).

13 Also see Kevin Dawson, *Undercurrents of Power: Aquatic Culture in the African Diaspora* (Pittsburgh: University of Pennsylvania Press, 2018) for a discussion of how dominant (re: white) groups came to rely on the aquatic knowledges, skills, and Maritime cultures that flourished among the African diaspora in a variety of geographic locations. By tracing histories of swimming, diving, paddling, and even surfing, Dawson confirms that enslaved and freedmen used bodies of water to assert agency and experience moments of freedom.

14 Mooney, *Race Horse Men*, 13.

15 Nuttall, *Entanglement*, 25.

16 Ornella Nzindukiyimana and Eileen O'Connor, 'Let's (Not) Meet at the Pool: A Black Canadian Social History of Swimming (1900s–1960s)', *Loisir et Société / Society and Leisure*, 42 no. 1 (2019): 150.

17 Nuttall, *Entanglement*, 11.

18 Frank Andre Guridy, 'What's Good for Boyle Heights Has Been Good at the Los Angeles Coliseum', *Kalfou* 4, no. 2 (2017): 211–227.

19 Kimberle Williams Crenshaw, 'Mapping the Margins: Intersectionality, Identity Politics, and Violence Against Women of Color', *Stanford Law Review*, 43 (1990): 1241–1300. For an overview of the

advent and use of intersectionality within sport studies including sport history see Susan J. Bandy, 'Gender and Sport Studies: An Historical Perspective', *Movement and Social Science* 86 (2014): 15–27; for a focus on intersectionality within historical and contemporary Canada see Simon Darnell, Janelle Joseph, Yuka Nakamura eds. *Race and Sport in Canada: Intersecting Inequalities* (Toronto: Canadian Scholars Press, 2012).

20 Amira Rose Davis, 'No League of Their Own: Baseball, Black Women, and the Politics of Representation' *Radical History Review,* 125 (2016): 74–96.

21 Dain TePoel, 'Mary Garber's Coverage of Black Sports in the US Segregated South, 1944–1964', *The International Journal of the History of Sport* 31, no. 13 (2014): 1598–1616.

22 Jaime Schultz, *Moments of Impact. Injury, Racialized Memory, and Reconciliation in College Football* (Lincoln: University of Nebraska Press, 2016). For another discussion of public memory, race, and racism see David Naze, *Reclaiming 42: Public Memory and the Reframing of Jackie Robinson's Radical Legacy* (Lincoln: University of Nebraska Press, 2019); for an overview of memory in sport studies, including sport history see Stephen G. Wieting ed. *Sport and Memory in North America* (Portland: Frank Cass, 2001) and Daniel A. Nathan, *Saying It's So: A Cultural History of the Black Sox Scandal* (Urbana: University of Illinois Press, 2010).

23 Schultz, *Moments of Impact.*

24 Rita Liberti and Maureen M. Smith, *(Re)Presenting Wilma Rudolph* (Syracuse: Syracuse University Press, 2015).

25 Nuttall, *Entanglement.*

26 Adrian Burgos, 'Left Out Afro-Latinos, Black Baseball, and the Revision of Baseball's Racial History', *Social Text* 27, no. 1 (98) (2009): 37–58.

27 Burgos, 'Left Out', 44.

28 Burgos, 'Left Out', 45.

29 Burgos, 'Left Out', 45.

30 Nuttall, *Entanglement*, 47.

20

SPORT IN POST-APARTHEID SOUTH AFRICA

The race to class

Ashwin Desai

The date 10 May 1994 marked the inauguration of Nelson Mandela as the first democratically elected President of the Republic of South Africa. It was a storyline that grabbed world headlines. Sport muscled into the fairy-tale narrative as the country won the 1995 Rugby World Cup on home soil, followed by victory in soccer's African Cup of Nations. It was at this time that 'Madiba (Mandela's) Magic' caught the public imagination and we came to believe that something exceptional was being born in South Africa. The promise was that the racial badges of apartheid would be dumped into the garbage can of history and class privilege on the nation's playing fields would be progressively levelled. This chapter is a contemporary conjunctural picture of where that promise stands 25 years after the 1995 moment, in what Patti Waldmeir called 'an orgy of reconciliation'.[1] I pay particular attention to rugby and cricket, which, together with soccer, are the most popular games in the country. Unlike soccer, which has a majority of Black players, the national composition of rugby and cricket for most of the nearly three decades of 'unity' was dominated by White players and was to come under increased scrutiny during the post-Mandela years. I interrogate how the chestnuts of race and class that have run through the long twentieth century have been addressed by the African National Congress (ANC) government and sports organizations. I do this against the background of a powerful strand of thought and practice in anti-apartheid resistance, that of non-racialism, which, in the 1970s, captured the imagination of Black sportspersons.

Fields apart

The boycott of apartheid sport that gained momentum in the 1970s is an incredible story of local roots and wide global resonance. Its rallying cry was 'no normal sport in an abnormal country'. Led by the South African Council on Sport (SACOS), it preached a selection system for national teams based on 'same opportunity' and a commitment to non-racialism.

The conditions in which Black sport were played as compared with White sport have been highlighted in a number of seminal works.[2] I had a ground level view of these two worlds in the late 1960s and early 1970s. Almost every summer weekend, I made the

DOI: 10.4324/9780429318306-23

journey from the centre of Durban to Springfield grounds. Springfield is now the site of business complexes and double-lane roads hemming it into the city sprawl, but in the 1970s it was still very much on the outskirts. Six or seven games of cricket were played, simultaneously, on ancient matting wickets according to rules first written in the eighteenth century. There were no sightscreens and irregular boundaries were marked by misshapen, whitewashed stones. Clumps of grass and mole-hills hid crevices that tested the most flexible of ankles. In a script that veered between comedy and tragedy, I could not wait to get the call to don my whites and be drawn into the drama of a Springfield middle.

Preparations before the game were a cross between Kafka and Monty Python. On a Saturday afternoon, you would arrive and fetch the mat from a wood and iron shed. The mats were crusty and mouldy and came in all sorts of grotesque shapes. The lime would be mixed so that the lines of the crease could be marked. But the line would never be straight, as the elements had created ruts and lumps all over. Still, measurements were taken with surgical care.

It was only then that the mat would be laid on the pitch. The holes were huge. If you tried for a quick single, more often than not you would get stuck, so you had to run alongside the pitch. This meant running in the direction of cover and then veering back to the pitch. We were playing cricket but running like baseball players. It was impossible to play driving shots down the ground. The turf was too spotted with holes and mounds and a square cut could bounce and scoot off to the wicket-keeper or simply just not carry beyond a yard or two. To score, one had to loft the ball.

Equipment was in short supply. As one batsman left the field, he would start changing, so that the next batsman could grab pads and 'the guard'. Guards were placed under your underpants; one size fitted all, jocks without straps. This was not village cricket but a game played in conditions where the very best Black provincial players plied their trade.

Occasionally, my father and I would go to Old Kingsmead, that cathedral of White cricket. Here was a completely different world of wonder: turf wickets, picket fences, sightscreens, a scoreboard that flashed lights while invisible hands moved the score. Everything was so beautifully white, pristine, and ordered. My father carved out a space under the clock for us to sit. A small blanket, two paper cups, and a bottle of cool drink forming our own boundary, within the tiny Non-White section.

During one provincial game against the Transvaal, my father, who was light of hue, snuck into the White area in search of a cup of tea. On his way back, he was man-handled and unceremoniously pushed over the fence, all the while trying to hold on to his tea. People on both sides of the divide clapped and laughed. He took his place on the blanket next to us, this most gentle of school teachers, and without saying a word, picked up the binoculars to follow Mike Proctor's run-up that started near the sightscreen. In one of my father's greatest gifts to me, C.L.R. James' *Beyond a Boundary*, I marked these words: 'The British tradition soaked deep into me was that when you entered the sporting arena you left behind the sordid compromises of everyday life. Yet for us to do that we would have to divest ourselves of our skins.'[3] We never went back.

Durban, my world, was a place where signs read European and Non-European in the 1960s, and then, as Afrikaner power consolidated in the 1970s, White and Non-White.

Fields of non-racialism

Despite the crude racial classifications and divisions, non-racialism as an idea took hold. While the actual content of what a non-racial society would look like was not given much attention, it was a lived feeling among people who played under the SACOS banner. It is only over the last decade, mining interviews with former rugby players and administrators in Makhanda (Grahamstown), that I have come to understand the depths of commitment to non-racialism and the sacrifices that people were prepared to make in order to ensure it was a way of life.[4]

Until the early 1970s, Black rugby in Makhanda was split into separate Coloured and African bodies. A new body was mooted, the South Eastern Districts Union (SEDRU) that united the two. SEDRU affiliated to the South African Rugby Union (SARU), which opposed carving up rugby into racial enclaves, consonant with apartheid's racial categories. All Blacks half-back, Chris Laidlaw, summed up South Africa's prevailing and changing rugby landscape in 1974 with incredible prescience:

> Apartheid, bringing with it multi-institutionalism, dictates that there must be separate Rugby unions for each racial group .... Besides the European South African Rugby Board, which naturally enough is the ruling body ... there exists a South African Rugby Federation for Coloureds, a South African Rugby Union for Bantu players, and most interestingly of all, the South African Rugby Union .... The SARU is so determinedly non-racial that in 1971, after twenty-one years, it dropped its annual test match against a national African team.[5]

The stunning assertion of a principled non-racialism embodied in this action takes a while to hit home. Barred by apartheid laws from playing against White teams, the only federation to persist with a non-racial vision for the game also refused to play an all-African team. This is the kind of politics that verges on the prophetic – a voice in the wilderness. One cannot but think of C.L.R. James' assertion that 'To establish his own identity, Caliban, after three centuries, must himself pioneer into regions Caesar never knew.'[6]

Talking to SEDRU stalwarts of the early 1980s, it becomes clear that non-racialism, as much as it was fuzzy, was a long-term vision that had to be lived in the present. Jon Soske's reflections on non-racialism are incredibly apposite, as one thinks of those rugby warriors of the 1960s, 1970s, and 1980s:

> As a multivalent 'structure of feeling', shared across ideological commitments, nonracialism resisted easy encapsulation in the form of a theory or doctrine .... Yet for many of the activists who internalized it through their participation in the struggle, it came to possess a power and clarity that approached self-evidence. At the same time, the translation of felt principle into reality proved deeply contentious.[7]

How would the rapidly changing political terrain of the early 1990s impact on sport, with its huge divide, encapsulated by the cricket grounds of Springfield and Kingsmead?

Turf wars

In 1990, as Nelson Mandela strode out of prison, the two worlds of sport edged closer. In 1991, they united, at the top at least, and international recognition quickly beckoned. By this time, a new sports organization, the National Sports Congress (NSC) had risen like a phoenix. It was seen as the sports arm of the ANC and effectively supplanted SACOS in the public domain.

A debate began to emerge in the sports movement. There was a strong lobby from SACOS associated sportspersons that international competition be embargoed until there was a commitment to level the playing fields. The ANC, with Mandela at the fore, leaned to an immediate return and were supported by the NSC. The players coming out of Springfield grounds would have to compete with players from Kingsmead.

Across the country, sportspersons, beholden to the idea of 'no normal sport in an abnormal society' and the ideals of non-racialism, began to turn on each other. In Makhanda, for example, the battle between SACOS and the NSC took its toll on the rugby-loving people as they struggled with ideas of non-racialism, allegiances born in the heat of struggle, and a new politics of power with its concomitant trappings of privilege. As in 1972, Black rugby in Makhanda faced divisions that bit deep into old loyalties and clubs. One of the rugby greats of the 1970s, with the passion of an old warrior asked to recount battles whose wounds still fester, George Lamani, remembered:

In 1989, Lilywhite split again. Swallows had divisions. We were again affected when the NSC people came. What was being preached to us was that the NSC wants a truly non-racial rugby. We asked ourselves, how could they want that? They said, if you look at the current South African Council on Sport, there are no Black people there. Then we asked them, 'Who are Black people?' They said, 'You are being controlled by the Coloureds'. This is what they were saying. At first, we couldn't decide which non-racialism is more right. Fortunately, at the time that this came, I was also in the management of the club. We were asking, 'Guys, if you want an organization that will be controlled by Blacks ... if you are looking at the demographics of this country ... why are you taking us away from what has been tried and tested? Because, you are now theorising to us that you are now going to be truly non-racial. Guys, we haven't seen these people in action. Why do you want to take us to where we don't know?' That's how we managed as a club to say, guys, let's stay where we are. That's where we were playing under SACOS, Lilywhite and Swallows.[8]

The politics of transition and the 'unity' of sports organizations have received attention in many publications.[9] In addition, the debate about this sports unity has been posed in binary terms; use resources to level the playing fields, or

race headlong into full international competition .... [T]he latter won out as the global capitalist sports system is too powerful for nations such as South Africa to resist. Additionally, Mandela and the ANC invested in sport with the role of reaching out to worried whites who feared what majority rule would mean to their 'way of life'.[10]

Of course, the story was linked to a rapidly changing political conjuncture. The ANC wanted to 'normalize' South African society after the long years of 'ungovernability'. Part of this process was to be achieved by being accepted rapidly into existing global organizations, whether it be the World Bank or International Olympic Committee (IOC). It was hoped by many in the NSC that the largesse from international competitions would then filter down to the grassroots.

Normal sport?

What is important to keep in mind for this particular narrative is how 'unity' played out in places like Makhanda. Overnight, Black clubs were asked to compete in open competition with White clubs. A century of basically two worlds; one with gravel fields and car head-lights acting as floodlights shared by four to five teams; the other of pristine fields and club houses. Black clubs scrambled and amalgamated to strengthen themselves. Rugby colours that survived through the tortured twentieth century were exchanged for the post-apartheid hoop. Those incubators of Black rugby talent, schools, were abandoned as the old private schools kept, if not improved, their standards, by recruiting Black rural talent.

This promise to redress the conditions of existence of those oppressed under apartheid came to be captured in a simple but evocative ANC slogan: 'A Better Life for All'. The party's Reconstruction and Development Programme (RDP) of 1994 promised a heady mix of measures to address the expectations of the majority of South Africans, for whom poverty and minimal life chances were still a daily reality.[11] The RDP specifically addressed sport and recreation, referring to it as '[o]ne of the cruellest legacies of apartheid' and signalling an emphasis on the 'provision of facilities at schools and in communities where there are large concentrations of unemployed youth'. As was the way with the RDP, the document tempered this commitment with the recognition that 'sport is played at different levels of competence and ... there are different specific needs at different levels'.[12]

In the aftermath of the 1995 World Cup, it appeared that everyone could be part of a 'talismanic club of equality',[13] but the challenges of redress and change would see sport become an arena of intense engagement, contestation, and dreams both broken and realized.

From top to bottom

In discussions and debates around policy formulation for the 'new' South Africa, two approaches that could broadly be labelled 'reformative' and 'transformative' emerged. The transformative project sought to fundamentally transform the way in which society was structured; its economic emphasis was best captured in the popular slogan 'growth through redistribution'. In sport, this would mean a bottom-up, mass-based approach. The reformative approach, on the other hand, prioritized reconciliation and cooperative governance, in the interests of economic growth and acceptance into a neoliberal world order. In this scenario, conditions best suited to facilitate an environment for doing business in South Africa would be created; the logic underlying this paradigm was that the benefits of economic growth would 'naturally' trickle down to the poorest members of society. This argument was encapsulated in the adage 'redistribution through growth'. In this model, state intervention would be key in de-racializing the uppermost reaches of class hierarchy through the pursuit of Black Economic Empowerment (BEE). In sport, this would be seen in the emphasis on high-performance centres and on the racial composition of national teams. Billions of rands would also be pumped into mega sports events, such as football's FIFA World Cup 2010.

It was the reformative project that won hegemony as the transition to democracy unfolded; encapsulated in economic policies whereby the 'twin objectives of restoring business confidence and attracting foreign investment seemed to swamp all other considerations'.[14] Still, the hope was that integration into the global economy and stable social relations would slowly produce dividends in order to redress the huge inequalities bequeathed by apartheid. In the first decade, the score line did not make great reading for the poor, while a small Black elite was making quick-fire gains.

Between 1994 and 2004, the number of South Africans who would be classified as 'super rich', in other words having assets in excess of US $30 million (approximately R300 million), increased from 150 to 600.[15] Included in this list were some well-known figures from the former liberation movement. The black elite had arrived, and the speed of wealth accumulation was astounding. Alongside this, there was an immediate post-apartheid rise in income and intra-race inequality.[16]

More recent figures do not make for any better reading. The Living Conditions Survey of 2014/2015 showed that approximately 40 per cent of South Africans were living below the upper-bound poverty line:

> the highest headcount of adult poverty is Limpopo (67,5%), Eastern Cape (67,3%), KwaZulu-Natal (60,7%) and North West (59,6%). For these four provinces, significantly more than half of their population were living in poverty. Gauteng and Western Cape had the lowest proportion of adults living in poverty at 29,3% and 33,2%, respectively.[17]

The trickle-down had not worked and change to people's lives is minimal.

In sport, while a tremendous amount of resources has been thrown into mega stadiums and the professionalization of sport, this has created a stratum of highly paid players of all colours, while doing little to redress the damage caused by 'one of the cruellest legacies of apartheid'.[18]

It is not difficult to discern that there are two sporting fields in South Africa, one represented in state-of-the-art, high-performance sports centres and incredible stadiums built in preparation for the 2010 World Cup. It is also to be seen in the old White schools, with four or five rugby fields, floodlights, Olympic-size swimming pools, and highly qualified coaches. The other sporting field consists of sandpits that pass for football pitches, a lack of even rudimentary equipment, and the erosion of organized school sports. In shack-lands across the country, footballers barely carve out a tiny piece of land that becomes 'home ground' for five to ten teams, before this is gobbled up by more shacks.

In cricket, for example, instead of a mass approach that concentrated resources on township clubs and schools, the emphasis was placed on ensuring that international teams were competitive. The majority of African players are now either middle class or have been removed from townships into middle-class or private schools, in order to provide them with the proper training, diet, and education. One might add that, in this environment, school sport in state schools is virtually non-existent. Siya Kolisi, the present Springbok rugby captain, sums up the state of play with brutal simplicity: 'Imagine if I hadn't gone to an English school. I wouldn't have eaten properly, I wouldn't have grown properly and I wouldn't have had the preparation that the other boys did.'[19]

Kolisi is one of the exceptions.[20] In African township schools across the country, sport as an organized activity remains mostly non-existent. The same is the case in Coloured and Indian schools in working-class areas. Black cricket clubs that survived apartheid have disappeared and schools' cricket in the townships has never really taken off. Part of the reason is that cricket cannot provide facilities on its own, and government, which cannot even provide toilets in schools, has opted for a numbers game, particularly in cricket. This model fits in with the ANC government's notion of Black Economic Empowerment (BEE), which has sought to foster a Black middle and upper class, often at the expense of the African poor.

Between race and class apartheid

With the failure to produce African cricketers by the late 1990s, and in the absence of facilities in townships, cricket administrators opted to place talented Black cricketers in elite former White Model C (government) or private (independent) schools. It is mostly Black players from these elite schools, with access to a privileged education, excellent diet, outstanding facilities, and high-level coaching, who are selected to meet 'race' quotas and are exhibited as proof of cricket's transformation.

In this regard, race and class remain at the forefront of discussions about cricket and rugby in South Africa. As long as the status quo remains, transformation will mainly be viewed as a race issue. Until facilities are extended into townships and the base of cricket and rugby expanded, the gap between the haves and have-nots will remain, if not widen. Meanwhile, this class bias is over-ridden by an almost messianic drive that is enveloping some cricket administrators to Africanize the game, but in the absence of massive spending in school sports and townships more generally, the pool of African players will continue to come from an elite-strata of society and schools. While quotas have facilitated the emergence of African players, this development fails to address the workings of class and privilege in sporting achievement. To effect real change, macro-economic structural change that leads to a more equitable redistribution of resources and equality of opportunity is required.

The different roads into national teams for Black players have been almost exclusively through ex-Model C schools or private schools. The downside of this model of transformation is that it removes the imperative to develop a culture of cricket in the townships.

At the dawn of South Africa's democracy, Mike Marqusee wrote:

> With the end of apartheid and the coming of democracy, will white and black in South Africa at long last share a level playing field? … Will development be aimed at producing showpiece players for the national squad, or will tend the grassroots? … How will the legacy of apartheid be redressed? Are electoral democracy and legal equality enough? Or will more radical solutions have to be found? The lesson of the years of isolation is that cricket cannot be an island. The tensions between the dictates of the market and the promise of democracy which will course through South African society in the years to come will also run through South African cricket.[21]

Marqusee's words are still prescient two decades later. Class apartheid can be witnessed in the very geography of South African cities and reinforced by a bountifully endowed private and semi-private school system, ranged against township schools which struggle with huge numbers and largely non-existent sporting facilities.

But, this is not to discount the heart-tingling changes that have taken place.

Grounds of hope?

Since those words were written, the reality of the South African transition has come in for critical scrutiny. Poverty and inequality have deepened and Mandela's ANC has been caught in a quagmire of corruption. As the years have unfolded, Maingard's summation of the victory in 1995 as an 'orchestration of national identity', an imposition, has come to have greater and greater resonance.[22]

The lifting of the cup by Siya Kolisi in 2019 felt more organic, more real. C.L.R. James, who was involved in the struggle to ensure that Frank Worrell became the first Black man to captain the West Indies in the 1950s in an entire series, noted that on the tour to Australia, what he found himself 'hoping for was that we would give a good account of ourselves, and that we would shed much ancient baggage to lighten ourselves for a long climb'.[23] James tells us that Worrell, through his leadership and post-match speeches, 'expanded' the 'conception of West Indian personality'.[24]

Kolisi, too, enlarges the idea of what it is to be a South African. In the name of transformation, by now quite organic, Big Brother still insists on dictating the exact composition of teams, obsessively trading in racial categories as any administrator of the old separate Coloured, White, and African rugby boards would have been versed in.[25] With the same no-nonsense approach with which he approaches a ruck, Kolisi confronted racial quotas, reaching beyond the tight sc(r)um of race, beckoning once more the militant non-racialism of the 1970s. In 1995, the ANC government provided some cover for rugby's racial make-up. In 2019, the ANC, dogged by a virulent African racial chauvinism, tailed behind the game with an oval ball.

Makhanda represents a microcosm of small-town experience in present-day South Africa. Anthony Lemon points out:

> The city's population was recorded as 62,640 in the 1996 census, but five years later the real figure was estimated to be about 100,000 .... The result of this growth, in the absence of significant economic growth, is an estimated unemployment rate of 60–70 per cent. Survival, for many families, depends upon old age pensions (often supporting younger members of the family as well as their recipients) and informal employment.[26]

Into the year 2020, by all accounts, unemployment and reliance on grants have increased. It is symptomatic of many an Eastern Cape town. In a seminal judgement, the Makana Municipality was ordered to dissolve for its lack of service delivery. In court papers, residents detailed a myriad of ways in which the Municipality had failed them, with the Judge responding that the Municipality should be 'hanging their heads in shame'.[27]

The Minister of Sport and Recreation, Makhenkesi Stofile, in 2004, promised:

> Our focus will be to build the right attitude and skills from below. In our view the starting place to achieve this is to get the basics right. Community clubs must be received and our children in townships and village schools must be assisted to do sport. There is no short cut to this .... Schools sport is the nursery for participants in senior competition .... We are strongly arguing here for a focussed attention on the schools and community clubs in building a broad base for talent scouting, developing and nurturing. This is the mass that will transform society and de-racialise it. We must go back to Wednesday afternoons as school sports days. But this cannot happen by chance.[28]

There has not just been a retreat from these lofty ideals come 2020, but what is seemingly a capitulation to an elite transition.[29] The June 2020 report on Transformation in Sport compiled by the Eminent Persons Group (EPG) revealed that fewer than 10 per cent of the 25,000 schools in the country participate in sport. The gap between private schools and township schools is widening rather than closing. Marqusee's question, posed in 1995, of whether 'development be aimed at producing showpiece players for the national squad, or will tend the grassroots?' can only be answered that sport remains at the level of 'showpiece players'.

Sport in post-apartheid South Africa

Old traditions, new times

What will be the spark for a new struggle to level the playing field?

Perhaps the idea of non-racialism of SACOS, which envisioned the 'free interaction of all human beings in all activities of society on the basis of total equality and opportunity without regard to race', and not the 'mere physical presence … of different races and colours on the … field', seems today almost a quaint idea, more for speechifying than having any real purchase.[30] But can the idea of a *militant* non-racialism be resurrected; an idea that places both the idea of racial transformation and class privilege centre-stage?

Whatever one thinks of the idealism of 'same opportunity', one can see how at the height of apartheid these words had such an evocative ring. Twenty-five years after unification, can they bring into sharper focus both race and class privilege? Is there an ability to move from the hollowness of transformation speak, which 'has been divested of radicalism and reduced to head counts'[31] to the idea of structural change that places redistribution and inequality at the centre of macro-economic policy?

Nevertheless, sport has come a long way since the days when my father was 'helped' over the barrier separating Whites and Non-Whites at Kingsmead, and top Black cricketers changed behind the trees at Springfield cricket grounds in Durban. But one still has a deep sense that the commitments made at the onset of South Africa's admittance into world sport, about taking the game to grassroots level, about firing up sport in township schools, about redressing past inequalities, have stalled.

As I write this article, the Eminent Persons Group in Sport released its report. In his foreword, Minister of Sport, Nathi Mthethwa concedes that 'the impact of increasing levels of poverty and inequality' is 'dividing the sports system in two – one for those who can afford to play, and another for those who cannot afford to play.' He goes on to argue that: 'It is, therefore, crystal clear that if we fail to administer tough reforms and find reliable partners in implementing the transformation agenda, we will be failing our society and future generations.'[32]

The central approach of these transformation efforts seems to be to closely monitor organizations running sport, demanding that they provide minute details of how they are ensuring progressive moves towards demographic representation at all levels of the organization. The emphasis is on self-policing and numbers. Witness the words of the Minister again:

> Transformation status is established by measuring actual federation performance in 18 categories (as defined by the Charter) against two sets of targets in scorecard format. The one scorecard is based on the achievement of the prescribed and one-size-fits-all targets of the Charter, and the other, the 'Barometer' (introduced in 2016/2017) is based on the achievement of a federation's own or self-set and forward-projected targets. Both sets of measures serve as milestones directing a federation's transformation journey towards 'an accessible, equitable, sustainable, demographically representative and competitive sport system'. As the adage goes, 'you can't improve what you don't measure'. Therefore, the quality of data collected and submitted by federations becomes integral to the audit process. Though there has been some improvement in the data submitted, more still needs to be done …. With all the barometer forecasts reviewed and changed where required, penalties will be rigorously applied in 2020. Four of the five pilot federations, namely rugby, cricket, football and netball, have all achieved their self-set Barometer targets in 2018/19.[33]

The responsibility of the government in providing basic facilities at schools in what, in the Minister's own words, is 'dysfunctional' is ignored. Sports administrators are reduced to Kafkaesque figures spending their time in filling in forms providing 'progress' reports on racial representation. The importance of growing the game, building township facilities, the progressive erosion of two systems of sport are not the priority. And so divides deepen as the racial complexion of sport changes.

The race game increasingly exposes the class game of the ANC. Travelling through the back-lands of South Africa, one sees the continuing power of the slogan 'no normal sport in an abnormal society'.

Notes

1 Patti Waldmeir, *Anatomy of a Miracle: The End of Apartheid and the Birth of a New South Africa* (London: Penguin, 1998), 270.
2 John Nauright, *Sports, Identities and Cultures in South Africa* (London: Philip, 1997) and Douglas Booth, *The Race Game: Sport and Politics in South Africa* (London: Frank Cass Publishers, 1998).
3 C.L.R. James, *Beyond a Boundary* (Durham: Duke University Press, 1963/2013), 66.
4 Ashwell Adriaan conducted most of these interviews. We are collaborating on a book entitled *Line-Breakers and History Makers: The Rugby Playing Sons of Makana and Stuurman*.
5 Chris Laidlaw, *Mud in Your Eye* (Cape Town: Howard Timms, 2004), 188.
6 James, *Beyond a Boundary*, Preface.
7 Jon Soske, 'African Nationalism, Nonracialism, and Pan-Africanism', in *The Oxford Handbook of South African History*, ed. D. Magaziner (online edition 2020), 16.
8 Interview by Ashwell Adriaan.
9 Booth, *The Race Game*; Samba Ramsamy (with E. Griffiths), *Reflections on a Life in Sport* (Cape Town: Greenhouse, 2004); Ashwin Desai, 'Introduction: Long Run to Freedom?' in *Race to Transform: Sport in Post-apartheid South Africa*, ed. Ashwin Desai (Pretoria: HSRC Press, 2010), 1–13.
10 Nauright, *Sports, Identities and Cultures*, 157–158.
11 African National Congress (ANC), 'Organizational Renewal: Building the ANC as a Movement of Power' (2012) http://www.anc.org.za/docs/discus/2012/organizational renewalf.pdf
12 ANC, 'Reconstruction and Development Programme' (Pretoria: Umanyano Publications, 1994), 72.
13 *Cape Times*, 26 June 1995.
14 Martin Murray, *The Revolution Deferred: The Painful Birth of Post-Apartheid South Africa* (London: Verso, 1994), 24.
15 *Sunday Times*, 9 May 2004.
16 Statistics South Africa, Men, Women and Children: Findings of the Living Conditions Survey 2014/2015 (2020) http://www.statssa.gov.za/?p=12075.
17 Statistics South Africa.
18 ANC, 'Reconstruction and Development Programme', 72.
19 *Sport 24*, 1 July 2019.
20 Jeremy Daniel, *Siya Kolisi: Against All Odds* (Johannesburg: Jonathan Ball, 2019).
21 Mike Marqusee, *Anyone but England: Cricket and the National Malaise* (London: Verso Books, 1995), 212.
22 Jacqueline Maingard, 'Imag(in)ing the South African Nation: Representations of Identity in the Rugby World Cup 1995', *Theatre Journal* 49 (1997): 17.
23 James, *Beyond a Boundary*, 257.
24 James, *Beyond a Boundary*, 260.
25 Christopher Merrett, Colin Tatz, and Daryl Adair, 'History and Its Racial Legacies: Quotas in South African Rugby and Cricket.' *Sport in Society* 14, no. 6 (2011): 754–777.
26 Anthony Lemon, 'Redressing School Inequalities in the Eastern Cape, South Africa', *Journal of Southern African Studies* 30, no. 2 (2004): 278–279.
27 *Maverick Citizen*, 22 May 2020.
28 Makhenkesi Stofile, Minster of Sport and Recreation Speech (2004), www.info.gov.za/speeches/2004/04061511451004.htm.
29 Patrick Bond, *Elite Transition* (Pietermaritzburg: University of KwaZulu-Natal Press, 2005).

30 Ashwin Desai, Vishnu Padayachee, Krish Reddy, and Goolam Vahed, *Blacks in Whites: A Century of Cricket Struggles in KwaZulu-Natal* (Pietermaritzburg: University of Natal Press, 2002), 351.

31 ANC, 'Organizational Renewal'.

32 Sports and Recreation SA, 2020: Sport and Recreation South Africa, EPG Comparative Sport Federation Transformation Status Dashboard, 5, https://www.srsa.gov.za/sites/default/files/Transformation%20Status%20Report%20-%202016-2017%20EPG%20-FINAL.pdf, and Sport and Recreation South Africa, EPG Individual Federation Barometer; Sport Transformation Charter Scorecards 2018/2019 (2020) https://www.srsa.gov.za/sites/default/files/Part%201%20SRSA%20EPG%20Individual%20%20Federation%20Barometer%20and%20Sport%20Transformation%20Charter%20Scorecards_LR_0.pdf.

33 Sports and Recreation SA, 5.

21
WOMEN'S SPORT HISTORY

Jaime Schultz, Michelle M. Sikes and Cat M. Ariail

The academic study of women's sport emerged in the late 1960s and early 1970s with the rise of social history, women's history, and sport history. At the same time, women's sport activism, feminist movements, civil rights movements, fitness booms, and the democratization of higher education set the stage for greater attention to the history of women's active physicality. Early academic efforts were often 'compensatory' or 'recuperative' projects that entailed 'adding female subjects to histories that did not include them'.[1] Sport historians first devoted isolated sections or chapters to 'the role of women in sports'.[2] Soon thereafter began the gradual, grinding effort to transform 'the history of women in sport' into what Reet Howell called 'her story in sport' and, later, to 'women's sport history', in the words of Catriona Parratt.[3]

Early works were often descriptive, progressive narratives that began with women's 'exclusion' from and 'controlled development' in sport.[4] Academics tended to focus on 'women worthies' or significant figures in institutionalized sport and physical education. These foundational studies were important political enterprises that attended to the hidden scripts of women's involvement in sport and demanded they be taken seriously.

In 1984, Nancy Struna urged historians to go 'beyond mapping' women's experiences and ask what remain crucial questions today:

> Has our literature moved beyond the parochial to the universal questions which historians ask; has it begun to suggest what ultimate difference woman's sporting experience makes in our total understanding of the human experience; is it contributing to theoretical debate and methodological innovation?[5]

Over the next two decades, a number of scholars answered Struna's call. At the forefront were those who utilized gender as a 'useful category of historical analysis', as Joan Scott persuasively argued.[6] Theorizing gender and, to a lesser extent, race, ethnicity, sexuality, religion, and social class, opened new possibilities for sources, methodology, periodization, and the conceptualization of sport. For example, in *The Eternally Wounded Woman*, Patricia Vertinsky provided a Foucauldian analysis of the medical discourse that shaped Victorian womanhood.[7] Four years later, Susan Cahn's 'landmark study', *Coming on Strong*, critically blended issues of gender, sexuality, race, and social class.[8] Adding to this were increasingly sophisticated critiques of health, physical education, exercise, recreation, and the body.[9]

Since the turn of the twenty-first century, scholars have sought innovative answers to new lines of inquiry, such as religious and spiritual differences, feminist analyses of power, and 'who counts as the subjects of women's history?'[10] Although there has been significant progress, there remains much to be done. Carol A. Osborne and Fiona Skillen note that the 'dedicated study of women in sport history remains a peculiarly neglected area of academic research in Britain'.[11] Daryl Adair similarly contends that 'the analysis of women in Australian sport history seems to have reached a hiatus'.[12] African women 'have long been on the periphery of methodological, theoretical and empirical discussion', according to Michelle Sikes and John Bale.[13] Moving women from margins to centre is exceedingly important. As Brenda Elsey and Joshua Nadel argue in *Futbolera: A History of Women and Sports in Latin America*, neglecting women's historical participation serves to 'naturalize gender differences in society more broadly and to justify the denial of resources to women athletes.'[14]

Women, sport, and identity

A prospective athlete's identity has often determined the opportunities available to her. Historians of twentieth-century women's sport highlight the complex ways in which identities – particularly racial, ethnic, and classed – influence opportunities across the American continent. From middle- and upper-class white women, often considered too fragile to play, to women of colour long excluded by 'mainstream' society, women have asserted their status as athletes as their performances raised questions about the socially constructed categories used to define and divide people.

Cahn's *Coming on Strong* is instructive for introducing how these differences operated. For example, her account of the tensions surrounding women's basketball at the turn of the twentieth century demonstrates how racialized class norms determined if, when, and where women could take the court.[15] Yet, many women challenged those norms. Martha Verbrugge describes how white women at elite colleges across the United States 'pushed back by creating forms of competition and ambition within the bounds of mass recreation'.[16] Various 'points of change' in the timeline of US women's sport, as Jaime Schultz argues in *Qualifying Times*, have also marked uneven development for women. For instance, changes in tennis fashion, the emergence of commercial tampons, the invention of the sports bra, the passage of Title IX, and the commercial fitness industry often benefited white, middle-class women more than others.[17]

Class position and politics likewise influenced African American women's opportunities. In contrast to their white counterparts, Black middle-class Americans increasingly understood sport as a space for enhancing young women's respectability, as well as the respectability of the race.[18] Nonetheless, as Rita Liberti highlights in her account of basketball at the historically Black Bennett College, women's sport in the early-to-mid twentieth century 'reveal[s] complexities of an on-going negotiation of boundaries surrounding female physicality in the African American community'.[19] Moreover, many of the racialized beliefs that prohibited white women's athletic pursuits opened up opportunities to African American women, especially in post-Second World War track and field. Through superlative performance and careful comportment, athletes representing institutions such as Tuskegee Institute and Tennessee State University earned national attention and admiration.[20] Even as they encountered enduring discrimination, they introduced new models of athleticism and American identity. This is particularly true of Tennessee State's Wilma Rudolph, winner of three gold medals at the 1960 Olympic Games. Still, as Liberti and Maureen Smith emphasize in their analysis of Rudolph's 'fairy tale', there are important distinctions between history, memory, and the past.[21]

Throughout the twentieth century, women from multiple racial, ethnic, and religious backgrounds cultivated their own sporting spaces, motivated by what sociologist Nicole Willms calls 'a push-pull phenomenon: the pull of shared culture – language, food, customs – and the push of being ostracized by the mainstream culture'.[22] Linda Borish, for instance, examines how Jewish American young women used sport to assert their religious and national identities.[23] In 1920s and 1930s California, Buddhist temples and Young Women's Buddhist Associations established basketball leagues and teams for Japanese American girls and women. During the Second World War, the US government enacted policy that interned over 110,000 people of Japanese descent, most of whom were American citizens. In those deplorable camps, documents Samuel Regalado, women's softball and other sports provided sources of identity, community, and much-needed morale boosts.[24]

The importance of sport for twentieth-century women is clear throughout the Americas, as young athletic women in Central and South America, as well as the Caribbean, contested the norms of nation, gender, race, and colour, as several scholars have begun to document.[25] The study of women's sporting experiences across period and place underscores the potential of these histories to provide insight into the construction of identities and communities.

Global perspectives and social change

A global narrative of women's sport history beyond the ambit of North America and parts of Europe has been slow to develop. Asian, African, and the Middle Eastern sportswomen have been absent from this historical record. Writing in 1990 about the physical activity of Asian girls in Malaya during the early twentieth century, Janice Brownfoot observed, 'Serious studies of the relationship of sport to issues of gender and social change for females in colonial societies are virtually non-existent.'[26] More than 30 years later, narratives of sport, women, and social change have advanced. The emergence of women's football (soccer) in China, Korea, and India; 'football feminine' and the development of the game in Africa; and Muslim women, sport, politics, and power have all received attention in edited collections.[27] Full anthologies, although not always historical, have been published on *Muslim Women and Sport* and *Women's Sport in Africa*.[28] What follows outlines some of the key texts and trajectories in this literature, with focus on China, the Muslim world, and South Africa.

Twentieth-century Chinese sportswomen excelled, and a growing number of sport historians began to challenge the assumption that elite sport was a male preserve.[29] Fan Hong's *Footbinding, Feminism and Freedom* explored the beginnings of the 'physical emancipation' of Chinese women, after which scholars shifted the debate from issues of 'sport as male' to those of women becoming, in Susan Brownell's words, 'symbolic figureheads in the revival of Chinese nationalism'.[30]

Historians concerned with Muslim sportswomen have grappled with how to balance oppression with agency, victimization with resistance, and gender with religion, nation, class, and ethnicity, while not treating 'Muslim women' as a homogenous category.[31] Studies such as Jennifer Hargreaves' work on the 'Muslim female heroic', Sharon Wray's investigation of Muslim Pakistani women's physical activity, Payoshni Mitra's examination of female boxers of Kolkata, and Gertrud Pfister's analysis of the opportunities for and barriers to participation in elite sport for women from Islamic countries, all share an interest in how Muslim women negotiated the tension evoked by involvement in Western styles of physical activity.[32]

Over the past 20 years, a growing body of historical work addresses the under-representation of women in African sport history by recognizing women's place in football, track and field, and other sports. Scholars have focused on sport in South Africa, particularly women's football, and in relation to race and class.[33] Led by Cheryl Roberts's *Against the Grain: Women and Sport in South Africa* and Denise Jones's 'Race and Gender Challenges', historians of sporting women in South Africa have heeded Susan Birrell's call for critical analyses of racial relations and sport, in common with the scholars detailed earlier in this chapter.[34]

Taken together, these writings demonstrate the significance and diversity of athletes previously marginalized within the annals of sport history. Yet we still know too little about the sporting pasts of too many groups of women. 'Diversity is part of the strength and richness and political power of sportswomen,' affirms Hargreaves, 'but only if communication across differences takes place.'[35] We urge scholars to continue this conversation, certain that addressing the gaps that remain, some of which are outlined below, will provide a rich seam of scholarship for anyone interested in relations of power, politics, and sport history.

The possibilities for power, politics, and women's sport history

Based on the review of literature, the following 'Top 10' list of possibilities suggests various turns that historians of women's sport might take in the future.

1 *Women 'without sport history'*: Too many groups and populations remain either under-represented or absent – women 'without sport history', to use Brownell's phrase.[36] Few scholars have addressed issues of age. The field lacks substantial information on the history of women with impairments and in para sport. Our scholarship on women of colour continues to grow but must do more to move beyond 'the Black–white paradigm' that shapes 'the popular narrative about race and sport in society'.[37] And historians continue to marginalize issues of social class, religion, sexualities, and migration.

2 *Intersectionality*: Although there are many populations, identities, and subjectivities that still need attention, analyses attending to these issues must not perpetuate 'single-axis frameworks'. More than three decades on from legal theorist Kimberlé Crenshaw's generative work, sport historians have yet to take an identifiable 'intersectional turn' to account for 'the intersections of racism, sexism, class oppression, transphobia, able-ism and more'.[38] Importantly, however, such a turn should not fall victim to the 'whitening' and depoliticization of intersectionality.[39]

3 *Geographical exclusions*: The field benefits from work that is both globally informed and locally grounded. What are the debates and challenges prevalent in specific regions when it comes to women and sport? How can this work speak to the concerns, contexts, struggles, and challenges of women's sporting pasts beyond the Global North?

4 *Transnational histories*: At the same time, the field remains wedded to the nation–state paradigm. Moving across national borders and taking a transnational turn, according to historian Lynn Hunt, 'promises to offer not just fresh perspectives on the past but truer accounts of it: it puts Africa and Asia back into the study of African and Asian Americans, the influence of competing empires back into the history of the early United States, the colonized back into the study of imperialism, diasporic peoples back into the study of trade networks, and so on'.[40]

5 *Theoretically informed analyses*: Feminist sport historians have been at the forefront of theoretical insight and innovation. Still, greater sensitivities to and engagements with

critical race theory, queer theory, crip theory, postcolonial feminism, literary criticism, borderland studies, cultural memory, and other perspectives can provide alternative ways of interpreting the past.

6 *Expansion of sources*: Scholars interested in women's sport have always had to be creative with their primary source material. They have made good use of visual and material culture, oral histories, estate inventories, court proceedings, census data, athletic fashions and equipment, memoirs, letters, and diaries, but more experimentation is needed to account for the complexities of women's sporting pasts.[41]

7 *Methodological innovation*: How is women's sport history being produced? How can sport historians better define the choice and application of methods, the interpretation and analysis of findings, and ultimately develop feminist methodological approaches to this topic?

8 *Representing the past*: Booth criticized sport historians for their 'tendency toward conformity and a stifling of experimentation'.[42] Feminist scholars offer exceptions to his critique by playing with text, form, style, and reflexivity.[43] What might historians do with genres of historical fiction and film, critical biography, public history, or digital technologies?

9 *Digital technologies*: Sport history has only recently joined the 'digital revolution' that began in the mid-1990s. There are exciting possibilities for decolonizing and diversifying traditional repositories. Moreover, digitization can democratize access to historical memories and artefacts, yet it is important to remain sensitive to the predominant use of 'first-world language' and to keep in mind who has access to computers and the Internet.[44]

10 *Politically-engaged histories*: Women's sport history is always already political. By attending to women's experiences, historians have disrupted sport history's dominant paradigms and troubled the field's disciplinary concepts. Parratt urges historians to 'talk back to the institutionalized power in sport that keeps its girls and women, keeps so many, from safely realizing their full humanity'.[45] For as Colin Howell asks, 'if history does not have emancipatory potential then what is its value'?[46] Jeffrey Hill provides an answer: 'if the study of sport and leisure is not "political" in the broadest sense of the term, then it isn't worth a damn'.[47]

These and other possibilities for ingenuity, innovation, and interpretation can keep the field moving forward in understanding what 'ultimate difference woman's sporting experience makes in our total understanding of the human experience'.[48]

Notes

1 Gerda Lerner, 'Placing Women in History: Definitions and Challenges', *Feminist Studies* 3, nos. 1–2 (1975): 5.

2 Joan S. Hult and Roberta Park, 'The Role of Women in Sports', in *Sports in Modern America*, eds. William J. Baker and John M. Carroll (St. Louis: River City Publishers, 1981), 115–128.

3 Catriona M. Parratt, 'From the History of Women in Sport to Women's Sport History: A Research Agenda', in *Women and Sport: Interdisciplinary Perspectives*, eds. D. Margaret Costa and Sharon R. Guthrie (Champaign, IL: Human Kinetics, 1994), 5–14.

4 Ellen Gerber, 'The Controlled Development of Collegiate Sport for Women, 1923–1936', *Journal of Sport History* 2, no. 1 (1975): 1–28; Joanna Davenport, 'The Women's Movement into the Olympic Games', *Journal of Physical Education and Recreation* 49, no. 3 (1978): 58–60.

5 Nancy Struna, 'Beyond Mapping Experience: The Need for Understanding the History of American Sporting Women', *Journal of Sport History* 11, no. 1 (1984): 121.

6 Joan W. Scott, 'Gender: A Useful Category of Historical Analysis', *The American Historical Review* 91, no. 5 (1986): 1053–1075; Patricia A. Vertinsky, 'Gender Relations, Women's History and Sport History: A Decade of Changing Enquiry, 1983–1993', *Journal of Sport History* 21, no. 1 (1994): 1–24.

7 Patricia A. Vertinsky, *The Eternally Wounded Woman: Women, Doctors, and Exercise in the Late Nineteenth Century* (Manchester University Press, 1990).

8 Susan K. Cahn, *Coming on Strong: Gender and Sexuality in Twentieth-century Women's Sport* (Harvard University Press, 1995); Linda J. Borish, 'Women in American Sport History', in *A Companion to American Sport History*, ed. Steven A. Riess (John Wiley & Sons, 2014), 511.

9 Roberta J. Park, 'A Decade of the Body: Researching and Writing about the History of Health, Fitness, Exercise and Sport, 1983–1993', *Journal of Sport History* 21, no. 1 (1994): 59–82; M. Ann Hall, *Feminism and Sporting Bodies: Essays on Theory and Practice* (Champaign, IL: Human Kinetics, 1996).

10 Elisa Camiscioli and Jean H. Quataert, 'Who Counts as the Subjects of Women's History?' *Journal of Women's History* 28, no. 4 (2016): 7–13.

11 Carol A. Osborne and Fiona Skillen, 'Introduction: The State of Play: Women in British Sport History', *Sport in History* 30, no. 2 (2010): 189–195.

12 Daryl Adair, 'Australian Sport History: From the Founding Years to Today', *Sport in History* 29, no. 3 (2009): 415.

13 Michelle Sikes and John Bale, 'Introduction: Women's Sport and Gender in Sub-Saharan Africa', in *Women's Sport in Africa*, eds. Michelle Sikes and John Bale (Routledge, 2015), 1.

14 Brenda Elsey and Joshua Nadel, *Futbolera: A History of Women and Sports in Latin America* (Austin: University of Texas Press, 2019).

15 Cahn, *Coming on Strong*, 55–109.

16 Martha H. Verbrugge, *Active Bodies: A History of Women's Physical Education in Twentieth-Century America* (New York: Oxford University Press, 2012), 109.

17 Jaime Schultz, *Qualifying Times: Points of Change in U.S. Women's Sport* (Urbana: University of Illinois Press, 2014).

18 Verbrugge, *Active Bodies*, 129–142.

19 Rita Liberti, '"We Were Ladies, We Just Played Basketball Like Boys": African American Womanhood and Competitive Basketball at Bennett College, 1928–1942', *Journal of Sport History* 26, no. 3 (1999): 579.

20 Cindy Himes Gissendanner, 'African American Women Olympians: The Impact of Race, Gender, and Class Ideologies, 1932–1968', *Research Quarterly for Exercise and Sport* 67, no. 2 (1996): 172–182; Jennifer H. Lansbury, *A Spectacular Leap: Black Women Athletes in Twentieth-Century America* (Fayetteville: University of Arkansas Press, 2014).

21 Rita Liberti and Maureen M. Smith, *(Re)Presenting Wilma Rudolph* (Syracuse, NY: Syracuse University Press, 2015).

22 Nicole Willms, *When Women Rule the Court: Gender, Race, and Japanese American Basketball* (New Brunswick, NJ: Rutgers University Press, 2017), 8.

23 Linda J. Borish, 'American Jewish Women on the Court: Seeking an Identity in Tennis in the Early Decades of the Twentieth Century', in *Beyond Stereotypes: American Jews and Sports: The Jewish Role in American Life*, eds. Bruce Zuckerman, Ari E. Sclar, and Lisa Ansell (West Lafayette, IN: Purdue University Press, 2014), 43–68; Linda J. Borish, 'The Philadelphia Jewish Y's: Sport and Physical Health in American Culture', in *Philly Sports: Teams, Games, and Athletes from Rocky's Town*, eds. Ryan A. Swanson and David K. Wiggins (Fayetteville: University of Arkansas Press, 2016), 113–126.

24 Samuel O. Regalado, 'Incarcerated Sport: Nisei Women's Softball and Athletics during Japanese American Internment', *Journal of Sport History* 27, no. 3 (Fall 2000): 431–444.

25 María Graciela Rodríguez, 'The Place of Women in Argentinian Football', *The International Journal of the History of Sport* 22, no. 2 (2005): 231–245; Claudia M. Guedes, 'Empowering Women through Sport: Women's Basketball in Brazil and the Significant Role of Maria Helena Cardoso', *The International Journal of the History of Sport* 27, no. 7 (2010): 1237–1249; Cat Ariail, 'Between the Boundaries: The Athletic Citizenship Quest of Carlota Gooden', *Journal of Sport History* 44, no. 1 (2017): 1–19; Claire Brewster and Keith Brewster, 'Women, Sport, and the Press in Twentieth-Century Mexico', *The International Journal of the History of Sport* 35, no. 10 (2019): 965–984; Elsey and Nadel, *Futbolera*.

26 Janice Brownfoot, 'Emancipation, Exercise and Imperialism: Girls and the Games Ethic in Colonial Malaya', *The International Journal of the History of Sport* 7, no. 1 (1990): 62.

27 See Fan Hong and J.A. Mangan eds. *Soccer, Women, Sexual Liberation: Kicking Off a New Era* (London: Frank Cass, 2004) for the following: Fan Hong and J.A. Mangan, 'Will the "Iron Roses" Bloom Forever? Women's Football in China: Changes and Challenges', 47–66; Eunha Koh, 'Chains, Challenges, and Changes: The Making of Women's Football in Korea', 67–79; Boria Majumdar, 'Forwards and Backwards: Women's Soccer in Twentieth Century India,' 80–94; Martha Saavedra, 'Football Feminine – Development of the African Game: Senegal, Nigeria and South Africa', 225–253. Jennifer Hargreaves 'Sport, Exercise, and the Female Muslim Body', in *Physical Culture, Power and the Body*, ed. Jennifer Hargreaves and Patricia Vertinsky (London: Routledge, 2007), 74–100.

28 Tansin Benn, Gertrud Pfister, and Haifaa Jawad eds. *Muslim Women and Sport* (London: Routledge, 2010); Sikes and Bale, *Women's Sport in Africa*.

29 Dong Jinxia, *Women, Sport and Society in Modern China: Holding up More than Half the Sky* (London: Frank Cass Publishers, 2003).

30 Fan Hong, *Footbinding, Feminism, and Freedom: The Liberation of Women's Bodies in Modern China* (London: Frank Cass, 1997); Susan Brownell, 'The Body and the Beautiful in Chinese Nationalism: Sportswomen and Fashion Models in the Reform Era', *China Information* 13, nos. 2–3 (1998): 41.

31 Jennifer Hargreaves, *Heroines of Sport: The Politics of Difference and Identity* (London: Routledge, 2000).

32 Hargreaves, *Heroines of Sport*, 46–77; Sharon Wray, 'Connecting Ethnicity, Gender and Physicality: Muslim Pakistani Women, Physical Activity and Health', in *Gender and Sport: A Reader*, eds. Sheila Scraton and Anne Flintoff (London: Routledge, 2002); Payoshini Mitra, 'Challenging Stereotypes: The Case of Muslim Female Boxers in Bengal', *The International Journal of the History of Sport* 26, no. 12 (2009): 1840–1851; Gertrud Pfister, 'Outsiders: Muslim Women and Olympic Games', *The International Journal of the History of Sport* 27, nos. 16–18 (2010): 2925–2957.

33 Cynthia Pelak, 'Women and Gender in South Africa Soccer: A Brief History', *Soccer and Society* 11, no. 1 (2010): 63–78.

34 Susan Birrell, 'Race Relations Theories and Sport: Suggestions for a More Critical Analysis', *Sociology of Sport*, 6 (1989): 212–227; Cheryl Roberts, *Against the Grain: Women and Sport in South Africa* (Cape Town: Township Publishing Cooperative, 1992); Denise Jones, 'Women and Sport in South Africa: Shaped by History and Shaping Sporting History', in *Sport and Women: Social Issues in International Perspective*, eds. Ilse Hartmann-Tews and Gertrud Pfister (London: Routledge, 2003), 130–144.

35 Hargreaves, *Heroines*, 232.

36 Susan Brownell, *Beijing's Games: What the Olympics Means to China* (Rowman and Littlefield, 2008), 20.

37 Adrian Burgos, Jr., 'Wait till Next Year: Sports History and the Quest for Respect', *Journal of American History* 101, no. 1 (2014): 179.

38 Kimberlé Williams Crenshaw, 'Demarginalizing the Intersection of Race and Sex: A Black Feminist Critique of Antidiscrimination Doctrine, Feminist Theory and Antiracist Politics', *University of Chicago Legal Forum* (1989): 139–167; Idem. (2015) 'Why Intersectionality Can't Wait', *Washington Post*, https ://www.washingtonpost.com/news/in-theory/wp/2015/09/24/why-intersectionality-cant-wait/?utm _term=.090672616d78.

39 Ange-Marie Hancock, *Intersectionality: An Intellectual History* (New York: Oxford University Press, 2016).

40 Lynn Hunt, 'The Future of the Discipline: The Prospects of the Present', *Perspectives on History* (December 2012), http://www.historians.org/publications-and-directories/perspectives-on-history/ december-2012/the-future-of-the-discipline.

41 Susan K. Cahn, 'Sports Talk: Oral History and its Uses, Problems, and Possibilities for Sport History', *The Journal of American History* 81, no. 2 (1994): 594–609; Nancy L. Struna, 'Gender and Sporting Practice in Early America, 1750–1810', *Journal of Sport History* 18, no. 1 (1991): 10–30; Linda J. Borish, and Murray G. Phillips, 'Sport History as Modes of Expression: Material Culture and Cultural Spaces in Sport and History', *Rethinking History* 16, no. 4 (2012): 465–477.

42 Douglas Booth, *The Field: Truth and Fiction in Sport History* (London: Routledge, 2007), 221.

43 Synthia Sydnor, 'A History of Synchronized Swimming', *Journal of Sport History* 25, no. 2 (1998): 252–267; Megan L. Popovic, 'A Voice in the Rink: Playing with our Histories and Evoking Auto-ethnography', *Journal of Sport History* 37, no. 2 (2010): 235–255; Carly Adams, '(Writing Myself into) Betty White's Stories: (De)constructing Narratives of/through Feminist Sport History Research', *Journal of Sport History* 39, no. 3 (2012): 395–413.

44 Paula Hamilton and Mary Spongberg, 'Twenty Years On: Feminist Histories and Digital Media', *Women's History Review* 26, no. 5 (2017): 673.
45 Catriona M. Parratt, 'A Testing Time', *Journal of Sport History* 41, no. 3 (2014): 493.
46 Colin Howell, 'Assessing Sport History and the Cultural and Linguistic Turn', *Journal of Sport History* 34, no. 3 (2007): 461.
47 Jeffrey Hill, *Sport, Leisure, and Culture in Twentieth Century Britain* (New York: Palgrave, 2002), 187.
48 Struna, 'Beyond Mapping', 121.

22
TROUBLING SEXUALITY AND SPORT
Early histories of queer athletic visibility

Judy Davidson

In the summer of 2019, at the FIFA Women's World Cup, soccer superstar Megan Rapinoe held the world in thrall as the US Women's Soccer team dominated the tournament with a combination of stunning athletic skill, political activism, and very pink hair. Rapinoe's unapologetic loud and proud lesbianism was put on full display in the mainstream media's representation of the US women's team captain, including a public Twitter fight with President Donald Trump. Similarly, at the 2018 Winter Olympics, the first out gay member of the US Olympic team, figure skater Adam Rippon, publicly flaunted his effeminate homosexuality overtly in ways that directly countered performatives of hegemonic athletic masculinity. Like Rapinoe, Rippon explicitly pushed back against homophobic comments made by Vice President Mike Pence. Both of these events can be hailed as major victories in the long march for freedom and equality for lesbian and gay athletes. After almost a century of homophobic repression and heterosexist discrimination, what are the early conditions of possibility that enable white athletes like Rapinoe and Rippon to be able to stand victorious, on their respective athletic pedestals, as out queer athletes? This chapter will briefly trace a particular history of sexuality and sport in North America and how the emergence of a nascent homosexual identity in the early twentieth century, up to the emergence of a gay and lesbian civil rights movement in the late 1960s and early 1970s, has both enabled and constrained certain normative kinds of (primarily) white queer athletic subjectivities to become representable in the current moment.

In queer sports studies, there has generally been a bifurcated approach to understanding sexuality and sport.[1] The first of these is to understand the experiences of athletes identified as queer, gay, lesbian, bisexual, or trans. In popular sport history, this has often taken the form of excavating, creating, and/or celebrating gay and lesbian athletic heroes throughout millennia.[2] Beyond a certain kind of revisionist and celebratory history, what this kind of approach obscures is the work of race and capital in both the historical production of what we now know as lesbian or gay identities, homophobia, and heterosexism in the Western context, and its role in how sport has contained and enabled certain kinds of lesbian or gay athletes through various historical periods. This chapter, then, follows the second approach often taken in queer sport scholarship, which is an analysis that

188 DOI: 10.4324/9780429318306-25

understands sport as a cultural form that is forged through powerful discourses of gender, sexuality, race, and capital. Perhaps ironically, I use three early iconic athletes, who have been produced as sporting heroes for gays and lesbians (Bill Tilden, Babe Didrikson, and David Kopay) to illustrate how sport and sexuality have been deeply constitutive of one another as discursive formations through the demands of gender, race, and capital. What I emphasize in this piece is that the earliest precursors of queer sporting identities were always already formed through systems of power, even as those realities have not necessarily been explicitly brought forward as constitutive for the field of sport and sexuality. This chapter is a contribution to reducing this lacuna.

The emergence of gay sporting identity (within white settler states)

Most sport historians are familiar with how modern athletics became possible with the establishment of capitalism, and emerged through the Industrial Revolution, the development of industrial leagues, the fall of class-based amateurism, and the rise of the professional player and leagues.[3] However, these same sport historians may not be as familiar with how modern white homosexual identities emerged in and through the same temporal and economic frame that professional sport was established. I want to start by sketching an argument for how modern non-normative sexual identities (such as lesbian or gay) have come to be known and legitimized. Historian John D'Emilio offers us one starting point to understand how homosexuality became an identity in the context of white settler states. Using colonial New England as his exemplar, he argues that the emergence and establishment of capitalism in eighteenth- and nineteenth-century America created possibilities for men and women to develop intimate and sexual relationships outside of the traditional procreative and economically independent family unit:

> As wage labor spread and production became socialized, then, it became possible to release sexuality from the 'imperative' to procreate .... In divesting the household of its economic independence and fostering the separation of sexuality from procreation, capitalism has created conditions that allow some men and women to organize a personal life around their erotic/emotional attraction to their own sex. It has made possible the formation of urban communities of lesbians and gay men and, more recently, of a politics based on a sexual identity.[4]

As it became possible for people to live as independent wage earners, new 'social space' was created for men and women to explore alternative relationships. In this way, following D'Emilio, the free market labour economy partially created the conditions for various leisure identities to develop, outside of strictly upper-class enclaves, for both athletic and sexual communities.

What D'Emilio fails to make explicit in his analysis of the relationship between capitalism and the emergence of a gay identity in America, is how such an identity becomes constituted through whiteness, class privilege, and nationalism, and it is through those constitutive relations of power that this form of gay identity becomes representable in its later athletic formations. The very existence of a 'New England' colony and the contemporary nation states of North America, with their sporting infrastructures and sexual communities, were and are an outcome of the *ongoing* processes of European settler colonization. Property theft and the systematic genocide of sovereign Indigenous nations and peoples made possible the early colonial settler communities. Part and parcel of the project of dispossession wrought by settler colonialism and racial capital was (and is) the systematic attack on Indigenous 'gender, political systems, and rules of descent'.[5] European values, mores, and practices, in the form of a 'civilizing' settler sexuality, were forcibly inculcated through legal and para-legal structures including, but not limited to, settler state law (e.g. the *Indian Act* in Canada), residential schools, and religious conversion. Inextricably, chattel slavery and the economy of the Black Atlantic, were (are) the wheels for an exploitative and extractive capitalism built on the dehumanizing slave labour of African Americans, and whose 'atmosphere of antiblackness' continues to regulate, confine, surveil, and criminalize black sexualities and kinships.[6]

In briefly charting this emergence of modern homosexualities, I want to underscore it as a deeply racialized and classed project (in addition to being a constitutively gendered enterprise) in order to disrupt a naturalized assumption in much of the literature on sport and sexuality, which often fails to account for its own tenacious whiteness in settler states such as Canada and the United States.[7] Situating how homosexualities became possible *through* a historicized, racialized capitalism helps the field account for how it is that a primarily homonormative queer athleticism, that is one that relies on whiteness, class privilege, and cisgendered erotic normativity for its intelligibility, has gained a contingent respectability in some sporting circles in the twenty-first century.

Paedophiles and mannish lesbians

Michel Foucault famously argued:

> Homosexuality appeared as one of the forms of sexuality when it was transposed from the practice of sodomy onto a kind of interior androgyny, a hermaphrodism of the soul. The sodomite had been a temporary aberration; the homosexual was now a species.[8]

This new form of categorization – the 'homosexual' – presages new dynamics for how men's and women's sport manages expectations about normative gender and sexuality in tenacious ways throughout the twentieth century. Fears about gender inversion saturate and haunt women's sport, through the powerful trope of the 'mannish lesbian'. The homosocial/homoerotic nature of men's (particularly physically aggressive team) sport requires the development of a virulently homophobic athletic culture to hold 'the homosexual' at bay. As the existence of nascent same-sex communities developed in the early twentieth century, this 'queer threat' was also ideologically naturalized through the production of a psychiatrized condition of homosexuality, which came to be understood as an essentialized nature.[9] These pathologized descriptions were widespread, impacting both the consciousness of lesbians and gay men, but also larger legal and social policies, wherein both criminalization and deviance were popularly ascribed.[10]

One of the earliest 'gay' heroes of sport (even though he himself never publicly identified as gay), tennis player Bill Tilden was caught up in some of these socio-legal apparatuses. During the 'Jazz Age' of the 1920s, Tilden reigned as the champion of men's tennis, winning Wimbledon multiple times, and being national US champion for seven years.[11] This era was marked by the earliest forms of quiet cultural acceptance of homoerotic attachments amongst certain privileged communities. While Tilden was rumoured to be a homosexual, and cultivated many young male protégés, he was able to self-style as a kind of 1920s sport celebrity, using his white masculine class privilege to good effect. Nathan Titman makes a compelling case for how Tilden challenged and changed the playing styles of men's tennis. Titman's analysis is noteworthy in that it considers how Tilden's whiteness and class privilege converged with his non-heteronormative style of play 'to express a gender and sexual identity that constituted an alternative to contemporary expectations regarding male bodies and movement'.[12] This act of resistance to the increasing demand for white men to perform a more aggressive, instrumental masculinity marks a shift in how athletic masculinities were represented. Along similar lines, Mary Louise Adams (2011) also charts how men's figure skating did not become a 'feminized' sport until the 1930s, as performative demands for athletic masculinities shifted.[13]

The freedom and openness of the 1920s were rapidly and conservatively shut down by the onset of the 1930s Great Depression, and the advent of the Second World War. By the late 1940s, rigid expectations about the deeply binarized roles of men and women, the return to stable post-war nuclear families, and the McCarthy-era witch hunts for 'sexual dissidents' of the 1950s ushered in a very repressive era for homosexuals. It is in this context that Bill Tilden's arrests in 1946 and 1949 for moral depravity highlight how even being a 1920s tennis celebrity could not insulate him from repressive apparatuses of sexual conformity and the policing of orthodox heteromasculinity. Interestingly, one of the rhetorical moves that Tilden mobilized in his legal defence was to suggest that he was suffering from a condition beyond his control. His claim was that it required rehabilitation and treatment, not incarceration. Clearly, Tilden attempted to mobilize the popularized, psychiatric ideological formation about how homosexuality was understood at the time.[14]

During the same time period, women's sport was also haunted by the corollary version of female homosexuality. Supported by the ideological work produced by sexologists and other medical experts in the early part of the twentieth century, Foucault's trope of 'interior androgyny' was applied to women as gender inversion – or more colloquially, a man trapped in a woman's body. As Susan Cahn brilliantly lays out in her book *Coming on Strong*, athleticism and womanhood did not coalesce easily. In mid-twentieth-century sports journalism there were only two possible, and utterly contradictory, positions for female athletes: 'beauty queen' or 'muscle moll'.

Arguably, the most famous female athlete of the first half of the twentieth century, Mildred 'Babe' Didrikson found herself straddling these two popular discourses used by sports journalists from the early 1930s until her death in 1956. In 1932, Didrikson burst onto the national athletics scene, competing as a one-woman team at the qualifying meet for the Los Angeles Olympics. She swept all of the events in which she competed, and went on to win three medals at the 1932 Games. Hailing from a white, working-class family in Texas, Didrikson was just 18 years old. She proceeded to make a name for herself in track, baseball, and basketball throughout the Depression:

> Didrikson's blunt, unpolished manner – both in speech and appearance – was cause for comment. She dressed in loose-fitting sweatsuits, wore her hair in a short, unstyled cut, and addressed the press with plain talk that pulled no punches .... these features intrigued reporters and fans who were fascinated by her unapologetic rejection of conventional femininity.[15]

Didrikson regularly suggested that she preferred the company of women to men, and her 'mannish appearance' and remarkable physical achievements attracted insinuations that she must be a lesbian.

In 1938, Didrikson married George Zaharias, and as Cahn suggests, it is not clear whether it was for love or convenience. In the late 1940s, Didrikson took up golf, donned pretty dresses, and put on weight for a more curvaceous figure. Relieved, the press was more easily able to represent her as a properly feminine athlete. In the later years of her life, Didrikson was accompanied by her devout companion, Betty Dodd – a younger golfer on the women's professional tour. It is rumoured that they were lovers, rooming together and playing on the circuit, and Dodd was Didrikson's caregiver in the last years of her life, as the aging star lived with the effects of cancer treatment. Didrikson was wildly popular and successful, and managed to maintain deep close friendships with women, under the cover of her marriage to Zaharias. As Cahn suggests, in a sexist and heteronormative culture, white women are not to be masculine.

The enterprise of sport often demanded bodily performances which involved demonstrations of aggression, strength, physicality, competition, and dominance. When a female-identified body performed these skills, they ran the risk of acting manly, and therefore being marginalized as a 'mannish lesbian'. Women's behaviour and actions were (and are) thus carefully circumscribed on and off the court, field, or arena to secure their heterosexual credentials as 'real' women. The transformation of Didrikson in the 1940s clearly highlights these dynamics, and how sport actively contributed to the dominant codes of conventional white femininity and the appearance of compulsory heterosexuality. The conservative and reactionary decades of the 1950s and early 1960s severely restricted many women's and men's choices and options to be who they were in athletic contexts. Gay men and lesbians who played sport carved out carefully coded and concealed lives and communities for themselves.[16]

Both Tilden and Didrikson offer us particular origin stories for the earliest accounts of modern gays and lesbians in sport. Their stories have often been mobilized as object lessons in unfair treatment, especially as their experiences include the ways in which normative expectations about gender and sexuality were enforced – formally and informally – in each of their contexts, through various oppressive relations of power. Over time, this singular focus on gendered differences and their sexualized inflections has had the effect of obscuring or sidelining the obdurate whiteness of the gentile, upper-class nature of tennis and golf, and its relation to settler colonialism.[17] In highlighting their differences from the settler norm of gendered comportment and sexual behaviour, the dissident performatives of Tilden and Didrikson counterintuitively continue to resediment the white heteronormativity of men's tennis and women's golf in the early and mid-twentieth century. As the fight for gay and lesbian recognition and visibility proceeds in the remaining decades of the twentieth century, this unitary focus on gender and sexuality effectively naturalizes the other violences upon which white supremacist capitalism consolidated settler sexuality, and how sport is an integral part of that disciplinary apparatus. Tilden and Didrikson, like Rapinoe and Rippon, were/are tremendously skilled athletes who captured the world's attention even as they defied gender expectations. While there has been close to a century of struggle to open up gender and sexual expression, the structural basis of sporting apparatuses and how sexual and gender transgressions are accommodated within those, has only changed very slightly. Rippon's explicitly fey gay masculinity, and Rapinoe's unabashed and overt celebration of sporting triumph still rankle expected gendered comportments, even in the twenty-first century. It appears that the only terms on which alternative sex/gender performatives can be legitimated, is to simultaneously adhere to the normative terms of white supremacy, racial capitalism, and patriotic nationalism paired with exquisitely exceptional performances of the physicality various sport formations demand.

Troubling sexuality and sport

The homoerotic paradox of men's sport

In 1975, retired pro football player David Kopay made American news headlines by being the first major league athlete to come out as gay. Kopay played for several NFL franchises over nine seasons between 1964 and 1972. After revealing his homosexuality, he was unable to secure any of the football coaching positions to which he applied. In 1977, he published a memoir, entitled *The David Kopay Story*. His coming out turned him into a somewhat reluctant gay rights advocate. He appeared on a television talk show, debated gay rights against the right-wing conservative Anita Bryant, and became a role model for many closeted athletes. 'Maybe what I am doing will help create some space so that people like my friend won't have to hide anymore.'[18]

In his book, Kopay explicitly highlighted the dynamics that perpetuate the stranglehold that homophobia has on men's competitive sport. 'I was out to prove that I was in no way less a man because I was a homosexual. It is also true that during most of my athletic career the physical outlet of the game was a kind of replacement for sex in my life.'[19] Brian Pronger walks us through the powerful paradox of sublimated desire at the centre of men's athletics:

> It's ironic that while sport is traditionally a sign of orthodox masculinity for men, emphasizing the conventional masculine values of power, muscular strength, competition and so on, it is a world that celebrates affinity among men, and therefore, a paradoxical experience.[20]

Sport has developed to be one of the key social institutions that requires and reproduces a rigid adherence to the mythic discourse of gender difference. One of the ways that gendered distinctions are reinforced is that men segregate themselves from women into athletic subcultures and they develop 'a greater affinity for other men than they do for women'.[21] Pronger continues:

> Competitive athletes are actually erotic accomplices ... men's sport is a bodily, carnal experience in which the myth of masculine struggle is actualized .... The hidden erotic paradox of orthodox sport is terrifying for some men. Homophobia in sport is the fear of the inherent slippage between orthodoxy and paradoxy realized in sporting scenes.[22]

In the 1970s, a different wave of feminist and gay resistance was powerfully disrupting the repressive notions of acceptable heterosexual gender relations. The virulent homophobia in men's sport at this time was (and is) required to maintain the heteropatriarchal power men's sport viciously guards, and this is maintained through the ritualistic denigration of women. For a male athlete, the worst epithet was (and is) to be labelled a woman, and therefore a penetrable homosexual. Men's need to repress the homoerotic dimension of athletic participation keeps such misogyny alive as it props up the illusion and preserves the structural privileges of patriarchal orthodox masculinity. In the early years of the post-Stonewall era, Kopay's coming out shook the bastion of pro football for a moment, opened the door a crack momentarily for gay and lesbian acceptance in sport, but ultimately made little difference in making the game more sexually progressive. Like Didrikson and Tilden, this coming out has also been taken up as an origin story. The focus of Kopay's case as object lesson was to highlight the discrimination he suffered solely as a result of his sexuality.[23] This was to become the ongoing (if inadvertent) strategy of an athletic lesbian and gay movement and focus for queer sports studies.

Coda: sport and lesbian and gay visibility politics

David Kopay's coming out heralded the advent of identity-based, LGBQ athletic activism, which started to combat the explicit homophobia and heterosexism rampant at all levels in sport. Over the last four decades, advocates have worked to help lesbians and gay men find their place in various sport contexts. Out of these efforts, for example, an international lesbigay sport movement emerged in the 1980s in the form of the Gay Games. It instantiated itself globally in the late 1990s as a neoliberal, queer athletic mega-event spectacle. The development of anti-homophobia advocacy groups and LGBQ public education projects for mainstream athletic contexts was also established in this time frame. At the heart of these initiatives was the political rationality of queer liberalism more generally, characterized by the struggle for recognition of lesbigay civil rights, and the profitability of a queer 'pink' market, which neoliberal capital aggressively courted. These strategies, clearly embedded in the exhortation for lesbian and gay athletes to come out, mobilized a queer visibility politics whose celebration of successful and marketable athletes reconsolidated 'sexual subjectivities [which] are rendered in isolation from the processes of racialization and capital accumulation through which they are constituted'.[24]

This returns us to Megan Rapinoe and Adam Rippon, with whom I opened this chapter. While each of them seemingly resisted dominant gendered and sexual identities (and perhaps, the US administration), the possibility for their legibility in mainstream media representation cannot be made explicit even as it relies upon white supremacy, neoliberal capital, and patriotic nationalism. As I have shown in this chapter, it has been ever thus, with the earliest 'heroes' of gay sport being produced through historical variations of these same apparatuses, effectively masking the relations of power required for white queer athletic recognition, however contingent such recognition may be.

Notes

1 Mary Louise Adams, *Artistic Impressions: Figure Skating, Masculinity, and the Limits of Sport* (Toronto: University of Toronto Press, 2011). Samantha J. King, 'What's Queer About Queer Sport Sociology Now? A Review Essay', *Sociology of Sport Journal* 25, no. 4 (2008): 419–442.

2 Patricia Nell Warren, *The Lavender Locker Room: 3000 Years of Great Athletes Whose Sexual Orientation Was Different* (Beverly Hills, CA: Wildcat Press, 2006).

3 Steven A. Riess, *Sport in Industrial America: 1850–1920* (Wheeling IL: Harlan Davidson, 1995).

4 John D'Emilio, 'Capitalism and Gay Identity', in *Powers of Desire: The Politics of Sexuality*, eds. Ann Snitow, Christine Stansell, and Sharon Thompson (New York: Monthly Review Press, 1983), 100–113.

5 Leanne Betasamosake Simpson, *As We Have Always Done: Indigenous Freedom Through Radical Resistance* (Minneapolis: University of Minnesota Press, 2017), 41.

6 Christina Sharpe, *In the Wake: On Blackness and Being* (Durham, NC: Duke University Press, 2016), 112; see also, Saidiya Hartman, *Wayward Lives, Beautiful Experiments: Intimate Histories of Social Upheaval*, New York: W.W. Norton & Company, 2019.

7 Mary G. McDonald,'Beyond the Pale: The Whiteness of Sport Studies and Queer Scholarship', in *Sport, Sexualities, and Queer Theory*, ed. J. Caudwell (New York: Routledge, 2006) 33–46; Mary, G. McDonald, 'Mapping Intersectionality and Whiteness: Troubling Gender and Sexuality in Sports Studies', in *Routledge Handbook of Sport, Gender, and Sexuality*, eds. Jennifer Hargreaves and Eric Anderson (London: Routledge, 2014), 151–159.

8 Michel Foucault, *The History of Sexuality, Volume 1: An Introduction*, trans. Robert Hurley (Vintage: New York, 1990), 43.

9 D'Emilio, *Capitalism and Gay Identity*, 105.

10 These persistent depictions include that homosexuals were/are immoral (especially in religious terms), unnatural, mentally ill, criminal, depraved, and therefore dangerous and predatory, especially in terms of protecting children from paedophiles.

Troubling sexuality and sport

11 John Carvalho and Mike Milford, '"One Knows That This Condition Exists": An Analysis of Tennis Champion Bill Tilden's Apology for His Homosexuality', *Sport in History* 33, no. 4 (2013): 554–567.

12 Nathan Titman, 'Taking Punishment Gladly: Bill Tilden's Performances of the Unruly Male Body', *Journal of Sport History* 14, no. 3 (2014): 448.

13 Adams, *Artistic Impressions*, 20, 27.

14 Carvalho and Milford, *One Knows That*, 562.

15 Susan K. Cahn, *Coming on Strong: Gender and Sexuality in Twentieth-Century Women's Sport* (Cambridge, MA: Harvard University Press, 1994), 115.

16 Cahn, *Coming on Strong*; See also Liberti, Rita, 'Queering Fields and Courts: Considerations on LGBT Sport History', in *The Routledge History of American Sport*, ed. Linda J. Borish (New York: Routledge, 2017), 240–251.

17 As a contemporary case in point, the 1990 uprising at Kanehsatake was centred on land theft from the Mohawk (Kanien'kéha:ka) people for a proposed golf course expansion.

18 David Kopay and Perry Deane Young, 'Homosexuality and Machismo Sport: A Gay Jock Speaks Out', in *Jock: Sports & Male Identity*, eds. Donald F. Sabo and Ross Runfola (Englewood Cliffs, NJ: Prentice-Hall, 1980), 92.

19 Kopay and Young, *Homosexuality*, 90.

20 Brian Pronger, *The Arena of Masculinity: Sports, Homosexuality, and the Meaning of Sex* (Toronto: Summerhill, 1990), 177.

21 Pronger, *Arena of Masculinity*, 178.

22 Pronger, *Arena of Masculinity*, 181, 182.

23 See also Liberti, *Queering Fields* for her excellent critique of this kind of analysis in regards to black MLB player Glenn Burke.

24 King, *What's Queer*, 420.

196

PART 3

Emerging themes

198

23

EMERGING THEMES

Introduction

Carly Adams, Douglas Booth and Murray G. Phillips

The field of sport history is constantly transforming as historians of sport take up new and emerging themes, perspectives, and methods.[1] As we discuss in Part 2, historians of sport are engaging and re-engaging ongoing debates central to the field. Arguably they are also pushing the field of sport history in new and exciting directions. The various 'turns' that mark the field have led to new questions and new areas of research and will continue to do so as historians of sport reach into more diverse substantive and methodological areas. The chapters in Part 3, 'Emerging Themes', capture the dynamic essence of the field of sport history as they engage with and feature emerging ideas, topics, approaches, and cross-disciplinary directions. The words of Douglas Booth still ring true in that 'the diversity of paradigms … is proof of the discipline's richness and creativity, its ability to adapt and accommodate fresh approaches and trends, and its development'.[2]

The concept of 'emerging' lies at the heart of Part 3. In 1977, Raymond Williams wrote:

> [b]y 'emergent' I mean, first, that new meanings and values, new practices, new relationships and kinds of relationship are continually being created. But it is exceptionally difficult to distinguish between those which are really elements of some new phase of the dominant culture … and those which are substantially alternative or oppositional to it: emergent in the strict sense rather than merely novel.[3]

The 'new' or 'emergent' as a cultural process then cannot be considered on its own, but rather in 'relation to' and within the context of discourses of power that underpin how we position scholarship or themes as 'new' or 'emergent'. Following Williams, imagining the 'new' or the 'emergent' in the field of sport history means considering our axiological assumptions, 'the often-unexamined, unrecognized, or mistakenly universalized values that influence our work'.[4] To confront the disciplinary assumptions of sport history, we must offer some kind of epistemological challenge to the field as we think about the 'new' and the 'emergent'. If we fail to do this, then the themes are novel and just different versions of the research we have always done. The contributors in Part 3 compel historians of sport to grapple with and expand their understandings of sport history, to engage with cross-disciplinarity at a deep(er) level, and to recognize and challenge their complicity in

DOI: 10.4324/9780429318306-27

reproducing the taken-for-granted assumptions of the field, assumptions that reverberate well beyond our conferences, classrooms, and publications. In this Introduction, we consider these chapters and draw connections between and among the axiological assumptions the authors interrogate through the headings of the digital; the affective; the (trans)national.

The digital

The digitization of research materials, online platforms, and the complicated growing phenomenon of social media have changed the nature of research and teaching. Jennifer Guiliano traces how historians of sport have engaged with digital technologies as a site for research and a research archive since the expansion of the Internet in the 1990s. In her exploration of the emergence and development of digital sport history (Chapter 24), she discusses the ways in which historians of sport have utilized technologies such as statistical software, spreadsheets, the Internet, and social media, pointing to the ways some sport history scholars have embraced digital technologies. She concludes that as a community of scholars, historians of sport have been slow to embrace new digital forms of dissemination beyond the traditional written journal articles and books. She calls for associations and journals to include digital projects as 'real' and meaningful forms of scholarship and she challenges historians of sport to embrace the digital realm of the future and move beyond the requirement for all sport history projects to have an analogue companion in order to be recognized as legitimate and credible.

In their chapters, Lu Zhouxiang and Tara Magdalinski observe that esports, online competitive gaming, and virtual fandom place us at the dawn of new areas of inquiry and methodological considerations in sport history. Magdalinski (Chapter 25) suggests that teachers and learners will both need to grapple with new technologies to produce and share digital histories, but they will also need to develop new methodological skills to contend with the ways sport engagement is transforming and is mediated through virtual, augmented, and simulated environments. Zhouxiang (Chapter 26) traces the histories of online competitive gaming and esports to the 1950s, suggesting that only recently have virtual sports taken a more prominent place in the global sports landscape. While scholars are grappling with the relationship between esports and non-digital sports as they situate the development of the esports industry and global communities, Zhouxiang suggests that more work needs to be done as historians of sport reckon with the development of virtual and digital sporting landscapes. Magdalinski advises that the COVID-19 pandemic is already pushing historians of sport rapidly in these directions as we face 'new normals' and embrace new challenges for teaching and learning.

The affective

While the history of emotions is a widely recognized field of study, in Chapter 27 Barbara Keys suggests it is another area of inquiry to which sport historians have devoted little attention, despite the copious amount of sport history scholarship on stadia, place, spectators, and fans. Gregory Ramshaw (Chapter 28) draws similar conclusions in his consideration of the social construction and cultural production of heritage and, in particular, sport-based heritage. In his chapter, through a discussion of the potential cross-disciplinary connections between sport studies, heritage studies, and sport history, Ramshaw emphasizes the meaning-making that occurs when tangible and intangible sport heritage is commodified as experiences, souvenirs, and memorabilia to commemorate and nostalgize events, places, and achievements.

Emerging themes

In their discussion of the new materialist turn, Holly Thorpe, Julie Brice, and Marianne Clark (Chapter 29) urge sport historians to think about relationality and all matter as lively 'to develop research practices that attend to the agentic capacities of matter rather than solely attending to the discursive or human'. How might we know objects of sport history differently if we 'live with' them, considering the entwined relations between object, bodies, discourse, and environment, and the affective flows and lines of flight? Thorpe, Brice, and Clark encourage sport historians to ask critical questions about 'more-than-human' histories to allow space for 'new lines of (ethically oriented) inquiry' working towards 'more equitable and sustainable futures'.

Although David Turner suggests that scholars working in the fields of disability history and the history of the emotions have had very little interaction,[5] in many ways, Danielle Peers' research crosses disciplinary boundaries to 'understand the complexities of emotions in relation to (in)active bodies' to tell more *just* histories.[6] Pointing to Indigenous and anti-colonial activists as an example, in Chapter 30, Peers reframes 'disability' as 'an historically constituted and deeply contested category of immense diversity' offering new insights and emerging themes to the histories of deaf and disability sport. The complexities and diversities of the histories we write, as Peers argues, must reflect the complexity and diversity of the communities about which we are writing. As historians we must acknowledge the words and meanings we use and the axiological assumptions and affect we perpetuate through these uses.

Keys (Chapter 27) observes that sport is intensely emotional. Yet, instead of engaging with emotion as a category of analysis, historians of sport 'cover emotions sporadically, implicitly, or as part of different categories' when exploring themes such as social control, gender norms, (inter)nationalism, and violence. To fully understand the affective dimensions of modern sport, Keys also advocates for cross-disciplinary engagements, arguing that we must look to the fields of psychology and sociology. To this end, Keys engages with debates about the definition of 'emotion' to explore how emotions are experienced by individuals and groups. She considers how not just events, but places, can have strong emotional affect through architecture and atmosphere. To this end, Thorpe, Brice, and Clark encourage sport historians to consider how new materialisms could push historians of sport 'to reimagine sources, to know artefacts differently, and to read knowledge through each other, in creative ways that prompt affect and political responses'.

The (trans)national

Tracing the development of borderland sport studies, Colin Howell and Daryl Leeworthy, in Chapter 31, discuss emerging themes in this area that go beyond 'trans-boundary physical spaces' to engage with 'complex transnational processes associated with the construction of cultural identities and other processes of production'.[7] While a borderlands approach has particular utility for sport historians, it has only been recently taken up. Howell and Leeworthy suggest that in recent years interest in borderlands has grown in light of rapid globalization, the flows of cultural, capital, and peoples between and across borders, and rising concerns with border security. Pointing to specific examples such as cross-border Mexican bullfighting in the late nineteenth century, Aboriginal influences on the development of Australian football, Anaulataq or Inuit baseball in the Arctic, and the history of lacrosse in Britain, Ireland, and First Nations communities spanning the Canadian–American border, they suggest transnational perspectives offer 'a view from the edge, a different way of seeing'. In this regard, they emphasize the particular relevance of borderland sport cultures when examining the complicated relationships between settler communities and Indigenous peoples around the world.

With this in mind, it is also important to note that we would be remiss if we did not position indigeneity, decolonization, settler colonialism, and Indigenous sport history as emergent themes in the field of sport history. Arguably, many sport historians continue to write colonial sport histories 'struggling to draw on Indigenous approaches to and understandings of movement cultures'.[8] In the *Handbook*, we have intentionally positioned the chapters on Indigenous sport as a separate Part (see Part 4). Yet, all of the chapters in Part 4 could also be meaningfully placed here in this Part. As Malcolm MacLean writes, we need to develop 'a more fluid dialogic approach to historiographical practice in a manner that not only enhances the usefulness of sport history to Indigenous movements for decolonization but also enhances academic tendencies that disrupt the frames of Eurocentric modernity'.[9] The chapters in Part 4 point to the ways in which we, as a community of scholars, must engage with the broader methodological, epistemological, and ontological debates in Indigenous studies. In this regard, we might follow Braden Te Hiwi and Carly Adams who write histories that encourage reflection on ongoing colonial effects and which decentre settler perspectives and colonial logic.[10]

Final thoughts

As Thomas King writes '[s]tories are wonderous things. And they are dangerous .... So you have to be careful with the stories you tell'.[11] Sport history is the work of sport historians, who actively shape, define, and (re/de)construct histories.[12] We need to think about the power of stories, how they are told and why, and whose voices are missing, purposefully silenced, or misrepresented. We must challenge ourselves to interrogate our research practices, our assumptions, to look beyond history for new methodologies or themes in order to address silences as we strive to write histories of sport that are, in the words of Williams, 'substantially alternative or oppositional' and not merely novel.[13] The authors in this Part encourage historians of sport to move away from shoring up the prevailing ways of conducting research and writing sport histories – to do this work differently. As we work towards 'new' and 'emergent' forms of sport histories, perhaps in the areas of focus from this Part or others, we must challenge the ontological and epistemological underpinnings of the field.

Notes

1 See Dave Day and Wray Vamplew, 'Sports History Methodology: Old and New', *The International Journal of the History of Sport* 32, no. 15 (2015): 1715–1724.
2 Douglas Booth, *The Field: Truth and Fiction in Sport History* (Abingdon: Routledge, 2005), 210.
3 Raymond Williams, *Marxism and Literature* (Oxford University Press, 1977), 123.
4 Danielle Peers, 'Engaging Axiology: Enabling Meaningful Transdisciplinary Collaboration in Adapted Physical Activity'. *Adapted Physical Activity Quarterly*, 35 no. 3 (2018): 268. See also Samuel L. Hart, 'Axiology: Theory of Values'. *International Phenomenological Society*, 32 no. 1 (1971): 29–41.
5 David M. Turner, 'Disability History and the History of Emotions: Reflections on Eighteenth-century Britain'. *Asclepio. Revista de Historia de la Medicina y de la Ciencia* 68, no. 2 (2016): 1–13.
6 Avner, Zoe, William Bridel, Lindsay Eales, Nicole Glenn, Rachel Loewen Walker, and Danielle Peers. 'Moved to Messiness: Physical Activity, Feelings, and Transdisciplinarity'. *Emotion, Space and Society* 12 (2014): 55–62.
7 See for example the November 2021 Special Issue of the *Sport History Review* entitled 'Issues in Transnational Sport History'.

8 Malcolm MacLean, 'Engaging (with) Indigeneity: Decolonization and Indigenous/Indigenizing Sport History,' *Journal of Sport History*, 46 no. 2 (2019): 204.
9 MacLean, 'Engaging (with) Indigeneity,' 205.
10 See Braden Te Hiwi and Carly Adams, 'Sports Histories, Timelines, and De-Centring Settler Colonial Perspectives,' in *Sport and Recreation in Canadian History*, ed. Carly Adams (Champaign, IL: Human Kinetics, 2021), 337.
11 Thomas King, *The Truth About Stories* (Toronto: House of Anasni Press, 2003).
12 See Booth, *The Field*.
13 Williams, *Marxism and Literature*, 123.

24

DIGITAL SPORT HISTORY

History and practice

Jennifer Guiliano

Each day, 2.5 quintillion bytes of data are created. More than 3.7 billion people surf the Internet. Sixteen million text messages are sent per minute. Four point seven trillion photos are stored each day.[1] The deluge of both digitized and born-digital materials is simply unceasing.[2] From the digitization of analogue physical materials, to the recovery of materials stored on early media formats like floppy disks, to the harvesting of web and social media platforms that document the hundreds of thousands of sports forums and events, sport historians of the future will certainly have to confront digital artifacts and platforms when they write sport history. In the last 25 years, sport historians have begun to fully integrate their analogue research methods with digital opportunities and methods. Full-scale digital repositories allow not only access to documents and artifacts-on-demand but also the ability to annotate, analyse, combine, and remix them into new forms of scholarship. Catalogues and search engines assist in identifying resources. The computer and its associated software can make organizing and producing research more efficient than previously able.

Digital sport history + quantification

The starting point for most digital sport historians is the act of turning on one's computer, connecting to the Internet, and opening a browser window. We eagerly jump onto a search engine and begin querying away. However, the roots of digital sport history lie not in the Internet but rather in quantitative and social histories of the 1980s and early 1990s. In 1980, Steven A. Riess published *Touching Base: Professional Baseball and American Culture in the Progressive Era*,[3] a cultural history of players, owners, and spectators in Atlanta, Chicago, and New York between 1900 and 1920. Riess surveyed living players who had played in the major leagues via a mailed questionnaire. He augmented the data returned with information gleaned from newspapers to assemble a dataset of players and their social and professional relationships. Riess then weighted the dataset to address issues of over and under-representativeness aligning his sample to the National Baseball Library's authoritative listing of baseball players and their demographic backgrounds (particularly their level of educational attainment). His adoption of the Statistical Package for the Social Sciences (SPSS), a computer program that allowed for statistical processing, facilitated the work that today's digital historians commonly utilize when assembling and processing their datasets.[4] Riess was

204

DOI: 10.4324/9780429318306-28

unique in his utilization of statistical software, and Melvin Adelman and Don Morrow would both lament that sport historians had not embraced quantification en masse given the proliferation of records that lent themselves to quantitative methods.[5] The lone bright spot within sport history were those who explored the economic aspects of sport.[6] Digital tools and methods were slowly creeping into practice through the adoption of the spreadsheet to track research and create datasets. Spreadsheets served as the most common form of quantitative analysis in part because they allowed sport historians to examine data over time, craft comparative analyses, and produce mathematical and graphical representations of information. Frequency distributions, charts, graphs, and line plots of change over time were all enabled by sport history's rich numerical record that could be culled from newspapers, game reports, business records including financial and salary documents, and player rosters.[7] Here sport history mirrored the larger historical discipline that embraced dataset creation and analysis to discuss social and economic history.[8] It also reflected the influence of sociology of sport scholars who were trained in quantitative methods and interested in establishing the existence of sporting cultures.[9]

Digital sport history + the Internet

Computers, the Internet, and the content that proliferated beginning from the early 1990s would dramatically shift sport history as it began to intersect with new media and communication technologies.[10] The widespread adoption of personal computing and the expansion of the Internet in the 1990s enabled historians to share and communicate much more rapidly. E-mail, listservs, file transfer protocols that allowed for the sharing of large datasets, and messages boards transformed sport history as it allowed sport historians to pool resources and communicate about potential avenues of research. It also facilitated discussions of the teaching of sport history.[11] The Internet would also serve as an abundant new research archive for the study of sport as it saw the digitization of analogue materials and the launch of born-digital sport in the new digital world.[12] Organizational websites,[13] fan sites and forums,[14] sports blogs,[15] fantasy leagues,[16] and even encyclopedias that incorporate sport history[17] have all proliferated since the wide adoption of the Internet. Fiona McLachlan and Douglas Booth provide an extensive overview of how sport historians have approached the Internet as an archival site.[18] Using swimming as a case study, they argue that sport historians need to recognize the Internet as a purveyor of sources, a context through which we can theorize about sport, and a form of historical representation that is itself subject to continual meaning-making.[19]

Perhaps unsurprisingly, the largest body of digital sport history literature is situated around blogging as both content and scholarly practice. Andrew McGregor, Andrew Linden, and Lindsay Parks Pieper have posited that blogging on the Internet offers immediate access to sporting communities and audiences that would otherwise be left by the wayside.[20] McGregor argues that blogging 'serves as an increasingly important meeting ground for scholars and interested publics' that allows sport historians to communicate to willing audiences.[21] Linden and Parks Pieper analyse who the authors of sport blogs are, what types of content they are creating, and whether the content aligns to scholarly practices in sport history. Using a corpus of 600 blogs drawn from six sites, they argue that the content of sport history blogs was most frequently exposition on current events (37.5 per cent) and reflections (25.4 per cent).[22] The corpus also revealed problems that mirrored the state of sport history and the academy: most contributors to sport history blogs were male with most content about men's sports and men's teams. It is not only blogging that the expansion of the Internet has enabled within sport history, it is also social networking.

Analysis of social media platforms like Facebook and Twitter has received attention from sport historians. In 2015, Mike Cronin asked, 'how do we, indeed should we, engage with Twitter and other social media?'[23] Using his own work on the Gaelic Athletic Association and Ireland's built sporting environment as a case study, Cronin argues that sport historians have to distinguish between three impulses in using social media: 1) social media as a network of potential individuals who can provide research assistance; 2) social media as an advertising platform that allows you to gather research materials from its community; and 3) social media content about sport generally.[24] The latter two are, in Cronin's articulation, in flux. As Gary Osmond argues in his analysis of Lesbian, Gay, Bisexual, and Transgender athletes on Twitter, the platform's development and uptake by users parallels the growth of 'out' athletes. As a result, it offers an opportunity for contemporary and recent sport historians to engage with social memory research.[25] His conclusion, that Twitter helped perpetuate memories of Australian rugby league player Ian Roberts, though, was tempered by methodological concerns about social media research in general: What are the legal and ethical implications of Twitter archives? How does a historian retroactively gain permission to use a 'tweet' in publication? Does the inability to systematically examine every tweet within a specific research query limit the conclusions that sport historians can reach? The question of limitations is one that Holly Thorpe explores in her analysis of Facebook memorial pages lamenting the deaths of surfer Andy Irons and freestyle skier Sarah Burke.[26] She argues that virtual memory carries with it many of the same concerns of power, authority, and agency that non-virtual mourning practices do. Ultimately, like Osmond, Thorpe concludes that sport historians must grapple with the contextualization of virtual and social media as a form of representation.[27]

Digital sport history + cultural heritage digitization

In the closing paragraphs of the foreword to the 2010 *Routledge Companion to Sports History*, Peter N. Stearns writes, 'one of the defining features of good sports history, along with its relationship with kindred disciplines and its deep interest in linking to other historical facets, involves its commitment to high-level analysis'.[28] For Stearns, the kindred disciplines were sociology and kinesiology that embraced the cultural turn in history which invigorated questions of race, gender, class, ethnicity, and lived experience. This conclusion was supported by S.W. Pope and John Nauright, who articulated the future of sports history as global in nature. This was accurate, yet it also elided an even greater turn in sport history that would surpass quantitative history: digitization and the representation of digital surrogates. The entry point for most sport historians to digital sport history is through the consumption of digital resources in the form of digital archives and digital libraries. Digital surrogates enable scholars to view Edward III's Proclamation banning football in 1363, coverage of the first ladies' Wimbledon Tennis Championship in 1884, and diaries from the 1936 Berlin Olympics.[29] Institutional digitization efforts allow researchers to browse the Avery Brundage Papers Collection held by the University of Illinois, the physical culture collection at the Stark Center at the University of Texas Austin, and the Sport Collection at the National Museum of Australia.[30] In the late 1990s and early 2000s, cultural heritage institutions, often backed by government initiatives, undertook a massive digitization effort to share local cultural heritage with potential audiences across the world.[31] Europeana, a 2008 initiative of the European Commission, provided access to 4.5 million digital objects from over 1,000 institutions.[32] They joined a landscape of digitization initiatives already populated by the Internet Archive, the Google Print/Google Books project, as well as national digitization initiatives from the governments of India, China, Norway, Australia, and the United States (to name just a few).

Books, manuscript collections, newspapers, and physical objects have all been fodder in the growing landscape of digital cultural heritage. Digitization of *Sporting News, Sports Illustrated, Sporting Life, Baseball Magazine, Spaulding Baseball Guides,* and hundreds of local, state, regional, and international newspapers nudged sport historians to embrace digital consumption as one of the first acts of historical research. Digital historian Roy Rosenzweig noted these opportunities in his 2004 'Sport History on the Web: Towards a Critical Assessment' article. Sport historians will be astonished at the 'gems they will find in a single afternoon of searching', including baseball cards from the Library of Congress, historical newspapers from the ProQuest digital resource, and secondary scholarship available through digital archives and associations.[33] Martin Johnes and Bob Nicholson illustrate how digitization of newspapers both enables a rapid research process and introduces a number of practical problems that sport historians must consider.[34] Optical character recognition technologies, search algorithms, and information disambiguation in addition to digital remediation can complicate using digital newspaper databases. Digitized materials available for download as datasets are quite valuable for sport historians.

Murray G. Phillips, Gary Osmond, and Stephen Townsend leveraged text analysis methods to explore and analyse newspaper coverage of Muhammad Ali, women's surfing in Australia, and homophobic language in coverage of Australian sport.[35] They conclude that the digital method of distant reading is dependent upon the quality of the original analogue material, the quality of the digitized surrogate, and the accuracy of the algorithm used in optical character recognition. These are common problems of textual analysis that Amanda Regan faced in her work on *Mind and Body*, a monthly publication on physical education that ran from 1894 to 1936.[36] Regan downloaded every issue and used optical character recognition to turn the printed issues into plain-text files. The plain-text files of *Mind and Body* then operated as her own personal research archive, allowing her to experiment with text analysis methods to analyse the corpus. Borrowing linguistic analysis methods from computer science, she ultimately used MALLET, a statistic analysis tool that identifies topics and trends within corpora, to uncover 60 themes that dominated *Mind and Body*.[37] These results then allowed her to understand shifts and continuity without having to read and characterize every single article within the publication.

Digitization has enabled the identification of sport history sources in far-flung locales through digital catalogues, finding aids, and digital repositories. Digitization has also allowed researchers to create their own personal digital archives that could be manipulated and shared electronically to support research communities. Rwany Sibaja, for example, uses the Omeka content management system to craft a personal research archive on Argentinean soccer.[38] Jennifer L. Schaefer, in her work on August 1973 and March 1974 political protests in Buenos Aires, created her own digital repository of primary source materials that she could augment through timeline and map tools.[39] Liz Timbs crafted her archive on the 2010 World Cup by gathering 'openly accessible texts, images, sounds, and videos that capture fans' perspectives and experiences at World Cup stadiums and fan parks'.[40] Ari de Wilde utilized digitized photographs of a six-day-long cycling race at Madison Square Garden to create a panoramic digital representation of the Garden from the perspective of someone who had attended the race.[41] Culling through materials has become a challenge for sport historians as the flood of analogue to digital and born-digital materials continues.

Digital sport history + the future

Mass digitization for all its potential has reproduced many of the biases and problems of analogue archival materials.[42] Similarly, as Dain TePoel has pointed out, digital sport history is complicit in the consumptive practice of digital media and Internet technologies that have steep ecological consequences.[43] Even as sport historians have embraced the consumption of digital cultural heritage resources and the utility of the computer and the Internet for the purposes of research, the discipline has been much slower to recognize its environmental impacts. Similarly, the embrace of analytical, productive, and experimental capabilities of digital sport history that result in anything other than a written peer-reviewed article or monograph has been slow to emerge. Most digital sport history arrives not in its digital form but as a scholarly article that justifies the digital product that exists on its periphery. In part, this is a result of the glacially slow pace of historical methods courses to embrace digital history as a relevant methodology.[44] But slowness also illuminates core questions that are largely unresolved for digital sport historians: Can a digital sport history project exist without a peer-reviewed companion article? What knowledge does a non-digital sport historian need to adequately engage with and review a digital history project? What explication must a digital history project do to validate as a quality piece of sport history scholarship?[45]

These questions are not trivial. There are dozens of digital methods that might be utilized by sport historians. Digital sport history scholarship to this point has concentrated on social media analysis, digital surrogate and repository creation, distant reading coupled with text analysis, and geo-spatial, geolocative, and image-based visualization. The possibilities are limitless, though, for digital sport history as digital methods become more commonplace in history programmes. For us to embrace that future though, we must be willing to meet digital sports history where it originates: in the digital realm. We cannot ask scholars to continue producing analogue companion works to support their digital sport history projects. We must instead transition our professional structures including our associations and journals to incorporate digital projects as de facto forms of scholarship. Digital project demonstrations at annual meetings, born-digital publications enabled by editors of press series and flagship journals, and the inclusion of peer-review of digital projects without hesitancy would go a long way to moving digital sports history from the periphery to the mainstream of our scholarly practice. And, as TePoel cautions us, we must do so with full awareness of the consequences of digital scholarship for the world around us.

Notes

1 Portions of this chapter appear in Jennifer Guiliano, *A Primer for Teaching Digital History*, Duke University Press, forthcoming. Bernard Marr, 'How Much Data Do We Create Every Day? The Mind-Blowing Stats Everyone Should Read', *Forbes*, https://www.forbes.com/sites/bernardmarr/2018/05/21/how-much-data-do-we-create-every-day-the-mind-blowing-stats-everyone-should-read/ (accessed 10 October 2017).

2 Born-digital materials originate in digital form in contrast to digitized materials which are reformatted from analogue to digital form. Common born digital materials include digital photographs, electronic records, and content created on the Internet and via software platforms.

3 Steven A. Riess, *Touching Base: Professional Baseball and American Culture in the Progressive Era*, rev. ed, Sport and Society (Urbana: University of Illinois Press, 1999), 227–228.

4 His utilization of an appendix to elucidate his methodology separate from analysis is one that continues to dominate scholarly production in digital history, much less digital sport history.

5 Melvin L. Adelman, 'Academicians and American Athletics: A Decade of Progress', *Journal of Sport History* 10, no. 1 (1983): 80–106; Don Morrow, 'The Powerhouse of Canadian Sport: The Montreal Amateur Athletic Association, Inception to 1909', *Journal of Sport History* 8, no. 3 (1981): 20–39.

Digital sport history

6 Arthur Padilla and Janice L. Boucher, 'On the Economics of Intercollegiate Athletic Programs', *Journal of Sport and Social Issues* 11, nos. 1–2 (1987): 61–73, https://doi.org/10.1177/019372358701100105.

7 Neil L. Tranter, 'The Patronage of Organised Sport in Central Scotland, 1820–1900', *Journal of Sport History* 16, no. 3 (1989): 227–247. A more recent critical perspective on quantitative history and its limits for sport history is Yago Colás, 'The Culture of Moving Dots: Toward a History of Counting and What Counts in Basketball', *Journal of Sport History* 44, no. 2 (2017): 336–349.

8 A useful review of social histories relationship to sport history generally is Nancy L. Struna, 'Social History and Sport', in *Handbook of Sports Studies* eds. Jay Coakley and Eric Dunning (London: SAGE, 2000), 188–204, https://doi.org/10.4135/9781848608382.

9 Wray Vamplew, 'In Praise of Numbers: Quantitative Sports History', *The International Journal of the History of Sport* 32, no. 15 (2015): 1835–1849. Vamplew advocated for sport historians to reexamine the utility of counting, spreadsheets, and databases.

10 On the history of the Internet and computing, see Joy Lisi Rankin, *A People's History of Computing in the United States* (Cambridge, Massachusetts: Harvard University Press, 2018).

11 Richard William Cox and Michael A. Salter, 'The IT Revolution and the Practice of Sport History: An Overview and Reflection on Internet Research and Teaching Resources', *Journal of Sport History* 25, no. 2 (1998): 283–302; Tara Magdaliniski, 'Into the Digital Era: Sport History, Teaching and Learning, and Web 2.0', in *Sport History in the Digital Era* eds. Gary Osmond and Murray G. Phillips (Chicago: University of Illinois Press, 2015), 113–131.

12 Brian Wilson, 'New Media, Social Movements, and Global Sport Studies: A Revolutionary Moment and the Sociology of Sport', *Sociology of Sport Journal* 24, no. 4 (2007): 457–477, https://doi.org/10.1123/ssj.24.4.457; Brett Hutchins and David Rowe, *Digital Media Sport: Technology, Power and Culture in the Network Society*, 1st ed. (New York: Routledge, 2013), https://www.routledge.com/Digital-Media-Sport-Technology-Power-and-Culture-in-the-Network-Society/Hutchins-Rowe/p/book/9780415517515.

13 Geoffrey Z. Kohe, '@www.Olympic.Org.Nz: Organizational Websites, E-Spaces, and Sport History', in *Sport History in the Digital Era*, 77–96.

14 Matthew Klugman, '"Get Excited, People!": Online Fansites and the Circulation of the Past in the Preseason Hopes of Sports Followers', in *Sport History in the Digital Era*, 132–156; Matthew Klugman, 'The Passionate, Pathologized Bodies of Sports Fans: How the Digital Turn Might Facilitate a New Cultural History of Modern Spectator Sports', *Journal of Sport History* 44, no. 2 (2017): 306–321; Deirdre Hynes and Ann-Marie Cook, 'Online Belongings: Female Fan Experiences in Online Soccer Forums', in *Digital Media Sport: Technology, Power and Culture in the Network Society* eds. Brett Hutchins and David Rowe, 1st ed. (New York: Routledge, 2013), 97–110, https://www.routledge.com/Digital-Media-Sport-Technology-Power-and-Culture-in-the-Network-Society/Hutchins-Rowe/p/book/9780415517515.

15 Rebecca Olive, 'Interactivity, Blogs, and the Ethics of Doing Sport History', in *Sport History in the Digital Era*, 157–179.

16 Luke Howie and Perri Campbell, 'Privileged Men and Masculinities: Gender and Fantasy Sports Leagues', in *Digital Media Sport*, 235–248, https://www.routledge.com/Digital-Media-Sport-Technology-Power-and-Culture-in-the-Network-Society/Hutchins-Rowe/p/book/9780415517515.

17 Stephen Townsend, Gary Osmond, and Murray G. Phillips, 'Wicked Wikipedia? Communities of Practice, the Production of Knowledge and Australian Sport History', *The International Journal of the History of Sport* 30, no. 5 (2013): 545–559, https://doi.org/10.1080/09523367.2013.767239.

18 Fiona McLachlan and Douglas Booth, 'Who's Afraid of the Internet?: Swimming in the Infinite Archive', in *Sport History in the Digital Era*, 227–250.

19 A useful summary of how sport historians encounter all three Internet activities is Noah Cohan, 'New Media, Old Methods: Archiving and Close Reading the Sports Blog', *Journal of Sport History* 44, no. 2 (2017): 275–286. Cohen uses born-digital Internet content in the form of blogs to analyse blogging as a communication medium. He also conducts an auto-ethnographic reflection of his own blog creation and its relationship to academic standards.

20 Andrew McGregor, 'The Power of Blogging: Rethinking Scholarship and Reshaping Boundaries at Sport in American History', *Journal of Sport History* 44, no. 2 (2017): 239–256; Andrew D. Linden and Lindsay Parks Pieper, 'Writing Sport Online: An Analysis of the Pitfalls and Potential of Academic Blogging', *Journal of Sport History* 44, no. 2 (2017): 257–274.

21 McGregor, 'The Power of Blogging', 239.

22 Linden and Parks Pieper, 'Writing Sport Online', 262.

23 Mike Cronin, '"Dear Collective Brain…": Social Media as Research Tool in Sport History', in *Sport History in the Digital Era*, 98.

24 Cronin, '"Dear Collective Brain…"', 102.

25 Gary Osmond, 'Tweet Out?: Twitter, Archived Data, and the Social Memory of Out LGBT Athletes', *Journal of Sport History* 44, no. 2 (2017): 322–335.

26 Holly Thorpe, 'Death, Mourning, and Cultural Memory on the Internet: The Virtual Memorialization of Fallen Sports Heroes', in *Sport History in the Digital Era*, 180–200.

27 Thorpe's work is an important extension of Mike Huggins' call to embrace the visual turn in sports history within the context of digitized photographic and film archives to expanding the potential source base for historical analysis. See Mike Huggins, 'The Visual in Sport History: Approaches, Methodologies and Sources', *The International Journal of the History of Sport* 32, no. 15 (2015): 1813–1830, https://doi.org/10.1080/09523367.2015.1108969.

28 Peter N. Stearns, 'Foreword', in *Routledge Companion to Sports History* eds. S.W. Pope and John Nauright (London: Routledge, 2010), xv.

29 'Sport History Collections', Institute of Historical Research, https://www.history.ac.uk/library/collections/sport-history (accessed 27 October 2019).

30 'Avery Brundage Papers and Audiovisuals (Digital Surrogates), 1929–1969 | Digital Collections at the University of Illinois at Urbana-Champaign Library', accessed 22 November 2019, https://digital.library.illinois.edu/collections/c5babd80-a24d-0131-4a3f-0050569601ca-f; 'E-Starkives Home', https://archives.starkcenter.org/ (accessed 15 January 2019); National Museum of Australia, 'National Museum of Australia – Sport', https://www.nma.gov.au/explore/collection/collection/sport (accessed 15 December 2019).

31 LIBER: Association of European Research Libraries, 'European Commission's Recommendation on Digitisation and Digital Preservation', *LIBER* (blog), n.d., https://libereurope.eu/european-commission-s-recommendation-on-digitisation-and-digital-preservation/; National Archives and Records Administration, 'Digitization at the National Archives', National Archives, 26 June 2017, https://www.archives.gov/digitization; Commonwealth of Australia, 'Digital Transformation Agenda', Digital Transformation Agency, n.d., https://www.dta.gov.au/what-we-do/transformation-agenda/.

32 Nanna Bonde Thylstrup, *The Politics of Mass Digitization* (Cambridge: MIT Press, 2019).

33 Roy Rosenzweig, 'Sport History on the Web: Towards a Critical Assessment', *Journal of Sport History* 31, no. 3 (2004): 371–376.

34 Martin Johnes and Bob Nicholson, 'Sport History and Digital Archives in Practice', in *Sport History in the Digital Era*, 53–74; See also Martin Johnes, 'Archives and Historians of Sport', *The International Journal of the History of Sport* 32, no. 15 (2015): 1784–1798, https://doi.org/10.1080/09523367.2015.1108307.

35 Murray G. Phillips, Gary Osmond, and Stephen Townsend, 'A Bird's-Eye View of the Past: Digital History, Distant Reading and Sport History', *The International Journal of the History of Sport* 32, no. 15 (2015): 1725–1740, https://doi.org/10.1080/09523367.2015.1090976.

36 Amanda Regan, 'Mining *Mind and Body*: Approaches and Considerations for Using Topic Modeling to Identify Discourses in Digitized Publications', *Journal of Sport History* 44, no. 2 (2017): 160–177.

37 Andrew Kachites McCallum, *MALLET: A Machine Learning for Language Toolkit*, 2002, http://mallet.cs.umass.edu/; For more on topic modelling generally, please see: Shawn Graham, Scott Weingart, and Ian Milligan, 'Getting Started with Topic Modeling and MALLET,' *Programming Historian*, 2 September 2012, http://programminghistorian.org/lessons/topic-modeling-and-mallet.html; David M. Blei, 'Topic Modeling and Digital Humanities', *Journal of Digital Humanities*, 8 April 2013, http://journalofdigitalhumanities.org/2-1/topic-modeling-and-digital-humanities-by-david-m-blei/; 'Topic Modeling for Humanists: A Guided Tour – the Scottbot Irregular', http://www.scottbot.net/HIAL/index.html@p=19113.html (accessed June 15, 2016).

38 Rwany Sibaja, 'Omeka to ¡Animales! Building a Digital Repository of Research on Argentine Soccer', *Journal of Sport History* 44, no. 2 (2017): 209–224; 'Omeka', https://omeka.org/ (accessed 23 May 2015).

39 Jennifer L. Schaefer, 'Mapping Politics into the Stadium', 2016, http://mappingpoliticsintothestadium.jenniferlschaefer.com/; Jennifer L. Schaefer, 'Mapping Politics into the Stadium: Political Demonstrations and Soccer Culture in Buenos Aires, Argentina, 1973–74', *Journal of Sport History* 44, no. 2 (2017): 193–208; Schaefer utilized the Neatline plugin for geospatial mapping within Omeka. See 'Neatline', Neatline: Geospatial & Temporal Interpretation of Archival Collections, http://neatline.org (accessed 23 July 2015).

40 Liz Timbs, *Imbiza 1.0: A Digital Repository of the 2010 World Cup*, 2014, http://imbiza.matrix.msu.edu/; Timbs used KORA and WordPress to create her archive. MATRIX and Michigan State University, *KORA*, https://kora.matrix.msu.edu/ (accessed 21 December 2019); 'WordPress.Com', *WordPress.Com* (blog), 2015, https://wordpress.com.

41 Ari de Wilde, 'Revisiting "Ghosts of the Garden": Sport History, Modernizing Technology, and the Promise and Perils of Digital Visualization', *Journal of Sport History* 44, no. 2 (2017): 225–238.

42 Thylstrup, *The Politics of Mass Digitization*.

43 Dain TePoel, 'Digital Sport History, with Costs: An Ecocentric Critique', *Journal of Sport History* 44, no. 2 (2017): 350–366.

44 Dave Day and Wray Vamplew, 'Sports History Methodology: Old and New', *The International Journal of the History of Sport* 32, no. 15 (2015): 1715–1724, https://doi.org/10.1080/09523367.2015.1132203.

45 Jennifer Guiliano, 'Toward a Praxis of Critical Digital Sport History', *Journal of Sport History* 44, no. 2 (2017): 146–159.

25
TEACHING/LEARNING SPORTS HISTORY

Tara Magdalinski

In university and college departments offering kinesiology, exercise science, and sport management programmes, the utility of teaching sports history is often unclear and, in many cases, hard to justify in the face of shrinking budgets and fewer specialist positions. Mirroring the foregrounding of STEM disciplines, sports historians have had to fight for the continued existence of their courses, often with the compromise that the socio-cultural disciplines (history, sociology, philosophy) are bundled into a single unit of study. Yet sport practices in the twenty-first century require contextualization, and here sports history can offer important insights for students. The significance of taking a knee during the national anthem to protest police brutality is enhanced when it is located within a legacy of Black protest in sport. Far from being a series of names, dates, and places, these techniques ensure that students appreciate how internal and external forces have shaped contemporary sporting practices, ideologies, and mythologies. Whether it is tracing the development of modern sport alongside industrialization and capitalism, or identifying how Victorian attitudes towards women's physicality continue to influence how cis female and trans athletes' bodies are regulated and controlled, the history of sport provides insight into, as well as potential solutions for, many of the challenges faced by governing bodies, commercial enterprises, athletes, and fans today.

In addition to exploring *why* sports history should be taught, this chapter also considers *how* sports history can be taught. Despite regular introspection on its precarious disciplinary foothold in the academy, the teaching of sports history has received significantly less academic attention. This field is well suited to a range of engaging pedagogies that enable students to not only understand, but experience, sport through different developmental stages. These include practical challenges such as making and using equipment from different eras to experience how technology influences sport and ponder the innovations yet to come; interviews with diverse communities to record personal experiences of sport as a participant or fan; or drawing upon digital humanities methods to create mixed-media or digital archives that capture online engagement for future sports historians. Sports history lends itself well to student-centred and authentic learning approaches, given most students have physical experience of sport and can bring their embodied experience to their study of sporting cultures and practices.

DOI: 10.4324/9780429318306-29

Sports history in the curriculum

Alongside broader crises in the study of history, including declining enrolments and an increasingly market-driven definition of what is 'valuable' in higher education, sports history has certainly struggled over the past decade, though its precarity is longstanding.[1] As a field of study, it has been caught in the nexus of neoliberal approaches to course design and delivery, the cessation of courses deemed too niche or esoteric, and an increasing focus on developing job-ready graduates. At the same time, the retirement of the pioneers of the field who have largely not been replaced by historians of sport has, in places, reduced advocacy for sports history within mainstream and sports-related degrees.[2]

Sports history has in some respects not found its secure academic home. Broad-based physical education programmes have given way to narrow exercise science or sports management degrees, where the history of sport has not always been regarded as core to a more scientific or business-focused curriculum. If a lone sports history course is built into an exercise science degree, it can be perceived as an unnecessary or irrelevant departure from 'real' science;[3] if it is an elective, this may signal the course is ancillary to the core mission of the degree. A 2010 survey of sports management programmes in the United States noted three-quarters do not offer any sports history courses, 14 per cent included it as a required course with only 6 per cent offering a sports history elective.[4]

There is often a mismatch between the content of the sports history course and the human sciences that the students have chosen to study. This is not to say there is no relevance, but how sports history is incorporated into these degrees is important. It can be difficult to understand how jousting in the Middle Ages is relevant to someone learning to improve cardiac fitness, but studying the emergence of exercise science and the influence of the Cold War to escalate evidence-based coaching systems can offer valuable context to the next generation of exercise physiologists and coaches. Projects that trace and critique the development of common health advice, such as drinking eight glasses of water per day, can help future fitness trainers critically investigate new health claims to better advise their clients. And finally, it is critical that students review changes in scientific methods, standards, and research over time to appreciate that exercise science is as influenced by dominant ideological positions, particularly in regards to race, gender, and sexuality, as is the production of historical narratives. These are genuinely critical transferable skills.

Similarly, sports history has often been considered either too obscure for history majors, too trivial for 'serious' history departments, or simply yet another vanity inclusion in an already crowded curriculum.[5] This is compounded by the fact that sports historians find it difficult to gain employment in mainstream history, with some told there is simply a 'limited audience' for sports-focused courses.[6] The dearth of sports historians was confirmed by a review of Australian academic sports historians nearly two decades ago, which noted at the time only nine were located in humanities departments.[7] Since then the number has dwindled. Nevertheless, utilizing sport as the lens through which to explore history can be highly effective.[8] Students are already intimately familiar with the ubiquity of sport either through fandom or as willing or unwilling participants. Even if they are not interested in sport or have had their own negative experiences, they understand its place in their society, its economic power, its foundational meritocratic and character-building philosophies, or its position as a fundamental social good or public health imperative. To take a social practice that is so naturalized and demonstrate its emergence to standardize and commodify physical activity, to subjugate and regulate bodies and its function as an ideological weapon is powerful.

Since the 1980s, there have been suggestions about how to reinforce sport history's place within physical education, exercise science or history courses and departments by weaving sports history more purposefully into the curriculum,[9] yet there are few examples that have charted curriculum changes where these goals have been realized. Moving forward, it is imperative that we capture the process of reviewing and changing course and programme designs to embed sports history so these can be shared with colleagues facing challenges at their institutions. At a course level, sharing examples of good practice can contribute not just to a capability uplift but to a strengthening of the position of sports history in the academy. The following section outlines some critical pedagogical approaches that can elevate sports history education in post-secondary institutions.

Teaching sports history

For many educators, designing a course typically begins with a reflection on its role and position in the curriculum, a set of learning outcomes identified by the teacher, and a set of institutional considerations, such as graduate attributes. Next, the teacher will usually select the content to be covered, broken down into weekly topics with required readings and learning activities. As a final step, the assessment is designed ostensibly to assess whether a student has understood the content and achieved the learning outcomes. The unit is then reviewed by peers and accredited by the institution and in some cases by an external professional body. Although replicated the world over, this top-down approach typically misses a key stakeholder – the learner.

Student-centred learning

Contemporary pedagogical practices focus less on teaching and more on learning as traditional didactic modes of teaching are replaced by pedagogies that position students at the centre of their learning experience. Student-centred approaches refocus the locus of learning from the teacher to the student so that learners shift from being recipients of information towards active and collaborative co-creators of knowledge.[10] Furthermore, student-centred approaches recognize that 'content' is no longer the exclusive domain of the cloistered academy and education is not simply 'content delivery'. Student-centred pedagogies embrace active learning where learners assimilate, co-design, and synthesize nuanced and creative responses to complex – or wicked – problems curated and supported by teachers. It provides a space where students, no longer passive recipients, construct and contextualize knowledge in ways that are meaningful for them. By presenting students with fully formed courses, the teacher is essentially trying to cajole them onto a pre-determined learning pathway rather than supporting them as they forge their own way to explore and interpret the core topic areas.

Decentring the transfer of content has important implications for sports history. Traditional survey courses that cover sport from ancient times to the modern era in a single semester can only offer a rapid flyby that may touch on a lot of events or moments, but do not provide enough time for students to develop analytical, reflective, or evaluative skills. Indeed, keeping up as the centuries whiz past may be a personal triumph. Similarly, courses that focus on a single phenomenon, such as the Olympics, also may try to cover both the ancient and modern Games as well as themes, such as politics, nationalism, race, gender, and economics, which can hinder students from deeply exploring or connecting with wider theoretical concerns and their application to contemporary events. Repositioning sports history as a process that can be reviewed, examined, and shaped creates a paradigm where students engage in, and appreciate the importance of, an exploration of the past to understand or inform action in the present.

Students as partners

Designing a student-centred learning approach can be confronting for academics who may feel that their disciplinary knowledge would be undervalued and that students 'don't know what they don't know'.[11] Students can also be suspicious when entrusted with the reins, as they too are enculturated into an education system that has conditioned their passivity. Importantly, a genuine student-centred approach to learning cannot be created without student involvement. Those starting on this path may reflect more deeply on student feedback or utilize focus groups to better understand the student experience. Asking a student from outside the programme to serve as a critical friend who attends classes to provide immediate feedback to the academic on engagement is another useful starting point for those seeking to include students in their course design and continuous improvement processes.

For those teachers looking to embed the student voice more meaningfully, adopting a 'students as partner' model, which invites students to contribute as equal partners to the curriculum design, can be transformative.[12] It replaces a proscriptive syllabus with a more adaptive version that can be customized for each instance of the course and even for each learner. Students might design the learning outcomes as a group or personalize them for their own learning; they might identify core themes and topics to be explored across the teaching period; or they might design projects or other assessments that align with areas of enquiry, personal experiences, or current events. This approach creates space for students to engage in a metacognitive reflection on the purpose of the course, their learning process and their role as a learner, and enables them to establish collective and/or personal goals. Viewing the learning process holistically inspires a deeper connection with their own motivations, strengths, and weaknesses and at the same time their understanding of their role in the co-constructing knowledge is sharpened. Sharing power in this manner can certainly be confronting for teachers, however creating genuine partnerships based on trust and mutual respect has been shown to lead to not just improved disciplinary outcomes but enhanced transferable learning skills.[13]

Authentic and experiential learning

If students are inspired and supported to take a more active role in their learning, then the type of activities they engage in must also be transformed to capture authentic and relevant opportunities to learn. Students who are empowered to co-create will not be satisfied with pop quizzes, tests, and other spurious 'measures' of learning. Indeed, 'assessment of learning' becomes redundant and even the increasingly fashionable 'assessment for learning' may inadequately decouple the learning from the assessment. In this context, 'assessment *as* learning' seems to be a better conceptualization, though taking this one logical step further means the notion of 'assessment' may be redundant. All activities that students undertake are learning, and it is the student learning, not the assessment of that learning, that should be foregrounded. A bold instructor might divorce themselves from the notion of assessment all together by enabling students to assign their own grades based on their own perceptions of improvement and achievement. The ultimate objective is to create the conditions whereby learning can flourish. To that end, an authentic and experiential project design aligns more closely with student-centred learning approaches.

Authentic learning invites students to find solutions to real-world challenges that are either modelled on those routinely encountered by professionals and practitioners or co-designed with industry and community partners or clients.[14] Students are able to apply their learning to these novel situations and generate new insights through their responses. The more authentic the activity, the more relevant the experience for students. Indeed, live client briefs with the expectation of implementation of the students' solution are highly motivating. Whether these projects are individual and self-sourced by the student or encompass the entire class, the ability of teachers and students to be agile enough to respond to roadblocks as they organically emerge is fundamental to the learning experience.

Whilst other disciplines offer ample opportunities to engage in practical or experiential learning, sports history has often been classroom-based, though many academics have started to embrace practice-based learning that engages students through physical experiences of ancient sports, the production of their own 'historical artefacts', or the collecting and analysis of oral histories. A good starting point is to consider the skills that are needed to produce sports histories and to reflect on how these might be designed into learning activities. Taking archival research as an example, a typical class might describe the different methods of dealing with primary sources, whereas a more experiential introduction might be to simply make a mix of primary and secondary documents and artefacts about a local sporting event or moment available to students to think about. Ask the students to write down the kinds of questions the materials provoke. Ask them to consider which materials are more authoritative and why. Ask them to construct a short narrative to describe what happened. And just as they start figure out 'the story', introduce more, perhaps confounding, materials to the mix. Ask them whether the new information or viewpoint changes the narrative and how they might weight the relative value of each item to the narrative. Sharing their narratives would also encourage students to reflect on how different subjectivities influence the construction of history. Trying to write a brief historical piece based on archival sources is a powerful learning experience and primes students for more theoretical debates about historical research methods.

Sports historians can also partner with external bodies to design mutually beneficial authentic projects. These might be one-off projects or an ongoing relationship to which students contribute each semester. Students could work with local sports clubs to produce rich, digital histories. An interactive website with video, interviews, photos, and written narratives could be a collaborative digital storytelling project that has meaningful social impact. Not only are students more motivated when they know their work has meaning in 'the real world', students also develop valuable skills by defining the scope, collecting primary data, triangulating with secondary sources, grappling with contested narratives, curating the source material, and producing a public-facing collection. Partnering with a local museum to curate a sports historical exhibition creates not just a service-learning project, but authentic engagement with and impact on the community.

Whilst the twenty-first century skills of planning, analysis, curation, reflection, iteration, evaluative judgement, social impact, and digital communication might be organically embedded in authentic projects, if designed as a collaborative project, each class can be dedicated to project planning, status reports, reviewing materials, assigning tasks, and reflecting on their progress. The teacher would not 'cover content' as much as guide students, provide advice and feedback, and, where needed, offer 'just in time' context, insight, or depth to the activities that students are about to undertake. For example, when students are about to conduct interviews, an introduction to ethical research, informed consent, and how to conduct interviews could be explored during class time. Students could pair up to role play an interview to experience the process as both interviewer and interviewee.

New skills for new histories

Although the production of sports historical narratives has typically drawn upon archival texts, documentary sources, physical artefacts, and oral histories, the explosion of esports and new forms of virtual fandoms place us at the advent of a new kind of sports history. Not only will our future sport historians need the technical skills to produce and share digital histories or the analytical skills to engage with digital and digitized archives, they will also need to be equipped with methodological skills to piece together intricate narratives from digital fragments. This presents exciting opportunities but also a sense of overwhelm as context, authenticity, and ethical practice differ considerably from more traditional sports historical scholarship.

Students will need to grapple with new ways of understanding sport, events, athletes, and fandom. Discussions about the place of 'local' sport in a digitally connected world or a time when athletes might be powered by the Internet of Things should be used to prompt reflections on the changing methods of the sports historian. Indeed, for many, engagement in sport as a spectator or participant is already a mediated, embodied experience that takes place in virtual, augmented, or simulated environments. It is a real experience with the same highs and lows, excitement and disappointments, but it is not staged on terra firma per se. And whilst the Internet never forgets, these types of experiences may not be recorded systematically or made available through centralized channels. Instead, they are likely to be fragmented and distributed through personally curated archives that are housed on publicly available but privately owned platforms. Whilst recovering the millions of digital breadcrumbs that point to a specific event will present new data mining and ethical challenges, it is likely that reconstructing and interpreting these experiences will require fluency in living through and across these immersive new worlds. Although we cannot overestimate their technological abilities, our current Generation-Z undergraduates could be well positioned to navigate through the complexity, and lead our understanding, of the nuances of lives lived and shared seamlessly in and across virtual and physical domains. As educators it nevertheless remains our responsibility to support these insights with fundamental research skills coupled with new digital literacies so that our graduates can critically engage with virtual worlds, sporting or otherwise, as they follow their career path to the middle of the century.

A COVID-19 epilogue

The original plan to close this chapter was to reflect on the changing role of technology in sports history teaching since my last overview six years ago.[15] I had planned to note the slow visible change, that despite ad hoc examples presented here and there, it was difficult to identify a move towards good technology-enhanced pedagogy or assessment within sports history internationally. I was going to call on scholars to engage with their pedagogies and report on their successes – and failures – to demonstrate how best to embrace the affordances of technology to enhance scholarship, disseminate outcomes, and to link sports history teaching with future-focused digital skills and literacies.

I still want to make those points, however, the global COVID-19 pandemic provoked the rapid shift from face-to-face teaching to remote delivery with very little notice. For many, this was a baptism of fire, and despite periodic reminders over the last 20 years or more to engage with technology and flexible learning modalities,[16] the pivot revealed gaps in institutional, academic, and student digital capability as well as a significant digital divide that has prompted many institutions to consider how they will design higher education moving forward. This 'new normal' must take a flexible learning approach that provides multiple ways for students to engage with their studies. We cannot simply replace 'like for like' when many students, and a not inconsiderable number of staff, do not have reliable access to the Internet. There is opportunity to be more creative in the design and support of our students' learning experiences, and where sports historians may have lagged in the past, it is time to embrace the challenge to vault into the future.

Notes

1 Doug Booth, 'Sports History: What Can Be Done?' *Sport, Education and Society* 2, no. 2 (1997): 191–204.
2 Daryl Adair, 'Australian Sport History: From the Founding Years to Today', *Sport in History* 29, no. 3 (2009): 405–436.
3 Rebecca Olive, 'Embodied Pedagogies in Human Movement Studies Classrooms: A Postgraduate Pathway into Teaching and Learning', *Review of Education, Pedagogy and Cultural Studies* 40, no. 3 (2018): 227–248.
4 Andrea N. Eagleman and Erin L. McNary, 'What Are We Teaching Our Students? A Descriptive Examination of the Current Status of Undergraduate Sport Management Curricula in the United States', *Sport Management Education Journal* 4, no. 1 (2010): 1–17.
5 Kausik Bandyopadhyay, 'Fighting Against Heavy Odds: An Indian Perspective on Sports History', *The International Journal of the History of Sport* 34, nos. 5–6 (2017): 320–325.
6 Martin Johnes, 'Putting the History into Sport: On Sport History and Sport Studies in the U.K.', *Journal of Sport History* 31, no. 2 (2004): 145–160.
7 Daryl Adair, 'Location, Location! Sports History and Academic Real Estate', *ASSH Bulletin* 36 (2002): 11–14.
8 See Robert F. Wheeler, 'Teaching Sport as History, History through Sport', *The History Teacher* 11, no. 3 (1978): 311–322; Johnes, 'Putting the History into Sport'; Murry Nelson, 'Sports History as a Vehicle for Social and Cultural Understanding in American History', *The Social Studies* 96, no. 3 (2005): 118–125.
9 Booth, 'Sports History: What Can Be Done?'; Martin Johnes, 'The Teaching-Research Nexus in a Sports History Module', *Journal of Hospitality, Leisure, Sport and Tourism Education*, 3, no. 1 (2004): 47–52.
10 Tara Magdalinski and Elizabeth Branigan, 'Student-Centred Learning', *The SAGE Encyclopedia of Higher Education* eds. Marilyn J. Amey and Miriam E. David (London: SAGE, 2020), 4: 1403–1406; Geraldine O'Neill and Tim McMahon, 'Student-Centered Learning: What Does It Mean for Students and Lecturers?', in *Emerging Issues in the Practice of University Learning and Teaching* eds. Geraldine O'Neill, Sarah Moore, and Barry McMullin (Dublin: AISHE, 2005), 27–36.
11 Magdalinski and Branigan, 'Student-Centred Learning'.
12 Alison Cook-Sather, 'Student–Faculty Partnership in Explorations of Pedagogical Practice: A Threshold Concept in Academic Development', *International Journal for Academic Development* 19, no. 3 (2014): 186–198.
13 Cook-Sather, 'Student–Faculty Partnership'.
14 Verónica Villarroel, Susan Bloxham, Daniela Bruna, Carola Bruna, and Constanza Herrera-Seda, 'Authentic Assessment: Creating a Blueprint for Course Design', *Assessment and Evaluation in Higher Education* 43, no. 5 (2018): 840–854.
15 Tara Magdalinski, 'Into the Digital Age: Sport History, Teaching and Learning, and Web 2.0', in *Sport History in the Digital Era*, eds. Gary Osmond and Murray Philllips (Urbana: University of Illinois Press, 2014), 113–131.
16 Magdalinski, 'Into the Digital Age'; Holly Thorpe, 'The Internet and the Future of Sport History: A Brief Commentary', *Journal of Sport History* 40, no. 1 (2013): 127–135. Richard W. Cox and Michael A. Salter, 'The IT Revolution and the Practice of Sport History: An Overview and Reflection on Internet Research and Teaching Resources', *Journal of Sport History* 25, no. 2 (1998): 283–302.

26

COMPETITIVE GAMING

Lu Zhouxiang

Competitive gaming, or esports, refers to 'competitive tournaments of video games, especially among professional gamers'.[1] A 2015 research report produced by gaming market research company Newzoo and global sports market analytics firm Repucom points out that worldwide esports market revenue totalled $194 million in 2014. The number of esports enthusiasts reached 89 million, with another 117 million people watching esports competitions occasionally.[2] Newzoo predicted that global esports revenue would reach $1.08 billion by 2021 and that esports enthusiasts and occasional viewers would total 234 million and 240 million respectively, which means competitive gaming has already become a popular spectator event with a fan base comparable to that of mid-tier traditional sports such as table tennis, baseball, rugby, and golf.[3]

The early years

The history of competitive gaming can be traced back to the 1950s and 1960s when the first generation of video games was developed by computer scientists and electronic engineers in order to explore and demonstrate the capabilities of computers. Pioneering games, such as Josef Kates' *Bertie the Brain* (1950), Alexander Shafto Douglas' *OXO* (1952), William Higinbotham's *Tennis for Two* (1958), and Steve Russell's *Spacewar!* (1962), were all based on the concept of competition, pitting players against each other or against the computer. The world's first competitive gaming event, the Intergalactic Spacewar Olympics, took place in Stanford University's Artificial Intelligence Laboratory on 19 October 1972, with some 20 participants fighting a virtual interstellar war for the title.

When commercial video games began to emerge in the United States and Japan in the early 1970s, game developers and manufacturers, consciously or unconsciously, forged a link between video games, competition, and sport. As early as 1974, Sega hosted Japan's first competitive gaming event, the Sega All Japan TV Game Championships. The tournament was designed to promote interest in video games and 'foster better business relationships between the maker-location-customer and create an atmosphere of sports competition on TV amusement games'.[4] Regional qualifiers were held throughout Japan and 16 of the 300 location champions were selected by lottery to take part in the grand finals in the Hotel Pacific, Tokyo.[5]

DOI: 10.4324/9780429318306-30

219

Starting in the late 1970s, coin-operated arcade distributors and operators in the United States began to organize video game events and competitions. In 1977 Atari's corporate newsletter, *Atari Coin Connection*, reported that local operators in Des Moines, Iowa had created special games rooms in hotels and motels for high school students who visited the city to attend sporting events. Atari advised operators in other cities to follow this 'profitable idea' and organize mini game tournaments 'to provide added incentive to the players'.[6] In early 1979, the Scores Arcade in Dallas organized a video game tournament during the Winter Pinball Olympics. Participants competed in some of the most popular games of the time, such as *Sea Wolf* (1976), *Laguna Racer* (1977), *Atari Football* (1978), and *Space Invaders* (1978).[7] In August and September, a Pinball Olympics and a game tournament were hosted by Pinball Pete's Arcade during the 'Games of Amusement' exhibition staged at the Impression 5 museum in Lansing, Michigan.[8] In October, New Hampshire entertainment centre Funspot organized a three-week *Space Invaders* tournament, with the top five players awarded trophies and prizes.[9]

The late 1970s also saw the arrival of video game contests on television. This started with *TV POWWW*, an interactive television game show that debuted in 1978 on Los Angeles station KABC-TV. Viewers called into the station to play *Shooting Gallery* (1976) on a modified Fairchild Channel F home video game console via a voice activation system. While watching the game live on television, contestants yelled 'Pow' over the phone to take a shot. As in traditional television game shows, the objective was to score points and win prizes. The show was an instant hit. In less than two years, it was picked up by some 79 television stations in the United States.[10]

The 1980s witnessed the simultaneous development of video arcade games, home video game consoles, and PC games. A three-pillar video game industry began to take shape. Assisted by the powerful Atari phenomenon, *Pac-Man* fever, and the Nintendo craze that swept the world, video games started to penetrate pop culture and gain mainstream acceptance. Against this background, competitive gaming entered its first golden age.

Manufacturers and developers started making efforts to build up the link between video games and the Olympic Games by producing games based on Olympic sports and organizing Olympic-themed video game tournaments. This gave birth to several important pioneering events, such as the Olympic Arcade Triathlon held during the 1980 Lake Placid Winter Olympics, the Activision Decathlon Lounge at the 1983 Baton Rouge Summer Special Olympics, and the 1984 March of Dimes International Konami/Centuri Track & Field Challenge. At the same time, video game fans began to suggest that competitive gaming should be made a part of the Olympic Games.[11]

Video game companies continued to popularize the idea of competitive gaming, using gaming tournaments to promote their products. Major events of this kind included the 1980 First National Space Invaders Competition, the 1981 Atari $50,000 World Championships, the 1982 Bally Midway National Tron Video Game Tournament, the 1983 Stop-N-Go Krull Tournament, the Atari *Swordquest* challenge of 1982–1984 and the Sega Challenge of 1987–1988. Besides manufacturer- and developer-sponsored tournaments, local operators, distributors, and video game magazines were also actively organizing gaming competitions to boost business.

Newly emerging video gaming organizations, notably the Twin Galaxies International Score Board in 1982, the US National Video Game Team in 1983, and the Amusement Players Association in 1986, played an instrumental role in organizing and developing competitive gaming events at local, regional, national, and international levels. These organizations were responsible for many firsts in the history of competitive gaming, including the first international video game high score list, the first star players, the first official rulebook for video game competitions, the first inter-state video game tournament, the first organized video game marathon, and the first professional video game players.

In addition, television became a platform for video game competition. The popular *TV POWWW*, the *That's Incredible!* Video Game Invitational (1983), and video game television shows *Starcade* (1982–1984) and *The Video Game* (1984–1985) not only introduced competitive gaming to a wider audience but also helped video games to achieve mainstream popularity.

The 1990s

The 1990s saw the further development and restructuring of the video game industry. Home console and PC games began to dominate the market while arcade games gradually lost their popularity. As the size of the global video game market continued to grow, gaming competitions and tournaments were widely used by video game companies and retailers for promotion and advertising purposes. In the first half of the 1990s, against the background of the console war between Nintendo and Sega, an increasing number of national and international gaming tournaments were held in North America, Europe, and Australia, with Nintendo PowerFest/World Championships (1990 and 1994), Sega's European Championships (1992 and 1993), and Blockbuster's World Video Game Championships (1994 and 1995) being the most influential events. At the same time, game developers and publishers made efforts to organize sports games competitions during real sporting events and use star athletes and celebrities to endorse their games. By the mid-1990s, public video game contests with large numbers of participants and featuring big cash prizes of up to tens of thousands of dollars, became increasingly common.

With the rapid development of computer and Internet technologies, video games have grown in complexity and diversity, providing a more immersive and challenging gameplay experience. These new generations of video games have transformed the competitive gaming landscape. First, Capcom's *Street Fighter II* (1991) and Midway's *Mortal Kombat* (1992) unleashed a fighting game fever and gave rise to gaming tournaments that focused exclusively on head-to-head, one-on-one contests.[12] Second, pioneered by Prodigy's *Baseball Manager* (1991), Access Software's *Links 386 Pro* (1992), Blizzard's *Warcraft: Orcs & Humans* (1994), Westwood Studios' *Command & Conquer* (1995), Activision's *MechWarrior 2* (1995), and id Software's *Doom* (1993) and *Quake* (1996), the new breed of PC games, which allowed gamers to compete against each other via LAN, dial-up modem connections and the Internet, emerged as an ideal platform for player vs player (PvP) gaming contests. Third, as fighting, sports, first-person shooter (FPS), and real-time strategy (RTS) games have turned PvP tournaments into the mainstream of competitive gaming, traditional player vs computer (PvC) and player vs environment (PvE) high-score competitions lost their popularity. Nevertheless, in the late 1990s, the newly formed retro gaming community started to organize classic high-score gaming contests to evoke a sense of nostalgia and bring back memories of the first golden age of video games in the 1970s and 1980s.[13]

When online PC gaming was taking off in the early 1990s, Nintendo and Sega also started to add online functions to home consoles and provided content streaming services through phone line, cable TV network, and satellite. Game tournaments were organized to attract subscribers for these dedicated gaming networks. From 1994, real-time, head-to-head online competitive gaming was made available for console gamers by matchmaking service XBAND.[14]

In the second half of the 1990s, online competitive gaming gained momentum. An increasing number of online contests were held across the world, with FPS and RTS games being the most popular games for competition. Game developers/publishers, online gaming service providers, and the online gaming community played a leading role in organizing these tournaments. Landmark events, such as DWANGO's Deathmatch '95, the annual QuakeCon, started in 1996, the 1997 Red Annihilation Quake Tournament, the Cyberathlete Professional League (CPL)'s FRAG series (1997–1999), the Professional Gamers League (PGL) seasons (1997–1999), Blizzard's StarCraft Ladder Tournament, Incredible Technologies' annual Golden Tee 3D Golf National Championships launched in 1997, Australia's 1998 Wireplay Invades Brisbane Tournament, Korea's '99 Sports Seoul Cup, and China's 1999 CBI National Computer Games Championships all contributed to the formation of a modern form of competitive gaming which involved players, spectators, game developers/publishers, event organizers, sponsors, media coverage, online gaming platforms/services, and game-based virtual clans and communities.

By the late 1990s, together with the widespread arrival of personal computers and the Internet, competitive gaming had developed into a popular leisure activity, a sport-like competition, and a new cultural phenomenon. Based in the rapidly growing online gaming community and stimulated by an ever-increasing prize pool, a cyberathlete culture took shape and the concept of esports and professional gaming began to spread internationally.

The esports age

Beginning in the early 2000s, an increasing number of esports organizations and international tournaments were launched in Asia and Europe. In South Korea, the World Cyber Games (WCG) was formed in October 2000 and organized the WCG Challenge in Yongin that same year. The initiative was supported by South Korea's Ministry of Culture and Tourism and the Ministry of Information and Communications, and was sponsored by Samsung. The WCG Challenge attracted 174 competitors from 17 countries.[15] The games selected for the event were *Quake III Arena* (1999), *FIFA 2000* (1999), *Age of Empires II* (1999), and *Star-Craft: Brood War* (1998).[16] The four gold medallists each took home $25,000.[17] A few months later, the first full World Cyber Games event was launched in March 2001. Approximately 389,000 players participated in national preliminaries which lasted for six months, with 430 winners making it to the grand final in Seoul in December 2001.[18]

In China, computer hardware company Asus launched the World Gamemaster Tournament (WGT) in May 2006. The event was sponsored by Intel, ATI, and ADATA. Thousands of players competed in *Counter-Strike* (1999), *Warcraft III* (2002), *FIFA 06* (2005), and *Need for Speed: Most Wanted* (2005) in regional qualifiers held in 12 cities, with 100 winners taking part in the finals in Beijing in July 2006.[19] In the following years, the WGT grew into one of the most important esports events in China.

In France, esports event management company Ligarena launched the Electronic Sports World Cup (ESWC) in 2003. Players first competed in national preliminaries in four games: *Counter-Strike*, *Quake III Arena*, *Warcraft III*, and *Unreal Tournament 2003*. A total of 358 competitors from 37 countries then took part in the finals in Poitiers in July 2003, which featured a total prize pool of $156,000 and attracted over 8,000 spectators.[20] The ESWC has since become an annual event, with continental and international tournaments held in Brazil, Canada, China, Morocco, France, and the United States.[21]

In Germany, businessman Ralph Reichert founded the Deutsche Clanliga (DeCL) in 1997 to provide servers for gamers to host online gaming competitions. In 2000, the DeCL was renamed the Electronic Sports League (ESL). In 2002, the ESL launched a German national league called the ESL Pro Series, with players competing in *Counter-Strike, Warcraft III, Jedi Knight 2* (2002), and *NASCAR 2002* (2002).[22] In subsequent years, the ESL Pro Series was held in Germany, France, Denmark, Spain, the UK, Poland, and Bulgaria, making it Europe's leading esports event.[23]

Entering the 2010s, with the rapid development of computer hardware and software technologies, and assisted by high-speed broadband networks and services, more and more players joined the ever-growing esports world, and a new generation of games began to arise. Traditional RTS games have been replaced by Multiplayer Online Battle Arena (MOBA) games, pioneered by *Defense of the Ancients (DotA)*, a modification for *Warcraft III* created by a player named Kyle 'Eul' Sommer in 2002. Soon after its release, *DotA* became extremely popular among *Warcraft III* fans and has been maintained and updated by *Warcraft* enthusiasts and map-makers. It has since been adopted by major esports events.[24]

Inspired by the overwhelming popularity of *DotA*, video game companies began to produce stand-alone MOBA games. Popular titles like Riot Games' *League of Legends* (*LoL*, 2009) and Valve's *Dota 2* (2013) started to dominate the world's competitive gaming scene and were featured in almost all major esports tournaments, such as the WCG, the Intel Extreme Masters (IEM), and the ESWC.

In 2011, Riot Games launched its *LoL* Season One World Championship. In June, the eight winning teams from the Asian, European, and North American regional qualifiers were invited to Jönköping, Sweden to compete in the grand finals. Subsequently, professional *LoL* leagues were set up around the world, many invested in and run by Riot Games and sponsored by multinationals like Intel, AMD, Red Bull, and Nike. In the same year, Valve launched its annual *Dota 2* tournament, The International. Sixteen professional *Dota 2* teams from China, the Czech Republic, Denmark, France, Germany, Malaysia, the Philippines, Russia, Singapore, Thailand, the United States, and Ukraine were invited to Cologne, Germany in August to compete in the final tournament. The *LoL* World Championship and the *Dota 2* International are now among the most important tournaments in the esports world.

By the mid-2000s, FPS pioneers *Quake* and *Unreal*, once the primary games used by gamers for one-on-one death match competitions, had been dropped by major esports tournaments. The team play-oriented *Counter-Strike*, on the other hand, has remained popular among competitive FPS fans, with the rest of the market shared by games that offer well-balanced, team-based multiplayer modes. Popular titles of this kind include Microsoft Game Studios' *Halo* series (2001–), Activision's *Call of Duty* series (2003–), EA's *Battlefield* series (2005–), Valve's *Team Fortress 2* (2007), and Blizzard's *Overwatch* (2016).

Bluehole's *PlayerUnknown's Battlegrounds* (PUBG, 2017) brought a revolutionary change to competitive FPS games. The game allows 100 players to fight in a last person standing death match. As an alternative to traditional competitive FPS titles that pit two teams of three to six players against each other, PUBG's unique 100-person battle royale concept was warmly welcomed by the esports community. Inspired by the highly successful *PUBG*, game developers are pumping out multiplayer battle royale games as fast as they can. Major titles include Epic Games' *Fortnite* (2017) and EA's *Apex Legends* (2019), each adding innovative features to the genre.

Mirroring the achievements of real sports

During the past two decades, esports have shown great potential and have begun to mirror real sports. An increasing number of regional, national, continental, and international tournaments have been held around the world, with major tournaments taking place in traditional sports venues. For example, in June 2014 the ESL organized the ESL One Frankfurt *Dota 2* tournament in a former World Cup soccer stadium, the Commerzbank Arena,[25] and in July 2018 the PUBG Global Invitational was held at the Mercedes-Benz Arena in Berlin.[26]

Alongside this, media networks started bringing esports to television platforms. In 2000, a cable television channel named Ongamenet was launched in South Korea to broadcast StarCraft matches and video game-related content.[27] In 2003, China's first dedicated video gaming television channel, GTV, was launched by state-owned television broadcaster Liaoning TV.[28] In 2005, German television channel Sport1 began to broadcast esports events.[29] In 2007, the UK's first dedicated esports television channel, XLEAGUE.TV, was launched on Sky channel 291.[30] In May 2015, US sports television channel ESPN aired Blizzard's Heroes of the Dorm event in primetime.[31] ESPN also launched a dedicated site in 2016 to keep up with the ever-growing esports industry.[32]

A third development is the advent of live streaming video platforms for video games and esports. Twitch (2011), Douyu (2014), Huya (2014), YouTube Gaming (2015), and Mixer (2016) are the major players in the market. They primarily focus on live streaming games, esports competitions, news, reviews, and other gaming-related information. For example, the LoL Season One World Championship in June 2011 attracted over 1.69 million viewers on Twitch; the 2018 LoL World Championship drew 74.3 million online spectators.[33]

As in traditional sports, esports prize money is now sky-high, matching that on offer in some of the world's richest traditional sporting events, such as the US Open tennis tournament, the FIFA Club World Cup, and the PGA Tour. The total prize pool for the International 2019 *DotA 2* Championship exceeded \$34 million, a new esports record.[34]

Since the mid-2000s, efforts have been made by various organizations to have esports accredited as a full sport. Non-profit and membership-based esports associations and federations have been launched in a host of countries, and traditional governing bodies for sport, including the Olympic Council of Asia (OCA), Sport Accord, and the Association for International Sport for All (TAFISA), have started to take esports seriously. In 2007, with the effort of the Macau E-Sports Federation (MESF) and the OCA, esports was included in the Second Asian Indoor Games as a demonstration discipline.[35] In 2013, the OCA included esports as an official discipline in the Fourth Asian Indoor and Martial Arts Games held in South Korea.[36] In 2018, the OCA cooperated with the Asian Electronic Sports Federation (AESF), the Indonesian Esports Association (IeSPA), and AliSports to include esports as a demonstration discipline at the Jakarta-Palembang Asian Games. In recent years, the International Olympic Committee (IOC) has also begun to review esports, hoping to find a way to link it with the Olympic Games. IOC President Thomas Bach commented in 2018, 'There is agreement we can't, and we should not, ignore the growth of the e-games industry and the interactivity of it for the young generation. That we should engage with this community.'[37] Subsequently, an agreement was reached at the 8th Olympic Summit in 2019 that the IOC should facilitate the integration of sports simulations into the Olympic Movement and International Federations should consider how electronic and virtual forms of sport could be governed. A year later, at the 135th IOC Session in Lausanne, Bach again highlighted the necessity and urgency of Olympic inclusion of esports: 'Whether they could one day be considered for the Olympic programme – the answer is yes. It depends when this day is coming.'[38]

Conclusion

Competitive gaming was born together with the first generation of video games produced by computer scientists and electronic engineers. When commercial video games began to emerge in the United States and Japan in the early 1970s, game developers and manufacturers started to build up the link between video games, competition, and sport. Coin-operated arcade distributors and operators organized gaming competitions to promote their products and increase sales. Competitive gaming entered its first golden age in the 1980s. Video game companies and the newly emerging video gaming organizations started to organize gaming tournaments. Television became a platform for video game competition. By the 1990s, public contests had become increasingly common and online competition began to rise. Moving into the twenty-first century, an increasing number of esports organizations and international tournaments have emerged. Esports has become a concept that gaming companies, PC hardware vendors, and online streaming platforms are eager to sell to gaming fans. Today, competitive gaming is widely regarded as a hobby, a leisure activity, a social media platform, and a new lifestyle choice in the computer age. It is mirroring the achievements of 'real' sports and changing the global sports landscape.

In recent years, due to its overwhelming popularity, competitive gaming has become an important academic topic, and an increasing number of book chapters, journal articles, and monographs have been published. Some focus on the definition of competitive gaming and discuss its relationship with real sport, some examine the esports industry and community from a social perspective, other published work concentrates on the management and business aspects of esports.[39] As a modern form of entertainment and sport-like competition, the nature of competitive gaming, and its complexity, needs to be explored further.

Notes

1 'esports', Dictionary.com, available at https://www.dictionary.com/browse/esports (accessed 5 February 2019).
2 Dan Pearson, 'Report: eSports Revenues to hit $465m in 2017', Gamesindustry.biz, 17 February 2015, available at http://www.gamesindustry.biz/articles/2015-02-17-report-esports-revenues-to-hit-usd465m-in-2017 (accessed 5 February 2019).
3 'Global Esports & Live Streaming Market Report 2021' *Newzoo*, 2021, 29–31; 'The World's Most Watched Sports', *Sport For Business*, 17 July 2017, available at https://sportforbuisness.come/the-worlds-most-watched-sports/ (accessed 12 May 2021).
4 'Sega Sponsors All Japan TV Game Championships', *Vending Times* 14 (1974): 69.
5 Sega Retro, 'Sega TV Game-ki Zenkoku Contest', Sega Retro, available at https://segaretro.org/Sega_TV_Game-ki_Zenkoku_Contest (accessed 19 February 2019).
6 Atari, Inc., 'Location Profile: A Special Game Room', *Atari Coin Connection* 1, no. 4 (1977): 3.
7 Keith Smith, 'Early Video Game Tournaments and Players', *The Golden Age Arcade Historian*, April 9, 2013, available at http://allincolorforaquarter.blogspot.com/2013/04/ (accessed March 3, 2019).
8 Atari Inc., 'Games Exhibited', *Atari Coin Connection* 3, no. 7 (1979): 3.
9 Funspot, 'A Quick Historical View of Funspot', Funspot, available at https://www.funspotnh.com/-Media-Kit/media-funspot-history.htm (accessed 5 March 2019).
10 Charles Erickson, 'TELEVISION/RADIO; When the Future of TV Was a Youngster Yelling "Pow!"', 9 June 2002, *New York Times*, available at https://www.nytimes.com/2002/06/09/arts/television-radio-when-the-future-of-tv-was-a-youngster-yelling-pow.html (accessed 5 March 2019).
11 Craig Kubey, *The Winners' Book of Video Games* (New York: Warner Books, 1982), 270.
12 'International News', *Electronic Gaming Monthly* 6, no. 10 (October 1993): 74–76.
13 'American Classic Arcade Museum … How It All Started', Funspot, https://www.funspotnh.com/-Media-Kit/media-museum-history.htm (accessed 15 March 2019).
14 'Madden 96 XBAND Challenge', *Electronic Gaming Monthly*, Issue 77a (December 1995): 236–237.

15 Ella McConnell, 'The End of the World Cyber Games', ESL, 7 February 2014, available at http://www.eslgaming.com/news/end-world-cyber-games-1912 (accessed 15 March 2019).

16 Alanna Yeo, 'World Cyber Games Asian Championships', Youth.SG, 12 August 2006, available at https://www.youth.sg/Peek-Show/2006/8/World-Cyber-Games-Asian-Championships (accessed 2 April 2019).

17 'World Cyber Games', Esports Earnings, available at https://www.esportsearnings.com/leagues/110-world-cyber-games (accessed April 7, 2019).

18 'World Cyber Games'.

19 'WGT 2006', Sina, 24 July 2006, available at http://games.sina.com.cn/e/n/2006-07-24/1013159813.shtml (accessed 12 April 2019).

20 Justin Calvert, 'Swedes Claim Electronic Sports World Cup', Gamespot, 14 July 2003, available at https://www.gamespot.com/articles/swedes-claim-electronic-sports-world-cup/1100-6071613/ (accessed 5 May 2019).

21 'ESWC Preliminaries Now Over in Five Countries', IGN, 6 June 2008, available at https://ie.ign.com/articles/2008/06/06/eswc-preliminaries-now-over-in-five-countries (accessed 8 May 2019).

22 Johannes Schiefer, 'A Trip Down Memory Lane: 12 Years of ESL Pro Series', ESL, 25 March 2014, available at https://www.eslgaming.com/article/trip-down-memory-lane-12-years-esl-pro-series-1811 (accessed 9 May 2019).

23 'Turtle Entertainment Polska', Gameindustries.biz, 7 January 2011, available at https://www.gamesindustry.biz/articles/turtle-entertainment-polska-new-electronic-sports-league-in-poland (accessed 15 May 2019).

24 'US Qualifiers for ESWC 2008', IGN, 20 March 2008, available at https://ie.ign.com/articles/2008/03/20/us-qualifiers-for-eswc-2008 (accessed 15 May 2019).

25 John Gaudiosi, 'Big Brands Gravitating towards eSports', *Fortune*, 24 July 2014, available at http://fortune.com/2014/07/24/esports-sponsors/ (accessed 18 May 2018).

26 'PUBG Global Championship Tournament Worth $2,000,000', Esports Bite, available at http://esportsbite.com/pubg-2019-global-championship-tournament-worth-2-million-dollars/ (accessed 27 May 2018).

27 Annie Pei, 'South Korea Esports Network OGN to Invest at Least $100 million in North America, Plans Big Partnership with Battle Royale Giant PUBG', CNBC, 11 October 2018, available at https://www.cnbc.com/2018/10/10/esports-network-ogn-to-invest-at-least-100-million-in-north-america.html (accessed 27 May 2019).

28 'GTV Competitive Gaming', available at http://www.tvyan.com/tiyu/gtvyouxi/ (accessed 27 May 2019).

29 Jack Stewart, 'Sport1's German-Language Esports Channel Launches in January 2019', Esports Observer, 28 November 2018, available at https://esportsobserver.com/sport1-german-esports-channel/ (accessed 27 May 2019).

30 Sam Espensen, 'XLEAGUE.TV Discovers World Champion', Games Industry, 15 October 2017, available at https://www.gamesindustry.biz/articles/xleaguetv-discovers-world-champion (accessed 27 May 2019).

31 Eddie Makuch, 'People React to ESPN Airing eSports Tournament', Gamespot, 27 April 2015, available at http://www.gamespot.com/articles/people-react-to-espn-airing-esports-tournament/1100-6426920/ (accessed 2 June 2019).

32 Danny Cowan, 'ESPN Rolls Out eSports-focused News Site', Digital Trends, 15 January 2016, available at https://www.digitaltrends.com/gaming/espn-now-hosts-dedicated-esports-coverage/ (accessed 6 June 2019).

33 Jeff Eisenband, 'Riot Games Wants Non-Endemic Brands that Buy into Creative Approach', Front Office Sports, 11 June 2019, https://frntofficesport.com/riot-games-non-endemic-brands/ (accessed 16 July 2019).

34 'T19 Prize Pool Exceeds $34,000,000', VPESPORTS, 24 August 2019, available at https://www.vpesports.com/dota2/ti9-prize-pool-exceeds-34000000 (accessed 12 May 2021).

35 'Electronic Sports', Olympic Council of Asia, available at http://www.ocasia.org/Sports/SportsT.aspx?AMPuohtNGyxFinVzEIKang (accessed 12 June 2019).

36 'e-Sports Included in the Asian Games', GameZone, 21 November 2012, available at http://www.mweb.co.za/games/view/tabid/4210/Article/4433/e-Sports-included-in-the-Asian-Games.aspx (accessed 14 June 2019).

37 'Can eSports Still be Itself in the 2019 SEA Games?', Fox Sports, 8 December 2018, available at http s://www.foxsportsasia.com/esports/993711/can-esports-still-be-itself-in-the-2019-sea-games/ (accessed 28 June 2019).

38 'Zoom In – Esports and Gaming', Olympic World Library, available at https://library.olympics.com/default/esports-gaming.aspx?_lg=en-GB (accessed 12 May 2021).

39 T.L. Taylor, *Raising the Stakes E-Sports and the Professionalization of Computer Gaming* (Cambridge: MIT Press, 2012); Tobias Scholz, *eSports is Business* (Cham, Switzerland: Palgrave Pivot, 2019); Seth E. Jenny, R. Douglas Manning, Margaret C. Keiper, and Tracy W. Olrich, 'Virtual(ly) Athletes: Where eSports Fit Within the Definition of "Sport"', *Quest* 69, no. 1 (2017): 1–18; Mariona Rosell Llorens, 'eSport Gaming: The Rise of a New Sports Practice', *Sport, Ethics and Philosophy* 11, no. 4 (2017): 464–476; Lu Zhouxiang, 'From E-heroin to E-sports: The Development of Competitive Gaming in China', *The International Journal of the History of Sport* 33, no. 18 (2016): 2186–2206; David Ekdahl and Susanne Ravn, 'Embodied Involvement in Virtual Worlds: The Case of eSports Practitioners', *Sport, Ethics and Philosophy* 13, no. 2 (2019): 14–27; Margaret C. Keiper, R. Douglas Manning, Seth Jenny, Tracy Olrich, and Chris Croft, 'No Reason to LoL at LoL: The Addition of Esports to Intercollegiate Athletic Departments', *Journal for the Study of Sports and Athletes in Education* 11, no. 2 (2017): 143–160; Paul Chaloner, *This Is Esports (and How to Spell It): An Insider's Guide to the World of Pro Gaming* (London: Bloomsbury Sport, 2020); William Collis, *The Book of Esports: The Definitive Guide to Competitive Video Games* (New York: RosettaBooks, 2020).

27

SPORT AND EMOTION

Barbara Keys

Sport is intensely emotional. The passions it generates account for its centrality in modern societies around the world – the millions spent on stadiums, the high salaries paid to elite athletes, the levels of time and energy many fans invest, and corporate eagerness to capitalize on sport to sell products. Fans experience more intense feelings around sport than around almost any other social activity. As one adult male American football fan wrote, 'I love fall and college football so much I can burst out in tears at the very thought of it all.'[1] Sportswriter Rob Steen explains it this way:

> For all the times [sport] falls short, for all the times it disappoints and dismays, offends and outrages, I love it because of what it *can* be: it can be beautiful, it can be dramatic, it can defeat prejudice and disadvantage, and it can bring together disparate, even warring peoples. And also because, in a world where the only certainty is uncertainty, it consistently gives us, in the shape of the final score, something absolutely, utterly, gloriously unarguable.[2]

To unpack the emotional dimensions of modern sport, this chapter first surveys the theoretical approaches from psychology and sociology that address emotions and sport and then discusses how emotions appear in current writing about the history of sport.

Dimensions of emotion in sport: theoretical understandings

What is emotion? The term lacks a clear definition in any field: psychologists, neuroscientists, philosophers, anthropologists, sociologists, and historians disagree among themselves about how to define emotion.[3] What most scientists agree on today is that, in neurological terms, reason and emotion are deeply interlinked. Cognition is profoundly influenced by feelings, and emotions are often shaped by cognition: we are afraid when a lion approaches us because we access cognitive information about the dangers lions pose. Rationality and emotion therefore operate together. In popular thinking, rationality without emotional 'contamination' is often seen as a goal, but in terms of how the human brain works, reason and emotion are neither opposite nor separate.[4] Most scholars also now agree that emotions are not culturally universal but instead are historically constructed. Debate continues over

228   DOI: 10.4324/9780429318306-31

Sport and emotion

whether core ('basic') emotions exist that are interpreted in different ways in different cultures, but the current consensus holds that culture has unique rules and vocabularies for perceiving, expressing, and giving meaning to senses and emotions.[5]

The emotional power of spectatorship derives from its social or shared characteristics. According to social psychologists, emotion is not merely an individual experience limited to neurological and physiological changes in a single body. Emotion can also be experienced by groups. Any individual has multiple identities, which come to the fore depending on social context. A person might identify primarily as a bartender at work, a mother at home, and an Arsenal fan in the stadium. For fans, group identification is powerful. When watching a game, fans often feel like an interchangeable part of a whole, so they experience collective emotions. The phenomenon of group-based emotions explains why a fan may feel pride in her team even when she had no role in their success.[6]

Interaction ritual theory, first developed by sociologist Randall Collins, offers a fruitful lens for understanding why sports fans experience such intense emotions. According to this theory, interaction rituals are group activities – such as prayers in church or singing the national anthem in a stadium – that give people positive emotional energy. When these rituals succeed, individuals experience a sense of connection and solidarity, along with feelings of confidence, elation, and trust. Four ingredients combine to create this emotional energy: bodily co-presence, mutual focus of attention, shared mood, and a barrier to outsiders. Individuals must be physically co-present in order to 'monitor each other's signals and bodily expressions', allowing 'human nervous systems to become mutually attuned'. They must have an object or an activity that draws their shared attention. They must experience a common mood or emotion, such as when individuals get 'into shared rhythm, caught up in each other's motions and emotions'. Finally, they must have a sense of 'who is taking part and who is excluded'. These conditions amplify the original emotional condition among participants, leading to exaltation or 'electricity', feelings that bind the group and generate solidarity. 'Whoever has experienced this kind of moment wants to repeat it,' Collins notes.[7]

It is not only watching a sports competition in the stadium or on television, with real or virtual co-spectators, that generates an interaction ritual leading to positive emotional energy; conversations around the water cooler at work can also become a resource that starts and sustains future interaction rituals. Remembering past sports events or wearing a team jersey can recall the emotional energy originally associated with the ritual of spectatorship. Such memories or souvenirs function as 'batteries' that store the emotional energy originally generated by the sports event and reignite that energy in the individual even in the absence of the original group. As Collins writes, 'individuals are motivated to enact or reject conversational rituals with particular persons to the extent that they experience favorable or unfavourable emotional energies from that interaction'.[8] In other words, people seek out ritualized interactions, including talking about sports, that yield emotional solidarity.

Sports fans everywhere know that the emotions elicited by competitions are sometimes positive and sometimes negative. Intense highs are matched by intense disappointment. Sports spectatorship brings pleasure but also depression and even sometimes aggression towards others. Among some fans, a culture of frustration applies, in which fans interact with sports events in a mode of strong and visceral angst. Such fans can become so irate that they appear to lose control, swearing and hurling abuse even when the targets of the abuse cannot hear it. The culture of frustration is one way that sport fan culture appears to differ from other fan cultures, say, in music. Scholars have suggested two possible explanations for why sports fans continue to participate in events that cause them anguish: first, that frustration offers an excuse for antisocial behaviour, including violence; and second, that the frustration offers a cathartic outlet for tension.[9] Yet another explanation is offered by psychologists, who suggest that some fans develop obsessive passion that results when the sense of excitement that comes from engaging in spectatorship becomes uncontrollable. Obsessive fans feel excessive identification with a team or other object of passion, which leads them to feel a compulsion to engage in spectatorship and often experience negative feelings because of it.[10]

Places, too, can be strongly emotional. Stadiums and other venues in which sports competitions occur, like courtrooms and circuses, can be considered emotional arenas – a space that reveals a community's expressive capacity. In any particular stadium, cultural norms dictate what emotional styles are acceptable. Beyond how the people in the stadium – both athletes and spectators – express emotions and interpret the emotions of others, the physical site can itself elicit emotions. Architecture and other aspects of a stadium produce aesthetic judgments and sensory inputs that in turn elicit emotions. Sports marketing professionals have defined atmosphere in sport stadiums as the characteristics of the surroundings that create mood. Sports marketers are now investigating how atmosphere produces emotional readiness to buy tickets, souvenirs, and food and willingness to pay particular prices for them.[11] Fans' emotional attachment to stadia is not dependent on comfort or beauty but on shared memory and symbolism. Boston's Fenway Park, for example, is an inefficient and uncomfortable stadium with limited seating capacity and expensive prices, but many patrons feel fierce pride, veneration, and loyalty to the place and its 'aura'.[12]

Sports broadcasters can develop a deep emotional bond with fans. Ronald Reagan, for example, honed this skill in his early career as a radio baseball announcer. The convention in television broadcasting is to provide two commentators operating in tandem, one doing a play-by-play analysis, the other providing 'colour'. In Lemann's words,

> the play-by-play man tells you what just happened, and the color man offers up your feelings; your own reaction and that of your friends, gathered in front of the screen, are cued and shaped by the intricate interplay of their reactions.

The announcers mediate and intensify the relationship between the sports event and the audience.[13] Howard Cosell was the most famous and most controversial radio and television sports broadcaster in the United States from the 1950s through the 1970s. He never played professional sports but was inducted into the Boxing Hall of Fame for the drama and excitement he imparted to the sport.[14]

Historical developments

Surprisingly little scholarship on the history of sport has attended explicitly to its emotional dimensions, and no overarching history of emotion in sport has been attempted. Although most histories of sport naturally touch on emotion because it is so pervasive, sport historians rarely treat emotion as a category of analysis. Instead, sport histories cover emotions sporadically, implicitly, or as part of different categories, such as aggression or gender norms. Because a thorough accounting of emotion in the history of sport is as yet impossible, what follows is a survey of some of the major issues that sport historians identify as key areas where sport and emotion have intersected.

Social control

Governments and social reformers have a long history of promoting sport to potentially problematic social groups in order to teach emotion regulation. Athletes are influenced by emotion, and today a huge subfield of sport psychology analyses how emotional elements such as competitive anxiety, anger, joy, burnout, and 'flow' influence athletic performance.[15] When modern governments came to see the potential of sport to change the 'character' of participants, they began to embrace sport and physical education programmes. When sport became widely popular in Europe and North America in the nineteenth century, it was partly due to the efforts of social reformers who believed that competitive activities offered a way to channel potentially harmful working-class emotions into healthy pursuits.[16] This new way of thinking constituted a striking shift, for previously the authorities had seen popular recreations as mostly harmful. In Britain especially, the nineteenth century saw an expansion of sport driven largely by perceptions that sport would foster positive emotional qualities such as discipline and courage.[17]

One example of the use of sport and physical recreation programmes to inculcate socially useful emotion is Nazi Germany's mass tourism organization, Kraft durch Freude (Strength through Joy). This Nazi organization offered a variety of affordable leisure activities to German workers. Its sports and fitness programme was intended to strengthen the nation physically and to foster emotions that enhanced communal values rather than competition. Designed for both men and women, Strength through Joy courses taught a range of sports, from boxing to tennis to sailing.[18] Impressed by the results of such programmes, other governments followed suit. The French government, for example, appointed its first Minister for Sport in 1936; he declared his mission to be allowing 'the masses of French youths to find in the practice of sport joy and health'.[19]

Gender norms

Sport has long been a vector for societies to inculcate gender norms, including those having to do with the expression of emotion.[20] Gendered expectations about how men and women should express emotions shape fan and athlete behaviour, as well as media coverage of sport. For example, one study showed that when tennis greats Martina Navratilova and Jimmy Connors faced off in the 'Battle of Champions' in 1992, media commentators frequently described Navratilova as subject to emotions that made her vulnerable, while they rarely mentioned Connors' emotions. The coverage of this event replicated a longstanding pattern in which journalists suggested that women athletes were unusually susceptible to stress and might collapse due to emotional instability. Journalists tended to describe male athletes as driven by competitive zeal, passion for the game, and aggression, while foregrounding women's cooperation and self-sacrifice.[21] As author Henry Jenkins observes, the rules of emotional expression have long shaped fan behaviour, too: 'social conventions [in modern Western societies] have traditionally restricted the public expression of sorrow or affection by men and of anger or laughter by women'.[22] Gender can determine who gets into the stadium, as in Iran, where women were prohibited from attending for decades after the 1979 Revolution. In Australia, women have long attended Australian rules football games, and many have felt free to yell angry comments at players throughout the game, expressing their sense that athletes must exert themselves to bring pleasure to fans. Historian Matthew Klugman argues that in recent years, despite Australian football's inherent sexism, 'Aussie Rules allows women to judge players not for who they are but how they perform, to demand that footy players sacrifice their bodies for them, and to publicly abuse them when they fail.'[23]

Nationalism

Especially in international competitions, sport has long been intimately linked to the growth of nationalism, a phenomenon built on emotional attachment. As Benedict Anderson wrote in his classic study, nationalism 'claims emotional legitimacy' and arouses 'deep attachments'.[24] The success of a national team in the Olympic Games can bring pride and elation to much of the country's population, and for smaller postcolonial countries the spectacle of a national team when it first marched in the opening parade was a proud assertion of identity and independence. Historian Mark Dyreson argues that in the early twentieth century, Americans 'developed an intense athletic nationalism – the devotion of emotion and energy to the state through sport – by participating in the [Olympics]'.[25] Hosting a sports mega-event has also long been a source of nationalist pride, as the 2008 Beijing Olympic Games vividly illustrated. Many Chinese were angered, for example, when protests over human rights problems in China erupted in some Western countries as the Olympic torch relay passed through. Historian Xu Guoqi commented at the time: 'The arrogant attitude of the Western politicians to use the torch relay and the coming Games to humiliate and shame Chinese was treated by many Chinese at home and abroad as a collective insult.'[26] More often, international sports competitions have offered a way for nations to garner respect – an emotion-laden term. Since the early twentieth century, participating, hosting, and winning at international competitions have been seen as signals that the international community respects and values one's country.

Internationalism

If the emotions of sport have fed nationalism, they have also propelled internationalist feelings. In 1998, the International Olympic Committee sought to 'protect, build, and leverage' the Olympic brand by identifying its unique aspects and its power. The research showed that people associate Olympic values with specific emotional qualities, including hope, inspiration, friendship, and joy in effort.[27] International sports mega-events such as the Olympic Games have likely had significant influence on how people around the world feel about global society. The dramatic and competitive elements in sport, and sport's homologies with what are perceived to be universal elements of human struggle – loss, disappointment, failure, achievement – make it appear universally readable. This assumption of sport's cross-cultural emotional readability may in turn have allowed international sports events to promote a shared understanding of humanity. In this way sport may have had a role in expanding humanitarian sentiment in the last century, for we are more likely to feel concern and responsibility for other people if we believe we share their emotional responses to events.[28]

Fan violence

The long-debated question of the relationship between sport and violence – does sport provide an outlet for the harmless release of pre-existing aggressive feelings or does it foster and foment such feelings? – is rooted in emotion. Emotional dynamics are important to understanding football (soccer) hooliganism, for example. Hooligans feel an intense 'buzz' or adrenalin rush during confrontations that is tied to anticipation but also to overcoming fear. One Chelsea hooligan confessed that 'fear is a drug'. What gives the fighting a pleasurable emotional arousal is the suppression of fear or the capacity to act in spite of it.[29]

Such hooliganism has resulted in tragic events, such as the 1985 Heysel stadium disaster in Brussels. Thirty-nine people died when Juventus supporters tried to flee when Liverpool supporters charged toward them across a terrace, leading to a stampede and the collapse of a wall. Spectator violence has long been common in English football, but beginning in the 1960s the pattern shifted from attacks on match officials and rival players to attacks on rival fans. Historians attribute this shift to the rise of segregated youth seating, which exacerbated the class and age stratification of fans and the cultivation of norms of aggressive masculinity. However, the circulation of social emotions explains why social stratification intensified the feelings of anger, resentment, and antipathy that fostered violence. Once young fans were physically separated from other fans, their sense of ingroup solidarity and resentment of outgroups strengthened. Segregation moved the violence away from football stadia to the streets, pubs, and railway stations. The decline in fan violence in Britain since the 1990s is likely due to a variety of measures, including the spatial transformation of football stadia that reduced the prospect for virulent emotional contagion.[30]

Emotions analysis offers a powerful tool for studying the history of sport. Love and hatred, pride and envy, fear and hope, joy and sorrow: sport calls forth the full range of passions. Those passions in turn influence how people decide what to buy, how to dress, who they care about, where they live, which communities they join, and how they think about gender, class, race, nation, and even humanity. More explicit – and explicitly theorized – approaches to the emotional dimensions of sport history promise to enhance our understanding of long-studied phenomena and to reveal new ones. A key challenge to integrating the study of emotion more thoroughly into the history of sport is that it overlaps and intersects with so many other categories of analysis. As social psychologist Margaret Wetherell rightly asks, 'How can we engage with phenomena that can be read simultaneously as somatic, neural, subjective, historical, social and personal?'[31] Thanks to sharp growth in interest in emotion among psychologists and neuroscientists in recent decades, historians are increasingly taking up the study of emotion. In the age we live in, when emotion seems to play an outsized role in politics, such interest will surely expand.

Notes

1 John Clendening, *Love Letters to Sports: Moments in Time and the Ties that Bind* (Bloomington: iUniverse, 2011), 109.

2 Rob Steen, *Floodlights and Touchlines: A History of Spectator Sport* (London: Bloomsbury, 2014), 1.

3 See Barbara Rosenwein and Ricardo Cristiani, *What Is the History of Emotions?* (New York: Polity, 2017), ch. 1.

4 Rose McDermott, 'The Feeling of Rationality: The Meaning of Neuroscientific Advances for Political Science', *Perspectives on Politics* 2, no. 4 (2004): 693.

5 Keith Oatley, 'Social Construction in Emotions', in *Handbook of Emotions*, eds. Michael Lewis and Jeannette M. Haviland (New York: Guilford, 1993), 341–352.

6 Eliot R. Smith and Diane M. Mackie, 'Dynamics of Group-Based Emotions: Insights from Intergroup Emotions Theory', *Emotion Review* 7, no. 4 (2015): 349–354.

7 Randall Collins, *Interaction Ritual Chains* (Princeton: Princeton University Press, 2004), 32–39, 47–49, 64. Collins draw on Emile Durkheim's study of religious ceremonies.

8 Randall Collins, 'On the Microfoundations of Macrosociology', *American Journal of Sociology* 85, no. 5 (1981): 1012.

9 Matthew Klugman, "'My Natural Environment Has Provided Me with about Fifty Different Ways of Expressing Frustration": Mining the Visceral Angst of Australian Rules Football Followers', *Emotion, Space and Society* 12 (2014): 24–31.

10 Robert J. Vallerand et al., 'On Passion and Sports Fan: A Look at Football', *Journal of Sports Sciences* 26, no. 12 (2008): 1279–1293.

11 Chen-Yueh Chen, Yi-Hsiu Lin, and Hui-Ting Chiu, 'Development and Psychometric Evaluation of Sport Stadium Atmosphere Scale in Spectator Sport Events', *European Sport Management Quarterly* 13, no. 2 (2013): 200–215.

12 Michael Ian Borer, 'Important Places and Their Public Faces: Understanding Fenway Park as a Public Symbol', *Journal of Popular Culture* 39, no. 2 (2006): 205–224.

13 Nicholas Lemann, 'The Voice of Big-Time Sports', review of Mark Ribowsky, Howard Cosell: *The Man, the Myth, and the Transformation of American Sports*, in *The New York Review of Books*, 22 March 2012, 14.

14 John Bloom, *There You Have It: The Life, Legacy, and Legend of Howard Cosell* (Boston: University of Massachusetts Press, 2010).

15 See, for example, Andrew Friesen, 'Managing Own and Others' Emotions in Sport', in *Sport and Exercise Psychology*, ed. Andrew M. Lane (New York: Routledge, 2015), 144–177.

16 Norbert Elias and Eric Dunning, *Quest for Excitement: Sport and Leisure in the Civilizing Process* (New York: Basil Blackwell, 1986).

17 Barbara Keys, *Globalizing Sport: National Rivalry and International Community in the 1930s* (Cambridge: Harvard University Press, 2006), 20–1.

18 Shelley Baranowski, *Strength through Joy: Consumerism and Mass Tourism in the Third Reich* (Cambridge: Cambridge University Press, 2004), 96–98.

19 Quoted in Mihir Bose, *The Spirit of the Games: How Sport Made the Modern World* (London: Constable, 2012).

20 See, for example, Michael A. Messner, Michele Dunbar, and Darnell Hunt, 'The Televised Sports Manhood Formula', *Journal of Sport and Social Issues* 24 (2000): 380–394; and Danielle M. Soulliere, 'Wrestling with Masculinity: Messages about Manhood in the WWE', *Sex Roles* 55 (2006): 1–11.

21 Margaret Carlisle Duncan, 'Gender Warriors in Sport: Women and the Media', in *Handbook of Sports and Media*, eds. Arthur A. Raney and Jennings Bryant (New York: Routledge, 2006), 258–259.

22 Henry Jenkins, *The Wow Climax: Tracing the Emotional Impact of Popular Culture* (New York: New York University Press, 2007), 80.

23 Matthew Klugman, 'Gendered Pleasures, Power, Limits, and Suspicions: Exploring the Subjectivities of Female Supporters of Australian Rules Football', *Journal of Sport History* 39, no. 3 (2012): 415–429.

24 Benedict Anderson, *Imagined Communities: Reflections on the Origin and Spread of Nationalism* (London: Verso, 1991), 4.

25 Mark Dyreson, *Making the American Team: Sport, Culture, and the Olympic Experience* (Urbana: University of Illinois Press, 1998), 32.

26 Xu Guoqi, 'Beijing Olympic Torch Relay and Its Implication for China and the Rest of the World', 22 May 2008, at harvardpress.typepad.com/off_the_page/2008/05/beijing-olympic.html.

27 Holger Preuss, *The Economics of Staging the Olympics: A Comparison of the Games, 1972–2008* (Cheltenham: Edward Elgar, 2004), 8–9.

28 Barbara Keys, 'Senses and Emotions in the History of Sport', *Journal of Sport History* 40, no. 1 (2013): 401–417. On the emotions of internationalism in general, see Ilaria Scaglia, *The Emotions of Internationalism: Feeling International Cooperation in the Alps in the Interwar Period* (Oxford: Oxford University Press, 2020).

29 Ramón Spaaj, *Understanding Football Hooliganism: A Comparison of Six Western European Football Clubs* (Amsterdam: Amsterdam University Press, 2006), ch. 1.

30 Spaaj, *Understanding Football Hooliganism*, ch. 3.

31 Margaret Wetherell, *Affect and Emotion: A New Social Science Understanding* (London: Sage, 2012), 11.

28

SPORT HERITAGE

Gregory Ramshaw

Heritage and sport share an important relationship. Sporting events and achievements generate memories and important touchstones for individuals and communities alike, while sporting traditions, rituals, and superstitions become part of the behaviours and activities of both spectators and competitors. Famous sporting sites, such as arenas, stadiums, sporting routes, and sport landscapes are recognized and conserved by heritage societies, organizations, and public agencies as important places and can become magnets for devoted sporting pilgrims. Sports museums and halls of fame are catalysts for preserving sporting artefacts and venerating athletes, while also becoming important anchors of tourism development. Sport heritage is frequently commoditized into experiences, souvenirs, and memorabilia for a wide variety of consumers, while sporting moments are commemorated, replayed, and nostalgized through media outlets and social media channels. Chants and cheers at sporting events regularly reflect and espouse particular heritage values and viewpoints, and often become heritage in and of themselves for supporters and teams, while the very act of playing a particular sport by a particular person or group of people can represent a type of dissonant heritage performance. Sport often plays a role in broader national heritage moments and events, frames contemporary debates and discussions, and is used as a tool of both power and resistance. In short, there is little doubt that heritage is integral to sport, and sport is integral to heritage. This chapter therefore explores the concept of sport heritage and the types of sport heritage.

Heritage and sport

Heritage is a complex and frequently misunderstood term. Often, heritage is castigated as 'bad history'[1] when, in fact, heritage and history – though related – have very different tasks, audiences, and outcomes. Peter Howard further emphasizes the differences between history and heritage, noting that 'heritage is an applied humanity, whereas history is a pure one; history is interested in the past, heritage is interested in how the past might be conserved and interpreted for the benefit of the present'.[2] This is not to suggest that history and heritage do not overlap or share common concerns. Clearly, sport history plays a vital role in the understanding of sport heritage, not only in terms of providing content and context but also in understanding how sport heritage – particularly in its focus on the present – may mask,

DOI: 10.4324/9780429318306-32

obscure, or misrepresent the factual past. However, sport heritage also needs to be understood as a broad topic area with many component parts, including perspectives ranging from management and marketing to anthropology and archaeology. In addition, sport heritage is strongly related to areas such as museums, nostalgia, or tourism – though these topics are not synonyms for sport heritage. As such, sport heritage intersects with a variety of interdisciplinary topics and concepts, including (though not exclusively) history.

In terms of what heritage is, then, Dallen Timothy succinctly argues that heritage is 'what we inherit from the past and use in present day'[3]. Similarly, Rodney Harrison emphasizes that heritage is a present consideration, noting that heritage is both current circumstances *and* inherited concerns.[4] Emma Waterton and Steve Watson further describe heritage as 'a version of the past received through objects and display, representations and engagements, spectacular locations and events, memories and commemorations, and the preparations of places for cultural purposes and consumption'[5]. Although this definition reflects the popular understanding of heritage as both tangible (buildings, objects) and intangible (traditions, language), it also reflects heritage as a discursive practice which has led some scholars such as Laurajane Smith[6] and Gregory Ashworth[7] to suggest that all heritage is ultimately intangible. However, Rodney Harrison's[8] exploration of heritage argues that, though heritage remains a discursive practice that is defined through language, it is also rooted in tangible places, objects, and people. Furthermore, as a discursive practice, heritage reflects notions of power which may legitimize and delegitimize various viewpoints and perspectives; what Smith[9] terms the Authorized Heritage Discourse. As such, because heritage is frequently a source of dissonance and disagreement,[10] the idea of a singular, unified heritage narrative has largely been discredited and, rather, heritage is often understood through a range of competing agendas and narratives.

Both heritage and sport are evolving concepts. Certainly, many places and practices that are now termed 'heritage' may not have been considered as such even a decade ago, while one need only look at the listings for any number of sports networks to see that what constitutes 'sport' is also undergoing significant changes. Looking at lifestyle sports such as snowboarding or, more recently, the growing interest in eSports, it is evident that contemporary sport is evolving. A definition for sport heritage must therefore recognize these changes and evolutions. As such, sport heritage can be understood as the recognition and use of a variety of sporting pasts as a means of addressing or illuminating a variety of contemporary social, cultural, and economic processes and practices.[11] This definition recognizes that there are many bodies of knowledge which inform contemporary constructions of sport heritage, that there are many different forms and types of sport heritage, and that sport heritage is often interpreted in the present differently by different actors to achieve different objectives. It also recognizes heritage as a discursive process which may create, enshrine, and legitimize any number of sport-based places and activities under a heritage-banner for a variety of contemporary reasons.

The relationship between heritage and sport may also be viewed from two broad perspectives: the *heritage of sport* and *sport as heritage*.[12] The *heritage of sport* perspective views the heritage/sport relationship primarily as self-contained within a sport's specific culture and history. In other words, this view considers the important records, achievements, artefacts, and places of a sport as being important to the athletes, fans, and administrators of that sport, but which may not transcend that sport into broader public heritage discourses. An example of the *heritage of sport* might be the championship records of a particular team, or the goal scoring record of a particular athlete, each of which may be vitally important to the supporters of that sport, particularly in terms of understanding the history and heritage of a

Sport heritage

particular sport or athletes, but which may not necessarily have any broader heritage implications outside of the sport itself. The other perspective, *sport as heritage*, considers sport heritage which transcends sport and becomes part of a broader heritage discourse. For example, some athlete 'firsts' – such as the first African-American in a sport or the first openly LGBTQ+ athlete in a sport – is certainly important to the *heritage of sport*, although often these become part of *sport as heritage* discourses as they become touchstones of larger cultural moments.

The sport heritage typology

The sport heritage typology[13] considers different forms and manifestations of sport heritage. Specifically, the sport heritage typology includes:

- Tangible immovable sport heritage
- Tangible movable sport heritage
- Intangible sport heritage, and
- Goods and services with a sport heritage component.

The sport heritage typology offers a useful framework for exploring the major facets of sport heritage. Below, each type is explained in more detail.

Tangible immovable sport heritage

Tangible immovable sport heritage refers to a material form of sport heritage that normally remains *in situ*. Perhaps the most notable forms of tangible immovable sport heritage are sports stadia and sporting venues. As Sean Gammon notes, 'the stadium has grown in importance, from an often aesthetically indifferent utilitarian structure into an iconic symbol of place, team, sport and/or event'.[14] As such, many sporting venues have become important heritage resources in and of themselves, as well as important tourist attractions for sports fans from around the world. Sports stadia such as Yankee Stadium in New York, Lord's Cricket Ground in London, and Camp Nou in Barcelona are not only symbolic of a particular sport, place, or team, they are also locations which have become part of tourists' itineraries, whether they are supporters or not. At an individual or community level, sporting venues are often linked to personal or family heritages, while losing a beloved stadium is often expressed by supporters as akin to a form of bereavement for a loved one.[15] As such, sporting venues have increasingly been understood as possessing many forms of heritage value.

Sporting monuments and memorials are another form of tangible immovable sport heritage. Although monuments and memorials will sometimes move (such as when a sport organization moves to a new venue), often they are inexorably linked to a specific location or space. Most sport heritage markers recognize important sporting people, such as players, coaches, and administrators – and sometimes even supporters and fans[16] – as well as famous sporting places, feats and accomplishments, and events. At times, they also intersect with other types of public monuments and memorials, such as war memorials. Beyond celebrating and recognizing the sporting past, sport heritage markers and memorials may also be vehicles for a addressing a variety of contemporary needs, from demonstrating the authenticity and legitimacy of a particular sporting space or venue, to a sense of social cohesion and shared identities for supporters, to connecting a suitable (and marketable) past to a sport organization.

Sporting landscapes are a final type of tangible immovable sport heritage. In sport, there are many different types landscapes, some of which (such as stadia, golf courses, and the like) are created primarily – if not exclusively – for sport. In some instances, sport heritage plays a role, often in terms of design. On the other hand, there are many landscapes – such as parks – where sport is one of many activities which creates and ascribes meanings to particular spaces.[17] Some sport landscapes are organic, in that a specific space becomes a culturally important reference point for a particular sporting practice, although it was not originally designed for sport. The Southbank Skatepark in London, for example, was an unused concrete undercroft that has become an iconic location for British skateboarding.[18] Other sporting landscapes may appear organic and naturalistic, but are imbued with cultural meanings. The 'village green' for cricket and the 'outdoor pond' in ice hockey create and maintain particular heritage associations about their meaning and use. Many sporting landscapes recreate and replicate elements of natural and cultural heritage in their design, both as a cultural reference to the sporting past as well as to create a distinctive and unique sports spectating experience. Natural heritage, such as the sandy dunes of the Scottish coast, are replicated at every golf course in the world. Some sport landscapes are also temporary, but overlap with other, non-sport, heritage landscapes (e.g. marathon routes) Of course, sport heritage landscapes are also contested, including which sports can be played and by whom, or whether the landscape may even be used for particular sporting practices.

Tangible movable sport heritage

Tangible movable sport heritage refers to a material form of sport heritage that need not necessarily remain *in situ*. Most often, tangible movable sport heritage is composed of the sporting objects, artefacts, and memorabilia housed in sports museums and halls of fame.[19] Individuals and organizations may acquire sporting objects and exhibit them, sell them, put them in storage, loan them to other museums, or use them as part of a travelling collection. Although some sports museums and halls of fame are inexorably connected to a specific community or location – such as the National Baseball Hall of Fame and Museum in Cooperstown, New York[20] – others are more mobile, particularly if they need to move to reach a larger audience. For example, both the College Football Hall of Fame in the United States (moving from South Bend, Indiana to Atlanta, Georgia) and the National Football Museum (moving from Preston to Manchester) moved, in part, for commercial reasons.

Heritage is also integral to sporting events. Although some certain heritage-based sporting events such as Wimbledon or the Kentucky Derby remain in one location, many others which use heritage as part of their events – such as the Olympics and World Cup – are mobile. The uses of heritage at sporting events can vary. While some events use heritage as a secondary component to the actual competition, others are primarily heritage-based performances which include elements of sport. Folk football matches in Orkney and Florence or the Running of the Bulls in Pamplona are as much (if not more) about the continuation of cultural traditions and rituals (as well as, perhaps, tourism development) as they are about competition. Similarly, heritage organizations such as UNESCO are actively preserving traditional sports and sporting practices, part of which includes having regular World Traditional Games events, which display and perform aspects of traditional sports from around the world. Certain professional leagues also host regular or one-off heritage-based events. These events explicitly refer to the heritage traditions, rituals, and landscapes of the sport while, at the same time, creating 'new' heritage products and spectacles, which organizations can market as a different (and often premium) product.[21] Many other events, such as civic events (where a local athlete is honoured and presented with a public monument such as a statue), artistic events (such as sport heritage-themed plays, operas, gallery exhibitions), and memorabilia shows (where sporting collectables are bought, sold, and traded) are just a few of the other types of events which use sport heritage. Some sporting events are memorialized in more permanent ways. Many Olympic host cities, such as Lake Placid and Lillehammer, have museums dedicated to their past hosting duties, while many annual sporting events also have their own museums, such as a museum at the Indianapolis Motor Speedway, site of the Indianapolis 500 motor-race,[22] the Wimbledon Lawn Tennis Museum, site of the Wimbledon tennis tournament,[23] and the Centrum Ronde Van Vlaanderen, museum of the Tour of Flanders cycling race.[24]

Intangible sport heritage

Many forms of sport heritage cannot necessarily be touched or catalogued as a building or artefact might. Normally, intangible heritage is related to cultural practices such as language, tradition, and ritual, although it could potentially be connected to any number of non-material practices. Memories, knowledge, time, and sensory perceptions of sport heritage all play a role in its creation and construction. The chants from the crowd, the smell of the ground, and even the taste of certain foods at sporting events can all evoke a sense of heritage, particularly if they are considered a strong part of the rituals and history of watching or participating in a particular sport. Certain traditions, such as those practised by a team before a match, are also a kind of sport heritage, as are the rivalries between teams (and their supporters) which may call on broader notions of identity and belonging. Even how particular sports and sporting practices are connected with time or a sense of continuity could be considered a form of intangible sport heritage, as could the transmission of sporting knowledge between generations. Indeed, one of the challenges of encapsulating the relationship between intangibility and sport heritage is that it could potentially involve an almost innumerable number of rituals and practices. Of course, the rituals and traditions of intangible sport heritage are not without their politics. How a sport is played – and, most importantly, by whom – are often defended as a point of 'tradition', which may marginalize or entirely omit many participants.

However, the intangibility of sport heritage is not only in the historic rituals and traditions of sport. Social institutions, such as the media, church, government, educational system, and through sport's own governing bodies and agencies, often use sport heritage as a form of recognition, legitimacy, and continuity. Mike Cronin and Roisin Higgins, for example, examine the relationship between sport, heritage, and institutions in Ireland, finding that institutions such as the church and educational system generated intangible sport heritage through values, ideologies, and rules systems related to sport, while also creating tangible sport heritage places through establishment of playing fields, sporting venues, and offices and buildings which housed sports' governing bodies.[25] However, the links between institutions and sport heritage are not benign, as institutional structures reinforce particular ideologies through sport and sport heritage. Many institutional sport heritages are created, promoted, and reinforced institutional structures related to colonialism, racism, class, and gender inequity.

Finally, sport heritage can also be an existential heritage practice. The notion of 'being' a part of a sporting heritage often reflects more hereditary elements of heritage. Numerous examples in sport exist where the children of athlete parents go on to become star athletes themselves. In baseball for example, the father–son duos of the Griffeys (Ken Sr. and Ken Jr.)

and the Bonds (Bobby and Barry) are legendary in the sport. Mother–daughter sporting duos are also common, including in martial arts (AnnMaria De Mars/Ronda Rousey), athletics (Liz and Eilish McColgan), and archery (Jessie and Brenda Wadworth). The most recognizable and celebrated example of hereditary heritage in sport is in horseracing. Champion horses are often known as much for their offspring as they are for their on-track accomplishments. However, 'doing' a type of sport also demonstrates existential sport heritage which can be performed as an embodied cultural practice as well as an activity to be experienced with others. A particular style of play, for example, might be viewed as expressing or embodying a particular national character. From an interpersonal point of view, personal sport heritage identities can be created and reinforced through connections with others. Mementos and souvenirs, such as from past games and events, can be personal artefacts and reminders of times spent with friends and family. Sport-based travel, particularly in travelling with a group, can also help to create, re-enforce, and perform personal and collective sporting heritages, particularly amongst diasporic communities.

Goods and services with a sport heritage component

Sport heritage can be a commodity. This can be most clearly be seen in the use of sport heritage in tourism. The form and type of sport heritage attractions are varied, though they often include locations such as sports museums and sports halls of fame, famous or historic sports stadia, as well as experiences such as sport fantasy camps, or historic or heritage-based sporting events. Sport heritage is also often used in broader forms of tourism development. American cities such as Baltimore and Cleveland employed heritage-based baseball stadia as key features of their tourism development, while American communities such as Charlotte (NASCAR Hall of Fame) and Atlanta (College Football Hall of Fame) have added large-scale sports museums to their tourist attraction mix in recent years. Similarly, heritage-based sporting events can attract tourists to communities outside of regular tourist seasons. The 2003 Heritage Classic outdoor ice hockey event in Edmonton, Canada, which relied heavily on heritage and nostalgic images of outdoor ice hockey in Canada, attracted a significant number of international visitors to the city in November, which is traditionally a low-leisure tourism month in that community.[26] Tourism demand for sport heritage experiences remains a relatively understudied phenomenon though the desire for nostalgic consumption appears to be one of the main motivations for heritage sport tourists. Sheranne Fairley and Sean Gammon suggest that it is the duality of nostalgia for artefacts (such as the stadium) and the nostalgia for social experience (nostalgic interaction with others through sport) as the main motivations,[27] though Heetae Cho, Gregory Ramshaw, and William Norman found that tourist motivation for sport-based nostalgia is multifaceted, encompassing experience, socialization, group identity, and personal identity.[28]

Beyond its use in tourism, sport heritage is increasingly an important marketing resource. Team names and logos often use local or regional heritage as part of branding initiatives, thus helping to link the identity of the team to local supporters and businesses in that community. Sport organizations may also use heritage items and events in their promotions in order to drive ticket sales and sponsorship and may create particular forms of souvenirs or apparel which incorporate heritage designs or historic logos. Organizations may also use heritage in their social media feeds, such as including highlighting historic victories or performances, in order to strengthen fan affiliation and engagement. The in-game experience may also include heritage components, including in-venue design, music, and staging. Non-sport organizations, such as businesses and corporations, may also use sport heritage in marketing initiatives. Products which use heritage in their marketing may create strategic alliances with sport heritage brands in order to increase brand awareness and legitimacy.

Sport heritage is increasingly managed both as a cultural and commercial resource. Many organizations from both sport and heritage agencies will plan for forms of sport heritage, particularly when a sport heritage venue is slated for abandonment or when a sporting anniversary approaches or an important sporting moment is anticipated (such as a player retirement or a sporting achievement being accomplished). Capturing sport heritage therefore becomes part of its management, as many sporting activities – particularly sport events – will generate documents, artefacts, memories, and other material which may be used for both academic and commercial interests. Similarly, managing sport heritage also concerns forms of protection, lest a vital sport heritage resource – be it tangible or intangible – is lost and therefore cannot be used as a future cultural or commercial heritage resource.

Conclusion

There is little doubt that heritage and sport share a strong and enduring relationship. Sporting moments, achievements, and people are celebrated, venerated, and commodified in various ways and in different locations, while sport heritage has transcended the field of play and entered broader discourses about the recognition of our collective heritage. Although sport heritage scholarship is relatively new in both sport studies and heritage studies fields, it is undoubtedly an emerging and important field. Although sport was once largely ignored in broader heritage debates, the evidence of sport as a topic of interest is undeniable and is now largely embraced as part of heritage studies scholarship. Similarly, many sport studies fields and disciplines had not necessarily linked sport and heritage together. However, the use of heritage in public history, geography, tourism, and marketing – among other areas – has placed heritage as a growing feature of contemporary sport scholarship. Perhaps most of all, there appears to be a public appetite for sport heritage, whether through public heritage recognition (such as through heritage plaques, statues, or museums), through sport heritage-based products and services, and through broader forms of heritage recognition, including sport heritage ceremonies, events, and festivals.

Notes

1 David Lowenthal, *The Heritage Crusade and the Spoils of History* (Cambridge: Cambridge University Press, 1998).
2 Peter Howard, *Heritage: Management, Interpretation, Identity* (London: Continuum, 2003), 21.
3 Dallen Timothy, *Cultural Heritage and Tourism: An Introduction* (Bristol: Channel View, 2011), 3.
4 Rodney Harrison, 'Forgetting to Remember, Remembering to Forget: Late Modern Heritage Practices, Sustainability and the 'Crisis' of Accumulation of the Past' *International Journal of Heritage Studies* 19, no. 6, (2013): 579–595.
5 Emma Waterton and Steve Watson, 'Heritage as a Focus of Research: Past, Present and New Directions', in *The Palgrave Handbook of Contemporary Heritage Research* eds. Emma Waterton and Steve Watson (London: Palgrave-Macmillan, 2015), 1.
6 Laurajane Smith, *Uses of Heritage*, (London: Routledge, 2006).
7 Gregory Ashworth, 'Paradigms and Paradoxes in Planning the Past' in *Selling or Telling? Paradoxes in Tourism, Culture and Heritage* eds. Mark Smith and Leander Onderwater (Arnhem: ATLAS. 2008) 23–34.
8 Rodney Harrison, *Heritage: Critical Approaches.* (London: Routledge, 2012).
9 Smith, *Uses of Heritage.*
10 Brian Graham, Gregory Ashworth, and John Tunbridge, *A Geography of Heritage: Power, Culture & Economy* (London: Arnold, 2000).

11 Gregory Ramshaw, *Heritage and Sport: An Introduction* (Bristol: Channel View, 2020).

12 Gregory Ramshaw and Sean Gammon, 'More than Just Nostalgia? Exploring the Heritage/Sport Tourism Nexus' *Journal of Sport & Tourism* 10, no. 4 (2005): 229–241; Gregory Ramshaw and Sean Gammon, 'Towards a Critical Sport Heritage: Implications for Sport Tourism' *Journal of Sport & Tourism* 21, no. 4 (2017): 115–131.

13 Ramshaw, *Heritage and Sport*.

14 Sean Gammon, '"Sporting" New Attractions? The Commodification of the Sleeping Stadium' in *Tourism Experiences: Contemporary Perspectives*, eds. Richard Sharpley and Phil Stone (London: Routledge, 2011), 115–126.

15 John Bale, *Sports Geography* (2nd edition), (London: Routledge, 2003).

16 Chris Stride, Ffion Thomas, and Gregory Ramshaw, 'Standing Out from the Crowd: Imaging Baseball Fans through Sculpture' *The International Journal of the History of Sport* 32, no. 14 (2015): 1611–1638.

17 Simon Inglis, *Played in London: Charting the Heritage of a City at Play* (Swindon: English Heritage, 2014).

18 Gregory Ramshaw, 'Subaltern Sport Heritages' in *Engaging Heritage, Engaging Communities*, eds. Bryony Onciul, Michelle Stefano, and Stephanie Hawke (Martlesham: Boydell & Brewer, 2017), 179–187.

19 Murray Phillips, ed. *Representing the Sporting Past in Museums and Halls of Fame* (London: Routledge, 2013).

20 Gregory Ramshaw, Gregory, Sean Gammon, and Felipe Tobar, 'Negotiating the Cultural and Economic Outcomes of Sport Heritage Attractions: The Case of the National Baseball Hall of Fame', *Journal of Sport & Tourism* 23, nos. 2–3 (2019): 79–95.

21 Gregory Ramshaw and Tom Hinch, 'Place Identity and Sport Tourism: The Case of the Heritage Classic Ice Hockey Event', *Current Issues in Tourism* 9, nos. 4–5 (2006): 399–418.

22 Jean Williams, 'The Indianapolis 500: Making the Pilgrimage to the "Yard of Bricks"', in *Sport, History, and Heritage: Studies in Public Representation* eds. Jeffrey Hill, Kevin Moore, and Jason Wood (Woodbridge: Boydell Press, 2012), 247–262.

23 Honor Godfrey, 'Upping Our Game: The New Wimbledon Lawn Tennis Museum' in *Sport, History, and Heritage*, 161–182.

24 Gregory Ramshaw and Tim Bottelberghe, 'Pedaling through the Past: Sport Heritage, Tourism Development, and the Tour of Flanders', *Tourism Review International* 18, no. 1 (2014): 23–36.

25 Mike Cronin and Roisin Higgins, *Places We Play: Ireland's Sporting Heritage* (Wilton: The Collins Press, 2011).

26 Ramshaw and Hinch, 'Place Identity and Sport Tourism: The Case of the Heritage Classic Ice Hockey Event'.

27 Sheranne Fairley and Sean Gammon, 'Something Lived, Something Learned: Nostalgia's Expanding Role in Sport Tourism' *Sport in Society* 8, no. 2 (2005): 182–197.

28 Heetae Cho, Gregory Ramshaw, and William Norman, 'A Conceptual Model for Nostalgia in the Context of Sport Tourism: Re-Classifying the Sporting Past' *Journal of Sport & Tourism* 19, no. 2 (2014): 145–167.

29

TOWARDS NEW MATERIALIST SPORT HISTORY

Holly Thorpe, Julie Brice and Marianne Clark

Given the growing engagement with new materialisms across the social sciences and humanities, and increasing focus within sport sociology and physical cultural studies, it is somewhat surprising that sport historians have yet to take the new materialist turn seriously.[1] However, some historians are exploring the potential of new materialisms. For example, Hans Schouwenburg asks: 'Is new materialism applicable to the study of the past? Is there a new materialist history?'[2] In this chapter we consider such questions in relation to sport history. We begin by providing a brief introduction to new materialisms and consider how such approaches may be taken up to expand the ethico-onto-epistemology of sport history. In the remainder of the chapter we offer two key new materialist concepts – lively matter and spacetimemattering – that we suggest have potential to expand the field towards a more-than-human sport history.

A brief introduction to new materialisms

Referred to variously as the ontological or posthuman turn, vitalist theories, and 'more-than-human' approaches, new materialisms refer to an evolving scholarly tradition that confronts the assumed boundaries between nature and culture and counters humanist approaches to contemporary thought.[3] Prompted by increasing dissatisfaction across the social sciences and humanities with the privileging of language, culture, and discourse as arbiters of meaning, new materialisms acknowledge the agentic capacities of matter and its role in shaping experience and meaning. This emerging body of knowledge is informed by an eclectic array of disciplinary foundations and draws upon the work of contemporary thinkers such as Karen Barad, Rosi Braidotti, Jane Bennett, Gilles Deleuze (with Felix Guattari), Donna Haraway, Bruno Latour, and Brian Massumi, among others. Despite many different interpretations and applications over the past decade, Nick Fox and Pam Alldred provide a succinct summary of the key tenets of new materialisms, including: i) rejecting the notion of discrete boundaries between the social and natural worlds, ii) assuming the material world is contingent, relational, and uneven, iii) re-imagining the concept of agency beyond the human domain, iv) conducting socially, politically, and materially oriented research with the aim to improve the social world, and v) dissolving the binary between ontology and epistemology.[4] Over the past five years, sport sociologists have increasingly considered the implications of new

DOI: 10.4324/9780429318306-33

243

materialisms for their field, with considerable debate emerging as to what is 'new' about new materialisms for sport sociology and related disciplines.[5] In our new book, *Feminist New Materialisms, Sport and Fitness: A Lively Entanglement*, we build upon and extend such work by offering a detailed explanation of how these key tenets have been, and might be, taken up for scholars of sport, physical culture, and the moving body.[6]

While the tenets of new materialisms provide scholars with ways for theorizing and thinking differently about various phenomena, they also require us to revisit our research methods. Some have identified a dissonance between new materialisms and familiar anthropocentric qualitative methodologies (i.e. interview, focus groups, observations, media and textual analysis) that are strongly rooted in humanism and rely on language and discourse. Consequently, some are 're-engineering' familiar qualitative methods,[7] whereas others are developing more innovative and creative approaches that align with the ethico-onto-epistemology of new materialisms.[8] Despite widespread uptake regarding both its ontological and epistemological implications, sport historians have been slow to grapple with new materialisms. Arguably, new materialisms have the potential to encourage radically new lines of flight in the thinking about, and *doing*, sport history. In the remainder of this chapter we offer two of many such possibilities.

Lively matter: rethinking sporting artefacts

New materialist thought is concerned with the material processes of the world and with the lively capacities of matter itself. In response to humanist ontologies that assume matter as passive and grant meaning only through the determining forces of the human and culture, new materialist ontologies acknowledge matter as agentic, indeterminate, and constantly 'becoming' in unexpected ways.[9] According to Diana Coole and Samantha Frost, new materialisms envision matter as 'something more than "mere" matter: an excess, force, vitality, relationality or difference that renders matter active, self-creative, productive, unpredictable'.[10]

Recognizing the vitality of nonhuman matter, new materialist approaches push back against human exceptionalism, which has long placed the intentionally acting human at the centre of meaning and experience. In so doing, new materialisms reimagines agency as a feature and potentiality of all non-human and human entities.[11] Through this, bodies (both organic and non-organic), environments, ecologies, technologies, and objects emerge as vital forces that demand our attention as they become part of the unfolding of the world.[12] Thinking about agency in a more relational manner and all matter as lively urges scholars to develop research practices that attend to the agentic capacities of matter rather than solely attending to the discursive or human. As Coole prompts us to consider: 'is it not possible to imagine matter differently: as perhaps a lively materiality that is self-transformative and already saturated with agentic capacities and existential significance that are typically located in a separate, ideal, and subjectivist, realm?'[13]

Sport sociologists are increasingly taking up such questions. For example, in the introduction to their anthology focused on new materialisms, sport, physical culture, and moving bodies, Joshua Newman, Holly Thorpe, and David Andrews explore the agentic capacities of gold, and particularly the gold medal won by the late Muhammad Ali (then Cassius Clay) at the 1960 Summer Olympic Games.[14] Also in this book, leading feminist sport scholar, Samantha King proposes a multispecies sport studies to explore protein powder as vital matter.[15] Sport historian Douglas Booth explores the agency of geomorphological features (i.e. Bondi's big rock),[16] feminist sport scholar Kiri Baxter examines the intra-actions between women boxers and the boxing glove,[17] and Gavin Weedon, and Rosalind Kerr and Camilla Obel, use Actor–Network Theory to trace the workings of various human and non-human actants in Tough Mudder events and gymnastics migration (i.e. Skype, leotards, work visas) assemblages, respectively.[18, 19] In our own work we have engaged with Karen Barad's theory of agential realism to explore the vitality of mundane and often taken-for-granted objects of fitness cultures, including the sports bra.[20] Engaging with Barad, we embarked on a theoretically driven project of 'living with' this object, and in so doing, came to know them differently, noticing the various agentic forces that emerged through the entangled relations between fitness objects, bodies, gendered discourse, and environments.

While socio-cultural sporting scholars have begun to grapple with the relational vitality of objects, scholars within history are also increasingly engaging with material artefacts as alternatives to textual sources.[21] More recently, some historians are drawing upon new materialisms to move beyond the cultural turn and to rethink relations with material culture. According to Schouwenburg, for historians, the 'new' in new materialisms is 'not so much an increased engagement with the material world, but rather a new conceptualization of developing theory and reading texts, which cuts through established dichotomies between matter and meaning or culture and the social'.[22] Referring to new materialisms as a 'movement that rejects the episteme of the cultural turn', Schouwenburg describes the 'analytical toolbox' of new materialisms as based on the metaphor of 'reading' (or what he refers to as re-reading and transversal readings), with 'new materialist readings ... result [ing] in surprising and challenging conceptions of matter and the agency of objects'.[23] While acknowledging (as we do) that 'notions of matter as generative force and nonhuman agency may seem foreign to many historians' – many of whom continue to treat objects as 'cultural artefacts made and modified by humans',[24] Schouwenburg concludes that a new materialist history can help 'solve some of the problems associated with the cultural turn and the turn to material artefacts'.[25] Here Schouwenburg is referring specifically to the tendency among historians to focus on the human-meaning associated with material artefacts. While he acknowledges such approaches have political underpinnings, with the material turn initially embraced by historians in the 'search for traces of marginalized people whose voices had escaped the official records in the archives',[26] he sees much potential in new materialisms for re-reading artefacts as always relational, material-discursive, vital, and more-than-human.

One such example of a historian turning to new materialist theory to rethink material artefacts can be seen in Bronwyn Davies' work in 'animating' a letter written in 1799 by her great (×3) grandfather, Thomas Bloomsfield. Rather than exploring what the letter represents, Davies shows how

> the words on the page of a letter ... invite us ... into different forms of existence ... the letter is not an entity that must be represented, but diffractive movements, capable of effecting us – animating us – of working on our own indefinite boundaries.[27]

In a traditional account, information from the letter might be mapped, a 'reality of a particular individual, a reality that exists independent of the one who searches the archives and assembles the facts'.[28] But in this new materialist-inspired approach, Davies came to understand the letter as 'alive, animating me, affecting me. The boundaries between me and Thomas, and between me and the letter, are blurred'.[29] Acknowledging the material artefact of the letter (and Thomas Bloomsfield) as lively (and therefore irreducible to cultural forces),

245

she traces the various affective flows and lines of flight that permeate the boundaries of the page and transcend time.

For sport historians whose focus of study often includes sporting artefacts (i.e. letters, newspapers, balls, uniforms, trophies, stadium, statues), new materialisms encourage a rethinking of sporting objects of past and present as agentic in their relations with, and beyond, the human. One such 'approach' that offers potential for sport historians is post-qualitative inquiry (PQI). Developed by feminist education scholar, Elizabeth St. Pierre, PQI rejects the constraints of methodology, the logic of representation and anthropocentrism of qualitative research.[30] Instead, PQI calls for a deep engagement with new materialist theory and invites an iterative dialogue between theory and process in an effort to move towards more-than-human ways of knowing. Rather than being guided by familiar processes of doing qualitative research, PQI asks researchers to think deeply with theoretical concepts in order to 'create something new and different that might *not* be recognizable in existing structures of intelligibility'.[31] Across many disciplines, scholars are taking up PQI to imagine more-than-human methodologies.[32] For example, Brian Kumm and Lisbeth Berbary explore the implications of PQI for reimagining '"data," "theory," "analysis," and "representation" within non-humanist onto-epistemologies of post-qualitative research' in leisure studies.[33] Various sport and physical cultural scholars have advocated the potential in PQI for radically rethinking the research process on/with moving bodies.[34] Some have embraced PQI approaches in their empirical studies, including Cathy van Ingen in her work on boxing, in which she leans into the processes of 'getting lost' in her data,[35] and Marianne Clark and Holly Thorpe in their collaborative experiment of wearing a FitBit while reading Baradian theory.[36] In so doing, these scholars are engaging with the ethico-onto-epistemological challenges of new materialisms. For sport historians, PQI could offer endless possibilities and creative freedom to explore the vibrancy of artefacts and historical objects, using theory as a conceptual research guide. Such approaches might include 'living with' particular sporting artefacts, using new materialist theoretical concepts to prompt new noticings or diffractively 're-reading' sporting artefacts, sources, and texts through each other.

Spacetimemattering: sporting histories of past-present-future

A leading figure in new materialist theorizing, Karen Barad is a feminist physicist whose theory of agential realism offers new ways of conceptualizing the material-discursive complexities of phenomena. Working at the intersection of quantum physics, science studies, the philosophy of physics, feminist theory, and poststructuralist theory, Barad offers a unique framework for exploring the complex relationships between humans and nonhuman matter.[37] Encompassing several key concepts (i.e. entanglement, intra-action, diffraction, apparatus), her theory of agential realism 'provides a posthumanist performative account of technoscientific and other naturalcultural practices'.[38] In this section we consider how a Baradian approach may encourage alternative ways of thinking about space, time, and matter, that could open up new possibilities for sport historians.

Of course, sport historians have extensively explored the complex relationship between time and space.[39] Acknowledging such important contributions, herein we consider how Barad's concept of spacetimemattering might extend upon such work. Barad's onto-ethico-epistemological framework explicitly rejects time as linear and instead insists 'ideas around time and space are created through intra-actions which themselves matter to the making/marking of space and time .... Time is out of joint. Dispersed. Diffracted. Time is diffracted through itself'.[40] For Barad, past-present-futures are always entangled: 'there is no moving beyond, no leaving the "old" behind. There is no absolute boundary between here-now and there-then. There is nothing that is new; there is nothing that is not new'.[41] In other words, what is 'old' always lives in and transforms that which is continuously emerging. This conceptualization of time has implications for how we think and understand unfolding practices and how they emerge in, through, and across space and time. According to Barad, time, space, and the 'practice of mattering' are always entangled, 'infinitely overlapping, interlaced, and co-constitutive'.[42]

Karen Barad's concept of spacetimemattering has been a useful theoretical concept for many scholars, particularly those working within educational fields.[43] While few sporting scholars have engaged with the concept, Julie Brice has used spacetimemattering to explore the athleisure phenomenon and the construction of femininity within societies past-present-future.[44] Bringing together feminist historical literature, archival sources, activewear advertising, and quotes from her interviewees, she emphasizes how diffractively reading women's contemporary experiences through past events means recognizing how the 'simple' act of wearing leggings is 'not simply here-now' but is 'always already threaded through with anticipation of where it is going but will never simply reach and of a past that has yet to come'.[45]

As noted above, new materialisms encourage methodological innovations aligned with its ontological and theoretical foundations. Diffraction is one such approach that has been used to explore spacetimemattering and has the potential to extend historians' ways of doing research. Barad describes diffraction as a process of 'reading insights through one another for patterns of constructive and deconstructive interference'.[46] In a diffractive approach, different disciplines, concepts, theories, and/or data sources can be brought into 'conversation with one another', such that we 'engage aspects of each in *dynamic* relationality to the other'.[47] Schouwenburg sees value in diffraction for history, advocating that the greatest strength in new materialisms for the discipline is the critical engagement with 'fresh ideas from other disciplines, including the natural sciences … without rejecting the work of previous generations of humanities scholars'.[48] For sport historians, new materialisms may offer alternative approaches for entering into new dialogue across the disciplines, or for diffractively reading artefacts, text, literature, and sources (both human and non-human) from past-present-future through each other. Furthermore, if we take up Karen Barad's understanding of the present as 'not simply *here-now*', but also a dis/continuous enfolding of heterogeneous *there-then*, sport historians might also find history lurking in strange new places.[49]

New materialisms and sport history: a critical conclusion

To date, few sport historians have taken up new materialisms. Thus, in this chapter we presented the key tenets of new materialism and discussed how these have been engaged and advanced across an array of fields, including history and sport sociology. While it was beyond the scope of this chapter to offer a more comprehensive examination, we hope the tentative offerings presented herein are enticing enough such that some sport historians will be inspired to read more new materialist theory, to live with the concepts, and to begin imagining the many possibilities for rethinking what and how we *do* sport history. How might the ethico-onto-epistemological implications of new materialisms prompt sport historians to reimagine sources, to know artefacts differently, and to read knowledge through each other, in creative ways that prompt affective and political responses?

Despite our optimism for the potential in new materialisms for opening new lines of flight within sport history, we also remain critical in our engagement. Some have expressed concerns about the lack of acknowledgement and the limited engagement of some new materialisms with post-colonial and queer scholarship and Indigenous ways of knowing.[50] Working explicitly in such tensions, some scholars are experimenting with the entangled relations between Indigenous, intersectional, queer, feminist politics, and posthumanist practices, and in so doing are 'explicitly grappling with the political and ethical ambivalences, contradictions, and failures of more-than-human research' in highly productive ways.[51] Thus, sport historians taking up new materialisms must continue asking critical questions about more-than-human histories. Grappling with such tensions, while reading matter and knowledge of past-present-futures through each other, has the potential to inspire more ethical sporting histories for humans and non-humans alike. Furthermore, it also offers radical political possibilities for sport historians as new materialisms radically rejects and seeks to disrupt human-centred approaches to knowledge and the formation of meaning. Doing so destabilizes many of our historical tropes, creating both uncertainty and new spaces for new lines of (ethically oriented) inquiry that understand the past in new ways, and thus revitalizes our efforts towards more equitable and sustainable futures for all.

Notes

1 Joshua Newman, Holly Thorpe, and David Lawrence Andrews, *Sport, Physical Culture and the Moving Body: Materialisms, Technologies and Ecologies* (New Brunswick, NJ: Rutgers University Press, 2020).

2 Hans Schouwenburg, 'Back to the Future? History, Material Culture and New Materialism', *International Journal for History, Culture and Modernity* 3, no. 1 (2015): 66.

3 Stacy Alaimo and Susan Hekman, eds. *Material Feminisms* (Bloomington, IN: Indiana University Press, 2008); Diana Coole and Samantha Frost, eds. *New Materialisms: Ontology, Agency and Politics* (Durham, NC: Duke University Press, 2010); Rick Dolphijn and Iris van der Tuin, *New Materialism: Interviews and Cartographies* (Ann Arbor, MI: Open Humanities Press, 2012).

4 Nick Fox and Pamela Alldred, 'New Materialism', in *The Sage Encyclopedia of Research Methods* eds. P.A. Atkinon et al. (London: SAGE, 2018).

5 Newman, Thorpe, and Andrews, *Sport, Physical Culture and the Moving Body*; Pirkko Markula, 'What Is New About New Materialism for Sport Sociology? Reflections on Body, Movement and Culture', *Sociology of Sport Journal* 36, no. 1 (2019); Javier Monforte, 'What Is New in New Materialism for a Newcomer?', *Qualitative Research in Sport, Exercise and Health* 10, no. 3 (2018): 378–190.

6 Holly Thorpe, Julie Elizabeth Brice, and Marianne Clark, *Feminist New Materialisms, Sport, and Fitness: A Lively Entanglement, New Femininities in Digital, Physical and Sporting Cultures* (Palgrave Macmillan, 2020).

7 Nick Fox and Pamela Alldred, *Sociology and the New Materialism: Theory, Research and Action* (Thousand Oaks, CA: Sage, 2017).

8 Bronwen Davies, 'The Persistent Smile of the Cheshire Cat: Explorations in the Agency of Matter through Art-making', *Qualitative Inquiry* 26, no. 7 (2020): 707–715; Anna Catherine Hickey-Moody, 'New materialisms, Ethnography and Socially Engaged Practice: Space-Time Folds and the Agency of Matter', *Qualitative Inquiry* 26, no. 7 (2020): 724–732; Jessica Ringrose, Katie Warfield, and Shiva Zarabadi, eds. *Feminist Posthumanisms, New Materialisms and Education* (Oxon, UK: Routledge, 2019). For a detailed discussion of new materialist methods, see Thorpe, Brice, and Clark. *Feminist New Materialisms, Sport and Fitness.*

9 Diana Coole and Samantha Frost, 'Introducing the New Materialisms', in *New Materialisms.*

10 Coole and Frost, 'Introducing the New Materialisms', 9.

11 Jane Bennett, *Vibrant Matter: A Political Ecology of Things* (Durham, NC: Duke University Press, 2010); Bruno Latour, *Reassembling the Social: An Introduction to Actor-Network Theory* (New York, NY: Oxford University Press, 2005).

12 Karen Barad, *Meeting the Universe Halfway: Quantum Physics and the Entanglement of Matter and Meaning* (Durham, NC: Duke University Press, 2007); Rosi Braidotti, *The Posthuman*, (Cambridge, UK: Polity Press, 2013); Donna Haraway, *Manifestly Haraway* (Minneapolis, MN: University of Minnesota Press, 2016).

13 Diana Coole, 'The Inertia of Matter and the Generativity of Flesh', in *New Materialisms*, 92.

Towards new materialist sport history

14 Joshua Newman, Holly Thorpe, and David Lawrence Andrews, 'Introduction: Sport, Physical Culture, and New Materialism', in *Sport, Physical Culture and the Moving Body*, chap. 1.

15 Samantha King, 'Towards a Multispecies Sport Studies', in *Sport, Physical Culture and the Moving Body*.

16 Douglas Booth, 'Bondi's Big Rock: Explanations and Representations in Coastal Geomorphology', *Geographical Research* 54, no. 4 (2016): 357–364.

17 Kiri Baxter, 'The Politics of the Gloves: Finding Meaning in Entangled Matter', in *Sport, Physical Culture and the Moving Body*, chap. 7.

18 Gavin Weedon, 'Camaraderie Reincorporated: Tough Mudder and the Extended Distribution of the Social', *Journal of Sport and Social Issues* 39, no. 6 (2015): 431–454.

19 Roslyn Kerr and Camilla Obel, 'The Migration of Gymnastics Coaches from the Former Soviet Union to New Zealand: An Actor–Network Theory Perspective', *Leisure Studies* 37, no. 5 (2018): 615–627.

20 Julie Elizabeth Brice, Marianne Clark, and Holly Thorpe, 'Feminist Collaborative Becomings: An Entangled Process of Knowing through Fitness Objects', *Qualitative Research in Sport, Exercise and Health* (2020), doi:10.1080/2159676X.2020.1820560.

21 Karen Harvey, ed. *History and Material Culture* (London, UK: Taylor and Francis, 2009).

22 Schouwenburg, 'Back to the Future?', 59.

23 Schouwenburg, 'Back to the Future?', 63.

24 Schouwenburg, 'Back to the Future?', 66.

25 Schouwenburg, 'Back to the Future?', 59.

26 Schouwenburg, 'Back to the Future?', 61.

27 Bronwyn Davies, 'Animating Ancestors: From Representation to Diffraction', *Qualitative Inquiry* 23, no. 4 (2017): 268.

28 Davies, 'Animating Ancestors', 269.

29 Davies, 'Animating Ancestors', 268.

30 Elizabeth St. Pierre, 'Practice for the "New" in the New Empiricisms, the New Materialisms and Post Qualitative Inquiry', in *Qualitative Inquiry and the Politics of Research*, eds. Norman Danzin and Michael Giardina (London: Routledge, 2015); Elizabeth St. Pierre, 'Post Qualitative Inquiry in an Ontology of Immanence', *Qualitative Inquiry* 25, no. 1 (2019): 3–16.

31 St. Pierre, 'Post Qualitative Inquiry in an Ontology of Immanence', 4.

32 Deborah Lupton, 'Toward a More-Than-Human Analysis of Digital Health: Inspirations from Feminist New Materialism', *Qualitative Health Research* 29, no. 14 (2019): 1998–2009; Margaret Somerville, 'The Post Human I: Encountering "Data" in New Materialism', *International Journal of Qualitative Studies in Education* 29, no. 9 (2016): 1161–1172.

33 Brian E. Kumm and Lisbeth Berbary, 'Questions for Postqualitative Inquiry: Conversations to Come', *Leisure Sciences* 40, nos. 1–2 (2019): 71.

34 Michael D. Giardina, '(Post?)Qualitative Inquiry in Sport, Exercise, and Health: Notes on a Methodologically Contested Present', *Qualitative Research in Sport, Exercise and Health* 9, no. 2 (2017): 258–270; Simone Fullagar, 'Post-Qualitative Inquiry and the New Materialist Turn: Implications for Sport, Health and Physical Culture Research', *Qualitative Research in Sport, Exercise and Health* 9, no. 2 (2017): 247–257.

35 Cathy van Ingen, 'Getting Lost as a Way of Knowing: The Art of Boxing within Shape Your Life', *Qualitative Research in Sport, Exercise and Health* 8, no. 5 (2016): 472–486.

36 Marianne Clark and Holly Thorpe, 'Towards Diffractive Ways of Knowing Women's Moving Bodies: A Baradian Experiment with the Fitbit/Motherhood Entanglement', *Sociology of Sport Journal* 31, no. 1 (2020): 12–26.

37 Barad, *Meeting the Universe Halfway*.

38 Barad, *Meeting the Universe Halfway*, 32.

39 John Bale, *Running Cultures: Racing in Time and Space* (New York, NY: Frank Cass Publishers, 2004).

40 Karen Barad, 'Diffracting Diffraction: Cutting Together-Apart', *Parallax* 20, no. 3 (2014): 180.

41 Barad, 'Diffracting Diffraction: Cutting Together-Apart', 168.

42 Jessica Ringrose and Victoria Rawlings, 'Posthuman Performativity, Gender and "School Bullying": Exploring the Material-Discursive Intra-Actions of Skirts, Hair, Sluts, and Poofs', *Confero* 3, no. 2 (2015): 90.

43 Malou Juelskjaer, 'Gendered Subjectivities of Spacetimematter', *Gender and Education* 25, no. 6 (2013): 754–768; Linnea Bodén, 'Dexter Time: The Space, Time, and Matterings of School Absence Registration', *Discourse: Studies in the Cultural Politics of Education* 37, no. 2 (2016): 245–255.

44 Julie Elizabeth Brice, 'Women's Bodies, Femininity, and Spacetimemattering: A Baradian Analysis of the Activewear Phenomenon', *Sociology of Sport Journal* (under review).

45 Karen Barad, 'Quantum Entanglements and Hauntological Relations of Inheritance: Dis/Continuities, Spacetime Infoldings, and Justice-to-Come', *Derrida Today* 3, no. 2 (2010): 244.

46 Malou Juelskjær and Nete Schwennesen, 'Intra-Active Entanglements: An Interview with Karen Barad', *Kvinder, Køn og Forskning* 1, no. 2 (2012): 12.

47 Barad, *Meeting the Universe Halfway*, 92–93.

48 Schouwenburg, 'Back to the Future?', 69.

49 Barad, 'Quantum Entanglements and Hauntological Relations of Inheritance', 244.

50 Sara Ahmed, 'Open Forum: Some Preliminary Remarks on the Founding Gestures of the "New Materialism"', *European Journal of Women's Studies* 15, no. 1 (2008): 23–39; Jerry Lee Rosiek, Jimmy Snyder, and Scott L. Pratt, 'The New Materialisms and Indigenous Theories of Non-Human Agency: Making the Case for Respectful Anti-Colonial Engagement', *Qualitative Inquiry* 26, no. 3 (2019): 1–16; Kyla Wazana Tompkins, 'On the Limits and Promise of New Materialist Philosophy', *Lateral* 5, no. 1 (2016).

51 Eve Mayes, 'The Mis/Uses of "Voice" in (Post)Qualitative Research with Children and Young People: Histories, Politics and Ethics', *International Journal of Qualitative Studies in Education* 32, no. 10 (2019): 1202; Alyssa D. Niccolini, Shiva Zarabadi, and Jessica Ringrose, 'Spinning Yarns: Affective Kinshipping as Posthuman Pedagogy', *Parallax* 24, no. 3 (2018): 324–343; Stephanie Springgay and Sarah Truman, *Walking Methodologies in a More-Than-Human World: Walkinglab* (New York, NY: Routledge, 2017).

30

DEAF AND DISABILITY SPORT

Danielle Peers

If you have heard any history of disability sport, it is probably the one about how Dr Ludwig Guttmann, medical director at Stoke Mandeville Hospital, created the first disability sports competition in 1944, and how this grew to become the Paralympic Games.[1] The story is a compelling one, but it is by no means the whole story, and it is not uncontested. Like any other history, sport histories are written by those with the most privilege. In the case of disability sport, this translates to stories that most often celebrate and justify the actions of non-disabled white doctors saving passive-yet-empowered men with mobility-related injuries.[2] In this chapter, I will weave together claims from these dominant histories with some more rarely discussed archives to tell a more complex and diverse history filled with more disability agency and struggle.

Tracing disability histories carefully

To tell any history of disability, one must first acknowledge that 'disability' is an *historically constituted* and *deeply contested* category of *immense diversity*. To say that 'disability' is historically constituted is to argue that the way we name, categorize, understand, and self-identify around what Westerners would now call disability has varied immensely across cultures and across historical periods.[3] Indeed, numerous Indigenous and anti-colonial activists and scholars have argued that contemporary concepts of disability as pathology did not exist within their cultures prior to colonization.[4] This, along with the colonial erasure of traditional (his) stories might explain the lack of records we have about non-Western disability sport. Further, the kind of people that Westerners deem to have a disability changes over time with some becoming de-pathologized (e.g. homosexuality) and others becoming newly pathologized (e.g. 'attention deficit disorder'). With this in mind, this history focuses on Western sport programmes since the late nineteenth century that were developed specifically by or for people who were widely understood to have disabilities.

To say that disability is deeply contested is to acknowledge that some individuals and communities have fought hard to be de-pathologized. LGBTQ2S communities and deaf communities, for example, have both argued that there is nothing wrong with them, and that their cultures and ways of being should be celebrated not fixed.[5] The terminology used to refer to pathologized communities has also been widely contested. For example, many

DOI: 10.4324/9780429318306-34

251

activists – particularly in the United Kingdom – consider themselves *disabled people* (i.e. people actively disabled by ableist structures) rather than *people with disabilities* (those whose bodies or minds are inherently problematic).[6] To acknowledge this contestation, the language used by the communities discussed is prioritized, including speaking about deaf histories as distinct from disability.

Finally, disability is internally diverse in that it can refer to forms of social marginalization, medical diagnoses, generative social identities, and a wide range of bodily sensations and capacities. We come to experience disability in relation to how we move, communicate, process information, perceive and process sensations, socialize, learn, breathe, digest, heal, age, and appear to others. It is important to note that only a very small portion of these disability experiences have been met with the kinds of specialized, segregated, and highly structured sports programming that histories such as this one set out to trace.

Micro-histories of deaf and disability sport emergence

The first historical record we have of disability or deaf sport is a deaf football (soccer) club in Glasgow that was formed in 1871.[7] Numerous other deaf sports clubs followed, including the Berlin Deaf Gymnastics Association, which hosted gymnastics, bowling, and chess competitions from 1888.[8] A Parisian club for deaf cyclists started in 1899.[9] Gallaudet – an American University for deaf and hard of hearing students – first participated in inter-collegiate athletics in 1883.[10] Deaf communities were the first to create structured sport likely because both familial inheritance patterns and segregated deaf schooling created strong linguistic, cultural, and social traditions that were passed on through generations often within strongly knit, self-governed communities with strong activist traditions.[11] Some of these clubs, like the one in Berlin, were led initially by non-deaf advocates, teachers, or doctors. However, by the early to mid-twentieth century many deaf and 'silent' sport clubs, competitions, and leagues were run by deaf leaders. Arthur Kruger, for example, was a successful deaf athlete at Gallaudet who went on to organize regional deaf sports leagues and national deaf sports teams in the United States in the mid twentieth-century. Most notably, Eugène Rubens-Alcais was an accomplished deaf cyclist and the leader of France's Deaf Sports Federation. In 1924 he collaborated with deaf athlete Antoine Dresse of Belgium to host the first International Silent Games, in Paris. The event drew nearly 150 European deaf athletes, led to the founding of the International Committee of Sports for the Deaf (CISS), and continues every four years as the Deaflympics.[12]

Similar pockets of impairment-specific sports emerged within schools for the blind in the early twentieth century. Pennsylvania's Overbrook School for the Blind's students, for example, played competitive baseball, football, gymnastics, and track and field since 1909.[13] Blind football (soccer) dates back to Spain's school playgrounds in the 1920s, while the 5-per-side version played in the Paralympics emerged in Brazil in the 1960s.[14] Goalball – a unique sport developed specifically for athletes with visual impairments – was created in 1946 by Austrian Hanz Lorenzen and German Sepp Reindle to support the rehabilitation of injured Second World War veterans.[15] Although blind sport had been practised in numerous countries since the turn of the twentieth century, the International Blind Sports Federation was not established until 1981.

The first recorded international event for athletes with physical disabilities was the 'Cripples Olympiad' held in the United States in 1911.[16] The high skill level noted by media coverage suggests that sport opportunities for these athletes significantly predates our earliest records.[17] Early twentieth-century polio epidemics as well as two World Wars significantly

Deaf and disability sport

increased the number of young people with mobility impairments, and often led to them recovering in hospital wards where shared sporting activities could be developed and practised. British soldiers with amputations, for example, took up cycling and rowing around rehabilitation hospitals during the First World War, apparently more for the social benefits than rehabilitation.[18] The first recorded 'wheelchair games' were held at the Royal Star and Garter home in Richmond, Surrey in 1923, and included bowling and wheelchair races between patients with spinal cord injuries and medical staff.[19] Wheelchair basketball was invented and largely led by injured American veterans with both spinal cord injuries and amputations, first in rehabilitation hospitals in 1945, then through a national league in 1949.[20] Canada's first multi-sport competition for patients with physical impairments was held in 1947 at Deer Lodge Hospital in Manitoba, followed in the early 1950s by formal wheelchair basketball and skiing programmes, in which polio survivors were known to participate, and sometimes lead.[21] Polio survivors were self-organizing, national-level recreation clubs across South America throughout the 1950s and 1960s. The Cororación Argentina de Discapacitados, for example, was formed in 1956, and played a significant role in Argentina's disability rights movement in the 1980s.[22]

It is in this larger context that sporting programmes and competitions emerged at Stoke Mandeville Hospital for spinal cord injury in the United Kingdom. Some historical records suggest that medical director Dr Ludwig Guttmann first came up with the idea for the competitions after seeing veterans in his hospital playing a series of sports that they had adapted and organized themselves.[23] After four years of mandating sport for rehabilitation, Guttmann organized the first annual Stoke Mandeville Games in 1944, in which 16 veterans with spinal cord injuries competed in several sporting activities at the same time as the 1948 London Olympics.[24] In 1952 some Dutch veterans joined the games, followed by an increasing international presence each year. In 1960, the games were moved to Rome to use the same facilities as the Olympic Games, a strategy Guttmann attempted, with limited success, to repeat every quadrennial.[25] The same year, Guttmann founded and presided over the International Stoke Mandeville Games Federation (ISMGF), with a mandate to govern sport for those with 'paraplegia' worldwide.

Guttmann fought vehemently to ensure the Stoke games, his federation, and the early Paralympics remained solely for those with spinal cord injury.[26] As such, in 1961, the World Veterans Federation pushed for the creation of an international organization to support veterans with other common war injuries, most notably amputation and visual impairment. In response, the International Sports Organization for the Disabled (ISOD) was established in 1964; Dr Guttmann was president of ISOD between 1968 and 1979.[27]

Those diagnosed with cerebral palsy, intellectual disabilities, and many other conditions considered congenital, genetic, developmental, or degenerative are largely absent within these celebratory mid-twentieth century histories. At the same time as rehabilitation-based sports were being developed to support returning war veterans, those with more congenital conditions were often being institutionalized against for most of their lives, sometimes eugenically sterilized or lobotomized, within 'schools' that neither offered the freedom to experiment with producing sporting cultures, nor the education to write about whatever sports were invented and played therein.[28] For example, despite the science behind eugenics being thoroughly debunked in the 1930s,[29] it was not until 1966 that some researchers took seriously the possibility that physical activity and sport could have benefits for people diagnosed with intellectual disabilities.[30] Canadian researcher, Dr Frank Hayden, was a significant leader in this research, arguing that it was lack of opportunity, not lack of capacity that was the major fitness and health issue. Eunice Kennedy Shriver, having had a sister who

253

had been institutionalized and eventually lobotomized, had already begun running recreation programmes for people diagnosed with intellectual disabilities in the United States. She hired Dr Hayden, and her family foundation financially backed the first Special Olympics competition in 1968 in Chicago, incorporating Special Olympics, Inc. that same year.[31]

People with cerebral palsy (CP), as well as various congenital and developmental conditions that impact mobility, often experienced similar histories of institutionalization and neglect as those with intellectual disabilities during the eugenic era. Organized sports programmes for athletes with CP are first documented in the 1960s in the UK, emerging from Tonbridge's segregated school.[32] The first international governing body – The Cerebral Palsy International Sports and Recreation Association (CPISRA) – formed in 1969, hosted their first international games in 1972. Other athletes with mobility-related impairments that tended not to result from war injuries – such as those with short stature, congenital limb difference, post-polio complications, muscular dystrophy, or Osteogenesis imperfecta – came under the governance of the International Sports Organization for the Disabled in the late 1970s, grouped together in a category officially called *les autres* (the French term for 'the others').[33] Having always been sidelined within international disability sport culture, a number of these communities continue to run national and international championships that fully celebrate the breadth of athletes in their impairment categories (e.g. CP World Games, Dwarf World Games).

Institutional histories of disability's mega sport events

By the late 1960s, early versions of the Special Olympics, the Deaflympics, and the Paralympics were fast-growing international competitions with significant links to the Olympic movement. The Deaflympics (previously the International Silent Games and the World Silent Games) was the first of these to develop, and the first to be officially recognized by the International Olympics Committee, in 1955.[34] Over its 95-year history, it has grown to serve 113 countries, to host summer and winter games with hundreds of athletes, and to support 24 summer sports and 5 winter sports.[35] Its core mandate of cultural exchange, and the kinds of athletes it serves, have remained largely unchanged over its long history, despite a few decades of an attempted collaboration with Paralympic sport, to be discussed in detail below.

The Special Olympics demonstrated the quickest growth in terms of numbers. Within a decade of the first Games, they boasted Summer Games with 3,500 athletes, large crowds, and mainstream television coverage.[36] By the end of the 1980s, they acquired official recognition from the International Olympic Committee (IOC), and grew from a largely American phenomenon to an international event, representing over 50 countries.[37] Significant shifts in the 1990s and early 2000s include programmes to increase the role of former athletes in officiating and organizational leadership, as well as the addition of integrated programmes where non-disabled athletes participate alongside those with diagnoses.[38] The core focus of Special Olympics on participation, health, and stigma reduction has remained constant throughout their first five decades, leading to an emphasis on local and regional annual competitions alongside their large quadrennial events. At last count, the Special Olympics had over 5.3 million athlete members participating in over 100,000 different competitions across more than 165 countries; their 2015 Summer Games hosted over 6,200 athletes from 165 countries, playing 25 different sports.[39]

The Paralympics has undergone significant changes and challenges since its first quadrennial event in 1960, including a change from a rehabilitation to elite sport focus as well as the near constant changing of their name until 1988 (e.g. Torontolympiad, Olympics for the Disabled, World Wheelchair Games).[40] Far from being an international, multi-disability festival, 'The Paralympic movement, at this time, was certainly European, promoted by the patriarchal weight of Ludwig Guttmann,' who fought vehemently for decades against athlete leadership, and refused to allow the participation of anyone other than those with spinal cord injuries.[41] Despite Guttmann leading the International Sports Organization for the Disabled since the late 1960s, it was not until 1976 – 30 years after the first Stoke Games, that athletes with amputations and visual impairments would be introduced into the Paralympics. Blind athletes, however, were always only marginally included for most of the next 30 years (e.g. no braille on medals, not chosen for Olympic demonstrating events), leading the International Blind Sports Association to threaten to leave the Paralympics on multiple occasions, and to try to convince Paralympic funders to remove their funding.[42] Not without significant internal dissent, the Paralympic Games added sport for athletes with cerebral palsy to the 1980 Paralympic Games.[43] Similar to blind athletes, athletes with cerebral palsy have often found themselves marginalized within the Paralympic movement, including being shunned from Olympic demonstration sports, having their events cancelled or amalgamated, and overall being treated as less valuable, athletic, and marketable than their amputee and wheelchair-using peers.[44]

In the early 1980s, the IOC started using both the threat of legal action around the use of Olympiad-style terminology and the promise of core funding to coerce these three international sport movements to become one. This led to four of the international disability sport organizations discussed above – International Stoke Mandeville Games Federation, International Sports Organization for the Disabled, International Blind Sports Association, and Cerebral Palsy International Sports and Recreation Association – founding the International Co-ordination Committee of World Sports Organizations for the Disabled (ICC) in 1982.[45] Due to ongoing pressure from the IOC, the International Committee of Sports for the Deaf joined the ICC in 1985, and from the start endured a tumultuous relationship. The ICC not only refused to support deaf participants in the Paralympic Games for many years, and kept many important votes to their four founding members, they also refused to pay for sign language interpretation at meetings: a point that was especially important given that deaf sports organizations mandated deaf leadership.[46] Regardless, the International Committee of Sports for the Deaf stayed with the ICC as it morphed into the International Paralympic Committee (IPC) in 1989, finally leaving the organization in 1995, because the IPC decided to enable non-deaf members to speak and vote on behalf of deaf sport.[47] The International Committee of Sports for the Deaf continues to run both the summer and winter Deaflympics, and continues to prioritize deaf leadership in its constitution and governance.[48]

In 1986, the ICC decided to also invite the newly formed International Association of Sport for Persons with Mental Handicap (INAS-FMH) to join them. This choice was intended to address the IOC's demands that they include all impairment groups, while not joining up with the far more established Special Olympics, which ICC members feared would exert significant power and influence in decision-making.[49] INAS-FMH was much smaller and thus the ICC was able to ignore their demands for inclusion in the Games for decades, on the grounds that, as Stan Labanowich of ISMGF put it, 'admission of mentally retarded persons to a Paralympic competition would be detrimental to the sports movement of the disabled'.[50] In short, the addition of INAS-FMH was not a move to include athletes with intellectual disabilities, but a way to ensure they could continually be excluded. Nearly a decade later, in 1996, athletes from INAS-FMH participated for the first time in the Paralympic Games, but their inclusion was short-lived. A large media scandal broke about athletes faking intellectual disabilities at the 2000 Paralympic Games. Although classification scandals are a relatively regular occurrence in a number of impairment groups at the Paralympics, and sometimes lead to single athlete disqualifications or four-year suspensions, the IPC voted to discontinue all events for INAS-FMH athletes for another 12 years, reintroducing them for the London 2012 Paralympics.[51] The International Sports Federation for Persons with Intellectual Disability (INAS), as the organization is now called, continues to run world championships for over 15 sports and 4,000 athletes, while still working with the International Paralympic Committee to support their athletes' competitions at the Paralympic Games. Although the impairment groups that INAS serve overlap significantly with the Special Olympics, they continue to differentiate themselves from the much larger and well-known organization by their explicit focus on elite sport competition.

Closing thoughts

In this chapter, I have given a very short overview of the emergence and institutionalization of some of the most widespread segregated disability sport programmes in the Western world. Although large multi-sport events have emerged from these programmes, many of these began as small, local clubs – sometimes led by well-meaning doctors and advocates, other times created and led by disabled and deaf athletes themselves. The complexity and diversity of these histories mirror the complexity and diversity of disability communities, and their histories more broadly. Further, far from being a history made up exclusively of empowerment, disability sport histories offer a glimpse into some of the more troubling, deeply unjust social structures that disabled and deaf people have and continue to face, including their forced institutionalization, hierarchies of disability privilege and valuation, as well as the undermining of disability and deaf self-determination.

Notes

1 Robert Steadward and Cynthia Peterson, *Paralympics: Where Heroes Come* (Edmonton, AB: One Shot Holdings, 1997).
2 Danielle Peers, '(Dis)empowering Paralympic Histories: Absent Athletes and Disabling Discourses', *Disability & Society* 24, no. 5 (2009): 653–665.
3 Shelley Tremain, 'On the Government of Disability', in *The Disability Studies Reader*, 2nd edition, ed. L.J. Davis (New York: Routledge, 2006): 185–196.
4 James Charlton, *Nothing About Us Without Us* (Berkeley, CA: University of California Press, 2000).
5 David Stewart, *Deaf Sport: The Impact of Sports within the Deaf Community* (Washington: Gallaudet University, 1991).
6 Danielle Peers, 'Say What You Mean: Rethinking Disability Language', *Adapted Physical Activity Quarterly* 31, no. 3 (2014): 265–282.
7 Vanessa Haggie, 'Long Before the Paralympics there was the Paralympics', *The Guardian*, https://www.theguardian.com/science/the-h-word/2012/sep/05/paralympics-deaflympics (accessed 3 July 2019).
8 David Legg et al., 'Historical Overview of the Paralympics, Special Olympics, and Deaflympics', *Palaestra* 20, no. 1 (2004): 30–35; 56.
9 Didier Séguillon, 'The Origins and Consequences of the First World Games for the Deaf: Paris, 1924', *The International Journal of The History of Sport* 19, no. 1 (2002): 119–136.
10 Gallaudet University, 'Athletics', https://www.gallaudet.edu/academic-catalog/services-and-activities/student-activities/athletics (accessed 3 July 2019).
11 Stewart, *Deaf Sport*.
12 Legg et al., 'Historical Overview of the Paralympics'.
13 Steve Bailey, *Athlete First: A History of the Paralympic Movement* (Chichester, UK: John Wiley & Sons, 2008), 14.

14 International Paralympic Committee, 'Sport Week: History of Football 5', https://www.paralympic.org/news/sport-week-history-football-5 (accessed 3 July 2019).

15 Ian Gregson, *Irresistible Force: Disability Sport in Canada* (Victoria, BC: Polstar, 1999).

16 Bristol Street Versa Mobility Solutions, 'Pioneers of Disability Sport', https://www.bristolstreetversa.com/news/pioneers-of-disability-sport/ (accessed 3 July 2019).

17 For example, a 1913 article in the *Thames Star* celebrated the many success of Welsh athlete Walter William Francis at the Cripple's Olympiad and beyond, including winning medals on behalf of the United Kingdom in both wrestling and running. In this same article he is celebrated for setting a record for swimming the 15-mile Bristol Channel. See Thames Star, 'Skipper Francis at Thames', https://paperspast.natlib.govt.nz/newspapers/THS19131017.2.25 (accessed 14 February 2020).

18 Arthur Pearson, *Victory over Blindness: How It Was Won by the Men of St. Dunstan's and How Others May Win It* (London: Hodder and Stoughton, 1919).

19 Buckinghamshire County Council, 'Mandeville Legacy', http://www.mandevillelegacy.org.uk/category_id__21_path__0p4p14p.aspx (accessed 3 July 2019).

20 Bailey, *Athlete First.*

21 Gregson, *Irresistible Force*, 108.

22 Diane Driedger, *The Last Civil Rights Movement: Disabled People's International* (New York: St. Martin's Press, 1989), 18.

23 Joan Scruton, *Stoke Mandeville: Road to the Paralympics* (Aylesbury, UK: Peterhouse, 1998).

24 Scruton, *Stoke Mandeville.*

25 Bailey, *Athlete First.*

26 Steadward and Peterson, *Paralympics.*

27 Bailey, *Athlete First.*

28 Danielle Peers, 'Sport and Social Movements by and for Disability and Deaf Communities: Important Differences in Self-determination, Politicisation, and Activism', in *Palgrave Handbook of Paralympic Studies*, eds. I. Brittain and A. Beacom (Basingstoke: Palgrave Macmillan, 2018), 71–97.

29 Ladelle McWhorter, *Racism and Sexual Oppression in Anglo-America: A Genealogy* (Bloomington, IN: Indiana University Press, 2009), 245.

30 A.E. (Ted) Wall, 'The History of Adapted Physical Activity in Canada', in *Adapted Physical Activity*, eds. Robert D. Stedward, Garry D. Wheeler, and E. Jane Watkinson (Edmonton, AB: University of Alberta Press, 2003), 27–44.

31 Special Olympics, 'The Beginning of a Worldwide Movement', https://www.specialolympics.org/about/history/the-beginning-of-a-worldwide-movement (accessed 3 July 2019).

32 Cerebral Palsy Sport, 'Our History', http://www.cpsport.org/about-us/our-organisation/our-history/ (accessed 3 July 2019).

33 Bailey, *Athlete First.*

34 International Committee of Sports for the Deaf, 'Time-line', http://www.ciss.org/icsd/time-line (accessed 3 July 2019).

35 International Committee of Sports for the Deaf, 'Home', http://www.ciss.org/; http://www.ciss.org/icsd/time-line.

36 Special Olympics, 'A Joyful New Movement Gains Momentum', https://www.specialolympics.org/about/history/a-joyful-new-movement-gains-momentum (accessed 3 July 2019).

37 Special Olympics, 'Recognition and Growth Around the World', https://www.specialolympics.org/about/history/recognition-and-growth-around-the-world.

38 Special Olympics, 'Pushing for Inclusion and Improved Health for People with ID', https://www.specialolympics.org/about/history/pushing-for-inclusion-and-improved-health-for-people-with-id (accessed 3 July 2019); Special Olympics, 'The Sun Never Sets on the Special Olympics Movement', https://www.specialolympics.org/about/history/the-sun-never-sets-on-the-special-olympics-movement (accessed 3 July 2019).

39 Special Olympics, 'Building an Inclusive World', https://www.specialolympics.org/about/history/building-an-inclusive-world (accessed 3 July 2019).

40 Steadward and Peterson, *Paralympics.*

41 Bailey, *Athlete First*, 21.

42 Bailey, *Athlete First*, 21.

43 Bailey, *Athlete First*, 21.

44 P. David Howe, *The Cultural Politics of the Paralympic Movement: Through an Anthropological Lense* (London: Routledge, 2008).

45 Bailey, *Athlete First*.
46 Steadward and Peterson, *Paralympics*.
47 Legg et al., 'Historical Overview of the Paralympics'.
48 International Committee of Sports for the Deaf, 'Constitution', http://www.ciss.org/icsd/constitution (accessed 3 July 2019).
49 Bailey, *Athlete First*.
50 Bailey, *Athlete First,* 95.
51 Bailey, *Athlete First*.

31

SPORTING BORDERLANDS

Colin Howell and Daryl Leeworthy

Over the years the field of sport studies has become increasingly interdisciplinary, having established early roots in departments of kinesiology and physical education before branching out to include historians, geographers, and sociologists, as well as scholars in literature, film, and cultural studies. More recently, the fields of sports psychology, management, and marketing have begun to address sport as one of the leading social technologies of our contemporary world. As specific disciplines confront the theoretical challenges that complicate interdisciplinary forms of explanation, moreover, older fixed categories of analysis, including class, gender, race, and ethnicity have given way to the idea of intersectionality: the way that each of these categories folds over upon and shapes the rest.[1] In addition, the traditional rendering of both imperial history and the globalization process has gradually shed its metropolitan bias in favour of a more nuanced approach to how imperialism and globalization was (and continues to be) received in colonial and other non-metropolitan spaces.[2] Sociologist Roland Robertson speaks of 'glocalization', a process in which metropolitan power is shaped to meet the needs of local communities, giving 'agency' to people on the ground working to mediate the process of cultural influence in ways that make sense to them.[3] This widespread crossing of theoretical and disciplinary boundaries within the field of sport history, moreover, mirrors the growing interest in borderland studies which, in its widest application, involves not just discrete trans-boundary physical spaces, but complex transnational processes associated with the construction of cultural identities and other processes of production.

The borderlands model has a lengthy pedigree going back to Herbert Bolton's presidential address to the American Historical Association meetings in Toronto in 1932 and even before. Reacting to Frederick Jackson Turner's argument that the 'frontier' was a crucible of American democracy and exceptionalism, Bolton lamented the tendency towards national chauvinism in writings about the past, and suggested that historians give greater attention to the importance of borderlands in the wider sweep of transnational history. According to Bolton each borderland history 'will have clearer meaning when studied in the light of others'. Convinced of the possibility for a synthetic history of the Western hemisphere, Bolton considered national histories mere threads of a larger strand. Although his primary focus was on the 'Spanish borderlands' and the American southwest, he was equally aware of the unique history of the northeastern border and its connection to the imperial influences of Britain and France.[4]

DOI: 10.4324/9780429318306-35

Whereas borderlands have always been the subject of attention from a small cadre of historians, as evidenced in academic journals such as the *Journal of Borderland Studies* established in 1986 and in occasional special issues in the *American Historical Review* (*AHR*) and *Journal of American History* (*JAH*), interest has grown in recent years in the face of rapid globalization, the international flows of peoples and capital, and concerns about border security.[5] Large research initiatives such as the $4.8 million Borders in Globalization (BIG) project funded by the Social Science and Humanities Research Council of Canada beginning in 2013 exemplify the renewed interest in the social, economic, and cultural history of borderlands and include among other things the study of borderland sporting life.

Of course, it matters a great deal where and when historians cast their gaze, and upon whom. We have argued for some time that a borderlands approach has particular utility for sport historians. Rather than putting sport history in the service of nation or empire, we are interested in a multi-directional process of ludic diffusion and a globalized sport culture. In ways reminiscent of Bolton, giving careful attention to sport in various cross-border settings allows for an alternative to top-down, uni-directional metropolitan analyses of the sporting (and wider cultural and social) past and what we have called the 'metropolitan fallacy'.[6]

Another thing worth considering is that a borderlands analysis can be applied across the sweep of sport history from earlier centuries to the twenty-first century. It is also applicable to different transnational settings and easily applied to a range of sporting forms. From the earliest development of sport in local, national, and international contexts to the contemporary realities of global sport, the borderlands model offers a distinct and novel way to investigate sporting culture. Whether we are looking at the pre-Revolution enthusiasm of Benjamin Franklin for cricket, bullfighting on both sides of the Mexican border in the late nineteenth century, aboriginal influences on the development of Australian football, Anaulataq or Inuit baseball in the Arctic, or the history of lacrosse in Britain, Ireland, and First Nations communities spanning the Canadian–American border, addressing shared cultural influence and local adaptation in borderland regions offers a view from the edge, a different way of seeing, an alternative gaze to the predominant metropolitan approach to sporting life. Of course the relationship of settler communities to aboriginal or Indigenous peoples around the world is especially relevant to discussions of borderland sporting culture.[7]

But just what constitutes a borderland? In North America there are a number of easily identifiable cross-border regions, from the Maritimes and New England in the northeast, to Cascadia in the Pacific Northwest, to the Mexican–American borderlands that are the source of such politically charged debates at present. One can replicate this in virtually every part of the world, and on every continent, not least on the island of Ireland in the age of Brexit. Borderlands are in some cases just as identifiable as nation states, and like Benedict Anderson's notion of nations as 'imagined communities',[8] one can understand borderlands as spaces of cultural exchange that imply a sense of identity and shared experience to the people who inhabit them.

Of course, territorial borderlands across landed borders jump easily to mind. It is perhaps just as important, given that cultural transmission often took place by sea, to investigate maritime or oceanic borderlands. Our most recent work thus considers the Atlantic as both a highway of cultural transmission and as a sporting borderland, sharing the insights of other historians of the Atlantic World who speak of the Black (Slave), the Green (Irish), the Queer (LGBT), the Red (Revolutionary), the Criminal, and the Military Atlantic. Common to all this work, and that of the 'new' Imperial History, is a focus on cultural exchange, the existence of multi-directional cultural connections, networks, and random interactions.[9] In general, the trend of this scholarship runs counter to the privileging of nation and empire in

Border games

In the popular imagination, baseball and lacrosse are as alien to British and Irish culture as cricket and soccer are to those of North America. In a recent article for the *New York Times*, journalist David Waldstein reported on the limited contemporary and historic enthusiasm for baseball in the United Kingdom just as Major League Baseball prepares to launch its new London series.[11] This follows in the wake of the National Football League's similar efforts, which have run since 2007. Such reports, accompanied by the prevailing diffusionist ideas of many sport historians, serve to present American and British sporting cultures as distinct from each other. Yet there has always been crossover, both commercially manufactured, as these latest examples suggest, and more organically as migrants and tourists move from one side of the Atlantic to the other, and back again. Mass digitization, particularly of the newspaper press, but also of a range of day-to-day cultural ephemera and archival documentation, which has taken place over the last decade, allied to the theoretical and historiographical insights of the borderlands approach, enables significant recovery of those cultural and material crossovers.

To begin with cricket. With its origins in eighteenth-century England and close association with the former British Empire, particularly India and Australia, cricket is readily identified as the preeminent imperial game. Nevertheless, as Keith Sandiford has noted, 'fashions and models are seldom replicated exactly as intended … imperial models carry the defects of the metropolis and these warts also assume peculiarly local characteristics when transplanted'. As a result, he suggests, 'the story of imperial cricket is really about the colonial quest for identity in the face of the colonisers' search for authority'.[12] Such contestation is not so far from the perspective we have adopted in our work on sporting borderlands; the multiplicity of cultures within which a sport such as cricket developed meant that different traditions emerged regardless of the original source of transmission. This is readily seen in Canada, as one of us noted in *Northern Sandlots*[13] and as John and Robert Reid have recently demonstrated in their own studies, and in the United States – which is our focus here.[14]

References to cricket in the Americas date from the colonial period, translated by migrants, along with a range of other games common to the different parts of England, Scotland, and Wales from whence they came. The American cricketing tradition survived the War of Independence and the revolutionary period, and the making of a distinctive liberal American society and culture by the first generation born in the United States.[15] In 1889, for example, the *Salt Lake Herald* in Utah reported that 'the game of cricket has not been entirely snuffed out in America by baseball', although it did acknowledge that by then 'the American game is so popular that cricket necessarily is obscured'.[16] Nearly 20 years later, the *New York Tribune* pondered the fin-de-siècle revival in the sport's fortunes noting its uptake amongst a group of young women from Brooklyn who formed the Prospect Park Ladies' Cricket Club in 1904.[17] And in the early 1920s, the same paper noted that 'New York cricketers number thousands' with teams playing in the Metropolitan District Cricket League and the New York Cricket Association. Many of those involved were Afro-Caribbean migrants whose cricketing enthusiasms were established in the West Indies, but who nonetheless created a cricketing culture in the Bronx, which continues to the present day.[18]

New York City was by no means the only centre of cricket playing, either, with working-class cricket a feature of life in Newark, New Jersey, in Massachusetts, and in other industrial centres such as Baltimore, Pittsburgh, Detroit, Chicago, Denver, St Paul, and San Francisco. In the latter, the local press enthused that 'cricket thrives in California'.[19] The regularity of British naval vessels arriving in Hawaii meant that cricket was a popular and widespread pastime in nineteenth- and early twentieth-century Honolulu, with the sport providing an avenue for anti-American attitudes in the build up to annexation in 1898.[20] Perhaps most ironically, the heart of American cricket was Philadelphia, the centre of the American revolution. Home to the leading American journal dedicated to the sport, the *American Cricketer* (1877–1929), cricket was widely played in the city's schools, colleges, and universities, and the most elite clubs regularly hosted their English counterparts, including the Marylebone Cricket Club.[21] In the mid-1890s, attendance at matches in Philadelphia was as high as 20,000.[22] This activity can easily be mischaracterized as conservative or absent an American character, but the breadth of cricket playing within American society into the twentieth (and twenty-first) century cannot be comfortably encapsulated in those terms: understood through intersectionality and the borderlands, the remarkable survival of cricket in the United States points to the nuances of sporting culture. To borrow an apposite phrase: what do they know of America who only America know?

A similar pattern is apparent in the development of soccer. Long regarded as the historical 'exception that proves the rule', one need only step away from the traditional historiographical presentation of American exceptionalism to quickly uncover a far richer past. New York City was a notable soccer centre: similarly, Chicago and other industrial cities, as well as the northeastern borderlands. As Thomas Cahill, the editor of the annual *Spalding's Soccer Guide*, observed in 1922,

> soccer in this country is in a far more advanced state than any of its most optimistic advocates dreamed ... its players today are more numerous than were players of baseball when it had been no longer on an organized basis than is soccer today.[23]

Cahill was remarking on the tenth anniversary of the formation of the United States Football Association (USFA) (of which he was secretary) in April 1913. The early 1920s saw the advent of the American Soccer League, the first national professional competition, albeit one dominated by the existing heartlands of soccer in the northeast. The USFA, nevertheless, had a much wider reach, with members including the state football associations of California, Colorado, Illinois, Missouri, and Wisconsin.

Key to the development of soccer in those states (and others such as Utah) was European immigration, of course, which rendered soccer the 'natural' footballing code in many communities, rather than American Football. It was a similar story in the southwestern borderlands, but with soccer sustained by a cross-border Hispanic culture as much as a transplanted European one. By the mid-1920s, Texas had two well-organized leagues covering the northern and southern parts of the state, with many of the teams in Houston, for example, established and largely rostered by Mexican-Americans. In the neighbouring state of New Mexico, soccer developed in similar circumstances and flourished with the support of the High School Athletic Association.[24] Much as in the United States, soccer's association with Britishness in Canada – and thus a form of conservatism normally reserved for discussions of the Maritime provinces and their cultures – has tended to mask its significance. It was nevertheless widely played and followed amongst English-speaking, French-speaking, and immigrant communities alike.

Sporting borderlands

On Prince Edward Island, Canada, soccer began to compete with rugby football for popularity in the aftermath of the First World War: in the words of the *Charlottetown Guardian*, 'many of our boys played this game when overseas and many of them prefer it to Rugby which has been the regular game here'.[25] At Dalhousie University in Halifax, Nova Scotia, soccer was taken up in the early 1930s and the university team successfully competed in the Halifax City League. One unique feature of the team, as the campus newspaper the *Dalhousie Gazette* noted, 'was its cosmopolitan personnel. On the team were representatives from Canada, Newfoundland, Ireland, [the] West Indies, South Africa and China'. Soccer, the paper concluded, 'is not classified as Canadian, American or British'.[26] The multicultural nature of the interwar Dalhousie sides was subsequently mirrored at neighbouring Saint Mary's University, which adopted soccer after the Second World War. That immigration into the United States and Canada brought with it a range of cultural traditions is hardly a novel insight, or rather it ought not to be, but this does not mean that these processes of glocalization and the cultural agency of those who live in the borderlands should be taken for granted and subsumed into a narrative which gives priority to the national, the metropolitan, and the commercially powerful.

The case for diffusion rests substantially on the movement of sporting culture from Britain – in practice, from England – outwards through imperial and commercial frameworks. As Mike Huggins has put it: 'The British pioneered many of the sports which later spread around the world.'[27] In this reading, Britain was an exporter rather than an importer of sporting culture and sports which were imported have generally been written off as thinly based commercial endeavours.[28] As in the United States, British 'exceptionalism' has a tendency to prioritize a singular – usually white, male, and 'native' born – form of cultural capital. Sports such as lacrosse and baseball, as well as ice hockey and basketball, which have been played in Britain for more than a century, have been minimized in a historiography dominated by soccer, cricket, and rugby, though the latter to a lesser extent (since it is itself divided into two codes).

Lacrosse, of course, has its origins in First Nations culture but was appropriated to Anglophone Canadian nationalism in the 1860s and codified by the Montreal dentist W.G. Beers before being 'spread' to the United States and to Britain and Ireland in subsequent decades. The earliest lacrosse matches played in Britain and Ireland were part of organized tours from Canada, but by the 1870s clubs and leagues had been established across England, Scotland, and Ireland, albeit with the Welsh showing little interest, with a few exceptions such as in the town of Pontypool, until the late 1890s.[29] Baseball had a similar flourish, with tours from the United States prompting the uptake of the sport in Britain with clubs and leagues developing soon afterwards. In various guises lacrosse and baseball leagues survived long into the twentieth century. In both cases, there was some divergence between the American-Canadian style of play and the British and Irish style, with amendments to the laws and playing equipment also taking place. What was, for instance, a summer game in Canada (in the case of lacrosse) became a winter one on the other side of the Atlantic. The divergence in baseball was more significant, particularly in the 1890s when the National Rounders Association adopted the name 'English baseball' after finding 'there was so much prejudice against the name of the game'.[30] As a result, baseball in England and Wales used flat bats, laid out bases 22 yards apart rather than 30, and had 11 players a side rather than 9.[31]

But not all baseball clubs in England or Wales adopted the 'English' rules: the American code remained popular in the Midlands, and in the northern counties, Cardiff had its own American Baseball Club, and within a decade or so the British Baseball Association had been formed which adopted a codebook and playing style identical to that of American baseball.[32] Its members included leading soccer clubs such as Arsenal, Tottenham Hotspur, and Fulham, and by 1908 there were renewed efforts to spread American rules into Wales, providing a direct competitor to 'Welsh Baseball'.[33] These efforts continued into the period of the First World War, with visiting American forces providing further exhibitions in Cardiff and neighbouring Barry, and were periodically revisited in the interwar years – notably in 1939.[34] That year saw no fewer than seven American baseball clubs established in and around Cardiff, including two from the Royal Air Force camps and one from the staff of the *Western Mail and Echo*. There also were fleeting efforts to form an American league in the coalfield.[35] In neither case was 'Americanness' a barrier to establishing activity, nor was there a sense that the sport was alien to local culture. Rather it belonged to a borderlands society absorbent of a range of influences and peoples.

Diffusion and multi-directionality

Although we have concentrated here on the transnational trajectories of cricket, baseball, lacrosse, and football, the approach we champion can be applied to a wide array of sporting activity including ball and net games, racing over land and sea, Nordic competitions involving ice and snow, and water sports of various kinds. Recently, for example, Stephen Hardy and Andy Holman have written a compelling synthesis of hockey's diverse manifestations. *Hockey: A Global History* moves effortlessly through the 'convergence and divergence' of Canadian, American, Soviet, and European hockey.[36] Although not operating explicitly within a borderlands framework, the authors are familiar with the approach, and conscientiously avoid proprietary and chauvinistic assumptions of ownership from those who unequivocally claim it as 'Canada's Game'. Almost two decades ago we raised the following questions: 'To what extent can or should we disconnect sport history from narratives of nation-building or metropolitan dominance? Does sporting life in hinterland or borderland regions simply replicate the experience of sport in metropolitan centers, as some have suggested?'[37] More recent trends in historical scholarship have fleshed out our understanding of imperialism and globalization and underscored the multi-directionality of transnational influences in sport. Increasingly we have come to a more informed understanding of how hinterland regions and local communities shape metropolitan culture to meet their own needs. Investigating sport from the perspective of the borderland is thus an increasingly fruitful pursuit: indeed, a view from the 'edge' provides a more textured understanding of the diffusion process and of sportive nation-building.

Notes

1 The term intersectionality was first used by Kimberle Crenshaw, 'Mapping the Margins: Intersectionality, Identity Politics and Violence against Women of Color', *Stanford Law Review* 43, no. 6 (July 1991): 1241–1299. Intersectionality addresses the inter-connections between race, ethnicity, class, and gender, and underscores the indeterminate nature of borders and boundaries when applied to identities.

2 Kathleen Wilson, ed. *A New Imperial History: Culture, Identity and Modernity in Britain and the Empire, 1660–1840* (Cambridge: Cambridge University Press, 2004).

3 Roland Robertson, 'Glocalization: Time-Space and Homogeneity-Heterogeneity', in *Global Modernities*, eds. Mike Featherstone, Scott Lash, and Roland Robertson (London: Sage, 1995), 25–44.

4 Herbert Bolton, 'The Epic of Greater America', *American Historical Review* 38, no. 3 (1933): 448–474. See also David Weber, 'Turner, the Boltonians, and the Borderlands', *American Historical Review* 91 (1986): 66–81.

5 See, for example, the discussion of borderlands, regional and local identities, and alternatives to national narratives in both the *AHR*, 104 (1999) and *JAH*, 86 (1999).

6 Colin Howell and Daryl Leeworthy, 'Borderlands and Frontiers in the Writing of Sport History: Confronting the Metropolitan Fallacy', in S.W. Pope and John Nauright eds. *The Routledge Companion to Sport History* (London: Routledge, 2010), chapter 4.

7 A recent issue of the *Journal of Sport History* (Summer, 2019) 46, no. 2 addresses this topic from various vantage points.

8 Benedict Anderson, *Imagined Communities: Reflections on the Origin and the Spread of Nationalism* rev. ed. (London: Verso Books, 1991).

9 Colin Howell and Daryl Leeworthy, 'Playing on the Border: Sport, Borderlands and the North Atlantic, 1850–1950', *Sport in Society* 20, no. 10 (2017): 1354–1370; Leeworthy and Howell, 'Observing from the Border: Sport, Borderlands and the Margins of the Transnational in the North Atlantic World', *Yearbook of Transnational History* 1 (2018): 229–244. Such an approach is equally applicable as well to the spread of sporting culture through the Pacific region. See, for example, Erik Neilson, *Sport in the British World, 1900–1930: Amateurism and National Identity in Australia* (New York: Palgrave Macmillan, 2014); Joseph A. Reaves, *Taking in a Game: A History of Baseball in Asia* (Lincoln: University of Nebraska Press, 2002).

10 Maarten van Bottenburg, 'Beyond Diffusion: Sport and its Remaking in Cross-Cultural Contexts', *Journal of Sport History* 37, no. 1 (2010): 41–54; Cf. Allen Guttmann, *Games and Empires: Modern Sports and Cultural Imperialism* (New York: Columbia University Press, 1994).

11 David Waldstein, 'Baseball in London? It's a Real Thing, Even When the Yankees Aren't Visiting', *New York Times*, 26 June 2019. Available online: https://www.nytimes.com/2019/06/26/sports/yankees-red-sox-london-.html (accessed 27 June 2019).

12 Keith Sandiford, 'Introduction', in Brian Stoddart and Keith Sandiford eds. *The Imperial Game* (Manchester: Manchester University Press, 1998), 1.

13 Colin D. Howell, *Northern Sandlots: A Social History of Maritime Baseball* (Toronto: University of Toronto Press, 1995).

14 John Reid and Robert Reid, 'Diffusion and Discursive Stabilization: Sports Historiography and the Contrasting Fortunes of Cricket and Ice Hockey in Canada's Maritime Provinces, 1869–1914', *Journal of Sport History* 42, no. 1 (2015): 87–113.

15 Joyce Appleby, *Inheriting the Revolution: The First Generation of Americans* (Cambridge, MA: Harvard University Press, 2000).

16 'Philadelphia Cricketers', *Salt Lake Herald*, 20 July 1889, p. 2.

17 'Cricket More Popular', *New York Tribune Illustrated Supplement*, 24 July 1904, p. 3.

18 Arthur James Pegler, 'Ebony Cricketers with an English Accent', *New York Tribune*, 11 September 1921, p. 4.

19 'Old English Game of Cricket Thrives in California', *San Francisco Call*, 20 June 1903, p. 10.

20 'Local and General', *Evening Bulletin* (Honolulu), 15 November 1897, p. 5; 'Sports', 24 February 1909, p. 7; 'Cricket Season Opens Today', *Pacific Commercial Advertiser* (Honolulu), 16 April 1904, p. 5.

21 *Rand, McNally & Co's Handy Guide to Philadelphia and Environs* (New York: Rand, McNally and Company, 1905), 137.

22 Frank Hamilton Taylor, *The City of Philadelphia as It Appears in the Year 1894* (Philadelphia: G.S. Harris & Sons, 1894), 165; John Ashby Lester, *A Century of Philadelphia Cricket* (Philadelphia: University of Pennsylvania Press, 1951).

23 Thomas W. Cahill, 'Foreword', in Thomas W. Cahill (ed.), Spalding's Official Soccer Football Guide (New York: American Sports Publishing Company, 1922), p. 5.

24 'State Athletic Association for Highs Organized', *Belen News* (Belen, NM), 25 November 1915, p. 1.

25 'Sports', *Charlottetown Guardian*, 19 June 1920.

26 'Dal to Have Soccer Team', *Dalhousie Gazette*, 12 October 1933, p. 4.

27 Mike Huggins, *The Victorians and Sport* (London: Bloomsbury, 2004), ix.

28 Mike Huggins and Jack Williams, *Sport and the English, 1918–1939* (London: Routledge, 2006), 67–68.

29 Pro Bono Publico, 'A Recreation Ground for Pontypool', *Pontypool Free Press*, 27 June 1890, p. 2; 'Lacrosse: The Game in South Wales', *Western Mail*, 28 September 1899, p. 7; 'Lacrosse: Exhibition Games in South Wales', *South Wales Daily News*, 28 September 1899, p. 7.

30 'Baseball', *South Wales Echo*, 10 April 1893, p. 2.

31 The Welsh having adopted the English Baseball code at their annual meeting in April 1893. 'South Wales Baseball Association', *Western Mail* (Cardiff), 27 April 1893, p. 7.

32 For the Cardiff club see, 'Baseball' *South Wales Daily News*, 5 May 1893, p. 6.

33 *Evening Express* (Cardiff), 'American Baseball', 12 June 1907, p. 3; 'American Baseball', 1 January 1908, p. 4; 'American Baseball', 4 January 1908, p. 3.

34 *Barry Dock News*, 'American Baseball at Barry', 5 April 1918, p. 3; *Western Mail*, 'Grand Baseball Match', 4 July 1918, p. 4; 'A Sportsman's Notebook', 1 March 1939, p. 4; 'Wageless Players on the Open to Transfer', 22 April 1939, p. 5; 'Welsh Rugby Cap Wants to Come Home', 14 June 1939, p. 3; 'Long-Serving Official', 22 July 1939, p. 5; 'Baseball', 14 August 1939, p. 4.

35 *Western Mail*, 'Baseball', 25 May 1939, p. 4; 'Whitsun', 15 June 1943, p. 3; 'Grand Fete and Gala', 4 August 1943, p. 2; 'Baseball', 29 March 1944, p. 3.

36 Stephen Hardy and Andrew C. Holman, *Hockey: A Global History* (Urbana, IL: University of Illinois Press, 2018). See Andrew C. Holman, 'Playing in the Neutral Zone: Meaning and Uses of Ice Hockey in the Canada-US Borderlands, 1895', *American Review of Canadian Studies* 34, no. 1 (Spring 2004): 33–57; and Daryl Leeworthy, 'Skating on the Border: Hockey, Class and Commercialism in Interwar Britain', *Histoire Sociale/Social History* 48 (2015) for a borderlands approach to hockey.

37 Colin D. Howell, 'Borderlands, Baselines and Bearhunters: Conceptualizing the Northeast as a Sporting Region in the Interwar Period', *Journal of Sport History* 29, no. 2 (2002): 251.

PART 4

Indigenous sport history

32
INDIGENOUS SPORT HISTORY
Introduction

Murray G. Phillips, Douglas Booth and Carly Adams

Sport has been, and continues to be, a very significant component of Indigenous lives. While conditions varied markedly across places that became known as Aotearoa/New Zealand, Australia, Canada, and the United States of America, sport was prominent for Indigenous peoples in all cases. Sport was central to life on missions, reserves, and settlements in Australia, and at residential, boarding, and industrial schools and on reserves in Canada and the United States of America. In Aotearoa/New Zealand, Brendan Hokowhitu argues (Chapter 34) that Māori similarly 'faced limiting racist structures' and that they also 'succeeded in sport more than any other colonial institution'.

Sport was popular in Indigenous communities for two reasons. First it was accepted, condoned, and encouraged by administrations whose capacities of control extended, in some contexts, to nearly every facet of the lives of Indigenous people during the twentieth century. Sport was an integral part of larger social, cultural, and political practices that were initially framed by discourses about disciplining the 'savage', and then by assimilation practices which stripped Indigenous people of virtually everything that made them Indigenous, forcing them to live as subjects in their own country. Second, sport was popular because it provided opportunities for Indigenous people to exercise various levels of agency: to promote their identities, to engage in forms of resistance, to continue, reimagine, and reassert their cultures, to pursue political aspirations, and to endorse Indigenous self-determination. In this way, the experiences of Indigenous people in settler colonial communities demonstrate the Janus-face of sport.

Given the importance of sport to Indigenous lives, it is telling that there are few Indigenous sport historians. Settler colonial states can take full responsibility for this situation. The denial of basic human rights, including very limited educational opportunities that focused on non-academic education with a low ceiling for employment, followed by chronic underinvestment in secondary and higher education, resulted in delayed entry of Indigenous scholars to universities. This situation is slowly being addressed, and there is an emerging and powerful Indigenous presence in many spheres of the academy, but for niche subdisciplines like sport history there are very few historians who identify as Indigenous. Fortunately, we are privileged that several Indigenous scholars who work in sport history contributed to this Part of the *Routledge Handbook of Sport History*.

DOI: 10.4324/9780429318306-37

These Indigenous scholars, along with their non-Indigenous allies, have a vision for sport history that extends its contemporary boundaries, conceptual frameworks, and theoretical perspectives. This vision encourages sport historians, either trained in schools of history or through kinesiology programmes, to take up the methodological, epistemological, and ontological challenges to work effectively with Indigenous communities. As Linda Tuhiwai Smith argues, this includes devising ways that facilitate Indigenous people to tell their own stories, write their own versions, in their own ways, for their own purposes.[1]

The challenges start with the organizing concepts and theories used in critical Indigenous studies and history. Critical race theory, postcolonial studies, settler colonialism, whiteness, along with other strands of Indigenous studies and decolonizing methodologies, all make meaningful contributions to understanding the relationship between sport and Indigenous peoples.[2] In Chapter 33, Murray Phillips focuses on settler colonialism as a theoretical framework that helps comprehend the unique, but considerably different, experiences of Indigenous peoples in Aotearoa/New Zealand, Australia, Canada, and the United States of America. He argues that sport historians have overwhelming embraced colonialism as a theoretical paradigm to understanding sport and Indigenous identity without differentiating it from a more pertinent and distinctive formation: settler colonialism. The consequences of sport historians conflating settler colonialism with colonialism is that there is little appreciation of the specific qualities of settler colonialism and how this formation shaped the lives of Indigenous peoples. In the sport history literature, the problem is compounded as race and racism are the primary and popular analytical concepts, often describing the experiences of those who suffered not only under colonialism and settler colonialism, but also from slavery, as if these historical phenomena can be merged without diminishing their differences and uniqueness. In this conflation – slavery, colonialism, and settler colonialism – Indigenous sport history has been stifled under the weight of sporting imperialism, African-American experiences, and apartheid sport.

The challenges continue with reframing the concept of sport history. The vast majority of sport historians work through the lens of post-contact sport without acknowledging physical activities that were inseparable from life prior to settler colonial states and continue to have cultural influence into the present.[3] As Jennifer Guiliano and Beth Eby argue in Chapter 37:

> Dissolving the use of 'modern' and its associated focus on competitive sport as intrinsic to sporting history allows us to challenge dominant narratives that tie sporting culture to modernity, capitalism, consumption, regulation, and the colonial and imperial aims of Western Europe.

Eschewing the value-laden term of modern sport, and the temporal framework of prehistory, which depreciates cultural practices prior to modernity, opens up the capacity to examine the continuation of traditional games, their complex meanings, and their cultural importance. Rather than positioning these activities through the lens of what Malcolm Maclean calls twentieth-century salvage ethnography (a form premised on racial theories predicting the ultimate demise of Indigenous people and their cultures),[4] physical activities are being analysed and understood for their distinctiveness, their cultural continuity, and their value to the contemporary Indigenous world.[5]

As several authors have articulated, and Christine O'Bonsawin and Janice Forsyth explain in Chapter 36, Indigenous movement and physical culture activities are structurally and functionally different from settler sport and are enmeshed in land-based, and water-based, lifestyles and firmly rooted in spiritual beliefs.[6] Consider, for example, the physical activities

Indigenous sport history

and games of the Dene, the First Nations people who inhabit an extensive territory stretching across the Canadian western Subarctic. Dene were required to travel constantly for survival, which ensured their strong connection to the land. Crucial basic physical characteristics – strength, endurance, speed, and accuracy – that were necessary for travel and survival were developed and reinforced through playing traditional games.[7] These physical activities straddle both pre and post settler colonialism and, as such, have always been central to Dene existence. Since the 1970s, these activities have been part of multi-community events, larger regional games. Dene winter events – finger pull, stick pull, snowsnake, pole push, and hand games – along with traditional Inuit Arctic sports, are part of the Arctic Winter Games. The position of these traditional activities in larger sporting festivals such as the Arctic Winter Games, the North American Indigenous Games, and the World Indigenous Games not only reinforces Indigenous ways of knowing, being, and doing, but promotes cultural continuity and cultural identity, pushing back at narrow modernist versions of sport and sport history.[8]

The epistemology of empirical history is not ideal training for sport historians wishing to work in Indigenous history.[9] The issue is especially pronounced in the archives which empirical historians conceive as a site of knowledge retrieval where historical research is an extractive exercise providing the documentary evidence of dates, facts, people, and events that are the building blocks of narrative development by an objective scholar, whose desire is to establish the past-as-it-happened. Sport historians have leaned heavily into the archive as an extractive resource. This version of the archive provides insights about Indigenous people from the perspectives of settler colonial administrators, politicians, and media, but the voices of Indigenous people are often missing, as their perspectives and opinions were deemed not worthy enough to solicit, record, or retain. The colonial archive delivers a cacophony of settler voices, but it reeks of Indigenous silence.

The consequences of solely relying on the archive as a site of knowledge retrieval is at the heart of Barry Judd and Gary Osmond's analysis of the origins of Australian Rules Football (Chapter 35). They contest the national organization's official narrative that Australian Rules Football was created exclusively through British sporting traditions because 'these conclusions rest on the critical question of empirical evidence in the form of written documents in the colonial archive'. The archive-driven, official narrative is framed by chronological time and notions of linear progress, which exclude Aboriginal perspectives of history making that are based on oral traditions that 'prioritize ethics and morality over empirical facts, and privilege place and conformity over time and change'. At the heart of the debate about the origins of Australian Rules Football is the challenge to Western historical empiricism through the insertion of Indigenous knowledge systems, issues that are magnified in settler colonial discussions about identity, culture, history, nationhood, and reconciliation.

The debate about the origins of Australian Rules football shines a light on the emergence of Indigenous research paradigms. These paradigms help sport historians to critically consider asymmetrical power relations in colonial institutions, to read against the grain of official documents, and assess the silences of the archive. On a grander scale, Indigenous research paradigms raise methodological, epistemological, and ontological issues. Epistemological and methodological issues, in particular, are addressed in this Part of the *Handbook* through attention to Indigenous-focused methodologies – specifically yarning and the Kitchen Table Methodology. Barry Judd and Gary Osmond advocate yarning, a form of Indigenous communication, which is similar to other storytelling mechanisms common in oral communities. This culturally appropriate methodology often takes the form of unstructured or semi-structured group discussions, most effectively led by Indigenous Elders who control the topics, engagement, and practices. Indigenous facilitation and flexible time schedules allow unhurried exploration of topics where researchers, both Indigenous and non-Indigenous, are required to deeply listen to what is discussed, how the discussions are negotiated between the participants, and what remains unspoken. Christine O'Bonsawin and Janice Forsyth (Chapter 36) provide another Indigenous-centred method of recording, remembering, and truth-telling, the Kitchen Table Methodology. Like yarning, this methodology focuses on Indigenous voices and practices which encourage ways of listening, talking, and learning. The 'kitchen table' provides a safe space, where trust develops over time, ensuring knowledge-sharing feels natural, and the process of storytelling is often slow, measured, and incremental.

Yarning and the Kitchen Table Methodology have the capacity to change accepted historical narratives. In the case of Australian Indigenous sport, the official archival record reflects the relationship between assimilationist practices and settler colonial sport, but Indigenous yarning by people who lived through this period and participated in sport stress 'stories of agency, identity, pleasure, pride, resistance and sorority'. Similarly, the Kitchen Table Methodology suggests that sport was enmeshed in assimilationist agendas but, for participants, sport provided an avenue of personal agency 'because they saw its physical, cultural, and spiritual value and because it provided an opportunity to be on and connect with the land'. Stories derived from Indigenous-centred methodologies that prioritize Indigenous voices are central to re-telling, re-framing, and re-storying the sporting past.

Indigenous methodologies demonstrate how many sport historians have pigeon-holed their work into one dimension of the grand narrative of settler colonialism. This dimension focuses on the marginalization, dispossession, assimilation, and attempted elimination of Indigenous people, and the employment of sport by the state to achieve these goals. Often buried deep in these histories are stories of Indigenous people resisting sports or appropriating them for their own purposes or visions. In the context of the United States, Jennifer Guiliano and Beth Eby (Chapter 37) cite foot running amongst the Hopi nation, Indian horse relay races, the up tempo 'Rez ball' played by women on Native reserves, and the Wabanaki who hosted their own tribal baseball league for 50 years as examples of Indigenous people using sport for their own means, creating sports in their own visions, and pursuing sport to further goals and aspirations about cultural revitalization.

These redemptive capacities of sport are extended in Allan Downey's award-winning book, *The Creator's Game: Lacrosse, Identity, and Indigenous Nationhood*, which details the role that lacrosse has played in facilitating identity formation, political advocacy and self determination. Downey explores the relationship between Indigenous people, most notably the Haudenosaunee, and the appropriated version of lacrosse, one of settler colonial Canada's prominent sports. By looking at lacrosse through Indigenous lenses, he uncovers the ways in which Indigenous players have made the most of the settler colonial version of their game, earning income, generating pride and prestige, and maintaining their cultural traditions. Equally powerful are the Indigenous voices that describe how lacrosse initiates and fulfils political aspirations, promotes Indigenous self-determination, and subverts the goals and aspirations of the settler colonial state.[10] Christine O'Bonsawin and Janice Forsyth commend Downey's approach to history making: 'The history of Iroquois participation in global lacrosse is not one that revolves around narratives of dispossession, segregation, and extermination. Instead, it is a history premised on survival, revival, decolonization, and the resurgence of Haudenosaunee nationhood.'

In Chapter 34, Brendan Hokowhitu acknowledges this approach to Indigenous sport history, but is less sanguine than other contributors about its efficacy in an Aotearoa/New

Zealand context. He cautions against employing positivist approaches to sport history in Indigenous studies. He recognizes the merits in investigating Indigenous agency, for example, when Māori leadership in early rugby had international implications and, more recently, as increased Māori access to sport has produced successes and notable role models. He also identifies a key site for productive research. This site is the interface between indigeneity and urbanization that was created when Māori moved from rural settings to the cities of Aotearoa/New Zealand. The role of sport, in particular rugby, rugby league, softball, and netball, among urbanized Māori 'remains under-investigated and under-analysed and ripe for interdisciplinary and multidisciplinary examination'. Overall, however, his analysis is pessimistic about postcolonial studies and Indigenous ontologies, which he argues do not escape ongoing assimilation discourses and, in the long run, just end up reinforcing the power, reach, and success of settler colonialism.

Instead, Brendan Hokowhitu argues, it is far more useful in the Aotearoa/New Zealand context to focus on how sport aligned with assimilatory policies to produce a certain type of 'brown citizen'. Sport is viewed as a powerful component of the colonial machine, along with other institutions, which created compliant Māori. Using Foucault as his theoretical touchstone, and employing a genealogical approach, Brendan Hokowhitu examines the Māori sportsperson as a discursive formation. This discursive formation is generated through what Foucault refers to as 'dense transfer points'[11] with multiple discourses intersecting through Māori bodies. 'Physicality' is identified as the dense transfer point and Hokowhitu argues 'physicality is the axis to a centrifugal force that has produced the Māori sportsperson as a discursive formation'. Understanding the Māori sportsperson as a discursive formation cannot be achieved through a narrow framework of contextualizing sport, but rather through an expansive approach that draws from multiple disciplines including anthropology, history, sociology, education, gender, and popular culture. Adopting this approach, he concludes: 'the Indigenous sportsperson is not merely an ethereal concept, rather Indigenous bodies are the materialization of discourse'.

The chapters in this Part of the *Handbook* point to a particularly productive and enriching potential for Indigenous perspectives in sport history. While there are a range of competing ways to add to the understanding and scope of Indigenous sport history, there are a number of themes that emerge. Indigenous sport history will be enriched by disentangling the relationship between sport, colonization, and settler colonialism in a way that recognizes the uniqueness of settler colonialism as a political formation, but also the diversity of forms it took in places that have become known as Aotearoa/New Zealand, Australia, Canada, and the United States of America. Likewise, sport historians will benefit from reading and assessing emergent approaches in Indigenous/Native/Aboriginal Studies and Indigenous/Native/Aboriginal History. In contradistinction to traditional approaches to sport history, these fields provide insights into methodologies, epistemologies, and ontologies that contribute to history-making about Indigenous sport. In these ways, sport history can contribute in some small way to the project of decolonization.

Notes

1 Linda Tuhiwai Smith, *Decolonizing Methodologies: Research and Indigenous Peoples* (London: Zed Books, 2012): 72.
2 Murray G. Phillips and Gary Osmond, 'Australian Indigenous Sport Historiography: A Review', *Kinesiology Review* 7, no. 2 (2018): 193–198.
3 Samuel M. Clevenger, 'Sport History, Modernity and the Logic of Coloniality: A Case for Decoloniality', *Rethinking History* 21, no. 4 (2017): 568–560.

4 Malcolm Maclean, 'Engaging (with) Indigeneity: Decolonization and Indigenous/Indigenizing Sport History', *Journal of Sport History* 46, no. 2 (2019): 189–207.
5 Murray G. Phillips, Russell Field, Christine O'Bonsawin, and Janice Forsyth, 'Indigenous Resurgence, Regeneration, and Decolonization through Sport History', *Journal of Sport History* 46, no. 2 (2019): 143–156.
6 See for example, Michael Heine, *Dene Games: An Instruction and Resource Manual*, 2nd edition (Yellowknife, Northwest Territories, Canada: Sport North Foundation, 2006); Michael Heine, *Inuit Games: An Instruction and Resource Manual*, 3rd edition (Yellowknife, Northwest Territories, Canada: Sport North Foundation, 2007); Vicki Paraschak, '"Reasonable Amusements": Connecting the Strands of Physical Culture in Native Lives', *Sport History Review* 29 (1998): 121–131.
7 Audrey R. Giles, 'Women's and Girls' Participation in Dene Games in the Northwest Territories', in *Aboriginal Peoples and Sport in Canada: Historical Foundations and Contemporary Issues*, eds. Audrey R. Giles and Janice Forsyth (Vancouver: University of British Columbia Press, 2013), 145–159.
8 Janice Forsyth and Kevin B. Wamsley, '"Native to Native … We'll Recapture our Spirits": The World Indigenous Nations Games and North American Indigenous Games as Cultural Resistance', *The International Journal of the History of Sport* 23, no. 2 (2006): 294–314.
9 The reliance of sport historians on empirical history is discussed in Douglas Booth, *The Field: Truth and Fiction in Sport History* (London: Routledge, 2005); Murray G. Phillips ed. *Deconstructing Sport History: A Postmodern Analysis* (Albany: SUNY Press, 2006); Richard Pringle and Murray G. Phillips eds. *Examining Sport Histories: Power, Paradigms, and Reflexivity* (West Virginia: FIT, 2013).
10 Allan Downey, *The Creator's Game: Lacrosse, Identity, and Indigenous Nationhood* (Vancouver: University of British Columbia Press, 2018).
11 Michel Foucault, *The History of Sexuality: An Introduction,* vol. 1 (Camberwell, Australia: Penguin, 2008), 103.

33
SETTLER COLONIALISM AND SPORT HISTORY

Murray G. Phillips

> A growing body of literature has characterized settler colonial phenomena as 'distinct', and called for the establishment of dedicated interpretative tools. 'Distinct', however, begs the question: distinct relative to what?[1]

The answer to Lorenzo Veracini's question, posed above, is that settler colonialism is distinct from colonialism. The development of settler colonialism as an autonomous scholarly field has, in the main, bypassed most sport historians.[2] Settler colonial studies began in the 1990s and, in the new millennium, has emerged as a unique discipline covering many fields, hosting conferences, publishing edited collections, and establishing the *Journal of Settler Colonial Studies*.[3] The consequences of sport historians not engaging with this new field is that colonialism is often conflated with settler colonialism, and analyses of sporting imperialism are framed under colonialism with little appreciation of the specific qualities of settler colonialism. While both forms routinely coexist and reciprocally define each other, there are structural differences, as Patrick Wolfe has clearly articulated, which require settler colonialism and colonialism to be understood as conceptually discrete phenomena.[4]

Colonialism and settler colonialism share the feature of exogenous domination over their destinations, but the differences are stark in relation to population structure, claims of sovereignty, colonial and settler mindsets, and narrative making.[5] Colonialism seeks to establish a community that is temporary and built on unequal relations, often a master–servant hierarchy, principally to exploit labour and resources. Settler colonialism, on the other hand, is not primarily established to extract surplus value from labour, rather settlers attach to and exploit the land, seeking to eliminate and replace Indigenous peoples. Different communities underpin particular versions of sovereignty. Colonists are sojourners who intend to return 'home'; settlers, as the term implies, intend to stay and claim sovereignty over the land. Sovereignty is premised on displacing Indigenous people and building regenerative communities. What goes with the population structure and sovereignty is a settler colonial consciousness and specific forms of narrative making. The settler colonial mindset disavows the violent displacement of Indigenous people from their lands, discourses of denial that continue today in many forms, producing narratives that serve two interrelated functions: to legitimize 'the suppression or effacement of the Indigenous peoples' and 'to perform the concomitant indigenization of the settler'.[6]

DOI: 10.4324/9780429318306-38

Distinguishing settler colonialism from colonialism has significant outcomes. The characteristics of settler colonialism help draw attention to the ambiguity about what constitutes Indigenous identity.[7] For example in the sport history literature about sporting imperialism, Indigenous identity is understood in the following way:

> [C]olonial officers (administrators, clergy, educators, military personnel) took cultural practices with them overseas and effectively 'sold' them to the indigenous whom they conscripted into their service. The indigenous – primarily cosmopolitan upper-class types presumably at one with their masters – were the early adopters of the foreign cultural form which typically followed trade and other capitalist routes of global entrepreneurialism. The vertical diffusion of the cultural formation followed later and was the result of lower-class appropriation.[8]

This passage might appropriately describe some colonial situations, but it does not depict settler colonialism and the sporting experiences of the Indigenous peoples of the lands that we now call Aotearoa/New Zealand, Australia, Canada, or the United States of America. In contrast, the logic of settlers was to eliminate and replace, rather than exploit Indigenous people for commercial purposes under the colonialism model. As Elkins and Pedersen argue, settlers 'wished less to govern Indigenous peoples or to enlist them in economic ventures than to seize their land and push them beyond an ever-expanding frontier of settlement'.[9] Settler colonial states employed genocidal practices – violence, murder, displacement, isolation, cultural erasure and assimilation – to displace Indigenous peoples from their lands. As a consequence, sporting experiences in settler colonial settings are inextricably linked to the effacement of Indigenous people and claims of sovereignty, including narratives that legitimize these processes.

Equally importantly, the distinctiveness of settler colonialism draws attention to the way race and racialization have been interpreted and engaged by sport historians. Race and racialization are concepts that are employed to analyse sporting experiences of non-white Others, whether their history is shaped by slavery, colonialism, or settler colonialism. Not surprisingly, given the scale of North American sport, the number of scholars in the United States of America, and centrality of African-American people to national, international, and global sport, the sport history literature on race is dominated by the experiences of African-American people. Google Books, for example, recognizes 297,000 titles that focus on African-American sport.[10] Second on the list of sport and race books is apartheid sport, which has 99,100 titles.[11] One of the unintended consequences of the richness of the story of race and sport in the twentieth and twenty-first centuries is that Indigenous experiences are marginalized in the cacophony generated by African-American and apartheid sport. Indigenous experiences are further marginalized in the scholarship about sport and race.

In reviews of the field of sport history and in monographs about sport and race, racialization is often conflated with colonialism and settler colonialism. Racism in all of its forms – cultural, enlightened, individual, institutional, scientific, and structural – is blended together under the conceptual framework of sport and race. Daniel Widener's chapter on 'Race and Sport' in *The Oxford Handbook of Sports History* endorses 'the value of viewing European and American colonialism alongside domestic patterns of racial exclusion'. He uses this context to explain the demise of 'traditional' Hawaiian sports, the development of baseball in the Philippines and Cuba, and concludes that 'cricket would serve as a crucial carrier of Victorian values, while football would spread through military and commercial circuits into Africa, South American, Asia, and the Middle East'.[12] Similarly in *Cricket and Race*, Jack Williams muddies three systems of dominance – racialization, colonialism, and settler colonialism – in his treatment of the sport that was widely embraced throughout the British Empire. Race is the conceptual umbrella that frames the Australian Aboriginal nineteenth-century tour to the United Kingdom, exclusion of South Africans from world cricket, allegations of Pakistani cheating, the successes of West Indian teams of the late twentieth century, and experiences of non-white immigrants – those of African-Caribbean and South Asian descent – in England.[13] As these examples indicate, racialization, colonialism, and settler colonialism are often entangled and undifferentiated in sport history.

It is not too difficult to understand why race, colonialism, and settler colonialism are conflated in sport history. All three have simultaneously and collaboratively worked, as Byrd argues, 'to other and abject entire peoples so they can be enslaved, excluded, removed, and killed in the name of progress and capitalism'.[14] In this conflation, the world is divided according to what Charles W. Mills refers to as the 'racial contract', where white and non-whites are the fundamental categories for analysis.[15] The racial contract, which most sport historians have adopted in their work, often trades away indigeneity. It is this contract that enables scholars to produce coherent and engaging narratives, such as Widener's 'Race and Sport' and Williams' *Cricket and Race*, about the experiences of a potpourri of non-white athletes with contrasting histories. In this scholarship, however, Indigenous people are categorized as non-white colonized people, which effaces their indigeneity by failing to recognize the unique processes intrinsic to settler colonialism. As Veracini summarizes, 'the racist ideologies that insist on the dichotomy between white and non-whites and their adversaries transfer indigeneity away'. He adds: 'it is unsurprising that the relationship between indigenous activism in settler locales and civil rights agendas has been a contrasted one'.[16]

The solution for some critical scholars is to explore Indigenous history by analytically separating racism from colonialism and settler colonialism or, at least, decentring race within Indigenous studies. This approach has a number of benefits: it recognizes Indigenous peoples as seeking decolonization and sovereignty, rather than a racialized minority group seeking emancipation; it acknowledges thousands of years of pre-settler history and Indigenous peoples' priorities which are not necessarily focused on inclusion or exclusion, but aligned more to sovereignty; and it avoids conceptualizing Indigenous peoples as just one of several internal ethnic/racial minorities struggling for social, financial and political gains in white settler societies.[17] Within this framework sport history works less to decentre racism, and more to understand the process of settler colonialism. The theoretical and political project for sport historians shifts from an antiracist framework, which has dominated the discipline, to decolonialism that privileges Indigenous ontologies, epistemologies, and voices.

There are consequences for conflating racialization, colonialism, and settler colonialism and ignoring Indigenous identity. This is most obvious in recent significant scholarly books about the discipline of sport history, which were commissioned by major international publishers and edited by leading scholars. Both the *Routledge Companion to Sports History* and *The Oxford Handbook of Sports History* are testament to a flourishing sport history discipline, but attention to Indigenous history in these works is almost non-existent. The *Routledge Companion to Sports History* published in 2010 has 38 chapters extending over 650 pages, but has no chapter dedicated to Indigenous sport history. In fact, the index reveals there is a total of 17 pages attributed to Aborigines (3), First Nations (1), Indigenous (9), and Maori (4).[18] Similarly, the most recent tome, Edelman and Wilson's *The Oxford Handbook of Sports History* published in 2017 has 34 chapters extending over 560 pages, with no chapters dedicated to Indigenous sport history. Only 10 pages are attributed to Indigenous sports (8) and marngrook (2) in the index.[19] Based on these prominent scholarly sources, it is not too hard to make a rational and convincing case that sport historians are contributing to settler colonialism by erasing the histories of Indigenous people from our collective memory.

Murray G. Phillips

Notes

1 Lorenzo Veracini, 'Understanding Colonialism and Settler Colonialism as Distinct Formations', *Interventions International Journal of Postcolonial Studies* 16, no. 5 (2014): 615.
2 For some recent exceptions see: Craig Fortier, 'Stealing Home: Decolonizing Baseball's Origin Stories and their Relations to Settler Colonialism', *Settler Colonial Studies* 6, no. 1 (2016): 1–22; Audrey R. Giles and Janice Forsyth eds. *Aboriginal Peoples and Sport in Canada: Historical Foundations and Contemporary Issues* (Vancouver: University of British Columbia Press, 2013); and Murray G. Phillips, Russell Field, Christine O'Bonsawin, and Janice Forsyth eds. *Journal of Sport History* (Special Issue) 46, no. 2 (2019), 324 pp.; as well as a considerable body of work by Victoria Paraschak (https://scholar.google.com.au/citations?user=nYwjXIsAAAAJ&hl=en&oi=ao).
3 Lorenzo Veracini, 'Settler Colonialism': Career of a Concept', *The Journal of Imperial and Commonwealth History* 41, no. 2 (2013): 313–333.
4 Patrick Wolfe, *Settler Colonialism and the Transformation of Anthropology: The Politics and Poetics of an Ethnographic Event* (London: Cassell, 1999).
5 Lorenzo Veracini, *Settler Colonialism: A Theoretical Overview* (New York: Palgrave Macmillan, 2010).
6 Veracini, *Settler Colonialism*, 95.
7 Ken S. Coates, *A Global History of Indigenous Peoples Struggle and Survival* (London: Palgrave Macmillan, 2004).
8 See S.W. Pope, 'Imperialism', in *Routledge Companion to Sports History*, eds. S.W. Pope and John Nauright (New York: Routledge, 2010), 231–232.
9 Caroline Elkins and Susan Pedersen, 'Introduction: A Concept and its Uses' in *Settler Colonialism in the Twentieth Century: Projects, Practices, Legacies*, eds. Caroline Elkins and Susan Pedersen (New York: Routledge, 2012), 2.
10 Search term 'African American sport', https://www.google.com/search?tbm=bks&q=African+American+sport (accessed 8 April 2019).
11 Search term, 'Apartheid sport', https://www.google.com/search?tbm=bks&q=Apartheid+sport (accessed 8 April 2019).
12 Daniel Widener, 'Race and Sport' in *The Oxford Handbook of Sports History*, eds. Robert Edelman and Wayne Wilson (New York: Oxford, 2017), 462.
13 Jack Williams, *Cricket and Race* (Oxford: Berg, 2001).
14 Jodi A. Byrd, *The Transit of Empire: Indigenous Critiques of Colonialism* (Minneapolis: University of Minnesota Pres, 2011), xxiii.
15 Charles W. Mills, *The Racial Contract* (Ithaca: Cornell University Press, 1997).
16 Verancini, *Settler Colonialism*, 48.
17 For a synopsis of the complexity of these issues see Stephanie Nohelani Teves, Andrea Smith, and Michelle H. Rahaja eds. *Native Studies Keywords* (Tuscon: The University of Arizona Press, 2015), 271–300.
18 See S.W. Pope and John Nauright eds. *Routledge Companion to Sports History* (New York: Routledge, 2010).
19 See Robert Edelman and Wayne Wilson eds. *The Oxford Handbook of Sports History* (New York: Oxford, 2017). Marngrook (or marn-grook) is an Aboriginal ball game that emerged in Southern Australia with many of the same characteristics that define Australian Rules Football (see Chris Hallinan and Barry Judd, 'Duelling Paradigms: Australian Aborigines, Marn-grook and Football Histories', *The International Journal of the History of Sport* 15, no. 7 (2012): 975–986 for the historiographical debate about the relationship between the two activities).

34

MĀORI AND INDIGENOUS SPORT HISTORIES

Hero/ine or dupe?

Brendan Hokowhitu

There are at least two ways to think about historicizing Māori and Indigenous sport. First, where sport is viewed as an important cog of the colonial machine, dedicated to the production of compliant brown citizens. This historical analysis or genealogical reading centralizes 'physicality' as a core concept that primarily enabled the Māori sportsperson to be produced as a recognizable entity amidst other cartesian *'enunciations'*.[1] Second, what could be thought of as a 'counternarrative' in terms of historical method; a method primarily focused on displaying Indigenous agency, whether that be in the earliest days of Māori rugby where Māori leadership influenced the global game,[2] or more recently where Māori have been able to break down participation barriers and, as a consequence, have created a space where young Māori have been exposed to role models and have been able to succeed.

Although both these approaches to Indigenous sport history recognize racist colonial structures, they are very much competing methods. However, they do not compete in the sense that the material history and *contre-histoire* were synchronously implausible. Rather, in the sense that if we view colonial subjugation/resistance as a spectrum, they view the possibility of sport at least as operating or producing on/at opposite ends of this spectrum. Where one method is dedicated to telling the story of Indigenous agency overcoming racism, the other describes the Indigenous athlete as an enunciation within a system of discourse that goes far beyond sport. Writing previously on these two competing approaches I have argued: 'For the sport historian, it is unclear whether the historical figure of the Indigenous athlete is hero or dupe.'[3]

Indigenous *contre-histoire*

[W]e came out of the shadows, we had no glory and we had no rights, and that is why we are beginning to tell of our history … the misfortune of ancestors, exiles, and servitude. It will enumerate not so much victories, as the defeats to which we have to submit during our long wait for the promised lands and the fulfilment of the old promises that will of course re-establish both the rights of old and the glory that has been lost.[4]

DOI: 10.4324/9780429318306-39

The facticity of Indigenous existence (i.e. the unremitting conditions of being Indigenous) is that colonization wrought and continues to wreak havoc on Indigenous people's lives and epistemologies. For instance, the Māori population in general had radically decreased from pre-colonial estimates of as high as 500,000 to a population of just 56,000 in 1857–1858, so that by 1874 Māori had become 'only fourteen per cent, a minority in their own country'.[5] It is hard to fathom such devastation and inhumanity. Indeed, the task for most, if not all, Indigenous people since has been to reclaim their humanity; to re-make themselves as fully human yet within the confines of the colonizer's definition of what humanity entailed. The project of re-establishing humanity in the eyes of the colonizer in part demanded a 'contre-histoire'.

In the quote that begins this section, it is important here to note Foucault's focus on 'defeats' as the course to 're-establish both the rights of old and the glory that has been lost', which is both referring to the Western academy's 'tradition of dissent'[6] and the tendency of historians of subjugated groups to rationalize rights discourses based on the oppressive acts of their, in this case, colonizers. This is no less the case for Indigenous Studies scholars who have turned to methods and practices of 'decolonization', leading to the development of decolonial theory, which has become the panacea for the pan-Indigenous movement and reasserts the centrality of colonization to the emerging discipline. Whilst decolonization, dissent, and the focus on rights discourses may appear righteous (and they are), they nonetheless re-centre the defeats at the hands of their conquerors to re-new access to rights, resources, and discourse.

As an example, for some, sport acts as a barometer of equity in society. Hence, the prominence of Māori and now Pasifika New Zealand based players in codes such as rugby, rugby league, and netball have often been highlighted by white New Zealanders as indicative of good 'race-relations' particularly in comparison to Aotearoa/New Zealand's[7] greatest sporting rivals, Australia and South Africa. Speaking directly to this point, popular rugby writer T.P. McLean, speaking of the 1888/89 'Native' Tour of New Zealand, Australia, and Britain, suggests:

> That surely, was one of the romantic developments of all sport − the mingling, within so short a space, of natives and newcomers in an expedition which, while not truly representative, identified New Zealand Rugby to the world long before any other nation's game had become known outside its own shores. How different might have been the history of South Africa, one cannot help thinking, if the peoples native to that country had been permitted and encouraged, as were Maoris, to join the sport brought in by the foreign settlers.[8]

McLean's linear history of racial harmony in New Zealand is not exactly a counternarrative and such claims have been debunked several times over generally and in relation to Māori rugby,[9] however, the history of the heavy involvement of Māori in sport and rugby in particular has been consistently used by both Māori and Pākehā to speak to the possibilities of Māori rights in a broader political context.

That is, where sport history is employed to uncover racialized boundaries and to reveal structural bias (nationally, locally, in certain sports, in certain teams, and in relation to particular individuals); to present examples of athletes who have overcome these boundaries and, thus; to employ a historical method that affirms the re-establishment of rights of an oppressed group as a certitude of truth. Such certitude is neatly outlined below by Mike Marqusee who sees sport as a symbolic site of creative resistance for oppressed groups:

On sport's level playing field, it is possible to challenge and overturn the dominant hierarchies of nation, race and class. The reversal may be limited and transient, but it is nonetheless real. It is, therefore, wrong to see black sporting achievement merely as an index of oppression; it is equally and index of creativity, collective and individual.[10]

This intent to employ sport history in relation to subjugated racialized groups as a positivist approach to history more generally is seemingly the *modus operandi*.

In New Zealand, for Māori the index of collective creativity was markedly different as colonization went through its numerous stages. How sport shaped postcolonial Māori identities, for instance, morphed as the majority of Māori moved from rural to urban environments. Rural Māori sport was generally localized and *hapū* (i.e. the core Māori social unit; a large extended family) centric. It, thus, was employed to strengthen *hapū* collectiveness and connectivity with other *hapū*. For instance, prior to urbanization it was common for Māori sporting clubs to travel on buses to play other clubs in multiple sports, such as rugby, netball, and tennis, enabling both collectivism and connectivity using sport as a medium. Therefore, sport was a postcolonial avenue to observe a pre-colonial cultural practice.

In contrast, Māori sporting participation in the cities produced new cultural formations. The official narrative of Māori urbanization is quite well known in Aotearoa/New Zealand at least. Prior to the Second World War, 90 per cent of Māori were rural;[11] by 1956 'nearly two-thirds of Māori lived in rural areas; by 2006, 84.4 percent of Māori lived in urban areas'.[12] Urbanization and the developing need for labourers in urban centres meant Māori were increasingly trained in trades for jobs in cities. The search for employment forced many young Māori men and women, and consequently young Māori families, to leave their *hapū*.

While it is true that Māori and Pākehā were, in the main, discrete cultures prior to urbanization, the intermeshing of culture brought by Māori to the city and culture developed once there meant that, by Bhabha's definition at least, urbanization provided the space for the liminal negotiation of cultural identity; urbanization effected a third culture.[13] Noted Māori academic Sir Mason Durie argues, 'from 1945 urbanisation became the unmarshalled force which called for fresh understandings of what it meant to be Māori'.[14] Given sport has become a postcolonial 'tradition' amongst Māori, the production of a third culture at the interface between indigeneity and urbanization was almost certainly partly indebted to sport, and in particular rugby, rugby league, softball, and netball. It is here that the dialogue between Indigenous Studies and Sport History, Sport Sociology and Sport Cultural Studies becomes important and yet remains almost totally under-investigated and under-analysed.

There are two important components here in relation to the Indigenous urban third culture generated. First, the urbanization of Māori eventually led (i.e. particularly in the late-1960s and 1970s) to an international politicalization[15] of Māori as Māori displaced from their *kāinga tipu* (ancestral home) interacted with civil-rights discourses particularly coming out of the Black Power movement in the United States. Second, Māori through urban sport became increasingly subject to sports' dominant enunciations: egalitarianism; meritocracy; an even and objective playing field; and the pursuit of individual glory. It is possibly not a coincidence then that one of Māori's most famous All Blacks of all time but particularly of the 1960s was Waka Nathan, aptly nicknamed 'the Black Panther'.

The latter of these enunciations is particularly important because the achievement of Indigenous individuals chorused with narratives about overcoming odds and barriers common to sporting tropes.[16] Hence, the Māori sportsperson who achieved against the odds of their race, background, and economic status provided a fertile ground for producing a popularist historical counter-narrative, which sat at ease next to Māori political con-scientization, and particularly the rights-based discourses underpinning Māori protests sur-rounding injustices related to the Treaty of Waitangi. Accordingly, popular New Zealand rugby writer and creator of historical popular memory, Spiro Zavos relayed a history where rugby could be held up to be the beacon of 'racial democracy':

> The concept of the team, of every man in it being equal, of the physical and racial democracy of the game in New Zealand ... has been one of the most constant themes of rugby talk and behaviour ... the very essence of our English game and pastimes must be, that rich and poor, high and low, mix together on terms of per-fect equality in them .... Before Jim Bolger [New Zealand's Prime Minister from 1990 to 1997] enunciated the doctrine of the 'politics of inclusion', rugby was practising – successfully – that same doctrine ... the rugby community was the one important force in New Zealand life that behaved in the proper way by practicising [sic] the doctrine of inclusion.[17]

The cultural juncture between the familiarization of Māori with the international civil-rights movement, misconceived notions of 'Indigenous rights' (voiced here as 'politics of inclu-sion'), and the alignment with popularist sports discourses restresses Gayatri Spivak's (1996) scathing definition of postcoloniality as 'the failure of decolonization'.[18]

Spivak's overwhelmingly defeatist conclusion is in stark contrast to the utopian desires of the typical sport historian of subjugated peoples, who predictably claim that the victories of the subjugated on the sportsfield determine a 'win' for humanity in general. I am less hopeful; the subsuming of postcolonial or 'new' Indigenous ontologies within synthesizing assimilatory discourses simply demonstrates the successes of colonization. That is, to para-phrase Foucault (2003) in relation to biopower, the purpose of the neo-colonial state with the complicity of some Indigenous agents has been to 'make live and let die'.[19] Those sub-jectivities that have 'lived' (i.e. are given authority) often function to let alternative Indi-genous subjectivities die, literally in the sense of exclusion from communities and the will to definitionally exclude often based on markers of authenticity. As eluded to above, the Māori sportsperson represents the emergence of a new ontology; a 'new' Māori tradition.

Indigenous sport as an enunciation

A genealogy of Māori sport complicates the banal historical machinations surrounding sport described above, which either romanticize sport as the racial harmonizer, or narrate a story of Māori overcoming odds to become elite sportspeople. Although it is clear that Māori have faced limiting racist structures, it is also true that Māori have succeeded in sport more than any other colonial institution. This would suggest that a significant part of the colonial machinery in New Zealand employed sport to produce 'brown citizens'.

Given that sport is merely one aspect of society that regulates the body, and Foucault's clear direction to determine heterogeneity and discontinuity in the production of discursive formations, it is evident that the sport genealogist cannot hope to understand the production of the trope of the Māori sportsperson via sporting analyses alone. To delve into such a construction the genealogist must cross disciplinary boundaries including anthropology, his-tory, sociology, education, gender, and popular culture. As I have written elsewhere,[20] for Māori and indeed for other Indigenous peoples by degrees, I suggest that 'physicality' equates to what Foucault refers to as 'dense transfer points', one: 'endowed with the greatest

Māori and Indigenous sport histories

instrumentality: useful for the greatest number of manoeuvres and capable of serving as a point of support, as a lynchpin, for the most varied strategies';[21] a terminal hub where competing, contrasting, synthesizing, and dissident concepts hover to make possible the various ways that the Māori body is made real/authentic; a lynchpin that strategically enables the imprint of history upon the Māori body; the axis to a centrifugal force that has produced the Māori sportsperson as a discursive formation.

The Indigenous objects of colonization that emerged (i.e. the postcolonial discursive formations) in conjunction with the biopolitical management of Māori were dependent on producing colonial apparatuses designed to dialogue with Māori via physical statements, and to produce Indigenous bodies recognizable through their natural physicality. Crucially, and obviously then, the 'general economy' of colonial power[22] included Cartesian Dualism as a strategic statement that helped effect the various discursive formations of colonization, including the physiognomy of the Māori body. The profound weave of mind/body duality into the fabric of colonialism has in part enabled the 'biopolitical management of life' within the normalizing neo-colonial state. Evolutionism and anthropology provided the scientific taxonomy to facilitate the fragmentation of the human continuum into a hierarchy of social development, where Indigenous peoples were pin-pointed along the continuum from ape to the Enlightened rationalism of the European.

The Māori soldier was heralded for his domesticated savagery in the service of the Commonwealth. The 'ignoble' violent resistance to colonial domination by various *hapū* in the 1860s civil land and sovereignty wars was an example of Māori physicality that needed to be quelled. 'For the good of the colony', then, it was essential that the violence of Māori men was domesticated (i.e. noblised) in the service of the British First and Second World War efforts. Colonization, in New Zealand at least, did not attempt to drive the subversive violence out of Māori, realizing this was impossible given the immutability of the savage; rather Indigenous subversion was assimilated into the service of Imperialism itself.

Likewise, in the particular case of Māori rugby, sport was seen as an appropriate avenue where Māori savagery could be tamed and controlled. Sport provided the 'natural outlet' for Māori physicality or, as the late New Zealand historian, Michael King, once suggested, 'Apart from warfare, the national activity to which Maoris contributed in a measure resembling their full potential was rugby football.'[23] Similarly, Māori sports historian Hemi Nikora, argues: 'Rugby is one sport where Maoris succeed. It is the sport in which the natural instincts of the individual complements team combatant skills. It is said that rugby is the natural outlet or activity substituting for the days of tribal warfare.'[24]

The education system as a crucial component of the 'technology of power'[25] supplied the State mandated physical curricula, which invariably forced Māori into physical vocations. What I've described elsewhere as a 'physical education'[26] or a non-academic education was designed so that the Māori citizen would be primarily located in the trades, as manual labourers and more recently (i.e. with the advent of tourism as New Zealand's primary industry) in the service industries. Consecutive Ministers of Education from 1880 deemed education suitable for Pākehā children as 'too academic' for Māori. In 1866, the Inspector of Native Schools, James Pope, outlined what he thought a Māori masculine education should entail: 'Maori boys could be taught agriculture, market gardening, stock farming, poultry keeping and bacon curing.'[27] By 1910 Reverend Butterfield, the headmaster of a Gisborne Māori boarding school, told the Young Māori Party that Māori were:

> not fitted to the various professions. About 999 out of 1000 could not bear the strain of higher education. In commerce, the Maori could not hope to compete

with the Pakeha. In trades the Maoris were splendid copyists, but not originators. As carpenters they would cope under a capable instructor but not otherwise. Agriculture was the one calling suitable for Maoris .... It was therefore necessary to teach them the *nobility of labour*.[28]

This not so 'hidden curricula' continued as formal educational policy until the 1950s, and continues informally to this day. As a consequence, Māori communities were to be 'reduced to serving as a reserve army of wage labour for Europeans'.[29] By 1965, 'nearly 90 percent of Maori men [were] employed as farmers, foresters, labourers, transport operators, factory workers, or in other skilled and unskilled occupations'.[30]

From vocations, to sport and leisure, to dysfunctional violence, to health disparities, the statistics are clear surrounding Māori physicality as a dense transfer point. However, what is less discussed is multi-generational biopower where Māori, as compared with non-Māori, acquired different relations to their bodies as a necessary effect of a physically intensive life. Thus, Māori sub-cultures developed based on relationships with a physically labouring and active body that, in turn, came to symbolize authentic postcolonial ontologies (i.e. the 'new Māori traditions' referred to above). In the context of the present chapter then, it could be argued that the conditioning of Indigenous sportspeople throughout colonization has not only a symbolic genealogy but a material existence also. A genealogical analysis would suggest then, that the overrepresentation and media prominence of Māori athletes in sport witnessed today are the advent of a genealogy that in-part helped constitute and tune the Indigenous body to reproduce dominant historical discourses. Foucault's conception of biopower, where individuals become aware of themselves and their place in the world through the disciplined nature of their own body, speaks to the material depth of colonization and, as referred to above, the forlorn nature of a decolonial project. From a Foucauldian perspective then, the Indigenous sportsperson is not merely an ethereal concept, rather Indigenous bodies are the materialization of discourse.

Conclusion

There remains a third Indigenous sports history that I have not covered here, which is of course the possibility that the material presence of Indigenous bodies in sites like sport can disrupt colonial narratives by being situated beyond the disciplinary complex. The seminal work of C.L.R. James (1963) on Caribbean cricket proffered essentially the notion that the art and style of Black cricketers was subversive and unsettled dominant colonial narratives. Taking the Trinidadian Marxist's lead, I have similarly written about how, in the past at least, Māori rugby demonstrated a capacity for subversion, an unorthodox 'style' that did not adhere to the disciplinary regime in colonial sport;[31] where game-plans, for instance, governed by master-plans based on safety and efficiency were replaced with an aesthetics of the body. However, I have become entirely dubious as to whether sport can be a subversive site for Indigenous peoples, simply because of its inherent tithing to physicality as that critical dense transfer point, which has so effectively served to produce brown citizens. It is certainly possible that sport was once incendiary for Indigenous people but those days are long gone, and the fact that the flash of a bat or a 'Māori sidestep' has done little to quell neo-colonialism and neo-capitalism suggests the aesthetics of the Indigenous have meant very little in terms of undermining the general economy of colonial power; indeed the aesthetic has probably been on-sold to a multi-national company.

As an Indigenous scholar, I cannot ignore the historical inscription upon the Indigenous body, especially as a material occupier of colonized space. As Bourdieu argues: 'It is quite illusory to believe that symbolic violence can be overcome with the weapons of consciousness and will alone, this is because the effect and conditions of its efficacy are durably and deeply embedded in the body in the form of dispositions.'[32] Hence, rather than a historical analysis focused on racialized structural limitations,[33] what is more useful in the Aotearoa context at least is a focus on how sport aligned with assimilatory policy in producing a certain type of brown citizenry that was at once the same but different. The implication here that postcolonial Indigenous traditional subjectivities are 'produced', and that the production of an Indigenous *contre-histoire* alongside the rising profile of Indigenous politics in the settler (read 'invader') State has, in turn, led to the production of Indigenous subjectivities replete with authenticating power. To be an 'authentic' Indigenous person is to be one with the prevailing, and I would say State induced, discourses that construct indigeneity. Therefore, certainly the Māori sportsperson can be heroic, but the heroism is materially duplicitous.

Notes

1 Michel Foucault, *The Archaeology of Knowledge*, trans. A.M. Sheridan Smith (London, UK: Routledge, 2002), 155.

2 For further reading see Brendan Hokowhitu, 'Rugby and *Tino Rangatiratanga*: Early Māori Rugby and the Formation of Māori Masculinity', *Sporting Traditions: Journal of the Australian Society for Sports History* 21, no. 2 (2005): 75–95.

3 Brendan Hokowhitu, 'Foucault, Genealogy, Sport and Indigeneity', in *Examining Sport Histories: Power, Paradigms, and Reflexivity*, eds. R. Pringle and M.G. Phillips (West Virginia: FIT Publishers, 2013), 225.

4 Michel Foucault, *Society Must Be Defended: Lectures at the Collège de France 1975–1976*, trans. D. Macey (New York: Picador, 2003), 70–71.

5 Mason Durie, *Te Mana, Te Kāwanatanga: The Politics of Māori Self-determination* (Auckland: Oxford University Press, 1998), 53.

6 Lloyd Spencer, 'Postmodernism: Modernity and the Tradition of Dissent', in *The Routledge Companion to Postmodernism*, ed. S. Sim (London: Routledge, 2001).

7 I use 'New Zealand', 'Aotearoa/New Zealand', and 'Aotearoa' interchangeably depending on the sentence. For example, when referring to the State government, I will use 'New Zealand'.

8 Terry P. McLean, 'Maori Rugby Emerging as a Force', *Tu Tangata* 9 (1982): 18.

9 Brendan Hokowhitu, 'Māori Rugby and Subversion: Creativity, Domestication, Oppression and Decolonization', *International Journal of the History of Sport* 26, no. 16 (2009): 2314–2334.

10 Mike Marqusee, 'Sport and Stereotype: From Role Model to Muhammed Ali', *Race and Class* 36, no. 4 (1995): 5.

11 Ranginui Walker, *Ka Whawhai Tonu Matou: Struggle Without End* (Auckland: Penguin, 1990), 197.

12 Te Puni Kōkiri, *Historical Influences: Māori and the Economy* (Wellington: Government Printer, 2007), 7.

13 Homi K. Bhabha, *The Location of Culture* (London: Routledge, 1994).

14 Durie, *Te Mana, Te Kāwanatanga*, 54.

15 Māori have always been politicized but, until urbanization, Māori politics were largely based on organic philosophies.

16 Colin Tatz, *Obstacle Race: Aborigines in Sport* (Sydney: University of New South Wales Press, 1995).

17 Spiros Zavos, 'Kea Kaha', *Metro Magazine* 127 (1992): 77–80.

18 Gayatri C. Spivak, 'Diasporas Old and New: Women in the Transnational World', *Textual Practice* 10, no. 2 (1996): 249.

19 Foucault, *Society Must Be Defended*, 241.

20 Hokowhitu, 'Foucault, Genealogy, Sport and Indigeneity'.

21 Michel Foucault, *The History of Sexuality: An Introduction*, vol. 1 (Camberwell, Australia: Penguin, 2008), 103.

22 Michel Foucault, *Security, Territory, Population: Lectures at the Collège de France 1977–1978*, trans. G. Burchell (New York: Picador, 2004), 117.

23 Cited in Zavos, 'Kea Kaha': 78.

24 Hemi Nikora, 'Maori Rugby: Otaki and Districts', *Historical Journal, Otaki Historical Society* 11 (1988): 35.

25 Foucault, *Security, Territory, Population*, 117.

26 Brendan Hokowhitu, 'Physical Beings: Stereotypes, Sport and the 'Physical Education' of New Zealand Māori', in *Ethnicity, Sport, Identity: Struggles for Status* eds. J.A Mangan and A. Ritchie (London: Frank Cass, 2004), 192–218.

27 John M. Barrington, 'Learning the Dignity of Labour: Secondary Education Policy for Maoris', *New Zealand Journal of Educational Studies* 23, no. 1 (1988): 47.

28 Barrington, 'Learning the Dignity of Labour', 49 (emphasis added).

29 Judith Simon, 'The Place of Schooling in Maori-Pakeha Relations' (unpublished PhD thesis, University of Auckland, 1990), 88.

30 John Watson, *Horizons of Unknown Power: Some Issues of Maori Schooling* (Wellington: New Zealand Government Printer, 1967), 6.

31 Hokowhitu, 'Māori Rugby and Subversion'.

32 Pierre Bourdieu, *Masculine Domination*, trans. R. Nice (Cambridge: Polity Press, 2001), 39.

33 Which is not to say that New Zealand sport did not structurally discriminate. For instance, until 1970 the New Zealand Rugby Union and the New Zealand Government colluded with their South African counterparts in enacting the policy of 'whites only' rugby tours to South Africa.

35

A CRITICAL DISCUSSION OF HISTORY AND INDIGENOUS SPORT IN AUSTRALIA

Barry Judd and Gary Osmond

While Indigenous research paradigms increasingly guide scholarly collaborations and engagements with Aboriginal and Torres Strait Islander people, they are uncommon in Australian sport history. Such paradigms emphasize the importance of Indigenous epistemologies and methodologies, prioritize oral histories, Indigenous perspectives and voice, and value Indigenous-driven scholarship and co-construction of knowledge. While these ethical, epistemological, and methodological principles are not completely absent in Australian sport history, research relies on documentary evidence and analytical empiricism, which seldom admits and often dismisses Indigenous oral histories, voices, and perspectives.

This chapter analyses this tension. *Marngrook*, a traditional form of football played by Aboriginal nations in south-eastern Australia, offers an example of the dominance of empiricism and the reluctance to consider, let alone embrace, Indigenous perspectives. While Western historical epistemologies and methodologies reign, a move towards incorporating Indigenous research paradigms in Australian sport history is discernible. We examine this shift in direction via examples where Aboriginal storytelling as a methodological approach has been privileged in the co-construction of knowledge.

Since the 1970s, Australian historians increasingly have questioned the viability of research based in forms of empiricism and methodologies that preference documentary evidence and chronological reconstructions of the past. Histories of interactions between settler-colonists and Indigenous peoples have been constructed traditionally from records contained in the colonial archive. Australian understandings of race and cross-cultural relations between settler-colonists and Indigenous peoples since 1770 have been exclusive of Indigenous perspectives and based only in the stories of former colonists. Aboriginal academic Marcia Langton has therefore observed that 'most Australians do not know how to relate to Aboriginal people. They relate to stories told by former colonists'.[1] In 1968, anthropologist W.E.H. Stanner drew attention to the limitations inherent in what might best be described as archive-based empiricism and challenged historians to end what he called 'the great Australian silence'.[2] This challenge was first taken up by Charles Rowley in the 1970s and later, most notably, by Henry Reynolds who, from the 1980s, dedicated his career to reconstructing the Australian past in ways inclusive of Indigenous peoples and perspectives. Although he set out to interrogate the national past

DOI: 10.4324/9780429318306-40

287

from the 'other side of the frontier', Reynolds' methodological approach remained grounded in empiricism.[3]

More recently, Bain Attwood has attempted to survey the limits of historical studies in Australia by drawing attention to the position of history as a Western academic discipline. What becomes clear in his work is that the discipline of history reconstructs representations of the past in very particular ways. History is therefore capable of telling only particular truths that emerge from and reflect the processes through which the discipline reconstructs the past. Attwood contrasts the empirical methods that define history with Aboriginal recall of the past and concludes that history largely ignores Aboriginal ways of knowing and understanding past time. He notes that while history confirms its truth through collections of empirical facts, figures, and dates framed by chronological time and notions of progress, Aboriginal recall of the past prioritizes ethics and morality over empirical facts, and privileges place and continuity over time and change.[4]

Such differences have been demonstrated most clearly by Deborah Bird Rose, whose work documents Aboriginal recall of James Cook, a figure proclaimed by Anglo-Australian history as 'discover' of Australia.[5] Rose shows that Cook is widely memorialized throughout much of northern Australia, despite the fact that he never visited most of the Aboriginal peoples who continue to recall his incursion and disruption of their country. The Cook sagas demonstrate how Aboriginal reconstructions of the past emphasize morality over fact, as the figure of Cook represents Anglo-Australian colonialism, dispossession of Aboriginal lands, and the imposition of foreign and unjust laws.

Although many historians recognize the negation of Aboriginal recall of the past as being problematic in a supposedly 'post-colonial' contemporary Australia, some have rejected the need for inclusion of Aboriginal perspectives and memorialization of the past in the history of the settler-colonial state.[6] The reaction against efforts to reconstruct national histories to include both the empirical-based traditions of the discipline and Aboriginal recall of the past erupted in the 1990s in what became known as the History Wars. These 'wars' functioned to divide Australian historians into diametrically opposed camps. Historians who sought to reconstruct a national past inclusive of Aboriginal peoples' perspectives and sympathetic to their experience of settler-colonialism were labelled 'black armband' historians. The scholarship of 'black armband' historians became the subject of destructive and often unfair critique because their brand of history allegedly questioned the achievements of the Anglo-Australian settler state. Critics alleged that the construction of national histories that emphasized the impact of settler-colonialism on Aboriginal peoples required the reassessment of both the benign nature of British imperialism and the nation-building achievements of the Australian settler-colonial state. Those who opposed questioning the past in this way became known as holding the 'white blindfold' view of Australian history. Those in the 'white blindfold' camp who sought to undercut the inclusion of Aboriginal peoples and perspectives in national histories did so by retreating into a dogmatic form of empiricism that both aligns and limits history to the documentary contents of the colonial archive.[7]

Dominant empiricism – The case of *marngrook*

The emergence of revisionist histories, the fallout of the History Wars, and the ongoing debates about the place of Aboriginal methods for recalling the Australian past have impacted Australian sport history. In many ways, current methodological debates within Australian sport history mirror those that have occurred within Australian history more broadly. This is best illustrated with reference to the debate and controversy surrounding the origins of the popular sport, Australian (rules) football. Until recently, the history of this sport held that it began in 1858 at Melbourne and that it is best understood as a hybrid offshoot of British forms of football, namely association football (soccer) and rugby football (rugby union). This origin story became orthodoxy after Geoffrey Blainey published his influential history of the sport, which focused much attention on its recognized inventor, Thomas Wentworth Wills.[8]

Although Wills was Australian-born and spent much of his childhood on the colonial frontier, Blainey's portrayal of Wills focuses attention on his formal education in England. Wills attended the Rugby School, playing a form of schoolboy football that would evolve into rugby union and captaining in cricket. After leaving school, supported by his wealthy father, Wills became an amateur 'gentleman' cricketer playing first-class cricket throughout England. When he returned to Australia in the mid-1850s he did so as the first cricketing hero of the colonies. He used his influence to argue for the formation of a football club to keep cricketers fit in the off-season.[9] The Melbourne sporting public supported the idea and a number of scratch matches soon followed. In 1859 the Melbourne Football Club was formed and Wills met with other club members to devise rules. These became known as the Melbourne Rules, which form the basis of contemporary Australian (rules) football. Blainey emphasizes the Englishness of meeting attendees, with the chosen rules a compromise between members, such as Wills, who favoured rugby football and others who favoured the rules of association football.

While the influence of British sporting tradition on the origins of Australian (rules) football is indisputable, since the late 1980s some Australian sport historians have been compelled to explore the possible influence of Aboriginal sporting traditions on the sport. These scholars, including Jim Poulter, Graham Atkinson, Jenny Hocking, Barry Judd, and the sports journalist Martin Flanagan, have emphasized that Wills was not born in England but on the frontier of colonial Australia. Between 1840 and 1846, Wills spent his childhood on his family's pastoral property in western Victoria. During this period, his only playmates were children of the local Kulin Aboriginal clans known as the *Djabwurrung* and he demonstrated an exceptional ability to learn Aboriginal songs, mimic their voice and gestures, and 'speak their language as fluently as they did themselves'.[10] Wills' father, Horatio, noted his son's kinship with Aborigines.[11] During this time it is likely that Wills came to know about and witness Aboriginal forms of football that were played widely by Aboriginal peoples throughout south-eastern Australia, including by the *Djabwurrung*. Today, these traditional forms of football are collectively known as *marngrook*, from the *Gunditjmara* language.

Wills' childhood entanglement with *Djabwurrung* people was followed by positive and negative interactions with Aboriginal people. In 1861, he accompanied his father to Queensland to establish another pastoral station. The pair unwittingly arrived in the midst of a land war, and Horatio Wills and 18 of his party were killed. Wills' response to the murder of his father was unusual in that he refused to be part of the reprisal party and the killings that followed. Even more unusual was his later decision to coach an all-Aboriginal cricket team.

Those who have drawn attention to Wills' interactions with Aboriginal peoples have questioned why historians of the sport have rendered these facts, which were so fundamental in shaping his personal identity and life story, marginal to the critical role he played in founding Australian (rules) football. The first to do so was Poulter, who hypothesized that the codified game had in part originated in *marngrook*. According to Poulter, Wills likely witnessed and perhaps participated in the Aboriginal game as a child living among the *Djabwurrung* people, which led him to incorporate specific elements into Australian (rules) football.[12]

Sport historians who have engaged with the *marngrook* thesis have subsequently developed a more subtle and nuanced approach to the question of Aboriginal influence on the origins of Australian (rules) football. Flanagan suggests that Wills' engagement with *Djabwurrung* culture gave him insight into a games culture that existed beyond that of British sporting tradition. According to Flanagan, Wills' experience of both sides of the colonial frontier provided him with the confidence to break with that tradition and envisage 'a game of our own'.[13] Judd makes similar arguments, suggesting that it is highly probable that Wills' significant involvements with Aboriginal peoples did influence his worldview, including his role in codifying Australian (rules) football.[14]

Despite the more nuanced questions about Wills' relationships with Aboriginal peoples and how this may have influenced his role as an originator of Australian (rules) football, efforts to reinsert Aboriginal people and Wills' own knowledge of their cultural practices into the story of the Australian game have met with resistance by those sport historians who seek to maintain the sport as an historical offshoot of purely British sporting traditions. Whereas Blainey conceded that the overhead mark may have its origins in *marngrook*, others have been firmer in denying any connection between Aboriginal sporting traditions and the origins of Australian (rules) football. Gillian Hibbins, a key contributor to an officially sanctioned history of the sport, categorically rejects an Aboriginal influence in Wills' sporting life. She says that 'while endeavouring to make recompense for the errors of the past, falsifying history does that endeavour no favours'.[15] Significantly, these conclusions rest on the critical question of empirical evidence in the form of written documents in the colonial archive.[16]

Hibbins' dismissal of the *marngrook* thesis rests on a strict understanding of empiricism. In her effort to categorically discount the Aboriginal influence on the origin of Australian (rules) football, she limits valid recall of Australia's sporting past to that which can be reconstructed by referencing the colonial archive. Hibbins' categorical rejection of the Aboriginal connection is highly problematic in the context of the broader discussions about historical methodologies over the past two decades. Her insistence that the history of Australian sport be restricted to empiricism ignores the consequences of colonialism and maintains an understanding of historical method that differs little from that devised by Ranke in the nineteenth century.[17] While the History Wars have resulted in conscious efforts to rework historical method to accommodate Aboriginal perspectives, the *marngrook* case study suggests the approach to Australian sport history remains resistant to considerations of Aboriginal recall of the past.

Emerging Indigenous research paradigms – the case of yarning

While sport history has resisted Aboriginal perspectives, it is not entirely immune. Oral histories, for example, have been an essential tool for many sport historians.[18] The stories extracted, however, were interpreted almost entirely from the perspective of the historian in ways that sometimes leached their content of its full range of meanings and disempowered the storytellers. In an admirably self-reflexive admission, historian Richard Broome noted that although he had interviewed many former Aboriginal tent boxers, he not only excluded them from his initial publications on the topic but also missed their inflections of agency and power in favour of more obvious deficit readings.[19] On reflection, Broome added, he has 'developed a stronger sense of power from below and the agency held by Aboriginal historical actors'.[20] In some ways, Broome's changing position mirrors that of sport history, which is beginning to show a willingness to recognize Indigenous experiences, perspectives, and voices.

History and Indigenous sport in Australia

The work of Lawrence Bamblett provides an exemplar for incorporating Aboriginal voices not only for factual detail and memory recall but also for enunciations by Aboriginal people of meanings of their sporting pasts. Bamblett, a Wiradjuri man from New South Wales, writes about his home community, the former mission of Erambie, and the importance of sport and storytelling to cultural identity for Aboriginal people. He argues that sport offers opportunities to explore discourses beyond 'straight-line stories' that emphasize tragic tropes like racism.[21] Racism, as important as it is, is not the only story. Behind the dark curtain of racism as experienced through sport lies a rich and complex range of community stories about sport that reveals its integration with individual, community, and cultural identity. By exploring such stories through an emphasis on community voice and storytelling, Aboriginal communities can be strengthened by 'an expanding discourse that tells more about Aborigines as people (individually and collectively) than only the sum of our grievances'.[22]

For researchers who are interested in following Bamblett's inspiration, yarning may offer a useful methodology. In Indigenous Australia, yarning is a commonly used term for storytelling. Over recent decades, researchers have formalized the concept as a research methodology. It is a flexible methodology, one adaptable to different purposes, but commonalities include un-structured or semi-structured group discussion and storytelling, Indigenous facilitation and flexible time schedules that allow unhurried exploration of topics. Accordingly, it has been defined as 'informal and relaxed discussion through which both the researcher and the participant journey together visiting places and topics of interest relevant to the research study' in a 'culturally safe' way.[23] To date, yarning has been used predominantly in health contexts.[24] Its advantages are its appeal as a culturally appropriate methodology and its potential to yield findings that are not possible via traditional archive-based research.

Recent scholarship has differentiated between various types of yarning.[25] Cross-cultural yarning is perhaps most relevant here because it acknowledges the intersections of traditional storytelling with formal protocols necessary for academic research (ethics processes, recording, etc.). Anthropologist Nonie Sharp, who yarned with Torres Strait Islanders, referred to the 'asymmetry' of combining the narrators' lived experiences and stories with the 'requirements and expectations of the university'.[26] Rather than see this as a weakness, she accepted that this is an inevitable dimension of a powerful research tool for gathering and making sense of others' stories. The language that she used to articulate this process reflects something of the repetitive, circular, emphasized nature of oral enunciation and the demanding requirements for proper listening to spoken tales: 'Listening to yarning, yarning, yarning. Yarning is reflecting. And yarn too and listen; not just to the words, but to quiet judgement.'[27]

The co-author of this chapter has experienced the power of yarning in Aboriginal communities as part of a collaborative sport history research project with Elders in Cherbourg, a former government-controlled Aboriginal settlement in Queensland. Following various sport history projects with the community, the potentially transformative potential of collective yarning became apparent.[28] The specific context was the historical accomplishments of teams of precision marchers – known as Marching Girls – in the 1950s and 1960s. Invited by the aunties, now aged in their seventies, to 'tell our story', we collaborated with them in three separate yarning sessions. These involved two dozen women, facilitated by an Aboriginal elder from Cherbourg who had also been a marcher. In addition to this Indigenous facilitation, the sessions aligned with other standards of yarning via semi-structured group discussion and storytelling and unrushed time schedules.

291

These yarning sessions prioritized Indigenous perspectives and voices and respected Indigenous-driven scholarship and the co-construction of knowledge. In doing this, they were transformative not only in the sense that Aboriginal informants were involved in ways uncommon in sport history research but also in the knowledge that was produced. The value of this was immeasurable. Prior to the yarning, we had collaborated with the women to research their experiences via the archive. This had detailed the full extent of their sporting involvement and had contextualized marching within the government policy of assimilation; from the 1950s onward this policy aimed to expose young Aboriginal people to white settler-colonial society through education, social, and sporting experiences. From this research, we published a paper analysing these official meanings associated with marching.[29] In many ways, this was a representative sport history project in that it narrated a history of this sport reconstructed from documentary evidence that bypassed Aboriginal voices and meanings. As with most empirically based histories, those voices are absent in the vestigial records. What yarning did was make available those missing voices, and allowed for a lengthy and detailed examination and exploration of memories, stories, and perspectives from the participants themselves.

The result of these sessions was a profoundly different history from that derived from the archive. Whereas the official record stressed assimilation, compliance, and Western-focused sporting achievement, yarning revealed stories of agency, identity, pleasure, pride, resistance, and sorority.[30] Giving voice to these alternative meanings was powerful for the women themselves, who had told these stories amongst themselves but had never had their experiences valued and validated through a research process. But it was also powerful from a sport history perspective because it offered an alternative reading to the official record and revealed the possibilities of direct engagement with research methodologies like yarning that fit within an Indigenous research paradigm. Kamilaroi woman and educator Cheree Dean noted this power a decade ago: 'Where once Aboriginal knowledges and voices competed and often lost against the outside influence and voices of research, yarning now permits these voices to become the authority of their knowledges and sets the responsibilities of its use with others.'[31] The opportunity for sport historians to collaboratively engage likewise with communities remains open.

Concluding thoughts

The example of yarning demonstrates how engaging with Indigenous memories can be both powerfully affective for Indigenous people and important to academic historians in revealing alternative versions of the past. Refusing to seriously engage with Indigenous historical memories and perspectives shows a faith in reconstructionist empiricism that is not borne out by recent scholarship of history, is dismissive of Indigenous knowledges and epistemologies, and denies sport history of the richness of alternative perspectives on the past.

Until recently, Indigenous storytelling traditions that recall the past, made famous by anthropologists Baldwin Spencer and Frank Gillen via the term 'Dreamtime' (translated from the Arandic word *alcheringa* meaning eternal, uncreated) were considered analogous to European fairy tales in both academic and popular understandings of Aboriginal cultures.[32] Emerging archaeological evidence, however, reveals that many traditional Indigenous stories accord with scientific facts of global climatic change, confirming Aboriginal knowledge of rising sea levels held in stories that are at least 12,000 years old.[33] Such emerging knowledge has significant implications for how we understand oral-based evidence that derives through storytelling and yarning. The ability of Indigenous peoples to convey knowledge of events that occurred millennia ago with a high degree of accuracy through oral means alone suggests that efforts to discount these methods of recalling the past are based in nothing more than a persistent eurocentrism. The challenge therefore remains for all researchers, sport historians included, to pay greater attention both to Indigenous research paradigms and to how its tenets can be explored.

Notes

1 Marcia Langton, 'Beyond the Myths', http://www.shareourpride.org.au/sections/beyond-the-myths/ accessed 27 May 2019.
2 W.E.H. Stanner, *White Man Got No Dreaming: Essays 1938–1973* (Canberra: Australian National University Press, 1979).
3 Henry Reynolds, *The Other Side of the Frontier: Aboriginal Resistance to the European Invasion of Australia* (Melbourne: Penguin, 1995 [1981]).
4 Bain Attwood, *Telling the Truth about Aboriginal History* (Sydney: Allen & Unwin, 2005).
5 Deborah Bird Rose, 'The Saga of Captain Cook: Morality in Aboriginal and European Law', *Australian Aboriginal Studies* 2 (1984): 24–39.
6 Keith Windschuttle, *The Fabrication of Aboriginal History: Van Diemen's Land, 1803–1847* (Sydney: Macleay Press, 2002).
7 Anna Clark, 'History in Black and White: A Critical Analysis of the Black Armband Debate', *Journal of Australian Studies* 26, no. 75 (2002): 1–11.
8 Geoffrey Blainey, *A Game of our Own: the Origins of Australian Football* (Melbourne: Black Inc., 2003).
9 *Bell's Life in Victoria*, 10 July 1858.
10 H.C.A. Harrison, Anne Mancini, and Gillian Hibbins, *Running with the Ball: Football's Foster Father* (Melbourne: Lynedoch, 1987), 79.
11 T.S. Wills Cooke, *The Currency Lad*, 4th edition (Stephen Digby, 2012), 37–39.
12 Jim Poulter, 'An Old, Old, Ball Game', *Australasian Post*, 4 August 1983, 8; Jim Poulter, 'Marn-Grook – Original Australian Rules', In *This Game of Ours: Supporters' Tales of the People's Game*, eds. Peter Burke and Leo Grogan (Melbourne: EATWARFLEMSD, 1993), 64–67.
13 Martin Flanagan, *The Call* (Sydney: Allen & Unwin, 1998).
14 Barry Judd, *On the Boundary Line: Colonial Identity in Football* (Melbourne: Australian Scholarly Publishing, 2008).
15 Gillian Hibbins, 'A Seductive Myth', In *The Australian Game of Football since 1858*, ed. Geoff Slattery (Melbourne: Geoff Slattery Publishing, 2008), 45.
16 Hibbins, 'A Seductive Myth', 45.
17 Chris Hallinan and Barry Judd, 'Duelling Paradigms: Australian Aborigines, Marn-Grook and Football Histories', *Sport in Society* 15, no. 7 (2012): 975–986; Barry Judd, 'The Question of Indigenous Origins and the Unlevel Playing Fields: Outside the Boundary of the Dominant Paradigm', *Sport in Society* 15, no. 7 (2012): 1026–1033.
18 Kenneth David Edwards, 'Black Man in a White Man's World: Aboriginal Cricketer Eddie Gilbert' (PhD diss., The University of Queensland, 1992).
19 Richard Broome, 'Theatres of Power: Tent Boxing circa 1910–1970', *Aboriginal History* 20 (1996): 1–2.
20 Broome, 'Theatres of Power', 1.
21 Lawrence Bamblett, 'Straight-Line Stories: Representations and Indigenous Australian Identities in Sports Discourses', *Australian Aboriginal Studies*, no. 2 (2011): 17.
22 Bamblett, 'Straight-Line Stories', 16.
23 Dawn Bessarab and Bridget Ng'andu, 'Yarning about Yarning as a Legitimate Method in Indigenous Research', *International Journal of Critical Indigenous Studies* 3, no. 1 (2010): 38, 37.
24 See, for example: Larry Maxwell Towney, 'The Power of Healing in the Yarns: Working with Aboriginal Men', *International Journal of Narrative Therapy and Community Work*, no. 1 (2005): 39–43; Lynore K. Geia, Barbara Hayes, and Kim Usher, 'Yarning/Aboriginal Storytelling: Towards an Understanding of an Indigenous Perspective and its Implications for Research Practice', *Contemporary Nurse* 46, no.1 (2013): 13–17.

25 Gary Osmond and Murray G. Phillips, 'Yarning about Sport: Indigenous Research Methodologies and Transformative Historical Narratives', *The International Journal of the History of Sport* 36, nos. 13–14 (2019): 1271–1288.

26 Nonie Sharp, *Stars of Tagai: The Torres Strait Islanders* (Canberra: Aboriginal Studies Press, 1993), 15.

27 Sharp, *Stars of Tagai*, 14.

28 Chelsea Bond, Murray G. Phillips, and Gary Osmond, 'Crossing Lines: Sport History, Transformative Narratives and Aboriginal Australia', *The International Journal of the History of Sport* 32, no. 13 (2015): 1531–1545.

29 Murray G. Phillips and Gary Osmond, 'Marching for Assimilation: Indigenous Identity, Sport, and Politics', *Australian Journal of Politics and History* 64, no. 4 (2018): 544–560.

30 Gary Osmond and Murray G. Phillips, 'Indigenous Women's Sporting Experiences: Agency, Resistance and Nostalgia', *Australian Journal of Politics and History* 64, no. 4 (2018): 561–575; Rebecca Olive, Gary Osmond, and Murray G. Phillips, 'Sisterhood, Pleasure and Marching: Indigenous Women and Leisure', *Annals of Leisure Research* 24, no. 1 (2021): 13-28.

31 Cheree Dean, 'A Yarning Place in Narrative Histories', *History of Education Review* 39, no. 2 (2010): 10.

32 Baldwin Spencer and F.J. Gillen, *Native Tribes of Central Australia* (London: Macmillan, 1899).

33 *First Footprints* [film], dir. Bentley Dean, 2013.

36
INDIGENOUS SPORT HISTORY IN CANADA
Past and future considerations

Christine O'Bonsawin and Janice Forsyth

> Indigenous histories have always existed. Indigenous notions of the past that connect people to places, events, peoples, and memories help Indigenous peoples define their place in the created world and explain its shapes, wonders, and human relations (like other kinds of history).[1]

Indigenous sport history, then and now

We open with a quote by White Earth Ojibway scholar, Jean M. O'Brien, to call attention to the fact that Indigenous people have always held their own ways of remembering the past. The histories of Indigenous people, cultures, and nations are often rooted in oral transmission as well as memory methods and technologies (e.g. pictographs, wampum, coppers, etc.), helping them to understand and assert their place in the world according to narrative. Although Indigenous people have been documenting their lives since time immemorial, the histories they produced were habitually dismissed as folklore, myth, and legend. Consequently, Indigenous-led histories were not only rejected within history as a discipline, but when taken up by settler scholars Indigenous histories were wedded to colonial narratives that reinforced the legitimacy of settler dominance.[2]

Yet, O'Brien explains there is reason to be hopeful: 'The long-standing marginality of [Indigenous history] has produced a situation of rich possibilities for transforming Indigenous histories, and, if there is a will, national narratives as well.'[3] This transformative work, she suggests, is both challenging and rewarding since it requires scholars to consider innovative approaches, interventions, and worldviews to better illuminate the needs, interests, and experiences of Indigenous people. It also urges scholars to use interdisciplinary approaches that provide a deeper understanding of Indigenous histories and to broaden their view of what constitutes evidence so as to shed new light on the past, especially from Indigenous perspectives. This approach is transformative because it requires scholars to reflect on and articulate if and how their methodologies support or challenge settler colonialism.

Indigenous sport history sits at the intersection of Indigenous history and sport history. As an area of study, the history of Indigenous sport in Canada received its impetus in the

DOI: 10.4324/9780429318306-41

1960s,[4] as scholars drew primarily from mainstream repositories, and thus mainly from the perspectives of wealthy white male settlers, to reconstruct histories of Indigenous sport in Canada. Consequently, early Indigenous sport history is mostly wedded to national narratives that reinforce the marginalization of Indigenous people by focusing on the pre-contact era, European exploration and discovery, and Canada's assertion of sovereignty over Indigenous people and their lands – frames that privilege settler ways of understanding Canadian–Indigenous relations.

Indigenous sport history has grown significantly since then, with scholars mapping the varied and complex role of sport in Indigenous lives.[5] This body of research shows that Indigenous people do not necessarily see sport as a form of Canadian nation-building. Instead, they see it as a way to enhance their identities and to support their claims to nationhood, views that were often at odds with those of the nation-state.[6] Therefore, Indigenous sport history can provide critical insights into how Indigenous people see themselves in relation to the state, which is significant today given the complex legal relationships that underpin Indigenous rights in Canada and Indigenous sovereignty.

Recently, a growing number of historians and scholars are relying less on mainstream repositories and more on the people who are responsible for preserving such histories according to Indigenous-centred methods of recording and remembering. This approach allows us to see that some of the most meaningful 'repositories' in the field of Indigenous sport history exist within Indigenous communities, with the stories shared amongst Indigenous families, friends, and community members. These 'kitchen table' conversations are where people take the time to listen, talk, and learn from one another as they discuss and analyse the past and its relationship to the present, as well as imagine a better way forward.[7] In other words, histories of Indigenous sport can be found in the daily storytelling and truth-telling practices of Indigenous people, where the stories of historical actors and events are remembered, retold, reframed, rerighted, and reclaimed.[8]

To describe the field as Indigenous 'sport' history is somewhat misleading since it implies the body of research focuses almost exclusively on sport, which is a specific type of movement culture. Sport in Canada emerged in the mid-nineteenth-century, during the first industrial revolution, and is recognized by an emphasis on competition and winning, as well as a highly organized structure that is overseen by governing bodies that police what happens in sporting spaces. Broadening our understanding of sport to encompass 'movement' or 'physical' culture allows us to see how different groups of people weave movement (not just sport) into their lives and use it to relate to one another. It can also tell us a great deal about how people relate to the land, about their belief systems, and even their views on labour and economics, in addition to their ideas about class, race, gender, etc.

Prior to colonization, Indigenous physical culture was tied to their land-based lifestyles as well as their spiritual beliefs. By engaging in their old-time practices Indigenous people were training for survival on the land, reaffirming their place in their community, establishing political alliances, calling on the spirits to assist with such things as hunting – basically any physical practices that served their collective needs.[9] Indigenous physical practices were dramatically different from settler-based sports, which were rule-bound, secular contests that aligned with values that supported the growing capitalist economy. For instance, many traditional Indigenous practices, especially ones rooted in spirituality, involved sharing and reallocating resources among the group. Since their physical practices were structured to support that way of life, they challenged the idea of individual ownership and thrift that lay at the heart of settler economies. Therefore, traditional Indigenous practices were fundamentally different from settler sport practices.[10] Researchers need to attend to this cultural

Indigenous sport history in Canada

backdrop when writing about Indigenous sports, especially as it relates to settler (read: mainstream) sports, even in modern contexts.

Increasingly, scholars who are writing about Indigenous sport history in Canada are beginning to 'restory' dominant versions of history by adopting Indigenous storytelling and truth-telling methodological practices.[11] These approaches can tell us a great deal about why Indigenous people view sport as an important cultural practice and can shed much needed light on how and why Indigenous people use sport as a form of resistance, revitalization, resurgence, and self-determination. From this vantage point, we come to see more clearly that the history of Indigenous sport in Canada is less about the triumphs and challenges of athletes and teams, and more about the aspirations of Indigenous people, communities, and nations to keep their cultures alive as they try to address ongoing threats to their identities, cultures, and land bases.

Patterns in the literature

When people think of Indigenous sport in Canada, the history of lacrosse likely comes to mind. The sport has always enjoyed a prominent place in the Canadian imaginary, a status no doubt aided by the passing of the National Sports of Canada Act in 1994, which identified lacrosse as Canada's official summer sport and hockey its official winter sport. While lacrosse does not enjoy the same media interest, financial support, or participation rates as hockey, its Indigenous heritage offers a type of symbolic value different from that of hockey, representing, for instance, ideas about peaceful Indigenous–settler relations in Canada. The Canadian Lacrosse Association's interpretation of the sport is a good example of how sport history can be used to mythologize a nation's past by obscuring the way sport was used to advance settler colonialism, thus removing settler responsibility for decolonizing sport.[12] On its website, under the section labelled 'Our Sport', the Association explains:

> The roots of our country lay in many cultural soils, and Canadian society has grown and benefited from the contributions of people of many cultural backgrounds. The English and French are recognized as the dominant influences in the creation of this country and the foundation of our nation.[13]

The website then tells readers that 'Canadian society' embraced Indigenous lacrosse and 'together' they worked with Indigenous people to produce the game we know today:

> It is one of the rare examples of the culture of the First Nations being accepted and embraced by Canadian society. To the religious and social rituals of the first North Americans, the settlers brought the European concepts of structure and rules, and together they produced one of the first symbols of the new Canadian nation, the sport of Lacrosse.

It is a sad irony that such narratives continue to exist in spite of the findings of numerous national investigations into Indigenous–settler relations in Canada that clearly show how sport is imbricated with Indigenous dispossession, segregation, and extermination.

Scholars have documented a radically different history of lacrosse from the one promoted by the Canadian Lacrosse Association. Relying mostly on archival sources, scholars have demonstrated how the settlers appropriated the game from the Haudenosaunee (Iroquois Confederacy), whose territory spans the border of Canada and the United States in the northeast regions of the continent, divested the game of its traditional significance, and then banned Indigenous players from championship matches, all the while refashioning the game to reflect the settler values, belief, and practices. The game that the Association celebrates as 'our' sport is really a celebration of white, male, English, settler sport couched in self-redeeming narratives, which conceals Canada's history of colonial violence.[14] By exposing the myths that surround lacrosse, we can see how the sport was, and continues to be, an important site where people promote, reinforce, and challenge ideas about Indigenous–settler relations in Canada, even if they are not doing this intentionally.

As important as the scholarship on lacrosse is, it nevertheless mirrors a weakness that can be found in the larger body of literature on Indigenous sport history: it documents how sport remains a tool for colonization. In other words, research on lacrosse, as well as Indigenous sport history generally, tends to highlight what the settlers did to Indigenous people with little corresponding emphasis on how Indigenous people responded to those efforts. When we take a step back to examine the larger pattern in the literature, we can see that Indigenous sport history is primarily a history of marginalization, dispossession, and assimilation. The numerous stories of racism and other forms of discrimination, in addition to the stories of cultural dislocation and loss, are merely two prominent themes that align with this body of literature. To be sure, these histories are valuable because they provide evidence of the way sport is entangled with larger colonial forces that continue to make life a struggle for Indigenous people in Canada. Yet, a focus on Indigenous agency, which analyses the capacity of Indigenous people to act independently, is needed, as positive social change is made possible with this kind of evidence.

We know that Indigenous people did not accept new sport forms into their lives unconditionally. As with any population, they made choices, whether consciously or not, about what aspects of sport to keep, change, or throw away, in addition to determining how they wanted to participate in sport. Some Indigenous people went even further, adapting their traditional physical practices to modern sporting contexts, which is no small feat considering that some traditional Indigenous values are at odds with competitive sport values. In the far northern regions of Canada, for instance, the Inuit and Dene people transformed the physical practices that once sustained their land-based lifestyles into sport in an effort to keep their culture and values alive by appealing to youth interests in sport. One of the challenges they faced was addressing the emphasis on competitive comparisons and winning that underpins mainstream sport; these mainstream sport values went against their beliefs founded on cooperation in subsistence production and life more generally.[15] Historical research has helped us better understand what value Indigenous people see in sport today and how they have adapted their cultures in order to make sport work for them, culturally speaking.

This is not to say that Indigenous people have complete control over decisions about how sport should fit into their lives. As marginalized people, they sometimes had sport forced upon them, as when Indian agents and missionaries used sport in an attempt to replace outlawed spiritual practices, or when sport was taught to students in the Indian residential school system in an effort to assimilate them into white, mainstream society.[16] In addition, they did not get to decide how sport should be organized and funded, which meant settler society retained this control. The problem of control is relevant today. Indigenous people often do not have the luxury of deciding if they would like to stick with their customs or experiment with the dominant culture's traditions for fun, or decide on how their programmes should be funded and evaluated.[17] Therefore, doing Indigenous sport history means developing a keen awareness of the asymmetrical power relations that characterize settler domination, which continues to provide some groups of people with more opportunities than others to shape sport in their preferred way.

The future of Indigenous sport history

There are various examples in the study of Indigenous sport in Canada, whereby historians as well as Indigenous studies and sport studies scholars, are utilizing new and exciting approaches, interventions, and perspectives. Rather than accept the outcome of the assimilatory intentions of the colonizer, some scholars working in the area of Indigenous sport history are adopting Indigenous-centred methods often found in the storytelling and truth-telling practices of Indigenous people. Michael A. Robidoux's *Stickhandling through the Margins: First Nations Hockey in Canada*, for example, provides valuable direction, reminding scholars to reconsider how Indigenous people are positioned in settler colonial frameworks. Robidoux explains the importance of the game of hockey to many Indigenous people, communities, and nations throughout Canada.[18] To understand the centrality of hockey within such realms, Robidoux cautions scholars against viewing Indigenous people as colonized people who took up settler Canada's national winter sport unassumingly. Instead, he encourages scholars to recognize Indigenous people as autonomous self-determining peoples, communities, and nations who freely brought hockey into their lives because they saw physical, cultural, and spiritual value in the game. The repositioning of Indigenous people in the scholarly record, and thus national narrative, requires that scholars – Indigenous and non-Indigenous – adopt Indigenous research methodologies, similar to Robidoux, where we are encouraged to listen, talk, and learn from one another.[19]

Another example of what it means to listen, talk, and learn in an Indigenous-centred research context is considered using the work of the first author, Christine, who wrote a graduate thesis on the history of two Indigenous athletes. The study began as an exercise in data collection and analysis on the experiences of Sharon and Shirley Firth, Gwich'in and Métis sisters who represented Canada at the highest levels of cross-country skiing between the 1960s and 1980s.[20] The hope was that the thesis would record and assess the achievements of these women and that their successes would be entrenched permanently in the historical record. The end product mostly achieved these objectives; however, through the research process, Christine learned what it truly means to listen, talk, and learn in an Indigenous-centred research process. As their relationship developed, Sharon sometimes called Christine in the early morning hours to share new stories or to correct her understanding of an event or story. These were their kitchen table conversations, where (Christine hopes) Sharon found a safe space to share her experiences, perspective, and knowledge, and where some of Christine's important learning occurred.

Christine decided to title her thesis 'Failed TEST: Aboriginal Sport Policy and the Olympian Firth Sisters'. The Territorial Experimental Ski Training programme did not fail, in her estimation, because the Firth sisters were unsuccessful in capturing Olympic and world championship medals. Rather, this loosely designed integration programme failed because it was unable to assimilate the Firth sisters (and others) into the broader mainstream society through this sport process. Further, as exposed through this Indigenous-centred research process, we learn that the Firth sisters did not participate in cross-country skiing because they were forced to do so through assimilatory measures; they participated in the sport because they saw its physical, cultural, and spiritual value and because it provided an opportunity to be on and connect with the land.

Allan Downey's *The Creator's Game: Lacrosse, Identity, and Indigenous Nationhood* is a prominent example of how Indigenous perspectives can dramatically change our understanding of the past.[21] In it, he explores how the Haudenosaunee, as well as the Skwxwú7mesh people situated in Coast Salish territory on the Pacific Northwest Coast, used lacrosse to enhance their identity claims and assert their Indigenous rights. He opens with the story of Sky Woman, a Haudenosaunee creation story that signals to the reader the central importance of lacrosse to the Haudenosaunee worldview. As the chapters progress, the story shows us how the settler version of lacrosse is different from the Haudenosaunee version and, by implication, the Skwxwú7mesh version. It also shows us how Indigenous people viewed their involvement in mainstream lacrosse: why they played, what meanings they attached to the game, and what value they saw in it politically. Such a history was made possible by paying close attention to Indigenous perspectives and their epistemologies, that is, by attempting to restory an Indigenous history of lacrosse.

In the closing chapter, Downey provides an overview of the Iroquois Nationals (men's) and Haudenosaunee Nations (women's) lacrosse teams, which have participated as representatives of a sovereign Haudenosaunee nation at the World Lacrosse Championships beginning in 1990 and 2009, respectively. Through this restorying process, we learn that the history of Haudenosaunee participation in international lacrosse is not wedded to national narratives of settler colonialism.[22] Rather, the re-emergence of these inter-reservation all-star teams served the Confederacy in very particular ways as it was considered to be an investment in future generations, it afforded young people opportunities (e.g. athletic scholarships, healthy lifestyles, confidence, etc.), instilled pride in their identities, and assisted in unifying the Confederacy. The Haudenosaunee refused to be received in international sport as settler colonial subjects, avowing that national and international bodies recognize them as 'representatives of the distinct and sovereign Haudenosaunee Nation – or not at all'.[23] Taken from this vantage point, the history of Iroquois participation in global lacrosse is not one that revolves around narratives of dispossession, segregation, and extermination. Instead, it is a history premised on survival, revival, decolonization, and the resurgence of Haudenosaunee nationhood.

As scholars and community members, we are only beginning to scratch the surface in our efforts to write about the rich history of Indigenous sport in Canada. The literature on Indigenous sport is not only growing, it is also theoretically and conceptually robust, which makes it fertile ground for understanding the complex nature of sport in Canada, in both Indigenous and settler Canadian contexts. Nonetheless, there is much work left to be done. Indigenous sport history, as applied to Canada and beyond, is a vibrant and dynamic area and its scholars are well-positioned to rewrite narratives using Indigenous methodologies.[24] This requires sport historians to not only broaden their approaches and sources, but equally importantly, to listen to the needs, interests, and experiences of Indigenous people. Such approaches ensure that the history of Indigenous sport in Canada recognizes and respects, fully, that 'Indigenous notions of the past that connect people to places, events, peoples, and memories can help Indigenous people define their place in the created world and explain its shape, wonders, and human relations (like other kinds of history)'.[25]

Notes

1 Jean M. O'Brien, 'Historical Sources and Methods in Indigenous Studies: Touching on the Past, Looking to the Future', in *Sources and Methods in Indigenous Studies*, eds. Chris Andersen and Jean M. O'Brien (New York: Routledge, 2017), 15.

Indigenous sport history in Canada

2 O'Brien, 'Historical Sources and Methods in Indigenous Studies'.

3 O'Brien, 'Historical Sources and Methods in Indigenous Studies', 18.

4 Don Morrow, 'Canadian Sport History: A Critical Overview', *Journal of Sport History* 10, no. 1 (1983): 67–79.

5 To date, the most comprehensive collections on Indigenous sport history as it relates to Canada are Janice Forsyth and Audrey R. Giles eds. *Aboriginal Peoples and Sport in Canada: Historical Foundations and Contemporary Issues* (Vancouver: UBC Press, 2013) and Murray Phillips, Russell Field, Christine O'Bonsawin, and Janice Forsyth, *Journal of Sport History – Indigenous Resurgence, Regeneration, and Decolonization through Sport History* 46, no. 2 (2019).

6 Christine O'Bonsawin, 'Failed TEST: Aboriginal Sport Policy and the Olympian Firth Sisters', Master's thesis (University of Western Ontario, 2002); Janice Forsyth and Victoria Paraschak, 'The Double Helix: Aboriginal People and Sport Policy in Canada', in *Sport Policy in Canada*, eds. Lucy Thibault and Jean Harvey (Ottawa: University of Ottawa Press, 2013).

7 The Kitchen Table Methodology is an emerging Indigenous-centred research methodology that is considered to be a natural way of listening, talking, and learning from one another. As Cathy Mattes and Sherri Farrell Racette explain: 'The kitchen table is where some of the best learning occurs. When we gather with friends and family around food and tea, we relax into easy conversation, lending to safe space for dialogue and knowledge sharing.' See Cathy Richardson and Christina Löwenborg, 'Ellen-Maria Ekström and the Stories That Connect Us', *Genealogy* 3, no. 2 (2019): 6.

8 The term 'rerighted' is used by Maori scholar, Linda Tuhiwai Smith in *Decolonizing Methodologies: Research and Indigenous Peoples* (London: Zed Books Ltd., 1999), 28.

9 For example, see Ann Hall, *The Girl and the Game: A History of Women's Sport in Canada*, 2nd edition (Toronto: University of Toronto Press, 2016), xvi1–26ii-xx. Michael Heine, *Arctic Sports: A Training and Resource Manual* (Yellowknife, NWT: Arctic Sports Association and MACA (GNWT), 1998); and Michael Heine, *Dene Games: A Culture and Resource Manual, Traditional Aboriginal Sport Coaching Resources, Volume 1* (Yellowknife, NWT: Sport North Federation and MACA (GNWT), 1999).

10 Michael Heine, 'Performance Indicators: Aboriginal Games at the Arctic Winter Games', in *Aboriginal Peoples and Sport in Canada: Historical Foundations and Contemporary Issues*, eds. Janice Forsyth and Audrey Giles (Vancouver: UBC Press, 2013), 160–181.

11 Jeff Corntassel, Chaw-win-is, and T'lakwadzi, 'Indigenous Storytelling, Truth-Telling, and Community Approaches to Reconciliation', *English Studies Canada* 35, no. 1 (March 2009): 137–159; Paulette Regan, *Unsettling the Settler Within: Indian Residential Schools, Truth Telling, and Reconciliation in Canada* (Vancouver: University of British Columbia Press, 2011).

12 Recent monographs, which also document Indigenous responses to nation-building activities and discourses, include Janice Forsyth, *Reclaiming Tom Longboat: Indigenous Self-Determination in Canadian Sport* (Regina: University of Regina Press, 2020); Michael A. Robidoux, *Stickhandling through the Margins: First Nations Hockey in Canada* (Toronto: University of Toronto Press, 2012).

13 'History – Lacrosse: Canada's National Summer Sport', Canadian Lacrosse Association, accessed 26 November 2019, http://cla.pointstreaksites.com/view/cla/our-sport/history.

14 For examples, see Don Morrow, 'The Institutionalization of Sport: A Case Study of Lacrosse, 1844–1914', *The International Journal of the History of Sport* 9, no. 2 (1992): 236–251; Nancy Bouchier, 'Idealized Middle-Class Sport for a Young Nation: Lacrosse in Nineteenth-Century Ontario Towns, 1871–1891', *Journal of Canadian Studies* 29, no. 2 (Summer 994): 89–110; Donald M. Fisher, *Lacrosse: A History of the Game* (Baltimore: The Johns Hopkins University Press, 2002); Michael A. Robidoux, 'Imagining A Canadian Identity Through Sport: A Historical Interpretation of Lacrosse and Hockey', *Journal of American Folklore* 115, no. 456 (2002): 209–225; and Gillian Poulter, 'Snowshoeing and Lacrosse: Canada's Nineteenth Century National Games', *Culture, Sport, Society* 6, nos. 2–3 (2003): 293–320.

15 Heine, 'Performance Indicators', 164–165.

16 Janice Forsyth, 'Bodies of Meaning: Sports and Games at Canadian Residential Schools', in *Aboriginal Peoples and Sport in Canada: Historical Foundations and Contemporary Issues*, eds. Janice Forsyth and Audrey Giles (Vancouver: UBC Press, 2013), 15–34; Evan Habkirk and Janice Forsyth, 'Truth, Reconciliation, and the Politics of the Body in Indian Residential School History', *Active History* (January 2016), available, http://activehistory.ca/papers/truth-reconciliation-and-the-politics-of-the-body-in-indian-residential-school-history/; and Janice Forsyth, 'The Indian Act and the (Re)Shaping of Canadian Aboriginal Sport Practices', *International Journal of Canadian Studies* 35 (2007): 95–111.

17 Forsyth and Paraschak, 'The Double Helix'.

18 Robidoux, *Stickhandling through the Margins*, 3–4.
19 Richardson and Löwenborg, 'Ellen-Maria Ekström and the Stories That Connect Us'.
20 O'Bonsawin, 'Failed TEST'.
21 Allan Downey, *The Creator's Game: Lacrosse, Identity, and Indigenous Nationhood* (Vancouver: UBC Press, 2018).
22 Downey, *The Creator's Game*.
23 Downey, *The Creator's Game*, 213.
24 O'Brien, 'Historical Sources and Methods'.
25 O'Brien, 'Historical Sources and Methods', 21.

37

AMERICAN INDIAN SPORT HISTORY

Jennifer Guiliano and Beth Eby

More often than not, the history of sport in what became the United States of America begins in the colonial period of the eighteenth century with games of chance, horse-racing, cockfighting, and other leisurely pursuits.[1] These 'modern' sports were governed by organized rules and parameters including specialized roles, uniforms, publication of results, and record keeping, particularly for national competitions.[2] Swimming, cycling, and golf were modern as were the newer sports of baseball, basketball, and American football that would rise to public attention in the nineteenth and early twentieth century. What was not modern were Indigenous sporting histories that existed both well before contact and that would evolve through their incorporation with British, French, Spanish, and finally American sporting traditions. Dissolving the use of 'modern' and its associated focus on competitive sport as intrinsic to sporting history allows us to challenge dominant narratives that tie sporting culture to modernity, capitalism, consumption, regulation, and the colonial and imperial aims of Western Europe.[3] One of the continuing effects of this tie is the preferential status of competitive sports like baseball, basketball, and football that were forced upon Native students, athletes, and communities. Lesser known sports as well as those with fewer professional opportunities have been overshadowed by considerations of how Natives fit into 'the big three'. Instead, this chapter demonstrates that expressions of religious, cultural, and communal ways of knowing through sport allowed Indigenous peoples the space to articulate their own worldview.

Sports, be they games of wagering, chance, or physical activity, were enmeshed in Indigenous tradition, ritual, and ceremony. As early as 1636, Jesuit missionary Jean de Brébeuf noted that the games of cross [lacrosse], dish, and straw, were ordered by Wyandot-Huron tribal healers to assist sick individuals in regaining their health. Players participated in ceremonial cleansings led by tribal leaders who would consecrate the playing field, the equipment, and serve as arbitrators of any game disputes. Tribal leaders would also determine the rules and equipment uses for male and female players, which sometimes differed. For example, Cherokee women played the game with their hands, rather than sticks as did Shawnee women.[4] Variations of lacrosse abounded with men dominating play in some communities and women participating in others: the Onandaga played dehunshegawaes ('they hit a round object'); the Ojibwe played bagaa'atowe ('they hit something'); the Potawatomi played lacrosse as did Kasaskia Illinois peoples and also Plains Cree and

DOI: 10.4324/9780429318306-42

303

Nippising north of what would become the US national border.[5] Cayuga Haudenosaunee would play the 'Creator's Game' and tie its existence to the creation of Turtle Island and the founding of the nation by Sky Woman, Hadoui, and other pivotal spiritual ancestors.[6] Its importance remains as the Haudenosaunee-Iroquois are consistently ranked in the top five teams in the world in lacrosse. In 2022, they will compete in the World Games despite being denied a place in the tournament by officials who do not recognize the team as a sovereign nation.

Lacrosse games historically were hosted to honour the dead, encourage fertility, and as signs of faith to placate spirits. Betting with beaver robes, porcelain collars, and other goods, clans would compete against one another not only for victory but also to gain favour for their family and village.[7] Games could demonstrate friendship between communities visiting for council or they could be used to settle disputes. They also served as training for war and even a distraction. Winnebago players, for example, would share their successes in war before play to intimidate opponents.[8] In 1763, Ojibwe players invited British troops at Fort Michilimachinac [now Fort Mackinac] to watch a game of lacrosse. They used play to disguise warriors who rushed the gates and overwhelmed British troops, securing use of the fort as they fought against colonial invaders. Despite interest in the game of lacrosse and other Indigenous sports, Western colonizers often lamented that Indigenous peoples' play did not conform to Western value systems. The religious rituals associated with sport were perceived as forms of paganism. Women were not supposed to exert themselves in mixed-gender company. Gambling was certainly never to be allowed.

Lacrosse was not the only game that interested Natives. René Goulaine de Laudonnière recorded the Timucua playing a game where they lobbed a ball into a reed mat placed atop a tree in the 1560s. Mississippian Natives played chunkey, which involved rolling a disk or hoop across a playing field in the fifteenth and sixteenth centuries.[9] Native communities also played shinny, a ball and stick game with the main objective to get the ball in the opponent's goal. The size of the playing field and materials used to create the sticks and balls varied; some played the game on ice while others used level ground as a playing field. Players could hit, or even kick the ball, but could not use their hands in any way. Although not as elaborately religious as lacrosse, shinny still operated as an important community ritual. The Makah, for example, celebrated the successful capture of a whale that would feed and support community survival with a game of shinny.

Shinny crossed racial and gender divisions: soldiers in the American Revolution played shinny at camp; enslaved children on South Carolina plantations played shinny prior to the Civil War.[10] It could be played against other Native women, against Indigenous men, or both.[11] It displaces basketball or baseball which most sport historians credit as being the first organized women's sports in the United States; Native women enjoyed far greater access to athletic opportunities than their white counterparts who were constrained by Protestant gender norms. Unmarried women could play double-ball where two balls tied together with a string where thrown and caught upon a stick, scoring points against one's opponents. They could also compete in games like kicking the ball, which Crow woman Pretty Shield remembered playing with her female friends growing up.[12] Despite these opportunities for Indigenous women, the sports Indigenous women played have long been underexplored by scholars, particularly those prior to the twentieth century. In part, this is a function of contemporary archival practices that have preserved written and photographic evidence from boarding schools, colleges and universities, and progressive organizations. Much less attention has been payed to pre-twentieth-century sports that require navigating oral histories, physical artifacts, and other generational forms of knowledge transfer in Indigenous communities.

Along with these ball games, Native communities also organized around physical activities like running and horse-racing. Seneca Louis 'Deerfoot' Bennett would gain international recognition in the 1850s and 1860s as a competitive runner.[13] Pawnee Big Hawk Chief would, in 1876, run the world's first recorded (but unofficial) sub-four-minute mile at the Sidney Army Barracks in Nebraska. Narragansett Ellison Brown Sr. won the Boston Marathon in both 1936 and 1939, challenging detractors who had panned his withdrawal at the 1936 Berlin Olympics as a result of injury. Oglala Lakota Tamakoce Te'Hila [Billy Mills] would become the first Native to win the 10,000-metre run at the 1964 Tokyo Olympics drawing on the training he'd received at Haskell Institute and the University of Kansas. Running was a not just individual, it was also a matter of tribal identity. Historian Matthew Sakiestewa Gilbert eloquently documents the significance of running within the Hopi Nation, stating, 'since the beginning of Hopi time, Hopis have been in a constant state of movement to and away from home'.[14] For the Hopi, running was not just a sport that relied on fixed times and lengths of runs – it was and remains a significant cultural practice that underlines Hopi ways of knowing and being. Running in this manner often confounded white sportsmen who viewed the sport of running as requiring a finish line and a clear, sole winner. This ideology was on full display during the 1904 Anthropology Days in St. Louis, Missouri where white anthropologists devised a number of athletic competitions for Indigenous peoples participating in the World's Fair. When, during a footrace, the athletes waited to cross the finish line together, director of Physical Culture James Sullivan attributed this practice to a sign of mental weakness rather than recognizing an alternative conception of running.[15] Natives, particularly those who lived within the US Plains and the Southwest, turned to running and horse-racing as both a sport and as a means of survival. Shoshone, Bannock, Crow, Ute, Diné, and other Native peoples acquired horses from Spanish colonizers reinvigorating the horse-trading network that had arisen prior to the eighteenth century in the lands that would become Mexico.[16] Pi-Kániwa (Piegan Blackfoot), Gros Venture, and Apache participated in horse races between tribal communities, including those hostile to one another. Spiritual ceremony including protective medicines would be utilized to enhance both the horse's performance and that of its rider as well as to guard against those who might wish the horse or rider harm. Warfare was also tied to horse-racing as men, including race attendees, would boast of their prowess at war before and during races. Racehorses themselves were also valuable commodities that were carefully protected. Acquiring a racehorse through raiding was considered an impressive feat. Despite the suppression of horse-racing and its associated betting by colonizers, its importance to Native communities remained consistent historically. It was incorporated into Independence Day festivals, Native fairs, and other communal events like rodeo.[17] Today's Indian Relay competitions serve as a modern manifestation of this historical ritual.[18] Competitors often connect their own sporting experience to those of tribal or familiar Elders. This acts as an expression of both cultural continuity and Indigenous agency. Participating is a way to honour one's history and one's community.

When the Office of Indian Affairs (later known as the Bureau of Indian Affairs) started constructing off-reservation Native American boarding schools in the latter half of the nineteenth century, sports emerged as curricular focal point. US administrators were guided by Progressives who believed sports could assist with assimilation activities within Native communities.[19] The athletic culture created and fostered at Native boarding schools permeated the boundaries of the schools. It provided a literal training ground for Native athletes who would find success in professional sports of running, boxing, baseball, and football.[20] Sport offered the opportunity for athletes to support themselves and their communities. It provided community where colonialism impinged on Native life.[21] It also, dependent on the sport, was met with Native students' own belief systems about which sports were appropriate based on gender. Tennis, for example, was not embraced by male students at the Cherokee Seminary as they felt it a 'sissy' sport that violated their own sense of gender roles.[22]

Football, arguably the most well-known sport that Natives participated in, began at the Carlisle Indian Industrial School in 1893. It was not until Superintendent Richard Henry Pratt hired famous football coach Glenn 'Pop' Warner in 1899 that football would become synonymous with Carlisle. Seneca Bemus Pierce (1894–1898), Laguna Pueblan Frank Hudson (1895–1899; first all-American and one of the first non-white coaches in college football), Oneida Martin Wheelock (1894–1902), and Stockbridge-Munsee Jimmy Johnson (1899–1903) each contributed to the Carlisle teams along with Albert Exendine (Delaware) and Gus Welch (Chippewa). Sac and Fox athlete Jim Thorpe would letter in track and field, football, baseball, and lacrosse. A two-time all-American, Olympic gold medallist, professional football hall of fame inductee, and professional baseball player, Thorpe was voted greatest athlete of the first half of the twentieth century by sportswriters and broadcasters. Often dubbed the 'Carlisle of the West', Haskell Institute, one of the nation's largest Native American boarding schools located in Lawrence, Kansas, was also renowned for its football programme. The game generated inter-tribal relations and solidarity amongst athletes and their Native fans. While school officials and administrators within the Bureau of Indian Affairs used sport as a tool for assimilation and US citizenship training, Native athletes engaged in sport to escape the harsh realities of the boarding school setting.[23] Boarding school sport histories are a particularly rich vein of Indigenous sporting history. Boarding school archives offer significant archival collections around sport including Native letters, diaries, and publications where Native athletes expressed their own ways of understanding sport. Importantly, though, like all archival holdings tied to the settler-colonial state, we must understand the complexity of those records. While students might express joy at the sporting opportunities, it was also a form of coercive activity that inserted non-Indigenous values and ways of play into Native worldviews.

Carlisle and Haskell were not the only boarding schools that encouraged sport as a means of 'civilizing' Native students. Hopi students who attended Sherman Institute in Riverside, California participated in track and cross country.[24] Hopi runner Louis Tewanima would participate in both the 1908 and 1912 Olympics, garnering silver in the 1912 10,000-metre event. Women at the Fort Shaw Indian School competed in, and won, the women's basketball tournament at the 1904 St. Louis World's Fair. Basketball, which could be played indoors during the winter, had been introduced to the Montana school after student Josephine Langley visited Carlisle. Just a little over a decade old, their exhibition games at the Fair not only generated significant public interest, it also allowed the women to demonstrate their physical abilities. They played full court, 20-minute halves, with no timeouts – rules that were used by their male counterparts unlike the modified game played by white women.[25] Like the women's team at Fort Shaw, Haskell women basketballers competed against local colleges, high schools, and Young Women's Christian Association teams, affording the students the chance to travel to and from school grounds (a privilege often afforded few students). References to women's basketball appear with relative frequency within Native newspapers. Students often wrote home to family members about their passion for the new sport. Sports at Native boarding schools served anticolonial purposes by allowing them a measure of community and autonomy that they would not have had otherwise. Sport allowed them to travel locally, regionally, and in some cases nationally. It also allowed them time set aside from the strict authoritarian rules of Superintendents and other white administrators. Yet, these moments of joy were tempered by the reality that many Natives had been torn from their families and communities and forced into a coercive system of education that was dehumanizing.

The opportunities of Native sport were further mitigated by the rampant discrimination athletes faced.[26] Racial sensationalism from sportswriters captured the football and baseball games as battles between Indian 'savages' seeking revenge against civilized whites. Fans lamented that the athletes looked too much like their own [white] boys with their short hair, trousers, and lack of face paint or war bonnets. They were also held to standards of sportsmanship and decorum on the field and off that were not shared by their white counterparts. Native players were treated as objects of curiosity that reinforced stereotypes of Indian peoples. Penobscot Louis Sockalexis would debut for Major League Baseball's Cleveland Spiders in October 1871 after attending the College of the Holy Cross and Notre Dame University. Six years later, *Sporting Life* recorded that Sockalexis' taking the field was greeted with 'war whoops, yells of derision … and demonstrations border[ing] on extreme rudeness'.[27] These taunts echoed those heard by minor league Native player Sioux Henry Legg whose manager invented a mock-Sioux name for him in the Central State league, 'Rats-in-the-Garrett'.[28] This racism would contribute to twentieth-century mascot movements that depicted racist stereotypes of Indians.[29] Beginning in the late 1920s, colleges, universities, and professional teams would develop Indian-themed athletic brands that drew on colonial tropes of conquest and subjugation. Using headdresses, breech clothes, feathered capes, and other supposedly Native imagery, white institutions would reenact stereotypes of Indians. This would include war whoops, quasi-fancy dancing, and the adoption of music that composers believed best represented Indian life. Drawing vaudeville performances as well as fictional narratives of American conquest, Native mascots served as a primary site of how sporting fans learned about Indians. Importantly, this was supported by cultural organizations including the Boy Scouts of America, the Young Men's Christian Association, and other social groups who inculcated young white men and women with stories of success through American conquest. Importantly, beginning in 1971, Native students and activists would begin an almost six-decade long battle to prohibit the use of these by college and professional teams.

Seneca Jacob Jimeson would lead more than a dozen other Carlisle baseball players into the Major league including Chippewa-Ojibwe pitcher Charles Bender, Thorpe, Stockbridge-Munsee Louis Leroy, Cheyenne Michael Balenti, Ojibwe Frank Jude and Charles Roy, and Ho-Chunk Winnebago George H. Johnson.[30] Still more boarding school baseball players from Haskell Institute, Chilocco Indian School, Flandreau, Sante Fe, and others would actively participate in major, minor league, and collegiate baseball. The lure of baseball, with its regular income as well as the opportunities for education and career, encouraged the participation of Native athletes. Charles Bender, for example, would coach the Chicago White Sox (1925–1926), the US Naval Academy (1924–1928), and the Philadelphia Athletics where he scouted and managed their minor league team. Charles Mayo Guzon, graduate of Carlisle, would use his baseball experience as a minor league player to serve as the first Native umpire before joining the A.G. Spaulding Company as a regional director for sales. Like lacrosse and other ball games, baseball would serve individual and communal purposes. The Wabanaki, for example, hosted their own tribal league play from the 1890s through the 1940s. It served as a means of generational transmission with MicMac language rules, musical performances, and gender roles as fathers trained their sons to play.[31] While baseball and football began as white men's games, Native communities adapted the culture of sport to support their own cultural and social survival.[32]

307

The dominance of boarding schools and the associated sports of baseball and football have overshadowed other sporting histories in the early to mid-twentieth century. While Native men adapted baseball and football, Native women developed their own sporting experiences that were tied to their own sense of community identity. Navajo women embraced basketball in the early 1920s well before Church of Latter-Day Saints (Mormon) missionaries brought the game to the reservation in the 1940s. Lillian Nelson would play the game with her friends at both the Shiprock and the Riverside boarding schools. Her daughter Georgia would play for the Shiprock Cardinals, a team that would collect over a thousand trophies in state, regional, and national tournaments from the 1960s to the 1980s.[33] Reservation basketball would take on a decidedly different tone from that of games played under the control of boarding school and missionary officials.[34] Clandestine games were an opportunity to shed the rules of play enforced on Native students. 'Rez ball', a style of basketball noted for its up-tempo style of play where every player is treated as a shooting threat, likely draws its origins from unsupervised games held by students at boarding schools. Shoni Shimmel (Umatilla), Tahnee Robinson (Northern Cheyanne), and Angel Goodrich (Cherokee) would participate in Rez ball prior to their careers in collegiate and professional women's basketball. They followed in the footsteps of Ryneldi Becenti (Navajo), who was the first Native American athlete to play in the Women's Basketball Association. Rez ball games are accompanied by communal meals, spiritual rituals, and large-scale crowds that resonate with tribal identity.[35] Importantly, it is not only youth play where basketball has flourished on reservations; many hosted adult leagues where tribal Elders could compete.

Native communities off the mainland participated in their own sporting experiences. Kanaka Maoli Duke Paoa Kahanamoku popularized the Hawaiian sport of He'e nalu (surfing). He'e nalu was an expression of the kapu system of political and religious structures that organized Indigenous life. Commoners could not surf with tribal chiefs, certain surf breaks were reserved for royalty, and boards themselves were equated to one's political and social status.[36] Ranking chiefs would compete against one another, demonstrating their knowledge of ocean currents as well as their physical skills. Like Indigenous ball games, which missionaries and colonizers feared would lead to gambling and laziness, surfing was also perceived by missionaries in the 1820s as potentially corruptive. Despite its prohibition, surfing, along with canoeing and hula, remained a vital part of Kanaka Maoli culture as it not only served as a form of resistance to white colonizers but also became a way for Native Hawaiians to build industries around tourists who would journey to Hawaii after its annexation. Similarly, Inuit, Iñuiat, Yupik, and other Alaska natives would develop their own sporting culture around circumpolar life. Stick pull games simulated common activities in daily life including grabbing a slippery salmon from rushing water (the Indian Stick Pull) and pulling seals from holes in ice (the Eskimo Stick Pull).[37] Other games mimicked skills competitors would need to hunt seals or carry animals across long distances as a result of successful hunts, and contests of balance represented practice needed when moving over ice floes. Dog mushing, cross country and downhill skiing, as well as curling, ice hockey (known as ricket prior to the eighteenth century), and other sports appropriate for ice play also encouraged Native athleticism. Natives also adopted games from the lower 48 including baseball and basketball. These sports tied into, and continue to profit from, tourism efforts.

Indigenous religious, political, and communal practices are enmeshed within sport and as such this reveals a richer and more progressive history than its white US counterpart. Native communities were deeply invested in sport as uniquely Indigenous. Even when adopting sports developed by white colonizers, Indigenous communities adapted games to incorporate their own value systems. Dependent on tribe, this could include using one's Native language

American Indian sport history

to organize play, participating in religious or spiritual ceremonies, or incorporating communal knowledge, Native dress, and performance into events surrounding game play. This disruption altered the meaning of sport by co-opting it to fit Indigenous culture and community. That disruption has manifested in a continuing tension between sports as familial, communal, and sacred, and sports as a way for Native athletes to achieve notoriety and opportunity outside of their tribal communities.[38] Contemporary Native athletes who compete professionally often speak of their relationship to sport as generational knowledge transfer. Others, like Madison Hammond (Navajo, San Felipe), note that their success as a professional athlete provides an opportunity for tribal youth to see others with similar backgrounds and experiences succeed.

Centring Indigenous experiences in sport requires the recognition that Native voices and interpretations are silenced in many archival spaces. Archives within the settler-state purview either wholesale fail to incorporate Native experiences and voices or reproduce archival silences by neglecting to challenge dominant discourses around Indigenous sports and athletes.[39] Decolonial approaches might include incorporating Native forms of knowledge, questioning archival practices and approaches to preserving Native sporting pasts, expanding studies of the relationship between sport and settler-colonialism, and exploring Indigenous resistance and activism. Such an approach should also include contemporary engagement with Native communities and foreground their efforts in furthering Native sporting traditions. Native sport offers the opportunity to consider a variety of structural obligations between Indigenous communities and settler-colonial governments, be they treaty-based, legal, or cultural.[40] There is ample space for scholars to reinterpret colonial records by incorporating Native knowledge and interpretations. This, though, requires recognition that Native ways of knowing may challenge dominant sporting discourses of sports as pleasurable, civilizing, and capitalist. As sport history currently stands, this chapter represents an overview of how sport histories have been expressed in relationship to Indigenous peoples. However, what it also illustrates is a shortcoming within sport history where there is little existing scholarship on the inverse: how is sport transformed by its relationship to Indigeneity? A decolonial approach to US Indigenous sport history might encourage the partnership of sport historians with Indigenous communities to tell their sporting histories. It also might expand its efforts to recruit Indigenous scholars to join the field.

Notes

1 Elliott J. Gorn, *The Manly Art: Bare-Knuckle Prize Fighting in America* (Cornell University Press, 2012); Randy J. Sparks, 'Gentleman's Sport: Horse Racing in Antebellum Charleston', *The South Carolina Historical Magazine* 93, no. 1 (1992): 15–30; Steven Riess, 'The Cyclical History of Horse Racing: The USA's Oldest and (Sometimes) Most Popular Spectator Sport', *The International Journal of the History of Sport* 31, nos. 1–2 (2014): 29–54.

2 Melvin L. Adelman provides a chart to distinguish between 'pre-modern' and 'modern' sport. See Melvin L. Adelman, 'Modernization and the Rise of American Sport', in *Major Problems in American Sport History: Documents and Essays*, ed. Steven A. Riess (Boston: Houghton Mifflin, 1997), 5–6.

3 Malcolm MacLean, 'Engaging (with) Indigeneity: Decolonization and Indigenous/Indigenizing Sport History', *Journal of Sport History* 46, no. 2 (2019): 189–207, doi:10.5406/jsporthistory.46.2.0189. For an example of a comprehensive list and description of Indigenous games see: Stewart Culin, *Games of the North American Indians*, volume 2, Twenty-fourth Annual Report of the Bureau of American Ethnology (Lincoln: University of Nebraska Press, 1992).

4 Vennum, *American Indian Lacrosse*, 185.

5 Thomas Vennum, *Lacrosse Legends of the First Americans*, Illustrated Edition (Baltimore: Johns Hopkins University Press, 2007). See also Kenneth Cohen, 'A Mutually Comprehensible World? Native

Americans, Europeans, and Play in Eighteenth-Century America', *American Indian Quarterly* 26, no. 1 (2002): 67–93.

6 Allan Downey, *The Creator's Game: Lacrosse, Identity, and Indigenous Nationhood*, Reprint Edition (Vancouver: University of British Columbia Press, 2018).

7 Joseph B. Oxendine, *American Indian Sports Heritage* (Lincoln, NE: University of Nebraska Press, 1995); Vennum, *American Indian Lacrosse*.

8 Oxendine, *American Indian Sports Heritage*; Vennum, *American Indian Lacrosse*.

9 Anthony Michael Krus, 'Bridging History and Prehistory: The Possible Antiquity of a Native American Ballgame', *Native South* 4 (2011): 136–45, doi:10.1353/nso.2011.0004.

10 Bonnie S. Ledbetter, 'Sports and Games of the American Revolution', *Journal of Sport History* 6, no. 3 (1979): 29–40; David K. Wiggins, 'The Play of Slave Children in the Plantation Communities of the Old South, 1820–1860', *Journal of Sport History* 7, no. 2 (1980): 21–39.

11 Stewart Culin, *Games of the North American Indians*, Volume 2, *Games, of Skill*, Twenty-fourth Annual Report of the Bureau of American Ethnology (Lincoln: University of Nebraska Press, 1992), 449–450.

12 Frank B. Linderman, *Pretty-Shield: Medicine Woman of the Crows* (Lincoln: University of Nebraska Press, 1972), 61.

13 Oxendine, *American Indian Sports Heritage*.

14 Matthew Sakiestewa Gilbert, *Hopi Runners: Crossing the Terrain Between Indian and American* (Lawrence: University of Kansas Press, 2018), 5.

15 Nancy J. Parezo, 'A "Special Olympics": Testing Racial Strength and Endurance at the 1904 Louisiana Purchase Exposition', in *The 1904 Anthropology Days and Olympic Games: Sport, Race, and American Imperialism*, ed. Susan Brownell (Lincoln: University of Nebraska Press, 2008), 92. Brownell's edited collection on the 1904 Anthropology Days offers an extensive look at how pseudo-scientists and cultural anthropologists sought to define and categorize Indigenous strength and physicality.

16 Peter Mitchell, '"A Horse-Race Is the Same All the World Over": The Cultural Context of Horse Racing in Native North America', *The International Journal of the History of Sport* 37, nos. 3–4 (2020): 337–356, doi:10.1080/09523367.2020.1758672.

17 Ben Chavis, 'All-Indian Rodeo: A Transformation of Western Apache Tribal Warfare and Culture', *Wicazo Sa Review* 9, no. 1 (1993): 4–11, doi:10.2307/1409249.

18 Chavis, 'All-Indian Rodeo'.

19 John Bloom, *To Show What An Indian Can Do: Sports at Native American Boarding Schools* (Minneapolis: University of Minnesota Press, 2005).

20 Philip J. Deloria, *Indians in Unexpected Places* (Lawrence: University of Kansas Press, 2004), 128.

21 Beth Eby, 'Building Bodies, (Un)Making Empire: Gender, Sport, and Colonialism in the United States, 1880–1930', (PhD, University of Illinois at Urbana-Champaign, 2019), http://hdl.handle.net/2142/105606.

22 Devon Mihesuah, 'Out of the "Graves of the Polluted Debauches": The Boys of the Cherokee Male Seminary', *American Indian Quarterly* 15, no. 4 (1991): 512, doi:10.2307/1185367.

23 For examples of boarding school histories see: David Wallace Adams, *Education for Extinction: American Indians and the Boarding School Experience, 1875–1928* (Lawrence: University of Kansas Press, 1995); Brenda Child, *Boarding School Seasons: American Indian Families, 1900–1940* (Lincoln: University of Nebraska Press, 2000); Matthew Sakiestewa Gilbert, *Education Beyond the Mesas: Hopi Students at Sherman Institute, 1902–1929* (Lincoln: University of Nebraska Press, 2010); K. Tsianina Lomawaima, *They Called It Prairie Light: The Story of Chilocco Indian School* (Lincoln: University of Nebraska Press, 1994); Myriam Vučković, *Voices from Haskell: Indian Students Between Two Worlds, 1884–1928* (Lawrence: University of Kansas Press, 2008).

24 David Wallace Adams, 'More Than a Game: The Carlisle Indians Take to the Gridiron, 1893–1917', *Western Historical Quarterly* 32, no. 1 (2001): 25–53; Matthew Sakiestewa Gilbert, *Hopi Runners: Crossing Between Indian and American*; 'Hopi Footraces and American Marathons,' *American Quarterly* 62, no. 1 (2010): 77–101; 'Marathoner Louis Tewanima and the Continuity of Hopi Running, 1908–1912', *Western Historical Quarterly* 43, no. 3 (Autumn 2012): 325–346; Linda Peavy and Ursula Smith, *Full-Court Quest: The Girls from Fort Shaw Indian School, Basketball Champions of the World* (Norman, OK: University of Oklahoma Press, 2014), Benjamin Rader, '"The Greatest Drama in Indian Life": Experiments in Native American Identity and Resistance at the Haskell Institute Homecoming of 1926', *Western Historical Quarterly* 35, no. 4 (Winter 2004): 429–450; Raymond Schmidt, 'Lords of the Prairie: Haskell Indian School Football, 1919–1930', *Journal of Sport History*

28, no. 3 (Fall 2001): 403–426; Keith Sculle, '"The New Carlisle of the West": Haskell Institute and Big-Time Sports, 1920–1932', *Kansas History* 17, no. 3 (Autumn 1994): 192–208; Kim Warren, 'All Indian Trails Lead to Lawrence, October 27–30, 1926', *Kansas History: A Journal of the Central Plains* 30 (Spring 2007): 2–19.

25 Mark Dyreson, 'The 'Physical Value' of Races and Nations: Anthropology and Athletics at the Louisiana Purchase Exposition', in *The 1904 Anthropology Days and Olympic Games: Sport, Race, and American Imperialism*, ed. Susan Brownell (University of Nebraska Press, 2008), 127–155.

26 Michael Oriard, *Reading Football: How the Popular Press Created an American Spectacle*, Cultural Studies of the United States (Chapel Hill: University of North Carolina Press, 1993).

27 Jeffrey P. Powers-Beck, *The American Indian Integration of Baseball* (Lincoln, NE: University of Nebraska Press, 2004).

28 Powers-Beck, *The American Indian Integration of Baseball*.

29 Jennifer Guiliano, *Indian Spectacle: College Mascots and the Anxiety of Modern America*, Critical Issues in Sport and Society (New Brunswick, NJ; London: Rutgers University Press, 2015).

30 Powers-Beck, *The American Indian Integration of Baseball*.

31 Powers-Beck, *The American Indian Integration of Baseball*.

32 Another example of Native cooption of colonial sport contemporarily is Douglas Miles and his Apache Skateboards Company. For more on Miles and Native relationships to Skateboarding, see David Martínez, 'From Off the Rez to Off the Hook!: Douglas Miles and Apache Skateboards', *American Indian Quarterly* 37, no. 4 (Fall 2013): 370–394.

33 Ann M. Cummins, Cecilia Anderson, and Georgia Briggs, 'Women's Basketball on the Navajo Nation: The Shiprock Cardinals, 1960–1980', in *Native Athletes in Sport and Society: A Reader*, C. Richard King (University of Nebraska Press, 2005), 143–169.

34 Wade Davies, 'How Boarding School Basketball Became Indian Basketball', *American Indians and Popular Culture: Media, Sports, and Politics* 1 (2012): 263–278.

35 *Basketball or Nothing*, 2019, https://www.netflix.com/title/80245353.

36 Jérémy Lemarié, 'Debating on Cultural Performances of Hawaiian Surfing in the 19th Century', *Journal de La Société Des Océanistes*, nos. 142–143 (2016): 159–174.

37 'Competitive Events | Cook Inlet Tribal Council' (accessed 24 September 2020), https://citci.org/partnerships-events/nyo-games/competitive-events/.

38 Natalie Michelle Welch, 'Completing the Circle: Native American Athletes Giving Back to Their Community' (PhD, University of Tennessee, 2019), https://trace.tennessee.edu/utk_graddiss/5342/.

39 Murray G. Phillips et al., 'Indigenous Resurgence, Regeneration, and Decolonization through Sport History', *Journal of Sport History* 46, no. 2 (2019): 143–156.

40 Victoria Paraschak, '#87: Reconciliation, Sport History, and Indigenous Peoples in Canada', *Journal of Sport History* 46, no. 2 (2019): 208–223.

312

PART 5

Sport history journals

314

38

SPORT HISTORY JOURNALS

Introduction

Murray G. Phillips, Douglas Booth and Carly Adams

[A]cademic history is defined primarily, then, in terms of the heavyweight, textual monograph ... journal articles are highly regarded, especially if published in professionally approved (and) epistemologically sound journals. Finally, conference papers published in 'influential journals' or part of book collections are also, generally, 'safe and sound' professionally.[1]

As Munslow describes, there are disciplinary approved practices that make historical scholarship different from other academic pursuits in the arts, humanities, social sciences, and sciences. Munslow implies that there is a hierarchy of scholarly achievements in the historical discipline with single-authored monographs recognized as the gold standard followed by journal articles, chapters, and edited books. In many ways, the subdiscipline of sport history has followed this articulation. Single-authored monographs published by elite university presses are crucial to scholarly careers. Less merit is achieved through other professionally approved outlets. This hierarchy of esteem is exemplified in the award system created by sport history societies. The first awards for scholarship were exclusively for books. This formally acknowledged the prime place of monographs in sport history scholarship, ahead of edited books, journal articles, and presentations. The North American Society for Sport History (NASSH) instituted its Book Award in 1989, Edited Book Award (Anthology) in 2007, and Journal Article Award in 2015.[2] The British Society for Sport History (BSSH) Book Award stretches back to at least 1994 while the Journal Article Award began in 2007.[3] The Australian Society for Sport History (ASSH) created its Book Award in 2007, and Edited Book Award in 2013, but there are no awards for journal articles.[4]

Notwithstanding the status of scholarly monographs in sport history as the most esteemed outputs, we argue that journals have played a crucial role establishing, defining, and strengthening the emergence and ongoing existence of the subdiscipline. Journal articles represent the breadth and depth of scholarship as well as the international dimensions of the subdiscipline as they are produced in multiple languages and across several continents, often exceeding the reach of most single-language monographs. Journals are a critical forum of scholarly discourse, particularly in the digital age with online, pre-publication access that accelerates distribution and circulation. The relatively quick publication process for journal articles has helped junior untenured scholars and emerging scholars gain tenure or secure

DOI: 10.4324/9780429318306-44

Table 38.1 Sport history journals[5]

Journal	Year initiated	Country	Status	Language/s
Canadian Journal of the History of Sport and Physical Education; renamed *Canadian Journal of History of Sport/Revue canadienne de l'histoire des sports* (1981); renamed *Sport History Review* (1996)	1970–1996 1996	Canada United States	Ongoing	English and French
Journal of Sport History	1974	United States	Ongoing	English
STADION: Journal of the History of Sport and Physical Education; renamed STADION: International Journal of the History of Sport (1984)	1975–2016; 2019	Germany	Ongoing	German, English, French
The Sports Historian; renamed *Sport in History* (2003)	1984	United Kingdom	Ongoing	English
British Journal of Sports History; renamed the *International Journal of the History of Sport* (1987)	1984	United Kingdom	Ongoing	English
Sporting Traditions: The Journal of the Australian Society for Sports History	1984	Australia	Ongoing	English
The Japan Journal of Sport History	1988	Japan	Ongoing	Japanese, English
Nikephoros: Journal for Sports and Culture in Antiquity	1988	Germany	Ceased 2014	English, German, French, Italian, Modern Greek
Iron Game History: The Journal of Physical Culture	1990	United States	Ongoing	English
NINE: A Journal of Baseball History and Culture	1992	United States	Ongoing	English
Olympika: The International Journal of Olympic Studies	1992	Canada	Ongoing	English
Citius, Altius, Fortius; renamed *Journal of Olympic History* (1996)	1992	Europe	Ongoing	English
Ludica: Annali di storia e civiltà del gioco [LUDICA. Annals of History and Civilization of the Game]	1995	Italy	Ongoing	Language of author, plus three language translation
European Sports History Review	1999	United Kingdom	Ceased 2003	English
Annual of the European Committee for Sport History; renamed *European Studies in Sports History* (2008)	2000	France	Ongoing	All European languages
Materiales para la Historia del Deporte	2002	Spain	Ongoing	English, Spanish, and Portuguese
Recorde: Revista de História do Esporte [Recorde: Journal of Sport History]	2008	Brazil	Ongoing	Portuguese, Spanish, English, and French
Journal of Olympic Studies	2020	United States	Ongoing	English
Asian Journal of Sport History & Culture	2020	United Kingdom	Ongoing	English

positions, particularly in departments, such as kinesiology and sport management, which do not prioritize single-authored monographs. Equally importantly, journals provide an opportunity for contributing professional service duties, such as editing and reviewing, that can allow scholars to earn peer recognition and esteem. Indeed, we argue that the health and vibrancy of sport history is founded on speciality journals.

This is a persuasive argument that runs through the chapters on individual sport history journals in this Part of the *Handbook*. Beyond this central narrative, the chapters coalesce around several key themes: publishing practices; the gendered workforce; the developmental trajectory of sport history journals; and the scope, language, and assessment of sport history journals.

Publishing practices

As indicated in Table 38.1, the first dedicated sport history journal was the *Canadian Journal of the History of Sport and Physical Education* established in 1970 under the auspices of the Canadian Association for Health, Physical Education, and Recreation. This journal, established by Alan Metcalfe from the University of Windsor, was the leading-edge of publishing opportunities for sport historians. Nevertheless, the production of the *Canadian Journal of the History of Sport and Physical Education* was primitive by contemporary standards. As M. Ann Hall (Chapter 40) and Rob Hess (Chapter 45) describe in their chapters, sport history journals in their early years were artisanal in nature, 'do it yourself projects' in many ways, that were heavily reliant on an individual or a small group working in tandem with sympathetic university departments willing to share their resources and the costs of publication and dissemination.

Prior to the establishment of the *Canadian Journal of the History of Sport and Physical Education*, historians interested in the emerging subdiscipline of sport history were limited to publishing in mainstream history journals, generic physical education journals, and multidisciplinary kinesiology journals. The early work of now-noted names in sport history were published in journals that ranged from *Past & Present*, *The Journal of American History*, *The Physical Educator*, *Journal of Physical Education*, *Quest*, *Journal of Health, Physical Education, Recreation*, and *Research Quarterly*. The *Canadian Journal of the History of Sport and Physical Education* heralded the emergence of the new subdiscipline of sport history.

The *Canadian Journal of the History of Sport and Physical Education* was ultimately joined by a number of journals aligned to national associations established to foster sport history. The *Journal of Sport History* was launched in 1974 two years after the formation of NASSH, and the *Sports Historian* and the *British Journal of Sports History* were created in 1984 five years after BSSH was established. *Sporting Traditions: The Journal of the Australian Society for Sports History* published its first issue in 1984, a year after the formation of ASSH. In Chapter 45, Rob Hess explains the influence of NASSH and BSSH: 'in terms of the formation of societies and the publication of scholarly journals, there were models for ASSH to follow during the "take-off" period for the academic study of sport'. Even though *STADION: Journal of the History of Sport and Physical Education*, founded in 1975, was never officially affiliated to the International Association for the History of Physical Education and Sport (1973), as Manfred Lämmer and Markwart Herzog detail in Chapter 42, 'the journal was in fact a publication organ of this association'. Adding to this list of association journals is *The Japan Journal of Sport History* published by the Japan Society of Sport History, the *Journal of Olympic History* created by the International Society of Olympic Historians, *Materiales para la Historia del Deporte*, which is associated with the Andalusian Association of the History of

Sport, and *European Studies in Sports History*, which is an outlet of the European Committee for Sports History.

These journals are either published 'in-house' with no commercial company involvement, or by university presses and commercial publishers. In the last two decades, several journals have shifted to university presses and commercial publishers. As Andrew Linden and Alison Wrynn detail in Chapter 41, the *Journal of Sport History* was published in-house for 41 volumes before signing with the University of Illinois Press in 2015. Association journals benefit from the support of their aligned organizations, and a guaranteed subscription base and readership, both of which provide a level of security for their continuation.

There are, however, just as many journals that are not aligned with sport history associations. The remaining organizations and publishing outlets are quite diverse. *The International Journal of the History of Sport*, the *Asian Journal of Sport History & Culture*, and *Sport History Review*, for example, have contracts with commercial publishers.[6] The former two journals are with the large global company Taylor and Francis, while the latter is published by the US-based, kinesiology-focused company, Human Kinetics. University presses including the University of Nebraska Press and the University of Illinois Press publish *NINE: A Journal of Baseball History and Culture* and the *Journal of Olympic Studies* respectively. Other journals such as *Iron Game History: The Journal of Physical Culture*, *Olympika: The International Journal of Olympic Studies*, *Ludica: Annali di storia e civiltà del gioco*, and *Recorde: Revista de História do Esporte* are generated and published by research centres, foundations, and institutional organizations with no involvement from commercial companies.

The diversity in the management, vision, and publishing strategies of sport history journals, alluded to above, is epitomized by two of the older journals that originally emerged from BSSH and are currently published by Taylor and Francis: *Sport in History* and *The International Journal of the History of Sport*. The former is an association journal, while the latter is a commercial venture. *Sport in History*, like other society-based journals, services the membership with the latest scholarship and information, as well as promoting the sub-discipline where and when appropriate. Dave Day and Kay Schiller, in Chapter 43, capture this aspect of the journal. *Sport in History*, they contend, 'has always remained first and foremost a members' journal and the BSSH, working with its journal editor, will continue to use its pages to work towards an ever greater acceptance of sports history by the mainstream historical profession'. In contrast, *The International Journal of the History of Sport*, as Wray Vamplew argues in Chapter 44, was from its early days 'a commercial operation not a society journal'. Given this rationale, *The International Journal of the History of Sport* produces an incredible 18 issues a year (while *Sport in History* produces four) and dominates the quantity of journal articles from sport history outlets.[7]

Notwithstanding the complexity of the management, vision, and publishing strategies in sport history, the journals from the 1970s have provided dedicated outlets for aspiring sport history scholars in Asia, Australia, Brazil, the United Kingdom, Canada, Germany, Italy, Japan, Aotearoa/New Zealand, Spain, and the United States. As a result, these journals have played a critical role in announcing, establishing, defining and building a subdiscipline of sport history.

The gendered workforce

When the early sport history journals were established from the 1970s, the gender imbalance of both editorial staffs and editorial boards was stark. In the first editions of *Canadian Journal of the History of Sport and Physical Education*, *Journal of Sport History*, *The Sports Historian*,

STADION, British Journal of Sports History, and *Sporting Traditions*, there were 58 men involved in their publication (over 90 per cent) as opposed to five scholars who identified as women (less than 10 per cent).

The gender breakdown in sport history journals almost 50 years later in 2020 reveals three notable changes. First, the number of gatekeepers has expanded considerably from 63 to 414, indicating the growth of sport history journals and the associated intellectual workforce needed to maintain these journals. Second, the number and proportion of editors and editorial board members who identify as women has also increased. There are currently 35 women as editors and 91 as editorial board members. The proportion of women editors and editorial board members has also increased from 10 per cent to 30 per cent. Third, there are women who are currently managing or lead editors of five journals: *Sport History Review, Journal of Sport History, Olympika, Materiales*, and the *Asian Journal of Sport History & Culture*. There have been no female managing or lead editors in *Sport in History, The International Journal of the History of Sport*, or *Sporting Traditions*, although women have served as associate, regional, and academic editors.

In terms of women-identified authorship, data is a challenge to compile. But as Teresa González-Aja and Rodrigo Pardo report in Chapter 46 on *Materiales*, over 65 per cent of all contributors identify as men. Similarly, Andrew Linden and Alison Wrynn (Chapter 41) note that men appeared as authors in roughly 75 per cent of articles in the *Journal of Sport History*. They conclude: 'this is not surprising as history departments remain primarily male and sport continues to be a male-dominated purview'. This suggests that although the opportunities for women have expanded over the last half century, there is some way to go to achieve parity. Until then, it is hard to argue against M. Ann Hall's position in Chapter 40 that 'sport history generally is a male-dominated field'.[8]

The developmental trajectory of sport history journals

While gender inequity is an ongoing issue, sport history journals have faced additional challenges as they adapted to the changing conditions: problems with in-house publishing; incompetent or overzealous editors; battles between prominent identities; professional tussles between scholars from kinesiology/physical education departments and those from history schools; struggles to reconcile the needs of amateur and professional historians; financial pressures; and the transition to online management, publishing, and circulations systems. Few journals have avoided these problems and controversies. Virtually all have experienced volatile periods when their futures appeared uncertain.

Sport history journals, nevertheless, have proved to be quite resilient, with 17 of the 19 continuing to publish (see Table 38.1). These were established across a number of decades: three were formed in the 1970s, five in the 1980s, six in the 1990s, three in the 2000s, and two new journals in 2020. Sport history journals peaked in the last two decades of the twentieth century, although the recent creation of two new journals and other existing online scholarly forums is a positive sign for the future.[9]

Scope, language, and assessment

As Table 38.1 indicates, sport history journals are quite cosmopolitan, with ten nations publishing journals.[10] They are predominantly from the Northern Hemisphere, with six published from European countries (Germany, Italy, Spain, and France), five from the United States, one from Canada, four from the United Kingdom, and one from Japan.

Southern Hemisphere publications include one from both Australia and Brazil. While journals are published from a number of nations, English functions as the *lingua franca* in sport history, like it does more broadly in the sciences, social sciences, and the humanities. All sport history journals publish articles in English, while the majority (60 per cent) publish exclusively in English, and a minority (40 per cent) publish in languages other than English.

Contributors in this Part of the *Handbook* argue that the status of English as the *lingua franca* creates numerous challenges for non-English speaking scholars. *Sport History Review, STADION, The Japan Journal of Sport History, Ludica, Materiales, European Studies in Sports History*, and *Recorde* offer articles in a range of languages to contest the notion that English is the only language that can shape the intellectual agenda in sport history. As Rafael Fortes and Victor Andrade de Melo explain in Chapter 47: 'we launched *Recorde*, in part, to address the question of English hegemony in scholarly publications in the history of sport'. In a similar vein, *Sport History Review* has recently internationalized its editors to include an associate editor from France to help increase the French content. Manfred Lämmer and Markwart Herzog (Chapter 42) challenge the universality of the English language, addressing the relegation of provinciality to other languages in their chapter. As they argue, *STADION* is specifically positioned

> as an alternative to the purely English-language journals for sports history in the United States, Canada, and Great Britain. To this day, the journal adheres to the principle of tri-lingualism, which corresponds to the European academic tradition and offers French and German-speaking colleagues the opportunity to publish in their mother tongue.

Whether in English, French, German, Italian, Japanese, Portuguese or Spanish, most sport history journals publish a broad range of historical topics linked to virtually any sport-related topic that constitutes appropriate disciplinary knowledge. The exceptions are single sport and event-based journals such as *Iron Game History* (Physical Culture), *NINE* (Baseball History and Culture), and *Olympika, Journal of Olympic History*, and *Journal of Olympic Studies* (Olympic and Paralympic Games). A closer look at the general sport history journals, however, reveals a pattern of publication of articles from within or nearby the countries of origin. North American content is often published in the *Journal of Sport History* and *Sport History Review*, British material is found in *Sport in History*, European content is published in *STADION, Ludica, Materiales*, and *European Studies in Sports History*, Ibero-American material is evident in *Materiales* and *Recorde*, Asian content in the *Asian Journal of Sport History & Culture*, Japanese topics are found in *The Japan Journal of Sport History*, and Australian and Aotearoa/New Zealand material dominates *Sporting Traditions*. While, in theory, sport history journals will publish material related to all dimensions of the subdiscipline – local, national, and international – the *International Journal of the History of Sport* is the only truly global journal. As Wray Vamplew argues in Chapter 44, *The International Journal of the History of Sport* has the largest reach with an extensive, international editorial structure regularly producing regionally focused issues on the Americas, Africa, Asia, Australasia and the Pacific, Europe, and the Middle East.

As much as sport history journals have been publishing for almost half a century, in multiple languages and across several continents, Murray Phillips argues in Chapter 39 that the context in which they are situated has changed considerably. The key dynamic is the way in which universities have succumbed to neoliberalism and its key tenets of globalization, privatization, deregulation, and competitiveness. Neoliberalism has given rise to an audit

Sport history journals

culture that is increasingly shaping the careers of individual academics, intellectual disciplines, and scholarly outputs. With regard to journals, it has manifested in sites that calculate library holdings as well as a complex web of metrics and, more recently, altmetrics. As Murray Phillips contends, metrics and altmetrics are applied unevenly to sport history journals for a host of reasons, but what does emerge is that the subdiscipline performs well in relation to mainstream journals with several sport history journals being recognized as quartile one history journals. He concludes that the sport history journal culture is indicative of a subdiscipline that has matured, with a level of modest confidence, about its place in the scholarly landscape.

Based on the information we currently have about sport history journals, which includes their establishment, life span, affiliation/non-affiliation to sport history societies, language choices, geographical bases, library holdings, metrics and altmetrics, we commissioned a single chapter on evaluating sport history journals and eight chapters on specific journals: *Sport History Review* (founded in 1970), *Journal of Sport History* (1974), *STADION: Journal of the History of Sport and Physical Education* (1975), *Sport in History* (1982), *The International Journal of the History of Sport* (1984), and *Sporting Traditions: The Journal of the Australian Society for Sports History* (1984), *Materiales para la Historia del Deporte* (2002), and *Recorde: Revista de História do Esporte* (2008). They are all broad-based journals in that they do not explicitly focus on a single sport, activity, or event. They span the globe from the United Kingdom, Europe, North and South America, and Australia. Most are English journals; we include *STADION, Materiales,* and *Recorde* precisely because they generate sport history scholarship in languages other than English.

Notes

1 Alun Munslow, *Narrative and History* (London: Palgrave Macmillan, 2007): 66.
2 http://sporthistory.org/assh-book-award-prizes/.
3 Email correspondence from Malcolm Maclean (6 June 2020).
4 http://sporthistory.org/assh-book-award-prizes/.
5 These details were determined through information derived from journals, publishers, and editors.
6 *Sport History Review* adopted this title in 1996 after formerly being known as the *Canadian Journal of History of Sport/Revue canadienne de l'histoire des sports* (1981–1985) and the *Canadian Journal of the History of Sport and Physical Education* (1974–1980).
7 See Murray G. Phillips, 'Sizing Up the Journals: Metrics, Sport Humanities and History', *The International Journal of the History of Sport* 37, no. 8 (2020): 692–704.
8 The gendered nature of sport history journals raises a key issue not addressed in any of the chapters: how well represented in the management, administrative, and editorial boards are minority groups? A very selective example drawn exclusively from the *Journal of Sport History* demonstrates that there have been fewer than ten African-American, Indigenous, and Hispanic scholars involved in the journal throughout its history. This situation points to the necessity of measures to promote diversity in the subdiscipline of sport history and more specifically in the journal workforce.
9 For example, one prominent academic sport history blog, established in 2014, is 'Sport in American History' (http://ussporthistory.com).
10 Determining what constitutes a sport history journal, as opposed to another form of sport humanities or social science journal, can be as simple as the way journals are named. The majority of sport history journals declare their hands in their titles. Other journals require a more detailed analysis. Some titles are more opaque, representing a focus on a sport, or a physical activity or a sporting event, with no designated emphasis on historical aspects such as *Olympika: The International Journal of Olympic Studies* and the *Journal of Olympic Studies*. These journals are included in the list of sport history journals because they have chosen to follow the disciplinary practices shared by historians. The referencing systems used by all of the journals in Table 38.1 demarcate historical scholarship from other parts of the sport humanities and social sciences. These practices, as Hyland argues are 'not abstract and

disengaged beliefs' but 'reveal something of the sanctioned social behaviours, epistemic beliefs, and institutional structures of academic communities' (Ken Hyland, *Disciplinary Discourses* (Michigan: Michigan University Press, 2013), 1–2). In this context, journals such as *Olympika. The International Journal of Olympic Studies* and the *Journal of Olympic Studies* publish research about both contemporary and historical issues related to the Olympic and Paralympic Games, but their referencing systems indicate they see themselves as primarily historical journals. There are two exceptions to this framework – *Sport in Society* and *Soccer and Society* – which at some time in their life spans have referenced sources using historical practices, but are widely perceived as social science, rather than historical journals. Furthermore, there are a range of sport humanities and kinesiology journals – *Leisure Studies, Sport, Education and Society*, and *Quest* for example – that publish historical papers, but their referencing systems indicate they see themselves primarily as social science or science journals. Social science or science journals that publish historical material were not included in Table 38.1.

39
SPORT HISTORY JOURNALS AND NEOLIBERALISM
Auditing the subdiscipline

Murray G. Phillips

Since the 1970s, a mixture of academic and commercial publishers and professional organizations have produced 19 scholarly journals dealing with the history of sport. Of these, 17 remain active, which I suggest is a strong measure of the strength of the subdiscipline. Journals serve important functions. They provide a scholastic medium – through articles, forums, research notes, review essays, and editorials – for evaluations of the subdiscipline and historiographical debates between scholars; they provide access to contemporary concepts in the field (e.g. class, gender, ethnicity, race, nationalism, modernization, and globalization) as well as histories of local, regional, national, and international sports. With their relatively fast publication timelines, which are speeding up with online pre-print publishing technology, journals circulate scholarly discourses much more quickly in comparison with the timeframe to research, write, and publish single-authored monographs.

As much as journals are outlets for the latest scholarship, they also provide a range of service-related content, alongside sport history societies' bulletins and newsletters. Particularly in times when communication networks were slow and fragmented, journals provided an abundance of detailed information about upcoming conferences, recent dissertations, degree programmes, and new books. One long-standing feature of several sport history journals was the surveys of recent works published in mainstream journals, thereby widening the circulation of scholarly information about emerging scholarship. Information included both citation details as well as full abstracts of articles. Book reviews have always been central to sport history journals. They provide reader insights into the latest monographs and encourage critical discourse about the standards and achievements of particular monographs. The volume of this service-related material in the journals was not inconsequential, often taking up equal or more print space than scholarly articles. The *Journal of Sport History*, for example, has always dedicated a significant amount of each issue to book reviews. In these ways, journals have been a crucial form of communication making significant contributions to sport history's community of practice.

The content, structure, and components of sport history journals have not remained stagnant over the last 50 years. In many cases, discourses have become more sophisticated as sport historians embrace, reframe, or contest broader historical ideas, themes, and debates.

DOI: 10.4324/9780429318306-45

This is evident in articles published in the journals as well as the broader scope of content. For example, journals have extended their purview to include reviews of sport films, museums, and media. This content is an important reminder of the willingness of sport historians to engage with these scholarly fields. On the other hand, the digital age is changing the nature of service spaces traditionally provided by the journals. Information about upcoming conferences, recent dissertations, degree programme, and in some cases book reviews, have shifted to journal websites and/or publishers' websites, as well as associated social media. Social media is increasingly the main communication channel for sport history organizations.

Neoliberalism

As much as journals have always be a crucial part of scholarly communities of practice, and independently acknowledged for their contributions, the context in which they exist has significantly changed. The emergence of neoliberalism from the 1970s and 1980s has shaped academia in a multitude of different ways. Trying to provide a consensus definition of neoliberalism is difficult, but it is inextricably linked to globalization, privatization, deregulation, and competitiveness, which have become salient features of the university environment and which have manifested in the commodification of knowledge, market-driven strategies, and a profit motif.[1] Scholars in the neoliberal university are recast as service providers in a knowledge economy who engage with 'clients' and 'consumers', formerly students, training them to function in the global workforce. At the institutional level, neoliberalism endorses competition, managerialism, and an audit culture that takes many forms including state, national and international teaching, research, and overall university league tables.[2]

This audit culture shapes the careers of individual scholars in both teaching and research. In the research space, databases about scholarship, initially established to monitor academic knowledge, have been reshaped according to the precepts of neoliberalism. Journals are assessed, scored, and ranked in a number of databases through a range of metrics and, more recently, altmetrics. The consequences for scholars, as Feldman and Sandoval contend: is that "the familiar 'publish or perish' motto has been rewritten. It is no longer enough to just publish; one must publish in the 'right' formats, with the 'right' presses, in the 'right' journals in the 'right' timeframes".[3] Since the advent of institutional neoliberalism, scholars have been assessed in a competitive environment that creates hierarchies based on grant income, h-indexes, and altmetric scores. Scholars applying for positions, promotion, and tenure at institutions in many national systems will be acutely aware of the requirements to present themselves in a way that is acceptable in the age of the neoliberal university.

Neoliberalism has not been an ally of the humanities. While it is too simplistic to blame neoliberalism for the decline of the humanities experienced at many institutions, it has intensified tendencies that pre-existed in many national university systems.[4] The transformation of knowledge from a form of public service – which enriches individuals, generates intellectual skills, and contributes to creating a more humane society – to a private resource and a commodity, which produces graduates ready for the market economy, is a widely recognized consequence of neoliberalism. This process has devalued the humanities. Shumway's assessment is blunt:

> Because neoliberalism rejects the very idea of 'not-for-profit' and insists that all values must be measured by the market, the humanities appear valueless. This has been a problem both for humanities enrollments and for the status of humanities disciplines within the university'.[5]

At my university, I watch with dismay at the decline of the humanities from a position in a kinesiology school where, ironically, my future is more secure than that of my colleagues in the school of history.

At a more micro level, neoliberalism and its audit culture has perpetuated inequalities through the emergence of performance metrics that are used to assess, compare, and reward individual careers and academic disciplines. Metrics, which function differentially for individuals and disciplines, have in the main disadvantaged the humanities, particularly when they are used by managers to compare the performance of scholars and journals across different academic disciplines. This is not surprising given the origins of metrics which were tied to understanding, evaluating, and disseminating scientific research through specialized journals. Humanities research, with its unique forms of knowledge production and scholarly dissemination – books, book chapters, journal articles, audio files, book reviews, compositions, creative writing, digital forms, exhibition catalogues, images, musical scores, textual datasets, translations, and videos – were not the focal points when metrics were conceived and designed. As Stacy Konkiel argues, metrics have been 'grafted onto the humanities and social sciences from the hard sciences, rather than developed from the ground up in order to meet humanists' needs'.[6] In essence, metrics were not intended to capture the diversity of the outputs from humanities scholars, or to accommodate different referencing practices and circulation patterns, and the challenges escalate from this starting point.

I share concerns that metrics feed both neoliberalism and the audit culture, and my inclinations side with the considered positions of various recent declarations, manifestos, and reports that argue metrics need to be critiqued and can only be worthwhile if they are contextualized, informed, and responsible.[7] Not surprisingly, I do not advocate the extensive use of metrics in this chapter. Nonetheless, I recognize that metrics are integral to many parts of the neoliberal university: management, librarians, scholars, and disciplines. They are unlikely to disappear in the foreseeable future.

For humanities scholars, metrics about journals fulfil important functions. They can constitute a significant part of building an academic profile for a position, and for garnering promotion and for tenure. For humanities disciplines, metrics can be informative, if used responsibly. Metrics are instructive if they compare and contrast journals from the same discipline, in this case history, as there are compatible forms of knowledge production, scholarly dissemination, and patterns of citation. This context enables and justifies the evaluation of many of the journals that constitute the subdiscipline of sport history. More importantly, metrics are valuable for subdisciplines because they have the capacity to assess the performance of sport history journals in regard to the larger canvas of mainstream history and, where appropriate, legitimize the quality of scholarship in the subdiscipline.[8]

Library holdings, metrics, and altmetrics

Traditionally, journals have been assessed by scholars in a myriad of ways: through surveys conducted by relevant scholarly communities, through institutional and national research assessments, and through expert panels in academic societies, universities, and government departments.[9] Following the development of neoliberalism and innovations in academic publishing, the introduction of quantitative measures, including metrics and altmetrics, have contributed to a reshaped understanding of the effectiveness of journals. As discussed earlier, these measures are problematic but when used discretely along with library holdings – another way of determining the circulation and readership of journals – they can provide a useful snapshot of sport history journals.

One marker of the reach of journals is library holdings. The assumption is that the number of holding libraries equates to the influence and importance of the journal.[10] The digital platform *Worldcat* provides the worldwide holdings for sport history journals and, with the exception of *Nikephoros*, all are found in libraries across the globe.[11] The sport history journal currently held in more libraries than any other is *NINE: A Journal of Baseball History and Culture* (1009). This is surprising until you consider baseball's importance in the United States where the number of potential libraries is high compared with other continents: over 85 per cent of all holdings of *NINE* (875/1009) are in North America. Another single interest journal, *Olympika*, is also held widely across libraries (589) reflecting the popularity and significance of the Olympic Games as a global sporting phenomenon. However, the *Journal of Olympic History*, a less academically orientated journal than *Olympika*, is not as widely held in libraries (123), and the *Journal of Olympic Studies* (1) has only recently been launched. The final single interest journal, *Iron Game History*, is available in only 73 libraries.

The collective holdings of broad-based sport history journals outstrip single interest journals in the libraries of the world. The *Journal of Sport History*, probably benefitting from the intersection between the cultural status of American sport and the nation's extensive college system, leads with holdings in 957 libraries, followed by *The International Journal of the History of Sport* (573), *Sport in History* (407), *Sport History Review* (407), *Sporting Traditions* (179), *STADION* (98), *European Sports History Review* (32), and *European Studies in Sports History* (15). Perhaps surprising to the English-speaking world are the wide holdings of the Brazilian journal *Recorde: Revista de História do Esporte* (616), ranking it as the second highest holding for broad-based sport history journals, and to a lesser extent *Materiales para la Historia del Deporte* (275), *The Japan Journal of Sport History* (73) and *Ludica. Annali di storia e civiltà del gioco* (60). These library holdings are indicative of a wide non-English scholarly engagement in sport history.

While library holdings are indicative of a journal's status, assessment of the scholarly publishing landscape has become more quantitatively focused in the new millennium. Beside personal subscriptions, library holdings used to provide the only access point for scholars for the best part of the twentieth century. The emergent measure of scholarly journals is metrics that, ironically, were developed by librarians to help determine the journals to which they would subscribe.[12] Metrics measure the relationship between a journal and the level of citations of the articles they publish. They do not necessarily confirm the *quality* of the articles or the journal. Metrics involve a complicated analysis and, particularly in the humanities, are a contested space. There are multiple databases – Thomas Reuters' Web of Science, Elsevier's Scopus, and Google's Google Scholar – that create a variety of metrics ranging from Impact Factor, Eigenfactor, h-indexes, SCImago Journal Rank (SJR), Source-Normalized Impact per Paper (SNIP), and CiteScore. Each is configured slightly differently. They should not be used to compare journals across disciplinary areas (for example between history, sociology, health, or science) because each area is characterized by considerably different referencing practices and citation patterns. Comparisons of these sorts do not account for historical practices and preference for citing books rather than journal articles, and fail to acknowledge that the age of cited sources is much older in history than in other disciplinary areas. This reduces citations of contemporary scholarship.[13] The Web of Science and its metrics – Impact Factor and Eigenfactor – are not very informative in sport history as only one journal, *The International Journal of the History of Sport*, is measured by these metrics. Google Scholar is more valuable through its h-indexes as it captures the metrics for both English and non-English sport history journals. One limitation of Google Scholar is the inability to probe the database for additional details and analysis of h-indexes. The most

Sport history journals and neoliberalism

Table 39.1 Sport history journal Scopus average metrics (2015–2019)[14]

Journal	SJR	SNIP	CiteScore
Sport in History	.32	.89	.86
The International Journal of the History of Sport	.29	.64	.94
Journal of Sport History	.29	.69	.56
Sport History Review	.12	.27	.18
European Studies in Sports History	.14★	N/A	N/A

Note: ★no value for 2017.

valuable database for sport history journals is Scopus because it offers a range of metrics and provides access to the algorithms and data that drive the metrics.

Three prominent metrics in Scopus – SJR, SNIP, and CiteScore – compare and contrast sport history journals. Metrics are highly selective and are not fully representative of the field of sport history. Scopus metrics currently represent only one third of the continuing sport history journals. *NINE: A Journal of Baseball History and Culture, Recorde: Revista de História do Esporte, Olympika: The International Journal of Olympic Studies*, and others are not included in Table 39.1 yet are widely distributed in libraries around the world, as are, to a lesser extent, *Materiales para la Historia del Deporte* and *Sporting Traditions*.

The limited coverage is a consequence of the selection criteria used by Scopus. Journal editors and publishers have to apply to the Scopus Content Selection and Advisory Board which, through both quantitative and qualitative measures, vets new title applications before inclusion. Multi-lingual sport history journals are further disadvantaged as there are English language requirements in the selection criteria. As Hammarfelt argues, 'this is a major issue when using established databases such as Web of Science or Scopus to study research fields in the humanities'.[15] Consequently, sport history journals in languages other than English do not exist in Scopus, but they are recognized in other databases such as Google Scholar. Both *Materiales para la Historia del Deporte* and *Recorde: Revista de História do Esporte* are cited as widely as are some of the English journals in Table 39.1.[16] Acknowledging the biases, selectivity, and distortion inherent in databases, Scopus does allow a limited comparison of the citation metrics of several long-standing and prominent sport history journals. As indicated in Table 39.1, *Sport in History* is recognized as the leading sport history journal in two of the Scopus metrics, with *The International Journal of the History of Sport* and the *Journal of Sport History* battling for second position. As contemporary as metrics appear, the algorithms used to generate them are retrospective: they are based on various citation periods from previous years. As such, there is a delay between current utilization of a journal and the metrics generated. That lag can be months, but is more commonly an entire year.

The most current information about scholarship in journals is actually derived from web-based altmetrics,[17] which provide the capacity to measure and monitor the attention, and potential downstream impact, of scholarship and research through online interactions.[18] Altmetrics provide reports on online engagement as found in social media, blogs, Wikipedia, policy documents, Q&A mentions, videos, and traditional media. They are most productively employed in assessment activities as a complement to citation-based metrics.

There are two major forms of altmetrics: those generated by peer networks that serve as repositories of work (such as *Academia.edu, ResearchGate*, and *Social Science Research Network*) and harvesters that surf outside repositories and aggregate mentions (*ImpactStory, PlumX*, and *Altmetric.com*). The most valuable altmetrics for journals are harvesters because

Table 39.2 Sport history journal altmetrics[22]

Journal	Total mentions	Twitter	Facebook	News	Policy	Wikipedia	Blog	Other
The International Journal of the History of Sport	3,774	3,428 (91%)	80	108	20	105	25	5
Sport in History	3,500	3,363 (96%)	69	19	3	37	5	1
NINE: A Journal of Baseball History and Culture	190	124 (65%)	7	33	0	22	3	1
Journal of Sport History	153	131 (86%)	0	16	0	5	1	0
Sport History Review	77	68 (88%)	5	1	0	2	1	0
Materiales para la Historia del Deporte	3	2 (66%)	1	0	0	0	0	0

they gather information from external sources and aggregate online attention, providing their own data for comparative analysis.[19] The harvester that dominates the journal market is *Altmetric.com*. One of *Altmetric.com*'s products, *Altmetric Explorer*, is 'primarily designed for publishers wishing to sift through altmetrics data to learn more about attention and use of their journals'.[20] Scholars may be familiar with the *Altmetric.com* donut that features different colours showing the range and volume of altmetrics activity. The colour depicts the type of online attention while the number in the middle of the donut indicates the volume of activity level.[21]

As indicated in Table 39.2, the altmetrics coverage of sport history journals, like metrics, is very selective. While the majority of sport history journals are registered in *Altmetric Explorer*, as they have an ISSN number, only six sport history journals generate altmetrics. It is likely that online traffic about sport history journals is under-represented because *Altmetric Explorer* only registers altmetrics from sources with either a digital object identifier (DOI) or uniform resource locator (URL). For example, mentioning a journal by name on Twitter or Facebook, without a URL or a DOI, will not be recorded by *Altmetrics Explorer*. Similarly, *Altmetric Explorer* does not record all online attention. The *Journal of Sport History*'s Facebook site, for instance, with many posts is not acknowledged in altmetrics.

Another important issue is the strong correspondence between large commercial companies and high altmetrics traffic. Those journals affiliated with the international company Taylor and Francis (*The International Journal of the History of Sport* and *Sport in History*) generate the most altmetrics, while journals published by smaller organizations such as the University of Illinois Press (*Journal of Sport History*), University of Nebraska Press (*NINE*), and Human Kinetics (*Sport History Review*) have significantly less or no online attention. This is likely to be directly related to publishers' capacity to market their journals through dedicated staff as well as those journals being included in 'big deals' that bundle journals and provide them to institutions whether or not they want them. Bundling can raise metrics figures because the journal is included in the search engines of the aggregated repository rather than

Sport history journals and neoliberalism

via its own website. Finally, it is possible to game online attention and artificially inflate altmetrics for journals, something all harvesters acknowledge and actively work to combat.[23]

Altmetrics should be interpreted through this filter and critically assessed like metrics. In the case of sport history journals, there are some defining features. The most popular digital platform that provides public attention to sport history journals is overwhelmingly Twitter. A very high percentage of all online attention (93 per cent) about sport history journals and their articles is driven by tweets and retweets. A fine-grained examination of these quantitative measures reveals that tweets, similar to Facebook mentions, often originate from the journals, their publishers, their sport history associations, and enthusiastic individuals. As the altmetrics literature cautions, attention does not necessarily equate to quality or impact. News, policy, and Wikipedia mentions more specifically refer to citations of journals articles and directly infer some sort of impact. In this context, the *International Journal of the History of Sport* stands out. The combination of the resources of Taylor and Francis and a genuinely international authorship and readership generates online attention that collectively outperforms all other sport history journals in news mentions, policy documents, and Wikipedia articles.

Library holdings, metrics, and altmetrics are helpful because of their capacity to generate a composite picture about sport history journals. In essence, we can determine aspects about the journals based on these categories, which provides insights into the relative strengths and weaknesses of sport history journals. While this is interesting and important to a certain degree, what is far more significant for the subdiscipline is how sport history journals rank in comparison with other history journals. Metrics, rather than library holdings or altmetrics, is the only category that makes large-scale comparisons possible.

There are several metrics that can be used to compare journals.[24] The most accessible and widely acknowledged metric is the SCImago Journal Rank (SJR). SJR assesses on average over 1,100 historical journals per year. Journals are individually ranked based on their SJR assessment and then positioned in quartiles relative to all history journals. Sport history journals with a SJR ranking – *Sport in History, Journal of Sport History, The International Journal of the History of Sport, Sport History Review*, and *European Studies in Sports History* – are provided with quartile positions each year (see Table 39.3). For the last five years (2015–2019), *Sport in History* and *Journal of Sport History* are quartile one journals in every year, *The International Journal of the History of Sport* is a quartile one journal in four of the five years, and *Sport History Review* and *European Studies in Sports History* oscillate over the years between

Table 39.3 Sport history journals SJR quartile rankings (2015–2019)

	2015	*2016*	*2017*	*2018*	*2019*	*Average quartile*
Sport in History	1	1	1	1	1	1
Journal of Sport History	1	1	1	1	1	1
The International Journal of the History of Sport	1	1	1	1	2	1.2
Sport History Review	2	2	4	3	3	2.8
European Studies in Sports History	4	3	4	1	2	2.8

different quartiles. The production of journals that are regularly ranked as quartile one journals is a notable achievement of the subdiscipline of sport history.

Concluding thoughts

In many ways, the health of a subdiscipline is measured less by outstanding monographs, as important as they are, and more by its supporting community of practice. One important marker of the state of a scholarly community of practice is the journal culture that constitutes the subdiscipline. In the case of sport history, there are 17 ongoing journals, with new journals initiated in every decade since the 1970s, which are published in English, French, German, Italian, Japanese, Portuguese, and Spanish across all continents except Africa and Antarctica.[25] Library holdings, metrics, and altmetrics are informative about the performance of these individual journals, but more revealing about the subdiscipline is how the journals compare with the range of history journals throughout the world. Impressively, sport history has three journals that are regularly ranked as quartile one journals in metrics. Based on the number of continuing journals, the diverse geographical origins of these journals, the range of manuscripts published in different languages, and, most importantly, the high calibre of several journals, the subdiscipline of sport history is surviving in the age of neoliberalism. Indeed, the subdiscipline has exceeded the expectations of the pioneering sport historians who struggled to find outlets for their work over half a century ago.

Notes

1 Camille B. Kandiko, 'Neoliberalism in Higher Education: A Comparative Approach', *International Journal of Arts and Sciences* 3, no. 14 (2010): 153–175.
2 Zeena Feldman and Marisol Sandoval, 'Metric Power and the Academic Self: Neoliberalism, Knowledge and Resistance in the British University', *tripleC* 16, no. 1 (2018): 214–233.
3 Feldman and Sandoval, 'Metric Power and the Academic Self', 221.
4 David R. Shumway, 'The University, Neoliberalism, and the Humanities: A History', *Humanities* 6, no. 4 (2017): 83; https://doi.org/10.3390/h6040083.
5 Shumway, 'The University, Neoliberalism, and the Humanities', 83.
6 Stacy Konkiel, 'Approaches to Creating 'Humane' Research Evaluation Metrics for the Humanities', *Insights* 31 (2018): 44; http://doi.org/10.1629/uksg.445.
7 See, for example, the Declaration on Research Assessment (https://sfdora.org/), the Leiden Manifesto for Research Metrics (http://www.leidenmanifesto.org/), and Metrics Tide (https://responsiblem etrics.org/the-metric-tide/).
8 For an extended application of a comparative approach see Murray G. Phillips, 'Sizing up Sport History Journals: Metrics, Sport Humanities, and History', *The International Journal of the History of Sport* 27, no. 8 (2020): 692–704.
9 C. Michael Hall, 'Publish and Perish? Bibliometric Analysis, Journal Ranking and the Assessment of Research Quality in Tourism', *Tourism Management* 32, no. 1 (2011): 16–27.
10 Bjorn Hammarfelt (2016), 'Beyond Coverage: Toward a Bibliometrics for the Humanities', in *Research Assessment in the Humanities*, eds. M. Ochsner, S. Hug, and H.D. Daniel (Cham: Springer, 2016); https://doi.org/10.1007/978-3-319-29016-4_10.
11 Library holdings are derived from WorldCat (https://www.worldcat.org/). There are often multiple holding records for these journals in WorldCat and the largest single holding is included in this table, rather than an accumulation of all of the individual records. This approach provides the most current record of holdings, but may disadvantage journals that changed their names or publishers (all accessed 1 August 2020).
12 Robin C. Roemer and Rachel Borchardt eds. *Meaningful Metrics: A 21st Century Librarian's Guide to Bibliometrics, Altmetrics, and Research* (Chicago: Association of College and Research Libraries, A division of the American Library Association, 2015).

13 Anton J. Nederhof, 'Bibliometric Monitoring of Research Performance in the Social Sciences and the Humanities: A Review', *Scientometrics* 66, no. 1 (2006): 81–100.
14 Average data is calculated from the Scopus site: https://www-scopus-com.ezproxy.library.uq.edu.au/sources.uri (accessed 8 April 2020).
15 Hammarfelt (2016), 'Beyond Coverage: Toward a Bibliometrics for the Humanities'.
16 Phillips, 'Sizing up Sport History Journals'.
17 Roemer and Borchardt, *Meaningful Metrics*, 100.
18 See http://www.whatarealtmetrics.com/what/ (accessed 5 August 2020).
19 Roemer and Borchardt, *Meaningful Metrics*, 117.
20 Roemer and Borchardt, *Meaningful Metrics*, 136.
21 Roemer and Borchardt, *Meaningful Metrics*, 135.
22 https://www.altmetric.com/ (accessed 27 September 2020).
23 Roemer and Borchardt, *Meaningful Metrics*, 138.
24 In addition to SJR, Scopus and also CiteScore rank journals and provide them with a quartile position. SJR was chosen because of its popularity and ease of access (see SJR: Scientific Journal Rankings (scimagojr.com)).
25 While South Africa does not produce a specific sport history journal, the country has a vibrant community of sport historians who have published important monographs and edited collections, and who are now organizing regular conferences. Some historical work has been published in the *South African Journal of Research in Sport, Physical Education and Recreation*.

40

FIFTY YEARS OF *SPORT HISTORY REVIEW*

M. Ann Hall

Sport History Review was the first journal published in any language that was devoted exclusively to the history of sport and physical education. It was the brainchild of Alan Metcalfe, physical education graduate from England's Loughborough College and first-generation immigrant to Canada. After continuing his education at the University of British Columbia, then the University of Wisconsin-Madison, he took up a faculty position in 1968 at the University of Windsor in Ontario, Canada. Metcalfe's academic work focused on sport and social class in nineteenth-century Canada.[1] Sport history was a nascent field then, certainly in North America, and he was determined to create a means to share the growing research. In 1969, at a meeting of the History Section of the Canadian Association of Health, Physical Education, and Recreation (CAHPER), Metcalfe convinced a somewhat sceptical group to support a new venture.

The first issue of what was then called the *Canadian Journal of the History of Sport and Physical Education* was published in May 1970. It contained articles by pioneers in the development of sport history such as Peter McIntosh, Uriel Simri, Earle Zeigler, Max Howell, and of course, Metcalfe himself. In his inaugural editorial, Metcalfe explained that while the journal was being published under the auspices of CAHPER and aimed primarily at a Canadian audience, he hoped it would also be of interest to colleagues in the United States and elsewhere. The new journal was published bi-annually through the University of Windsor with considerable assistance from Metcalfe's colleague, Lorne Sawula, who also acted as associate editor until May 1972.

By December 1973, an editorial board was in place, consisting of some well-known academics in Canadian sport history: Gerald Carr, Kevin Jones, Mary Keyes, Jean Paul Massicotte, Gerald Redmond, 'Sandy' Young, and Earle Ziegler.[2] Mike Salter, a colleague at Windsor, assumed the role of associate editor in December 1972, becoming joint editor in December 1973, and from 1974 to 1977 the actual editor, while Metcalfe took over the editorship of the new *Journal of Sport History* published by the North American Society for Sport History (NASSH). Upon Metcalfe's return, they divided the responsibilities, and Salter took on the increasingly important task of book review editor, developing it into one of the strongest elements of the journal. Metcalfe was also indebted to another Windsor colleague, Gerald Booth, who assisted in editing submissions from authors whose first language was not English.

332

DOI: 10.4324/9780429318306-46

Fifty years of Sport History Review

Metcalfe's wife Heather was an additional force behind the production of the journal. She initially typed all the manuscripts, did the bookkeeping, looked after correspondence, and mailed out the journal to subscribers. Heather became a familiar figure at NASSH annual conferences where she publicized and distributed copies of the journal. Her work was officially recognized with the December 1988 issue, where both she and Gerald Booth were listed as associate editors for the first time.

Beginning in 1981 (Vol. 12, No. 1), and with no explanation, 'Physical Education' was dropped from the title and the journal became the *Canadian Journal of History of Sport/Revue canadienne de l'histoire des sports*. According to Metcalfe, the term 'physical education' was slowly disappearing from university degree programmes as faculties, schools, and departments changed their name to Human Kinetics, Human Movement, Kinesiology, and the like. Therefore, keeping 'physical education' in the journal title was too restrictive.[3] The change in title also clearly signalled that the journal would become more bilingual, since up to this point only four articles had been published in French. Between 1981 and 1995, ten more French language articles were published, mostly from sport historians in Quebec.

French sport historian Thierry Terret, a long-time member of the *Sport History Review* editorial board, described this period in its life as 'very artisanal in its functioning'.[4] In other words, the *Canadian Journal of History of Sport/Revue canadienne de l'histoire des sports* was a high-quality journal, assembled by hand on the Metcalfe's kitchen table, with a subscription list of between 400 and 500 distributed in 50 countries.[5] It worked well. The journal was economically stable and survived for all those years without experiencing too many problems. Over that time, 287 articles and 246 book reviews were published. Among the articles, 31 per cent were about Canadian sport history, 22 per cent concerned the United States or North America, and 47 per cent were 'international', meaning they were about somewhere else in the world or focused on a topic with no national boundaries.[6] Fourteen articles appeared in French, representing almost 5 per cent of the total.

After 25 years, Metcalfe decided it was time to look for alternatives to editing and publishing the journal. Don Morrow, at the University of Western Ontario (now Western University), sat on the editorial board for a number of years and he assumed the editorship, with the proviso that the journal needed a commercial publisher. After contacting several Canadian publishers who were not interested, Morrow came to terms with Human Kinetics, based in Champaign, Illinois.[7] In their view, having *Canadian* in the journal title gave the distinct impression that its content and focus was on Canada, and not North America or the world. Eventually, the new editor and Human Kinetics agreed on *Sport History Review* (*SHR*) as the rebranded title, and the first issue appeared in May, 1996.[8]

SHR's mandate clearly stated (and still does) that

> the editor and editorial board are committed to addressing topics and issues of international interest. Therefore, articles whose method of analysis or application and appeal is more universally or fundamentally relevant to an international readership are of particular interest to *SHR*.[9]

How has this worked out? Of 172 original articles published between 1996 and 2015 – Don Morrow's tenure as editor – 39 per cent were about Canadian sport history, 20 per cent concerned the United States, and 41 per cent could be classified as 'international' in their focus. There were 25 articles in French, almost all from authors in France, representing 14.5 per cent of the total. A more thorough content analysis of *SHR* articles outlining, for example, dominant themes, sports, countries, methodological frameworks, and theoretical perspectives would certainly be informative. However, without abstracts and key words, it would be a formidable task to research. Only in recent issues (beginning with Vol. 48, no. 2, 2017) does each article contain an abstract and the relevant key words.

After 20 years as *SHR*'s editor-in-chief, Morrow stepped down as editor but before leaving the journal he decided that a retrospective look at what had been published over those years would be instructive and interesting. He then attempted to select the 'best' articles published under his two-decade tenure; however, he soon realized this was a daunting and intensive undertaking so he limited his focus to some 89 articles published between 2005 and 2014. He also called upon two long-time, editorial review board members – Colin Howell and Ann Hall – to help identify the top articles.[10] After some debate, we arrived at seven articles considered to be the best representatives of the previous ten years and at the same time reflected *SHR*'s breadth of interest and diversity of approach. The topics of these articles were: 1) rethinking sport and American 'exceptionalism' ideology; 2) historiographical reflections on sport and physical education in France (in French); 3) imaginings of women and the body in socialist China; 4) contested memories associated with Paavo Nurmi's 1925 tour of the United States; 5) early manifestations of the cyclists' rights movement in Canada; 6) exploring US–French relations through the Tour de France and the Iraq War; and 7) reflections of one immigrant family's ethnic identities and their relationship to sport. The authors were invited to write a reflective piece on how their article represented what they do as a historian. Also included were short, retrospective articles by both Howell and Hall. Howell pointed to the absence of articles in French relating to Quebec, and noted that sport historians need to be more attentive to the questions that are most prominent in the discipline of history itself. I presented some statistical data pointing to some deficiencies in the range of articles published in the journal since its inception, one of which I now discuss.

Feminist sport historians, including myself, have complained over the years about the slow inclusion of women and gender within the field of sport history. Generally, women's history is about girls and women, whereas gender history takes gender, as a social category of power relations, centrally into account. Women's history has not been displaced by gender history, but there is an overlap and interplay between the two. With these definitions in mind, how has *SHR* fared? Again, of the 172 original articles published between 1996 and 2015, 28 per cent were either written or co-authored by a female scholar, but not all of these wrote about women or gender. Next, it should be noted that only 19 (11 per cent) of the articles were about girls or women, and only 17 articles (10 per cent) were even partially about gender. However, this was certainly an improvement over the 1970–1995 period of the journal when only 19 per cent of the articles were written by women, 7.5 per cent were about females, and 2.5 per cent were about 'gender' (very broadly defined). Sport history generally is a male-dominated field, but this information demonstrates the potential opportunities available for women sport historians and others whose research is about gender or females to present new studies to the readership. Improving the quantity and level of scholarship by women, or about females and gendered sport, is a priority for *SHR*.

As a tribute to Don Morrow's 20 years as *SHR* editor-in-chief, a special issue in the form of a *Festschrift* was published in 2017, edited by Nancy Bouchier and Carly Adams.[11] It contained several articles written by Morrow's colleagues and former students. Colin Howell provided an introductory essay pointing out that, as an historian, Morrow was somewhat of an enigma because he had 'an affinity for the liminal rather than the categorical, probing the blurred boundaries involving identities of all kinds: amateur and professional, proletarian and bourgeois, rough and respectable, masculine and feminine, ethnic and national, metropolitan and local, individual and social'.[12] Morrow's work, according to Howell, was always

Fifty years of Sport History Review

reflexive and he understood that the historian has three important responsibilities: 1) interrogate one's sources and oneself; 2) place both in the context of the time; 3) and realize the emancipatory potential that exists in historical knowledge. Each of the essays included in the *Festschrift* in some way addressed one or more of these indispensable historical qualities.

Over the past 50 years, *SHR* has attracted a remarkably loyal group of academics to serve as members of its editorial review board. During Alan Metcalfe's tenure as editor (1970–1995), 18 individuals served in this capacity.[13] Beginning in 1996, when Don Morrow became the editor, 33 individuals have served on the review board, and of these, 7 are still members.[14] The gender split on the current 18-member board is 6 women and 12 men. About one-third of these individuals are based in Canada, with the others situated in the United States, Australia, New Zealand, Europe, and South Korea. Since 1996, five individuals have served as book review editor: Victoria Paraschak (1996–2004), Greg Gillespie (2005–2007), Carly Adams (2007–2013), Toby Rider (2014–2019), and Colleen English (2019–).

SHR's third and current editor-in-chief is Carly Adams, a Kinesiology and Physical Education professor at the University of Lethbridge, Alberta, Canada. Having previously served as book review editor and a member of the editorial board for several years, as well as having a stellar reputation as a sport historian, she is entirely suited to this role. In her inaugural editorial, she stated:

> We have many high-quality journals in the field of sport history. One of our challenges at *SHR* is to distinguish ourselves from the others while continuing to contribute to the vibrant and diverse discussions in the field of sport history and history more broadly. First and foremost, we remain committed to promoting a diversity of approaches and topics of international interest. It is my hope that we can remain cognizant of earlier directions and legacies while also making space for new perspectives and approaches.[15]

Adams called upon researchers and scholars 'to experiment, transform, and embrace new ways of writing to push the boundaries of our sport work; to engage more centrally with current debates; to consider the possibilities of interdisciplinary and cross-disciplinary conversations; and to imagine new directions'. One initiative promoted by Adams included a call for scholars to submit a special issue proposal, which would be the responsibility of a guest editor. Several excellent proposals were received, and two were chosen. 'International Federations and National Governing Bodies: The Historical Development of Institutional Policies in Responses to Challenging Issues in Sport' edited by Jörg Krieger, Lindsay Parks Pieper, and Ian Ritchie was published in the May 2020 issue. The second one, 'Issues in Transnational Sport History' edited by Rob Lake and Simon Eaves will appear in Spring 2021, and another call for special issue proposals has been issued.

Other recent innovations by Adams include a redesigned and eye-catching journal cover through the use of dynamic photos. Adams also started a Twitter account (https://twitter. com/SHR_HK) to increase the journal's visibility and keep readers informed about the latest developments in the field of sport history. Of the nine issues published under Adams' editorship at the time of writing, almost every issue has contained at least one article in French, although all from scholars in France. Recently, an Associate Editor, whose main responsibility is to deal with French-language articles, has been appointed. He is Pierre-Olaf Schut, a professor at the Université Gustave Eiffel in France. Although several articles have been authored or coauthored by female scholars, only ten (out of 52) articles are about women or gender. One recent issue, however, included a special forum about women's cycling history.

335

The latest operational statistics for *SHR* show an increasingly healthy journal that defies some of the industry-wide trends. For instance, many journals have experienced declining subscriptions in recent years as university budgets decreased and libraries were required more regularly to justify journal subscriptions. However, *SHR* steadily avoided a significant drop in subscriptions. In fact, in 2017 it saw an almost 8 per cent increase in total institutional subscriptions.[16] Also important is the fact that institutions may have access to *SHR* through, for example, the SPORTDiscus database from EBSCO. Institutions can also purchase a site licence from Human Kinetics that grants access to all their journal titles at one low cost.

Consumers of journal content have steadily migrated to online access, which has motivated publishers to improve their web-based user experience. In 2016, Human Kinetics launched a new web publishing platform that provided users with tools to easily share articles of interest, use a smartphone or tablet to access the journal, and enhance the search function. The new publishing platform also meant that DOIs were assigned to every article, which makes content more 'findable'; all content was searchable on Google Scholar; *SHR* content was more accessible (and searchable) on the *SHR* website; and *SHR* content was now indexed in many additional databases.[17] As a result, article downloads jumped dramatically in 2017, almost double the previous year. Full-text access refers to the number of times an article is accessed via the *SHR* website and SPORTDiscus. In 2018, *SHR* articles were accessed more than 12,000 times via these sources.[18] In order to further improve the visibility and usability of their journals, Human Kinetics moved to yet another new web platform in the summer of 2019.

SHR published its fiftieth volume in 2019. The steadily improving manuscript submission rate was the highest it had been in five years.[19] Human Kinetics has improved their production processes for *SHR* with fully copyedited, formatted, and author proofed/approved article versions appearing on the website ahead of print. Human Kinetics has also partnered with Kudos, a platform designed to help authors maximize the visibility and reach of their published journal articles, and subsequently measure the impact of their work.

SHR is currently indexed in Thomson Reuters' *Arts and Humanities Citation Index* and in their *Web of Science*. It is also indexed in Elsevier's *Scopus*. This allows for some comparison between journals of sport history with regard to their 'impact' through various metrics.[20] For example, *Scopus* calculates a CiteScore, which measures the average citations per document that a journal title receives over a three-year period. As of 2020, there were six journals related to sport history indexed in the *Scopus* database: *Sport History Review, Sport in History, International Journal of the History of Sport, Journal of Sport History, STADION: International Journal of the History of Sport*, and *European Studies in Sports History*. The CiteScores for all of these journals are low (less than 1) because they are being compared with all other history journals in the database (over 1,000). However, their comparative CiteScores have been relatively stable for the past five years. Ranking on top is either the British journal *Sport in History*, with four issues per year, or the *International Journal of the History of Sport*, which publishes a staggering 18 issues annually. *Sport History Review* (two issues per year) and the *Journal of Sport History* (three issues per year) vie for third and fourth place depending on the year. Both *STADION: International Journal of the History of Sport* and *European Studies in Sports History* are relatively new to *Scopus*, and so far, they rank below the others.[21]

What always needs to be remembered is that, whatever the journal impact factor, it only measures the relationship between papers published and the level of citations they receive; it does not say anything about the *quality* of the articles cited. That, of course, is for the reader to decide. Perhaps a more significant indicator is the availability of these journals as measured by the number of libraries worldwide that own copies. A check through the database

Fifty years of Sport History Review

WorldCat (in mid-2020) shows that the *Journal of Sport History* tops the list at 960 libraries with the *International Journal of the History of Sport* second at 573. *Sport in History* is next at 407, followed by *Sport History Review* at 225, whereas *STADION: International Journal of the History of Sport* and *European Studies in Sports History* ranked at 98 and 15 respectively.

Sport History Review has been published for 50 years, longer than any other sport history journal. This continuity, across the years, has allowed it to develop properties of character, content, and community as an entity in its own right.[22] Character arises collaboratively between the publisher, editor, and editorial board. For half of its life, *SHR* did not have a publisher, but it did have a familiar layout and design, all recognizable by those who read its scholarly articles, books reviews, and sometimes interesting letters to the editor. *SHR's* character did not change that much over the next 20 years, although acquiring a commercial publisher allowed for a more professional layout and design, and certainly made the editor's life easier. Nonetheless, it was still the same interesting, scholarly, and high-quality journal to which readers were accustomed. As *SHR* moves forward into an ever-changing publishing world of primarily online access, journal impact metrics, and perhaps even open access, its character may of necessity be somewhat redefined.

The content of any journal begins with the articles submitted. External reviewers then become involved, which extends the content beyond those who are committed to the success of the journal, namely, the editor, editorial review board, and of course, the publisher. Through these processes, a community for scholarly dialogue is created among specialists, and hopefully, general-interest readers. In the case of sport history, several journals are competing for the attention of a relatively small group, and journals affiliated with a scholarly society have an advantage. *SHR* has never had this benefit, and yet it thrives and survives. To continue to do so, however, it must constantly evolve and not remain static in its character, content, or community.

Notes

1 For an interesting look at some of Alan Metcalfe's early influences and work, see C.A. 'Tony' Joyce, 'Alan Metcalfe: Maverick, Marx and Methodology', *Canadian Journal of History of Sport/Revue canadienne de l'histoire des sports* 18, no. 2 (1987): 59–69.

2 The following were members of the editorial board during Alan Metcalfe's tenure as editor: Gerald Carr (1973–1976), Kevin Jones (1973–1977, 1989–1995), Mary Keyes (1973–1988), Jean Paul Massicotte (1973–1977, 1989–1995), Gerald Redmond (1973–1976, 1991–1995), 'Sandy' Young (1973–1976, 1982–1988), Earle Ziegler (1973–1981), Jean Leiper (1976–1988), Brian Mutimer (1976–1988), Bim Schrodt (1973–1995), Bob Barney (1977–1995), Pierre Demers (1977–1979), Arthur Sheedy (1979–1981), Don Morrow (1980–1995), Bruce Kidd (1981–1995), Morris Mott (1982–1995), Tony Mangan (1984–1995), and Victoria Paraschak (1989–1995).

3 Telephone interview by author with Alan and Heather Metcalfe, 7 February 2019.

4 Thierry Teret, 'Finding the Path: Academic Journals in the Field of Sport History', in *Making Sport History: Disciplines, Identities and the Historiography of Sport*, ed. Pascal Delheye (London and New York: Routledge, 2014), 135.

5 'Editorial', *Canadian Journal of History of Sport/Revue canadienne de l'histoire des sports* 26, no. 2 (1995).

6 See also Don Morrow's critical analysis of the *Canadian Journal of History of Sport/Revue canadienne de l'histoire des sports* in 'Canadian Sport History: A Critical Essay', *Journal of Sport History* 10, no. 1 (1983): 67–79. He examined 25 issues published between 1974 and 1982. By general topic, he found the following in percentages: Canadian sport (23.1), American sport (20.9), Ancient, Medieval and Preliterate sport (20.9), and Other (35.1).

7 For information about the history of Human Kinetics, go to https://us.humankinetics.com/pages/a bout-human-kinetics (accessed 11 March 2019).

8 'A Note from Don Morrow, *SHR* Editor', *Sport History Review* 45, no. 2 (2014): 95. A tribute to founding editor Alan Metcalfe appeared a couple of years later. See 'Festschrift Issue: A Tribute to

Alan Metcalfe', edited by Nancy B. Bouchier and Victoria Paraschak, *Sport History Review* 29, no. 1 (1998).

9 Human Kinetics Journals, Sport History Review, About SHR, Mission, https://journals.humanki netics.com/page/about/shr (accessed 26 February 2019).

10 For more information on this process, see L. Donald Morrow, 'Special Issue of *Sport History Review*: A Ten-Year Retrospective on "the Best" of *SHR*', *Sport History Review* 46, no. 1 (2015): 1–4.

11 'Festschrift issue: A Tribute to Don Morrow', *Sport History Review* 48, no. 2 (2017).

12 Colin Howell, 'Realizing Sport History's Emancipatory Potential: Don Morrow and the Maturation of Canadian Sport Studies', *Sport History Review* 48, no. 2 (2017): 121–125.

13 See Note 2 above.

14 Since 1996, present and past members of the Editorial Review Board in alphabetical order are: Carly Adams (2011–2015), Douglas Booth (1996–), Nancy Bouchier (1996–), Douglas Brown (2000–2014), Tim Chandler (1996–2014), Russell Field (2014–), Jacques Gleyse (2015–), Ann Hall (1996–), Andrew Holman (2020–), Colin Howell (1997–2014), Annemarie Jutel (2000–2011), Bruce Kidd (1996–2014), Joo Youn Kim (2020-), Jörg Krieger (2020-), Stacey Lorenz (2019-), Tara Magdalinski (1996-), Fred Mason (2014–2019), John Nauright (1996–2019), Gary Osmond (2014–), Tina Parratt (1996–2019), PearlAnn Reichwein (2007–), Toby Rider (2019–), Jamie Schultz (2014–), Chad Seifried (2014–), Heather Sykes (2006–2007), Thierry Terret (1996–2019), Gertrud Pfister (1996–2019), Wray Vamplew (1996–2015), Michel Vigneault (1996–), Theresa Walton-Fisette (2015–), Kevin Walmsley (1996–), Stephen Wenn (1996–2015), Sandy Young (1996–1999).

15 'Editor's Note', *Sport History Review* 47, no. 1 (2016): 1–2.

16 Human Kinetics Journals, *Annual Publisher Report, Sport History Review*, 28 May 2018, 6.

17 Human Kinetics Journals, *Annual Publisher Report*, Sport History Review, 28 May 2018, 8.

18 Human Kinetics Journals, *Sport History Review 2018 Annual Report*, 8.

19 Human Kinetics Journals, *Sport History Review 2019 Annual Report*, 6.

20 For a more thorough analysis of all sport history journals, see Murray G. Phillips, 'Sizing up Sport History Journals: Metrics, Sport Humanities, and History', *International Journal of the History of Sport* 37, no. 8 (2020): 692–704.

21 An analysis using Harzing 's 'Publish or Perish' software by running three-year (2015–2018) Google Scholar metrics for each of the journals showed much the same result. However, by calculating the 'h-index' and 'g-index' (both representing a relationship between papers published and citations received), the results were more definitive with the *International Journal of the History of Sport* ranking first by a substantial margin. *Sport in History* and the *Journal of Sport History* were tied with *Sport History Review* next and *European Studies in Sports History* last.

22 Marie McVeigh, 'A Journal Is as a Journal Does: Four Emergent Properties of Journals in Scholarly Communication', published 19 April 2018 on https://clarivate.com/blog/science-research-connect/ journal-journal-four-emergent-properties-journals-scholarly-communication/ (accessed 11 March 2019).

Acknowledgements

This chapter is a revised and expanded version of M. Ann Hall, '*Sport History Review*: A Retrospective', *Sport History Review* 46, no. 1 (2015): 5–7. I wish to thank Alan and Heather Metcalfe, Don Morrow, Carly Adams, and Chad Seifried for their assistance in the preparation of this version.

41

THE *JOURNAL OF SPORT HISTORY*

Andrew D. Linden and Alison M. Wrynn

Introduction

In 1974, the North American Society for Sport History (NASSH) published the first issue of the *Journal of Sport History* (*JSH*). Since then, 46 volumes of the journal have contained peer-reviewed, primary-sourced, or historiographical articles; book, film, and museum reviews; research notes; and forums dedicated to the history of sport and physical culture.

This chapter 1) outlines a brief timeline of sport history scholarship; 2) explains the beginnings of the *JSH*; 3) provides an overview of editorship; 4) examines scholarship; and 5) discusses current issues and future directions. What began as a short volume of 90 pages that focused on peer-reviewed works, article reviews of related journals, and summaries of dissertations now is an international platform and among the foremost venues for scholarly research on the history of sport.

Sport history as an academic discipline

While the *JSH* first appeared in 1974, the discipline began nearly a century beforehand. In the 1880s and 1890s, physical educators published some of the first works when they began documenting the lineage of their professions. These included descriptions of the role of sport and contests from the ancient world to the contemporary. It should not be surprising that sport history emerged in this era. There was a rising interest in sport in the United States and Great Britain, particularly on college campuses; the modern Olympic movement was also emerging. These histories did not critically assess the *why* or *how* sports emerged, but they did perform one of the first steps needed in any body of literature – they wrote down early stories.[1]

For the next half century, few historians wrote on sport. In 1917, Frederic Paxon, a student of Frederick Jackson Turner, wrote 'The Rise of Sport' in *The Mississippi Valley Historical Review*. Paxon drew on Turner's 'frontier thesis' to argue that sport provided nineteenth-century Americans 'a partial substitute for pioneer life' after the frontier had closed.[2] In 1940, Foster Rhea Dulles published *America Learns to Play: A History of Popular Recreation*, which considered sport from colonial America through the early twentieth century.[3] Little else appeared in the scholarly literature.

DOI: 10.4324/9780429318306-47

A decade later, John R. Betts published his work, 'A Technological Revolution and the Rise of Sport, 1850–1900', also in *The Mississippi Valley Historical Review*, arguing that sport was not an antidote to, but an effect of the industrialization of the United States; he expanded this work to book-length form in 1974.[4] The limited volume of scholarship on sport history available to scholars by the end of the 1960s and into the early 1970s, according to Melvin L. Adelman, allowed 'an American sport historian at this time ... [to] easily keep abreast of the latest research'.[5]

However, the field was beginning to grow. In 1973, the editors of the *Maryland Historian*, assisted by Marvin Eyler, devoted an entire issue to sport. The editors signalled that 'sport history' was a new field of inquiry that deserved study as a significant area of research alongside conventional and emerging topics. The articles within the volume mirrored this focus including a historiographical piece by Adelman that focused on scholarly developments in American sport history.[6] Despite the limited scale of such work, these publications provided the academic impetus for the formation of NASSH and the establishment of the *JSH*.

NASSH and the *JSH*

The field expanded in the 1970s. Steven A. Riess argues that this was a result of cultural and structural change.[7] The historical profession was gradually becoming more democratic as younger scholars entered academia. A new 'social history' emerged in the broader field, drawing on the works of E.P. Thompson and Robert Wiebe, which allowed for the study of leisure pursuits.[8] Students, in general, began to demand 'more relevant curriculum' that included the stories of people of colour, women, and other groups that had traditionally been marginalized or excluded. Ultimately, academics began to recognize 'that sport and its interplay with society could inform us about the American experience'.[9]

Academic recognition of the role of sport in the American experience took institutional form with the establishment of the NASSH. Historian Guy Lewis had recently taken his PhD by finishing a dissertation at the University of Maryland in 1964 and, after beginning at the Pennsylvania State University as a faculty member in the department of physical education, he broached the concept of establishing an academic organization dedicated to sport history. Over the next several years, Lewis – with the assistance of his doctoral advisor – Marvin Eyler, historians from history and PE departments – such as Seward Staley and Earle Ziegler – and a contingent of graduate students at the University of Massachusetts – where Lewis began as an assistant professor in 1967 – formed NASSH in 1972 and held its first meeting at the Ohio State University the following year.[10]

At that gathering, Eyler, who was then the dean of the College of Physical Education, Recreation, and Health at the University of Maryland, brought up the idea of publishing a journal at the first meeting of the Steering Committee on 24 May.[11] The group agreed and unanimously passed the motion to create both a journal and a newsletter; Eyler became the chair of the publications board. Two days later, at the first membership meeting, Ronald A. Smith argued 'that a journal would be the focus of the society and that increased institutional membership would result from such a venture'.[12] After passing through the membership, more discussion occurred during the first meeting of the Executive Council on 26 May. At that meeting, NASSH council members decided to house the journal at Radford College (who would also assist in the proofreading process) thanks to the suggestion of the college's chair of their history department, Margaret Woodhouse.[13] A year later, the first issue of the *Journal of Sport History* appeared.

The Journal of Sport History

Editorial challenges

During the tenure of the 11 people who have served as editor or interim editor of *JSH*, several common issues have emerged. All have been deeply concerned about the quality of the journal. They have also attempted to provide a variety of unique features to secure a wider readership. Finally, there have routinely been concerns about the timely publication of the journal.

As the inaugural editor, Alan Metcalfe, wrote on the first page of the first issue: 'The publication of the *Journal of Sport History* is a result of the dedicated efforts of a number of people over a twenty-year period and a changing concept of what constitutes history.'[14] Metcalfe's influence on the structure of the journal lasts into the present as he proposed many of the standard features at the NASSH Council Meeting in May 1974. For example, the Council agreed that the journal editor should be given wide latitude to carry out tasks related to the journal, a tradition that carries into the present day.

In the first few years, editors made a conscious effort to bring together ideas about sport history, rather than simply historiographical debates about the academy. As Metcalfe declared in 1976:

> The *Journal of Sport History* will continue to encourage both the innovative and more traditional approaches to sport history. We do not wish to get embroiled in a discussion of 'What is History' but rather give support to the presentation of material and ideas which achieve a high scholastic level. Hopefully the first five issues fulfill this requirement and serve as a guide to future directions.[15]

In an editorial in his final volume as editor, Metcalfe declared that although the topics of the articles under his editorship might not have appealed to all historians, they were included as exemplars of strong historical scholarship. The success of the journal in the future would, in Metcalfe's assessment, be based on resistance to 'any attempts to make the journal subservient to any one particular view of history'.[16]

Jack Berryman stepped in as the second editor in 1978. He praised the work of the previous staff, but called for more historiography. 'The majority of space in the *Journal* will continue to be devoted to scholarly articles and it should be noted that the current editorial staff is especially anxious to encourage more hypothetical and theoretical sport historiography in the future.'[17] That same year, however, Berryman was concerned about the quality of submissions. The year's third issue was delayed 'due to a lack of publishable manuscripts'. His concerns focused on

> the major reasons for revision, resubmission, or rejection have been the failure to ask important and meaningful questions and the lack of careful research based upon primary source materials. Rarely has an article been rejected because of the topic chosen. It has ususally [sic] been rejected because of the way the topic was treated. That is, the editorial board demands that researchers conform to the canons of historical methodology and high standards of scholarship. Additionally, the board expects that authors will follow the submission guidelines which are clearly stated in each issue.[18]

These early years helped dictate the future course of the *JSH*.

Editorial terms were not fixed at the outset and inaugural editor Metcalfe served four years. He was followed by Berryman who served six years. During Steven Riess' seven-year term, several special issues appeared, including a retrospective in 1993 that examined recent topics in sport history.[19] Joe Arbena was appointed in 1993 to a four-year term. In 1995, the journal had begun to fall behind in its publishing dates and a few volumes came out several months late. Despite this issue, Arbena shared with members the hard work that he and his colleagues had undertaken to try to bring the journal back to a timely schedule. He also expressed the need for additional manuscript submissions.[20]

Arbena stepped down after three years due to health issues.[21] During David K. Wiggins' six-year term, an agreement was reached with the Amateur Athletic Foundation of Los Angeles (now the LA84 Foundation) to publish back issues of the journal and NASSH *Proceedings*. This relationship, which continues to the present day, brings the journal to a wider audience and provides a small amount of funding to NASSH.[22] In his four-year term, originally scheduled for 2002 to 2006, Melvin L. Adelman took the reins in order

> to evoke changes in the journal. ...[making] every effort to give *JSH* a greater international, non-North American flavour both in terms of content and in the background of authors, and [creating] an environment in which our non-North American colleagues feel comfortable sending us their works for consideration.[23]

One feature that Adelman added was a 'Forums' section that included a group of papers on a focused topic.

In this era, concerns emerged that the journal had fallen even further behind in its publication schedule. The Publications Board recommended that NASSH investigate a number of potential solutions, including: hiring a managing editor, using special editors for several issues, or securing a contract with a university or commercial publisher.[24] In response, Tom Jable stepped in as interim editor for a year and a half towards the end of Adelman's scheduled term. One issue that Jable spearheaded focused on work produced by graduate students.[25] During his five-year term, Wray Vamplew began to bring the journal back to a regular publishing schedule and expanded the regular features to include a section on 'Sources and Methods', as well as the publication of select Honour Addresses.[26] Additionally, in 2010, the decision was made to publish the journal online with Project MUSE.[27]

Table 41.1 JSH Editors

Years	Name	Institution
1974–1977	Alan Metcalfe	University of Windsor [Canada]
1978–1984	Jack Berryman	University of Washington [United States]
1985–1992	Steven Riess	Northeastern Illinois University [United States]
1993–1996	Joe Arbena	Clemson University [United States]
1996–2002	David Wiggins	George Mason University [United States]
2002–2006	Melvin Adelman	Ohio State University [United States]
2005–2006	Tom Jable (int.)	William Patterson University [United States]
2007–2012	Wray Vamplew	University of Stirling [Scotland]
2012–2015	Alison Wrynn	California State University [United States]
2015–2018	Murray Phillips	The University of Queensland [Australia]
2018–	Maureen Smith	California State University, Sacramento [United States]

The Journal of Sport History

The three most recent editors have each served a single three-year term (Wrynn, Phillips, and Smith) and this has been established as the editorial term by the NASSH Publications Board. Additionally, since 2007, at least one Associate Editor has served in the hopes that they will transition to the Editorship. During the editorial term of one of the authors of this chapter (AW), the journal was brought back to a regular, on-time publishing schedule. It was also during Wrynn's term that the decision was made by NASSH to publish the journal with the University of Illinois Press. During Phillips' term as editor, the idea of a 'best article' from each year, which had been recommended several times over the course of the journal's history, finally came to fruition. Additionally, the *JSH* also introduced the position of Past-Editor to provide structural continuity for the Journal. Maureen Smith has continued to keep the journal on a timely publication schedule and has planned for a number of special issues.

Scholarship in the *Journal of Sport History*

Like the field at large, authors in the *JSH* have produced histories on a wide array of topics related to sport. This began slowly. In the first issue, three of the four articles covered American baseball – David Voight's 'Reflections on Diamonds' the first – with the fourth article on methodology.[28] However, authors covered a wide array of topics for the remaining years of the journal's first decade.

For the remainder of the 1970s, authors wrote on ancient sport history, women in sport, and Russian physical education, just to name a few topics.[29] The 1980s saw sport in Cold War Germany and the history of the rodeo.[30] In the 1990s, authors wrote on sport in colonial America and the early United States, judo in Japanese culture, and the professionalization of ice hockey; in the 2000s, they wrote on gender and the Turners, the Joe Louis-Max Schmeling bouts, and British Olympic teams of the early 1900s.[31] Recently, authors have looked at early American physical education and 'play days', Falconry in Eastern Han China, and tennis's Davis Cup.[32] These represent a small sample of topics.

The journal has followed the timeline of the historical profession since the 1970s' social history turn through the cultural and postmodern turns of recent decades. In addition, sport historians drew on theory, such as those who worked on modernization in the 1980s.[33] Others, such as Roberta J. Park in 1987, built off Gregory Bateson, Erving Goffman, Victor Turner, and John MacAloon – who theorize the reading of texts – to better understand debating teams at Harvard and Yale.[34] In a 1996 article, Glenn Moore studied media representations of baseball by drawing on the works of Peter Golding and Noam Chomsky to recognize the 'silent power' of the media in helping normalize the capitalistic pursuits of baseball magnates.[35] Likewise, in 2004, Darcy Plymire studied the running boom beginning in the 1970s to problematize connections between health, sport, fitness, and theories of Foucauldian bio-power.[36] These are just a few examples of the ways in which authors connected theory with sport.

Methodological debates have existed since the launch of the *JSH*. Many of these have occurred outside of the journal; however, the scholarship in the *JSH* represents a mirror of the field and the ways in which scholars have engaged with questions of epistemologies and ontologies.[37] The first issue, for example, included an article by Eyler in which he questioned the veracity of historical truth, arguing: 'The historian deals with a synthetic recreation of past actuality.'[38] Numerous discussions of the field and its place within the various historical 'turns' appeared for the next four decades.[39]

Sport historians have continued into the twenty-first century to adopt theories and discuss historical methods through their writings. Many of these appear not as general historiographical or methodological pieces, but rather through topics that engaged innovative forms of scholarship. For example, in 2013, Cathy van Ingen used postmodernists Alun Munslow, Murray G. Phillips, and Keith Jenkins while theorizing black women boxers.[40] Likewise, Bieke Gils drew on Roland Barthes' discussions of body theories for her 2014 article on trapeze and physical culture.[41]

JSH authors also highlight interdisciplinarity. Sport history can draw on methodological and ontological debates in other disciplines and vice versa. For example, in 2017, editors devoted an issue to the question of sport history in the digital age, organized by Jennifer J. Sterling, Murray G. Phillips, and Mary G. McDonald.[42] In 2018, Josh Howard argued for discussions into sport history's function as public history, Ari de Wilde and Chad Seifried discussed the merging of sport management and sport history, and Wray Vamplew revisited entrepreneurship as a model.[43] There is little doubt that inaugural editor Metcalfe's call for a journal that resisted 'using a narrow definition of what comprises acceptable or good history' has come to fruition.[44]

Issues and conclusion

Since 1974, the *JSH* has been the home to sport history, particularly in the United States and Canada. However, the journal has been susceptible to broader academic issues. Gender inequality, for instance, persists. From 1974–2016, men appeared as authors on approximately 75 per cent of articles.[45] This is not surprising as history departments remain primarily male and sport continues continue to be a male-dominated purview. Fortunately, the generations following Title IX in the United States are showing shifts in the gender demographics. In addition to gender inequality, the editorship of the journal has had virtually no racial or ethnic diversity. We are hopeful that as NASSH brings in a more diverse membership that this will change.

Data on journal subscriptions and citation metrics have fluctuated over the past few decades. After seeing growth in subscriptions toward the first half of the journal's existence, the *JSH* has seen retreating subscriptions over the past decades. Much of this has to do with falling library and institutional subscription. However, individual NASSH membership (including a copy of the *JSH*) has remained stagnant. For the first 41 volumes (and the first issue of volume 42) the journal was published in-house by NASSH, which occasionally led to an irregular publication schedule, like that which occurred in the 1990s and early 2000s. Even with these issues, the journal has ranked near the top of citation metrics when related to other sport journals, and even against so-called mainstream history. Although it does not have an impact factor (only the *International Journal of the History of Sport* has one in the area of sport history), in systems like the Scopus rating metric, the *JSH* ranks highly among sport journals, in addition to being in the top quarter of rankings compared with mainstream history journals. As Murray G. Phillips showed in an examination of sport history journal metrics of 2019, the *JSH* received top billing in two of the three metrics in Scopus.[46]

These topics and issues demonstrate broader (and concerning) trends in both the humanities and academia at large. The issues with impact factors and other quantifiable metrics are also of concern. The drive for metrics is of uneven concern in various countries and at different levels of universities. Stagnant numbers and a retreat to quantifiable scholarship is a worry for both the *JSH* and the broader field of sport history. An assessment of the field in 2014 found that higher percentage of NASSH members worked in kinesiology or similar departments (42.5 per cent) compared with other academic departments, and as Jaime Schultz warned, as scholars working in sport history retire, 'shortsighted administrators will

The Journal of Sport History

fail to replace them with similarly inclined scholars' because they 'may see little value in bringing aboard individuals who do not contribute to the department's statistical prominence'.[47]

In the past five years the journal has been published by the University of Illinois Press. Furthermore, the journal has attempted to raise its place in the academy through measures such as instituting a 'Best Article of the Year Award' and creating a communications team, including the launch of a new website and social media platforms.

The *Journal of Sport History* has been fortunate that it has been a part of NASSH, which is a financially robust scholarly society. The fiscal strength of NASSH has allowed *JSH* to weather any number of storms over the past 46 years. As *JSH* approaches the half-century mark, it continues to be a leader in publishing high-quality, innovative scholarship.

Notes

1 Mark Dyreson, 'Sport History and the History of Sport in America', *Journal of Sport History* 35, no. 3 (Fall 2008): 405–414.

2 Frederic L. Paxson, 'The Rise of Sport', *The Mississippi Valley Historical Review* 4, no. 2 (September 1917): 167.

3 Foster Rhea Dulles, *America Learns to Play: A History of Popular Recreation, 1608–1940* (New York: D. Appleton-Century Company, 1940).

4 John Rickards Betts, 'The Technological Revolution and the Rise of Sport, 1850–1900', *The Mississippi Valley Historical Review* 40, no. 2 (September 1953): 231–256; John Rickards Betts, *America's Sporting Heritage: 1850–1950* (Reading, PA: Addison Wesley Publishing Company, 1974).

5 Melvin L. Adelman, 'Academicians and American Athletics', *Journal of Sport History* 10, no. 1 (Spring 1983): 80.

6 Editors, 'Introduction', *Maryland Historian* 4, no. 2 (Fall 1973): 69; Melvin L. Adelman, '"Academicians and Athletics": Historians' Views of American Sport', *Maryland Historian* 4, no. 2 (Fall 1973): 123–137.

7 Steven A. Riess, *Major Problems in American Sport History*, 2nd edition (Stamford, CT: Cengage Learning, 2015), 1.

8 E.P. Thompson, *The Making of the English Working Class* (New York: Alfred A. Knopf, 1966); Robert H. Wiebe, *The Search For Order, 1877–1920* (New York: Hill and Wang, 1967).

9 Riess, *Major Problems in American Sport History*, 1.

10 Robert K. Barney and Jeffrey O. Seagrave, 'From Vision to Reality: The Pre-History of NASSH and the Fermentation of an Idea', *Journal of Sport History* 41, no. 3 (Fall 2014): 381–400.

11 NASSH Steering Committee Meeting Minutes, 24 May 1973, https://www.nassh.org/about-nassh/by-laws-minutes/.

12 NASSH Business Meeting Minutes, 25 May 1973, https://www.nassh.org/about-nassh/by-laws-minutes/.

13 NASSH Council Meeting Minutes, 26 May 1973, https://www.nassh.org/about-nassh/by-laws-minutes/.

14 'Editorial', *Journal of Sport History* 1, no. 1 (1974): 1.

15 'Editorial', *Journal of Sport History* 3, no. 2 (Summer 1976): 110.

16 'Editorial', *Journal of Sport History* 4, no. 3 (Summer 1977): 245.

17 'A Note from the Editor', *Journal of Sport History* 5, no. 1 (Spring 1978): 5.

18 'A Note from the Editor', *Journal of Sport History* 5, no. 1 (Spring 1978): 5–6.

19 Steven Riess, Editor's Note, *Journal of Sport History* 20, no. 3 (Winter 1993), no page.

20 Annual Business Meeting Minutes, North American Society for Sport History. *Proceedings and Newsletter*, 1995, 91.

21 Annual Business Meeting Minutes, North American Society for Sport History. *Proceedings and Newsletter*, 1996, 109.

22 NASSH Council Meeting Minutes, 22 May 1998 North American Society for Sport History. *Proceedings and Newsletter*, 91–94.

23 Melvin Adelman, Editor's Note, *Journal of Sport History* 29, no. 1 (Spring 2002), no page.

24 Annual Business Meeting Minutes, North American Society for Sport History. Proceedings and Newsletter, 2005, 176–179.

25 Thomas Jable, Editor's Note *Journal of Sport History* 33, no. 3 (Fall 2006), no page.

26 'Editor's Note', *Journal of Sport History* 34, no. 1 (Spring 2007), no page. The JSH had always invited the Graduate Student Essay awardee to submit their essay for consideration for publication – this had not been typically done with the Honour Addresses.

27 Annual Business Meeting Minutes, North American Society for Sport History. Proceedings and Newsletter, 2009, 200–202.

28 D.Q. Voigt, 'Reflections on Diamonds: American Baseball and American Culture', *Journal of Sport History* 1, no. 1 (1974): 3–25.

29 Emelia-Louise Kilby, 'Á Cock to Asclepius', *Journal of Sport History* 6, no. 2 (Summer 1979): 28–36; Ellen Gerber, 'The Controlled Development of Collegiate Sport For Women, 1923–1936', *Journal of Sport History* 2, no. 1 (Spring 1975): 1–28; James Riordan, 'Pyotr Franzevich Lesgaft (1837–1909): The Founder of Russian Physical Education', *Journal of Sport History* 4, no. 2 (Summer 1977): 229–241.

30 G.A. Carr, 'The Involvement of Politics in the Sporting Relationships of East and West Germany, 1945–1972', *Journal of Sport History* 7, no. 1 (Spring 1980): 40–51; Mary Lou LeCompte, 'The Hispanic Influence on the History of Rodeo, 1823–1922', *Journal of Sport History* 12, no. 1 (Spring 1985): 21–38.

31 Nancy Struna, 'Gender and Sporting Practice in Early America, 1750–1810', *Journal of Sport History* 18, no. 1 (Spring 1991): 10–30; Kevin Gray Carr, 'Making Way: War, Philosophy and Sport in Japanese "Jûdô"', *Journal of Sport History* 20, no. 2 (Summer 1993): 167–188; Daniel S. Mason, 'The International Hockey League and the Professionalization of Ice Hockey, 1904–1907', *Journal of Sport History* 25, no. 1 (Spring 1998): 1–17; Annette R. Hofmann, 'Lady "Turners" in the United States: German American Identity, Gender Concerns, and "Turnerism"', *Journal of Sport History* 27, no. 3 (Fall 2000): 383–404; Lane Demas, 'The Brown Bomber's Dark Day: Louis-Schmeling I and America's Black Hero', *Journal of Sport History* 31, no. 3 (Fall 2004): 253–271; Matthew P. Llewellyn, 'A Nation Divided: Great Britain and the Pursuit of Olympic Excellence, 1912–1914', *Journal of Sport History* 35, no. 1 (Spring 2008): 73–97.

32 Sarah Jane Eikleberry, 'More than Milk and Cookies: Reconsidering the College Play Day', *Journal of Sport History* 41, no. 3 (Fall 2014): 467–486; Leslie V. Wallace, 'Representations of Falconry in Eastern Han China (A.D. 25–220)', *Journal of Sport History* 39, no. 1 (Spring 2012): 99–109; Simon J. Eaves and Robert J. Lake, 'Dwight Davis and the Foundation of the Davis Cup in Tennis: Just Another Doubleday Myth?' *Journal of Sport History* 45, no. 1 (Spring 2018): 1–23.

33 Melvin L. Adelman, 'The First Modern Sport in America: Harness Racing in New York City, 1825–1870', *Journal of Sport History* 8, no. 1 (Spring 1981): 5–32.

34 Roberta J. Park, 'Muscle, Mind and "Agon": Intercollegiate Debating and Athletics at Harvard and Yale, 1892–1909', *Journal of Sport History* 14, no. 3 (Winter 1987): 263–285.

35 Glenn Moore, 'Ideology on the Sportspage: Newspapers, Baseball, and Ideological Conflict in the Gilded Age', *Journal of Sport History* 23, no. 3 (Fall 1996): 228–255.

36 Darcy C. Plymire, 'Positive Addiction: Running and Human Potential in the 1970s', *Journal of Sport History* 31, no. 3 (Fall 2004): 297–315.

37 For 'turns', see Jack W. Berryman, 'Sport History as Social History?' *Quest* 20, no. 1 (1973): 65–73; Catriona M. Parratt, 'About Turns: Reflecting on Sport History in the 1990s', *Sport History Review* 29, no. 1 (1998): 4–17; Douglas Booth, *The Field: Truth and Fiction in Sport History* (London: Routledge, 2005); Allen Guttmann, 'The Ludic and the Ludicrous', *International Journal of the History of Sport* 25, no. 1 (2008): 100–112; Jaime Schultz, 'Leaning into the Turn: Towards a New Cultural History', *Sporting Traditions* 27, no. 2 (November 2010): 45–59; Jaime Schultz, 'Sense and Sensibility: A Pragmatic Postmodernism for Sport History', in *Examining Sport Histories: Power, Paradigms, and Reflexivity*, eds. Richard Pringle and Murray G. Phillips (Morgantown, W.V.: Fitness Information Technology, 2013), 59–78; Murray G. Phillips, ed. *Deconstructing Sport History: A Postmodern Analysis* (Albany: State University of New York Press, 2006); Amy Bass, 'State of the Field: Sports History and the "Cultural Turn"', *Journal of American History* 101, no. 1 (June 2014): 148–172.

38 Marvin H. Eyler, 'Objectivity and Selectivity in Historical Inquiry', *Journal of Sport History* 1, no. 1 (1974): 74.

39 Patricia A. Vertinsky, 'Gender Relations, Women's History and Sport History: A Decade of Changing Enquiry, 1983–1993', *Journal of Sport History* 21, no. 1 (Spring 1994): 1–24; Murray G. Phillips,

The Journal of Sport History

'Deconstructing Sport History: The Postmodern Challenge', *Journal of Sport History* 28, no. 3 (2001): 327–343; Colin Howell, 'Assessing Sport History and the Cultural and Linguistic Turn', *Journal of Sport History* 34, no. 3 (Fall 2007): 459–465; Dyreson, 'Sport History and the History of Sport in America'.

40 Cathy van Ingen, '"Seeing What Frames Our Seeing": Seeking Histories on Early Black Female Boxers', *Journal of Sport History* 40, no. 1 (Spring 2013): 93–110.

41 Bieke Gils, 'Flying, Flirting, and Flexing: Charmion's Trapeze Act, Sexuality, and Physical Culture at the Turn of the Twentieth Century', *Journal of Sport History* 41, no. 2 (Summer 2014): 251–268.

42 'Doing Sport History in the Digital Present', *Journal of Sport History* 44, no. 2 (Summer 2017): 135–366.

43 Josh Howard, 'On Sport, Public History, and Public Sport History', *Journal of Sport History* 45, no. 1 (Spring 2018): 24–40; Ari de Wilde and Chad Seifried, 'Sport History and Sport Management in the United States: Opportunities and Challenges', *Journal of Sport History* 45, no. 1 (Spring 2018): 66–86; Wray Vamplew, 'Products, Promotion, and (Possibly) Profits: Sports Entrepreneurship Revisited', *Journal of Sport History* 45, no. 2 (Summer 2018): 183–201.

44 'Editorial', *Journal of Sport History* 4, no. 3 (Summer 1977): 245.

45 Andrew D. Linden and Lindsay Parks Pieper, 'Writing Sport Online: An Analysis of the Pitfalls and Potential of Academic Blogging', *Journal of Sport History* 44, no. 2 (Summer 2017): 263.

46 Murray G. Phillips, 'Sizing up Sport History Journals: Metrics, Sport Humanities, and History', *International Journal of the History of Sport* 37, no. 8 (2020): 692–704.

47 Jaime Schultz, 'Kinesiology, Genealogy, and An (Ephemeral) Quantitative Turn', *President's Forum,* NASSH.org, https://www.nassh.org/blog/2016/04/17/kinesiology-genealogy-and-an-ephemeral-qu antitative-turn/.

42

STADION

International Journal of the History of Sport

Manfred Lämmer and Markwart Herzog

The founding and development of *STADION: International Journal of the History of Sport* can only be adequately understood from the political and educational context of sport and its institutionalization in the 1960s. Until then, there was no comparable institution in Germany that systematically dealt with the history of sport from the perspective of research, perhaps with the exception of the Deutsche Sporthochschule Köln (DSHS, German Sport University Cologne), established in 1947.[1] Even within the parent discipline of history, sport history was positioned on the margins of acceptability.[2] The reluctance of historians to write about sport as the subject of scholarly study was founded not least in the reservations of the established academic community who defined what was deemed worthy of academic research. But by the early 1970s, a turnaround could be observed. Many Institutes of Sport Science at German universities, in which history of sport, physical education, and body culture had long been cornerstones,[3] began establishing chairs and other academic positions in sport history.

Two major sporting events held in Germany were decisive in these changes – the 1972 Summer Olympics and the 1974 FIFA World Cup.[4] These events put sport at the centre of German public interest, but it was the terrorist attack on the athletes of Israel at the Munich 1972 Games which generated a world audience who engaged with the political dimensions of international sporting competitions.

In 1973, the founding of the International Association for the History of Physical Education and Sport (HISPA) in Zurich, on the initiative of Swiss military historian Louis Burgener, gave another important impetus to institutionalizing the historiography of sport at an international level. In forming and gradually expanding HISPA, which organized annual international conferences, the DSHS played a decisive role. The lectures were given in German, English, and French, paving the way for the trilingual characteristic of *STADION*.[5] From its early days, all articles in *STADION* have been summarized in German, English, and French abstracts, regardless of the language they are written in. In this way, *STADION* has seen itself as an alternative to the purely English-language journals of sport history in the United States, Canada, and Great Britain. To this day, the journal adheres to the principle of trilingualism, which corresponds to the European academic tradition, offering French- and German-speaking colleagues the opportunity to publish in their mother tongue. In recent years, the number of French-language contributions has risen considerably.

In the formative years of HISPA, Europe was over-represented, with a significant proportion of German members. This preponderance probably relates to the strong academic tradition of sport history in Germany and the location of the General Secretariat of HISPA in Cologne under the direction of Manfred Lämmer (DSHS). Subsequently, the number of members, mainly from North America and Asia, increased considerably. In 1989, HISPA and the International Committee for the History of Sport and Physical Education (ICOSH), founded in Prague in 1967, were dissolved and merged into the International Society for the History of Physical Education and Sport (ISHPES) in Olympia. Günther Wonneberger from Leipzig (ICOSH) and Manfred Lämmer from Cologne (HISPA) had previously undertaken the first steps towards a formal cooperation between the two (at times competing) institutions from 1977 onwards, which ultimately resulted in ISHPES.

By the early 1970s, an academic and political climate had developed that decisively favoured the founding of *STADION*. Its initiators, Manfred Lämmer and Wolfgang Decker, were both established at the Department of Sport History at the DSHS. From 1985 onwards, Manfred Lämmer had sole responsibility of publishing *STADION*, until he was joined from 2008 by Maureen Smith (University of Western Michigan) and Thierry Terret (Université Claude-Bernard-Lyon 1). Since 2019, Manfred Lämmer and Markwart Herzog (Schwabenakademie Irsee) are the editors of *STADION*.

Since its establishment, *STADION* has had three publishers. From 1975 to 1979 *STADION* was published by E.J. Brill in Leiden (Netherlands), a publishing house specializing in international scientific publications; from 1980 to 2018 the journal was published by Academia-Verlag, St. Augustin; and since 2019 at Academia within Nomos Publishing House, Baden-Baden. Throughout this time, the journal has adhered to a carefully supervised double blind peer-review process and has published in two issues per year, totalling about 400 pages.

Although *STADION* was never officially affiliated to HISPA, the journal was in fact a publication organ of this association. The relationship between HISPA and *STADION* marks the beginnings of international cooperation in the field of sport history. When HISPA merged with ICOSH to form ISHPES, the relationship with *STADION* was formalized. Since late 1995, *STADION* has been known as 'affiliated to the International Society for the History of Physical Education and Sport (ISHPES)'. Financially, *STADION* was initially supported by the Bundesinstitut für Sportwissenschaft (BISp, Federal Institute for Sports Science) in Bonn and, from volume 7 on, by the Minister für Wissenschaft und Forschung des Landes Nordrhein-Westfalen (Secretary of Science and Research of North Rhine-Westphalia) and the Gesellschaft der Freunde und Förderer der DSHS (Society of Friends and Patrons of the DSHS) and, from volume 11 (1985), by the Deutsche Forschungsgemeinschaft (DFG, German Research Foundation). These organizations recognized that sport was growing in its economic, cultural, and political influence, and a specialist historical journal at an international level was a worthy enterprise. Similar to journals dedicated to the history of medicine, music, technology, business, science, and art, there was a need for a scholarly journal about sport history. This journal needed to be interdisciplinary, transnational, and comprehensively designed to engage with all epochs of history.

The first volume (then subtitled *Journal of the History of Sport and Physical Education*) was dedicated to Prof Dr Werner Körbs, head of the Sport History Department at the DSHS, to mark his sixty-fifth birthday and retirement. During the early years, the Advisory Board consisted of Henning Eichberg (University of Stuttgart), Zdzisław Grot (University of Poznań), Richard D. Mandell (University of South Carolina, Columbia), Roland Renson (Catholic University of Leuven), and Hans Langenfeld (University of Münster). From 1984, the Advisory Board was expanded. The new board consisted of Gilbert Andrieu (University of Nanterre), Henning Eichberg (University of Copenhagen), Heiner Gillmeister (University of Bonn), Rosella Isidori Frasca (University of L'Aquila), Donald G. Kyle (University of Texas at Arlington), Hans Langenfeld (University of Münster), Jan Lindroth (University of Stockholm), Gertrud Pfister (Free University of Berlin), Roland Renson (Catholic University of Leuven), and James Riordan (Bradford University). From 1986–1987, Werner Meyer (Basel) and Günther Wonneberger (Deutsche Hochschule für Körperkultur und Sport, Leipzig) were added to the Advisory Board, as was Karl Lennartz (DSHS, Cologne) from 1997.

In 2008, the Advisory Board was repositioned again. The board included Irina Bykhovskaya (Moscow City University), Dittmar Dahlmann (University of Bonn), André Gounot (University Marc Bloch, Strasbourg), Richard Holt (University of Leicester), Lic Leena Laine (Vantaa, Finland), Gertrud Pfister (University of Copenhagen), Murray Phillips (University of Queensland, Brisbane), Roland Renson (Catholic University of Leuven), Otto Schantz (University Marc Bloch, Strasbourg), Patricia Vertinsky (University of British Columbia, Vancouver), Stefan Wiederkehr (Berlin-Brandenburgische Akademie der Wissenschaften, Berlin), Christopher Young (University of Cambridge), and Leif Yttergren (GIH, The Swedish School of Sport and Health Sciences, Stockholm). As *STADION* joined the Nomos Verlagsgesellschaft in 2019, the Advisory Board was re-established, comprising 20 personalities from varying disciplines of history and sports science.[6]

From the very beginning, the range of topics covered by the contributors was broad. Topics encompassed all historical epochs and cultures, with a focus on Europe, North America, and East Asia and, thanks to the cooperation of ethnologists and anthropologists, also embraced traditional movement cultures and sports in the so-called 'Third World'. In addition to essays, *STADION* has published reviews of important works on the history of sport and games, physical exercise, and body culture.

A special feature of the first two decades was the relatively high proportion of studies on early high cultures and Greco-Roman antiquity. This focus was not surprising given that both of the journal's initiators were classical philologists and historians, while Wolfgang Decker was also an Egyptologist. The strong connection to studies about classical antiquity made it possible to demythologize the romantic image of the ancient Olympic Games, which was widespread in sports federations, textbooks, and public discourses.[7] According to this new research, myths about Greek sporting festivals, including those attributed to the Olympic Games, were exposed. Scholars in *STADION* challenged the claims that the ancient Olympics Games were egalitarian; particularly that they were open to athletes of all walks of life and female participants, that athletes did not receive any rewards, and that the games contributed to international understanding and peace. The journal published articles which demonstrated that the ancient Olympic Games did not include women or athletes from all walks of life, they did not demonstrate an understanding of fairness in competition, and winners received prize money and gifts in numerous competitions. In essence, scholars debunked perceptions about the ancient Olympic Games which were central to the ideologies that underpinned the modern Olympic Games.

Another focus of early *STADION* research papers examined the development of physical exercises and sport since the end of the eighteenth century in Central Europe, especially in German-speaking and neighbouring countries. It also explored the beginning of systematic physical education among philanthropists, medieval festivals and tournaments, Far Eastern martial arts, as well as British sport and its global prevalence. In addition, *STADION* helped to bring topics, which had previously only been dealt with in Germany, to the attention of an international public. This prompted historians in North America and Europe to examine these subjects. Popular topics included German gymnastics and national movement, as well as the politicization and instrumentalization of sport during the Nazi era and in divided Germany during the so-called 'Cold War'.

More recently, *STADION* has worked to document its repository of articles and ensure this scholarship is widely distributed. In 2004, the journal published an index volume containing a complete table of contents and English abstracts of all issues published up to that time. By 2019, *STADION* became part of the Nomos Publishing House, and it had published a total of 42 issues, some of them as double volumes. *STADION* has also collaborated with Sport Und Recherche im Focus: Das Sportinformationsportal des Bundesinstituts für Sportwissenschaft – SURF (Focus on Sport and Research: The Sport Information Portal of the Federal Institute of Sports Science) to help disseminate scholarship.[8] The bibliographical data of all essays from the first year of publication onwards are listed on SURF, abstracts included, providing access to this body of scholarship.[9]

In addition, *STADION* has published several volumes as special issues with a thematic focus. These have included proceedings of HISPA, ISHPES, and other conferences including the *Proceedings of the XIIth HISPA Congress* (Gubbio, Italy, 1987). Other special issues focus on specific topics such as *Sport and Tradition – Tradition in Sport* (Asilomar, California 2005), edited by Thierry Terret and Patricia Vertinsky, *Sport and Religion* (2009), and national sports cultures including *Beiträge zur Geschichte des Sports in Nordeuropa* (1993/94), edited by Henning Eichberg and Jørn Hansen, and *Le Sport en France de 1870 à 1940: Intentions et interventions* (2001), edited by André Gounot.

One particularly notable issue focused on revised lectures from the 1988 conference, Die jüdische Turn- und Sportbewegung in Deutschland, which was held on the occasion of the fiftieth anniversary of the November 1938 pogroms in Nazi Germany. This thematic issue, which was also published as a standalone book,[10] provided historians Hartmut Becker, Hans-Jürgen König, Gertrud Pfister, Hajo Bernett, and Hans Joachim Teichler with the opportunity to publish their groundbreaking research on Jewish sport, sport under the Nazi regime and the exclusion of athletes of non-Aryan origin from German gymnastics and sports clubs. Up until the 1988 special issue, this topic had not been comprehensively addressed by sport historians.

In some instances, scholarship from conferences aligned to the quadrennial Olympic Games were published as volumes of *STADION*. In 1980, *STADION* published *Beiträge zur Geschichte der Olympischen Spiele* and, four Olympiads later, published *Studien zur Geschichte der Olympischen Spiele* (1995–1996), which drew attention to the 100th anniversary of the first modern Olympic Games. This volume was dedicated to the pioneer of contemporary history of sport in Germany and member of the Advisory Board of *STADION* in the 1970s and 1980s, Prof Dr Hajo Bernett. In 2003, Andreas Höfer, Manfred Lämmer, and Karl Lennartz, edited *Olympische Spiele*, and in 2012–2013 Daphné Bolz and Florence Carpentier edited the special edition of *STADION, Olympism and International Sport Relations*.

STADION is the only tri-lingual academic journal of sport history at international level. It serves as a scholarly platform for well-known historians, but also scholars of other disciplines, such as anthropology, archaeology, education, sociology, and philosophy. *STADION* is aimed both at experts and at all those who strive for a deeper and more differentiated understanding of sport, play, physical education, and physical culture from a historical perspective, including journalists and publicists.

Notes

1 Its forerunner, the Deutsche Hochschule für Leibesübungen (DHfL, German University of Physical Education), founded in Berlin in 1920 by Carl Diem and August Bier, had already dedicated itself to the recent field of sport science; see Jürgen Court, *Deutsche Sportwissenschaft in der Weimarer Republik und im Nationalsozialismus. Vol. 2: Die Geschichte der Hochschule für Leibesübungen 1919–1925* (Berlin: Lit, 2014).

2 Christiane Eisenberg, 'Die Entdeckung des Sports durch die moderne Geschichtswissenschaft', *Historical Social Research* 27, nos. 2–3 (2002): 4–21; Wolfram Pyta, 'Nicht mehr im Abseits. Fußball als Gegenstand bundesdeutscher Geschichtswissenschaft', in *Jahrbuch 2006 der Deutschen Gesellschaft für Geschichte der Sportwissenschaft*, eds. Jürgen Court, Arno Müller, and Christian Wacker (Berlin: Lit, 2007), 65–77; Markwart Herzog, 'Forschung, Märchen und Legenden. Von den divergierenden Perspektiven auf den Fußballsport in der NS-Zeit', in *Fußball, Macht und Diktatur. Streiflichter auf den Stand der historischen Forschung*, eds. Johannes Gießauf, Walter M. Iber, and Harald Knoll (Innsbruck, Wien, and Bozen: Studien Verlag, 2014), 91–116, here 91–94.

3 Arnd Krüger, 'Puzzle Solving. German Sport Historiography of the Eighties', *Journal of Sport History* 17, no. 2 (1990): 261–277; Kay Schiller and Christopher Young, 'The History and Historiography of Sport in Germany. Social, Cultural and Political Perspectives', *German History* 27, no. 3 (2009): 313–330; Michael Krüger and Hans Langenfeld, 'Sportgeschichte im Rahmen der deutschen Sportwissenschaft', in *Handbuch Sportgeschichte*, eds. Michael Krüger and Hans Langenfeld (Schorndorf: Hofmann, 2010), 12–19.

4 Kay Schiller and Christopher Young, *The 1972 Olympics and the Making of Modern Germany* (London: University of California Press, 2010); Kay Schiller, *WM 74. Als der Fußball modern wurde* (Berlin: Rotbuch, 2014).

5 For the relations between *STADION* and HISPA discussed in this chapter, see Roland Renson, 'Shaping the International Bodies for the History of Physical Education and Sport', in *Internationale Aspekte und Perspektiven des Sports. Prof. Dr. Walter Tokarski zum 65. Geburtstag*, eds. Jürgen Buschmann, Manfred Lämmer, and Karen Petry (St. Augustin: Academia, 2011), 201–212.

6 *STADION* – Editorial Board, www.stadion.nomos.de/en/editorial-board (accessed 22 January 2020).

7 For examples of the deconstruction of the mythology of peace and other romantic beliefs in the Olympic movement of modern times, see Manfred Lämmer, 'Der sogenannte Olympische Friede in der griechischen Antike', *STADION. International Journal of the History of Sport* 8/9 (1982/83): 47–83; Bernd Wirkus, 'Olympismus als Geschichtsphilosophie und Ideologie. Koordinaten einer philosophischen Standortbestimmung', *STADION. International Journal of the History of Sport* 18 (1992): 302–325; Christoph Ulf and Ingomar Weiler, 'Der Ursprung der antiken Olympischen Spiele. Versuch eines kritischen Kommentars', *STADION. Journal of the History of Sport and Physical Education* 6 (1980): 1–38.

8 The Federal Institute of Sports Science, www.bisp-surf.de (accessed 22 January 2020); *STADION. International Journal of the History of Sport*, www.stadion.nomos.de (accessed 22 January 2020).

9 The Federal Institute of Sports Science, 'STADION meets SURF', 16 September 2019, www.bisp.de/DE/WissenVermitteln/Aktuelles/Nachrichten/2019/Stadion_trifft_SURF.html (accessed 22 January 2020).

10 Manfred Lämmer, ed., *Die jüdische Turn- und Sportbewegung in Deutschland 1898–1938* (Sankt Augustin: Academia, 1989).

43

THE *SPORT IN HISTORY* JOURNAL

Dave Day and Kay Schiller

Introduction

In 1982, The British Society of Sports Historians changed its name to the British Society of Sports History (BSSH), whose declared mission was 'to stimulate, promote and co-ordinate interest in the historical study of sport, physical education, recreation and leisure with special reference to the British Isles'.[1] In January 1984, Richard Cox edited the first *Bulletin* of the BSSH, which replaced the former *Newsletter*, with the intention of providing a platform for research articles as well as communicating with the Society's membership. Included in this first issue were details of the BSSH third conference to be held at Chester College of Higher Education between 29 June and 2 July 1984, on the theme of 'Women, Sport and History', which included keynote presentations from Roberta Park and Jennifer Hargreaves. The 74 paid up members of the BSSH as at 31 December 1983 included many names that would be familiar to anyone interested in sports history in 2020, such as John Bale, Allen Guttmann, Richard Holt, John Lowerson, Tony Mason, Wray Vamplew, and Peter McIntosh.[2] This *Bulletin* marked the first stage in three key iterations that resulted in the *Sport in History* journal that is now recognized as a leading publication in the field of Sports History.

The *BSSH Bulletin*

The two issues of the *Bulletin*, produced in 1984 and edited by Richard Cox, consisted primarily of information for members, including details of complementary organizations, conferences, and sources, with little in the way of research, although the July 1984 *Bulletin* did highlight ongoing research projects being undertaken by Wray Vamplew, Richard Holt, and Chris Dodd, among others.[3] The BSSH launched a more research-focused publication in May 1984, *The British Journal of Sports History* (*BJHS*) (later to become the *International Journal of the History of Sport* in 1987), which, according to the then BSSH Chairman J.A. Mangan's report at the Chester conference, had been 'well received in many parts of the world' resulting in its editorial board being extended by including overseas academics, including Arnd Kruger from Germany.[4] The first issue of the *BJHS* included an article by James Walvin about the state of sports history and the need for a serious journal,[5] and co-founding editor of this journal, Richard Cox, believes this to have been the 'first initiative to

DOI: 10.4324/9780429318306-49

create a more scholarly publication to win academic respectability'. For him, it represented an attempt to appeal to the academic community that was developing around the field of sports history to supplement the *Bulletin*'s appeal to physical educationists, antiquarians, statisticians, collectors of ephemera, and revival groups, but it seems the BSSH struggled to reach the target circulation of 200 within three years that was required by the potential publishers Cass in order to demonstrate its long-term viability.[6]

The January 1985 issue of the *Bulletin* was the first to feature a detailed research article, giving the 71 members of the BSSH an opportunity to read a substantial piece on 'Sport in Surrey', written by archivist Dr D.A. Robinson. However, the July issue returned to giving members useful information about publications and events, as well as a programme for the BSSH conference, held at Jordanhill College of Education in Glasgow from 29 June to 1 July 1985.[7] In his introduction to the January 1986 issue of the *Bulletin*, Tony Mason, who took over as BSSH chair in late 1986, observed that the Bulletin fulfilled an important function for members in keeping them in touch with the Society and up-to-date with all the 'important tools of the trade for the historian of sport' and he urged members to keep the new editor, Jack Williams, informed of any developments.[8] This issue contained a transcript of a lengthy conversation between Tony Mason and Dennis Brailsford, together with a list of recent publications and details of the 94 BSSH members for 1985–1986. The July issue of that year featured an article from Peter Reed from the Liverpool Museum about Museums and the History of Sport and commentary on the A Level in Sport Studies, alongside the now standard material relating to sources and ongoing research projects.[9]

While the *Bulletin* had previously been produced in an A5 pamphlet format, two issues, the volumes for 1988 to 1991, were published in A4 and only once in the year. These volumes also marked a significant change in content, reflecting a response to the failure of the attempt in 1984 to create a long-lasting academic journal that would be permanently associated with the BSSH and provide a platform for academic research outputs. The 1988 volume combined traditional *Bulletin* content with papers delivered at the BSSH conference at the South Glamorgan Institute of Higher Education between 11 and 13 September 1987, by E. Allen, Peter McIntosh, and Alan Tomlinson, with five 'Research Reports' and several abstracts relating to the social history of physical, education, sport, and recreation.[10] In many respects, the editor, Jack Williams, was developing something that had much more of the feel of an academic journal, and John Lowerson, who took on the editorial responsibilities for volume 9 in 1989 and volume 10 in 1990, and Russel Potts, who took responsibility for volume 11 in 1991, continued to adopt that approach. The 1989 volume included the Aberdare Prize-winning essay on inter-war cricket from 1987 by Joe Thackway alongside research articles on topics ranging from Black Country bullbaiting to fifteenth-century tournament regulations.[11] The 1990 volume 10 presented all but one of the papers from the 1989 BSSH workshop on the 'Economics of Sport', held at Warwick University, the research ranging from football and cricket to television and sports sponsorship. The marriage between membership-related material and research that was a feature of the *Bulletin* in these years was reflected in the foreword to this volume, which noted that sports history had shown a 'marked capacity for development' within the last decade and advised members to communicate directly their research and other information to the *Bulletin* as often as they could.[12] A significant feature of membership publications over the years, both newsletter and bulletins, were Richard Cox's efforts in compiling data on archival holdings, together with recent publications and dissertations via the annual bibliographies, which grew year on year reflecting the growing interest and output. The bibliographies published in the *BSSH*

The Sport in History *journal*

Bulletin that transitioned into *The Sports Historian* dealt with everything published on Britain by a range of sports statisticians, antiquaries, chroniclers, and independent researchers.[13]

The final volume printed in A4 format, number 11 in 1991, published papers emanating from the 1990 annual meeting that had 'Sport and the Armed Forces' as its theme and introduced a new feature on lesser-known sports starting with Sean Creighton writing on the roller-skating boom of 1909. The foreword to this volume illustrated the depth of strategic thinking that characterized the BSSH with plans for conference topics now being discussed three years in advance, and it was at this point that the BSSH committee decided to separate its publications, keeping one format for issues related to members and launching a second publication, an academic journal, this time titled *The Sports Historian*.[14] In Spring 1992, the BSSH revived its *Newsletter*, starting with no. 1, as a mechanism for communication with the membership. Editor Dave Terry essentially retained the structure of the *Bulletin* but without the research articles that had become a central feature of the publication, which were now being transferred to the academic journal. That is not to say that articles of interest were completely ignored, but the *Newsletter* now provided an outlet primarily for non-academic communications, starting in this first issue with observations on chess, films on boxing, surfing, and an interview with an Olympian's daughter. These research articles represented some interesting original research and, although not historiographically grounded, the *Newsletter* did ensure that non-academic enthusiasts had a forum for their outlet.[15] The articles were accompanied by information on conferences, sources, and a full list giving the names and addresses of the Society's now 102 strong membership.[16] From this point onward, the *Newsletter* served its function of communicating with the membership annually until *Newsletter* no. 15, published in the Spring of 2002, and the content of these volumes documents the growth and consolidation of the BSSH and the field of sports history. Membership stood at 160 in April 1997, 194 in February 1998, 204 by March 1999, and 230 by April 2000.[17]

The Sports Historian

Newsletter no. 2 in Spring 1993 reiterated that the purpose of the BSSH was:

> To promote, stimulate and encourage study, collection, research and publication on sporting tradition; to organise meetings and to issue publications so as to advance interest and scholarship in this area of study; to liaise with individuals and institutions who have an interest in the aims of the society.[18]

A logical extension of these aims was the establishment of an academic journal, and the 1993 *Newsletter* announced to the membership that the *Bulletin* was being renamed *The Sports Historian* (rather than being called *Sporting Heritage, Sporting Legacy, Sports History Today*, or *Sporting Historian*, which had all been considered).[19] The first issue of *The Sports Historian* appeared in May 1993, although in recognition of the work that had gone on before with the *Bulletin*, its volume number was 13. The *BSSH Newsletter* no. 3 in Spring 1994 recorded 'Journal Editor' among the committee positions, a role occupied at that point by Russell Potts,[20] who edited the May 1993 (volume 13), May 1994 (volume 14), and May 1995 (volume 15) editions, the latter two with the assistance of an editorial board of John Lowerson, Tony Mason, Alan Tomlinson, Wray Vamplew, Jack Williams, and Gareth Williams, supported by Richard Cox as book reviews editor. Starting with the May 1996 volume 16, Benny Peiser took over as editor, assisted by associate editors Tony Mason, Sir Derek Birley,

355

and Richard Cox. In 1997, the same team, with the addition of Wray Vamplew, moved to producing two issues a year, in May and November, starting with volume 17, issues 1 and 2, volume 18, issues 1 and 2 in 1998, and then volume 19, issues 1 and 2 in 1999. The extended editorial board included many well-known British and international names such as Dennis Brailsford, Grant Jarvie, Jeffrey Hill, Richard Holt, John Lowerson, Catriona Parratt, Gertrud Pfister, Joachim Rühl, Alan Tomlinson, Patricia Vertinsky, Jack Williams, and Gareth Williams. While Benny Peiser, with the help of Tony Mason and Martin Polley, handled issue 1 of volume 20 in May 2000, Martin then took over editing the journal for the November issue that year and the May 2001, volume 21, issue 1, before handing over to Tony Collins for the November issue. Tony Collins and Jeff Hill then edited the May and November issues for 2002 (volume 22) before overseeing several important changes for the journal, not least a change of name and an association with a leading publishing house. For anyone wishing to access articles published in *The Sports Historian*, most of the volumes (1993, 1995, 1996, 1997, 1998, 2000, and 2001) are archived and freely available on the LA84 Foundation Digital Library website.[21]

Sport in History

The editorial for the *Newsletter* volume numbers 16 and 17 in Winter 2002–2003 announced that the *Newsletter* would be changing its name to the *Bulletin* and *The Sports Historian* would be changing to *Sport in History*, in the hope that 'the new names will project a new image more in line with their contents'.[22] Issue 18 of the *BSSH Bulletin*, previously the *Newsletter*, in the Summer of 2003 retained the A5 format, although it was now produced in white with a front illustration. Dave Terry, who been responsible for the *Newsletter* for several years, continued as editor and the *Bulletin* included short articles, in this case on billiards and on teaching sport history in America, alongside its conference reports and information for members.[23] Frank Galligan took on the editorship of the *Bulletin* in 2005 and it continued to appear once or twice annually up to issue 27 in the Spring/Summer of 2009, fulfilling its primary function of providing a platform for membership interaction with the BSSH.[24]

The first volume of the renamed *Sport in History* (volume 23) was edited by Tony Collins and Jeff Hill in 2003, when two issues were produced as normal. According to Martin Johnes, the shift in name to *Sport in History* was meant to convey a journal that was about history rather than sport. It was to be a signal of academic seriousness, partly influenced by the desire to establish the credibility of the journal and reflective of the tensions within the Society about whether it was for academics or for independent researchers. The pressure created by the Research Excellence Framework (or Research Assessment Exercise as it was then) was also part of this story.[25] The change of name conjoined with a series of colloquia at De Montfort University, organized chiefly by Dick Holt and Mike Cronin, known as 'Historians on Sport'.[26] Only one issue of the journal was published in 2004 (Summer, issue 1), which was probably the result of the negotiations taking place that would lead to radical changes to the profile of the journal. The *Bulletin* for the Summer of 2005 included within its back cover an advert for the *Sport in History* journal, 'New to Routledge for 2005', with Tony Collins and Jeff Hill, both of De Montfort University, as editors. The journal, starting with volume 25, was due to be produced three times a year and was described as 'a history journal that publishes original, archivally-based research on the history of sport, leisure and recreation. The journal encourages the study of sport to illuminate broader historical issues and debates'.

The Sports Historian had previously been produced in-house at Manchester Institute of Science and Technology by Richard Cox but this alliance with an external publisher in 2005

The Sport in History *journal*

marked the point at which the journal adopted a more traditional, professionalized approach to academic publication. It was also a recognition that the demands being made on volunteer time and effort as the Society expanded were not sustainable, not least in terms of the distribution of material to the membership.[27] Despite establishing this relationship with Routledge, the BSSH Executive remained adamant that the journal should remain a benefit of member of the Society and that has been the case ever since.[28]

Volume 25, issues 1, 2, and 3 were published by Routledge in April, August, and December 2005 respectively and edited by Tony Collins and Jeff Hill. Reflecting the move to a formal publishing platform, the extended editorial board was augmented by several well-respected academics, including Julie Anderson, Mike Cronin, Paul Dimeo, Philip Dine, Charlotte MacDonald, Martin Johnes, Malcolm Maclean, and Dave Russell. This was a process repeated over the following years. In 2007, Mike Huggins was added to the extended editorial board, Christopher Young in 2011, Brad Beaven, Christiane Eisenberg, Emma Griffin, Susanna Hedenborg, Shohei Sato, Ross McKibbin, and Carol Osbourne in 2014. In 2006, Dilwyn Porter replaced Jeff Hill as an editor and he and Tony Collins edited the three issues per annum of the journal for volume 26 (April, August, and December 2006). Interest in the journal had reached the stage at the end of 2006 that there were enough submissions to extend each volume to four issues, and in 2007 Tony Collins and Dilwyn Porter edited issues 1 to 4 in March, June, September, and December respectively, repeating the pattern again with volume 28 in 2008 and establishing the pattern that still exists today. Although there have been discussions subsequently about increasing the number of issues per year, consecutive editors, with the whole-hearted support of the BSSH Executive and Trustees, have always vigorously resisted any dilution of the journal's quality of content that would almost inevitably accompany any further expansion in the number of issues.

An important factor in maintaining continuity in the operation of the journal has been the practice of ensuring that incoming editors always have an experiential period as part of the editorial board before taking on a leadership role. For volume 28, issue 4, in December 2008, Paul Dimeo and Martin Johnes joined Dilwyn Porter as editors and they went on to edit the four issues for volume 29 in 2009. They were joined for the year by Matthew Taylor while Neil Carter took on the book reviews role for the journal, a position that Richard Cox had filled ever since the journal's inception. For volume 30 in 2010, Matthew Taylor took on the chief editor role, assisted by Paul Dimeo and Martin Johnes as associate editors, a team that also dealt with volume 31 in 2011, although Martin Polley replaced Paul Dimeo for issue 4 in December. This editorial group remained stable throughout 2012 (volume 32, issues 1 to 4) and 2013 (volume 33, issues 1 to 4) and for volume 34, issue 1, in March 2014. The impact of making the *Sport in History* journal available online in this period was significant, with a steady increase in downloads from 11,374 in 2012, to 16,769 in 2013, 26,407 in 2014, and 30,823 in 2015.[29]

As from issue 2 in 2014, Neil Carter took over as editor-in-chief, assisted by Martin Johnes, Martin Polley, and Matt Taylor as associate editors with Dave Day replacing Matt Taylor for issue 4 in December, at which point Samantha-Jayne Oldfield took over Neil Carter's role as book reviews editor. The same team dealt with all four issues of volume 35 in 2015 and the first two issues of volume 36 in 2016 but several editorial changes took place as from the September issue, with Dave Day taking over as editor-in-chief, assisted by Dean Allen, Martin Polley, and Kay Schiller as associate editors. This team went on to handle all the submissions for volume 37 in 2017 and the first three issues for volume 38 in 2018 before Kay Schiller took over as editor-in-chief, as from the December issue. Increasingly, social media was being used to enhance the reach of the journal and this has become an important publicity source for the journal, as highlighted by late-2019 Altmetric scores, which showed total mentions of 2,946, of which 2,826 were from Twitter, related to 265 research outputs.[30]

Under Kay's direction, and reflecting contemporary concerns within the sports history community, the emphasis since his taking over as editor-in-chief in October 2018 has been on diversity. This means diversity in terms of journal outputs with varying formats, including an increased number of special issues on topics ranging from 'Hemingway and Sport' (volume 39, issue 3) to 'Masculinities in Martial Arts and Combat Sports' (volume 40, issue 3, 2020) to types of article and article lengths from 6,000 words to 12,000 words, and to diversifying the board of editors in terms of gender, ethnicity, career age, and location. This is to allow for the journal to become more reflective of the interests and make-up of the historical profession and student body as it is today both in the UK and abroad. Kay's efforts, and those of the BSSH Trustees, to turn what for a long time was an all-male and white intellectual undertaking into a more inclusive venture, have been informed by the findings of the Royal Historical Society's 2019 reports on race and gender. Whereas the journal is still waiting for its first female editor-in-chief, there has been progress in getting on board both established and early career historians like Samantha Oldfield, Lisa Taylor, George Kioussis, and Souvik Naha, alongside the more experienced Rob Lake, who is based in Canada.

The focus on inclusivity has also partly informed the special issues that have become a feature of *Sport in History*. For example, in 2019 the journal published two issues (volume 39, issues 2 and 4) on women's football entitled *Upfront and Onside: Women, Football, History and Heritage*, edited by Jean Williams et al. on the occasion of the FIFA Women's World Cup. Volume 40, issue 4 (December 2020), edited by Carol Osborne and Fiona Skillen, provides orientation on *Women in Sports History: New Directions* on the occasion of the tenth anniversary of their first special issue on women's sport history. High-quality special issues, for which the journal always welcomes proposals, represent useful opportunities for scholars to bring together colleagues to work under a common theme and demonstrate the advances made in specific fields in a much quicker fashion than book publications allow for. They also make the journal stand out in what for better or worse has become a very crowded field of journal publications in sport history. *Sport in History* has always remained first and foremost a members' journal and the BSSH, working with its journal editor, will continue to use its pages to work towards an ever greater acceptance of sports history by the mainstream historical profession, so that its scholarly outputs are recognized for what they are, that is, extremely important contributions to the broader field of cultural history.

Notes

1 *BSSH Bulletin*, no. 1 (January 1984): 1.
2 *BSSH Bulletin*, no. 1 (January 1984).
3 *BSSH Bulletin*, no. 2 (July 1984).
4 *BSSH Bulletin*, no. 3 (January 1985): 43.
5 Email correspondence between Martin Johnes and Dave Day, 25 November 2019.
6 Email correspondence between Richard Cox and Kay Schiller, 5 June 2019.
7 *BSSH Bulletin*, no. 3 (January 1985): 2–35; *BSSH Bulletin*, no. 4 (July 1985): 1–2.
8 *BSSH Bulletin*, no. 5 (January 1986): 1.
9 *BSSH Bulletin*, no. 5 (January 1986); *BSSH Bulletin*, no. 6 (July 1986), no page numbers.
10 *BSSH Bulletin*, no. 8 (1988).
11 *BSSH Bulletin*, no. 9 (1989).
12 *BSSH Bulletin*, no. 10 (1990).

The Sport in History *journal*

13 Email correspondence between Richard Cox and Dave Day, 25 November 2019.
14 *BSSH Bulletin*, no. 11 (1991).
15 Email correspondence between Martin Johnes and Dave Day, 25 November 2019.
16 *BSSH Newsletter*, no. 1 (Spring 1992).
17 *BSSH Newsletter*, no. 6 (Winter 1997): 3; *BSSH Newsletter*, no. 8 (Autumn 1998): 3; *BSSH Newsletter*, no. 10 (Autumn 1999): 4; *BSSH Newsletter*, no. 12 (Autumn 2000): 5.
18 *BSSH Newsletter*, no. 2 (Spring 1993): 6.
19 *BSSH Newsletter*, no. 2 (Spring 1993): 4.
20 *BSSH Newsletter*, no. 3 (Spring 1994): 6.
21 Go to https://digital.la84.org/.
22 *BSSH Bulletin*, nos. 16/17 (Winter 2002–2003): 2.
23 *BSSH Bulletin*, no. 18 (Summer 2003).
24 *BSSH Bulletin*, no. 18 (Summer 2003): 3.
25 Email correspondence between Martin Johnes and Dave Day, 25 November 2019; For contemporary concerns around journals see Martin Johnes, 'Putting the History into Sport: On Sport History and Sport Studies in the U.K.', *Journal of Sport History* 31, no. 2 (2004): 145–160.
26 Email correspondence between Jeffrey Hill and Dave Day, 26 November 2019.
27 Email correspondence between Martin Johnes and Dave Day, 25 November 2019.
28 Email correspondence between Richard Cox and Kay Schiller, 5 June 2019.
29 Email correspondence between Alejandra Black of Taylor and Francis and Dave Day, 25 November 2019.
30 See *Sport in History* altmetric highlights at https://www.altmetric.com/explorer/report/1f7b2e65-8b71-4e75-84cc-81c4306e0caf.

Acknowledgements

We would like to thank Jeff Hill, Dilwyn Porter, Martin Johnes, Richard Cox, and Alejandra Black for their comments on earlier versions of this chapter.

44

THE INTERNATIONAL JOURNAL OF THE HISTORY OF SPORT 1984–2020[1]

Twenty-four million words and still counting

Wray Vamplew

Firm foundations with shaky leadership

As this chapter reaches completion, *The International Journal of the History of Sport* (*IJHS*) is about to publish its 305th issue, over 24 million words in aggregate. It has become the premier truly international sports history journal. Credit for establishing this behemoth goes to J.A. 'Tony' Mangan, though he must also take the blame for the subsequent debacle that befell the journal.

The *IJHS* began life in 1984 as the commercially produced *British Journal of Sports History* (*BJSH*). Due to internal political division and a reluctance by the publisher Frank Cass to reduce subscription fees for Society members, it had no connection with the British Society of Sports History. Its mission was 'to stimulate, promote and co-ordinate interest in the history of sport, recreation and leisure … and to advance scholarship in the study of these various aspects of social history by providing a forum for the discussion of new approaches, ideas and information'.[2]

In 1987, still under the Foundation Editorship of Mangan, it adopted its present title, but there was little comment on the change from the now newly titled Executive Editor, though he later claimed that this had been the intention all along.[3] The immediate impact was an expansion of the 13-member editorial board to 24 and the appointment of three editors under Mangan as well as regional editors for Australasia, Canada, Western Europe, Eastern Europe and the USSR, Japan, Latin America, and the United States. Additionally women, society, sport (as an entity), English language and foreign languages, and bibliographic editors were announced.

Mangan had astutely realized that a commercial publisher offered more opportunity to become international in outlook than did a society-based journal and articles began to cover sports history in every continent and even a one-off, two-part, German language historio-graphy.[4] Under his entrepreneurial leadership, *IJHS* introduced special issues dealing with major themes in sports history, beginning in 1995 with a self-edited collection of articles on nationalism and sport in Europe and followed before the turn of the century by compilations on European heroes, sport in Nordic countries, and a double issue on the Fascist body as a

360   DOI: 10.4324/9780429318306-50

political icon.[5] Ultimately, such special issues of *IJHS* formed the basis of Routledge's book series Sport in the Global Society: Historical Perspectives.

The 1990s were halcyon years for *IJHS*. A glance at the volumes for that decade reveals papers by almost every sports history scholar with an existing or emerging international reputation and several articles that have become seminal in the field, including ones by John Bale, Fan Hong, Catriona Parratt, S.W. Pope, and Steven Riess.[6] However, there was trouble on the horizon.

Mangan progressively expanded the journal from three issues a year when it began its new life to four in 2000, five in 2004, six in 2005, eight in 2006, and two more each year until it reached 18 in 2010. The author remembers the astonishment with which this figure was greeted at a round table of Routledge journal editors in Liverpool. Although the journal was expanded at his request, Mangan could not cope with the resultant pressure to fill its pages, which was accomplished only by devoting whole issues to book manuscripts and reprints of books, creating a meaningless annual review, and publishing some very thin issues both intellectually and physically. He also lost control of the editorial process, which seemingly overwhelmed him. This was not surprising as simultaneously he was responsible for the *IHJS* and three other academic journals that he had founded, the *European Sports History Review*, *Soccer and Society*, and *Culture, Sport, Society*. Indicative of the pressure he was under was his failure to correctly identify the starting dates of *BJSH* and *IJHS* when reviewing the progress of *IJHS* in 2006.[7] In 2007 Mangan introduced annual regional issues, each with its own editor, beginning with North America, South Asia, North and South East Asia, followed by Europe in 2008 and Australasia and the Pacific in 2009. This may have lessened Mangan's workload, though he insisted on adding the titles of Regional Consultant Editor for three of the issues to his portfolio.

By 2009, the journal was in crisis and Mangan was asked to relinquish his role as what he now termed Senior Executive Academic Editor. Academic credibility was low and the journal was held in disdain by many senior academics including, as Mangan's successor found out, members of its own International Advisory Board. The journal was seen as having become a vehicle for personal aggrandisement in which materials extolling his virtues were inserted by Mangan into articles and whole issues (four of them) devoted to singing his praises.[8] Some of this was merited given his contributions to sports history, but the place to do it was not a journal that you edited.

When he was eased out by the publishers he left a chaotic situation in which the refereeing process was opaque; some articles had not been reviewed a year after submission; many authors had not been informed whether their articles had been accepted or rejected; commitments to publish were inadequately documented and the backlog of articles was unknown; forward planning was insufficiently detailed; the page budget was not being adhered to leading to the postponement of a whole issue in 2010; the journal website was out of date, over two years in some instances, and contained submission instructions geared to a non-electronic age; and the editorial structure was over-heavy, convoluted, and without job specification. The meagre files that Mangan handed over to the publishers revealed not a single mention of any referees or their comments, and plans for future special issues were just titles without information on editors or authors. *IJHS* was flying by the seat of Mangan's pants, which was no way to run a journal.

Moving forward but falling behind

Wray Vamplew, Emeritus Professor of Sports History at Stirling University, was approached by Jonathan Manley from Routledge, who now published *IJHS*, to become Managing

Editor (effective from mid-2010) with the objective of restoring the journal's academic credibility. A secondary aim was to have *IJHS* dominate the sports history journal market. He was chosen primarily because of his experience in turning around the *Journal of Sport History*, the journal of the North American Society for Sport History, which had fallen many issues behind schedule. Vamplew faced some suspicion (though not hostility) from the existing editorial team, all of whom had been appointed by Mangan. They had proposed an editorial collective but Vamplew argued that such a cooperative approach was too risky in a commercial operation. He stressed the need for a Managing Editor to co-ordinate activities, control budgets, ensure that deadlines and page limits were adhered to, liaise with the publishers, and be the ultimate decision taker. Open discussion and a willingness from both sides to give and take led to the establishment of a good working relationship. Vamplew ceded a clause forbidding Academic Editors to publish their own work in *IJHS* (though he insisted that they must be double blind reviewed) and accepted their opposition to a particular appointment. In turn, he learned that several of the editorial team had become disillusioned with Mangan and welcomed most of the planned developments. All but one of the existing Academic Editors were reappointed to fixed-term contracts but of varying lengths so as to stagger any changeovers. The positions were sold to the incumbents on the basis of editorial freedom, the ability to choose their own editorial teams to ease the workload and delegate whatever tasks they wished, the potential to create a high-quality academic output, and an opportunity to influence the direction of sports history. Vamplew created an Editorial College comprising himself and the Academic Editors to discuss policy, develop strategic and operational plans, agree on editorial responsibilities, and ratify the publication schedule.

Vamplew's immediate tasks were to streamline the cumbersome editorial and advisory structure, to develop an electronic system for receiving and peer-reviewing submissions, and to set up a fully documented publishing schedule with the focus on original articles. He abandoned the complicated Mangan structure of titled positions such as International consultant editors, regional consultant editors and the like in favour of a simple Editorial Board (nominated by the Editorial College), which was to be a group drawn on for referees rather than merely a collection of figureheads to attract attention. Each Academic Editor was given autonomy to recruit and appraise their own editorial teams, delegating whatever tasks they chose to members of that team. All these positions were on a two-year basis so that new blood could be introduced over time. In order to reduce processing time, Vamplew changed the conventional peer-review requirements from three to two referees and introduced the ScholarOne system for organizing submissions and reviews. Although, because of elderly scholar resistance and the pipeline effect, this took until 2015 to be fully implemented, it has streamlined the process. The main problem has been the one-off Guest Editors who could not really learn by doing. Moreover, iFirst has enabled contributors to have their work placed in the public domain earlier than the actual publication issue. All commitments that could be traced were honoured, though some of these stretched into 2013.

Vamplew's appointment did not go down well with Mangan and his followers, the latter rightly concerned that the previous automatic acceptance of their papers would disappear. A cell of Mangan acolytes attempted to entrap Vamplew in a dispute over a paper twice as long as permitted, which had been rejected by another journal but accepted by Mangan. They planned to denounce him to the Head of Taylor and Francis, the publishers of *IJHS*, but their scheme backfired when they inadvertently included him in the conspiratorial email discussing their strategy. Vamplew took his petty revenge by publishing the paper as a commentary rather than a formal article with a note saying that it had been accepted by the old regime, something he did not do for other articles in the pipeline when he took over. In fairness, the journal continued to publish contributions from the Mangan clique if they were recommended by neutral referees. Mangan persistently attempted to intervene in the running of the journal. He bombarded both the Managing Editor and the publishers with complaints about production delays while refusing to acknowledge that much of this stemmed from his own actions, including a failure to deliver what he had committed to several years before. He refused to follow *IJHS* procedures in regard to the use of ScholarOne, article length, and deadlines. He sent out unapproved pre-publication flyers on special issues (for which he had previously appointed himself Guest Editor) even before the papers had been accepted; some of these flyers contained serious misstatements. He fought unsuccessfully and acrimoniously to have workshop funds allocated to conferences he had organized using the *IJHS* imprimatur but without Editorial College approval. When the Editorial College rejected a proposal for yet another special issue in his honour he mounted a campaign to undermine the College and have the decision reversed. Throughout the early years of the new regime he communicated to third parties denigratory, possibly libellous, comments comparing the current state of the journal with what it was when he was in charge. He was, as acknowledged even by an admirer who edited a special issue in his honour, 'a man of no little ego'.[9] Ultimately some leaked emails brought matters to a head and in late 2013 the Editorial College and the publishers agreed that his relationship with the journal had become irrevocably dysfunctional and, while continuing to acknowledge his role in establishing *IJHS*, he was informed that all links would be severed.

Although he was unable to persuade the publishers to rebrand the journal with a new title, Vamplew had some successes. He felt that the publishers were trying to run five or six journals within one and wanting to do so relatively cheaply. His point was that *IJHS* was a commercial operation not a society journal and he negotiated a budget – though he obtained only about two-thirds of what he requested – by which the publishers gave a prize for the best article each year thus attracting annual publicity;[10] provided money for the Academic Editors to attend conferences and part-fund workshops the contributions from which formed the basis of special issues; and offered limited funding to assist contributors whose first language was not English in expression and formatting. As Managing Editor, Vamplew had some significant achievements. He added Africa (2011) and the Middle East (2012) to the list of regional issues, though on an alternating biennial basis. *IJHS* was not formally associated with any learned society which may have adversely affected its marketing but Vamplew developed a relationship with the International Society for the History of Physical Education and Sport which involved the publishers funding a keynote lecture at ISHPES conferences and devoting a special issue to papers from such conferences. Most significantly, he gained citation status for *IJHS*, a vital factor for authors in this academic age of metrication. However, his idea for a special issue devoted solely to book reviews did not catch on. Book reviews remain a weakness of *IJHS* compared with other journals, especially the *Journal of Sport History* which can allocate up to half an issue to such matters. Vamplew's immediate successor, Rob Hess, did make the book review process more transparent for authors, publishers, and reviewers and developed a page devoted to such reviews on the *IJHS* website.

Vamplew had instigated a succession plan involving temporary promotions of regional Academic Editors. This came into operation in July 2014 when he decided to retire from the Managing Editor position six months early. The publishers had set up a new production team and it seemed appropriate to have them bed in with a new Editor. Consequently, Rob Hess from Victoria University in Melbourne, a major centre of sports research in Australia, stepped up from his role as Academic Editor for Australasia and the Pacific for a three-year stint. In turn, he was succeeded by Mark Dyreson, Academic Editor for the Americas and

Professor of Kinesiology at the Pennsylvania State University, another important centre of sports research. Hess made several innovations. He tidied up the website; refreshed and trimmed the editorial board; excluded the publication of research notes; changed the rejection terminologies to 'unsound' and 'unsuitable'; and reduced the resubmission time for major revisions from six months to 60 days. As part of its international remit, *IJHS* published translated abstracts in several languages but Vamplew made non-English abstracts online only as he felt they took up too much space in the journal. However, under Hess, translation of abstracts ceased and readers were left to utilize Google Translation.

Vamplew did little to assist *IJHS* in terms of social media. This was partly a generational distaste for such communication but mainly because he gave it a low priority among more pressing tasks to clean up the disorganization he had inherited. Hess, however, was more attuned and he appointed a Social Media Editor and, with her, promoted and publicized the journal. Hess had the unenviable task of introducing a new style guide. Rolling this out while there were so many manuscripts in the system in various states of review and revision inevitably led to frustration on the part of authors, editors, and production staff. At times Hess could have parts of up to 14 issues on his personal computer. However, the journal began to fall behind schedule. Vamplew had been pragmatic and had traded off presentational quality control for keeping to the publication schedule, believing the latter had more importance for subscribers and contributors. Prior to his appointment Vamplew had noted the poor standard of proofing in several issues. He appointed an Associate Editor to bring manuscripts into shape but she resigned after dealing with one issue, claiming that the task was way above her pay grade. Vamplew then took on the task himself but soon gave it up as too onerous and unwinnable a contest. It was not the quality of the content that was the trouble but the academic presentation. However, neither Hess nor Dyreson was prepared to be so lax and they were determined to improve the presentational quality of the final copy. Almost inevitably Hess and Dyreson found themselves devoting more and more time to micro-editing in order to create acceptable copy. In contrast to the backlog faced by Vamplew, which was a build-up of unprocessed submissions, that confronting Hess and Dyreson was output based. Contributing to a perfect storm of publication delay were changes in the copyediting team, the introduction at the publishers' insistence of a new style guide, a rise in the proportion of submissions from Asia to over 20 per cent of accepted papers, many of whose authors had little familiarity with academic English, and, of course, the floods in India which severely disrupted the production process.

Restructure and recovery

When Dyreson took over, *IJHS* was running over ten issues behind and he spent a year treading water rather than catching up. In 2018 Dyreson, fearful that *IJHS* (and possibly also the Managing Editor!) was heading for meltdown, undertook a root and branch review. His analysis revealed that a culture had developed in which authors and Guest Editors took little responsibility for the presentation of manuscripts. These editors were accepting articles for publication which too often were deficient in regards to referencing, house style, and basic scholarly standards of grammar and readability. Corrections were left for the Academic Editors to do and, sad to say, on many occasions certain editors did not vet the work adequately. Nor did it appear that the publisher's copyeditors were always up to the task. Hence, a pile of accepted articles was accumulating which still needed enormous amounts of editing, a task that fell to the Managing Editors, leaving them, as full-time academics, with little time to actually manage *IJHS*. The appointment of a new copyediting team in the summer of 2018 improved matters but bedding them in delayed production by several more months. Dyreson drew up a plan to get the journal back on schedule which, after input from the Editorial College, was accepted by the publishers for instigation in 2019. Put simply, the problem was a combination of too many issues and too few trusted editors. Publishing 18 issues per volume had been a contentious matter for several years but efforts to persuade the publishers to cut back continued to be fruitless. However, they were willing to fund an expansion in the editorial team with each editor taking full responsibility for one or two issues a year and making the final call on acceptance or rejection. Ironically, the new budget was roughly what Vamplew had requested almost a decade previously. Guest Editors are to be kept away from most of the intricacies of ScholarOne.

The backlog is now being reduced, which is vital in an academic world where metrics have become increasingly important.[11] As most citation indices operate on a two-year time frame, any delay in publication can have serious consequences. The growing emphasis on metrics has already caused problems for *IJHS* because of its unique position for a long time as the only sports history journal with citation status, which means that references in other sports history journals are ignored. *IJHS* thus runs the risk of having too large a proportion of self-citations, which could ultimately undermine its citation status. Additionally its impact factor has been adversely affected by its aggregate level of citations being diluted across so many issues. Fortunately, two developments in the citation indices are likely to aid *IJHS* provided that it gets back on track. One is the decision from 2017 to include references in books, previously eschewed because of the emphasis on science subjects which, unlike the humanities and social sciences, gave little research credit to books and monographs. Second, and probably much more important given the two-year citations window, is the establishment in 2015 of the Emerging Sources Citations Index, which allows journals of recognized quality but not yet of citation status to contribute to impact factor citations of those that have such status.

Despite its several crises, *IJHS* remains the world's premier sports history journal in terms of impact factors and library subscriptions with over 2,500 institutions having access. It is far more international in its coverage than any of its competitors but has sufficient regional material to challenge more locally oriented journals whilst maintaining its comparative advantage as the only truly international journal. It now has annual issues on Europe, Asia, Australia and the Pacific, and the Americas with alternating biennial ones on Africa and the Middle East. One potential production issue is whether hard print copy will be continued. The bulk of such copies go to members of the editorial teams whereas libraries these days much prefer electronic journals. This author for one likes to see the spread of copies along his office shelves but he is realistic enough to accept that their day is likely over. Anyway, the shelves are pretty full with 24 million words and still counting.

Notes

1 This chapter is generally unreferenced as it is based on confidential documents such as internal reviews and reports, correspondence between the publishers and the editors, and minutes from Editorial College meetings in the possession of the author (who was Managing Editor of *The International Journal of the History of Sport* from 2010 to 2014), some of which were supplied – again in confidence – by his successors Rob Hess and Mark Dyreson. Although it is not good academic practice to eschew references, the author trusts that the fact that he has been self-critical may lend support to his interpretation of the evidence.

2 J.A. Mangan, J. Lowerson, and R. Cox, 'Statement from the Editors', *British Journal of Sports History* 1, no. 1 (1984): iii.

Wray Vamplew

3 J.A. Mangan, 'A Personal Perspective: Twenty-five Years, IJHS', *The International Journal of the History of Sport* 23, no. 1 (2006): 1.

4 Arnd Krüger and Lothar Wieser, 'German Language Sport Historiography of the 1980s: Part 1: Reference Works and General Histories of Sport', *The International Journal of the History of Sport* 14, no. 1 (1997): 138–167; Arnd Krüger and Lothar Wieser 'German Language Sport Historiography of the 1980s: Part 2: Histories of National/Regional sport and Individual Sports', *The International Journal of the History of Sport* 14, no. 2 (1997): 122–162.

5 J.A. Mangan ed. *Tribal Identities: Nationalism, Europe and Sport* [*The International Journal of the History of Sport* 12, no. 2 (1995)]; Richard Holt, J.A. Mangan, and Pierre Lanfranchi eds., *European Heroes: Myth, Identity and Sport* [*The International Journal of the History of Sport* 13 no. 1 (1996)]; Henrik Meinander and J.A. Mangan eds. *The Nordic World: Sport in Society* [*The International Journal of the History of Sport* 14 no. 3 (1997)]; J.A. Mangan ed. *Shaping the Superman: Fascist Body as Political Icon: Aryan Fascism* [*The International Journal of the History of Sport* 16 no. 2 (1999)]; J.A. Mangan ed. *Shaping the Superman: Fascist Body as Political Icon: Global Fascism* [*The International Journal of the History of Sport* 16 no. 2 (1999)].

6 John Bale, 'Racing towards Modernity: A One-Way Street', *The International Journal of the History of Sport* 10, no. 2 (1993): 215–232; Mike Cronin, 'Fighting for Ireland, Playing for England? The Nationalist History of the Gaelic Athletic Association and the English Influence on Irish Sport', *The International Journal of the History of Sport* 15, no. 3 (1998): 36–56; Fan Hong, 'The Female Body, Missionary and Reformer: The Reconceptualization of Femininity in Modern China', *The International Journal of the History of Sport* 10, no. 2 (1993): 133–158; S.W. Pope, 'Amateurism and American Sports Culture: The Invention of an Athletic Tradition in the United States, 1870–1900', *The International Journal of the History of Sport* 13, no. 3 (1996): 290–309; Catriona M. Parratt, 'Little Means or Time: Working-Class Women and Leisure in Late Victorian and Edwardian England', *The International Journal of the History of Sport* 15, no. 2 (1998): 22–53; Steven A. Riess, 'Sport and the Redefinition of American Middle-class Masculinity', *The International Journal of the History of Sport* 8, no. 1 (1991): 5–27.

7 J.A. Mangan, 'A Personal Perspective: Twenty-five Years, IJHS', *The International Journal of the History of Sport* 23 no. 1 (2006): 1.

8 Scott A.G.M. Crawford ed. '*Serious Sport*' *J.A. Mangan's Contribution to the History of Sport* [*The International Journal of the History of Sport* 20, no. 4 (2003)]; Boria Majumdar and Fan Hong eds. *Modern Sport: The Global Obsession Politics, Class, Religion Gender: Essays in Honour of J.A. Mangan* [*The International Journal of the History of Sport* 22 no. 4 (2005)]; J.A Mangan ed. '*Manufactured Masculinity*' – *The Cultural Construction of Imperial Manliness, Morality and Militarism: Core Contributions of J.A. Mangan*' [*The International Journal of the History of Sport* 27 nos. 1–2 (2010)].

9 Scott A.G.M. Crawford, 'J.A. Mangan and *The International Journal of the History of Sport*', *The International Journal of the History of Sport* 20, no. 4 (2003): 6.

10 The first award was shared between Lai Kuan Lim and Peter Horton, 'Sport in Syonan (Singapore) 1942–1945: Centralisation and Nipponisation', *The International Journal of the History of Sport* 28, no. 6 (2011): 895–924 and Lauri Keskinen, 'Working-class Sports Clubs as Agents of Political Socialisation in Finland 1903–1923', *The International Journal of the History of Sport* 28, no. 6 (2011): 853–875.

11 For a synopsis of metrics as they relate to sport history journals see Murray G. Phillips, 'Sizing Up Sport History Journals: Metrics, Sport Humanities, and History', *The International Journal of the History of Sport* 37, no. 8 (2020): 692–704.

45

THE HISTORY OF *SPORTING TRADITIONS*

The Journal of the Australian Society for Sports History

Rob Hess

The biennial gatherings of the Australian Society for Sports History (ASSH) have always been designated as 'Sporting Traditions' conferences. The first two conferences were held in Sydney in 1977 and 1979, and papers from both events were subsequently published in book format by university presses, with a two-year time lag in each case.[1] However, the conferences actually pre-dated the formation of the Society and it was not until 1983 that there was sufficient momentum, and perhaps confidence, to both establish ASSH and set in train the publication of a dedicated journal bearing the title *Sporting Traditions: The Journal of the Australian Society for Sports History*, with the first volume appearing in November 1984. Other societies, notably the North American Society for Sport History, had preceded ASSH, and several journals dedicated to sport history also made their debut ahead of *Sporting Traditions*, notably the *Canadian Journal of History of Sport and Physical Education* (first published in May 1970) and the *Journal of Sport History* (first published in Spring 1974). Hence, in terms of the formation of societies and the publication of scholarly journals, there were models for ASSH to follow during the 'take-off' period for the academic study of sport.

In the case of Australia, however, there were some clear fault lines that emerged within the Society from the 1980s onwards, and the ASSH journal came to reflect these divisions. In summary, according to Cashman, there were three central issues which created some tension. First was the boundaries circumscribing sport history, since it was not clear if recreation or leisure should be included under the ASSH umbrella. Related to this was the question of the relationship of sports historians to other groups with an interest in the subject matter, especially scholars of human movement and so-called 'amateur' historians. Finally, there was little consensus on whether sport history should constitute its own separate area of study, or whether it should be part of the broader field of social history.[2] In the end, it was essentially historians from other fields, but with growing interests in sport, who took the lead in producing the Society's journal. This is evident in the Editorial Board of the first issue of *Sporting Traditions*, which consisted of just four individuals. The two key appointments were Wray Vamplew, the Lead Editor, a trained economist who had completed a PhD at Edinburgh University on the history of the relationship between railway development and the

DOI: 10.4324/9780429318306-51

367

Scottish economy, and subsequently became a Reader in economic history (and later a Pro-Vice-Chancellor) at Flinders University after he immigrated to South Australia in 1975,[3] and Richard Cashman, the Reviews Editor, then based in the History Department at the University of New South Wales, but who had been one of Monash University's first MA graduates in history in 1963, before moving to the United States and writing a PhD entitled 'The Myth of the Lokamanya: Tilak and Mass Politics in Maharashtraand' at Duke University. There were also two Associate Editors, namely Brian Stoddart from the Sport Studies Department at the Canberra College of Advanced Education, who had obtained his PhD from the University of Western Australia, focusing on nationalist politics in South India, and Ian Jobling, perhaps the odd one out, being an Australian who, after completing a teaching qualification, gained his Bachelor of Physical Education at the University of Alberta in Canada, before writing his MA and doctoral theses on aspects of sport history at the same institution and then returning home to a position in the Department of Human Movement Studies at the University of Queensland. In other words, Jobling was the only member of the Editorial Board who had a background in human movement and physical education.

The first issue of the journal, with a simple but bright wraparound cover in green and gold (the national colours of Australia), set out the contact details of the Editorial Board members, and also carried information about subscription rates for members of ASSH. As noted, members were 'entitled to receive one copy of each issue of *Sporting Traditions* plus periodic newsletters for the term of their subscription'.[4] The 'Editorial Preface', written by Vamplew, explained that the journal intended to provide 'an outlet for a serious, though not we hope humourless, look at sport, particularly Australian, both historical and contemporary'. He continued:

> It is hoped that readers and contributors will be drawn from all quarters; certainly it is not the board's intention to produce a journal solely for and by academics. Hence the range of books covered in our Reviews section and the establishment of our Barrackers' Corner for which we invite comments from our readers on the articles and reviews published in *Sporting Traditions* or on issues in sport or sports history.[5]

The inaugural issue contained four papers, including a short article from Vamplew himself, and two others from future presidents of the Society, namely Colin Tatz, a scholar of race and sport and at that time a Professor of Politics at Macquarie University, and Ray Crawford, Head of the Physical Education Department at the Phillip Institute of Technology and also national convenor of the Australian Council of Health, Physical Education, and Recreation special interest group concerned with the history and philosophy of physical education and sport.[6] An additional article was written by Chris McConville, a lecturer in Urban Studies at Footscray Institute of Technology, and all papers dealt with the history of Australian sport, although the material proffered by Tatz also contained some international perspectives on Black athletes. It was notable, however, that the issue was packed with book reviews (22 in number), as well as seven book notes (compiled by Cashman). In Cashman's wide-ranging introduction to the review section, he claimed it was important to make an initial policy statement 'in the interest of stimulating a continuing dialogue between the journal editors, the writers of reviews, authors, publishers and the general readership'.[7] He also asserted that his role was based on the assumption that readers 'would prefer a more extensive section on books than that which appears in many equivalent journals', a result that was achieved 'by casting ... the net much wider than some other journals'.[8] Summing up, he explained that 'The aim then is to produce a Reviews section which will be useful not only

The history of Sporting Traditions

to the specialist researcher but also for administrators, individual collectors, journalists, librarians and the general sports public,' claiming that 'There exists at present in Australia no such comprehensive and serious discussion of major books on sport,' adding 'We hope this section will fill this gap.'[9] Significantly, the issue was rounded out by 'Barrackers' Corner', with the first commentary provided by Chris Harte, consisting of a response to a review of one of his cricket books that had been reviewed in the first issue of the journal, indicating that Cashman had forwarded the review to Harte prior to the publication of the journal. From this brief overview of the context surrounding the formation of ASSH and the origins and initial content of the journal, it is apparent that there was a very conscious effort to be more inclusive of a wide readership, creating a template that has been a feature of both the Society and its journal since its inception.

On the practical side, as Vamplew later notes in his reflections on his role as Editor of the journal, 'In those pre-personal computer days everything had to be typewritten.'[10] Accordingly, the early issues of the journal contain no acknowledgement of a designer, proofreader, or printer, and no illustrations, yet are relatively devoid of typographical errors, a remarkable feat given the 'do-it-yourself' nature of producing the pioneering journal.

The second issue of the journal, published in May 1985, continued in the same vein as the first, with four articles by academics and one by a postgraduate student. There were also two review essays, 18 book reviews, and three book notes, as well as 'Barrackers' Corner', all adding up to an expanded issue. Vamplew's 'Editorial Preface' lauded the perceived success of the journal, but he rued the fact that almost all the manuscripts came from academic quarters, calling for some contributions from 'sport historians from other backgrounds',[11] a deficit that began to be corrected in future issues.

The intention here is not to produce an issue-by-issue analysis of the journal's development, but aspects of the third issue, published in November 1985, bear discussion. It seems, for example, that a survey of readership was conducted at some stage between the publication of the second and third issues. Vamplew dealt with some of the responses in an expanded 'Barrackers' Corner'. Here, he emphasized that 'although articles of general international interest are considered for publication, our emphasis is on Australasian sport'. He also added a reminder that 'All full-length articles are sent to referees for comment,'[12] but highlighted that 'this should not deter non-academics from submitting manuscripts as these are chosen from all categories of membership'.[13] His 'Editorial Preface' reflected further on this matter, when he applauded the fact that the issue featured an article by a 'non-academic sports historian'. Noting that the author in question had died before publication, he nonetheless expressed the view that 'It would be a fitting tribute to Radcliffe [Grace] if other amateur historians would now begin to contribute to our pages.'[14] This was a further manifestation of the conflicting desire of the Society, and its journal, to be inclusive, modelled on the notion that ASSH should be a 'broad church', against the view that the Society, and the journal, should be more rigorously academic in attitude and outlook. This potential schism has bedevilled the Society throughout its existence, with the variety of its publication programme an indicator of some of the tensions, as outlined below.

Sporting Traditions has always been the flagship publication of ASSH. However, several other publishing developments have had an impact, both positive and negative, on its status. As mentioned, the *ASSH Bulletin*, initially published irregularly from April/May 1985 onwards, settled into a regular biannual publication schedule. This much smaller publication enabled peripheral news and information to be siphoned out of *Sporting Traditions*, enhancing the overall academic status of the journal. The *ASSH Bulletin* also provided an outlet for shorter pieces that were not peer reviewed, such as conference reviews and opinion pieces, and over time it generally became acknowledged that, apart from editorials and book reviews, all material published in *Sporting Traditions* was of a peer-reviewed nature. A particular marker of this development was the fact that 'Barrackers' Corner' appeared for the final time in an issue of *Sporting Traditions* in May 2007.[15]

The instigation of the *ASSH Studies* series, a venture involving the publication of books, also had a direct influence on the journal. Pioneered in 1986 by the series editor, Wray Vamplew, *ASSH Studies* varied from book-length monographs, such as *Aborigines in Sport*, written by Colin Tatz and published in 1987, to anthologies such as *Crowd Violence at Australian Sport*, edited by John O'Hara and published in 1992, to collections of Honours theses, such as *Gender, Theory and Sport*, edited by Ian Warren.[16] While these publications were possible money-spinners for the Society, they also had the potential to restrict the flow of submissions to the journal, which continued to be published biannually, but sometimes found itself short of material. Accordingly, the *ASSH Studies* series went into abeyance in 2008, after the publication of the twenty-fifth volume, *Centenary Reflections*, an anthology of rugby material edited by Andrew Moore and Andy Carr.[17] The fact that ASSH conferences were only held biennially also helped create a potential lag in the flow of material to the journal, with a flood of submissions in conference years sometimes followed by a famine in non-conference years.

Positive aspects of the development of *Sporting Traditions* include the fact that there have been several long-serving lead editors,[18] bringing stability and experience to the position, although perhaps surprisingly there have been no lead female editors, apart from those who have guest edited the occasional special issue.[19] The arrangement of having a lead editor, a reviews editor, and two associate editors overseeing the journal remained in place for almost a decade, but in 1993 Richard Cashman introduced an expanded structure. As he explained, 'Following the example of other sports history journals an Editorial Review Board has been introduced.' 'The purpose of this initiative,' he stated, 'is to acknowledge the contributions of those who have assisted the journal in the past by refereeing articles. A second objective is to make more formal a long-standing informal practice that journal articles are refereed.' On this basis, he declared, 'It will now be the practice to state, in each issue, that *Sporting Traditions* is a fully refereed journal.'[20] As such, 15 persons from a variety of institutions were listed as being members of the inaugural Editorial Review Board, although only two were from universities outside the Australasian region. In the next issue (May 1994), Cashman also took the opportunity to assess the first decade of the journal, where he was able to proclaim, with evident satisfaction, that 'some 100 articles and more than 1,000 book reviews' had been published in that period, not to mention 20 issues of the *ASSH Bulletin* and 10 volumes of the *ASSH Studies* series.[21]

Thematic issues of the journal have appeared on an irregular basis, although it took until 1994 for the first one to appear, at Cashman's instigation. In this case, Cashman edited an issue which marked Sydney's successful Olympic bid with a range of articles devoted to Olympic topics.[22] However, the theme of the next special issue in 1999 was somewhat contentious, as Douglas Booth and Annemarie Jutel were invited to edit the contributions from ten speakers featured in debates at the Queenstown (New Zealand) 'Sporting Traditions' conference. The special issue, entitled 'The End of Sports History?', featured papers from an array of delegates, including John Nauright, Colin Tatz, Joseph L. Arbena, Amanda Smith, Joan Chandler, Murray Phillips, J.A. Mangan, David Andrews, Stephen Hardy, and Charlotte Macdonald. As Booth and Jutel noted in their introduction, the theme of their conference (and the special issue) seemed a good one 'in light of current institutional stresses endured by the academic discipline of history and its sub-fields, and in view of the questions

The history of Sporting Traditions

raised by Francis Fukuyama's "The End of History?" thesis a decade ago', although they admitted they were initially taken aback by some of the consternation expressed about their conference theme.[23] In terms of positive developments, this issue also carried the news that an arrangement had been made with the Amateur Athletic Foundation of Los Angeles to make back copies of the journal available on their website, a boon given that many early volumes of the journal were out of print and free access to back issues would increase the international reach of *Sporting Traditions*.[24]

On the back of a burgeoning membership base, which had passed the 400 mark in 1995, the journal underwent a makeover in 1996, with different shades of green used for the cover, different images appearing on the cover of each issue, and the adoption of a more attractive page design. By 2003, with a new Melbourne-based Editor appointed and a new designer and new printer contracted, the journal took on an even more contemporary, professional look, with the addition of full-colour images on glossier covers and an extensive re-design of the internal format. In 2004, covers of books were also reproduced in the review section for the first time, and in 2014 'Guidelines for Exercising a "Right-of-Reply" to Book Reviews Published in *Sporting Traditions*' became a fixture in the review section, with Matthew Klugman and Gary Osmond the first authors to take advantage of this policy in response to a review of their book by Braham Dabscheck.[25]

While these initiatives and practical enhancements to the look and feel of *Sporting Traditions* were received favourably by the readership, dark clouds had begun to gather across the horizon and the Achilles' heel of the journal was about to be exposed. In 2008, the Australian Research Council launched a consultation period on a draft journal ranking list, which was to be used as one of the indicators for a discipline-specific evaluation of research as part of the brief taken on by the Federal government's new body, known as Excellence in Research for Australia, and used accordingly as part of tertiary funding criteria. Journals were to be ranked as A★ (the top 5 per cent of journal outlets for a discipline), A (the next 15 per cent), B (the next 30 per cent), and C (the remaining 50 per cent). In most cases, the journals of parent disciplines were privileged, and journals of sub-disciplines such as sport history were either given a low ranking, or, in the case of journals such as *Sporting Traditions*, *Sport History Review*, and *Sport in History*, not ranked at all. This was a devastating blow for ASSH, as anecdotal evidence reveals that many academics employed in tertiary institutions were then explicitly instructed by their departments to seek publication opportunities in the highest ranked journals, meaning that *Sporting Traditions* was often eschewed as a viable publishing option. Despite a spirited rear-guard action by the ASSH Executive and other members of the Society to establish the case for recognition of their Society's journal (and their sub-discipline), the result was a foregone conclusion, with *Sporting Traditions* eventually ranked as a 'C' journal. While such rankings were later officially dispensed with by the government, the damage had been done, and in some cases the journal has struggled to win back those contributors who felt compelled to seek greener publishing pastures elsewhere.

In this context, it is fair to say that the membership more broadly, and the ASSH executive more specifically, are entitled to weigh up the future direction of the journal. There is no doubt that until recently *Sporting Traditions* has admirably met the needs of its members, particularly early career scholars who might have needed hands-on mentoring by a sympathetic editor to help produce their first publication, or non-academics who required some shepherding through the rigours of the peer-review process. The journal has also been a worthwhile forum and proving ground for a range of academic historians who have advanced not only their own careers, but the scholarship of sport in Australia and New Zealand, by their collective contributions to *Sporting Traditions* over many years. However, in an educational sector where metrics such as impact factors, and immediate electronic access to publications, seem to be valued above all else, there is the temptation to think that a commercial publisher for the journal may be a panacea that will heal all ills. With this scenario in mind, it is worth highlighting that the publications of ASSH have never been featured in citation indexes, such as those generated by Web of Science or Scopus, despite occasional agitation by some members wanting the Society to vigorously pursue such a path.[26] Contrary to this view is a perspective that the attraction of *Sporting Traditions* has always been the fact that it is a journal that has grown organically over time, adapting to changing circumstances while attempting to remain an inclusive publication for all its members, whether they be academics or not. Whether ASSH, faced with a shrinking membership, is willing to cede control of its flagship journal to commercial interests that may be able to lift its academic profile in an environment increasingly driven by metrics is still a question that is yet to be resolved.

Finally, it is worth noting that two indexes for *Sporting Traditions* have been produced. The first was a stand-alone publication, commissioned by John O'Hara and compiled in a thematic manner by Simon Best in 1992, and covering volumes one to eight. Another index was produced in 2014 as a special double issue of the *ASSH Bulletin*, but in this case the details of every item published in the journal (including editorial prefaces, reviews, items in 'Barrackers' Corner', and so on) are listed sequentially with full citation details for each issue, making it a useful bibliographic tool as well as a worthwhile historical record for a journal that is now in its fourth decade.[27]

Notes

1 See Richard Cashman and Michael McKernan eds., *Sport in History* (St Lucia: University of Queensland Press, 1979), and Richard Cashman and Michael McKernan eds., *Sport: Money, Morality and the Media* (Kensington: University of NSW Press, 1981). Several long-standing members have recently reflected in print on the pivotal role of Richard Cashman in instigating the initial conferences, and his influence in driving the formation of ASSH. See, for example, Rob Hess, 'The Preston "Confrontation": Revisiting Foundation Narratives of the Australian Society for Sports History', *Sporting Traditions* 34, no. 1 (May 2017): 75–86; Bill Murray, 'Forty Years of ASSH: A Personal Reflection on the Early Years', *Sporting Traditions* 34, no. 1 (May 2017): 87–92; and John O'Hara, 'Reflections on Richard Cashman and the Australian Society for Sports History', *Sporting Traditions* 34, no. 1 (May 2017): 93–97. For Cashman's own ruminations, published a decade after the first conference, see Richard Cashman, 'The Making of Sporting Traditions 1977–87', *ASSH Bulletin* (December 1989): 15–28.

2 As summarized in Hess, 'The Preston "Confrontation"': 78–79. For further commentary on the 'initial friction between those trained in physical education and those with a history background' during the early years of ASSH, see Wray Vamplew, 'Count Me In: Reflections on a Career as a Sports Historian', *Sport in Society* 19, no. 3 (2016): 300.

3 For Vamplew's musings on his own career path, including his later appointment as the first Professor of Sports History in the UK, see Vamplew, 'Count Me In': 297–312.

4 The first *ASSH Bulletin*, edited by Ian Jobling, was published with a cover date of April/May 1985. It featured a draft of the ASSH constitution, which was to be ratified at the 'Sporting Traditions' conference in Adelaide in August 1985. The *Bulletin* also contained a list of ASSH members and their postal addresses. There were 135 individual members, 20 student members, nine overseas members, and 25 institutional subscribers.

5 Wray Vamplew, 'Editorial Preface', *Sporting Traditions* 1, no. 1 (November 1984): np.

6 Colin Tatz, 'Race, Politics and Sport', *Sporting Traditions* 1, no. 1 (November 1984): 2–36; Chris McConville, 'Football, Liquor and Gambling in the 1920s', *Sporting Traditions* 1, no. 1 (November 1984): 38–55; Wray Vamplew, 'Australian Sports Review 1983 – A Personal View', *Sporting Traditions* 1, no. 1 (November 1984): 56–60; and Ray Crawford, 'Sport for Young Ladies: The Victorian Independent Schools 1875–1925', *Sporting Traditions* 1, no. 1 (November 1984): 61–82.

The history of Sporting Traditions

7 Richard Cashman, 'Book Reviews', *Sporting Traditions* 1, no. 1 (November 1984): 84.
8 Cashman, 'Book Reviews', 84.
9 Cashman, 'Book Reviews', 84.
10 Vamplew, 'Count Me In', 300.
11 Wray Vamplew, 'Editorial Preface', *Sporting Traditions* 1, no. 2 (May 1985): np.
12 This statement was the first overt reference to the peer-review process in the journal. See Wray Vamplew, 'Barrackers' Corner', *Sporting Traditions* 2, no. 1 (November 1985): 110.
13 Vamplew, 'Barrackers' Corner', 110.
14 Grace was a retired hospital administrator and the founder and first president of the Australian Cricket Society. See Wray Vamplew, 'Editorial Preface', *Sporting Traditions* 2, no. 1 (November 1985): np.
15 See J. Neville Turner, '"Change and Decay in All Around I See" (from Abide with Me)', *Sporting Traditions* 23, no. 2 (May 2007): 105–112.
16 Colin Tatz, *Aborigines in Sport* (Bedford Park: ASSH, 1987); John O'Hara ed. *Crowd Violence at Australian Sport* (Campbelltown: ASSH, 1992); Ian Warren ed. *Gender, Theory and Sport* (Melbourne: ASSH, 2005).
17 Andrew Moore and Andy Carr eds., *Centenary Reflections: 100 Years of Rugby League in Australia* (Melbourne: ASSH, 2005).
18 Editors have been Wray Vamplew (1984–1989), John O'Hara (1989–1992, 1999–2002), Richard Cashman (1993–1999), Rob Hess (2003–2007), and Lionel Frost (2007–present). Abdel Halabi has been a co-editor (2016–present).
19 Annemarie Jutel (1999), Clare Simpson (2005), Joyce Kay (2007). Reet Howell served a brief term as Reviews Editor in 1993.
20 Richard Cashman, 'Editorial Preface', *Sporting Traditions* 10, no. 1 (November 1993): 1.
21 Richard Cashman, 'Editorial Preface', *Sporting Traditions* 10, no. 2 (May 1994): 1.
22 See Richard Cashman, 'Editorial Preface', *Sporting Traditions* 11, no. 1 (November 1994): 1. Apart from the ASSH logo, which first appeared on the cover of the journal in November 1989, the 'Special Olympic Issue' of November 1994 was the first issue to feature a graphic, namely a sketch of an Olympic torch.
23 Douglas Booth and Annemarie Jutel, 'Why "The End of Sports History?"', *Sporting Traditions* 16, no. 1 (November 1999): 3. The cover of the special issue featured an illustration with the caption 'From a Puritan poster recounting the burning of the Book of Sports'. Another innovative special issue was devoted to 'Australian Sports Statuary', guest edited by Cashman. See Richard Cashman, 'Reflections', *Sporting Traditions* 33, no. 1 (May 2016): 97–100.
24 John O'Hara, 'Editorial Preface', *Sporting Traditions* 16, no. 1 (November 1999): 1. Many years later, a contract was also signed with RMIT Publishing, allowing issues from the journal to be made available on their platform, usually via packages that were sold to academic institutions.
25 See Matthew Klugman and Gary Osmond, 'Right of Reply to Braham Dabscheck's Review of *Black and Proud*', *Sporting Traditions* 31, no. 2 (November 2014): 105–106.
26 For discussion of the contested terrain surrounding the often problematic use of metrics to evaluate sport history journals, see Murray G. Phillips, 'Sizing Up Sport History Journals: Metrics, Sport Humanities, and History', *International Journal of the History of Sport* 37, no. 8 (2020): 1–13.
27 See the 'Preface' to Alexandre Joly and Rob Hess, 'Inside *Sporting Traditions*: The Contents of the Journal of the Australian Society for Sports History, November 1984 to November 2015', *ASSH Bulletin* 59/60 (February/August 2014): 1–2.

46

MATERIALES PARA LA HISTORIA DEL DEPORTE

The journal on the History of Sport, a reference for the Latin American world, with international scope

Teresa González Aja and Rodrigo Pardo

The journal *Materiales para la Historia del Deporte (Materiales)*[1] [Materials for the History of Sport] was created specifically for scholars in Spanish-speaking countries. It aimed to fill a gap which existed in the dissemination of research work in the history of sport as there was no journal written in Spanish in the field. In this regard, it continues to be the only one of its kind.

There have been different stages in its development which have influenced both its contents and format. Broadly speaking, we can distinguish the following stages.

Stage 1: The origins of the journal

The origin of *Materiales* is linked to the Instituto Andaluz del Deporte (IAD)[2] [Andalusian Institute of Sport], which around 1999 was organizing permanent seminars on research related to sport, simultaneously supporting different meetings and congresses at the national and international level. It was agreed to issue a periodic publication (annually) of these seminars with the title 'Serie Deporte y Documentación' [Collection Sport and Documentation] with a circulation of 1,000. Among these seminars, several educational and informative workshops focused exclusively on the history of sport under the title of 'Fuentes para el estudio del deporte en Andalucía' [Sources for the study of sport in Andalusia]. Specifically, between 2003 and 2005, four issues were published on this topic under the title of 'Materiales para la historia de la actividad física y el deporte en Andalucía' [Materials for the history of physical activity and sport in Andalusia].[3] As the entity responsible, the IAD covered the financial cost of the seminars and publications.

Among the key players during this stage were Jose Aquesolo Vegas, Head of the Documentation Department at the IAD, and editor of the first issues; José Manuel Zapico, director of the first issue of *Materiales*; and Juan Carlos Fernández Truan, who at that time was director of the seminars on the history of sport and would subsequently become

374

DOI: 10.4324/9780429318306-52

Director of the Journal. The Editorial Board of the first four issues was composed of the members of the Seminar on the History of Physical Activity and Sport in Andalusia, whose members varied every year according to the constitution of the Seminar. The texts were reviewed by the technical personnel of the Department of Documentation and Publications at the IAD.

Stage 2: Internationalization

The 10th International European Committee for Sports History Congress held in Seville in 2005 facilitated a meeting among national and international researchers in the history of sport, which revealed the need to formalize a publication that brought to light the research work carried out in the Spanish language. As the IAD stopped financing the seminars and publications on this topic, it was necessary to find new funding sources.

It was at this point that the *Asociación Andaluza de Historia del Deporte* (AAHD [Andalusian Association of the History of Sport]), chaired by Juan Carlos Fernández Truan, took charge of the publication. Thanks to the arrangements made by the President of the AAHD, the Universidad Pablo de Olavide in Seville (UPO) and the Wanceulen Publishing Company were involved, with the latter responsible for printing and distributing the journal. The publisher had an important position and distribution in Latin America, and its support was central to the aim of reaching the largest possible number of Spanish speakers, whether as readers or researchers. Support was also forthcoming from another academic institution, the *Facultad de Ciencias de la Actividad Física y del Deporte* (INEF) [the Faculty of Physical Activity and Sports Sciences] at the Universidad Politécnica de Madrid (UPM), through the lecturer in the history of sport, Teresa González Aja, and the Director of the Library, Pilar Irureta-Goyena Sánchez, both of whom became part of the Editorial Board of the journal.

The following issue, published in 2007, appeared with the name *Materiales*, which has been maintained up to the present. The new title excluded reference to the region of Andalusia in order to internationalize the publication. From this moment on, *Materiales* projected a clearly international character, with special attention on the area of Latin America. It is worth underlining the important impact of the journal in Cuba, Venezuela, Mexico, and, particularly, in Brazil. This expansion was reflected in the coverage of topics with a healthy mix of regional and international themes.

As part of this dynamic, manuscripts began to be accepted in Portuguese as well as Spanish. In addition, a scientific committee was formed with historians of international renown, such as: Eduardo Álvarez del Palacio, Victor Andrade de Melo, Arnd Krüger, Javier Olivera Beltrán, Marie-Helene Orthous, Xavier Pujadas, and Angela Teja, among others.

Stage 3: Looking for greater visibility

All of these changes led to a wider level of domestic and international recognition. To achieve greater presence and visibility on review platforms and systems for scientific journals, and in national and international databases, the journal continued as a publishing entity belonging to a University (in this case the UPO), as well as becoming an open access online publication.

These aspects were important for two reasons: first, the journal's academic rigour was reinforced by the endorsement of the University; second, online publication meant that peer reviewing was not only easier to administer, but the process was also completely transparent. With regard to open access, it constitutes a part, if not the most essential part, of the purpose of the journal. The aim is to provide the greatest dissemination of the research by enabling access to, and the ability to publish in, the journal at no cost for scholars interested in the history of sport.

The 2013 edition of *Materiales* marked the transition to an online open access format. During this transformational period, two new collaborators, Rodrigo Pardo from the UPM, as deputy director, and Manuel Peña Pulido from the UPO library, in charge of the online platform of the journal on Open Journal Systems (OJS), were important additions to the journal. This marked an important change towards the modernization and visibility of the journal.

In addition to regular journal editions, three special supplements were published from corresponding scientific congresses related to both the history of sport and the social sciences. In 2014 and 2016, abstracts were published of the presentations of the 4th and 5th International Congresses, 'Sport, Doping and Society', which were held at the UPM. The special supplement of 2015 published all the papers and presentations at the 1st International Congress of the History of the Olympic Movement organized by Conrado Durántez, the International University of Andalusia and the UPO.

Stage 4: The present day

The latest stage of *Materiales* began in 2019 as a result of the agreement between the AAHD, owner of the journal, and the UPM. This agreement facilitated the dissemination and maximization of *Materiales* by the UPM Research Group 'Humanist and Social Studies in Physical Education and Sport'[4] directed by Teresa González Aja, who together with Juan Carlos Fernández Truan (UPO), Vicente Gómez Encinas (UPM), Rodrigo Pardo García (UPM), Pilar Irureta-Goyena Sánchez (Director of the INEF-UPM library), and Andrés García Cubillo (INEF-UPM library), constitute the Editorial Board of the journal.

This development enhanced the quality of the journal as it became part of the Poli-Red (Polytechnic Digital Journals) of the UPM.[5] This situation made it possible, among other aspects, to obtain a DOI for the publication and greater institutional backing to request inclusion in databases like Scopus, an objective we hope will soon be achieved.

With regard to the editors, the journal has been structured to receive and evaluate texts in the language in which they are written. Specifically, there are three editors of international renown in the field of the history of sport, namely: Teresa González Aja (Spanish texts), Arnd Krüger (English texts), and Victor Andrade de Melo (Portuguese texts).

Nationality, language, gender in *Materiales*

The Scientific Committee continues to expand with the addition of international scholars. It is currently made up of 45 members from nine different countries[6] (Table 46.1). These two aspects, the reputation of the members of the Scientific Committee and their international profile, significantly contribute to the quality and visibility of the journal. With regard to their profiles, it is worthy to note that 48.8 per cent are Spanish and 51.2 per cent from other nationalities. The majority of the Scientific Committee belong to a range of high profile universities and have extensive experience as researchers in the history of sport.

Table 46.2 shows that in the 19 issues published between 2003 and 2019, with the exception of the special supplements, there was a total of 145 articles, of which a large majority 127 (87.6 per cent) were written in Spanish, with smaller contributions in Portuguese 14 (9.7 per cent), and in English 4 (2.8 per cent).

Materiales para la Historia del Deporte

Table 46.1 Nationality of the Scientific Committee membership

	Authors	*%*
Spain	21	48.8
France	9	20.9
Italy	7	16.3
Brazil	2	4.7
Germany	2	4.7
Portugal	1	2.3
Cuba	1	2.3
Argentina	1	2.3
Greece	1	2.3
TOTAL	45	100.0

Table 46.2 Language of articles

	Articles	*%*
Articles in Spanish	127	87.6
Articles in Portuguese	14	9.7
Articles in English	4	2.8
TOTAL	145	100.0

As Table 46.3 indicates, authors are affiliated to institutions in 20 countries: more than half to Spanish institutions (62.5 per cent), followed by affiliations to Brazilian (8.6 per cent) Portuguese (6.6 per cent), Cuban (6.2 per cent), and Argentinean (3.7 per cent) institutions. Scholars from French institutions (3.7 per cent) lead European contributions.

With respect to the gender, there is a considerable difference in relationship to authorship (Table 46.4) and leadership. In regard to authorship, 95 articles (65.5 per cent) are written exclusively by men, either as sole authors or sharing authorship with other men. Only 50 articles (34.5 per cent) include a woman among the authors, although not in all cases are the women the sole author, and they may share authorship with others.

With respect to leadership, the representation of women in different management and administration components of the journal (Table 46.5) is similar to authorship. Women almost reach parity with men in the Drafting Committee (44.4 per cent), constitute one third of the Editorial Board (33.3 per cent) as well as Section Editors (33.3 per cent), but the contribution to the Scientific Committee decreases significantly to 15.6 per cent.

Indexing and metrics[7]

Concerning international metrics, *Materiales* is indexed in Google Scholar, commonly acknowledged as the most popular database for individual scholars in the humanities and the only major database that prominently acknowledges non-English journals.[8] This database provides two specific h-indexes for journals: h5-index and h5-median. At present, *Materiales* has achieved an h5-index of 7 by publishing seven articles that have been cited at least seven

Table 46.3 National institutional affiliation of authors

	Authors	%
Spain	152	62.5
Brazil	21	8.6
Portugal	16	6.6
Cuba	15	6.2
Argentina	9	3.7
France	9	3.7
Czech Republic	3	1.2
Serbia	3	1.2
Italy	2	0.8
Chile	2	0.8
Mexico	2	0.8
Germany	1	0.4
United States	1	0.4
United Kingdom	1	0.4
Switzerland	1	0.4
Greece	1	0.4
Zimbabwe	1	0.4
Colombia	1	0.4
Uruguay	1	0.4
Pakistan	1	0.4
TOTAL	243	100.0

Table 46.4 Gender of published authors

	Articles	%
Articles signed by at least one woman	50	34.5
Articles not signed by women	95	65.5
TOTAL	145	100.0

Table 46.5 Gender of management and administration

	Men	Women	Total	Women %
Editorial Board	4	2	6	33.3
Section Editors	2	1	3	33.3
Drafting Committee	5	4	9	44.4
Scientific Committee	38	7	45	15.6

Materiales para la Historia del Deporte

times in the preceding five years.[9] The Google Scholar h5-median is the median number of citations for the articles that make up its h5-index. For *Materiales*, the h5-median is 9. These metrics indicate that *Materiales* 'competes quite well with both the *Journal of Sport History* and the field's oldest journal, *Sport History Review*'.[10]

Materiales is also included in the core collection of the Web of Science 'Emerging Sources Citation Index' (ESCI).[11] Although the journal does have an impact factor, citations are included in the citation counts for Journal Citation Reports. In addition, articles indexed in ESCI are included in an author's h-index calculation.

As regards other international databases, *Materiales* is also included in:

- SPORTDiscus: a prominent and specific bibliographic database for sports research.[12]
- Directory of Open Access Journals (DOAJ): a curated list of quality peer-reviewed open access journals.[13]

With regard specifically to Spanish language databases, *Materiales* is included in:

- Latindex v2.0 catalogue: composed of the highest quality journals published in Latin America, the Caribbean, Spain, and Portugal. It fulfils 34 of the 38 quality characteristics.[14]
- Dialnet: a free database devoted to making visible Spanish language scientific literature which predominantly focuses on the fields of human, legal, and social sciences.[15]

With regard to national metrics, *Materiales* is indexed in a good position given its specificity. In particular, in the Dialnet Metrics catalogue it has a 2019 IDR impact of 0.588 occupying the 16th position out of 43 (second quartile) for journals in the 'Sport' category.[16] It also appears in the *Matriz de Información para el Análisis de Revistas* (MIAR) [Matrix of information for the Analysis of Journals],[17] with a 2019 ICDS impact of 9.7 (first quartile) in the 'Physical Activity and Sports Sciences' category.

Conclusions

As we have seen, *Materiales* makes a significant contribution to research into the history of sport in the Latin American context. It is a conspicuous journal for historians of sport whose prominent language is Spanish and has the capacity to reach millions of Spanish speakers.[18] It is a visible platform for gaining information about important research on the history of sport in the Latin American world, often including other areas of study in the humanities and social sciences. The additional strength of *Materiales* is its inclusion of Portuguese and English languages, and its dissemination to countries where these languages are prominent. The trilingual capacities of *Materiales* have extended the breadth and range of published topics, as well as contributing to *Materiales*' metrics and indexing in several databases.

The project for the future of *Materiales* is twofold: first, to continue to provide a popular forum for Spanish-speaking authors with a special interest in sport in the Latin American area. Second, to reach out to authors from different countries to stimulate and facilitate comparisons, collaborations, and publishing on topics in the history of sport in all three languages from other geographical areas. In this regard, from the historiographic point of view, it is necessary to privilege the Hispanists who, in other areas of research, have consolidated their reputation but who do not have a specific forum related to the history of sport.

Notes

1 Official website of the journal *Materiales para la Historia del Deporte,*http://polired.upm.es/index. php/materiales_historia_deporte/index.

2 Official website of the *Instituto Andaluz del Deporte*, https://www.juntadeandalucia.es/turismoydep orte/opencms/areas/deporte/iad/.

3 This name was originally the idea of Jose Aquesolo Vegas, who states: 'I decided to use *materials*, as a word from the world of architecture: all the elements that helped to make a building grow until it was finished, were the materials with which it was built. It would depend on their quality and strength whether the construction would end up being a wonder or just another building with its cracks and signs of wear and tear. Thus, we returned by way of history to the ancient builders, masons, carpenters, stone cutters or glaziers who built constructions that are still standing today.' Personal interview carried out on 21 October 2020.

4 Official website of the Research Group 'Humanist and Social Studies in Physical Education and Sport': http://www.upm.es/observatorio/vi/index.jsp?pageac=grupo.jsp&idGrupo=375.

5 Official website of Poli-Red: http://polired.upm.es.

6 The complete list of the Scientific Committee can be consulted at: http://polired.upm.es/index. php/materiales_historia_deporte/about/editorialPolicies#custom-4.

7 For further information, the complete list of journal assessment platforms and bibliographical databases and thematic portals where *Materiales* is indexed can be found at: http://polired.upm.es/index.php/ma teriales_historia_deporte/pages/view/indexing.

8 Murray G. Phillips, 'Sizing up Sport History Journals: Metrics, Sport Humanities, and History', *The International Journal of the History of Sport* 37, no. 8 (2020): 692–704, doi: 10.1080/09523367.2020. 1796652.

9 Google Scholar metrics for *Materiales*, https://scholar.google.com/citations?hl=en&view_op=search_ venues&vq=materiales+para+la+historia+del+deporte&btnG= (accessed 31 October 2020).

10 Phillips, 'Sizing up Sport History Journals', 698.

11 Web of Science: Emerging Sources Citation Index, https://clarivate.com/webofsciencegroup/solu tions/webofscience-esci/.

12 EBSCO: SPORTDiscus, https://www.ebsco.com/products/research-databases/sportdiscus.

13 About DOAJ (Directory of Open Access Journals), https://doaj.org/about.

14 Latindex: Sistema Regional de Información en Línea para Revistas Científicas de América Latina, el Caribe, España y Portugal. Information about *Materiales*, https://www.latindex.org/latindex/ficha? folio=22994 (accessed 31 October 2020).

15 Dialnet, Universidad de La Rioja, https://dialnet.unirioja.es.

16 Dialnet Journal Index 2019, 'Sport', https://dialnet.unirioja.es/metricas/idr/2019/ambitos/2 (accessed 31 October 2020).

17 Matriz de Información para el Análisis de Revistas, 'Metrics for *Materiales*', http://miar.ub.edu/issn/ 1887-9586 (accessed 31 October 2020).

18 According to the *Instituto Cervantes*, in 2019, 580 million people in the world spoke Spanish, 7.6 per cent of the world population. Of these, 483 million – four million more than a year ago – are native Spanish speakers, which makes Spanish the second most important mother tongue in the world by number of speakers. In addition, it is studied by almost 22 million people in 110 countries. Spanish is the third most used language on the Internet, where it has a great potential for growth. https://www. cervantes.es/sobre_instituto_cervantes/prensa/2019/noticias/presentacion_anuario_madrid.htm.

47

RECORDE – REVISTA DE HISTÓRIA DO ESPORTE

A Brazilian, Latin-American, Ibero-American journal

Rafael Fortes and Victor Andrade de Melo

In Brazil, even though there have been sport-related studies dating back to the nineteenth century, the history of sport is a recent field of inquiry.[1] It was only from the 1990s, and particularly from the 2000s, that there has been a quantitative and qualitative increase in sport history research, an enterprise which has also attained a more organic character.[2]

At first, researchers sought a more intense dialogue with internationally renowned social scientists such as Pierre Bourdieu, Norbert Elias, and Michel Foucault, and those with national reputations, such as the anthropologist Roberto DaMatta. During that time, before the full development of the Internet, it was not easy to obtain information on international initiatives concerning the history of sport. Rarely were we aware of the organization of events or the publication of books and journals across Latin America, Europe, the United States, and other countries and continents.[3]

Initial contact began by inviting James A. Mangan to present at the 4th National Meeting on the History of Sport and Physical Education in 1996.[4] This acclaimed scholar introduced us to the *International Journal of the History of Sport*, and provided opportunities for the establishment of contacts and international exchange opportunities.

Subsequently, there was a progressive search for international engagement, through the acquisition of books and journals, and attendance at several events, particularly those organized by the International Society for the History of Physical Education and Sport and the European Committee for Sports History. The field in Brazil improved, expanded, and diversified with the publication of papers in conference proceedings and journals from other disciplines, notably physical education and history. The first publications explicitly engaged with concepts and advances in the larger field of historical research.

In this context, the 'Sport: Laboratory on the History of Sport and Leisure' was established as a research group within the Comparative History Graduate Studies Programme of the Federal University of Rio de Janeiro. Research funding was provided by the National Council of Scientific and Technological Development (CNPq), a funding agency of the Brazilian Federal Government.[5]

DOI: 10.4324/9780429318306-53

The guiding principle of the research group was to produce academic scholarship about the history of sport, to encourage graduate and undergraduate seminars, to organize scientific events, to publish books and research articles in scientific journals and conference proceedings, and, in 2008, to launch the first Latin American journal dedicated to the topic – *Recorde: Revista de História do Esporte*.[6]

The mission of *Recorde* is to contribute to the development and propagation of historical research centred around the institutionalized practices of the body. Although 'sport' is a key topic, the journal accepts research articles discussing physical education, gymnastics, capoeira, and other activities of leisure and entertainment from any period of history.

While Brazil does not yet have a professional association dedicated to the history of sport, *Recorde* is edited by members of the Sport: Laboratory on the History of Sport and Leisure research group. Rafael Fortes, Mauricio Drumond, Fabio Peres, and Cleber Dias have served as executive editors, alternating every year in tasks ranging from contact with authors, distributing research papers to reviewers, entering final papers into editing platforms, publication of full issues, and advertising of new editions. In the early years, these tasks were incumbent upon the first two scholars. Victor Andrade de Melo, as Editor-in-Chief, has been the leading figure in the conception of the publication and the assembly of its team and boards. He operates on both administrative and strategic fronts, representing the journal in multiple forums: the graduate unit that hosts it, the state and federal funding bodies, and the Federal University of Rio de Janeiro.

Recorde is a free-of-charge, biannual, open-access publication. There are no submission fees and no commercial company involved. Its board consists of a team of 27 scholars hailing from 11 different countries, among whom are some of the world's most acclaimed experts in the field. The consulting board consists of 40 researchers of national renown.

To emphasize its international character, the journal accepts research papers in four languages: Portuguese, Spanish, English, and French. In its 13-year trajectory, 26 issues have been released. Although most contributing authors are Brazilian, there are numerous articles from scholars from other countries, especially from universities in Latin America and the Iberian Peninsula.

A principal reason for the launch of *Recorde* was to increase the visibility of the sport-related research carried out by scholars in the Ibero-American space. An immediate and obvious explanation for the scarce knowledge of our research has often been explained by the fact that we mostly write in Spanish and Portuguese. The publication of *Recorde* is a response to English language hegemony in the history of sport.

The status of English as the *lingua franca* creates numerous challenges for non-English-speaking scholars. One key problem is that the majority of scholarship is published in English and this is compounded by English scholars rarely reading sport history literature in other languages. While *Recorde* has published and translated English sport history scholarship, reciprocity has not always been forthcoming.[7] As Giovani Levi argues in a larger context, many North American historians only resort to works published in English, even as they engage with topics in countries where there is abundant research published in local languages.[8] In effect, this positions English as the 'official language of globalisation', perpetuating the myth of the internationalization of scholarship, and relegates other languages to the status of local, parochial, and peripheral, diminishing the standing of scholars who publish in other languages.[9] 'The subaltern position of localism,' as Ortiz contends, effectively silences scholarly communities of knowledge, specifically those not communicating in English.[10]

The undisputed linguistic authority of English places pressure on non-English authors to translate their scholarship, if they want their work to be read and to contribute to debates in academic disciplines, including sport history.[11] Translating scholarship can be problematic. Not only are translations expensive, but meaning is often diluted, and complex concepts rarely cross linguistic barriers effectively. While translation in the sciences is practicable because they have a specific method, order, and structure of presentation as well as an accepted narrative form shared across the world, translating scholarship in the social sciences and the humanities is much more difficult. In the social sciences and humanities, there is a more nuanced, complicated, and intricate relationship to language and narrative.[12] Language is central to the intellectual historical craft from working with traces of the past, to developing concepts, frameworks, and theories, and then expressing everything through narrative. Language is integral to the complexity of narrative which is replete with metaphors, tropes, plots, arguments, and voice. Language and narrative do not sit outside of history, they are history.

Consequences of English as the *lingua franca* in sport history are considerable. It is worth noting that in international journals on the history of sport there are few works on Ibero-American countries – and even fewer on Latin American countries.[13] On many occasions, these studies are conducted by foreigners (which is not a problem in itself) and nationals that have lived several years overseas (which is also not a problem). The problem is when these circumstances become preconditions for the propagation of knowledge and scholarship. Furthermore, there is virtually no Latin American or Ibero-American contribution considered among wider debates in the history of sport. Even when research articles in Spanish or Portuguese are published in English in leading sport history journals, they are sparsely cited and rarely integrated in key debates in the subdiscipline. We argue that this minimal engagement is not caused by any lack of scholarly sophistication, but stems from a prejudice based on language that privileges English scholarship. Finally, the hegemony of sport history written in English influences how scholars approach their work in Latin American countries, which may inappropriately narrow or distort the research agenda. We acknowledge that this situation is not exclusively a matter of imposition from outside. Governments in our own countries often adhere, in an uncritical manner, to the trends and the fads of world powers, even in matters of scientific development and in policies of research publication.[14]

The regional/parochial/peripheral status of non-English scholarship extends to non-English journals, including sport history journals. This circumstance impacts *Recorde* in many ways. For one, bibliometric and indexing databases and their assessment metrics are conducted by corporations that control the editorial market, giving ample and often exclusive favour to journals published in English. Journals publishing in other languages are devalued. While *Recorde* appears in *Google Scholar*, as Phillips demonstrates, and performs quite well against other sport history journals, this database is commonly used for individual scholarship in the humanities, rather than evaluating journals.[15] In fact, journal metrics in Google Scholar are quite difficult to access. Journals are more commonly evaluated in international databases such as Elsevier's Scopus. However, *Recorde* does not appear in the Scopus database because there are English language requirements. These requirements serve as barriers to even being acknowledged as an academic journal in scholarly communities like sport history. In academic environments which are increasingly audited according to metrics, the lack of recognition in international databases deters scholars from contributing to journals like *Recorde*.

Funding

Because *Recorde* is an open-access journal, funding of the production and publication of the journal has not been a major problem. The journal is mostly the fruit of voluntary work.

Editors and reviewers receive no financial compensation for their service. Furthermore, as is the case with most Brazilian journals, which are stored on the websites of public institutions of teaching and research, the hosting of *Recorde*'s website is provided by the Federal University of Rio de Janeiro.

From its inception, *Recorde* has always been published online. This decision was not only motivated by a desire to ensure widespread access, but also by a shortage of resources to cover the costs of editing, printing, and distributing print-based editions. In the early years, *Recorde* relied on the assistance of members of the University staff who had ample knowledge of information technology, hosting, and publication of websites and were responsible for uploading individual PDF files (research articles, reviews, abstracts etc.). Later, the journal began to use a public platform, the Electronic Editing Service for Journals, developed by the Brazilian Institute for Science and Technology. Since then, each of the four executive editors utilizes this platform and is responsible for all pending tasks for a period of one year, which corresponds to two editions.

Resources secured from funding bodies, particularly the Rio de Janeiro State Foundation for Research Funding and Support, have allowed for the expansion of editorial initiatives, particularly the translation of articles published by the *Journal of Sport History*. Successive editors of the *Journal of Sport History* have kindly authorized the translation of articles in *Recorde*, allowing the distribution of the work of Anglophone authors in Portuguese.

Between 2010 and 2017, the editorial team published 31 translations of sport history articles written in English. In nearly all cases, they became the only texts of their respective authors available in Portuguese. We consider investing in translations to be a fundamental task for the effective development of the history of sport as a wider field of inquiry. As discussed previously, besides the linguistic, power, and diversity issues of scholarly experience, investment in, and attention to, publishing translations increases the visibility of research in our field of inquiry, and is a significant part of its development. Translations also minimize the repetition of knowledge through ignorance of research being carried out in other languages.

While *Recorde* has been very successful with limited resources, the editors are attempting to expand revenue for the journal to implement a number of initiatives that will develop its profile and reach. In optimal funding circumstances we would be able, for example, to offer compensation to our editors and reviewers; create and maintain professional social media profiles; professionalize the entire editorial process (possibly outsourcing to an established editorial group or commercial platform); and improve the website and its layout. All of these actions would also bring much relief to overburdened executive editors.

Quality of research articles

In the early years of the journal, every edition faced difficulties due to the limited number of submissions and the poor quality of many manuscripts. This was a reflection of the developmental state of the field that was still undergoing major transition in Brazil. In addition, the journal was relatively unknown and attracted few researchers. In the past four years or so, these difficulties have been overcome. We receive a healthy number of research articles, both from Brazilian scholars whose works have improved qualitatively following the maturation of the field, and from international colleagues who acknowledge *Recorde* as an appropriate medium for the publication of their research.

Recorde also faces other challenges. There is still a measure of prejudice against sport history in Academia – particularly in the overall field of history. The editors are aware that this

Recorde – Revista de História do Esporte

is not only an issue in Brazil or that it only affects our journal, but it is a relatively widespread situation in Anglophone scholarship and disciplines.

Indexing and assessment, particularly in the Qualis/CAPES system

Recorde has struggled to achieve the status in the ranking systems that appropriately represents the quality of the journal. There are several key reasons for this struggle. First, the history of sport does not fit easily into the two areas that could most adequately include it as a legitimate topic – physical education and history. Within physical education there is a long-standing and overt bias towards fields such as physiology, kinesiology etc., which has increased over the last decade. Within history, there are certain topics that are deemed prestigious and receive significant privilege – and sport is not recognized as one of those academic fields.

Second, the ranking systems both in Brazil and internationally have proved difficult for *Recorde*. For most of its existence, *Recorde* has been ranked B2 and B3, which is the intermediate strata of the Qualis/CAPES ranking system.[16] On two occasions, the editors argued that the journal did fulfil all requisites for a higher ranking. The ranking was queried, but the editors neither received an explanation nor a proper response to their attempts at addressing this issue. The editors were not provided with any assessment feedback or documentation justifying our ranking. Subject matter prejudice? We are unable to prove or disprove this bias.[17]

Internationally, the issues are different, but the editors experienced resistance when requesting indexation of the journal in other databases. As discussed earlier, there is a predisposition toward English language journals in the international databases and *Recorde* is part of the discrimination of journals that publish in languages other than English.

Scope and topics

In terms of scope, *Recorde* has a wide readership in both Spain and Latin America. As well as papers published in Portuguese, most editions feature articles in Spanish, including pieces authored by well-respected scholars of the history of sport in countries such as Argentina and Spain.

In terms of topics, *Recorde* publishes original research articles and reviews. Association football is the most popular topic from scholars seeking to publish with *Recorde*, averaging 35–60 per cent of all submissions. However, editors have worked to diversify topics. Other intermittently popular topics have included Brazil's hosting of the men's World Cup of Association Football (2014) and the Summer Olympic Games (2016). In recent years, interviews with foreign scholars have also been published that provide their perspectives on their own careers and trajectories, and the vicissitudes of the history of sport as a field of inquiry. Finally, there have been more articles submitted that engage with matters of historiography, a topic that is experiencing a resurgence in English language journals.

Conclusion

Recorde is a journal published on the periphery of the academic world, and this is where its goals are set. To openly claim our peripheral identity does not mean that we acquiesce to it, nor that we will always remain as such. Neither should we aspire to becoming central. It seems more interesting, utopian as it may sound, to envision a setting in which centre–periphery relations are no more, in which the potential of all poles is acknowledged, and there is no longer an insistence on the hierarchical relations that are so contradictory to what is expected of scientific endeavour.[18]

We may be peripheral but are fully aware of the potential, the originality, and the quality of the history of sport that is produced in Latin American and Ibero-American contexts. Always in dialogue with the centre with no room for prejudice or xenophobia, and in the face of all the limits and hardships we have encountered, the editors expect to keep opening venues for a wider diffusion of knowledge. Such is the mission of *Recorde*.

Notes

1 We employ the term 'history of sport' to indicate a field of inquiry that explores various institutionalized practices of the body: e.g. sport, physical education, gymnastics.
2 Victor Andrade de Melo and Rafael Fortes, 'Sports History in Brazil: An Overview and Perspectives', *Sport History Review* 42 (2011): 102–116.
3 Victor Andrade de Melo et al., *Pesquisa histórica e história do esporte* [Historical research and the history of sport] (Rio de Janeiro: 7 Letras, 2013).
4 This was the first scholarly event centred on this field of inquiry in Brazil. It was held for the first time in 1993 and has taken place regularly since.
5 Federal University of Rio de Janeiro, Compared History Graduate Studies Programme, 'Sport: Laboratory on the History of Sport and Leisure', www.sport.historia.ufrj.br. This website may be consulted for further information on the research group.
6 Federal University of Rio de Janeiro, Compared History Graduate Studies Programme, *Recorde: revista de história do esporte* [Recorde: Sports History Review] https://revistas.ufrj.br/index.php/Recorde. All editions are available from this website. In the Ibero-American context there is only one other journal dedicated to the topic, the Spanish *Materiales para la Historia del Deporte* [Materials for the History of Sport], with which we maintain a collaborative relation.
7 We wish to mention colleagues with whom we have established fruitful contact and collaboration, beginning with the aforementioned James Mangan. Among others, Douglas Booth, Murray Phillips, and Wray Vamplew have always been remarkably collegial and attentive to our initiatives. We also wish to mention our interchange with colleagues in South America (such as Pablo Scharagrodsky and Raumar Rodríguez) and in the Iberian Peninsula (such as Teresa Aja and Augusto Nascimento).
8 Giovanni Levi, 'O trabalho do historiador: pesquisar, resumir, comunicar' [The historian's work: to research, to summarize, to communicate] *Revista Tempo* 20 (2014): 1–20.
9 João de Pina Cabral, 'Língua e hegemonia nas ciências sociais' [Language and hegemony in the social sciences] *Análise Social* 62, no. 182 (2007): 233–237.
10 Renato Ortiz, 'As ciências sociais e o inglês' [The social sciences and English] *Revista Brasileira de Ciências Sociais* 19, no. 54 (February 2004): 5–22, 19.
11 There is a widespread idea that fluency in a second language is something positive, desirable, and necessary. In practice, it applies most often to those who do not have English as their main or first language, so that they may express themselves in this language – or at least consume bibliography published in it. It is rarely ever suggested, however, that native speakers of English should conform to the same principle, that is, of the fluency in a second language being a desirable or necessary quality for respectable careers as professors and scholars.
12 Ortiz, 'As ciências sociais e o inglês' [The social sciences and English], 5–22.
13 See Joseph Arbena, 'History of Latin American Sports: The End Before the Beginning?' *Sporting Traditions* 16, no. 1 (1999): 23–28; Victor Andrade de Melo, 'History of Sport in Brazil and in South America: Visibility for New Looks', *International Journal of the History of Sport* 34 (5–6) (2017): 399–404.
14 Rafael Fortes, 'Política científica no Brasil: dilemas em torno da internacionalização e do inglês' [Scientific policy in Brazil: dilemmas concerning internationalization and English] *Interfaces Brasil/Canadá* 16, no. 1 (2016): 142–180.
15 Murray G. Phillips, 'Sizing Up the Journals: Metrics, Sport Humanities, and History', *International Journal of the History of Sport* 37, no. 8 (2020): 692–704, 697.

16 Qualis is the Brazilian ranking of academic journals, and it is also used to rank graduate studies programmes and the output of individual scholars. It has been developed by the Coordination for Higher Education Staff Development (CAPES); a foundation controlled by the Ministry of Education. In terms of resources, it is the foremost funding agency for research in Brazil. In descending order, Qualis ranks journals as: A1, A2, B1, B2, B3, B4, B5, and C.

17 Rafael Fortes, 'Os estudos históricos do esporte no Brasil: avanços, limites, desafios' [Historical studies of sport in Brazil: advances, limits, challenges], in *História do Esporte: diálogos disciplinares* [The history of sport, interdisciplinary dialogues], eds. Victor Andrade de Melo et al. (Rio de Janeiro: 7 Letras, 2020). This text outlines further debate in the matter.

18 Victor Andrade de Melo, '15 anos de "Sport" – Investigando a periferia, investigando na periferia: reflexões e proposições' [15 years of 'Sport' – investigating the periphery, investigating in the periphery: reflections and proposals], in *História do Esporte: diálogos disciplinares* [The history of sport, interdisciplinary dialogues], eds. Victor Andrade de Melo et al. (Rio de Janeiro: 7 Letras, 2020).

PART 6

Conclusion

48

SPORT HISTORY

Past, present, future

Douglas Booth, Murray G. Phillips and Carly Adams

The *Routledge Handbook of Sport History* is testimony to a thriving academic field. Sport history's success rests on solid formal structures such as undergraduate and postgraduate programmes in institutions of higher education, book series published by university and commercial presses, long-running and emerging journals, and solvent professional associations. The field also benefits from an interest in the history of sport across the academy and the appearance of articles in virtually every discipline. For example, an important historical and political analysis of state-sponsored doping of athletes in the former East Germany can be found in the journal *Clinical Chemistry*.[1] The *Handbook* encapsulates the content and the form of sport history in the past and the present (time of publication). In these concluding comments we summarize the content and form of the contemporary field and offer some thoughts on the future. The *Handbook* is neither encyclopedic nor definitive; the chapters serve to introduce readers to a cross section of subjects rather than cover the entire field in detail. The *Handbook* does not contain chapters devoted to genres of representation, nostalgia and memory, oral history, public sport history, identity, and biography, in part because of the unavailability of experts.[2] Nonetheless, we believe that the overall content captures most critical elements of the field, including references to the aforementioned themes, as well as trends moving forward.

With regard to the elements of contemporary sport history, the content of the *Handbook*, as evident in the text, references, and citations, reaffirms that the field constitutes a broad church whose congregation subscribes to different – often competing – methods, theories, and interpretations, and whose interests cover a myriad of themes that seem to have no bounds. By definition, a broad church means constant change and ongoing debate among members about all manner of intellectual and professional matters.[3] Invariably, those debates are most intense when members critically examine established approaches and methods.[4] Notwithstanding the diversity and dynamism of the field, it remains firmly grounded in an empirical-analytical epistemology based on evidence from the past which typically takes, and implicitly assumes, a factual form. As historians of sport are ever alert to factual accuracy, as is evident in anonymous peer reviews of journal articles and published reviews of books, we argue that factual integrity remains a hallmark of accepted and acceptable practice.[5] Yet, while facts are the bedrock of the history of sport, there is little agreement – and even less discussion – about the presentation of facts. Like their colleagues across the discipline,

DOI: 10.4324/9780429318306-55

historians of sport typically present their facts in the form of either an argument or a narrative. The prime difference between an argument and a narrative is the existence of a plot in the latter. A plot is a mode of organizing the evidence as a genre of story (e.g. romance, tragedy, comedy, satire) in order to 'add meaning' and to 'wrap' the subject up 'in an account ... from which instruction can be derived'.[6] However, the line between argument and narrative is typically blurred. The philosopher of history Hayden White believes that any argument can be conceptualized as a form of story; he thus calls an argument a 'narrative impressionistic'.[7] Arthur Danto similarly argued that any non-narrative form (i.e. a statistic, a graph, an image) can be converted into a narrative and, indeed, that narrative exists at the heart of these forms.[8] Part 1 (History and Representing the Sporting Past) affirms a growing recognition that narrative structure is a critical element of the field.

Underscoring the contemporary broad church of sport history is a widely shared sentiment in which practitioners acknowledge that the practice of sport includes a political dimension and that it is grounded in contradictions and conflict, replete with structures and relationships of power, and riven with discrimination, subjugation, exploitation, and abuse. Many historians of sport are committed to highlighting these political dimensions; some are dedicated to challenging them. Political aspects of sport appear throughout the *Handbook* in analyses of structures and relationships of power, socio-economic and political contextualization, and the incorporation of the voices of ordinary people, and particularly minority groups, into arguments and narratives. One example, which we regard as particularly pertinent, concerns critiques of archives that have systematically silenced Indigenous voices. Collectively, these political sentiments and their associated methods and content present an academic field framed by democratic and emancipatory notions. None of this should surprise given that social responsibility is a prominent mandate of many traditional Western universities.

Of course, political sentiments and tendencies raise their own issues. Emancipation from structures and relationships of power is an ethical value which is not always easy to uncover in modernist-inspired empirical-analytical history founded on objective, typically written, and verifiable sources. In fact, the moral philosopher Emmanuel Lévinas argued that ethics resides first and foremost in the face-to-face encounter with the Other, and the choices that such encounters require. For the historian, any representation of an encounter with the Other involves choices about content (i.e. facts, concepts, context) and form (i.e. metaphors, emplotment, focalization). Moreover, Lévinas maintained that access to face-to-face encounters with the Other in the past more often than not exists only as a trace of unverifiable marks of the Other.[9] Taylor McKee and Janice Forsyth capture this point well in a recent account of team photographs taken in the 1950s from the St Michael's (Duck Lake) Indian Residential School in Saskatoon. At first glance the photographs of 'boys lined up in neat rows [and] dressed in uniform ... foster ... ideas about belonging, health, friendships, social networks, and economic well-being'. However, Eugene Arcand, a survivor of the school, presents a different interpretation. Pointing to swollen hands in several pictures, he recounted how boys were beaten with a strap, in some cases so badly that they could not even put on hockey gloves.[10]

One strength of the *Routledge Handbook of Sport History* lies in the number of contributors who are thinking about issues associated with witnessing the past and the responsibilities associated with presenting witnesses' accounts. This is most evident in Part 4 (Indigenous Sport History) where several authors seek out testimonies of Indigenous people, who have long been silent and silenced in mainstream narratives of sport, in order to bring new accounts and new stories to the fore. Yet, while we note the presence of Indigenous voices in the *Handbook*, we also echo Janice Forsyth, who asks, 'how can researchers do a better job of incorporating Indigenous histories?'[11] In this question is a reminder of the chasm between citing a voice and allowing that voice to tell its own story.

Questions of witnessing and responsibility are also apparent in the explicit discussions about the objectives and limitations of historical representations under the heading of reflexivity in Part 1 (History and Representing the Sporting Past). As editors, we suggest that these contributors are subtly shifting the field beyond the logic, reasoning, and methods of empirical-analytical, modernist-inspired history grounded in reconstructing the (political) sporting past. Although the contingencies in material and ideological life and the networks of relationships that make up social life make it impossible to identify the future, even the future of sport history, we believe that the *Handbook* offers clues. Here we are not suggesting, à la Arthur Keppel-Jones, the renowned liberal historian of South Africa, that studying the past is analogous to following a set of railway tracks which lead to a fixed terminus.[12] But it does appear to us that the field of sport history is slowly recognising the need to better contextualize the intersections between the historian researcher/author/narrator (and their implicit ideological inclinations, political proclivities, and emotional empathies) and their subject matter. Indeed, as many of the contributors to this volume point out, the very term history is undergoing a radical reformulation. Whereas once the term broadly denoted an attempt to reconstruct the past, today it increasingly connotes an authored representation of the past. Carly Adams captures the distinction well in her recent collection on the history of sport in Canada when she advises readers to shelve any expectations of a definitive history. 'There is no such thing as a "complete" history,' Adams writes, adding that '"history" is the work of historians' who 'make choices about the questions they ask, the sources they choose to examine, and the approach they take to their research'.[13]

It is not surprising to us then, to see more historians of sport delving into the relationships between the empirical-analytical and narrative-linguistic dimensions of historical representations, or as White puts it, the relationship between the content and the form of history.[14] This has been a slow journey begun some two decades ago by a small coterie of sport historians.[15] Nonetheless, in this journey perhaps lies the single most important lesson in the *Handbook*: our ability to reveal the past is inordinately complex. While every generation of sport historians has acknowledged the complexity of their practice, the depth of that complexity continues to grow. Logically, this means that no generation will ever cement the field in concrete; future generations will always question and challenge the assumptions, sentiments, approaches, and themes favoured by the current generation. As far as we are concerned, these are positive signs of a healthy subdiscipline, which is constantly shifting, changing, and adapting as the intricacy of the process of history making becomes more apparent.

Notes

1 Werner Franke and Brigitte Berendonk, 'Hormonal Doping and Androgenization of Athletes: A Secret Program of the German Democratic Republic Government', *Clinical Chemistry* 43, no. 7 (1997): 1262–1279.

2 Examples of these subjects include: genres of representation – Douglas Booth and Fiona McLachlan, 'Who's Afraid of the Internet? Swimming in an Infinite Archive', in *Sports History in the Digital Era* eds. Gary Osmond and Murray Phillips (Urbana: University of Illinois Press), 227–250; nostalgia and memory – Heetae Cho, Gregory Ramshaw, and William Norman, 'A Conceptual Model for Nostalgia in the Context of Sport Tourism: Re-classifying the Sporting Past', *Journal of Sport & Tourism* 19, no. 2 (2014): 145–167; oral history – Carly Adams and Mike Cronin eds., Sport and Oral History,

Special Edition, *The International Journal of the History of Sport* 36, 13–14 (2019); public sport history – Murray Phillips ed., *Representing the Sporting Past in Museums and Halls of Fame* (London: Routledge, 2012); identity – John Nauright, *Sport, Cultures and Identities in South Africa* (London: Leicester University Press, 1997); biography – John Bale, Mette Krogh, Christensen and Gertrud Pfister eds., *Writing Lives in Sport: Biographies, Life-Histories and Methods* (Århus: Aarhus University Press, 2004).

3 In this sense we conceptualize a broad church as a network of actors rather than a structural institution. See Bruno Latour, *Reassembling the Social: An Introduction to Actor Network Theory* (Oxford: Oxford University Press, 2005).

4 Carly Adams, 'Sport and Recreation Histories Matter', in *Sport and Recreation in Canadian History* ed. C. Adams (Champaign, IL: Human Kinetics, 2021), 5.

5 This statement simply acknowledges the practical reality of assessing historical scholarship which effectively operates independently of the philosophy of historical facts. For a classic engagement of the latter, see Edward Carr, *What Is History?* (London: Macmillan, 1961).

6 Hayden White, *The Practical Past* (Evanston, IL: Northwestern University Press, 2005), 83.

7 Hayden White, 'The Structure of Historical Narrative', *Clio* 1, no. 3 (1972): 6, 9, and 11.

8 Arthur Danto, *Narration and Knowledge* (New York: Columbia University Press, 1985).

9 Emmanuel Lévinas, *Totality and Infinity: An Essay on Exteriority*, trans. A. Lingis (Pittsburgh, PA: Duquesne University Press, 1969), and *Otherwise Than Being Or Beyond Essence*, trans. A. Lingis (Dordrecht: Kluwer Academic, 1978).

10 Taylor McKee and Janice Forsyth, 'Witnessing Painful Pasts: Understanding Images of Sports at Canadian Residential Schools', *Journal of Sport History* 46, no. 2 (2019): 175–176.

11 Janice Forsyth, 'Case Studies of Indigenous Sport', in Adams, *Canadian History*, 75.

12 See, for example, Arthur Keppel-Jones' dystopian novel, *When Smuts Goes* (Pietermaritzburg: Shuter & Shooter, 1947). In the early 1950s, Jones, who predicted the consolidation of legislative apartheid in South Africa, was widely hailed as something of a prophet, to which he replied, 'I am merely an historian'. Keppel-Jones' perspective might be viewed as a liberal version of that proposed more famously by Karl Marx. According to Marx, 'men make their own history, but they do not make it as they please; they do not make it under self-selected circumstances, but under circumstances existing already, given and transmitted from the past'. Karl Marx, 'The Eighteenth Brumaire of Louis Bonaparte', in *Karl Marx Selected Writings* ed. David McLellan (Oxford: Oxfxord University Press, 1977), 300.

13 Adams, *Canadian History*, xi and 4–5.

14 Hayden White, *The Content of the Form: Narrative Discourse and Historical Representation* (Baltimore, MD: The Johns Hopkins University Press, 1987). For a recent discussion, see Aaron Sachs and John Demos eds. *Artful History: A Practical Anthology* (New Haven, CT: Yale University Press, 2020).

15 See, for example, Synthia Sydnor, 'A History of Synchronized Swimming', *Journal of Sport History* 25, no. 2 (1998): 252–267, and Murray Phillips, 'A Critical Appraisal of Narrative in Sport History: Reading the Surf Lifesaving Debate', *Journal of Sport History* 29, no. 1 (2002): 25–40.

INDEX

Page numbers in **bold** indicate tables and page numbers in *italics* indicate figures.

Abala, Steve 67
Aboriginal Australians 61; *see also* Indigenous sport history; *see also* Australia; *see also* Cherbourg Aboriginal Settlement
Abrams, Phillip 29
academic oral history 62
Activision Decathlon Lounge 220
activism, sport and 3, 12, 82, 138–140; against apartheid 86; athlete activism 83–85; coalesced activism 84; diverse nature of 86–87; framing 83; OPHR programme 84–85; reforming of sports 84–85; on women's agitation for access to sporting opportunities 86–87
Actor–Network Theory 245
Adair, Daryl 181
Adams, Carly 334, 335
Adelman, Melvin 205, 340, 341
Adidas 157
African: National Congress (ANC) 169, 171–172, 174; sport history 183
African-American: athletes 70, 163; women 97, 164, 181
Afro-Caribbean identities 166;
Afro-Cuban players 166
Afro-Latino ball players 166
Age of Empires II (1999) 222
A.G. Spaulding Company 307
Ali, Muhammed 45, 70, 85, 244
AliSports 224
All-American Girls Professional Baseball League (AAGPB) 164
Alldred, Pam 243
Altmetric.com 328
Amateur Athletic Union 104

America: *American Cricketer* (journal) 262; American Baseball Club 263–264; Civil War (1861–1865) 105; American football 19, 105, 228, 262, 303; Indigenous sport history 303–309; sports literature 76
ancient Greece: athletic bodies in 119–120; sports in 2
Andrews, David 244
anthropological self 19
anti-apartheid movement 86, 140, 149
anti-homophobia advocacy groups 98, 194
anti-Olympic movement 138, 139, 140
antiquarians 26, 354
Aotearoa 270, 273, 281
apartheid sport 4, 13, 58, 85–86, 97, 122, 140, 149, 162–163, 169–170, 270, 276; *see also* non-racialism; South Africa
Arab Spring 87
Arbena, Joe 341
archival repertoires 62–63
archives 58–59, 62; institutional 58–59; notion of 'figured' 58; power and 59; as sites of knowledge, retrieval, and power 59; traditional conceptualization of 59
Arctic Winter Games 271
Arete: The Journal of Sport Literature 74
Ariail, Cat 93, 98
Arnold, Matthew 74
art history 18, 33, 131
Arthur, George 154
artifacts of sport 65–66
Aryan body 119
Ashe, Arthur 70, 71
Ashworth, Gregory 236

Index

Asian Electronic Sports Federation (AESF) 224

Asian Journal of Sport History & Culture 316, 319, 320

Asociación Andaluza de Historia del Deporte (AAHD) 375

Association for International Sport for All (TAFISA) 224

Atari: *Atari Coin Connection* (newsletter) 220; *Swordquest* challenge of 1982–1984 220; World Championships (1981) 220

Athens Olympics (1850, 1870, and 1875) 146

athletic masculinities 191

Atkinson, Graham 289

Atlanta (College Football Hall of Fame) 240

Attwood, Bain 288

Australia: Aboriginal cultures 62; Australian Rules football 231, 271; Society for Sports History (ASSH) 315, 367–370; sport history 288–289

Avery Brundage Papers Collection 206

Bach, Thomas 224

Baggataway 107

Bale, John 123, 181

Balenti, Cheyenne Michael 307

Bally Midway National Tron Video Game Tournament (1982) 220

Bamblett, Lawrence 291

Bandy, Susan 76

Barad, Karen 243, 246–247

Barnes, Sarah 13, 94, 97

Barthes, Roland 43

baseball 50–51, 105, 261, 263, 264

Baseball Manager 221

basketball 50

Bastow, Simon 27

Bateson, Gregory 343

Baton Rouge Summer Special Olympics, 1983 220

Battlefield series 223

Battle of Champions (1992) 231

Batts, Callie 87

Becenti, Ryneldi 308

Beers, George 107, 114, 144, 263

Beijing Olympic Games (2008) 157, 232

Bell's Life 153

Bender, Charles 307

Bend it Like Beckham (2002) 132

Bennett, Jane 243

Berbary, Lisbeth 246

Berger, John 129

Berlin: Deaf Gymnastics Association 252; Olympics (1936) 206, 305

Berryman, Jack 341

Bertie the Brain (Kates) 219

Betts, John R. 340

Black: 'black armband' historians 288; Black Lives Matter movement 87, 124; clubs 172; cricketers 174–175, 177, 284; Economic Empowerment (BEE) 173, 174; Economic Union 85; manhood and masculinity 163; rugby 171–173; sport 169

Blizzard's StarCraft Ladder Tournament 222

Blockbuster's World Video Game Championships 221

Block, D. 105

Bloomsfield, Thomas 245

boarding school sport histories 306

Bobel, Chris 83

body-as-machine metaphor 123

Booth, Douglas 20–21, 26, 36, 37, 43, 65, 101, 102, 105, 119, 124, 130, 162, 206, 244

border games 261–264

Borish, Linda 182

Bouchier, Nancy 334

Boucicault, Dion 129

Bourdieu, Pierre 5, 124, 285, 381

Braidotti, Rosi 243

Brébeuf, Jean de 303

Brice, Julie 201, 247

BRICS countries 138

Bright, Johnny 165

British Empire 102–103

British Journal of Sports History, The 316, 317, 319, 353

British Society for Sports History (BSSH) 315, 353; *Bulletin* of British Society for Sports History 353–355; *Newsletter* of British Society for Sports History 356

Broome, Richard 290–291

Brownell, S. 103

Brown, Jim 85

Brown, Narragansett Ellison, Sr. 305

Brundage, Avery 82, 122

Brutus, Dennis 85

Bundesinstitut für Sportwissenschaft (BISp) 349

Burgos, Adrian, Jr. 166

Burke, Peter 128, 131

Burke, Sarah 206

Butterfield, Reverend 283

Cahill, Thomas 262

Cahn, Susan 180, 191, 192

Call of Duty series 223

Canada: Canadian Association of Health, Physical Education, and Recreation (CAHPER) 332; *Canadian Journal of History of Sport/Revue canadienne de l'histoire des sports* 316, 333; *Canadian Journal of the History of Sport and Physical Education* 316, 317, 318, 332; female track and field team 78; national identity of

396

107; National Lacrosse Association 107, 297; sports history of 75
Carby, Hazel V. 163
Carlos, John 70, 85, 132
Carr, Gerald 332
Carter, T. 105
Cashman, Richard 367–368, 370
Cassioli, Giuseppe 132
cerebral palsy (CP) 254
Cerebral Palsy International Sports and Recreation Association (CPISRA) 254
Charlotte (NASCAR Hall of Fame) 240
Cherbourg Aboriginal Settlement 62
Cherokee 303, 306, 308, 310
Chicago White Sox 307
China 136
China's CBI National Computer Games Championships (1999) 222
Cho, Heetae 240
Church of Latter-Day Saints (Mormon) missionaries 308
CiteScore 326, 336
'civilizing process' discourse 18
Clark, Marianne 201
class *see* social class
Clough, Brian 132
Coakley, Jay 94
Cobley, A. 105
codified sport 35
Cohen, Thomas V. 33
Cold War 148–149, 156
College Football Hall of Fame, United States 238
Collins, Debbie 75
Collins, Randall 229
Collins, Shane 75
Collins, Tony 36
colonialism 275–277
Command & Conquer (1995) 221
Commons Preservation Society (Open Spaces Society) 115
competitive gaming 225; in 1990s 221–222; achievements 223–224; history of 219–221
Confederation of Independent Football Associations (CONIFA) 158
Connors, Jimmy 231
contre-histoire 279–282
Cook, James 288
Coole, Diana 244
Cororación Argentina de Discapacitados 253
corporate nationalism 157
Cosell, Howard 230
Coubertin Olympics 145, 148
Coubertin, Pierre de 145, 146, 148, 155
Counter-Strike 222, 223
COVID-19 pandemic 200, 217–218
Crenshaw, Kimberle Williams 164

cricket 2, 27, 67, 86–87, 102, 107, 115, 137, 154, 169–170, 174–177, 261–262
Cripples Olympiad 252–253
critical race theory 270
Croatian War of Independence 157
Cronin, Mike 10, 13, 27, 97, 153, 206, 239
cross-disciplinary work 18
Cuban nationalism 106
cultural heritage digitization 206–207
cultural identities, construction of 94
cultural imperialism 100
cultural turn 1, 3, 4, 6, 9, 12, 14n8
Curran, Sean 132
Cyberathlete Professional League (CPL)'s FRAG series (1997–1999) 222
Czech *Sokol* movement 154

Davidson, Judy 13, 97, 98
Davies, Bronwyn 245
Davis, Amira Rose 164–165
Davis Cup 86
Day, Dave 93
deaf and disability sport 252–254
Deaflympics 254
Defense of the Ancients (DotA) 223
Deleuze, Gilles 24–25, 28, 29, 243
Derrida, Jacques 129
Desai, Ashwin 13, 97, 98
Deutsche Clanliga (DeCL) 222–223
Deutsche Sporthochschule Köln (DSHS) 348
Dichter, Heather 12, 96
Didrikson, Mildred 'Babe' 191, 192
diffraction 247
digital object identifier (DOI) 328
digital sport history 3; cultural heritage digitization 206–207; digital tools and methods 204–205; future 208; Internet and 205–206; quantification 204–205; social media platforms 206
digital technologies 184
digitization 184, 200, 206–207
diplomacy 136–137
disability histories 251–252, 254–256
disabled sport 3
Djabwurrung people 289–290
Dodd, Betty 192
Donnelly, Peter 94
Doom (1993) 221
Dota 2 (2013) 223
Doubleday, Abner 52
Downey, Allan 107, 272, 300
Doyle, Jennifer 133
Dulles, Foster Rhea 339
Dunleavy, Patrick 27
Durie, Sir Mason 281
DWANGO's Deathmatch '95 222
Dyreson, Mark 232

397

EBSCO 336
Eby, Beth 270, 272
Edelman, Robert 1, 2
Ederle, Trudy 76
Edward III, Proclamation banning football (1363) 206
Edwards, Harry 84
Eichberg, Henning 123
Eigenfactor 326
Electronic Sports League (ESL) 223
Electronic Sports World Cup (ESWC) 222
Elias, Norbert 27
Elsevier's Scopus 326
Elsey, Brenda 181
Eminent Persons Group (EPG) 176–177
emotions in sport 228–230; fans and spectator violence 232–233; gender norms 231; historical development 230–233; hooliganism 233; humanitarian sentiments 232; internationalist feelings 232; nationalism 232; social control 231
English, Colleen 335
English football 45, 233
entanglements in sport history 13, 161–163; historical entanglements 163–164; inter-sectionality 164–165; memory and temporal 165–166; racial entanglements 161–162
epistemological certainty 18–20
ESL One Frankfurt *Dota 2* tournament 224
eSports 200, 217, 222–225, 236
ethnic nationalism 13, 156–157
European Sports History Review 316, 326
European Studies in Sports History 316, 318, 326, 329, 336, 337
Evans, Lee 85
exceptionalism 259, 262, 263, 334
experiential self 19
Extinction Rebellion 87
Eyler, Marvin 340, 343

Facebook 206, 230, 329
Facultad de Ciencias de la Actividad Física y del Deporte (INEF) 375
Fédération Internationale de Football (FIFA) 35, 104; *FIFA 06* 222; *FIFA 2000* 222; Women's World Cup 140; World Cup (1974) 348; World Cup (2010) 173; World Cup (2026) 140
Fédération Sportive Féminine Internationale (FSFI) 86–87, 148
feminism and sport history: *see* gender
fiction, sport 74; *Girl Runner* 78–79; on restricted possibilities for female athletes 78–79; *Sage Island* 75–77, 78–79
Field, Russell 12
First National Space Invaders Competition (1980) 220

First Nations people 271
Firth, Shirley 299
Fischer, David Hackett 20, 51
Fisher, D. 107
Flanagan, Martin 289–290
Flood, Curt 84, 85
Flower, Andy 87
folk games 102, 106, 114, 115
football 2, 19, 45, 50, 65, 70, 83, 102, 104, 114, 158, 165, 174, 177, 183, 193, 228, 231, 306
Forsyth, Janice 270, 272
Fortnite 223
Foucault, Michel 129, 191, 273, 282
Fourth Asian Indoor and Martial Arts Games 224
Fox, Nick 243
Freeman, Cathy 128
French Revolution 146, 153
Frost, Samantha 244
Frye, Northrop 53

Gaelic Athletic Association 154, 206
Gallaudet 252
gambling 3, 65, 101–102, 114, 304, 308
Games of the Newly Emerging Forces (GANEFO) 149
game-winning shots 50
Gammon, Sean 237
Garber, Mary 165
García, Sánchez 19
Gay Games 98, 194
gender 3, 5, 16, 29, 37, 41, 42, 52, 97, 98, 121–122, 124, 129, 132, 133, 154, 164, 180–183, 189–193, 201, 206, 213, 214, 230, 231, 233, 239, 259, 273, 282, 296, 304, 306, 307, 318, 319, 323, 334, 335, 343, 344, 358, 377, **378**; feminist methodological approaches 184; feminist sports history 10, 29, 34, 53; feminist sports historians 120–121, 183–184; feminism and sociology 29; push-pull phenomenon 182
Generation-Z undergraduates 217
geographical exclusions 183
German Turner Society 104
Ghobrial, John Paul A. 34, 35
Gibb, Alexandrine 79
Gillespie, Greg 335
Ginzburg, Carlo 37
Girl Runner 78–80
Giulianotti, Richard 45, 46
Give Our Athletes Level Salaries (GOALS) Act 96, 140
Gleneagles Agreement, 1977 86
Glennie, Paul 113
Global North 87, 98, 110
Global South 149–150
Goffman, Erving 343
Goldblatt, David 36

Index

Goldstein, Warren 104
González-Aja, Teresa 319
Goodes, Adam 87
Goodrich, Angel 308
Google Books 206, 276
Google Print/Google Books project 206
Google's Google Scholar 326
Gorn, Elliott J. 50, 51, 54, 104, 106
Gotass, Thor 36
Gottschall, Jonathan 52
Greek Olympics 36
Grossberg, Lawrence 17, 43
Gruneau, R. 101
Guattari, Félix 24–25, 28, 29
Guiliano, Jennifer 200, 270, 272
Guridy, Frank 164
Guttmann, Allen 27, 36, 124
Guttmann, Ludwig 253, 255
Guzon, Charles Mayo 307

Hall, M. Ann 317
Halo series 223
Hamburg Turner Society 104
Haraway, Donna 243
Hardy, Stephen 36, 65, 66, 106, 264
Hargreaves, Jennifer 95; gendered and racialized
   bodies 121; intersectional approach to
   understanding bodies 121; *Sporting Females* 121
Hargreaves, John 113
Harrison, Rodney 236
Hartmann, Douglas 85, 86
Harvey, David 111
Haudenosaunee 144, 272, 297–300, 304
Hayden, Frank 253
Heritage Classic outdoor ice hockey event (2003)
   240
Herodotus 51
Hess, Rob 317
heteromasculinity 191
heterosexual gender relations 193
Hibbins, Gillian 290
Higgins, Roisin 239
high-performance sport 83, 87, 174
Hill, Jeffrey 13
h-indexes 324, 326, 377
historical entanglements 162, 163
history *see* sport history
History of Physical Education and Sport (HISPA)
   17, 317, 348–349, 363, 381
History Wars 288, 290
Hoberman, J. 104
Hobsbawm, Eric 16
hockey 52, 69, 104, 106–107, 137, 263–264,
   297, 299, 308, 392
Hocking, Jenny 289
Hokowhitu, Brendan 272–273
Holman, Andy 106, 264

Holt, Richard 26
homosexual identity 98, 188
Hoosiers (1986) 132
Hopis 305, 306
horizontal diffusion 102
horse racing 114, 303, 305
hosting sporting events 138, 139–140
Howard, Josh 344
Howard, Peter 235
Howell, Colin 94, 106, 201
Howell, Max 332
Hudson, Laguna Pueblan Frank 306
Huggins, Mike 95, 131, 263
human body 94–95; ancient Greek athletic
   bodies 119–120; Aryan body 119; black body
   122; body-as-machine metaphor 123; gendered and racialized bodies 121–122; in locations and time periods 119–120; as object 123;
   religious beliefs and 120; socially conceived
   123–124; in sprinting 123
Hutcheon, Linda 10, 52

ice hockey 52, 69, 107, 114–115, 137, 148,
   238, 240, 263, 308, 343
Ichikawa, Kon 132
Impact Factor 47, 326, 336, 344, 365, 372,
   379
imperialism 100, 103, 105–107, 144, 146, 259,
   264, 275–276, 288
Incredible Technologies, Golden Tee 3D Golf
   National Championships (1997) 222
Indigenous sport history 5, 57–58, 61–62, 107,
   269–273, 277; brown citizen 273, 279, 282,
   284–285; in America 303–309; in Australia
   287–293; in Canada 295–300; as enunciation
   282–284; Rez ball games 308; spiritual
   ceremony 305
Indigenous sporting experiences 94
Indonesian Esports Association (IeSPA) 224
industrial capitalism 100, 103, 112
institutional racism 162
Instituto Andaluz del Deporte (IAD) 374
intangible sport heritage 200, 239–240
Intergalactic Spacewar Olympics 219
International Amateur Athletics Federation
   (IAAF) 122
International Association for the History of
   Physical Education and Sport 317
International Association of Sport for Persons
   with Mental Handicap (INAS-FMH)
   255–256
International Blind Sports Association 255
International Committee for the History of Sport
   and Physical Education (ICOSH) 349
International Committee of Sports for the Deaf
   (CISS) 252
international competitions 144

Index

International Co-ordination Committee of World Sports Organizations for the Disabled (ICC) 255
International Federation of Association Football (FIFA) 96
International Football Association Board (IFAB) 103
International Journal of the History of Sport, The 316, 317, 319, 326, 328, 329, 337, 360–365
International Olympic Committee (IOC) 35, 96, 104, 121–122, 136, 138, 140, 146–147, 149, 155, 172, 224, 254, 255
international relations and sports 144; Cold War and 148–149; interwar alternatives 147–148; isolation of apartheid South Africa 149; modern Olympic Games and 145–147; neo-liberalism 150; post-colonial relationships 148–149; racist exploitation and repression 149
International Silent Games 252, 254
international socialist movement 147
International Society for the History of Physical Education and Sport (ISHPES) 17, 349
International Sociology of Sport Association 17–18
International Sports Federation for Persons with Intellectual Disability (INAS) 256
International Stoke Mandeville Games Federation (ISMGF) 253
Internet 205–206
Internet of Things 217
intersectionality 38, 164–165, 183
Iron Game History: The Journal of Physical Culture 316, 318, 320
Irons, Andy 206
Iroquois 106, 272, 297, 300, 304

Jackson, Bruce 52
Jahn, F. L. 154
Jakarta-Palembang Asian Games 224
James, C. L. R. 170, 171, 175, 284
James, LeBron 82
Japanese body culture 19
Japanese martial arts 20
Japan Journal of Sport History 316, 317, 320, 326
Jedi Knight 2 223
Jenkins, Henry 231
Jenkins, Keith 344
jeux olympiques 146
Jim Crow laws 163
Jimeson, Seneca Jacob 307
jockeys 163
Johnes, Martin 207
Johnson, George H. 307
Johnson, Jimmy 306
Johnson, Mamie 'Peanut' 164
Johnson, Rafer 70
Jones, Kevin 332
Journal of American History 317

Journal of Olympic History 316, 317, 320, 326
Journal of Olympic Studies 316, 318, 320
Journal of Physical Education 317
Journal of Sport History 316, 318, 319, 320, 321, 326, 328, 329, 336, 337, 339–345; editorial challenges 341–342; editors **342**; scholarship in 343–344
Judd, Barry 271, 289, 290
Jude, Ojibwe Frank 307

Kaepernick, Colin 82, 87, 88
Kanaka Maoli culture 308
Kellner, Hans 10, 51
Kellogg, Robert 51
Kerr, Rosalind 245
Keyes, Mary 332
Keys, Barbara 200
Kidd, Bruce 96
Kimbadi, Prashant 32
King, Billie Jean 83–84, 85
King, Martin Luther 45
King, Michael 283
Klugman, Matthew 128
Knickerbocker Club 105
Kolisi, Siya 97, 174, 175–176
Kopay, David 193–194
Korea's Sports Seoul Cup (1999) 222
Kraft durch Freude (Nazi organization) 231
Krieger, Jörg 335
Kruger, Arthur 252
Kuhn, Bowie 84
Kulin Aboriginal clans 289
Kumm, Brian 246
Kurlansky, Mark 32

Lacan, Jacques 129
lacrosse 106–107, 114, 146, 261, 263, 297, 303, 304, 307; Winnebago players 304
Laidlaw, Chris 171
Lake Placid Winter Olympics (1980) 220
Lamani, George 172
Lämmer, Manfred 317
Langley, Josephine 306
Langton, Marcia 287
Lather, Patti 29
Latour, Bruno 243
Laudonnière, René Goulaine de 304
League of Legends(LoL) 223
Leeworthy, Daryl 94, 201
Lefebvre, Henri 111
Legg, Sioux Henry 307
Le Mans 132
Lerner, Gerda 20
Leroy, Stockbridge-Munsee Louis 307
lesbian, gay, bisexual, and transgender (LGBT): athletic activism 194; public education project 98; Q2S communities 251

Index

Lewis, Guy 340
Liaoning TV 224
Liberti, Rita 37, 181
library holdings 325–330
Lilesa, Feyisa 87
Linden, Andrew 206, 319
Links 386 Pro 221
Litchfield, Chelsea 13, 95
London Olympics: 1948 253; 2012 157
Longman, Jeré 82
Lorenzen, Hanz 252
Los Angeles Coliseum 164
Los Angeles Olympics (1984) 138, 149, 191
Louis, Joe 70
Loy, John 65, 94, 124
Ludica: Annali di storia e civiltà del gioco 316, 318, 326

MacAloon, John 343
Macau E-Sports Federation (MESF) 224
MacLean, Malcolm 9–10, 13, 86, 202
macrohistory 33, 34, 38; defined 34; use of big data 34
Maguire, Joseph 26
Major League Baseball 164–165, 166, 261
Major League Baseball Players Association 84
Makana Municipality 176
Makhanda 171, 172, 176
MALLET (statistical analysis tool) 207
Manchester United 45
Mandela, Nelson 169, 171, 172
Mandell, Richard 124
Mangan, J. A. 121
mannish lesbians 190–192, 194
Māori communities 273, 279–284; physicality 283; rugby sport 283; soldier 283; sport 282–283; sporting participation 281; sportsperson 281–282; sub-cultures 284; urbanization of 281
March of Dimes International Konami/Centuri Track & Field Challenge (1984) 220
marngrook 277, 287, 288–290
Marqusee, Mike 175–176, 280
Marshall, George 163
martial gymnastic movements 154
Maryland Historian (1973) 340
Marylebone Cricket Club 102, 262
Massicotte, Jean Paul 332
Massumi, Brian 243
material culture of sport 65; monuments 66; museums 68–70; objects and artifacts 66; sculptures at Sydney Cricket Grounds 67; special issue publications 66–67; sport historians and 66–68; visual culture 67
Materiales para la Historia del Deporte 316, 317, 321, 327, 374–379, **377–378**; gender of published authors **378**; institutional affiliation of

authors **378**; language and gender 376–377, **377**; management and administration **378**; metrics 377–379; origins 374–375
McComb, David G. 36
McDonald, Mary 13, 94, 97, 344
McGregor, Andrew 206
McIntosh, Peter 332
McKemmish, Sue 57
McLachlan, Fiona 206
McLean, Malcolm 270
McLean, T. P. 280
McMaster, Rowland 74
MechWarrior 2 (1995) 221
Meggyesy, Dave 83, 85
Melbourne Football Club 289
Messenger, Christian 76
Metcalfe, Alan 112, 114, 317, 332, 333, 341
methodological nationalism 19–21
#MeToo campaign 87
Mexico City Olympic Games (1968) 87, 122
microhistory 10, 32–38
militant non-racialism 176, 177
Miller, Marvin 84
Milliat, Alice 148
Mills, Charles W. 277
Miñoso, Orestes 'Minnie' 166
Mirzoeff, Nicholas 131
Mississippian Natives 304
Mitchell, W.J.T. 131
modern sport 94, 110, 111; characteristic differences between traditional and 101; evolution and diffusion of early British modern sport 102–103; growth of organizations and associations 103–104; North American context 104–106; origin and diffusion of 100–102; postcolonial cultural appropriation 106–107; rationalized sport 113; in reconstructed space and time 113–115
Montreal Lacrosse Club 107
Montreal Olympic Club 146
Mooney, Katherine: black talent and black subordination 163; stories of race horse men 163
Morgan, Connie 164
Morris, Alwyn 87
Morrow, Don 205, 333, 334; *Festschrift* 334–335
Mortal Kombat (1992) 221
Moscow Olympics (1980) 149
Mthethwa, Nathi 177
Mugabe, Robert 87
Multiplayer Online Battle Arena (MOBA) games 223
Munich Olympics (1972) 139
Munslow, Alun 20, 344
muscular Christians, development of 103, 120, 145
museums 68–70

Nadel, Joshua 181
Naismith, James 52
narrative/s in sport history 10–11, 51, 162, 217; functions of 52–53; human reliance on 52; knowledge sharing 53; representation of past 52–53; retrospective nature of 51–52; socially responsible historical narratives 13–14
NASCAR 2002 223
Nathan, Daniel 10, 11, 37, 67, 102
Nathan, Waka 281
National Baseball Hall of Fame and Museum, New York 238
national-based history 34
National Football League (NFL) 82, 193, 261
National Football Museum 238
National Holocaust Museum 70
nationalism and sports 97, 152–153, 232; Albania–Serbia soccer match 157–158; failure of internationalism 154–157; in global era 157–158; idea of nation 153–154; in ultra-competitive markets 157; masculinized nation state 35
nationalistic controversies 156
nationalist one-upmanship 156
National Museum of Australia, sport collection 206
National Olympic Committees (NOCs) 146–147, 149
National Rounders Association 263
National Sports Congress (NSC) 171
national symbolism 153, 157
nation branding 157
Native American boarding schools 60, 305–306
Nauright, John 1, 2, 3, 26, 206
Navratilova, Martina 231
Nazi Germany 70, 119, 138, 231, 351
Need for Speed: Most Wanted (2005) 222
Negro Industrial and Economic Union 85
Negro Leagues 164–165, 166
neo-liberalism 150, 320–321, 324–325
Newman, Joshua 244
new materialisms 243–244, 244–248
Newsletter 356
New York Cricket Association 261
New York Tribune 261
New Zealand *see* Māori communities
New Zealand rugby 149, 154, 282
Nicholson, Bob 207
Nike 88; Niketown stores 45
Niketown stores 45
NINE: A Journal of Baseball History and Culture 316, 318, 320, 326, 327, 328
Nintendo 220, 221
non-racialism 13, 97, 169, 170–171, 176, 177
Norman, William 240
North American Indigenous Games 271

North American Society for Sport History (NASSH) 315, 332, 339, 340, 344–345
Novick, Peter 10, 54
Nuttall, Sarah 13, 161–163
Nzindukiyimana, Ornella 163

Obel, Camilla 245
objective knowledge 16, 42
O'Bonsawin, Christine 87, 270, 272, 299
O'Brien, Jean M. 295
O'Connor, Eileen 163
Ojibwe players 303–304, 307
Olonga, Henry 87
Olympics: Arcade Triathlon 220; for the disabled 255; movement 85–86, 96; Olympic Council of Asia (OCA) 224; Olympic Games 66, 78, 138–139, 155, 182, 220, 232, 253; Olympic Internationalism 20; Project for Human Rights (OPHR) 84–85; solidarity 150
Olympika: The International Journal of Olympic Studies 316, 318, 319, 320, 326, 327
O'Mahony, Mike 129, 131, 132
Omeka content management system 207
online: gambling 3; PC gaming 221
ontology of sport history 16–18, 20
open-water swimming 12
optical character recognition technologies 207
oral history 58, 60, 62, 107; Kitchen Table Methodology 271–272, 296, 299, 301; orality vs written text 61; savage-orality-myth 61; yarning 58, 62, 272, 290–292
orality *vs* written text 61
organic knowingness 17
Oromo peoples 87
Osborne, Carol A. 181
Osborne, Jaquelyn 13, 95
Osmond, Gary 11, 37, 66, 67, 128, 131, 206, 207, 271
Overwatch (2016) 223
Owens, Jesse 70, 132
Oxford Handbook of Sports History (2017) 1–3, 276
OXO (1952) 219

Pākehā community 280–281, 283
Pan-Arab games 156
Paralympic Games 254, 255
Paralympic sport 123, 254
Pardo, Rodrigo 319
Park, Roberta 95, 121; adaptations of Muscular Christianity 121; gendered and racialized bodies 121; on sporting body 121
Pasifika New Zealand 280
patriotic nationalism 192, 194
Paxon, Frederic 339
Peers, Danielle 201
Pence, Mike 188

Index

Penn State-Sandusky scandal 54
Perry, Adele 61
Philadelphia Phillies 84
Phillips, Murray 37, 62, 67, 101, 131, 207, 270, 320, 343, 344
Physical Cultural Studies (PCS) 41; as an 'anti-relativist project' 43; approaches to sporting past **44**; constructionist and deconstructionist influences 43; contextualism for 43–45; effect of 45, 46; features 44; intellectual and political contexts of 41–42; observations 45–46; relations of power and progressive social change 46; self-reflexive approach 43; sports historians and 43–45
Physical Educator, The (journal) 317
Pieper, Lindsay Parks 206, 335
Pierce, Seneca Bemus 306
PlayerUnknown's Battlegrounds(PUBG) 223
player: *vs* computer (PvC) competition 221; *vs* environment (PvE) high-score competitions 221; *vs* player (PvP) gaming contests 221
Plymire, Darcy 343
politicization of sport 3, 95–98, 140
Pope, James 283
Pope, S. W. 1, 3, 93, 96, 206
popular historicization 17
post-apartheid South Africa 3, 169–178; class apartheid 174–175; income and intra-race inequality 174; reality of transition 175–178; reformative project 173–174; transformative project 173–174
postcolonialism 100
post-qualitative inquiry (PQI) 246
Poulter, Jim 289
POWWW 221
Pratt, Richard Henry 306
prehistoric cave pictograms 52
Pringle, Richard 10
Professional Gamers League (PGL) seasons (1997–1999) 222
Project MUSE 341
prolympic sport 111
ProQuest digital resource 207
Prospect Park Ladies' Cricket Club 261
Protect Our Winters (POW) 140
Prown, Jules D. 65, 66
PUBG Global Invitational 224
pugilism 153
Putin, Vladimir 139

Quake (1996) 221, 223
Quake III Arena (1999) 222
queer sports 188–189, 194; gay sporting identity 189–190, 193–194; mannish lesbians 191–192, 194; paedophiles 189–190
Quest 317

race 3, 4, 5, 11, 12, 13, 16, 18, 25, 37, 41, 52, 60, 65, 97, 98, 122, 124, 128, 129, 132, 161–167, 169–178, 180–184, 188, 189, 206, 213, 214, 259, 270, 276–277, 280, 281, 287, 296, 323, 358; racial contract 277; racial entanglements 161–162; racialized body in sport 121–122; racialized boundaries 280; racial sensationalism 307; *see also* Black
Race Men (Carby) 163
Raging Bull 132
Ramshaw, Gregory 200, 240
Rapinoe, Megan 188, 192, 194
Reagan, Ronald 150
real-time strategy (RTS) games 221
Reconstruction and Development Programme (RDP) 173
reconstructionist sport history 29
Recorde: Revista de História do Esporte 316, 318, 321, 326, 327, 381–386; funding 383–384; indexing and assessment 385; quality of research articles 384–385; topics 385
Red Annihilation Quake Tournament (1997) 222
Redmond, Gerald 332
Red Sport International 147
Red Star Belgrade 156
Regalado, Samuel 182
Reichert, Ralph 222
Reindle, Sepp 252
Rethinking History 67
Revolutionary War (1770) baseball 105
Reynolds, Henry 287
Rider, Toby 335
Riefenstahl, Leni 132
Riess, Steven 341
Rippon, Adam 188, 192, 194
Ritchie, Ian 335
Roberts, Ian 206
Robidoux, Michael A. 299
Robinson, Tahnee 308
Roman Republic and Empire 2
Rose, Deborah Bird 288
Rose, Gillian 131
Rosenberg, Alex 53
Rosenzweig, Roy 207
Rowe, Daivd 132
Rowley, Charles 287
Roy, Charles 307
Rudolph, Wilma 70, 166, 181–182
Rugby Football Union 102
Russell, Lynette 58

Saint Mondays 113, 115
Salter, Mike 332
Salt Lake City Winter Olympics (2002) 138
Salt Lake Herald 261
Samaranch, Juan Antonio 149

Index

Sands, Linda R. 36
Sands, Robert R. 36
Schaefer, Jennifer L. 207
Scholes, Robert 51
Schouwenburg, Hans 243, 245
Schultz, Jamie 37, 93, 95, 97–98, 131, 165
Schut, Pierre-Olaf 335
SCImago Journal Rank (SJR) 326, 329, **329**
Scopus database 336
Scott, Jack 84
Scott, James C. 60
Scott, Joan 180
Second World War 138, 145, 148, 156, 165,
    181, 182, 191, 252, 263, 281, 283
Sega 221; All Japan TV Game Championships
    219; Challenge of 1987–1988 220; European
    Championships 221
Seifried, Chad 344
self-reflexivity 9–10, 28, 95, 102
Seoul Olympics (1988) 149
settler colonialism 94, 275–277, 288
sexuality in sport 98
Sharp, Nonie 291
Shield, Pretty 304
Shimmel, Shoni 308
Shiprock Cardinals 308
Shooting Gallery 220
Shriver, Eunice Kennedy 253–254
Sibaja, Rwany 207
Sikes, Michelle 93, 181
Silva, Luiz Inácio Lula da 139
Simmons, Ozzie 165
Simri, Uriel 332
Sino–US relations 137
Skillen, Fiona 181
Smart, Aganetha 79
Smith, Laurajane 236
Smith, Linda Tuhiwai 270
Smith, Maureen 12, 37, 95, 131, 182
Smith, Ronald A. 54, 340
Smith, Tommie 70, 85, 132
Snyder, Carrie 78–80
Snyder, Jimmy 68
soccer: club badges and crests 133; televising of
    131
Sochi Winter Olympics (2014) 139
social class 3, 5, 25, 37, 41, 52, 86, 97, 101–103,
    106, 107, 114, 115, 121, 124, 129, 130, 132,
    145, 147, 164, 169, 173, 174–175, 177–178,
    180–183, 189, 190, 191, 192, 206, 231, 233,
    239, 259, 262, 276, 281, 296, 323, 332
Socialist Workers' Sports International (SWSI)
    147
Sockalexis, Penobscot Louis 307
Soja, Edward 111
Solms-Braunfels, Prince 155
Soske, Jon 171

Source-Normalized Impact per Paper (SNIP) 326
South Africa: South African Council on Sport
    (SACOS) 13, 169, 172, 177; South African
    Non-Racial Olympic Committee (SANROC)
    85; South African Rugby Union (SARU) 171;
    see also apartheid sport; non-racialism
Southbank Skatepark 238
South Eastern Districts Union (SEDRU) 171
sovereignty 275, 296
Soviet citizenship 156
Soviet Union 136
Spacewar! (Russell) 219
Spain: Spanish-American War (1898) 105;
    Spanish-speaking players 166
Spartakiads 147
Special Olympics 254
Spencer, Nancy 84
Spitzer, Alan 10, 55
Spivak, Gayatri 282
sport: borderlands 259–264; cultures 65; fans 50;
    landscapes and spatial representations 111–112;
    material culture 3, 65–71; new materialisms
    243–248; residual cultures 115; rivalries 104;
    social equality 26; social movements 83; social
    networking 205; sociology 24, 25–29
Sport Accord 224
sport-as-diplomacy 136–137
SPORTDiscus database 336
sport for development and peace (SDP)
    programmes 96, 137; sponsorship 138; Sport
    for All programmes 137
sport heritage 3, 130, 200, 235–237; goods and
    services 240–241; immovable 237–238;
    intangible 239–240; monuments and memor-
    ials 237; movable 238–239; notion of 'being'
    239–240; tangible immovable 237–238;
    tangible movable 238–239
sport history 162, 391–393; in curriculum
    213–214; as object of study 20–21; as a repre-
    sentation of the past 1, 9, 10, 12, 13, 55–56,
    205, 246, 392, 393; critical awareness in 10,
    19; epistemology of 18–20; introspective
    nature of 17; ontology of 16–18; periodization
    19–20; perspectives and conceptualizations
    11–12; responsible history 13; self-awareness
    16–18, 19; political form 26, 184, 392;
    women in 183 *see also* entanglements in sport
    history, intersectionality, narrative/s in sport
    history, self-reflexivity, sexuality in sport
sport history journals **2**, 5, 6, 17, 28, 47, 66, 94,
    130, 200, 208, 315–321, **316,327–329**; alt-
    metrics 327, **328**; circulation and readership of
    325; developmental trajectory of 319; editorial
    staffs and editorial boards 318–319; language
    319–321; library holdings and 325–330;
    metrics **327**; SJR quartile rankings 329, **329**
Sport History Review 316, 320, 321, 326, 329, 332

Index

Sporting Traditions 67, 317, 319, 321, 326, 327, 367–372
Sport in History 326, 329, 336, 356–358
Sport in the Movies (1982) 132
Sport Literature Association 74
Sports Historian, The 316, 318, 355–356
Sports Statues Project 131
Springfield 170
STADION: International Journal of the History of Sport 316, 317, 319, 320, 321, 326, 336, 337, 348–351
Staley, Seward 340
Stanner, W.E.H. 287
Starcade (1982–1984) 221
Star-Craft: Brood War (1998) 222
Statistical Package for the Social Sciences (SPSS) 204
Stearns, Peter N. 206
Steen, Rob 228
St. Louis Cardinals 84
Stoddart, Brian 103, 368
Stofile, Makhenkesi 176
Stoler, Ann Laura 58
Stone, Toni 164
Stop-N-Go Krull Tournament, 1983 220
'Stop the Seventy Tour' 86
storytelling 54–55
Street Fighter II (1991) 221
Stride, Chris 131
Struna, Nancy 180
student-centred learning of sport history 214–217; authentic and experiential learning 215–217; students as partner' model 215
Sullivan, James 305
Summer Olympic Games: 1936 70; 1960 244; 1972 348; 2020 139
Szijártó, István M. 37

Tatz, Colin 14
Taylor, A.J.P. 54
teaching, of sports history 212, 214
Team Fortress 2 (2007) 223
technological innovation 18
Tennis for Two (Higinbotham) 219
TePoel, Dain 208
tewaarathon 144
Tewanima, Louis 306
Thatcher, Margaret 150
That's Incredible! Video Game Invitational (1983) 221
theory in history 12–13
Third Reich 136, 138
Thomas Reuters' Web of Science 326
Thompson, E. P. 112–113, 114, 340
Thorpe, Holly 201, 244, 307
Thorpe, Jim 306
Thrift, Nigel 113

Tilden, Bill 191, 192
time, representation of 112–113
Timothy, Dallen 236
Tinkler, Jane 27
Title IX regulation, United States 87, 344
Tomlinson, Alan 28
Torontolympiad 255
Torres Strait Islander people 62, 287, 291
Touching Base: Professional Baseball and American Culture in the Progressive Era (Reiss) 204
Townsend, Stephen 207
transhumanism 36
transnational histories 183, 259
transnationalism 38
transnational perspectives, of sports 201–202
Trice, Jack 165
Trust and Technology project 59
Tudjman, Franjo 157
Turchin, Peter 34
Turner, David 201
Turner, Frederick Jackson 339
Turner (a form of gymnastics) movement 153–154
Turner, Victor 343
Twin Galaxies International Score Board 220
Twitter 82, 188, 206, 328–329, 335, 358
Tyus, Wyomia 85

uniform resource locator (URL) 328
Unitas, Johnny 67
United Nations Educational, Scientific and Cultural Organization (UNESCO) 238
United States (US): Football Association (USFA) 262; National Video Game Team 220; Olympic Committee 85, 122; Olympic movement 85; Open tennis tournament 84, 224; Title IX regulation 87
Universidad Pablo de Olavide in Seville (UPO) 375–376
Unreal Tournament 2003 222

Vamplew, Wray 27, 66, 68, 93, 367, 369
van Ingen, Cathy 344
Veracini, Lorenzo 275
vertical diffusion 102, 276
Vertinsky, Patricia 37, 46, 95, 120–121; biomedicalization of aging female bodies 120; *Eternally Wounded Woman, The* 120, 180; gendered and racialized bodies 121; religious bodies 120
Victorian values 276
video games 219, 220, 225; live streaming video platforms for 224; *Video Game, The* 221; video gaming organizations 220–221
Vienna Workers' Olympiad (1931) 147
village green 114, 238

Index

visuality in sports 95; approaches and methodologies 131–132; cultural constraints 133; as a discursive practice 129; photographs, films, and television 129–130, 132; range of visual representations 129–130; of soccer 131; in sport 130–131

Vito, Christian G. De 38

Vivier, Christian 131

Voight, David 343

Voros, Joseph 34

Vries, Jan de 33, 37

Wabanaki 307

Waldmeir, Patti 169

Waldstein, David 261

Warcraft III (2002) 222, 223

Warcraft: Orcs & Humans (1994) 221

Warner, Glenn 'Pop' 306

Warwick, Samantha 75, 76, 78, 79

Waterton, Emma 236

Watson, Steve 236

Weedon, Gavin 245

Weissmuller, Johnny 76

Wetherell, Margaret 233

Wheelock, Oneida Martin 306

White clubs 173

White, Hayden 102, 129

White, Spitzer 10

White sport 169

white supremacy 124, 192, 194

Widener, Daniel 276

Wiebe, Robert 340

Wiggins, David K. 341

Wilde, Ari de 207, 344

Williams, Jack 276

Williams, Raymond 199

Willms, Nicole 182

Wills, Thomas Wentworth 289

Wilson, Wayne 1, 2

Wimbledon Tennis Championship 206

Winkle, Jimmy 70

Winmar, Nicky 87, 128, 130

Winter Pinball Olympics 220

Wireplay Invades Brisbane Tournament (1998) 222

Women's Artistic Gymnastics 123

Women's Olympic Games 87

women's sport 180; African American women's opportunities 181; athlete's identity 181–182; Chinese sportswomen 182; history 183–184; Muslim sportswomen 182

Women's World Games 148

Workers' Olympiad (1937) 147

World Cyber Games (WCG) 222

World Gamemaster Tournament (WGT) 222

World Indigenous Games 271

World Wheelchair Games 255

Wrigley Ocean Marathon (1927) 75–76

Wrynn, Alison 319

Wyandot-Huron tribal healers 303

Xu Guoqi 232

Young, Christopher 28

Young Men's Christian Association (YMCA) 103, 105, 145, 307

Young, Sandy 332

Young Women's Buddhist Associations 182

Young Women's Christian Association 306

Zagreb, Dinamo 156

Zaharias, George 192

Zavos, Spiro 282

Ziegler, Earle 332, 340

Milton Keynes UK
Ingram Content Group UK Ltd.
UKHW051922120923
428563UK00008B/32